A SOLDIER'S LIFE IN

VICTORIAN TIMES

A SOLDIER'S LIFE IN
VICTORIAN TIMES

Fiona Corbridge

W
FRANKLIN WATTS
LONDON • SYDNEY

Illustrations by
Mark Bergin
Kevin Maddison
Lee Montgomery
Nick Spender
Peter Visscher
Mike White
Maps by Stefan Chabluk

First published in 2006 by
Franklin Watts
338 Euston Road
London NW1 3BH

Franklin Watts Australia
Hachette Children's Books
Level 17/207 Kent Street
Sydney NSW 2000

Series editor: John C. Miles
Art director: Jonathan Hair
Picture research: Susan Mennell

This book is based on *Going to War in
Victorian Times* by Craig Dodd © Franklin
Watts 2001. It is produced for Franklin
Watts by Painted Fish Ltd.
Designer: Rita Storey

A CIP catalogue record
for this book is available
from the British Library

ISBN 0 7496 6494 0
Dewey classification: 355.00941

Printed in China

CONTENTS

THE WORLD 1850-80

During the nineteenth century, soldiers were at war all over the world, especially in 1850–80.

Armies fought each other in Europe, the Balkans, India, Africa, the USA and the Far East. Thousands of men died in the fighting. Many thousands more died later of their wounds or from diseases caught in army camps and hospitals.

UNION STATES OF AMERICA

American Civil War

CONFEDERATE STATES OF AMERICA

Abraham Lincoln (1809–65) *Abraham Lincoln was the US president during the American Civil War. He led the Union states to win, but was shot dead by John Wilkes Booth.*

War in the Crimea, 1854

War broke out in the Crimea in Russia when the Russians decided to take over Ottoman (Turkish) land. France and Britain fought Russia to stop the Russians getting a way through to the Mediterranean Sea.

Mutiny in India, 1857

Indian soldiers who worked for the British East India Company were given bullets greased with cow and pig fat. This was against their religion. The soldiers had a mutiny which lasted for over a year.

Otto von Bismarck (1815–98)
Bismarck was the head of the government in the German state of Prussia. He built up his country's army and got the many German states to join together into one powerful nation.

RUSSIA

Crimean War

BRITAIN

PRUSSIA

FRANCE

Franco-Prussian War

MEDITERRANEAN SEA

OTTOMAN EMPIRE

ATLANTIC OCEAN

INDIA

Indian Mutiny

INDIAN OCEAN

WORLD MAP 1850–80

 Wars and fighting

Queen Victoria (1819–1901)
Victoria became queen of Britain in 1837. "Victorian times" means "during Victoria's rule". Britain managed to build a huge empire in these years.

The American Civil War, 1860

America was made up of states under a central government. The southern states (Confederates) broke away from the northern states (the Union). This started the American Civil War (US Civil War).

The Franco-Prussian War, 1870–71

The German state of Prussia went to war with France. After eight months, the French surrendered (gave up and agreed Prussia had won). Germany was now the most powerful country in mainland Europe.

JOINING THE ARMY

Some soldiers were volunteers – they decided to join the army. Others were conscripts – the government made them join. Conscripts served in the army for a fixed time before going back to their ordinary jobs. They could be called up to fight for their country at any time.

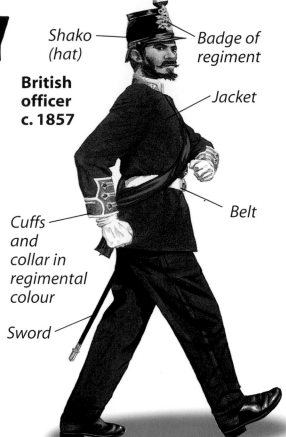

British officer c. 1857

Shako (hat)

Badge of regiment

Jacket

Belt

Cuffs and collar in regimental colour

Sword

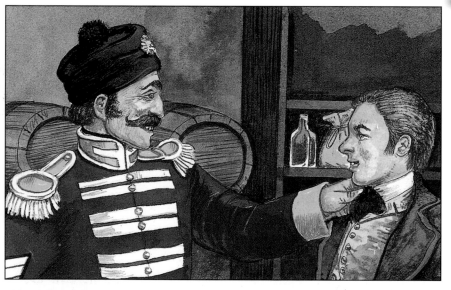

ARMY OFFICERS

Being an officer was a good career. In Britain, a rich family could buy their son a job as an officer.

Things were different in the USA. In the US Civil War, some groups of soldiers voted for their own officers.

REGIMENTS

In the nineteenth century, armies were organized into large groups of men called regiments.

The British army had regiments from different parts of the country.

Their names showed where they came from, for example the Lincolnshire Regiment.

Army recruiting sergeants sometimes visited village pubs to talk to young men and try to get them to join the army.

Regimental badge

CONSCRIPTS IN EUROPE

Prussia

In the 1860s, Bismarck (the ruler of Prussia) decided that all young men had to do military service. By the 1870s, Prussia had more than 700,000 conscripts who were trained and ready to fight.

France

France had a different system. Every man was given a number. If his number was chosen, he had to become a conscript for up to seven years. Some men paid someone else to take their place.

French soldier c. 1860

Prussian soldier c. 1870

Wide-brimmed hat

Blanket roll (for sleeping)

Musket (gun)

Water canteen (water bottle)

US Confederate conscript, 1862

AMERICA

Before the US Civil War, each state had a militia. Militiamen were part-time soldiers who met to practise fighting so that if a war began, they would be ready to fight.

AMERICAN CIVIL WAR

The two sides in the US Civil War were the Union and the Confederates.

Most soldiers were volunteers, but the Confederates started conscription in 1862. Union states had rules saying how many soldiers each state had to recruit.

COMMANDERS

The ruler of a country is often the head of the armed forces. In the USA, the president is the commander-in-chief of the armed forces.

During the US Civil War, President Abraham Lincoln was very busy commanding the soldiers of the Union states.

A British fusilier

WEST POINT

There is a famous US military academy called West Point. Many senior officers in the US Civil War trained there. They included Ulysses S. Grant, commander of the Union army, and Robert E. Lee, who commanded the Confederate forces.

Grant led the Union army to win and later became president of the USA.

A Union general in the US Civil War

RANKS

Armies are divided up into ranks. Commanders are the top rank and privates are the bottom rank.

Privates are known by a different name in some regiments – fusiliers, gunners, guardsmen or troopers.

(Right) Ulysses S. Grant

RANKS IN THE BRITISH ARMY, 1860

The highest rank was field marshal.
Field marshals commanded whole armies.

Field marshal

Below field marshals were generals.
Generals planned what the troops
would do on the battlefield.

General

Colonels commanded infantry regiments.
Lieutenant-colonels commanded artillery
and cavalry regiments.

Colonel

Majors and captains were in charge
of units in each regiment.
They were helped by junior officers,
such as lieutenants.

Major   **Captain**

The regimental sergeant-major was in
charge of discipline (rules and behaviour).
Sergeants led small groups of men and
made sure officers' orders were obeyed.
Next came corporals and lance-corporals.

**Regimental
sergeant-
major**   **Sergeant**   **Corporal**

The lowest rank was the private.

Privates

🔔 JOINING A REGIMENT

In the nineteenth century, armies in Europe and the USA were made up of regiments. Infantry regiments fought on foot. Artillery regiments used large mounted guns. Cavalry regiments rode horses.

In Britain, a regiment was usually divided into two. One part worked abroad while the other stayed in Britain.

During the US Civil War, many men joined their local militia. Militia units often became part of a larger regiment. Regiments were on active service (on duty) throughout the war.

UNIFORMS

Wearing a uniform helped soldiers to act as part of a team. It also made it easier for men to recognize other soldiers in their regiment in battle. That was why each regiment had a slightly different uniform.

Union soldier in the US Civil War

Kepi (cap)

Rolled blanket and backpack

Jacket

Cartridge pouch

Belt

Haversack

Tin mug

Musket

Wars and fighting in the nineteenth century

• *Crimean War, 1854. Russia against France and Britain.*

• *Indian Mutiny, 1857. Britain against Indian soldiers.*

• *US Civil War, 1860. Union states against Confederate states.*

• *Franco-Prussian War, 1870. France against Prussia.*

US UNIFORMS

In the US Civil War, Union soldiers wore dark blue jackets with lighter blue trousers. Confederate forces wore grey jackets and blue or brown trousers. Each regiment's uniform was slightly different. But as the war went on and it became hard to get materials, soldiers had to wear uniforms made out of rough brown cloth.

HATS AND HELMETS

Prussia

Prussian helmet

Prussian soldiers wore helmets with a spike on top. The French army copied these after it lost the Franco-Prussian War.

France

French soldiers wore a hat called a shako. It was made of leather, with a small peak and a coloured pompom on top.

Pompom

French shako

Confederate army kepi

America

Most Union soldiers wore a cap with a peak called a kepi. Confederate troops wore a hat with a wide brim, or a kepi with a blue band.

British cavalry trooper in a khaki uniform, 1850

THE COLOUR OF DUST

British troops in India wore lightweight khaki uniforms because it was so hot. The word "khaki" means "dust-coloured" in Urdu (an Indian language). Khaki uniforms merged into the landscape and made soldiers more difficult for an enemy to spot.

Victoria Cross

Medal of Honor

TOO BRIGHT FOR SAFETY

Soldiers in bright uniforms were easy for the enemy to see and shoot. By 1890, most countries had changed their soldiers' uniforms to duller colours.

MEDALS FOR BRAVERY

Britain's highest military medal is the Victoria Cross, named after Queen Victoria. The highest military medal in the USA is the Medal of Honor. These medals are given to soldiers who have shown great bravery.

Both medals were introduced between 1850 and 1880.

INFANTRY

In a battle, the infantry tried to break through the lines of enemy soldiers. In the early 1800s, they fired their guns then charged (rushed forward) at the enemy.

By 1870, armies had guns that were quicker to reload. Soldiers could keep firing and no longer needed to charge at the enemy.

A British infantryman loads his musket (gun)

Ramrod pushes the gunpowder cartridge down the barrel

US INFANTRY GEAR

Cutlery

Canteen

J. DUNBAR
C₀B
53ᵈPA

Backpack

Mug

Tin dish

Cartridge bag

Haversack for food

Infantry kit
Soldiers in the US Civil War had to carry a lot of equipment, including a rifle, cartridge bag, food and personal belongings.

MUZZLE-LOADERS
Guns used in the early 1800s were loaded from the muzzle (front end). The soldier pushed a cartridge containing gunpowder and a lead ball (the bullet) down the barrel with a ramrod. He risked being shot by the enemy while he did this.

Bolt and firing mechanism

Rear sight

Blade sight

Steel barrel

Wooden stock

Trigger
fires gun

Breech-loading rifle

BREECH-LOADERS
Breech-loading guns were loaded from the breech (rear) end of the barrel. The needle gun was a breech-loading rifle invented in 1837.

A cartridge contained the bullet, explosive and detonator. It could be fired and reloaded while lying down, so soldiers were in less danger from enemy fire.

French troops fire Chassepot rifles in the Franco-Prussian War

Johannes von Dreyse, inventor of the needle gun

CIVIL WAR RIFLES
In the USA, breech-loading rifles were used by both sides during the US Civil War. They were made by companies such as Hall, Joslyn and Jenks.

A BETTER WEAPON
The French made a breech-loading rifle called the Chassepot in 1866. It was much better than the Prussian needle gun. During the Franco-Prussian War, the Prussian army used Chassepots taken from captured or dead French infantrymen.

ARTILLERY

"Artillery" means "cannons and big mounted guns".

In the nineteenth century, some artillery was light enough to be mounted on gun carriages. These were pushed or pulled into position by one or two soldiers. Heavier guns were pulled by horses.

The Dictator

🔔 HUGE GUNS

Some big guns were so gigantic that they had to be mounted on railway wagons. One of these was the Dictator. This was a mortar (artillery that fired a shell) and it was used by the Union army during the US Civil War.

LOADING AND FIRING A CANNON

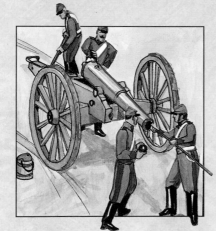

Ready...
A cloth bag of gunpowder and a cannon ball was rammed down the barrel of the gun.

Aim...
The gunner aimed the gun, poured the gunpowder charge into the touchhole and lit it.

Fire!
The gunpowder in the gun barrel exploded and the cannon ball flew towards the enemy.

AMMUNITION

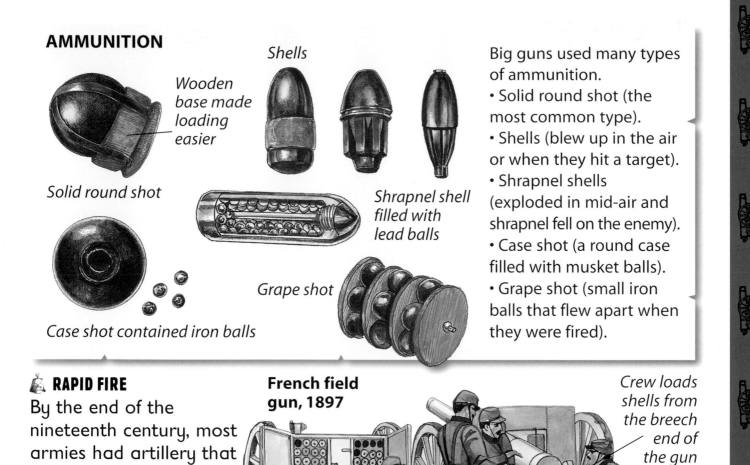

Shells

Wooden base made loading easier

Solid round shot

Shrapnel shell filled with lead balls

Case shot contained iron balls

Grape shot

Big guns used many types of ammunition.
• Solid round shot (the most common type).
• Shells (blew up in the air or when they hit a target).
• Shrapnel shells (exploded in mid-air and shrapnel fell on the enemy).
• Case shot (a round case filled with musket balls).
• Grape shot (small iron balls that flew apart when they were fired).

🔔 RAPID FIRE

By the end of the nineteenth century, most armies had artillery that could be loaded from the breech end and which fired quickly. The French had a field gun that could fire twenty rounds per minute.

French field gun, 1897

Crew loads shells from the breech end of the gun

🔔 THE GUNNERS

Many guns were pulled by horses. But gunners also had to be strong enough to move them.

Each time the gun was fired, it moved. The gunners had to push and pull the gun back into position and aim it again.

An 1870s Prussian gun crew aims a field gun

ON THE MOVE

In the early 1800s, armies often marched thousands of miles to battle. As the century went on, the network of railways grew and trains became important for moving troops around in war.

British troops went to the Crimea and India by ship.

FRANCO-PRUSSIAN WAR

The French were not very good at using railways to move troops. But the Prussian army made good use of trains and this helped it to win the war.

A French troop train

SAILING TO INDIA

The only way to get soldiers to India was by ship. It took two months and conditions were bad. Many men died on the way and were buried at sea.

AMERICAN RAILWAYS

There were more railways in the northern states than in the south. This helped the Union army to move men and artillery to where they were needed.

But the Confederate army used trains too, where it could.

STEALING THE GENERAL

Union soldiers stole a Confederate steam locomotive, the *General*. They drove it until it ran out of steam and they were captured by the Confederates. The soldiers were executed (killed).

The *General*

Steam trains

Steam trains were made up of a locomotive (engine) and some carriages.

The locomotive burned coal to make the steam that powered it.

Steam trains at this time could travel at speeds of up to 90 km/h.

ARMOURED MONSTER

New inventions made use of railways for war. The rail car below was used in the US Civil War. It had a cannon and armour plating to protect the crew.

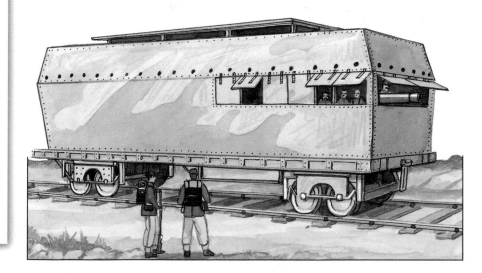

CAVALRY

The cavalry was made up of soldiers who rode horses. They helped to protect the infantry and artillery. Sometimes they charged at the enemy. At the end of a battle, they chased enemy soldiers who were running away. The cavalry was also used for reconnaissance – finding out what the enemy was doing.

Lord Raglan, commander-in-chief of the British army in the Crimea

THE LIGHT BRIGADE

In the Crimean War, the British Light Brigade (cavalry) was ordered to attack Russian guns at the Battle of Balaclava. The troops charged at the enemy but had to turn back. Nearly 250 men were killed or injured.

The Light Brigade charges at Balaclava

CAVALRYMAN'S KIT

Pistols and sabres

Cavalry troopers carried lots of equipment. They had weapons such as pistols and long swords called sabres.

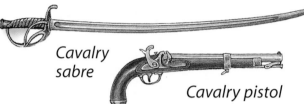

Cavalry sabre

Cavalry pistol

Officer's revolver

Blanket roll and canteen

Troopers had a blanket roll for sleeping and water in a canteen. They often carried a greatcoat to keep warm.

Saddlebags

Saddlebags were used to store a grooming kit for the horse, pen and paper, books and other personal items.

Canteen

Blanket roll

⚑ CHARGE!

To start a cavalry charge, the troops moved forward slowly. When they were about 700 metres from enemy lines, they started to trot. Just 180 metres from the enemy, they dashed forward in a charge.

⚑ CAVALRY IN THE US CIVIL WAR

Both sides had a large number of cavalrymen, but there were not many cavalry battles. Commanders mainly used horsemen for reconnaissance and for manoeuvres (army exercises) that were set up to confuse the enemy.

A Union cavalry trooper of the US Civil War

Cavalry regiments
There were three types of troops in a cavalry regiment – assault, support and reserve.

In battle, assault and support troops moved forwards and broke into a trot. Then the assault troops made the charge.

LIFE IN CAMP

In the Crimean War, there were only three major battles – Alma, Balaclava and Inkerman. But in the US Civil War, there were more than 230 battles.

When soldiers were not fighting, they lived in a camp. They spent their time eating, playing cards or simply waiting for the battle to start.

DRILLING

All soldiers had to do drill (practise manoeuvres). This helped to make them work well as a team and kept them ready to fight.

Prussian soldier drilling

OFF DUTY

Soldiers played games, read books and wrote letters home. Sometimes their families lived with them in camp.

A Union soldier and family at Camp Slocum, near Washington DC, in 1862

Flour

Fresh or salted meat

Hard bread

Beans Drink Salt Coffee Vegetables

A soldier's day

5.00 a.m. Drummer or bugler wakes everyone. Wash and dress.

5.15 a.m. Roll call.

5.30 a.m. Breakfast.

6.00 a.m. Chop firewood, clean camp and other duties.

8.00 a.m. Guard duty and drilling.

12 p.m. Dinner.

2.00 p.m. Drilling.

4.30 p.m. Get ready for evening inspection.

5.45 p.m. Roll call, inspection and parade.

6.30 p.m. Supper.

8.30 p.m. Last roll call.

9 p.m. Lights out.

FOOD

This picture shows the rations that a Union soldier was given each week. It was much better than the food of British soldiers in the Crimea – their usual meal was a thin stew of beef and potatoes.

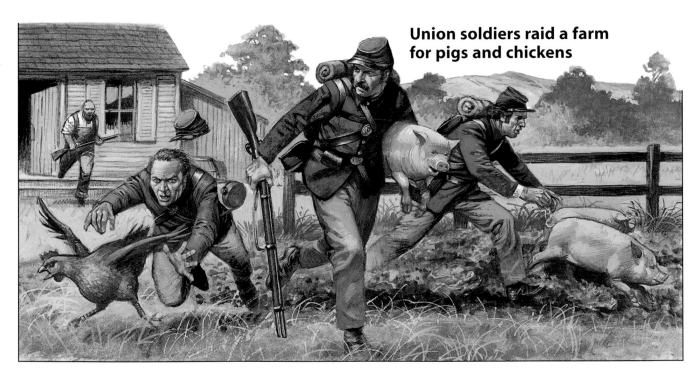

Union soldiers raid a farm for pigs and chickens

LIVING OFF THE LAND

Soldiers tried to find other things to eat when they could. Some hunted wild animals and birds. Others stole chickens and pigs from farms.

• **Rations**
Each soldier was given a certain amount of food each day or week. This was called his rations.

• **Inspections and parades**
Soldiers' appearance and equipment were checked at inspections and parades (marches).

WAR AT SEA

In the nineteenth century, the British navy was the strongest in the world. Prussia and France were more interested in building up their armies than their navies. So, in Europe, navies did not have much to do in 1850–80. But in the US Civil War, there was a lot of fighting at sea.

Britain's first ironclad: HMS *Warrior*, 1860

IRONCLAD WARSHIPS

Ironclad ships were very strong. They had iron plating to protect them. The first ones were the French *La Gloire* of 1859, and the British HMS *Warrior* of 1860.

IRONCLADS IN THE USA

In the US Civil War, Confederate forces captured a Union ship, the USS *Merrimack*. They covered it with iron plating and renamed it the CSS *Virginia*. They also fitted an iron ram and ten cannons.

The crew of an ironclad on deck during the US Civil War

BATTLE OF THE IRONCLADS

The citizens of Washington DC (part of the Union) heard that the Confederate navy had the CSS *Virginia*, an iron warship. They were frightened that it would shell their city. So the US navy built an ironclad of its own, the USS *Monitor*. The two ships went into battle in March 1862.

FOUR-HOUR FIGHT

The *Virginia* and the *Monitor* fired their big guns at each other for four hours. Then the ships' commanders decided to call it a draw and sailed off.

The battle between the *Monitor* and the *Virginia* in 1862

CSS Virginia

USS Monitor

Ironclads

• *"Ironclad" means "clad (covered) in iron".*

• *Iron is a metal that is often used for engineering (making engines, machines and bridges).*

• *HMS Warrior, the first British ironclad warship, never did any fighting. It can be seen today at the Historic Dockyard, Portsmouth, UK.*

THE MONITOR'S TURRET

The *Monitor* was armed with two huge cannons. These were in an armoured turret that turned round so the guns could be fired in any direction.

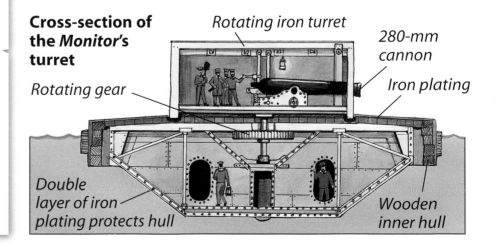

Cross-section of the *Monitor's* turret

Rotating iron turret

280-mm cannon

Iron plating

Rotating gear

Double layer of iron plating protects hull

Wooden inner hull

MEDICINE

More soldiers died of illnesses and infections than from being killed in battle. Military hospitals were filthy.

In the Crimean War, conditions started to get better when nurses such as Florence Nightingale and Mary Seacole went to the Crimea. By the end of the nineteenth century, medical care had improved a lot.

FLORENCE NIGHTINGALE
Florence Nightingale (above) went to the Crimea to nurse injured soldiers. She was horrified by the dirty conditions she found. She and her nurses worked very hard and death rates started to fall.

HOSPITALS
Conditions in military field hospitals were dreadful. Surgeons used dirty, bloodstained instruments. Anaesthetics (a way of stopping a patient feeling pain during an operation) were hardly ever used. Men who survived the operations often died later from fever.

A US Civil War military hospital

SURGEON'S KIT, 1850s

Army surgeons (doctors who did operations) had instruments for different types of injury. There were knives to cut through flesh, saws to cut bone, probes and bullet extractors to find and pull out bullets.

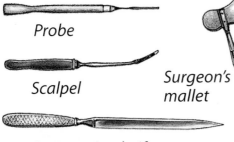

Bone saw

Surgical saw

Probe

Scalpel

Amputation knife

Surgeon's mallet

Tools to bore into bone

Bone crimper

Bullet extractor

Bone cutter

Henri Dunant with the flag of the Red Cross

THE RED CROSS

A Swiss man called Henri Dunant saw how soldiers suffered in war.

In 1862 he published a leaflet saying that a group was needed to care for wounded soldiers in wartime. The Red Cross started because of this.

LUCKY LOCALS

The British army in India had Indian soldiers called sepoys in it. They did not catch many of the illnesses that killed the British soldiers.

Indian sepoy of the 41st Regiment Bengal Native Infantry

Amputations
Sometimes soldiers had to have a badly injured arm or leg amputated (cut off). This was often done without an anaesthetic. Many died afterwards from infections because the hospitals were so dirty and full of germs. Little was known about germs at the time.

WAR NEWS

The fastest way to send news and messages was by telegraph. The sender used a machine to send pulses of electric current along telegraph wires. The pulses arrived at the other end as a pattern of dots and dashes. Telegraph operators could work out the message from the pattern.

People in Britain read about the Crimean War in *The Times*

Confederate troops lay a telegraph wire

WAR REPORTER

During the Crimean War, *The Times* newspaper sent a journalist called William Howard Russell to the Crimea. He was the first proper war reporter.

TELEGRAPH WIRES

At first there were not many telegraph stations and telegraph wires. But they soon spread across many countries.

By the US Civil War, there was a wide network of telegraph wires in the USA.

CRIMEAN HORROR

In the Crimea, Russell did not just write about who won the battles. His reports in *The Times* described the awful conditions that the soldiers faced.

A report from Russell: *"The men suffered exceedingly from cold. Some of them had no beds to lie on and none had more than their single regulation blanket. They dressed to go to bed, putting on all their spare clothing before they tried to sleep."*

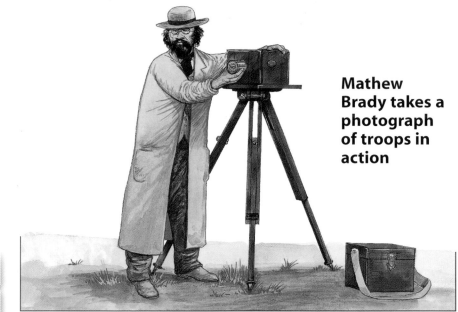

Mathew Brady takes a photograph of troops in action

PHOTOGRAPHING THE ACTION

During the US Civil War, a photographer called Mathew Brady was allowed to photograph army units. By the end of the war, he had taken more than 3,500 photographs. These showed civilians how horrible war was.

Photograph of Union troops by Mathew Brady, 1864

GLOSSARY

Artillery
The large guns (cannons and mounted guns) of an army and the men who use them.

The Balkans
The large peninsula in south-east Europe, between the Adriatic and Aegean Seas.

Bolt
A sliding bar in a breech-loading gun.

Union general

It ejects a used cartridge and guides a new one into the breech.

British East India Company
The company that ran India for the British government until just after the Indian Mutiny.

Cavalry
Soldiers on horseback.

c. (circa)
A Latin word meaning "about". It is used with a date to show that historians are not sure of the exact date.

Civilian
Non-military.

Confederate states
The southern states of the USA that broke away from the others in 1860, starting the US Civil War.

Conscription/ conscript
Compulsory military service (often, but not always, in wartime).

Crimea
A peninsula in Russia between the Black Sea and the Sea of Azov.

Empire
Group of states, countries or territories that were once independent (not controlled by another country or power), but now ruled by a single country or person.

Fusilier
A private in a British rifle regiment.

Guardsman
A private in a British Guards regiment.

Gunner
A private in Britain's Royal Regiment of Artillery.

Grape shot
Cannon ammunition made of small iron balls that scatter after firing.

Infantry
The foot soldiers of an army.

Kepi
A military cap with a circular top and a horizontal peak.

Manoeuvres
Military exercises for soldiers to practise what they have learned.

Military
Something that is to do with the armed forces.

Militiamen
Civilians who volunteer for military training so they can become a home defence force and increase army numbers in war.

Musket
A muzzle-loading shoulder gun used from c. 1650 to the mid-1800s.

Mutiny
A rebellion against authority (resisting it, rising up against it or fighting it).

Officer
A soldier above the rank of regimental sergeant-major.

Private
The lowest rank in any army.

Prussia
The most powerful German state in the nineteenth century. It wanted to make all independent German states into one country.

Ramrod
A rod used to push ammunition into the barrel of a gun.

Regiment
A large military unit, usually made up of battalions and often divided into companies and platoons.

Roll call
A register taken to check who is present.

Sabre
A long, curved, single-edged sword for use on horseback.

Shako
A peaked cap, also known as a "stovepipe", worn by soldiers of many countries throughout the nineteenth century until the introduction of the helmet (in Britain, around 1878).

Shell
Hollow artillery ammunition. It was

British soldier loading his musket

filled with explosives that exploded during flight or when it hit its target. It could also be filled with pieces of shrapnel.

Shrapnel
Small pellets or bullets in a shell, which explode before it lands. Or fragments from a shell.

State
An area with its own government.

Telegraph
Electric signals sent along a transmission wire. Used to send information.

Union states
The northern states in the US Civil War. They fought the Confederates (southern states).

INDEX

PHOTOGRAPHIC CREDITS

Peter Newark's American Pictures pp. 22, 29
Peter Newark's Military Pictures pp. 10, 17, 24, 26

SECOND EDITION

Sorensen's GUIDE TO POWERBOATS

How to Evaluate Design, Construction, and Performance

ERIC W. SORENSEN

FEATURING INSIGHTS AND RATINGS FROM J.D. POWER AND ASSOCIATES

BOAT COMPETITIVE INFORMATION STUDY

International Marine / McGraw-Hill

Camden, Maine • New York • Chicago • San Francisco
Lisbon • London • Madrid • Mexico City • Milan • New Delhi
San Juan • Seoul • Singapore • Sydney • Toronto

The McGraw·Hill Companies

1 2 3 4 5 6 7 8 9 DOC DOC 0 9 8 7

Copyright © 2002, 2008 Eric W. Sorensen

All rights reserved. The publisher takes no responsibility for the use of any of the materials or methods described in this book, nor for the products thereof. The name "International Marine," International Marine logo, and J.D. Power and Associates are trademarks of The McGraw-Hill Companies. Printed in the United States of America.

Library of Congress Cataloging-in-Publication Data
Sorensen, Eric W.
    Sorensen's guide to powerboats : how to evaluate design, construction, and performance / Eric W. Sorensen — 2nd ed.
          p.   cm.
    Includes index.
    ISBN-13: 978-0-07-148920-1 (pbk. : alk. paper)
    1.   Motorboats—Evaluation. 2.   Boats and boating.   I. Title.
    VM341.S646 2007
    623.82'31029—dc22

                                                2007041168

ISBN 978-0-07-148920-1
MHID 0-07-148920-7

Questions regarding the content of this book should be addressed to
International Marine
P.O. Box 220
Camden, ME 04843
www.internationalmarine.com

Questions regarding the ordering of this book should be addressed to
The McGraw-Hill Companies
Customer Service Department
P.O. Box 547
Blacklick, OH 43004
Retail customers: 1-800-262-4729
Bookstores: 1-800-722-4726
The author can be reached at info@sorensensguide.com

Photographs courtesy of Eric W. Sorensen unless credited otherwise. Page ii courtesy Betram. Part one opener courtesy Grady-White, part two opener courtesy Century.
Line art by Bruce Alderson unless credited otherwise.
Reproduction of any J.D. Power and Associates material in this publication is prohibited without the expressed written permission of J.D. Power and Associates.

Contents

Preface

Sorensen's Guide to Powerboats is intended as an aid for the prospective boat buyer and as a reference for the boatowner as well as the boating industry professional. The book is organized in two main sections: Part 1 explains powerboat design, construction, and performance. It has been updated to address advances in boat design and manufacturing, especially the discussions pertaining to propulsion systems (chapter 8). Part 2 surveys the market, describing specific boats in 27 different categories (e.g., pontoon boats, coastal fishing boats, and express cruisers).

A clear understanding of how a boat is designed and manufactured is critical to a buyer's ability to select the right boat. For example, if you understand why a pontoon boat is designed and manufactured the way it is, you will also understand why it would make an extremely poor choice as an offshore fishing boat. Because not all such comparisons are so obvious, part 1 explains the not-so-apparent differences between various hull configurations, materials and methods of construction, power plant options, bridge design choices, deck outfitting, interior accommodations, and other factors that determine a boat's suitability for its intended purpose. With a working knowledge of these subjects as you shop for a boat, you will understand the reasons behind the manufacturer's choices in design and construction, and you'll be better able to determine how well that particular boat suits your needs. If you are already a boatowner, you will gain a deeper understanding of your boat's strengths and shortcomings. This should enable you to use it more efficiently, safely, and enjoyably.

Much has changed since the publication of the first edition of this book in 2002. Most significantly, a revolution has taken place in marine propulsion systems so that what was the norm in 2002 is in many cases outmoded, while what was cutting-edge or even speculative technology has become mainstream. There have been less dramatic but in some cases equally important advances in composite hull manufacturing processes, exterior design, interior layout trends, and other areas of design and technology. And, of course, the boats have changed. Every boat that was new in 2002 is now an older model, while new models, incorporating many of the technical and design advances of the past few years, have been introduced, presenting a whole new world of choices for the boat buyer—boats that are faster, better-handling, more reliable, more fuel-efficient, sexier, safer, and more refined for their specific purpose, be it wakeboarding, fishing, overnight cruising, or entertaining.

Among outboard-powered boats, the market has shifted from being primarily composed of carbureted and electronically fuel-injected (EFI) two-stroke engines to being dominated by EFI four-stroke and direct-injected (DI) two-stroke outboards. This is great news for the boatowner since these modern outboards are so much more satisfying to own. They run cleaner with less smoke and fumes, they are more efficient and reliable, and they start easier and run quieter. Owning a modern EFI four-stroke or DI two-stroke outboard increases owner satisfaction with the boat as well as the engine, which translates to an overall enhancement of the boat ownership experience.

The big news in inboard propulsion is the advent of pod drives—starting with the Volvo Penta inboard performance system (IPS) and the Cummins-MerCruiser Diesel (CMD) Zeus systems. Pod propulsion has been around for decades in the commercial marine world, powering everything from tugboats to cruise ships, and happily they are now available for powerboats from about 30 feet and up. The IPS and Zeus are designed around steerable pods mounted on the bottom of the boat several feet forward of the transom. Both are powered by high-tech common rail diesel engines controlled and monitored by aerospace-derived electronics, use highly efficient counterrotating propellers, have streamlined low-drag pods analogous to the lower unit of a stern drive, and have propeller thrust lines parallel to the keel.

All of these elements combine to increase efficiency by as much as 30 percent over traditional inboards, while delivering unprecedented maneuverability at the dock using joystick controls. Pod propulsion takes up less interior volume, leaving more space for accommodations, so many boatbuilders are now designing boats around them. Pod-powered boats are so easy to handle that many women previously reluctant to drive a boat when docking are taking over at the helm, and couples are moving up to larger boats that would have been intimidating for them to handle with conventional power. (A number of the boat reviews in part 2 are of Volvo Penta IPS–powered boats. Zeus-powered boats were not available as of this writing.)

Diesel engines with common rail fuel injection technology are also becoming commonplace among larger inboard- and pod-powered boats. Common rail technology results in more efficient, smoother, quieter, and virtually smoke-free operation through sequential fuel injection, as you will see in chapter 8.

Part 2 includes photos and descriptive text of the reviewed boats, as well as full-length boat reviews of a select few of each category. The reviews cover boat construction, hull design, propulsion, a walk-through of the cockpit, topsides, helm station, and cabin, and a report of any sea trials conducted for that model, including information on boat speed and engine noise levels, and, in many cases, data on fuel consumption, economy, and range as well.

These reviews also contain details on a wide variety of other subjects, such as fiberglass resins, stringer systems, and hull-to-deck joints. Topside safety issues such as railing and cockpit height, toe kicks, and nonskid are addressed, as are accommodation layout specifications including berth length, headroom, and emergency egress. Performance considerations like porpoising, noise levels, bow rise, and helm station visibility are also covered.

This second edition also includes insights gained from studies done at J.D. Power and Associates on boats and marine engines based on thousands of surveys sent to boat buyers each year. The studies are designed to help boat and engine manufacturers improve customer satisfaction and loyalty, and to prioritize product improvement efforts based on what's most important to the boatowner. Key findings from these studies have been broken out and made available to you for the first time. See the introduction to part 2 for more information concerning these studies. (I was a director of the marine group at the consumer research firm J.D. Power and Associates, a position that I held for five years. Additionally, over the course the last few years J.D. Power and Associates became part of The McGraw-Hill Companies, which is also the parent of International Marine, the publisher of this book. These circumstances gave me and International Marine an opportunity to add this compelling data.)

The results derived from the J.D. Power studies are a treasure trove of information that will help you shop for your next boat with more focus and insight into what makes for a pleasurable boatownership. They will also help you prioritize your own dockside and sea trial inspection criteria. While at J.D. Power and Associates, I came to appreciate the importance of the boat and engine manufacturer both *listening* and *leading*: *listening* to the customer's input on what disappoints and what delights (and everything in between) in order to continually improve the product; and, *leading* the way by introducing new features and benefits the customer might never have imagined were possible.

The second edition of *Sorensen's Guide to Powerboats* aims to be the most comprehensive source of pleasure boat information available anywhere. Everything ranging from seaworthiness to sight lines, bass boats to motor yachts, rudders to anchor pulpits, even advice on how to conduct a sea trial—it's all here. I hope you enjoy the book and that it helps you to make the best possible choice when you buy your next boat. I welcome your feedback and questions at info@sorensensguide.com.

Acknowledgments

Updating this book was, much like writing it in the first place five years ago, a far more comprehensive and time-consuming enterprise than I had envisioned. You'd think I might have learned the first time around.

The process of creating this second edition was greatly facilitated by the support and friendship of Jon Eaton, the editorial director of International Marine, a division of The McGraw-Hill Companies. My editor, Bob Holtzman, an excellent writer and communicator, has been a pleasure to work with, offering sage counsel regarding substance, clarity, and flow.

My thanks to Pete Marlow and Jessica Migdol at J.D. Power and Associates who arranged for permission to use content from the company's annual boat competitive information study, and underwrote a number of the boat reviews in this edition (also available at www.jdpower.com).

I also thank my lovely wife, Sarah, who has been supportive through my many trips around the country sea-trialing and otherwise nosing around boats and during many late nights subsequently spent at home writing about them.

Part 1 How Boats Work

CHAPTER 1

Introduction

Nothing in life is so exhilarating as to be shot at without result.

—Winston Churchill

Welcome to the wonderful world of boating! You may be getting ready to buy your first boat, or maybe you've owned a series of yachts over the last forty years. But whether you're new to the game or an experienced boater, the more you understand about powerboats and yachts, the better. That's what this book is all about—helping you to better understand powerboat design, construction, and performance; in short, what *really* makes a boat tick. You'll learn more about the boat you own now—maybe why it porpoises at high speed, whether your hull is likely to blister, or why the bow rises excessively on plane. Or why a semidisplacement hull is really what you've been looking for all along, or the effect of bulwarks on dynamic stability. And of course my hope is that the reader will be a little more discriminating, and have higher expectations, next time around.

Choosing your next powerboat or yacht can be a perplexing process. There are hundreds of models to choose from, and most of the magazine ads say pretty much the same thing: that Brand X is the best, a revolutionary advance over the competition. Talk is cheap, however, and results speak volumes. Two boats, one well-designed and engineered and the other anything but, might look very similar during a quick tour at a boat show. But taking a closer look in the right places, asking the right questions, and insisting on a prepurchase sea trial will reveal the great gulf that may lie between the two boats' quality, performance, reliability, and longevity.

Even the smallest, simplest boats interact with wind and waves in complex ways. And even if it's basically a hull, an outboard, and a 6-gallon gas tank, you'll want your boat to perform well and to last a long time with minimal maintenance. The bigger the boat, the more complicated it gets with all the extra systems that make life afloat more enjoyable.

Whichever boat you end up buying, the more you know about the hull design's capabilities and limitations, the methods and materials used to build it, the propulsion system that makes it go, and the systems that provide fuel, ventilation, electricity, and fresh and salt water, the better off you'll feel about the experience. And feeling good is what owning a boat is all about.

Philosophy

The first half of the book, chapters 1 through 14, discusses the theory and engineering underlying good powerboat design, with plenty of illustrations to flesh them out. Here we explore questions such as what makes a boat seaworthy, and whether a displacement or planing hull is best for you, what propulsion system is most appropriate, and what to look for in topside safety, engine compartment access, helm station design, accommodations, and so on.

In places this book is opinionated. It reflects, among other things, the philosophy about boats I've developed and refined over recent years evaluating boats for consumers, magazines, and boatbuilders. And, perhaps more fundamentally, it reflects the twenty years I spent in the coast guard and navy, where safety was always the driving concern in our operations. Chapters 2 and 12 are dedicated to seaworthiness and safety afloat.

Not that I confuse a destroyer with a walk-around very often, but there are elements of design that are common to both, and there is much that the builders of pleasure craft can learn from military and commercial vessels. So the book is informed, among other things, by navy and coast guard design practices and assumptions, and ventures to say where they reasonably apply to your boat. Likewise, I will bring in standards applied to commercial vessels issued by regulatory bodies such as the American Bureau of Shipping (ABS) and the Maritime and Coast Guard Agency of Great Britain (MCA).

In a few places I may sound annoyed with boats that are, to put it charitably, unwisely designed—for instance with 18-inch-high bow railings that are placed just right to catch your ankle; with foredecks that slope like ski jumps; with an absence of flotation foam or compartmentation to limit flooding; or with helm stations designed by stylists rather than ergonomics experts. It *is* frustrating to see how close some models come to being really great boats—if just a little more thought and care had gone into their design. It generally doesn't cost any more to build a boat that's practical and safe as well as good looking. On the other hand, it's the rare boat that doesn't have at least a few positive traits going for it, and most have a lot going for them. Even with a problematic boat, it could be that the judicious investment of a relatively small amount of money could bring it up to snuff.

Perception and perspective are what I hope you will gain from this book. You can skim through the chapters in any order you like, of course. But, if you read it in order, from the Seaworthiness and Other Mysteries chapter (chapter 1) through the Finding Your Next Boat chapter (chapter 14), you'll find that each chapter, to some degree, builds on the last. For instance, it helps to understand the difference between static and dynamic stability (in chapter 2) before brushing up on weight distribution, propeller pocket design, and dynamic instabilities (in chapter 4).

Picking the right *type* of boat is also key to getting the most enjoyment out of it. Center consoles are great fishing boats, but you wouldn't want to spend a weekend on one. A deep-V is often the way to go offshore, but forget about cruising the Erie Canal in one. An express cruiser eliminates the ladder to the bridge, but you give up a climate-controlled saloon, and so on. As we'll see, it's important to first clearly define your expectations and needs, and then find a boat whose layout, features, and hull form best meet them.

Just like the foundation of a house, the hull of a boat, including its shape, is the entering argument as to its suitability for your purposes. A boat might have the perfect cabin layout, great helm visibility, and a family-safe topsides, but you'd better check out the hull design before making a decision. That 35-footer with the extra cedar-lined locker and bigger berth in the forward stateroom probably gained the extra cabin volume by widening the hull forward, and the result will be a really roomy boat with a rough ride. As you'll see in the planing hull chapter (chapter 4), you can't have the biggest, widest 40-footer in the marina *and* get a smooth ride. So the choice depends on your requirements and having realistic expectations; do you want to keep up with that Blackfin 33 and run comfortably at 25 knots in a 3-foot chop, or do you want the biggest cabin in your boat's class?

Boat speed depends on many things, but, along with available *horsepower*, *weight*, and *hull form* are at the top of the list. With few exceptions, a lighter boat goes faster than a heavier one of the same shape. To make a boat light is easy and cheap—you just use less fiberglass and smaller structural members. But to make it both light *and* strong takes time and costs money, as we learn in the chapters on construction. Weight aside, a boat with a flatter bottom goes faster than a deep-V, as we see in chapter 4. But while the 30-foot deep-V will slice through a stiff chop at 25 knots without spilling your coffee, the 50-foot flat-bottom boat will have to slow down to trolling speed to prevent serious injury, let alone discomfort, to its occupants. We'll also look at the relationship between *beam* and *ride quality*: given similar hull forms and propulsion packages, a longer, narrower boat will be consistently faster, smoother riding, and more fuel-efficient than one that has the same interior volume but is shorter and wider. Whether at displacement or planing speeds (assuming both have planing hulls), the longer, narrower boat is simply easier to push. The laws of physics and economy tell us that, in spite of those glossy brochures, you can't get something for nothing.

Reality

The second half of the book is a market survey in the form of boat reviews, where we take all the theory we have learned and apply it to actual boats. In addition, new data from the J.D. Power and Associates boat competitive information studies has been included. We will look at all the major powerboat types—from center consoles to pilothouse motor yachts—to see what each type does well (and not so well) and what to look for in each. You will find in-depth evaluations of representative boats, both new and old, to use as a starting point to assess design, construction, performance, comfort, and safety. All reflect my own independent analysis, judgment, and opinions. Some include performance data, and one may just be of the boat you're looking for. The inclusion of a boat means that I have a generally favorable impression of it, even though I am sometimes critical. Supplementing these full-length evaluations, you will find briefer "snapshot" reviews that cover related models.

A great many boatbuilders, kindly and without reservation, provided photos for use in this section of the book.

So what's the difference, really, between a name-brand and a no-name? It depends. The fact is, between large, premium-brand builders and their small, relatively unknown counterparts, modern manufacturing techniques and materials have tended to level the playing field to a large degree. Using advances like vinylester resins, core bonding putties, simplified vacuum-bagging techniques, and computer-aided design, the little guys can, and often do, turn out excellent products. (Construction techniques are discussed in chapters 6 and 7.) Some little-known boats—especially small boats powered by outboards and stern drives—are better than some of the pricier marquee names. So while that premium-brand cruiser may give an owner bragging rights with their dockmates, the shopper who takes the time to peer through the hype and haze can maybe buy a better boat for less money or a bigger boat for the same expenditure.

There is often a direct correlation between price and quality. Some well-known builders produce wonderful, long-lasting boats, and their prices reflect it. But their sticker prices also reflect the ego appeal and prestige of the *brand*, as well as the boat. A name-brand boat will tend to hold its value better over time, which is an important factor. Top-end boatbuilders may also have higher standards for their dealers than others and keep close tabs on buyers' selling and service experience through customer satisfaction surveys.

You should also factor the dealership into the equation. I'd rather have a decent boat backed by a good dealer than a better boat sold by one who's incompetent or indifferent. You'll feel the same when your starboard cooling pump breaks on a Friday morning just as all your relatives are arriving in town for a long weekend.

I'd even be prepared to pay more for a boat if it's sold by a good, reputable dealer. Dealers need to make a profit, without which they wouldn't be able to afford the people and facilities needed to get your boat back up and running by Friday afternoon. The same goes for working with a broker—find one with a good reputation, and he or she will stay with you and watch out for your interests as you trade up, or down, over the years. We cover boat shopping in chapter 14.

Finally, boatbuilders aren't just competing against each other for your discretionary income—they're also up against golf and ski resorts, travel agents, campgrounds, and motor home manufacturers. And whoever delivers the most satisfaction for harried, hurried, hard-working families gets the nod. The recreational boating industry is in the business of luring people to the boating world, so

it's not surprising that marketing and styling sometimes take on an inflated importance.

In the best boats, however, form and function blend seamlessly to make them safe, reliable, durable, attractive, and ergonomically engineered for the user's pleasure. Building safe and user-friendly pleasure boats isn't rocket science. It's a matter of applying common sense and care in their design and construction.

There are many terrific boats out there. Let's find out what makes them tick.

Sea Ray, the largest boatbuilder in the world, has its craft down to a science. Pictured is the boatbuilder's cruiser facility near Knoxville, Tennessee.

CHAPTER 2

Seaworthiness and Other Mysteries

Falling in love is not at all the most stupid thing that people do—but gravitation cannot be held responsible for it.

—Albert Einstein

A lot has been written about the subject of what makes a vessel "seaworthy," or literally "worthy of the sea." One legal definition says that a vessel is *seaworthy* if she can carry out the mission for which she was intended. Usually, the operative phrase is "fit for her intended purpose." Therefore, a coastal cruiser can be very seaworthy for coastal cruising, but not necessarily offshore voyaging. Yet she is still considered seaworthy for the use for which she is intended; it all depends on which "sea" we're talking about.

For our purposes, though, we apply a more stringent definition. The bottom line? Seaworthiness refers to a vessel's *survivability*, including its ability to resist capsize, and to its behavior, including its controllability and predictability, in rough water. When any vessel puts to sea, it must be able to provide its occupants a high degree of safety and security en route to its destination, and be able to take severe conditions of wind and sea in stride. The farther offshore a vessel travels, and the slower its speed, the higher the expectations for its seaworthiness, since safe haven may well be unreachable in time to avoid heavy seas and high winds. An adjunct to seaworthiness is the matter of *seakindliness*, as we discuss below, which acknowledges the importance of crew comfort to maintaining a vessel in a seaworthy condition.

Every vessel is the end result of a series of competing interests that must be compromised to

A Nordhavn 62 making way in heavy seas — an excellent example of a seagoing vessel built to withstand adverse conditions. The open bow sheds green water quickly, and the aft pilothouse is more comfortable in heavy seas than locations farther forward.

PACIFIC ASIAN ENTERPRISES

achieve the desired mix of qualities. To create enough interior volume to make a yacht attractive to some buyers, a designer may opt for a large deckhouse and full, blunt bow sections, both of which tend to make a vessel less seaworthy. In this and many other cases, a design objective may pull against the interests of seaworthiness. You can't have everything in a boat, no matter what the advertisers say.

Few vessels are designed with just one or two priorities, such as high speed or shallow draft. Most boats can accomplish several missions quite well but are utterly unsuited to some other purposes. By analogy, consider a sports car. A Ferrari can go 180 mph, but it would not be your choice to carry a load of plywood home from the lumberyard. Its utility is limited—and it costs a lot. You buy a Ferrari for speed, not for its climate-control system.

The SUV, on the other hand, represents a host of compromises and is much more useful. It can carry a load of passengers, it goes about half the speed of the Ferrari, it costs far less to buy and maintain, and it even pulls a trailer. But, it also guzzles gas and is far more susceptible to rollover than the Ferrari. Most pleasure vessels are more like the versatile SUV, representing a chain of compromises that produce a marketable product.

Ultimately, it is important that you understand and fully appreciate a boat's capabilities and limitations, and where compromises have been made that affect seaworthiness. In this chapter we look at the essential elements of seaworthiness and the effect on seaworthiness of the many competing design interests. We also point out a few important details to look for when choosing your next boat.

When heading offshore, and especially when your intended track takes you more than a few hours from the nearest safe refuge, safety considerations ought to be at the top of the priority list. For our purposes, *offshore capability* doesn't necessarily imply transoceanic range, simply the capability to operate with a high degree of security in the open ocean, many hours from shelter. For the run from Ft. Lauderdale to the Bahamas, for example, I for one would want offshore capability.

Range alone doesn't convey seaworthiness. Plenty of boats carry fuel enough to cruise hundreds of miles, but I personally wouldn't want to go offshore in them. When you're shopping for seaworthiness, range is important, but only one aspect. Hull design and construction quality are just two of the many other elements impacting seaworthiness.

Now let's consider how stability, roll damping, flooding resistance, steering, and speed, among other things, affect a vessel's seaworthiness. You'll see that naval architects have a language all their own, but the concepts are clear enough, so hang in there as we discuss a few of them.

Stability

For a vessel to be seaworthy, it must first of all resist capsizing under the most severe conditions that it can reasonably be expected to encounter. The term *stability* refers to the tendency of a hull to return to an even keel, or equilibrium, after an upsetting force is applied; stability is the result of the opposing forces of buoyancy and gravity working together. A boat *lists* when one side is more heavily loaded (by gear, equipment, fuel, or even green water on deck) than the other, and it *heels* when a dynamic movement, like a sharp turn or a wave or wind is introduced.

Seaworthy vessels have both *initial stability*, determined largely by the shape of the hull, and *ultimate stability*, governed more by weight distribution vertically within the boat. A boat derives stability from the *righting arm* (RA) created by the opposing forces of buoyancy and gravity. The longer the righting arm, and the greater the vessel's displacement, the more stable it will be.

If this is as clear as mud, don't worry: we'll return to it in a moment. First, however, let's have a look at a few key terms you'll need to understand to know what's going on when your boat rolls and pitches, and keeps coming back to an even keel.

Center of Gravity

Whether you're talking about a boat, an airplane, or a standard poodle, each has a *center of gravity*, called simply the CG (naval architects love acronyms). This is the exact point at which all the weights can be considered to be concentrated, or focused. A boat suspended from its CG would hang sedately in equilibrium, neither listing nor out of trim. So the CG is an absolute point within three dimensions—length, height, and breadth—and its position has three respective components: *vertical*

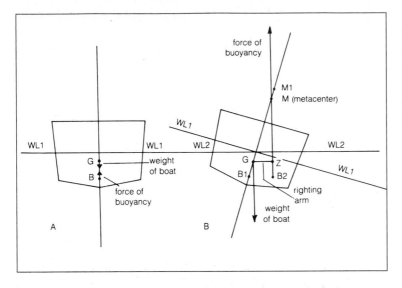

This diagram shows a boat on an even keel and at an angle of starboard heel. The center of gravity (G) does not move as the boat heels to 10 degrees, but the center of buoyancy (B) shifts to starboard (B2). If we were to draw a vertical line straight up from B2, it would intersect another line drawn up from the hull's centerline (like a mast) at a point called the metacenter (M). The amount of force available to return the boat to an even keel (the righting moment) is determined by the boat's weight and by the distance from G to Z, which is a point above B2 and level with G. Through the first few degrees of heel, M (an indicator of initial stability) falls in about the same place as B moves outboard. But as the boat heels beyond about 10 degrees, M ceases to be an indicator of stability since it no longer focuses about a single point above centerline. In other words, M1 migrates substantially from its consistent low-heel-angle position (M).

ADAPTED FROM ARMSTRONG, *GETTING STARTED IN POWERBOATING*

(VCG is usually measured from the keel or design *baseline*), *longitudinal* (LCG can be measured from either the transom or the bow at the waterline), and *transverse* (TCG is measured from a vessel's fore-and-aft centerline).

To get us thinking spatially, a typical express sportfisherman's LCG might be located 40 percent of the waterline length forward from the stern, the VCG will be near the top of the engines, and the TCG should be exactly on the centerline. In a planing powerboat, the VCG will be well above the waterline. On a deep-draft sailboat with a ballasted keel, the VCG will often be below the waterline. On a typical displacement hull, the CG will be farther forward and deeper than in the sportfisherman.

Designers list all the weights in a boat, including the hull, superstructure, engines, fuel, water, cabinetry, appliances, and so on, and record their centers of mass to determine precisely (from a sum of vectors) where the CG should be. Since the height of the VCG is so critical to stability, a builder can conduct an *inclining experiment* to confirm it; more on that in a moment. But to be considered seaworthy, a vessel's VCG has to be low enough to ensure adequate stability.

Buoyancy

Archimedes had it figured out in 250 B.C. The force of buoyancy acting on an immersed object equals the weight of the water displaced. So, just as gravity pushes down, buoyancy pushes up. In fact, a vessel floats because the pressure or buoyancy acting on the hull equals the weight of the boat. It doesn't matter whether the hull is made of wood, fiberglass, or steel; the buoyancy is determined by the *volume* of water the hull skin displaces. When a boat is at rest, gravity and buoyancy are in equilibrium. Add more weight, and the hull sinks lower until the added buoyancy, and upward pressure, reaches a new equilibrium.

Just as a boat has a center of gravity, it also has a *center of buoyancy*. If you were able to freeze the water your boat is floating in, and then lift the boat out with a crane, the hole your boat left in the ice would have a certain shape and volume. If you were to fill the hole in the ice with water and let *it* freeze, it would equal the weight of the boat. Now lift the frozen block of water out of the ice, and you will find that it, too, has a center of gravity, in three dimensions, just as the boat does. And that point corresponds to the center of buoyancy (CB), the exact point at which all buoyant forces acting on the hull are concentrated. The three dimensions of that point correspond to the hull's *longitudinal center of buoyancy* (LCB), *vertical center of buoyancy* (VCB), and *transverse center of buoyancy* (TCB), respectively.

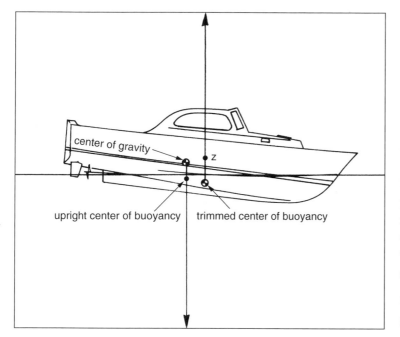

center of gravity

z

upright center of buoyancy   trimmed center of buoyancy

As the hull buries its bow or stern, B shifts and the hull finds its new equilibrium. The distance from G to ever-changing B determines the righting arm (GZ) that works to return the hull to equilibrium. Concentrating weight amidships results in a boat that buries its bow and stern less in rough water. Less pitching (and rolling) make a boat not only faster, but more comfortable (seakindly) in a seaway.

ADAPTED FROM LARSSON AND ELIASSON, *PRINCIPLES OF YACHT DESIGN*

Trim

Trim refers simply to the boat's fore-and-aft attitude, viewed from the side, with respect to the water surface. A boat is said to be at zero trim when it is floating on its design waterline. Trim can vary due to weight being added or removed in the bow or stern. It can also be affected by the dynamic lift of water flow along the bottom of a moving hull. A boat with a lot of extra weight aft is said to be trimmed down by the stern. A planing boat at cruising speed invariably runs with the bow raised

in relation to the stern—say at a 4-degree trim angle (with the bow angled 4 degrees upward)—since the *center of dynamic lift* (CDL; see page 28) is (or should be) forward of LCG.

LCG always corresponds with LCB, which means the total force of gravity is balanced with the total force of buoyancy, and the boat rests at a corresponding depth and trim angle in the water. As weight is shifted forward and aft or side to side inside the boat, the center of buoyancy shifts to match the new CG. If you haul a 900-pound tuna through the transom door, the boat's LCG shifts aft, and so does the hull's LCB as the volume of water displaced aft increases to compensate for the added weight. When a new equilibrium is reached, you'll be trimmed down by the stern a degree or two.

Longitudinal Center of Flotation

A couple more buoyancy terms, and we're ready to move on. The *longitudinal center of flotation* (LCF) is the center of the vessel's waterplane area, or "footprint" at the waterline. It's the point in the vessel longitudinally at which weight can be added without changing the fore-and-aft trim, and the point about which the hull rotates longitudinally when weight is added or removed fore or aft. LCF acts like the pivot point in the middle of a seesaw.

We already know that the LCB is the same as the center of gravity of the water displaced by the hull, or our block of frozen water, and the LCF is the center of the hull's waterplane. But unless we're talking about a floating shoe box, the LCB and the LCF won't line up at the same spot, since hull shape changes from the waterplane on down to the keel.

How much the hull immerses and trims (rotates) longitudinally with weight changes is also of interest to naval architects, so they've come up with a couple more catchy names for us to remember.

Adjusting Trim

Trim behavior may be intuitively obvious: add weight forward of the LCF and the bow trims down; add weight aft, and the stern settles. If the added weight is far enough forward, the stern will also come up, and vice versa. The effort, or moment (force times distance), that it takes to change the trim a total of an inch (adding up the changes forward and aft) is called the *moment to trim* an inch, or MT1. If the bow immerses 1 inch, and the stern emerges 1 inch, the trim has changed 2 inches. If a moment equal to MT1 is applied, the total change in trim is 1 inch, for instance when the bow goes up ½ inch the stern goes down ½ inch. The math is simple; moving 400 pounds 2 feet aft anywhere in the boat creates an 800-foot-pound moment. Knowing MT1 can help if you decide to relocate a heavy object in your boat, like a generator or water tank. When estimating MT1, a coefficient based on the hull form under consideration can also be used. For a rough approximation, you can multiply 0.38 by the waterplane squared divided by the waterline beam. Let's see how this works out for the 44-foot planing boat in the accompanying text. The waterplane area is an estimated 336 square feet. Square 336, divide by the 12-foot waterline beam, and multiply by 0.38, and you find that the MT1 is 3,575 footpounds. So, for example, adding a 500-pound weight 7 feet forward of the LCF will change the trim 1 inch. Since the LCF is roughly 36 to 40 percent forward of a planing hull's stern, weight added at the stern of a planing hull will raise the comparatively narrow bow more than it will sink the wide stern. In our example, the bow might rise 0.6 inch while the stern sinks 0.4 inch.

A figure called *pounds per inch immersion* (PPII) tells us how much weight has to be added at the LCF to make the boat settle an inch deeper in the water. Accurate PPII and MT1 figures should be available from the designer of your boat. It is a good idea to consult a naval architect before shifting or adding a significant amount of weight on the boat. To estimate PPII for a planing boat, you first need to estimate waterplane area. Multiply length times maximum beam (at the waterline) and multiply that product by 70 percent. So, a 44-foot boat with a 40-foot waterline length and a 12-foot waterline beam would have a waterplane of about 336 square feet (70 percent of a 40- by 12-foot rectangle). A cubic foot of seawater weighs 64 pounds, and a 1-inch-thick slice of that cubic foot weighs 5.33 pounds. Multiply 336 by 5.33 and we get 1,791 pounds-per-inch immersion for our 40-footer. For a displacement vessel, the figure to multiply the L × B rectangle by might be closer to 65 percent, yielding a waterplane of 312 square feet and a PPII of 1,163. The PPII usually goes up as a hull sinks into the water, as hulls tend to get wider above the design waterline.

Initial and Ultimate Stability

Now that we know some terminology, let's take a look at how stability works. The water supports the boat, at rest in calm water, with a buoyant force equal to the weight, or displacement, of the vessel. In the accompanying figure (page 8), as the hull rolls to one side, the center of buoyancy (B1) shifts outboard to B2, immersing the down side of the hull and raising the opposite side. Because the center of buoyancy shifts while the center of gravity does not, a righting arm (RA) is created that works to return the boat to an even keel. The righting arm is determined by the distance from the center of gravity to a point Z, which falls above the new center of buoyancy. For this reason, the righting arm is referred to on the stability diagram graphically as GZ (but mathematically it's the RA). Gravity pushes down and buoyancy pushes up, with both forces working to return the boat to an even keel. As the roll increases initially, so does the magnitude of the righting force represented by GZ.

Any seaworthy boat is stable to some degree. But it's important to understand the relationship among buoyancy, gravity, and the boat's VCG, and the two different but connected ways we speak about stability. It turns out that hull shape has the most to do with influencing stability as it starts to tip to one side; this early phase of the roll we call *initial stability*. But once the list reaches around 10 degrees or so, VCG starts to matter *more* (though hull *shape* still matters) since its height begins to have an increasing influence on stability; so *ultimate stability* refers to a vessel's tendency to right itself from more extreme angles of heel. A planing boat can *feel* deceptively stable when compared with a round-bilge displacement cruiser of the same size, but the latter will invariably be able to survive a far greater roll than the former.

The boat itself knows nothing at all about these arbitrary terms, and there is no magic point at which different laws of physics apply. It's just that with a dramatic shift sideways in CB, hull shape has the most effect on the hull's initial tendency to return to equilibrium with the water's surface. That's why a convertible sportfisherman *feels* so stable—it has a relatively flat, wide, and shallow bottom—in spite of its fairly high VCG. But as RA increases with greater angles of list, it's easy to see that the CG's height above the keel, or VCG, has a greater bearing on stability. That convertible will capsize when the displacement hull is still picking up righting moment.

So, naval architects refer to initial stability as the tendency of a vessel to right itself from small angles of heel due to the shape of the hull bottom. Initial stability is also referred to as *form* stability, because the length of the righting arm developed depends on the shape, or form, of the hull. It's called *initial* stability because hull form predominates in the stability equation only through the first 10 or 12 degrees of list. After that, weight distribution (VCG) starts to have relatively more to say about stability. Initial stability is usually calculated for a hull at rest or at slow speeds in calm water. It remains predictable at speed, but only as long as the wave train (the varying waterline created by the hull-generated waves along the hull) is known and does not substantially alter the buoyant forces.

The shape of the hull determines the height of its *metacenter*, commonly and cleverly called M for short, and M is the first thing to establish when determining initial stability. M is the point where lines drawn vertically from the upright center of buoyancy (CB) and the centers at various small angles of heel intersect. These lines tend to converge about the same point until the hull reaches 10 or 12 degrees of heel, and then they start to scatter and become useless as a stability indicator. M can be determined mathematically using the hull lines drawings, since the hull shape, or area exposed to the water at various angles of heel, can be calculated. The distance GM is called the *metacentric height*. The greater it is, the higher the initial stability.

Again, the horizontal distance from CG to a line drawn vertically from CB (a point called Z) represents the righting arm (RA) working to right the vessel. The magnitude of the righting arm, labeled GZ in the drawing, varies with the angle of heel.

Engineers conduct an inclining experiment to find, or verify, the height of VCG, just in case they miscalculated when adding up all the vessel's component weights prior to or during construction. In an inclining experiment, weights are placed off-center to make the vessel list to one side, usually up to 3 or 4 degrees. Knowing precisely how much the vessel displaces (weighs), how much the inclining weights themselves weigh, and how far off-center they're placed, the designer can calculate the effort the hull is making to resist listing. This effort is reflected in the hull's righting arm multiplied by the vessel's displacement, which equals the *righting moment*.

At this point the designer knows the magnitude of the righting arm and thus the length of GZ and can pinpoint the heeled center of buoyancy from hull shape. From this information the vertical center of gravity can be located so as to calculate the righting arm magnitude, GZ. Now the designer can calculate GM, which is the distance from M down to VCG, and once the height of VCG is

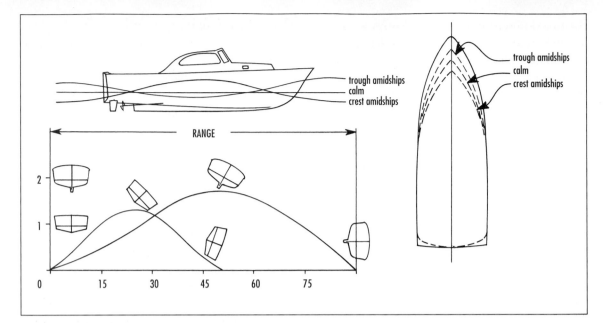

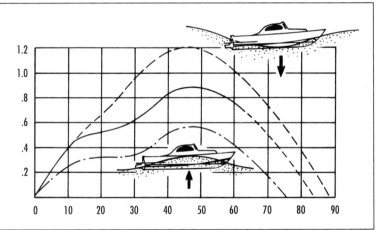

Above: A typical righting arm curve for a displacement hull that peaks at about 46 degrees and reaches its point of zero stability at some 85 degrees. If this vessel is heeled, say, to 60 degrees, the area to the right inside the curve represents the energy remaining to keep the vessel from capsizing. The planing hull's righting arm falls to zero at 50 degrees of heel or even less. **Right:** Shows the great difference between static stability calculations and actual dynamic stability, particularly when running downsea, in waves the same length as the hull (which will move at nearly the vessel's displacement hull speed, incidentally). Few owners, and, for that matter, not all boat designers, factor in the loss of (dynamic) stability that occurs when running in a seaway, straddling the crest of a wave.

TOP: ADAPTED FROM LARSSON AND ELIASSON, *PRINCIPLES OF YACHT DESIGN*

RIGHT: ADAPTED FROM MARCHAJ, *SEAWORTHINESS*

known with certainty, *ultimate stability* can be accurately calculated and displayed on a chart called the *curves of stability*.

Remember that GM is only useful in evaluating the vessel's *initial* stability. That's because M, the

spot where B intersects initially, starts to scatter at higher inclination angles.

Ultimate stability is also referred to as *weight stability* because vertical center of gravity (VCG), rather than hull shape, is most important at more extreme heeling angles. Beyond 10 degrees or so of heel, depending on hull shape in cross section, the metacenter starts to move. At this point, the naval architect uses VCG and the transverse center of buoyancy (TCB) to establish the righting arm (or RA, shown as GZ on the diagram on page 9). Then, RA is multiplied by the vessel's displacement to determine the righting moment (RM) at successive angles of heel. The stability curve is the product of those calculations, showing in graphic form the vessel's righting moment plotted successively through the stability range. Stability curves for ships and large yachts are usually drawn for light-, half-, and full-load displacements.

As the accompanying diagrams indicate, a vessel's stability curve is typically somewhat bell shaped, with the maximum righting arm developing about halfway to capsize. Some vessels' stability curves are irregular, reflecting the equally irregular shape of the hull and superstructure as they pick up buoyancy while listing. A vessel's ultimate stability, then, is the angle at which the righting arm retreats to zero. This point of no return, or point of vanishing stability, is the angle of heel at which neutral equilibrium is reached, and at which capsize is likely to occur; this point is represented by the right-hand side of the curve where the righting arm intersects the zero-righting arm line.

RM represents the energy available to return a hull to an even keel. Hence the importance of knowing a vessel's exact displacement when calculating its stability curves. And displacement is crucial to seaworthiness: all else being equal, a heavier vessel is more seaworthy than a lighter one of similar size and shape, since RM is a function of vessel weight. As mentioned, metacentric height is no longer a consideration when we're working with angles of heel past 10 degrees.

For some cruising sailboats and displacement trawlers, the range of positive stability can reach 130 or more degrees of heel. Some rescue craft and sailboats are stable at all angles of heel, even fully inverted, with a low center of gravity and a high, watertight and buoyant superstructure allowing them to roll 180 degrees and quickly return to an even keel. For navy destroyers, and many other ships, the figure is closer to 60 to 70 degrees. These displacement hulls have a low CG and moderate GM (metacentric height). Planing powerboats might have a range of stability as low as 45 degrees or even less.

Moderate GM

Depending on the hull, there is always an acceptable range of GM; it can be too low or too high. In fact, the most seaworthy vessel is one with moderate GM and low CG; too much GM is not a good thing for ultimate stability. Excessive GM indicates a hull that relies on great beam, rather than a low CG, for its stability. For that reason, ultimate stability in high-GM vessels drops off more quickly compared with those of moderate GM.

High GM makes a vessel follow wave slopes more closely, which means it will heel over farther as it rides up a wave crest, and then be more susceptible to capsize when hit broadside by the water jet produced by a breaking wave. High GM also makes for a stiff, uncomfortable motion with high roll and pitch accelerations. The snap roll created by these high accelerations can be dangerous as well as uncomfortable. Moderate GM, on the other hand, makes for a very long, deep roll period and low accelerations. The significant form stability of a high-GM hull is a double-edged sword, then, acting to make the hull conform more readily to wave action, and less resistant to capsizing in heavy seas.

As a general rule, seaworthy displacement hull vessels have moderate GM, a relatively narrow beam, deep draft, and heavy displacement, which results in a longer roll period, a greater range of stability, and the ability to resist capsize much better than other vessels.

Planing versus Displacement Hulls

Planing boats have relatively wide, flat, shallow bottoms with hard chines (the corners formed by the intersection of the hull sides and bottom) that create great initial stability, but their ultimate stability, the point at which the forces working to right the boat reach zero, generally occurs below 50 degrees. The ultimate stability of most planing vessels is limited by their relatively high VCG and shallow hulls. By contrast, as discussed, a well-designed displacement hull might have a range of positive stability of 130 degrees or more.

As a typical planing hull heels to one side, the hull's buoyancy outboard increases rapidly (more rapidly than a round-bilge hull) as the chine submerges. That's why a flat-bottom *planing* hull has a shorter, stiffer, less comfortable roll period than a displacement hull, and a deep-V will roll more than a modified-V. The flatter the bottom, and the beamier the boat (and the correspondingly greater the GM value), the stiffer the roll and the greater the initial stability.

Displacement hulls rock and roll more easily, because the shape of the bottom doesn't resist rolling nearly as effectively. Unlike a planing hull, there are no hard chines to create lots of buoyant force or lift outboard, just slack bilges (with a large, gentle radius at the bottom–hull side intersection) that are designed to minimize resistance to forward motion. In other words, because the hull is rounded in cross section, the volume of water displaced at the boat's extreme beam changes very little as the hull starts to incline to one side. Since the center of buoyancy doesn't shift outboard as dramatically in a roll, there's less righting moment created at small angles of heel to return the vessel to an even keel. But even though deep, narrow, round-bottom displacement hulls roll easily initially, they can, and usually do, have tremendous *ultimate* stability because of their lower centers of gravity.

Since a planing hull is relatively shallow, the VCG can only get so low in relation to total hull volume. A deeper-draft trawler-style displacement hull can use fuel, liquid ballast, machinery, and even fixed interior or keel-mounted ballast to make VCG very low. This creates a strong righting moment that, working with the hull's shifting center of buoyancy, results in tremendous ultimate and reserve stability. (When looking at a stability curve, the area to the right of the present angle of heel is *reserve stability*; this represents the energy, in the form of righting moment, that remains to prevent capsize.) Although a sportfisherman or express cruiser's stiff roll period makes it feel more stable, most displacement hulls keep gaining righting arm long after a planing hull's stability starts to drop off. Once again,

the center of gravity—not the hull shape—is the final arbiter of ultimate stability at angles of heel past 10 degrees. That's why it's important to keep heavy weight low in the boat and to minimize weight additions above the center of gravity.

Surviving a Roll

Rollover capability is touted by some displacement trawler builders, and the ability to survive a roll of 360 degrees certainly adds substantially to a vessel's seaworthiness. But this claim needs a reality check. Any vessel with a 360-degree range of positive stability must have a low center of gravity as well as significant buoyancy high in the hull and superstructure. To maintain this buoyancy as the vessel rolls to 180 degrees, windows, doors, and hatches must be watertight. They must remain watertight, too, and be able to withstand the significant forces caused by the static pressure and tremendous dynamic impact of seawater.

Most yachts have large windows in the saloon and pilothouse, and these are the most vulnerable during a rollover. And of course the larger the window, the more susceptible it is to breaking. Either the glass must be very thick, or they must be covered (before the rollover, obviously) with storm covers or shutters of fiberglass, metal, or acrylic. A better solution, from a seaworthiness perspective, is to keep the windows small and the glass thick, but unfortunately portholes in a dimly lit saloon don't sell boats. Nevertheless, smaller, thicker windows would eliminate the need for window covers, which would not likely be installed in time in the normal course of events, anyway.

Machinery must keep running after a rollover, and the amount of water shipped into the engine room must be limited by the aggregate volume of gooseneck combustion air intakes. Obviously, furniture and all other large objects must be secured to the deck, or storage space inside lockers must be provided in such a vessel, and seat belts should be provided for all passengers. Spare handheld radios and GPS receivers will also be a good idea, since their antennas are likely to be lost in a rollover.

The larger the window, the thicker the glass should be to resist breaking by wave impact. This Nordhavn's saloon windows are a full ½ inch thick. NORDHAVN

Storm windows made of impact-resistant Lexan are a great thing when the weather deteriorates at sea. These sheets bolt on from the outside, so it's important to get them mounted well before the strong winds hit. NORDHAVN

It's important to remember that initial and ultimate stability figures are applicable only to vessels in an *intact* condition, meaning they have suffered no structural damage that leads to hull flooding, like a hole in the bottom, that would affect stability. When a hull floods, even partially, significant stability and reserve buoyancy are lost. And, of course, initial and ultimate stability figures are only accurate for a vessel in the static condition—that is, when the vessel is not being tossed by seas and buffeted by wind.

Dynamic Stability

Static stability calculations are only the starting point when determining seaworthiness. *Dynamic stability* is an entirely different kettle of fish. The position of a hull on a wave, whether astride the peak (which diminishes stability) or in the trough (which increases stability); the area and shape of the hull exposed to tremendous breaking-wave energy; the synchronicity between a hull's roll period and the relative wave period; and the variation in trim as a hull pitches—all these are elements that affect a vessel's actual stability. They're also very difficult to predict accurately, which accounts, in part, for their relative obscurity. However, relying solely on static stability calculations to determine a vessel's seaworthiness can have disastrous results.

Dynamic stability can be defined as the tendency of a vessel, by virtue of its displacement, mass distribution, and shape, to return to equilibrium after being upset by the forces of wind and sea. It is possible for a vessel that has impressive static stability to be dangerously unstable dynamically. The stability curves produced by inclining experiments and hydrostatic calculations are a good start for determining a vessel's stability and seaworthiness, but they are useful mainly for comparing similar vessels to one another. They are not meant to be predictive of real-life vessel behavior. Broaching, rolling, and capsizing are *dynamic* events that have no sympathy for carefully calculated stability curves. When your boat is at sea in high seas and strong winds, that calculated 70-degree (or whatever it is) angle of vanishing (zero) righting arm in no way ensures that it will actually survive a dynamic roll to that angle without capsizing.

A hull with a very large, lightweight superstructure may be stable when inclined at the dock, but take it offshore and put it beam-to a 50-knot wind, and watch that windage go to work! In an 80-knot beam wind, a navy frigate will reach some 30 degrees of semipermanent heel, using up half its stability range even before wave action is taken into account. So while a vessel with a large superstructure may have as large a static righting arm as the low-profile trawler in the next slip, it'll be the first to capsize in extreme offshore conditions. Likewise, a wave is a moving force, and imparts its *inertia* (resistance to changing velocity or direction) to any hull it comes into contact with. Both wind and wave forces will diminish stability, making the stability curves, predicated on static conditions, unreliable in a seaway.

Another way of looking at it is that dynamic forces reduce reserve stability. Your yacht's stability curve may indicate that positive RA is present up to a 70-degree list. However, the inertia from a relatively small wave impacting the hull at the wrong time—say, when the hull is rolling away from the breaking wave at a 50-degree angle of heel at the time of impact—can easily capsize the vessel. If that same vessel was rolling *toward* that breaking wave when they met at 50 degrees of heel, its chances of surviving are greatly improved. Once again, the inertia created by the vessel's lateral movement opposes the inertia of the wave in this case, adding to its effective dynamic stability. Likewise, changing course induces a heeling moment as the rudder is put over, and the results are predictable in calm water. But when a boat turns to head upwind while running down the face of a wave in a quartering sea, the results can be anything but predictable or controllable. The same thing goes for a strong gust of beam wind at just the wrong moment.

It's important to distinguish between the two kinds of inertia at work in any vessel. *Mass inertia* is the energy stored as a result of the vessel's weight and weight distribution. *Waterplane inertia* results from the area, or the size and shape, of the hull at the waterline. Both influence vessel motion and seaworthiness.

Pitch, Roll, Yaw, Heave, Surge, and Sway

A boat is capable of a combination of six motions in a seaway. The first three are rotations about an axis: the bow (and stern) *pitches* up and down (about a transverse axis), the boat *rolls* from side to side (about a longitudinal axis), and the boat *yaws* about a vertical axis (the boat changes direction, or course, about a pivot point). The remaining three are linear, or nonrotational. *Heave* is a vertical movement, such as when a vessel is rising bodily on a wave. *Surge* is a fore-and-aft movement, and *sway* is a transverse or side-to-side movement. Combinations of these movements are felt at sea: riding up and over a wave would produce both heave and pitch; being hit by a wave amidships would create both roll and sway movements, for instance. A particularly exciting combination would be a roll and a yaw, which, when running down a wave, may result in a *broach*, with the stern being thrown ahead by a following sea while the bow digs in and stays put (relatively speaking).

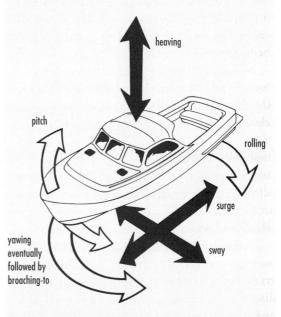

The vessel's motions in all these directions determine its seakindliness and controllability in a seaway.

ADAPTED FROM MARCHAJ, *SEAWORTHINESS*

A vessel's displacement has a great deal to do with its seaworthiness, for reasons of static stability as well as resistance to movement. As discussed, whereas a light, shallow boat will quickly conform to a wave gradient, and will be easily overwhelmed by a breaking wave, a heavy, deep vessel puts up a lot of resistance, through sheer mass and inertia, to being buffeted about. It conforms much less readily to a wave face. Grab hold of a 25-foot outboard and push it away from the dock, then do the same thing to a 60-footer. It takes a lot more effort to get the bigger boat moving, water and air resistance notwithstanding.

Another factor that plays a role in calculating capsize probability is the vessel's *roll moment of inertia* (RMI): its resistance to being rolled by outside, dynamic forces such as waves. The vessel's mass, and especially its mass distribution, is the main factor. In this regard, the boat behaves much like a flywheel. A larger-diameter flywheel resists changes in speed more than a smaller one of the same weight, and therefore is able to store more inertia in the form of rotational energy.

If significant weights are located well away from the center of gravity and the boat's roll axis, RMI increases. For instance, a tuna tower, though relatively light, extends a long way from the center of gravity, so it tends to add significantly to the roll moment of inertia, and can therefore work to resist a boat's initial roll movement caused by wave action. A hull with a larger RMI better resists roll *accelerations*, just as the larger flywheel does—it takes more effort to *start* it rolling.

A good analogy is in figure skating; when skaters pull their arms in, reducing the mass moment of inertia, the spin increases in speed. The 1979 Fastnet disaster, in which an offshore sailboat race was caught by a powerful storm, provides an illustration of the effect of *roll inertia* on dynamic stability. Severe weather caused many dismastings and—counterintuitively—it was discovered that dismasted yachts had a *greater* tendency to roll over than yachts with intact masts. Tank tests later confirmed this observation.

Roll Damping

All vessels have a certain amount of *damping* ability, which is the resistance to roll and pitch created by their mass and moment of inertia and by the drag of surrounding water. The more a hull is able to attenuate the energy from wave and wind action, the less it will roll, and the more stable it will be. Full keels, fixed bilge keels, fin stabilizers, paravanes, rudders, running gear, and, to a great extent, hard chines all dissipate roll. This is because of their mass and moment of inertia about the center of gravity, as discussed above, and because of their frictional drag underwater. A hull carries along with it a *boundary layer* of entrained water, known when headway is on as *frictional wake current*. This layer of water creates an additional damping effect caused by the frictional drag, or resistance, to the hull's movement. A hull with a larger underwater surface area carries more entrained water along with it, and this added drag makes the vessel less susceptible to wave action, and diminishes accelerations in all directions.

Planing hulls are susceptible to dynamic forces all their own, and the way in which a particular boat handles these forces has a direct bearing on its seaworthiness. The hull essentially flies on the surface of the water, with more of the vessel's weight supported by hydrodynamic pressure than buoyancy. Planing hull dynamics, stabilities, and instabilities are covered in more detail in chapter 4.

The brains and muscle behind an active fin stabilizer, viewed from inside the hull.

Complicating this matter of dynamic stability further, if the frequency with which waves impact a hull is in *resonance* with the vessel's natural roll period, a relatively low sea state can end up capsizing an otherwise seaworthy boat. If conditions produce a relatively modest sea on the beam every 4 seconds, and the vessel happens to have a 4-second roll period, this synchronous timing will roll the boat a little farther with each cycle. The same accentuated oscillations can occur in pitching as well as rolling. Fortunately, nature seldom delivers waves hullside with such regularity. The easiest way to avoid this condition is to aggressively alter course or speed to change the frequency with which waves are met. As mentioned, vessels can also either passively or actively reduce, or *dampen*, roll period and amplitude with their keels, fixed bilge keels, paravane "flopper stoppers," or active fin stabilizers.

Stability Works Both Ways

In a sense, stability can be your friend or your foe; it all depends. Within the range of positive RA, buoyancy and gravity are our friends; outside this range, past the angle of maximum righting arm, they work to cause capsize. The same forces that keep a hull on an even keel in calm water act to roll it when inclined on the surface of a wave. A hull beam-to a large wave will try to keep itself on an even keel in relation to the wave surface; a boat floating perpendicular to a 10-degree wave gradient is at equilibrium when heeling at 10 degrees. That's why the most seaworthy hulls have narrow to moderate length-to-beam ratios; they won't seek equilibrium with steep-faced waves as readily as wide-beamed hulls, resulting in a more moderate roll amplitude and, ultimately, a more stable vessel.

Seakindliness

I grew up fishing on semidisplacement boats, operated both planing and semidisplacement rescue boats as a coast guard coxswain and surfman, then spent the better part of fifteen years aboard displacement ships of 4,100 to 10,000 tons. I then started evaluating boats for a living—mostly high-speed,

hard-chine, planing boats. Then one day I found myself back on a semidisplacement Down East–style lobster yacht—a Dyer 40—in a stiff Narragansett Bay chop. The fact is, I'd forgotten how comfortable these semidisplacement boats can be. The Dyer rolled easily in the 2- to 3-foot seas, not too deeply, and certainly not stiffly like the average hard-chine planing hull with its pumped-up GM. The Dyer can't do some things as well as a modern planing hull, such as going fast with high efficiency, but it sure is a comfortable boat to go to sea in.

A seakindly yacht like our redoubtable Dyer 40 is, well, kind to her crew. A naval architect would say that *accelerations* in every direction are within a comfortable range. Such a boat does not pound or snap roll, and in general has an easy motion. It also won't roll too deeply or pitch too heavily. The amount of weight spread out on her waterplane (footprint at the waterline), called *bottom loading*, is within a certain range of moderation; a boat that is too light for its waterplane will bob and heave rapidly and dramatically, while one that is too heavy will lurch and surge about heavily and will require a prodigious power plant to plane. Heavier boats have an easier motion because of their added inertia, or resistance to movement, and diminished accelerations in all directions. Note that you don't see many lobstermen working all day from hard-chine, light hulls. Their round-bilge, moderate-beam (and moderate GM) boats have an easy motion that's lacking in their hard-chine, beamier cousins. Lacking accelerometers, seakindliness is difficult to quantify, but like a good performance of a Brahms piano concerto, you know one when you experience it—especially when you get out on different boat types.

As a rule of thumb, the wider, flatter, and lighter a boat is—or the more extreme in any one of those elements—the less comfortable it will be, at speed or at rest. If you want comfort and seaworthiness, there's just no substitute for a narrow, deep, and heavy vessel. Deeper hulls simply dissipate pitch and heave energy more effectively than shallow hulls. Heavy hulls, as we've seen, are more stable be-cause *ultimate stability* comes from the righting moment, a function of GZ times displacement, so it takes more energy to bring such a vessel to capsize. In terms of comfort, a heavier hull's greater mass is also less susceptible to the accelerations and inertia of wave action.

We talk about moderate length-to-beam ratios in the next two chapters, but keep in mind that a 40- by 12-foot boat, while having no more interior volume than a 32- by 14-footer, will deliver a much more comfortable ride, be a better sea boat, and run more efficiently.

The Kadey-Krogen displacement trawler yacht has great reserve (weight) stability, but less form (hull-shape) stability. The hull form of this long-range cruiser necessitates an easy turn of the bilge to reduce wavemaking resistance at its cruising speed of about 8 knots. Active fin stabilizers are designed to reduce rolling by 60 percent or more. KADEY-KROGEN YACHTS

A fine example of a seaworthy pleasure boat, made so by a sharp entry, ample deadrise throughout, and a moderate beam-to-length ratio (44 feet, 6 inches by 11 feet, 4 inches), this Dave Gerr–de-signed Westbourne 44 express yacht will keep steaming in a stiff chop when other boats head for the barn. She's also faster and more easily driven — much more so — than a shorter, wider boat of the same size (volume). The steering station is comfortably far aft, where vertical motions are less pronounced. DAVE GERR

Enhancing Stability

Now we know why hulls roll, but it's also nice to know something can be done about it, at least on displacement vessels. All roll-reducing devices work by introducing a *heeling* moment opposite to that created by sea conditions. The two most common are *paravanes*—mini wings suspended over the side from outriggers and towed through the water—and fixed or active *bilge stabilizers*. Nothing's free in life, though: any appendage added to the bottom of a boat or hauled through the water suspended from

outriggers will add drag, slowing the vessel and di-minishing propulsion efficiency. They are also sub-ject to impact damage from grounding or striking submerged objects.

Paravanes

Commonly seen on shrimpers and trawler yachts, paravanes, or flopper stoppers, passively reduce motion by creating a resistance to a vessel's natural tendency to roll. Suspended from long outriggers to create a significant lever arm, a pair of small para-vanes can work wonders. They even dampen roll with no way on—say, at anchor—but they steadily become more effective as speed is increased. The great advantage of paravanes is that there is no ma-chinery or hydraulics involved, so they're more reli-able than active stabilizers. Disadvantages include that you have to go on deck to deploy them, poten-tially a problem in rough water. They also slow the boat down, perhaps a half knot or so, which can be significant on a 6- or 7-knot vessel over a few thousand miles at sea. In rough conditions, they will also walk in toward the boat on the high side of the roll, and can actually make contact with the hull and get stuck against it by hydrodynamic

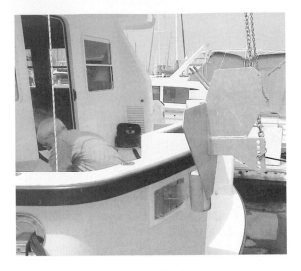

A paravane roll dampener taking a break.   NORDHAVN

pressure. In extreme conditions, especially if set too shallow, they can pull free of the water and go flying toward the boat.

Active Stabilizers

Mechanical bilge stabilizers act like adjustable wings to generate roll-reducing lift at the turn of the bilge. They're mounted at the turn of the bilge and linked to gyros that sense the vessel's motion and continuously adjust the *active* stabilizer fins to counteract roll. When the vessel rolls to port, for instance, the port fin changes its angle of attack to generate upward lift, and the starboard fin angles down to create a downward force. For active fin stabilizers to work effectively, the vessel must have headway on, and the more the better. Fin stabilizers jut out from the bottom of the hull, so they're susceptible to damage by grounding or striking an underwater object, and, like paravanes, they add some drag. They also are susceptible to mechanical failure. But both paravane and active bilge stabilizer systems help address the antiroll needs of a vessel with limited initial stability, which describes the typical full-displacement hull. Depending on the size of the vessel, a fin stabilizer might be 18 inches wide and 36 inches deep. Vosper, Naiad,

Wesmar, and Seabrace are a few prominent fin stabilizer manufacturers.

Bilge Keels

Fixed bilge keels or fins project at right angles from the hull at the turn of the bilge. They extend between one- and two-thirds the length of the hull and might be a foot or more deep on larger yachts. They aren't as effective as active stabilizers but, like paravanes, they reduce roll passively and with minimal drag if they are designed right, which they by no means always are. Bilge keels are generally considered more effective in large ships (about 10 percent dampening, according to some sources) than in small boats (closer to 3 to 5 percent dampening). The lever arm, or amount of useful work they do, is a function of the distance from the center of the bilge keels to the roll axis. Their effectiveness results from the hydrodynamic resistance they create while effectively being pushed sideways through the water as the hull rotates about its roll axis. Bilge keels can be hollow, allowing them to serve as auxiliary fuel tanks, or permitting the addition of lead ballast at their ends, which further reduces rolling through damping, thanks to the addition of mass well away from the roll axis and center of gravity.

Other roll-inhibiting methods include oversized transom-mounted trim tabs that flap up and down independently to minimize roll, and antiroll tanks that rapidly move mass (seawater ballast) from side to side out of phase with the vessel's natural rolling motion (see photo page 65). (Active tanks use pumps and passive tanks use sluice valves.) Icebreakers have tanks on either side of the ship that are rapidly filled and emptied sequentially to create a rolling action to help break up ice.

Whichever type of roll stabilization is selected, a boat with more initial stability will always roll more as it tries to remain square to the slope of the waves. A deep, heavy, long, and narrow displacement hull will have the more comfortable motion, since it is less reactive to wave slope influences. It is

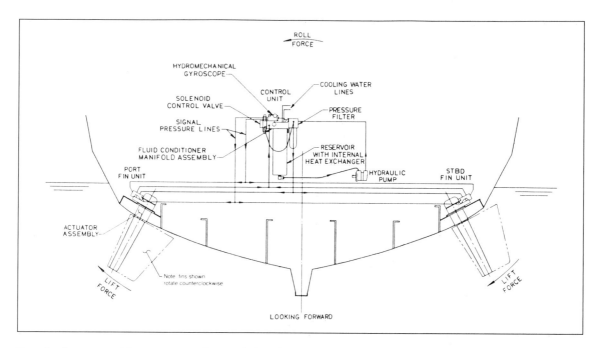

Example of an active stabilizing system. Working similarly to the ailerons on a plane, the fins can actually make a boat roll to either side, much as an airplane banks. A gyroscope senses true vertical and directs the fins to produce a counterroll opposing the natural roll induced by the hull's reaction to wave motion. The result is near-level cruising.

NAIAD STABILIZERS

also possible to add too much weight, or ballast, down low in a hull, resulting in a stiff, jerky motion and too-short roll period. Adding weight above VCG increases the roll period, whereas adding weight below has the opposite effect.

The Effect of Trim on Stability

Static stability calculations also assume that a vessel will not change its fore-and-aft trim as it rolls, but will rotate evenly around a longitudinal axis, like a roast on a spit. This isn't a valid assumption; unless the hull is perfectly balanced in displacement and cross section, trim will vary as a vessel heels. The imbalance is most significant when, for instance, a hull has a narrow bow and full, wide stern. This hull will initially trim by the bow when heeling because of the greater buoyancy in the stern as one side of the hull immerses and the other emerges. This tendency will significantly diminish ultimate stability.

This trimming effect is accentuated in boats that are overly beamy for their waterline length and asymmetrical forward and aft. Trimming moments, in fact, tend to *reduce* actual stability below the figures established using conventional static stability calculations. So, the most seaworthy hulls, while certainly not symmetrical, have well-balanced fore and aft sections, so that trim isn't dramatically altered as they heel over. In practice, the fore-and-aft asymmetry common to any hull form results in changing trim as a vessel heels, and this is usually taken into account in the righting arm curve.

The Effect of Freeboard on Stability

The lower the hull sides, the sooner they will be submerged on the low side of a roll. Higher freeboard picks up buoyancy as the hull rolls; low freeboard would result in buoyancy-derived stability dropping off when the gunwale submerges

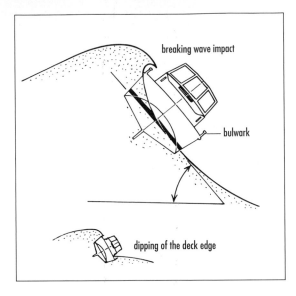

breaking wave impact

bulwark

dipping of the deck edge

There are many dynamic influences acting on a vessel's stability that aren't accounted for in a stability curve. A high-velocity, high-pressure wave jet from a breaker taken broadside can have calamitous consequences. The higher the freeboard, the more surface area on the up-wave side of the boat will be subject to the enormous force of a breaking wave. High freeboard on the down-wave side is a good thing, since the hull will better resist dipping its deck edge and be less prone to "tripping," which would hasten capsize. Should high bulwarks submerge, they may scoop up tons of seawater high on deck.   ADAPTED FROM MARCHAJ, *SEAWORTHINESS*

(assuming the absence of a full-beam, watertight superstructure). There is also a dynamic consideration when a steep wave rolls a boat and breaks against the hull side. Higher freeboard on the *low* side may allow the hull to slide sideways rather than tripping. The tripping effect of a submerged gunwale will make any vessel more susceptible to capsize, even if plenty of static weight stability remains (theoretically) in the righting arm curve. But this, too, is a double-edged sword: the higher freeboard that encourages the low side to slide down the wave rather than trip over it also exposes a larger surface that will absorb more energy of the breaking wave on the high side.

Bulwarks can be a mixed blessing, too. They do a good job of keeping water off the deck when running

into a sea, and add buoyancy initially in a roll. But if the top of the bulkhead is immersed in a roll, tons of water can be trapped temporarily before the scuppers have a chance to drain it overboard, dramatically, if temporarily, causing CG to rise. If a breaking wave jet upwind catches the hull when the lee bulwark is immersed, the tripping force, and lever arm, are intensified, increasing the chances of a capsize.

The same goes for the superstructure; the added buoyancy on the lee side is offset by the added surface area exposed to the breaking wave jet on the windward side. For the one to offset the other, the deckhouse has to be not only watertight, but built stoutly enough (including the doors and windows) to resist impact with solid water. The worst combination, from a dynamic stability perspective, is a combination of a wide beam (and high GM) and low freeboard, since the wider boat will more readily conform to the wave slope gradient, and therefore immerse its lee (low freeboard) gunwale sooner than a narrower hull of moderate GM.

Staying Afloat

The captain of one of the navy cruisers I served on liked to say that the ocean belonged on the outside of the ship, and it was our job to keep it there. I can appreciate his point! The fact is, unless certain precautions are taken during its design phase, a boat can sink very easily. When a hull is ruptured, usually through collision with an underwater object, the ocean will flow in until the water level inside and out is equalized, or the vessel sinks. Whether the hull stays afloat, although deeper in the water than usual, or sinks, depends on its built-in flooding resistance. If the hole, or crack, is of any significant size, don't count on the bilge pumps doing much more than slowly recirculating water from the bilge back into the ocean. So for any boat to have a chance of staying afloat despite a large hull penetration, it must be designed with adequate reserve buoyancy and stability. So, you ask, just how do designers build in flooding resistance to resist sinking in a damaged condition?

When floating normally, on its design waterline, the hull displaces an amount of water equal to its own weight, and so stays afloat. If water floods the hull, something inside the boat must create enough buoyancy to keep the boat from sinking, even with the added weight caused by flooding. So, positive flotation is built in by one or more clever methods.

It would be great if every boatbuilder took staying afloat and controlling free-surface effect as seriously as Ranger. Company founder Forest Wood and president Randy Hopper don't seem too concerned about this Ranger's ability to do both.   GENMAR HOLDINGS, INC.

Many small boats have low-density foam flotation pumped into the voids between the hull and deck liner during construction, so even with a hole in the bottom, the boat will only settle so far before finding equilibrium. The foam fills up the space, or at least enough of it, that flooding would otherwise fill. In fact, boats under 20 feet in length must have sufficient buoyancy, usually provided by foam, to keep the boat not only afloat, but floating *level* after being holed. All that foam, even though of low density, contributes to the hull's *impact resistance* well, and may prevent an underwater collision from penetrating the hull in the first place. Foam replaces belowdecks storage capacity, for sure, but maybe you only need to balance your family's security and your peace of mind with the ability to stow more junk onboard.

Compartmentation

Pumping a 50-footer full of foam is a different story. Foam is heavy, and a bilge space full of it represents lost storage space. Foam also prevents inspection of the hull's structural members and components, and hides problems like wood rot. Foam will also soak up liquids, especially if foam cells have been exposed by cutting. These are reasons why well-designed larger boats depend on *compartmentation* (watertight compartments). This represents another compromise: more watertight compartments make it harder to get around belowdecks.

From a survivability perspective, up to a point, the more compartments the merrier, since a single hole in the bottom will flood a correspondingly small percentage of the hull's volume. That leaves more reserve buoyancy, and stability, to keep you afloat. At one extreme, navy ships longer than 300 feet are "three-compartment ships," which means that any three adjacent compartments can flood completely and the ship will stay upright and afloat in moderate sea conditions. This might require ten watertight bulkheads, dividing the ship into eleven compartments.

Navy ships in the 200-foot range are usually two-compartment ships, since there's a practical limit to how small watertight compartments can be. Large oceangoing yachts settle for fewer watertight bulkheads to make getting around more practical, and those that meet shipbuilding standards organizations' requirements for commercial vessels will typically stay afloat with any one compartment completely flooded. Unfortunately, many oceangoing yachts do not meet a one-compartment standard, though they should by any reasonable standard.

Any larger boat not filled with foam should have, at a minimum, a collision bulkhead forward, watertight bulkheads forward and aft of the engine room, a watertight lazarette bulkhead, and watertight, dogged hatches in the cabin sole serving as a double bottom to contain flooding. This modified compartmentation arrangement will make a boat more apt to survive an underwater hull breach. In the engine room, the most likely location of failed through-hull fittings and hoses, watertight bulkheads will contain the flooding. The limited use of foam within each compartment further contributes to reserve buoyancy.

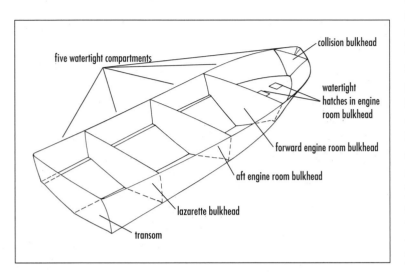

A seaworthy bulkhead configuration provides resistance to progressive flooding.

You can ask your boatbuilder if buoyancy and stability calculations, or real-world testing, have been done to determine if the boat would stay afloat with any one compartment completely flooded. I wouldn't head offshore without an answer, either in writing from the builder, through a design analysis, or by an inspection of the bulkhead arrangements. Otherwise, proceed with the understanding that any hull breach will likely sink your boat—either slowly or quickly, depending on the flooding rate.

The number of compartments, and how far apart the watertight bulkheads are separated, are reflected in a figure called *floodable length*, which is the length of the hull that can be breached and still maintain adequate reserve stability and buoyancy to remain afloat in moderate sea conditions.

The worst situation is to find yourself on a damaged boat that has no compartmentation and with little or no foam flotation built in. If the hole is larger than the bilge pumps can keep up with (and it doesn't take much of a hole to overwhelm even a pair of 5,000 gph bilge pumps), then the boat will sink. I've heard boat salesmen boast about being able to pour a cup of coffee in the bilge under the forward berth and have it drain quickly aft to the lazarette, where it gets pumped overboard. This is not a boat you want to head offshore in. Ironically, many boats come close to achieving subdivision, but builders often cut holes for shafts, wires, or plumbing in the otherwise basically watertight bulkheads. If the public demanded boats that were built with a higher level of survivability, and people were willing to pay for these improvements (which in some cases would require very little modification), all of this would change for the better.

Some will say that these are yachts we're talking about, after all—not coast guard or commercial ships—so what's all this fuss about compartmentation? The fact is, the recreational marine industry could learn much from the commercial and military sectors. When a boat is taking on water or has caught fire, the same principles of sound design would have obvious benefits.

Probably the biggest reason for Boston Whaler's continued popularity is the boats' quality of "unsinkability." Whalers have much to commend them, but they're no better built than some other similar brands. Whaler distinguishes itself from some of its competition by its generous use of structural foam that provides worst-case positive buoyancy. Look at the old ad for the 34-foot Defiance, settled in the water with seacocks fully open and a crowd onboard smiling at the camera. It's a good feeling to know that, no matter what you run into, or what runs into you, your boat is going to stay afloat.

Many trawler yachts have engine rooms that stretch a third or more of the hull's length, making it difficult or impossible for them to stay afloat in the event of major engine room flooding. Adding an athwartships watertight bulkhead somewhere in the middle of the engine room (essentially creating an engine room and an auxiliary machinery room) to such a vessel would make it much more able to survive flooding. It would also make routine maintenance less convenient. Deck hatches below the waterline must also be watertight to restrict flooding in the bilge.

On a boat with a large engine room, installing a bulkhead fitted with a watertight door would be a next-best solution, but make sure to keep the door dogged shut when it's not in use. The compromise is, then, one of habitability against seaworthiness. But few would disagree that the degree of subdivision, and its ramifications, ought to be a matter of intelligent consideration.

So what's reasonable for the average boatowner to expect? Boats smaller than 20 feet are required by the coast guard to have positive buoyancy, usually derived from low-density flotation foam pumped between the hull and deck liner, when swamped with a predetermined load onboard. A boat between 20 and 35 feet should have a combination of foam and compartmentation to keep it afloat. And larger boats can also be made unsinkable (at least from a single hull penetration) with a combination of compartmentation, foam, and watertight hatches and doors. Savvy boatbuilders make their boats unsinkable, then market their superiority to good effect.

Dewatering

Substantial pumping or dewatering capacity is highly desirable. Propulsion engine cooling pumps can have bilge suction pickups installed for dewatering. These two-way valves should be designed to prevent backflooding of the bilge by closing off the through-hull when the bilge suction is open (see chapter 10). Larger electric bilge pumps can have Y-valves for secondary use as backup fire pumps. Main drainage systems can remotely pump out watertight compartments using a common pump and remote-operated valves. In any event, many regulatory and advisory standards for dewatering capacity are grossly underprescribed, if they're mentioned at all, and do not take into account the real-world flooding rates of even small holes just below the waterline.

Four out of five boats that sink do so at the dock, for the excellent reason that that's where they spend most of their time, and there's no one on board to stop the leak. Not surprisingly, failed stuffing boxes and shaft logs, stern-drive seals, through-hull fittings, hoses and clamps, and self-bailing cockpits with scuppers plugged by pine needles, rain, or snow are among the leading causes of sinking dockside. Any through-hull on a powerboat that would be immersed when the boat heels 7 degrees or more should have a seacock. A single intake sea chest, which is essentially a distribution reservoir in the bilge of the boat with a through-hull supplying water to it, is a great way to go, since through-hull fittings are minimized. Engines, genset, air-conditioning, saltwater washdown, and other users can all tap into it.

Learn how to tie your boat up, since being caught under a dock on a rising tide is a surefire way to sink a boat. Make sure the freshwater system hooked up to a dockside connection is sound, or your boat could fill up with nice, clean, potable water and sink right to the bottom. You can install a bilge pump counter to find out how many times the bilge pump cycles on in a given period; excessive pump operation tells you to look for a persistent leak, and all it takes is for the float switch to stick on or the battery to drain to sink the boat. A manual bilge pump in the cockpit is a smart feature, since you can pump even if the bilge is flooded and inaccessible. Well-designed larger yachts have a main drainage system, which consists of a pipe running through the watertight compartments with remotely operated valves that allow, say, the engine-driven seawater pump to dewater the bilge under the forward accommodations. The Sea Key System, for example, can monitor bilge water levels and notify you if it gets too high.

Many small boats sink at sea because of low freeboard, particularly in the case of outboards. Transoms are so low that waves can board, or motor well drain holes are too small to quickly shed water. Worst case, of course, is a transom-mounted outboard without a motorwell. That welcomes boarding seas into the cockpit. That's why I like bracket-mounted outboards and full-height transoms. If the cockpit deck is too low, so is reserve buoyancy. The boat will have trouble surviving a big wave over the stern. Raw-water cooling system failure is another culprit, as is a missing drain plug on small baots.

If you think a 2,000 gph (gallons per hour) bilge pump is ample security against minor flooding, then consider that with typical static head pressure and hose restriction losses, you actually have a 1,000 gph bilge pump, which translates to 16 gpm (gallons per minute). All it will do is keep ahead of incidental leaks and accumulations, and many small cruisers have pumps of less than half that capacity. Bilge pumps are marketed and rated in gph rather than gpm because the higher figure sounds better. Commercial dewatering and firefighting pumps are rated in gpm. The accompanying chart gives approximate flooding rates in gpm versus hole size and depth below the waterline.

If you consider a hole as small as 2 inches in diameter, 2 feet below the waterline, the flow rate into the boat would be about 110 gallons per minute, or 6,600 gallons per hour! A boat equipped with

Approximate Flooding Rates in Gallons per Minute

Hole Size	Depth below Waterline			
	6"	12"	24"	36"
1/2"	4	5	7	18
3/4"	8	12	16	20
1"	14	20	28	35
2"	55	80	110	140
4"	220	320	450	550
6"	500	700	1,000	1,250

three 2,000 gph bilge pumps in the flooded compartment (allowing for their *actual* pumping rate) would only pump water over the side at half that rate. Now if this vessel is equipped with a bilge alarm (or Sea Key), it would at least be able to warn those on board (or ashore) and give them time to find and plug a hole that may have gone unnoticed until too late.

From the builder's perspective, the consumer has to demand that this equipment be installed and be willing to pay for it. If owners continue to put more emphasis on accommodations, furnishings, and storage volume than they do on seaworthiness, the status quo will continue unabated. Boatbuilders

A manual backup bilge pump can be a valuable commodity in the event of a power loss far offshore. NORDHAVN

are in business to sell boats, after all, not to be missionaries to an uninformed public with misplaced priorities. So don't condemn a boat that lacks this equipment or these design features—just pay to have them fitted on your next boat, preferably during construction, to the degree possible.

Other Seaworthiness Factors

Now that we've got concepts like stability, seakindliness, and flooding control down pat, we'll take a look at some of the other elements of seaworthiness. What follows applies to *any* boat, whether a full-displacement or a high-speed planing hull. Note the interactive relationship among such elements as freeboard, scupper or freeing port size and placement, bulwarks, free-surface effect, reserve buoyancy, and VCG, all of which contribute to a vessel's seaworthiness.

Reserve Buoyancy

Adequate *reserve buoyancy* is determined by compartmentation and the height of the watertight weather deck above the waterline. If you take green water on board, you can't have too much reserve

The Grady-White 225 tournament is a superb little offshore boat—the author once owned one—with a great ride delivered by its C. Raymond Hunt Associates–designed hull. Note the generous freeboard that adds seaworthiness while at the same time providing a high cockpit coaming *and* a self-bailing cockpit deck well above the waterline. GRADY-WHITE

buoyancy, since that's what keeps your boat floating while scuppers free this unwelcome ballast overboard. And a low VCG combined with a moderate GM will help keep you from rolling over while all that liquid weight on deck drains overboard. The higher the freeboard and watertight deck, and the greater the volume between the hull and deck liner, the more watertight volume or reserve buoyancy your vessel has built in. Competing interests are at work in a sportfisherman's cockpit, for instance, which must be low enough for a crew to comfortably handle gamefish close aboard, yet high enough to afford adequate reserve buoyancy aft in the event significant water is shipped over the transom.

This Trophy's motor well is integrated into the hull, extending its running surface for improved ride quality, seakeeping, and efficiency. What is effectively a full-height transom forward of the motor well adds seaworthiness.

Free-Surface Effect

When a hull floods, all that water has inertia that causes the vessel to lose stability as well as reserve buoyancy. As soon as the boat rolls slightly, all that liquid rushes to the down side, exaggerating the roll. This liquid movement is what naval architects call *free-surface effect*, and it wreaks havoc on a boat's ability to resist capsizing. The higher the liquid is in the vessel (and seawater on deck is a worst-case scenario, making big *scuppers* or freeing ports essential), the more stability is impacted. The stability-robbing inertia of free-surface effect is a function of the square of the beam, another seaworthiness argument for narrower vessels. If you've ever been in a dinghy or canoe half full of water, you've experienced free-surface effect firsthand.

Even worse is when the hole is off-center and water is free to flow in and out of the vessel as it rolls and pitches. Called *free communication*, this makes the stability situation even worse. Even if a yacht has enough reserve buoyancy to stay afloat with one compartment flooded, the lack of stability caused by free-surface effect and free communication can sink it if the ocean's rough. Stability-wise, a vessel is better off with a tank, or compartment, completely full of liquid rather than half full, since the free-surface effect will disappear when a tank is full. It's never a good idea to put a watertight bulkhead down the centerline of a boat. Uneven flooding would result, and risk of capsize would increase. The free-surface effect is also why fuel and large water tanks are baffled with inner, perforated walls to limit liquid movement; tons of liquid moving around unchecked would also create free surface.

Freeboard

A high *freeboard* (height of the hull sides and transom) combined with higher, watertight decks adds reserve buoyancy, helps keep solid water from reaching the deck, and can make for a drier ride. High freeboard can also help reduce tripping when beam-to a breaker; tripping is the effect caused by a gunwale submerging on the low side of a roll while a breaker impacts the opposite side. In modern convertible sportfishermen, the low cockpits needed for convenient handling of fish alongside reduce seaworthiness. At extreme angles of heel, low hull sides aft will allow water to ship into the cockpit, greatly reducing stability until the water drains back overboard, and reserve buoyancy aft is lost due to the cockpit's low deck. On the other hand, CG moves higher as freeboard increases, and there are the detrimental effects of excessive hull and superstructure exposure to wind and breaking waves to be considered.

Longitudinal Center of Gravity

A properly located *longitudinal center of gravity* (LCG) allows a vessel to float in trim on its design waterline. Weight must be distributed precisely from bow to stern so the boat floats neither bow- nor stern-high. This includes cargo, gear, stores, and liquid loads, including fuel and water. A bow-down trim angle, for example, can cause course-keeping instabilities.

Center of Dynamic Lift

For a planing hull, a well-positioned *center of dynamic lift* (CDL), or *center of pressure*, is crucial. A planing hull is supported by buoyancy when at rest or at slow speeds. But when a planing hull transitions "over the hump" to planing speed, vessel weight is supported predominantly by the dynamic lift generated by waterflow along the bottom of the hull. The center of this lifting force must be precisely located just forward of LCG so that the vessel runs at the proper trim, or bow-high attitude, for best efficiency (2 to 5 degrees of trim) or ride quality (0 to 2 degrees of trim). The shape of a planing hull and proper weight distribution are essential to achieving dynamic stability at all speeds and in all sea conditions.

Sail Area

Low *sail area*, or top hamper, in relation to the hull's underbody cross section, will help keep a boat from being too susceptible to the effects of wind. An above-water-to-underwater profile ratio of 2.5:1 or less is to be preferred for offshore vessels, and less is better. A boat with an excessively large, high superstructure and hull freeboard and shallow draft will be difficult to control, especially at slow speeds. Such a vessel has too little underwater lateral plane to offset the sail area exposed to the wind. A strong beam wind can cause such a ship or boat to heel dramatically, or even capsize, in severe conditions. On the other hand, a small-displacement vessel with a staysail rigged aft will be easier to steer into the wind and, as on a sailboat, will dampen the rolling effect of wind and wave.

Redundancy

A high degree of machinery and systems integrity, reliability, and redundancy is desirable. If it's man-made, it will eventually break, but some components are simply built better than others and will last longer before failure. To maximize reliability and longevity, machinery should be accessible so it's easy to work on properly. Mechanical systems should be well engineered with the best-quality water valves, pumps, hoses and pipes, compression-type fuel fittings and lines; heavy, well-supported and protected underwater gear; and so on. Bronze or stainless-steel through-hull and plumbing fittings and components can generally be expected to hold up better than synthetics. Although less economical to buy and operate, two engines and two shafts are, all else being equal, more reliable than one. In single-screw vessels, a backup means of propulsion is highly desirable, such as a generator that can be tapped electrically or mechanically to turn the shaft. It's very important that the auxiliary propulsion is powerful enough to make good headway in a strong wind. It is also a good idea to have an engine-driven generator or high-capacity alternator to back up the generator set—if not two gensets. Putting propulsion engines and backup auxiliary generators or engines in different watertight compartments increases reliability.

Adequate Scupper Size and Placement

The bigger the scuppers, the faster the deck drains. They should also be located where water is likely to collect, at the deck's low points. Larger scuppers are also less susceptible to clogging with debris. MCA regulations call for scuppers, or freeing ports, to be a certain size in relation to the length and height of the bulwark. Same goes for the drain lines in deck hatch gutters (which are, unfortunately, increasingly relied on for deck drainage); drain lines of under 1-inch inside diameter are far more likely to clog with debris ranging from striped bass scales to pine needles, which is why I recommend a minimum of 2-inch drain lines.

Directional Stability

Good *directional stability*, or *course-keeping ability*, refers to a boat's inclination to maintain its heading, in any orientation to the seas, with minimal helm input. A boat's ability to track well, or tendency to run in a straight line, is largely a function of hull form. A deep-V hull, with a large angle of deadrise at the transom, tracks better than a flat-bottomed, keel-less boat downsea. (We discuss deep-Vs in detail in chapter 4.) If a boat has a too-high VCG, it will yaw excessively. And if weight is concentrated too far forward, it will also cause excessive yaw or bow steer.

Most boats run straight enough in a head sea, but the true test is in a quartering sea. As discussed previously, a vessel with a fine bow and wide, buoyant stern will trim by the bow when rolling, especially with a hull that's wide for its beam. This works against directional stability, since the boat will tend to change its heading as it rolls. A moderate length-to-beam ratio also works to improve directional stability.

The Fairline Targa 47 Express has a deep-V, fine-entry hull form that delivers an exceptionally comfortable ride, the open-ocean speed potential for wave-avoidance in nasty weather, and a low profile to enhance stability.   FAIRLINE

A boat that is too directionally stable, though, will be hard to maneuver, with a very large keel providing great resistance to the rudder's turning effort. A balance must be found between directional stability and helm responsiveness.

In a following or quartering sea, wave speed relative to hull speed also has an impact on steering and on directional stability. As wave speed approaches or exceeds boat speed, the effectiveness of the rudder(s) and the directional stability of the hull are reduced; the relative speed of the water moving across the rudder(s) drops, reducing lift. A full keel can cause the boat to be thrown off course in these circumstances. And a hard-left rudder with a wave impacting it from astern can cause the boat's head to fall off to starboard. The only way to avoid this is to be in a boat that can travel faster than the waves coming from astern, which is not possible in a displacement hull when the wave is larger than the boat.

A deep-V is a better-running boat downsea than a flat-bottom boat because of its larger area of *lateral plane*, or the underwater area in profile (viewed from the side). When the center of this area of lateral plane corresponds with the boat's LCG, it will tend to track better. That's because the inertia of the vessel, centered on its LCG, as it tries to naturally resist being thrown off course by a passing wave, is balanced by the center of lateral plane directly below, and any yawing tendency is reduced.

Seaworthiness can have a direct correlation to speed capability. The Bertram 630 convertible, for example, is a well-regarded, time-tested modified-V planing hull with generous deadrise and a sharp entry that allows it to maintain relatively high speeds in rough water. This provides a measure of storm-system and local wave avoidance lacking in slower hulls. BERTRAM YACHTS

Speed and Maneuvering

Adequate speed and acceleration allow a vessel to better avoid approaching storm systems when offshore, as well as immediate hazards such as breaking waves. When trying to avoid bad weather or a sudden squall, there's no substitute for speed, and this speed capability must be usable in less-than-ideal conditions. It does little good to own a boat that will run fast in calm water, but, due to a poor hull design, must slow down to bare steerageway speeds in moderate to rough conditions.

Steering responsiveness should be proportional to the vessel's speed capability. The faster the boat, the more responsive (fewer turns lock-to-lock) the steering should be so that evasive maneuvers to avoid damage or personal injury can be carried out effectively. Steering should also take minimal effort, so that the boat can be operated for many hours without undue fatigue. Rudders should travel an arc of 70 degrees from full port to full starboard to provide an optimum turning

Trochoidal Wave Speed

Speed, knots	Length, feet	Speed, knots	Length, feet
6	20	12	80
7	27	14	109
8	35	16	142
9	45	20	222
10	55	25	347
11	67	30	500

This table illustrates the speed-to-length relationship of a wave in deep water. Note that the hull speed of a displacement vessel is identical to that of a wave of the same length. This explains why displacement hulls are limited in speed, since they start to create a bow wave that's longer than the hull and, by adding power, futilely try to climb up the back of it. PHILLIPS-BIRT, *NAVAL ARCHITECTURE*

Imagine coming alongside a canoe being paddled through the water. Give the bow a shove, and it veers off course. Same with the stern. But give it a shove amidships, and it merely slides sideways a few inches while pretty much staying on course.

rate, and rudder size should be proportional to the hull's dimensions, displacement, and speed. For more on steering systems, see chapter 9.

Deicing

For cold climes, *deicing capability* is important. This usually concerns only true passagemakers operating many hours or even days from safe harbor. When spray makes its way on board, and the seawater and air temperature are freezing, expect ice to start forming. CG will slowly start to rise as ice accumulates on deck, on the superstructure, and (especially dangerous) in the rigging, and the vessel will eventually capsize if stability is diminished sufficiently. If there is no exterior heating system installed, the only solution is to remove the ice manually with chipping tools, and minimize the amount of spray coming aboard by reducing speed or heading downwind. According to IMO recommendations, in extreme conditions, such as in the Bering Sea, adequate stability must be provided to compensate for ice accumulation of about 1.3 inches on deck and 0.33 inch on the superstructure and hull sides.

Scantlings

Structural members supporting well-built, high-strength hulls, decks, and superstructures have large enough *scantlings* to prevent heavy seas from causing structural damage (*scantling* refers to the *size* of the structural member). It's no good having the best design in the world if the vessel can't stand up to the stresses imposed by the worst conditions of wind and sea. Large scantlings ought to extend to any windshields, windows, and portholes (using thicker, high-strength glass, and intermediate window supports) and to any storm covers that might be subject to wave impact in severe sea conditions.

Fire Resistance

Fire protection or resistance is both passive and active in nature. Passive or structural resistance to fire results primarily from the construction materials used to build the vessel. A steel vessel is the most capable of surviving a fire, since it won't burn and won't melt until it reaches about 2,800°F. Aluminum, which melts at 1,220°F, is the next most heat-resistant common boatbuilding material, followed by fiberglass composite and wood, which, with combustion temperatures in the neighborhood of 500°F, are the least able to resist burning.

Compartmentation is also vital to a vessel's ability to survive a fire, regardless of its construction material. Any steel vessel that lacks watertight bulkheads also usually lacks fire boundaries and is susceptible to fire spreading throughout the vessel's length. Even if it doesn't sink, the result is a floating, burned-out steel hulk.

Active fire protection can be provided by several means. In its simplest form, fire extinguishing is provided by water hoses with which to cool and smother class A fires (wood, mattresses, or anything that leaves an ash residue). Class A materials should be broken up and resoaked to extinguish any embers remaining. A low-velocity water fog, when skillfully applied, can also be used in a pinch to put out class B fires (liquid fueled, usually fuel or lube oil). Water and foam should not be used on class C (electrical) fires due to the electrical shock potential.

Carbon dioxide (CO_2) fire extinguishers are effective on small class B fires, but best used on electrical fires, since they don't transmit electrical shock as water and foam will. CO_2 also won't permanently damage electrical equipment. Compared with water or foam, however, CO_2 is less effective at putting out class A fires since it dissipates quickly and has little residual cooling effect.

Dry chemical fire extinguishers are also commonly found aboard small boats, and they work well enough on class A and B fires. They leave a corrosive residue, though, so they're a last resort for electrical fires.

Active fire suppression is also created by fixed foam or water sprinklers; both act to cool hot surfaces and thereby prevent a fire reflash. Foam is especially effective at smothering class B fires, leaving an oxygen-depriving blanket over the fuel in the bilge or whatever the source of the fire may have been.

Gases that replace the now-banned Halon (such as Halotron and FE36) are commonly used in fixed and portable firefighting systems. These gases leave no residue and, if sufficient concentrations are maintained long enough, are very effective at putting out fires. Unlike water and foam, gas has little or no cooling effect of its own, so it must remain in high enough concentrations during the postfire cooldown period to prevent reflash. For this reason, gas is much better at putting out class B (liquid) and C (electrical) fires than class A fires; glowing embers retain heat. Halon replacements work by interrupting the free radicals in a fire triangle (heat, fuel, and oxygen), or inhibiting the chemical reaction of fuel and oxygen.

These systems ought to be carefully sized to provide concentration levels that will extinguish a fire and then prevent reflash for a long enough period of time for the space to cool down. The most effective gas systems in machinery compartments include audible and visual alarms to warn of impending discharge and automatic solenoids that shut down operating machinery and close air intakes in the affected space. These systems have time delays that shut down machinery and close ventilation sources and then automatically discharge the gas. Both flame and high-temperature sensors can be used to activate gas and foam or water bilge sprinkler systems.

As mentioned, it's important to keep in mind that even if the initial gas discharge is sufficient to put the fire out, sufficient concentration must remain for the fire to stay out in spite of hot metal surfaces that could otherwise reflash the fuel or whatever caused the fire initially. To this end, the space should not be entered for at least 15 to 30 minutes (according to some standards) after the fire has been extinguished; opening a door admits fresh oxygen and allows the gas to dissipate, creating a reflash potential. For the same reason, machinery—especially propulsion diesels that consume enormous amounts of air—must not be restarted too soon or left running, since to do so would quickly dissipate the remaining gas.

A Halon-replacement gas system has the advantage of being breathable, at least insofar as you won't lose consciousness after a couple of deep breaths, as would be the case with a fixed CO_2 flooding system. Higher gas concentrations are toxic, perhaps even carcinogenic, but that is probably an acceptable risk in return for surviving a fire. CO_2 is effective, but anyone caught in a CO_2-flooded space is liable to suffocate before they can escape.

It's important to know where all your vessel's fire extinguishers are located, to have frequent fire drills with varying fire type and location scenarios, and to make sure they're properly maintained. The same goes for fixed fire suppression systems—know how they work, what takes place before discharge (engine and ventilation shutdown, usually), and how the system is locally, remotely, and manually activated or overridden. Make sure your vessel is equipped with remote fuel shutoff valves so this potential fire source can be contained. When you eventually reenter a space after a fixed system has extinguished a fire, make sure you have a portable fire extinguisher with you in case of reflash. The longer you wait to reenter, the less the chance of a reflash.

Habitability

Habitability is the ability of the vessel to provide a safe and comfortable environment fit for human habitation. People require bunks that are actually long enough to stretch out on, heaters in cold climates, provisions for food storage and preparation, convenient and safe access to the boat's various compartments, a seakindly hull that produces low accelerations (comfortable motion) in a seaway, and so on. The *human factor* recognizes that the most seaworthy yachts in the world are ultimately only as good as their crews. An inexperienced, unfocused, inattentive, or just plain tired helmsman, in conjunction with adverse sea conditions, can capsize a boat in weather that it might well have ridden out comfortably otherwise. On the other hand, the most experienced, judicious, and attentive crew in the world can't make a manifestly unseaworthy vessel safe to put to sea.

CHAPTER 3

Displacement and Semidisplacement Hulls

Life's pretty good, and why wouldn't it be?
I'm a pirate, after all.

—Jack Sparrow

Choosing the right hull type for a boat is like building a house on a good foundation. Both are fundamental elements that help determine the success of the end product. No matter how pleasing the accommodations or how perfect the joinery, if your boat has a poorly designed hull or one that is not well suited to your purposes, you'll never be happy with it.

In this chapter we take a look at the capabilities and limitations of displacement and semidisplacement hulls. The next chapter, which covers planing hulls, builds on this discussion, so it's a good idea to read this one first.

There are three basic hull classifications: *displacement*, *semidisplacement*, and *planing*. Our focus here will be on monohulls, or single-hull vessels, mostly because of their popularity and dominance in the pleasure craft industry. We have a look at catamarans in chapter 5 and see why they are enjoying burgeoning popularity in pleasure, military, and commercial applications. These craft all have their advantages and disadvantages.

Displacement Hulls

Slow, heavy, and seaworthy, with deep draft and moderate beam—these are the qualities that typify a well-found displacement hull. A displacement vessel travels through the water rather than on top of it, displacing or pushing water to the side as it moves along—hence the name. With their slack, or rounded, bilges and gently upswept buttock lines aft, displacement hulls create little disturbance in the water at their low cruising speeds (see the accompanying figure). Displacement hulls, including trawler yachts, tugboats, and large ships,

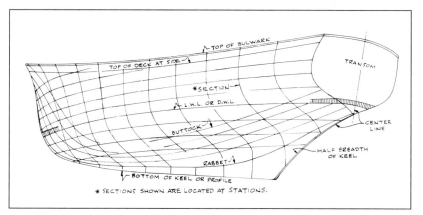

A typical deep-draft displacement hull, with round bilges and upswept buttock lines aft. The transom is mostly above the waterline, which minimizes drag at displacement speeds. Note the *stations, waterlines,* and *buttocks* used to define a hull's shape in three different planes.

STEWARD, *BOATBUILDING MANUAL*

are valued for their comfortable rides, easy motion, and, if well designed, their high ultimate stability and seaworthiness.

Displacement hulls excel at moving cargo, since added weight has relatively little impact on their resistance and efficiency. It takes only modest power to move a displacement hull at its design speed, so the propulsion plant can be quite small and inexpensive relative to the size of the boat. The downside (there's always a downside) is that a displacement hull's speed is limited by its waterline length, and although there are design tricks to squeeze a bit more speed out of a monohull of a given length—mostly involving a narrower hull with finer sections—there's no getting around this limitation.

Displacement Hull Power Requirements

Displ.	Length	bhp for 10 knots	Speed for 200 bhp
20	40	185	10.3 knots
20	45	140	11.0 knots
20	50	120	11.3 knots
27	50	185	10.3 knots

The advantage of length in a displacement hull. Listed are power requirements for 40-, 45-, and 50-foot, 20-ton hulls, and a 50-foot, 27-ton vessel to make the same speed, or achieve max speed with 200 hp. The longer the 20-ton hull, the less power it takes to drive it at 10 knots. And both the 20-ton 40-footer and the 27-ton 50-footer need 185 hp to make 10 knots. The same principle applies to planing hulls: longer-narrower is generally faster for a given power, as well as being more seakindly, than a shorter-wider boat of the same size and displacement.

ADAPTED FROM PHILLIPS-BIRT, *NAVAL ARCHITECTURE*

Wave Speed and Length

All waves, including the wake from a vessel, travel at a speed proportional to the wave length, which is the perpendicular distance from one wave crest to the next. An open-ocean wave travels at 1.34 times the square root of its length; thus, a wave that is 300 feet long will travel at 23.2 knots, and a 100-foot wave will travel at 13.4 knots. A vessel's wake, specifically the bow and stern waves generated

by a hull traveling through the water, propagates according to the same formula. Once any vessel (and its bow wave) is going fast enough for the length of the bow wave to equal the length of the hull, the boat cannot go any faster without *climbing up over* its bow wave, which is indeed what a semidisplacement or planing hull must do as it speeds up. That's why waterline length is the ultimate determining factor when it comes to a displacement hull's top speed. The longer the hull, the faster it can go before the bow wave reaches the length of the hull, but a displacement hull can't climb its bow wave. A displacement hull can travel at a speed-to-length (S/L) ratio of about 1.34, equivalent to the speed of a wave of the same length, and this is the point at which the bow is starting to rise and the stern to sink significantly. At S/L of 1.34, the hull will have one wave crest at the bow and a second at the stern, with the length of the wave the same as the underwater hull.

So hull speed-to-length ratios are based on the square root of waterline length; a 36-footer at 6 knots is running at a speed-to-length ratio of 1, at 12 knots the S/L ratio is 2, and so on. A displacement hull has a theoretical top hull speed of 1.34 S/L (1.34 times the square root of the hull's waterline length in feet), due to the hull's wavemaking characteristics (more to follow on this below). A displacement hull with a waterline length of 36 feet can be driven up to about 8 knots ($6 \times 1.34 = 8.04$). A vessel 64 feet long at the waterline could make 10.7 knots, and if you need to make 13.4 knots, set your sights on a hull that's 100 feet at the waterline. So, length is (nearly) everything when it comes to a displacement hull's speed potential.

You can look at it this way. A bow wave is pushed up and out as water is displaced by the hull. As the bow wave leaves the high-pressure area forward, gravity takes over and it starts to fall back into the surrounding water. In a short hull, the stern catches up to where the bow just was in short order, so the speed at which the hull tries to climb its bow wave is low. A longer hull can get away with producing a higher bow wave (generated by its higher speeds), since the wave has to travel farther to reach the stern. So the longer hull can be pushed faster before the bow-climbing tendency is manifested.

Driving a displacement hull faster than displacement speed is an exercise in futility, requiring exponentially more horsepower and reducing propulsion efficiency. Reaching somewhat higher speed-to-length ratios is possible with displacement monohulls that are designed to go fast, but you'll pay a penalty in load-carrying ability and form stability.

Resistance

At slow speeds, well below hull speed, the friction created by waterflow along the hull creates most of the propulsion resistance. A layer of water called the *frictional wake current*, or boundary layer, is dragged along with the hull, increasing in thickness aft and down along the hull. A clean bottom and faired underwater fittings and running gear appendages help reduce frictional drag.

Beam influences drag, since the wider the hull, the more surface area underwater and thus the greater the frictional resistance. A wider hull also increases the amount of water displaced, and therefore the amount of work the propulsion plant has to do to push the vessel. A short, wide hull requires more power to move through the water than a long, narrow hull of the same interior volume (or displacement).

In short, the less disturbance a hull makes as it runs through the water, including the water it drags along with it and the waves it generates, the less resistance it offers to forward motion. The smoother the hull, and the smaller the wake, the less the resistance.

Displacement Hull Characteristics

Let's see what characterizes an easily driven displacement hull. The accompanying figure shows a moderately deep-draft displacement hull drawn by Robert Beebe. There are three *views* in the *lines plan*, each one telling us something more about the design. In the *half-breadth view* (top), the curved lines above the fore-and-aft centerline are *waterlines*, representing horizontal slices through the hull. Counting outward from the centerline, the third waterline is the *design waterline*, on which the boat is intended to float; the other waterlines represent parallel slices through the hull above or below that one. In the *sectional view* (middle), the curved lines are transverse *sections*, or slices through the hull at regular intervals from bow to stern—like slices in a loaf of bread. In the *profile view* (bottom),

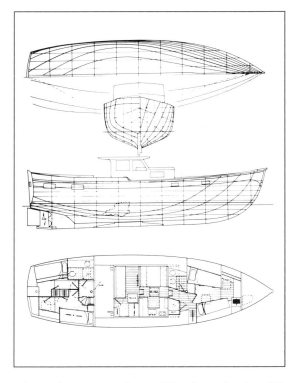

Robert Beebe's *Passagemaker*, an offshore boat with a deep, full-bodied displacement hull. BEEBE, *VOYAGING UNDER POWER*

the curved lines are *buttocks*, representing lengthwise vertical slices through the hull. These appear as straight lines in the sectional and half-breadth views; by the same token, the waterlines are straight in the sectional and profile views, and the sections are straight in the half-breadth and profile views. The round bilges seen in the sections deliver a comfortable, gentle motion in a seaway, and the easy waterlines and buttocks hint at how easily driven this hull would be at its sedate cruising speed. (At the same time, all three features testify to the futility of trying to move this hull above displacement speeds.) The hull's midsection is deep and full, and this mass low in the water is one of the qualities that make this type of vessel so seaworthy. The entry at the bow is fine, but not so sharp that a hollow waterline is created. By this we mean that, when looking down at the hull's *waterplane*, or footprint at the waterline, the bow should have slight convexity from the stem to the midships area of maximum beam. Otherwise, a secondary bow wave will be developed where a concave section creates a high-pressure region between the stem and the point of maximum waterline beam. For this reason, a hard-chine displacement hull's chines should, in the interests of reducing wavemaking drag, be entirely above or entirely below the waterline for the length of the hull. The deckhouse on this vessel is also low in profile, decreasing topside weight and improving stability, while minimizing windage for added seaworthiness.

Displacement hulls should have a certain amount of balance or geometric symmetry end to end, with buoyancy spread fairly equally as you work your way forward or aft from the midships area. This requires a gentle curvature to the buttock lines forward; hard curves there would indicate a blunt bow, which would cause excessive pressure (and a high bow wave), increasing resistance. The advantages of a balanced hull are also discussed in chapter 2. Aft, the buttock lines sweep up gradually to reduce drag and turbulence at the transom, which should be above the waterline. A submerged transom increases resistance as the smooth waterflow is interrupted at the stern, creating drag-inducing turbulence. It follows that a displacement hull that leaves less commotion behind is going to be easier to push

Speed/Length Ratio	Prismatic Coefficient
1.0 and below	0.525
1.1	0.54
1.2	0.58
1.3	0.62
1.4	0.64
1.5	0.66
1.6	0.68
1.7	0.69
1.8 and above	0.70

Optimal prismatic coefficient (Cp) as a function of hull speed.

BREWER, *UNDERSTANDING BOAT DESIGN*

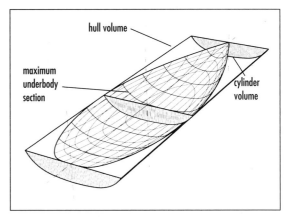

The prismatic coefficient is the ratio of the volume of a hull below the waterline to the volume of a "trough" having the same length as the hull and a uniform cross section matching the hull's fullest station. This coefficient is used to measure the fullness of a vessel at its ends. The fuller the ends, the larger the Cp. The most appropriate value depends on the desired speed of the vessel.

LARSSON AND ELIASSON, *PRINCIPLES OF YACHT DESIGN*

through the water. A waterline length-to-beam (L/B) ratio of four or higher is favored for propulsion efficiency and enhanced seakindliness.

These easy lines reflect a displacement hull's *prismatic coefficient*, which is the ratio of the actual below-the-waterline volume of the hull to the product of the hull's largest cross-sectional area below the waterline multiplied by its waterline length. A boat with fine ends and a correspondingly low prismatic coefficient (around 0.53) is best suited to slow hull speeds below a S/L ratio of 1.0. A semidisplacement hull will have fuller ends, and therefore a higher prismatic coefficient—generally in the 0.55 to 0.68 range. A planing hull with its deep, wide after sections will be in the 0.70 or higher region. The

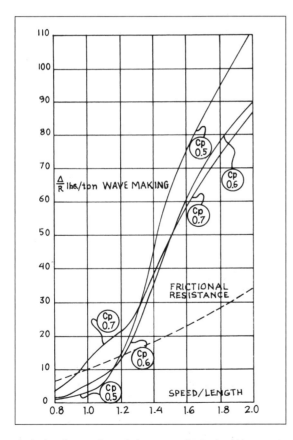

The higher the vessel speed, the greater the Cp should be to minimize wavemaking resistance.

PHILLIPS-BIRT, *NAVAL ARCHITECTURE*

hull form, and therefore its prismatic coefficient, is usually chosen to produce maximum propulsion efficiency at the design cruising speed.

The longitudinal distribution of weight in a boat has to be watched carefully as well. In an effort to open up more room amidships for accommodations, some builders shift heavy weights such as engines and fuel and water tanks into the ends of the hull. Although the overall weight distribution is the same, its effect at sea is a different matter. Too much weight forward results in excessive pitching and a tendency to bury the nose in a following sea. Too much weight in the stern, especially with fine lines aft, increases the risk of pooping. In general, boats that have their heavy weights concentrated more nearly amidships pitch less, handle better at sea, and have a more comfortable motion.

Tricks of the naval architect's trade include bulbous bows that decrease resistance and increase effective waterline length, adding speed potential (see sidebar next page). An overhanging counter stern, which allows the buttock lines to continue farther aft than they would in a squared-off transom stern, also adds waterline length, increases buoyancy aft in a following sea, and avoids the drag-inducing turbulence of an immersed transom.

So clearly, propulsion resistance isn't the only factor a naval architect must consider when designing a displacement hull. Load-carrying ability, initial stability criteria, volume for accommodations, and draft constraints are just a few elements that must also be considered.

In particular, a hull with fine lines forward may deliver an exceptional ride in a head sea. But with little buoyancy in the bow to balance a wide, buoyant stern, it may be squirrelly in a quartering or following sea. That fine entry with deep forefoot can turn into a fixed bow rudder (which is a lot more powerful than the rudders back aft) with a mind of its own when it digs into the back of a following sea, and it will lack the necessary buoyancy to lift the bow with the waves abaft the beam, making a

Bulbous Bows

Bulbous bows are definitely in with the big (over 70-foot, generally) displacement trawler crowd, and if nothing else, they impart a big-ship allure to a small boat. Bulbous bows add to the effective overall waterline length, even though they're below the waterline, increasing speed potential. If properly designed, they can reduce the height of the bow wave and move it forward off the stem. These appendages have been extensively tank-tested to come up the shape that offers the least resistance to forward motion. But few full-size boats spend much time in the calm waters of a test tank, preferring instead the open ocean, where drag is often a secondary concern after course-keeping ability and predictability in a heavy seaway. Since they are buoyant and have mass, bulbous bows can also reduce pitching in a head sea. However, they can create downsea handling problems if the bow effectively turns into a fixed rudder, working against the efforts of the movable rudder in the stern. Yawing can become more pronounced, and a broach more likely.

broach (slewing broadside to the waves), or even a *pitchpole* (somersault) in extreme conditions more likely. At the other extreme, a owner may insist on a roomy stateroom forward, but this will compromise ride quality when running into the seas at speed, since fuller sections forward are needed to provide a wider waterline beam. On the other hand, a full bow will tend to behave well downsea thanks to its greater buoyancy, which prevents deep immersion and loss of steering control.

The Result

A displacement hull's slack bilges and relatively narrow beam at the waterline make it quite comfortable in a seaway, with a longer roll period and deeper rolls. Accelerations in general are reduced (and comfort levels increased), thanks to its diminished form, or hull, stability, to the hull's finer ends, and to the vessel's greater weight for its waterplane area. A wider, lighter boat with hard chines or harder (more tightly radiused) bilges will be more

uncomfortable because the motion will be quicker and snappier, the roll of a shorter period, and the range of stability less. The displacement hull's greater roll amplitude belies its greater range of stability. And since it moves through rather than over the water, a displacement hull is not nearly as affected by added weight as a planing vessel.

These full-displacement Nordhavn trawlers have very deep forefoots and round bilges for enhanced seakeeping and a smooth ride offshore. Very little dynamic lift is developed forward (or aft) due to the shape of the hull. The high bows add significant reserve buoyancy, helping to make these hulls very seaworthy. NORDHAVN

Displacement powerboats have a few advantages over sailboats, which are also usually displacement vessels. A powerboat doesn't need a large keel to resist lateral movement due to wind pressure on the sails, or from which to suspend external ballast. So a powerboat's keel can be smaller, reducing frictional drag, which is the dominant power absorber below a S/L ratio of 0.90 or so. Nor do powerboats have to be as wide as sailboats, which must have sufficient initial stability to counter sail pressures, so the powerboat's narrower, more efficiently driven waterlines are an advantage.

The accompanying table shows the performance curves for the Krogen 39, a full-displacement trawler yacht; the relevant figures here are speed and nautical miles per gallon. This boat has a waterline length of 36 feet, 8 inches, or 36.66 feet, giving it a theoretical hull speed of 8.1 knots. A single,

115 hp diesel pushes this boat to a half knot higher than that, or 8.6 knots, at 1.4 nmpg. The Krogen takes less than half as much horsepower (look at the fuel flow to estimate horsepower output; a diesel develops roughly 20 hp for every gallon burned each hour) to make 7.7 knots, so above 8 knots the hull is starting to dig a hole in the water as it tries to climb its bow wave, with little success. You can see that it only takes about 36 hp (1.79 gph × 20) to drive the hull at 7 knots, a

Krogen 39 Trawler Performance Results

RPM	Speed, knots	Fuel Usage, gph	Nautical mpg	Range, nm
1,000	5.3	0.85	6.2	3,928
1,200	5.6	1.08	5.2	3,267
1,400	6.3	1.34	4.7	2,962
1,600	7	1.79	3.9	2,464
1,800	7.3	2.33	3.1	1,974
2,000	7.7	2.94	2.6	1,650
2,200	7.9	3.88	2.0	1,283
2,400	8.3	4.83	1.7	1,083
2,600	8.6	6.3	1.4	860

Tests are with a single, 115 hp John Deere diesel engine.

S/L ratio in this case of about 0.86. Drop down to 6 knots, and only 1.2 gph, or 24 hp, is required, and range goes up correspondingly.

Although the Krogen 39 conforms to the hull-speed rule, other displacement vessels can achieve speeds in excess of S/L 1.34. The Krogen has a hefty molded beam of 14 feet, 3 inches for increased accommodations and carrying capacity, and its L/B ratio of 2.7 holds it back in terms of speed. Trim the beam down to 10 feet or so and give the hull a lower

A typical full-displacement hull form, like this Krogen 44, easily makes hull speed — in this case, about 8 knots — but going any faster takes an exponential increase in power. All the power in the world couldn't get this boat to plane, with its emerged transom and highly swept buttock lines aft. But at displacement speeds, the same hull form characteristics make this yacht easily driven, with low wavemaking characteristics. 　　　　　KROGEN

prismatic coefficient with finer ends, and speed may well pick up by a couple of knots. Semidisplacement and planing hulls, as we shall see, require higher prismatic coefficients with fuller ends to achieve their higher speeds, but in a displacement hull—which lacks flatter buttock lines aft, an immersed transom, and a bottom shape that provides dynamic lift—finer ends reduce wavemaking resistance and help speed. The Krogen represents a design compromise: a marketable boat with the interior room and range people want and a top speed they can live with.

Semidisplacement Hulls

As the name suggests, a semidisplacement hull is capable of traveling in excess of hull speed by developing some hydrodynamic lift—enough to be partially supported by waterflow-induced pressure under the hull. It occupies a transition zone between displacement hulls, which even at top speeds are supported mainly by buoyancy, and true planing hulls, which, as we shall see in chapter 4, are largely supported by hydrodynamic lift at planing speeds. The semidisplacement (or *semiplaning*, if you prefer) vessel makes an excellent cruising yacht. It enjoys much of the full displacement hull's efficiencies at low speeds while offering reserves of higher speed to put more destinations within reach and to avoid bad weather.

Even a brick will plane with enough power, but the choice of hull form on a yacht ought to be appropriate to the owner's speed requirements. Here's what is nominally an 18-knot, semi-displacement, round-bilge, full-keel Maine-style hull being driven to just under 30 knots with twice the power it really ought to have under the deck. JONATHAN KLOPMAN

Another view of this Carroll Lowell—designed semidisplacement lobster yacht. The deep, fine entry prevents pounding, and the round bilges aft provide an easy motion. Oversized power plants are wasted, though; the planing surface aft is half of what it would be on a hard-chine planing hull; the full keel adds substantial drag, and the round bilges prevent efficient waterflow separation at speed.

The Maine-style lobster yacht, with its full keel and round bilges, is probably the best-known type of semidisplacement hull today. Semidisplacement hulls can often attain speed-to-length ratios of 2.5 or greater, so a semidisplacement hull with a 40-foot waterline length could reasonably be expected to achieve a speed of up to about 16 knots with moderate horsepower. Of course, larger engines can make it go faster still, but at the price of increased fuel consumption compared with a hard-chine planing hull. If you want to go fast—say, 25 knots—efficiently, you want a keel-less, hard-chine hull. A semidisplacement has fuller bottom sections than a planing hull and a shallower, flatter bottom than a displacement hull. A well-designed semidisplacement hull is seaworthy and has a more comfortable motion than a planing hull (if somewhat less so than a displacement hull).

A semidisplacement hull needs a larger waterplane than a displacement hull, in order to develop the necessary hydrodynamic lift to rise up on the surface of the water. This calls for a wider beam at the waterline, especially aft, and a fuller, flatter bow with chines that emerge from the water forward to increase dynamic lift. These hulls either have hard chines, or they have "hard" bilges with a smaller radius of turn from bottom to side than one sees in a displacement hull.

This widens the bottom's effective lifting surface and, in the case of the hard chine, contributes to waterflow separation, reducing drag at higher speeds. Hard chines or small-radius bilges also increase buoyancy outboard in the hull, increasing metacentric height (GM) and shortening the roll period. Back aft, the buttock lines are flatter than in a displacement hull, generally just 2 to 4 degrees from horizontal, and they

This round-bilge, full-keel, semidisplacement Down East cruiser built by Ellis Yachts in Maine is on plane at about 13 knots with a clean wake astern. At cruising speed, the stern is at about the same level as when stopped, and the bow is up a foot or so out of the water due to the dynamic lift forward. ELLIS YACHTS

terminate at a lift-generating submerged transom that prevents excessive squatting at speed.

The semidisplacement hull's prismatic coefficient is higher than that of a displacement hull, with more buoyancy (and dynamic lift at speed) in the hull's ends. Nothing's free in life, so the trade-off is a loss of efficiency at displacement speeds thanks to increased wetted surface and a higher wave-generating underwater shape.

Note that we said that semidisplacement hulls are speed limited. The fact is, if you put enough power in them, they'll go faster, all right. But to make a heavy 42-foot Maine-style hull move along at the same speed as a 42-foot planing hull is a questionable endeavor. It takes an inordinate amount of power to push the hull at planing hull speeds (above S/L 2.5), and dynamic instabilities can be a problem. Some of the working lobster boats entered in races along the Maine coast each summer achieve speeds well above 40 knots, but they do so by stripping all excess weight, adjusting trim, substituting souped-up power plants for their workaday engines, experimenting with exotic fuel mixes, and in general pushing the envelope any way it can be pushed. In the summer of 2001 one of these full-keeled boats flipped spectacularly during competition in a moderate chop—a graphic example of dynamic instability. (Fortunately, no one was seriously injured.)

Not long ago I had an opportunity to observe these limitations close up when I was asked to evaluate a high-end, nearly completed, 42-foot lobster yacht that was not performing up to expectations (see

The Krogen 49

The semidisplacement Krogen 49 measures 48 feet on the waterline, so its hull speed is about 9.3 knots. At 9 knots, she's using 5.1 gallons per hour of fuel, which translates into about 100 hp worth of propulsive power and an efficiency of 1.8 nmpg. Back off a knot and a half or so to 7.6 knots, and fuel consumption is cut in half to 2.5 gph, or a 50 hp output with 60 percent better mileage. On the other hand, if you want to take advantage of this Krogen's semidisplacement speed potential, crank it up to a fast cruise speed of 16.6 knots, at which point the hull is "semiplaning" at a S/L ratio of 1.8, and the 300 hp Cats are delivering about 550 hp between them while propulsion efficiency drops to 0.65 nautical mpg. This speed capability, in fact, is the biggest advantage of any semidisplacement hull.

A semidisplacement hull running essentially at planing speed. This Krogen 53 express cruiser leaves a clean waterflow down her side, a low wake astern, and runs at a moderate 3 to 4 degrees of bow rise, indicating an efficiently driven hull form. KROGEN

Krogen 49 Performance Results

RPM	Speed, knots	Fuel Usage, gph	Nautical mpg	Range, nm
800	5.7	1.6	3.6	1,924
1,000	7.6	2.5	3.0	1,642
1,400	9.0	5.1	1.8	953
1,600	9.8	8.0	1.2	661
1,800	10.3	11.9	0.86	467
2,000	12.4	15.7	0.79	426
2,200	14.2	19.9	0.71	385
2,400	16.6	25.5	0.65	351
2,600	18.4	30.3	0.61	328
2,780	19.7	35.5	0.55	300

Tested with twin 350 hp Caterpillar 3116 engines.

photo top right, opposite). The semicustom boat's builder started with a sound, well-known, Maine-style hull with a large, 15-foot beam, a gently radiused round bilge, a full hollow keel curving gently into the hull bottom, moderately fine entry, and flat sections aft. This boat would run well with a single 600 hp diesel at the speeds for which it was intended, in the S/L region of 2.5 to 3. But as we and the owner discovered, trying to make a semidisplacement hull perform like a planing hull with double that much power is a costly undertaking.

This semidisplacement hull was unsuited to meeting its advertised performance potential from the start; you can't just keep adding power to get satisfactory planing-hull performance. First, a radiused bilge combined with a hollow keel reduces the effective lifting surface (the flat area remaining between the radius of the keel and that of the bilge) to about half of what it would be on a true, hard-chine planing hull. This boat also had a full keel that was trimmed off back aft to reduce frictional drag and improve its turning characteristics. The problem is, since this hull is flat-bottomed aft, it needs a keel for directional stability, so it handled unpredictably in a quartering sea. Steering took a full 6.7 turns (3–4 turns is called for in a boat of this speed capability) lock-to-lock, which compounded the handling problem downsea.

Instead of the low, flat wake normally seen leaving the transom of a Maine-style hull, our boat's wake was much higher, due to an excessive running angle of 7 degrees and to the boat's heavy displacement. The high trim at speed was likely due to the LCG being too far aft, and to the minimal dynamic lift aft produced by the hull's relatively small planing surface. Filling the fuel tanks resulted in increased bow-down static trim, so as fuel is consumed, the bow will steadily rise in relation to the stern at speed. Ideally, the fuel is positioned over the *longitudinal center of flotation* (LCF) so trim remains constant regardless of fuel state. With the large trim angle, a 6-foot, 3-inch operator standing at the lower helm station couldn't see clearly over the bow at cruising speed. Plus, the boat pounded more in a head sea, since slamming loads increase as trim angle goes up.

Powered by twin 635 hp Cummins QSM11 diesels, this 38,500-pound lobster yacht had a top speed of 25.3 knots, at least 4 to 5 knots slower than all that horsepower led us to expect. It might be instructive to compare this semidisplacement boat to a similar-size planing hull like the ones we discuss in chapter 4. A Viking 43 convertible, with its bona fide hard-chine planing hull, makes for an interesting comparison. The Viking 43 is close to our lobster yacht in length and beam, and it's no lightweight, weighing in at a hefty 42,000 pounds, nearly 2 tons more than our lobster yacht. Nevertheless, with a pair of 625 hp Detroit Diesels, the Viking 43 reaches 33.6 knots at full throttle. Viking's modified-V hull design, with 15 degrees of deadrise (see chapter 4) at the transom, develops significant dynamic pressure at high speed, lifting the hull vertically a foot or more out of the water and reducing the wetted surface and frictional drag. The hard chines improve flow separation, further reducing drag at planing speed. The Viking also has a more efficient drivetrain and a flatter trim angle at speed.

The lesson learned here is that the boat should have been more moderately powered to achieve a below-20-knot cruising speed. A cruise speed of 18 knots at full load, possibly achievable with just one of those Cummins, would likely have produced a fine cruising yacht that would take full advantage of its hull shape's excellent rough-water ride and handling qualities. Push a semidisplacement hull shaped like this one too fast, a S/L of 4 in this case, and not only will fuel consumption be off the charts, but dynamic instabilities may well result. We cover planing hull design in depth in the next chapter.

This 50-foot wooden lobster boat has a classic semidisplacement hull form and a fine entry; round bilges with a full hollow keel produce a seakindly ride.

CHAPTER 4

Planing Hulls

Some people wonder all their lives if they've made a difference. The Marines don't have that problem.
—Ronald Reagan

You'll probably get more from this chapter if you read chapters 2 and 3 first. Many of the concepts discussed here are explained in those earlier chapters, and reading them will help you gain a more complete understanding of what makes a planing hull work.

Good planing hulls are amazing creations. They have to run reasonably well and handle predictably at displacement speeds *and* be capable of climbing up on plane and skimming along the water's surface. Besides the *static* pressure of buoyancy acting on any partially submerged body, planing hulls are subject to the *dynamic* forces of rapidly moving water. The ski boat, convertible sportfisherman, express yacht, and outboard-powered center console are all examples of planing boats.

Whereas displacement hulls can move huge amounts of cargo slowly while using very little fuel per ton of cargo, *planing* hulls can move small cargo loads, including people, very fast and very inefficiently, using a lot of fuel in the process. Though *semidisplacement* hulls can rise partially on plane, a planing hull can essentially fly on the surface of the water and reach tremendous speeds. We'll see why in this chapter.

Planing hull dynamics can be complex, and its study keeps some of our best naval architects and boatbuilders busy. Why the complexity? For one thing, unlike a displacement hull, a hull's behavior on plane is nonlinear and therefore hard to predict.

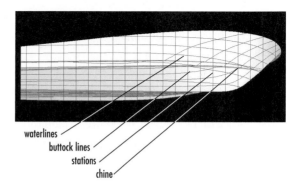

waterlines
buttock lines
stations
chine

A computer-generated rendering of the bottom of a Proteus Engineering–designed sportfisherman showing waterlines, buttock lines, stations, and chines. PROTEUS ENGINEERING

This means that steady changes in dynamic influences, like *trim*, have an inconsistent influence on the boat's behavior. Increasing trim by 2 degrees instead of 1 does not necessarily mean that lift is doubled, nor does dropping the bow a degree have the opposite effect of raising it a degree. A 1-degree increase in trim may suddenly cause a dynamic instability like *porpoising*, while a 3-knot increase in speed, say from 35 to 38 knots, may suddenly result in *chine walking*. So while the static buoyant forces acting on a displacement hull can be accurately predicted, *why* a planing hull acts the way it does under all conditions at high speed is another issue. We'll take a closer look at porpoising and chine walking on pages 70–71.

It would seem obvious, then, that designing a planing hull is a job for an expert with a thorough understanding of hydrostatics and hydrodynamics. But in fact many boats are designed by people who apparently rely on their boating experience and their intuition rather than on a comprehensive study of the principles of planing hull dynamics. The problem with this approach is that the behavior of planing hulls can be counterintuitive or evade intuitive powers altogether. So, while many planing boats are marvels of engineering, more than a few are inappropriately designed for their intended purpose. Others are designed to satisfy market demand for the roomiest possible boats for a given length, with wide, bottoms and full, blunt entries. These floating condos should never venture outside calm, sheltered waters.

Planing Speed

In chapter 3 we saw that a vessel is considered to be in the semidisplacement mode at speed-to-length (S/L) ratios between 1.34 and 2.5 (8.5 to 15.8 knots for a boat with a 40-foot waterline length, for instance). A boat is generally considered to be fully planing when traveling at speeds in excess of S/L 2.5 to 3 (for a boat 40 feet long at the waterline, that means over 15.8 to 19 knots). Concrete evidence of a boat on plane, though, is a noticeable rising of the hull relative to the water—that is, the boat has "emerged" from its hole in the water. A hull planes because it has a suitable shape and sufficient power; when going fast enough, it's supported primarily by dynamic rather than buoyant pressures. Dynamic lift (see below) tends to dominate the force of buoyancy at speeds over 25 knots in larger planing hulls.

Speed-to-length ratios notwithstanding, a heavily loaded boat may still be in semidisplacement mode at S/L 2.5, while the same hull lightly loaded may be on plane at a S/L ratio of 2.3. The speed at which a hull actually rises bodily out of the water depends to a large degree on its bottom loading.

If, upon achieving a certain speed, a 42-foot, 20,000-pound lobster boat rises vertically at the stern as well as the bow and leaves a clean wake

This fast-moving Mako 21 center console shows a rise in CG and a significant reduction in wetted surface, both of which define a hull on plane.

astern, is it on plane? The answer is yes, since there has been a rise in CG, and a clean wake indicates that significant dynamic pressures (lift) are being developed. But what about the same hull, now 18,000 pounds heavier with a load of fish on board and running at the same speed? Probably not, since the same dynamic forces acting on the bottom of the hull aren't likely to be sufficient to lift the hull vertically and make it plane. The only way to add dynamic lift is to add speed, and that requires more power. If it's available, the boat will plane.

So, although S/L ratios are useful for calculating wavemaking resistance, they aren't the whole story when it comes to predicting planing speeds; this is where the *volume Froude number* comes in. Naval architects use the volume Froude number, rather than the S/L ratio, or another Froude number based on length or beam, when evaluating planing craft. That's because the ability to plane is partly a function of the vessel's displacement, especially in the transition stages from semiplaning to planing.

Planing Hull Overview and Terminology

Let's consider first in broad-brush strokes how a planing hull works, and then we'll go into more detail with clear definitions of the terms used. Since boats have mass (weight), they have to be supported

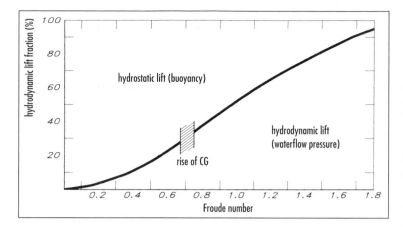

The faster a planing hull goes, the more it's supported by dynamic forces, and the less by buoyancy. This chart shows the relationship between speed (divide the Froude number by 0.298 to get S/L), the rise in CG (center of gravity), and the ratio of buoyancy-to-dynamic lift at various speeds. LARSSON AND ELIASSON, *PRINCIPLES OF YACHT DESIGN*

by something. An object that floats, including a planing hull, is supported by buoyancy when at rest, or at low speeds. When a planing (or semidisplacement) hull is moving above displacement speed, dynamic lift created by the pressure of moving water along the hull supports an increasing portion of the vessel's weight. Once a hull is moving fast enough, and this speed depends mostly on the hull's length and weight, dynamic water pressure predominates over buoyancy, doing most of the work of supporting the vessel. At this point we say a boat is "on plane."

We'll also see that a planing hull's overall dimensions mean little when it comes to its performance; what really matters is the *wetted* hull length and chine beam. And this wetted area, the part of the hull that's in regular contact with the water, is surprisingly small in relation to the boat's overall size.

Let's now define a few concepts that are critical to understanding how planing hulls work, and why some hulls perform much better than others.

Deadrise

Deadrise is the angle of the hull bottom (keel to chine) upward from the horizontal in station or cross-sectional view. The first place to look is the transom; a flat-bottom boat has no deadrise (0-degree deadrise) while a deep-V racing boat typically has 24 degrees of deadrise at the transom. The more deadrise, the smoother the ride. It's simple physics, based on the distribution of energy over time when a hull impacts a wave. When landing on a wave, a deep-V absorbs the energy incrementally, and decelerates slightly slowly than a flatter bottom, reducing the *vertical accelerations* felt by the boat and its human occupants. Larger angles of deadrise result in a smoother ride, allowing a hull to slice through the waves. However, as we shall see, this improvement in ride quality (see page 60 for ride quality explanation) comes at the expense of dynamic lift, propulsion efficiency, and form stability. The flatter the bottom, the more easily a boat is pushed along the surface of the water. But calm-water speed is gained at the expense of rough-water

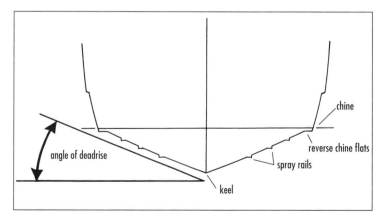

The angle of deadrise on a 65-foot Viking Sport Cruiser at station 4, or about 40 percent of the way aft of the bow. The convex sections above the waterline increase interior volume. BERNARD OLESINSKI

speed, because the low-deadrise boat will have to slow down sooner as the waves build to avoid pounding.

Transom deadrise, while an important at-a-glance indicator of how a boat will ride at speed, is by no means the whole enchilada. In fact, it's possible for a boat with 16 degrees of transom deadrise to ride better than the boat in the next slip with 22 degrees of transom deadrise, if the deadrise farther forward is greater. Deadrise in the bow and midship sections is important to ride quality because this is where the hull first meets the waves (except in ultra-high-performance racing boats, which can often become airborne and land stern-first). Planing hulls can have *constant-deadrise* or *warped-V* hulls, as we'll see.

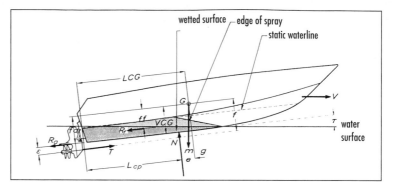

A side view of a planing hull at work, marked to show the major forces to be considered by the yacht designer. G is the center of gravity. The center of pressure caused by dynamic lift and buoyancy is N, and engine thrust is T. Resistance due to hull frictional drag is R_f; lower unit appendage drag is R_a. N, R_f, and R_a tend to trim the boat by the bow (bow down). The propeller thrust tends to trim the boat by the stern (bow up). The boat trims at an angle where all these forces cancel out. Compared to optimal trim (usually 2 to 5 degrees, depending on hull form), a lower trim angle reduces bottom pressure (spreads it out more evenly) but also increases wetted surface and frictional drag, and buoyancy will take more of the load. More bow rise reduces the wetted surface, but increases form drag, slowing the boat.   LARSSON AND ELIASSON, *PRINCIPLES OF YACHT DESIGN*

Longitudinal Center of Gravity

If one element is crucial to planing hull performance, it is *longitudinal center of gravity*. As we saw in chapter 2, LCG is defined as the precise location between bow and stern from which a boat would balance if suspended in the air. When a boat is designed, the weight of the hull, superstructure, decks, machinery, auxiliary equipment, fuel, water, furnishings, appliances, and everything else that will be placed in the finished boat must be precisely accounted for to ensure a well-balanced LCG. That's because the location of LCG is key to a planing hull's performance.

Longitudinal Center of Buoyancy (LCB) and Longitudinal Center of Flotation (LCF)

The *longitudinal center of buoyancy* (LCB) is the center of the buoyant forces acting on the hull; or to put it another way, it's the LCG of the water displaced by

the hull. An immersed body is buoyed up by a force equal to the weight of the displaced fluid, and the fore-and-aft center of buoyant force (LCB), determined by the underwater shape of the hull, lines up precisely with the fore-and-aft center of the boat's weight (LCG). If you add 500 pounds of weight aft, the LCG will move aft and so will the LCB, and the boat will trim down by the stern accordingly. The *actual* LCG must be located directly at the hull's design LCB, or center of the hull's submerged volume, for the boat to float properly at its design waterline.

The *longitudinal center of flotation* (LCF) is the longitudinal center of the hull's waterplane area (or *footprint* on the water's surface) about which the hull trims. Weight added *at* LCF will cause the hull to settle without any change in trim.

Center of Dynamic Lift

So a planing hull not only floats—it flies on the surface of the water. The pressure created by high-velocity water flow has a longitudinal center of effort

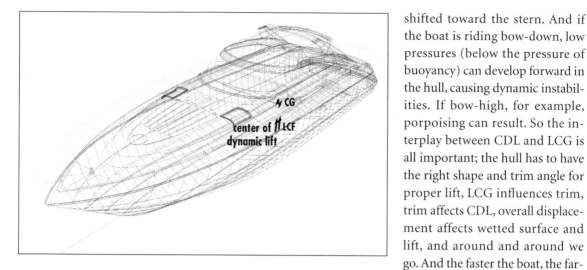

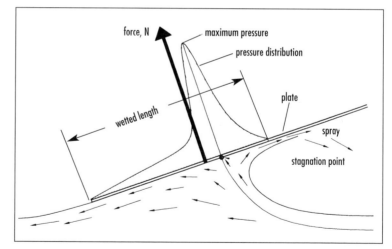

A port-bow computer rendition of a 65-foot Viking Sport Cruiser express yacht, designed by Bernard Olesinski. The center of gravity (CG), center of dynamic lift (CDL), and longitudinal center of flotation (LCF) are shown. These drawings can be fed to a computer-controlled 5-axis milling machine and turned into a flawless mold.   BERNARD OLESINSKI

that's called the *center of dynamic lift* (CDL). It's called *dynamic* lift simply because it depends on the constant motion of water flow to be present. The dynamic pressure acting on the planing hull varies from point to point along the bottom; it's high forward where the bottom first makes contact with the water, while back aft, near the propellers, it's quite a bit lower, in terms of pressure-per-square-foot of hull surface. CDL is determined by the shape of the bottom and the vessel's trim. Trim, in turn, is determined by CDL and LCG, so all these elements are interdependent.

If LCG is too far forward or aft in relation to CDL, the boat will run off trim, handling poorly and running inefficiently. CDL also changes with trim; it moves forward when weight is added at the bow, and aft when weight is

shifted toward the stern. And if the boat is riding bow-down, low pressures (below the pressure of buoyancy) can develop forward in the hull, causing dynamic instabilities. If bow-high, for example, porpoising can result. So the interplay between CDL and LCG is all important; the hull has to have the right shape and trim angle for proper lift, LCG influences trim, trim affects CDL, overall displacement affects wetted surface and lift, and around and around we go. And the faster the boat, the farther aft LCG should be to maintain control and prevent instabilities at high speed. That's why some repower jobs get into trouble; high-horsepower diesels are installed, LCG doesn't shift aft, and the boat becomes a performance and handling nightmare.

Bottom pressure concentration versus waterflow angle of incidence on a flat plate. N represents the center of pressure acting on the hull. From the hull's forward-most wetted surface to the transom, the peak pressure occurs just aft of the stagnation line. The sum of these pressures determines CDL. CDL (the focus of pressure) in relation to LCG (the focus of weight) helps determine running trim, with the weight of the hull balancing on the center of dynamic lift.

LARSSON AND ELIASSON, *PRINCIPLES OF YACHT DESIGN*

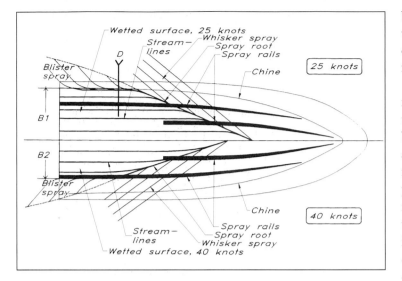

The bottom of a planing boat, showing the interaction between the hull and the water surface at 25 and 40 knots. Note how less of the hull is in contact with the water, but the pressures increase on the smaller area to support the weight of the boat. Forward is the spray developed by the hull's motion, and the immersed V-section shows the area of the hull in contact with solid water. Because of the "hump" in the bottom pressure curve, seen in the bottom illustration on page 47, the center of lift (CDL) is forward of the *center* of the waterplane area shown here.   LARSSON AND ELIASSON, *PRINCIPLES OF YACHT DESIGN*

Trim

Trim is the fore-and-aft inclination of the vessel, measured in degrees, and is often referred to as *bow rise* when on plane. A planing boat has a static trim (at the dock) and a dynamic trim (when on plane). When a boat runs with its bow raised 3 degrees higher than when floating (on its design waterline) at the dock, it is said to be running at 3 degrees of trim. For a given hull shape, static trim is determined by LCG. Dynamic trim is determined predominately by LCG, and also by CDL, with the latter in turn influenced by the direction and location of propeller thrust, and the shape of the hull, in particular its buttock lines. LCG is a moving target, since it changes as fuel is consumed (on most boats) and as people and gear move around.

Trim directly affects ride quality and propulsion efficiency. Planing hulls tend to run best in a trim range of 2 to 5 degrees (on warped-V and constant-deadrise hulls respectively), depending on

bottom type. The most efficient trim angle is, up to a point, the one that minimizes wetted surface, and therefore frictional drag.

But most efficient doesn't mean most comfortable; a bow-up attitude is more efficient than bow-down, but the latter delivers a smoother ride. The trick is to find the sweet spot, which will depend on how rough it is, what direction you're running in relation to the seas, and how fast you're going, that delivers a reasonable combination of efficiency and ride quality without causing instabilities and poor handling.

Excessive bow-high trim increases slamming loads (vertical accelerations), increases the tendency to porpoise, increases fuel consumption, and interferes with visibility from the lower helm station. Bow-down trim increases wetted surface and frictional drag, slowing the boat, although it produces a smoother ride in a chop. Bow-down trim also creates a tendency to bow-steer (a deeply immersed bow reduces the rudder's ability to control heading), so things can get out of control quickly in a following sea, and you'll be in for a wetter ride with spray developing farther forward. Running with a slightly bow-high attitude reduces drag by reducing wetted surface. Running with a degree or two less trim slows the boat a whisker, but reduces vertical accelerations in a chop. The longer a hull, and to an extent the greater the length-to-beam ratio, the flatter it tends to run. This make it easier to see over the bow of some 60-foot express cruisers than some 35-footers.

Buttocks

The shape of the buttock lines in profile can create or prevent dynamic instability, and in fact is the primary design factor distinguishing displacement,

Running with close to zero trim angle at high speed minimizes slamming loads, but it also increases wetted surface forward, slowing the boat and making for a wetter ride.　APREA MARE

Here's another relatively hard-riding hull, this time a small center console design with a flat and full entry forward.

This Sailfish 30-06 center console has a great rough-water ride, thanks to lots of deadrise, a sharp entry, and small chine flats forward.

A Bernard Olesinski–designed Viking Sport Cruiser's excellent ride is due to its refined forefoot, deep and fine, with high chines forward and radiused strakes and chines.

semidisplacement, and planing hulls. Waterflow at high speed very nearly follows the buttock lines, so their shape has a great deal to say about how a hull will perform. As we saw in chapter 3, a displacement hull's buttock lines sweep up aft to reduce the hull's wavemaking at slow speeds. The planing hull's buttock lines, on the other hand, must run parallel, or nearly so, to the waterline, in order to detach waterflow from the hull aft, to develop dynamic lift without an undesirable degree of bow-up trim, and to prevent the stern from squatting at speed.

Chines

The chine is the corner formed by the intersection of the hull's bottom and its sides. Planing hulls typically have "hard" chines, with true corners, although there are also round-bilge planing hulls. The gentle radius seen on displacement hulls and sailing boats is properly referred to as a *round bilge*, not a soft chine.

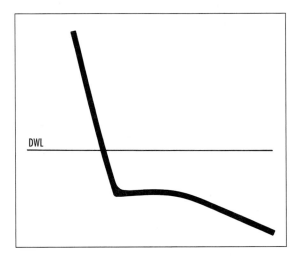

A gently radiused chine flat on a Viking Sport Cruiser deflects spray effectively and adds buoyancy high up and outboard for added form stability. BERNARD OLESINSKI

The hydrodynamic purpose of the chine is to provide waterflow separation from the bottom of the hull, which reduces frictional drag. And, since the chine forward projects farther outboard than the corresponding section of a round-bilge hull, the hard chine flattens the buttock lines forward, which helps prevent dynamic instabilities (see below). In a round-bilge hull, the intersection of hull side and bottom, seen in section, is a radiused curve. With no chine to separate the waterflow, when the round-bilge hull is running at high speed, water tends to flow outward around the turn of the bilge and up onto the hull sides, and negative pressures can result. If the hull is light enough and properly trimmed, this problem can be overcome and the hull will run perfectly well. Spray rails can be added

The chines and strakes on the bottom of a MasterCraft X-Star championship wakeboard boat are designed to channel waterflow, producing the wake geometry that wakeboarders favor.

forward to reduce spray and improve waterflow separation along the hull sides. For more information, see Round-Bilge Planing Hulls on page 62.

Some boats have double chines, which are intended to increase wetted beam at rest (with the upper chine submerged) and, once up on plane, reduce wetted surface and drag (with the upper chine clear of the water). Chine flats, in which the deadrise flattens out or even reverses downward a few degrees, like a flap, are de rigueur in modern planing hulls. These surfaces are usually 4 to 18 inches wide at the stern, depending on the size of the boat, and narrow toward the bow. They add buoyancy outboard, which increases form stability, and they deflect water and spray at planing speeds, increasing dynamic lift and contributing to a drier ride. The original deep-Vs, like the Bertram 31, which did not have chine flats, could run like the wind when slicing through a choppy sea, but were notoriously tender at rest since the chines were clear of the water at rest.

Forefoot

A hull's entry, or forefoot, plays a crucial role in determining both ride quality and course-keeping ability, which is the vessel's natural tendency to stay on course at all speeds and in all directions to the sea. Regulator, Buddy Davis, and Blackfin sportfishing boats have deep, fairly fine entries that essentially eliminate pounding in a head sea. It is possible for a forefoot to be *too* deep and fine, resulting in a boat that bow-steers in a following sea. A destroyerlike (long and narrow) bow with low displacement forward may develop too little buoyancy initially when immersed below its static waterline, such as when the stern is raised by a quartering sea. Especially when the stern is wide and fairly flat, this imbalance results in a boat that is difficult to keep on course when running downsea; the bow digs in, and the broad, buoyant stern gets thrown around.

A broad and shallow bow entry will often result in a faster, more easily driven hull, and one that handles well running downsea (since there's so little bow to dig in and trip the stern), but will also be far more susceptible to pounding in a head sea. A balanced hull has a moderately fine and deep entry to deliver a smoother ride in a head sea, but one that's not so deep and sharp that it scares the daylights out of you running downsea, or so full and blunt that it pounds your kidneys out upsea.

Boats powered by waterjets require special care in the shape of the entry: with no underwater gear aft to keep them going in a straight line, these hulls are inherently susceptible to fickle tracking downsea. A waterjet-propelled hull must have fairly shallow sections forward, with the hull radiused at the keel to help keep the bow from digging in downsea.

This walkaround carries very little deadrise forward where most wave impact will take place, thereby making it a rough ride in a chop at speed.

Boston Whaler's much improved hull designs have sharper entries, less Whaler smirk (which in older models produced excessive buttocks curvature forward), and more deadrise where it's needed for a smooth ride.

This Grady-White 360's excellent Hunt hull design and appropriate weight distribution provide a smooth ride offshore.

In addition to forefoot geometry, the overall hull shape, LCG, and rudder design are all factors in good course-keeping. Moderation is the key here: a boat that resists any course changes will be difficult to steer, and one that changes course too easily will require constant rudder corrections.

This Davis 45 has a superb, Don Blount–designed running surface with considerable flare, North Carolina style.

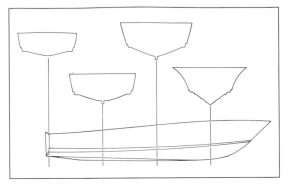

A Viking 52 profile with selected stations showing the change in shape from bow to stern. Viking uses double chines, which, when on plane at high speeds, reduce wetted surface by effectively narrowing the beam. The lower chines angle down a few degrees for added lift, and their buoyancy outboard improves form stability at rest. Note also Viking's flat "fairbody" sections along the keel aft, which add lift at speed, and also raise the hull's center of buoyancy slightly for added stability. The Viking 52, capable of speeds approaching 40 knots, has considerably more deadrise forward than its 1980s predecessors to accommodate the extra speed.

VIKING YACHTS

Flare

Flare is the concave curvature in a hull in section view: a hull with flare curves inward between the chine and sheer. Flare makes a boat look better, of course, but more importantly it adds buoyancy as the bow submerges; no amount of flare, though, can make seaworthy a hull that is too fine forward at the waterline to start with, or that has its LCG too far forward. And relying on flare alone to provide a dry ride is also an exercise in futility; the geometry of the bottom and the placement and shape of the bottom strakes and chines have a greater influence on whether a hull will deliver a wet or dry ride. Exaggerated flare sometimes hints at a boat's heritage, such as that of a North Carolina–built sportfisherman. Too much flare, though, and you only have to look at a few of the custom sportfishermen to find examples, just makes the boat look a little silly, though; a lot like a car with a huge tail fin. And pity the crew of such a boat that stuffs its inordinately wide foredeck in a following sea!

Section Shape

The shape of the hull bottom in cross section is also important to ride quality and dryness. Underwater hull sections can be *convex* in cross section, making for a ride that is smooth yet wet. *Concave* hull sections produce a dry ride but are hard-riding in a seaway, since water

gets trapped in the hollow sections, especially when the hull is heeled over. *Straight* sections are often a good compromise, offering a reasonable combination of smoothness and dryness. Some sophisticated hulls are bell shaped in cross section, with convex curvature near the keel (to soften wave impact) and concavity near the chines (to deflect spray), mixing the best of both worlds for a smooth and dry ride.

Hook and Rocker

Hook and *rocker* describe the curvature, in profile (viewed from abeam), in the aft 10 to 25 percent or so

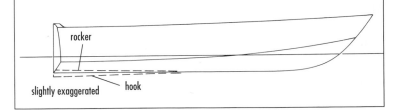

Hook and rocker (exaggerated).

of the boat's buttock lines. Hook is a concave curvature; rocker is convex. Adding hook or rocker is a good way to control trim. Hook makes a boat run flatter by shifting the center of dynamic lift (CDL) aft, thus raising the stern slightly. Rocker makes the hull run lower at the stern, trimming up the bow and shifting the CDL forward. A designer might add a little hook to compensate for a large amount of weight in the stern. Both hook and rocker can help correct dynamic instabilities, but some designers avoid rocker because it increases stern drag at lower speeds and its effects at higher speeds are not always readily predicted.

Length-to-Beam Ratio

This is the relationship between the boat's length and beam, usually at the waterline. Along with deadrise, displacement, and longitudinal center of gravity (LCG), the L/B ratio has a profound effect on ride quality in a seaway. A longer, narrower boat will have more comfortable motions and lower accelerations in rough water, and be more efficiently propelled, than a shorter, wider boat of the same size and displacement. The long and narrow vessel may not have a lot of room for its length, but it has ample room for its *displacement*. A short, wide hull may have more room for the LOA, but it will burn more fuel than its longer, narrower cousin and will have to slow down more and sooner when the going gets rough. The long-and-narrow advantage applies both to planing hulls and to displacement hulls. Unfortunately, market forces have driven the demand for shorter-wider boats, which is too bad since most people have no earthly idea how smoothly and efficiently a same-size, but longer-narrower, boat can run.

Speed-to-Length Ratio

The S/L ratio is the ratio of a hull's speed in knots to the square root of its waterline length. A boat that is 49 feet at the waterline makes 7 knots at a S/L of 1, or 21 knots at S/L 3. Maximum S/L is often used to define which category a hull belongs to; in general terms, with sufficient power, a displacement hull can reach S/L 1.34 and a semidisplacement hull S/L 2.5, while a planing hull theoretically has unlimited speed potential.

Resistance

The drag caused by a hull's interaction with the water is called *resistance,* which we break down into three types, just to make it interesting. *Frictional resistance* results in a boundary layer of water that the hull drags along with it due to the friction of the hull's surface disturbing water molecules in the immediate vicinity. This boundary layer gets thicker as a hull gets longer and deeper in the water, and may reach 4 to 6 inches on a sportfisherman and 18 inches on a navy destroyer. Where it contacts the hull, the boundary layer moves along as fast as the boat, but it slows gradually until at its outer edge the surrounding water remains undisturbed. Frictional resistance is largely a function of the immersed hull's surface area and roughness along with the size and shape of its appendages. *Wavemaking resistance* is caused by the hull's displacement of water as it moves along. Hull shape and trim have the biggest influences on wavemaking resistance. *Appendage drag* is the resistance caused by struts, shafts, rudders, and propellers sticking out into the waterflow. Then there's aerodynamic drag, caused by the above-water hull and superstructure moving through the air; a modestly proportioned displacement hull will hardly notice a stiff head wind, but a broad-beamed convertible with a flybridge brow and tuna tower might easily be slowed 4 or 5 knots by air drag when running upwind.

Hard-Chine Planing Hull Types

Planing hulls come in a variety of shapes that make each one well suited to a particular set of tasks and ill suited to others. Now that we've defined some terms, let's look at the boats. In this section we look at the various hard-chine planing hulls; in the next we compare these with the round-bilge planing hulls.

Flat-Bottom Hulls

Flat-bottom planing hulls are generally found on skiffs and other small craft that ply calm bays and lakes. Able to carry a lot of weight, the easiest to push through the water, and the most stable at small angles of heel, flat-bottom boats also produce a kidney-jarring ride in a chop.

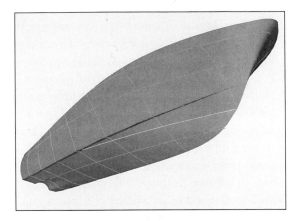

The hull lines of the Ward Setzer–designed Lyman Morse 74. The planing hull's 4:1 length-to-beam ratio, fine forefoot, and modified-V aft sections deliver excellent ride quality in rough water. Radiused, moderately proportioned prop pockets, also seen in the rendering, reduce draft and shaft angles without detracting noticeably from buoyancy, or dynamic lift at speed. WARD SETZER

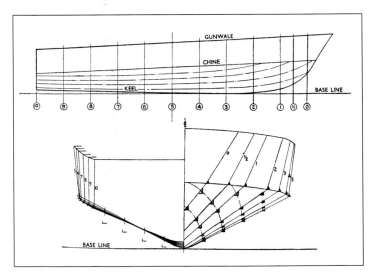

An early Ray Hunt–designed deep-V, the smoothest-riding planing boat around in its day. Modern refinements missing here include chine flats and a padded keel, which would add form stability and planing efficiency. This hull became an early Bertram and is the paradigm for all modern planing hulls.

BREWER, *UNDERSTANDING BOAT DESIGN*

Deep-V Hulls

The *deep-V* hull is the most common planing hull out there today. It is seen in its most basic form in the Bertram 31, the Ray Hunt hull that started it all. A deep-V typically has 20 degrees or more of deadrise at the transom, with 24 degrees a common standard on very high speed hulls. The deadrise angle on a deep-V is constant from the stern forward for over half of the boat's length, and then starts increasing from slightly forward of amidships, rising to the stem, where the chines start to rise out of the water and narrow up.

The great advantage of the deep-V is the smoothness of the ride in a rough chop at speed. A deep-V can keep on charging when a more flat-bottom boat has to slow to a crawl. That's because the *time* (in milliseconds) over which a hull impacts a wave is spread out over a longer period of time. A deep-V hull meets a wave incrementally—first the keel, then the garboard, then the midsection, and finally the chines. A flat-bottom hull, on the other hand, meets the same wave all at once—wham! Both boats follow the surface of the waves, but the deep-V adjusts to the contour of the water's surface with a lot more ease and finesse; the difference in terms of comfort between the physical effect of a deceleration that's spread out over a few milliseconds, and one that's virtually instantaneous, is significant.

The deep-V's high angle of deadrise, carried all the way back to the transom, allows a boat to slice smoothly through the waves. A deep-V can maintain speed without pounding in sea conditions that force boats with less deadrise to back off. On the flip side, all that deadrise tends to rob speed, because with more deadrise, less lift is developed. The best way to get some of that speed back is to reduce weight, and some builders have done a great job of doing so, without sacrificing strength, through the use of composite sandwich construction (see chapter 6). Deep-Vs can also gain speed through refinements that add lift, like reverse chines and padded keels (see below). But for two otherwise identical boats, the one with less deadrise will go faster in calm water since a flatter bottom is the more efficient lifting surface.

This deep-V hull is similar to the early Bertrams, with its chines emerged above the waterline at rest. Without the immersed reverse chines, or chine flats, seen on most modern V-bottom hulls, this boat will lack form stability and be on the tippy side at rest.

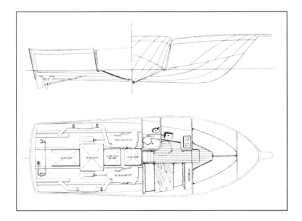

The Gerr 34's lines. That she's a smooth ride in rough water is apparent at a glance. A pair of 300 hp Cats pushes this 12-foot-beam, 19,000-pound sportfisherman to 32 knots and delivers a 28-knot cruise. The keel flat and radiused chines widen toward the transom, adding lift and stability.

GERR, *THE NATURE OF BOATS*

For high-performance craft that cruise fast enough to emerge most of the length of their bottoms on a regular basis, a deep-V bottom is the way to go. These very fast (50-knots-plus) hulls often become airborne in rough water, and when they land on the aft 30 to 40 percent of their bottoms, they need every bit of that 24-degree deadrise back there to smooth out the landings. The extra deadrise aft also helps a deep-V to track better downsea, since the hull shape tends to grab hold of those waves more tenaciously, creating its own railroad track as it goes. Well-known, superior deep-V hull designs include the original Bertrams, the Regulator- and Contender-type center consoles, and Formula's cruising and race boats.

Modified-V Hulls

Modified-V planing hulls typically have between 12 and 18 degrees of deadrise at the transom and 20 to 25 degrees amidships. This design works well with larger, heavier planing hulls that need all the dynamic lift they can get back aft and rarely come more than half their length out of the water at high speed. The flatter sections usually extend farther forward, as well, than in a deep-V hull. Deadrise is constant in the aft half of the hull, with the keel and chines running essentially parallel to the waterline. Buoyancy is centered higher in the hull, so the modified-V hull has greater initial stability than a deep-V, which helps on boats carrying a lot of weight topside. Unless a boat rides with half its length out of the water at cruising speeds, a modified-V is often a good choice for a designer.

Warped-V Hulls

The *warped-V* is so named because deadrise changes along the length of the vessel, lessening all the way to the transom. While the keel remains very nearly parallel to the waterline, the chine continues to run downhill as it approaches the stern, resulting in a *warp*, or twist, to the bottom. A planing hull with a warped-V bottom will run at a flatter trim than a constant-deadrise deep-V, since the CDL is farther aft, with more lift developed by the stern's flatter sections, thanks to the bottom's slightly twisting sections. And because the warped-V hull's

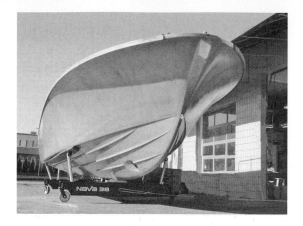

This Charlie Jannace–designed Nava 38 is a smooth, comfortable ride in a head sea, with a fine entry and deep deadrise forward. This boat has a single Yanmar 440 hp diesel powering a Power Vent surface-piercing drive. (Jannace designed many of the Blackfin boats.) NAVA COMPOSITES

chines are deeper in the water at the transom, LCB shifts aft as well, making this hull form an excellent candidate for an aft engine room with V drives. The warped bottom also produces an excellent lower-unit-powered boat, since the added buoyancy in the stern can easily accommodate the weight of a stern drive or a pair of big engines cantilevered off the stern on a transom bracket.

Warped-V hulls have gotten a bad rap because excessive warp, such as in some of the WWII PT boat designs, produces a lousy hull design with low

dynamic pressures aft in the hull on plane. Designers have since learned how to get it right. C. Raymond Hunt Associates of Boston, Massachusetts, in particular, has designed some of the finest warped-V planing hulls in the world. These designs are improvements on the original 1960s-era constant-deadrise deep-V hulls designed by Ray Hunt, since they combine the soft forward entry of a deep-V with the added buoyancy and lift aft of a moderate-deadrise hull. With their superb ride quality and excellent propulsion efficiency, Eastbay, Alden, Palmer Johnson, Grady-White, and some of the latest Chris Craft retro-yachts are examples of the

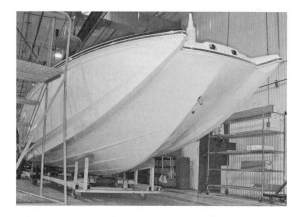

A glance at a hull provides a read on its abilities offshore. This MasterCraft X-80's hull has a "pickle fork" bow that opens up seating room forward. The modified sponson hull with moderate deadrise and wide chines forward delivers good propulsion efficiency and a decent ride in the light chop conditions for which it was designed.

The Hunt-designed Dettling 51 has a high-tech-construction, moderate-weight hull that rises well up on plane. The slight warp in the bottom produces a low trim on plane, improving ride quality, helm visibility, and running efficiency.

The Scout 35 Express, with a Michael Peters–designed deep-V step-bottom hull design provides a great ride offshore.

C. R. Hunt warped-V hull form done right. Trim tabs, incidentally, are to some degree superfluous with these hulls, since they climb on plane and run at a low trim naturally.

Stepped Hulls

Short, wide (high-aspect) surfaces are more efficient than long, narrow (low-aspect) ones in terms of frictional drag on water. Lift generation is just far more efficient with a large beam-to-length ratio surface. So, the idea behind a stepped bottom is to reduce wetted surface by allowing the hull to plane on two or three high-aspect planing surfaces rather than one large, low-aspect surface. And the popular notion that any added speed from a stepped bottom is due to a layer of bubbles blanketing the hull bottom is true to a degree but generally exaggerated. Entrained air bubbles undoubtedly reduce frictional drag to some extent, but the real saving is in minimizing the hull area in contact with the water, specifically by presenting two or three wide and short surfaces to the water instead of one long, narrow one.

Like any true design advance, though, the technology can be misapplied. While stepped bottoms work admirably on high-performance boats, they do little or nothing to improve performance on slower boats. In general, data indicate that if a boat can't cruise easily at close to 30 knots or more, it can't go fast enough to ride up on hull steps, so steps would only add drag. More specifically, this means that a gas-powered family cruiser with steps should be able to cruise fully loaded at 30 knots, not just reach this speed at full throttle. Otherwise, the extra cost of tooling and the added time and cost spent laying up a stepped hull is wasted, and the stepped bottom is just a marketing gimmick. Some runabout builders even carve out a little scoop at the chine amidships, which I suppose is

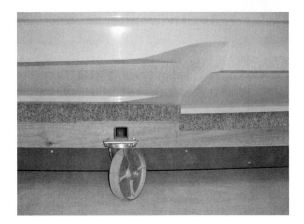

The Scout 35's hull step at the chine is large enough to keep airflow moving into the low-pressure area aft of the step, even in a hard turn when the chine is submerged.

meant to suggest that the bottom is stepped, when in fact the bottom is as straight as an arrow.

Assuming that it has enough power to cruise in the 30-knot range, what's the downside to a stepped

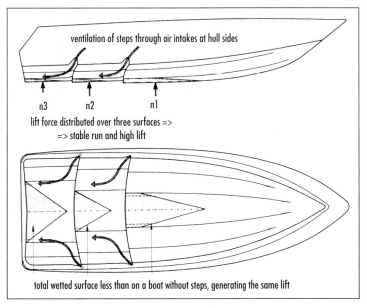

Bottom steps reduce wetted surface and drag, and pressure is distributed over three small, wide surfaces. Trim locks in at high speed, so trim tabs, lower unit angle, and changes in LCG have less effect than on a conventional hull. The stepped bottom tends to follow the water's surface (up and down waves) with great tenacity.

LARSSON AND ELIASSON, *PRINCIPLES OF YACHT DESIGN*

hull? Well, since stepped bottoms create localized areas of high pressure (dynamic lift) at the steps and at the transom, these boats tend to make up their own minds about trim angles. Fore-and-aft stability is significantly increased compared to a nonstepped hull, and stepped bottoms tend to follow wave contours more closely. Even in an outboard- or stern-drive-powered stepped-hull boat, at least at higher speeds, you can forget about raising the bow by trimming the lower units up in a following sea.

The area behind each step has to be adequately ventilated, and the airflow must not be cut off by waves, turns, or rolling. If airflow is lost, resistance is immediately created that can sharply reduce speed or, if airflow is cut off to one side of the hull only, the vessel may turn suddenly and unexpectedly. Builders often provide large inlets to the areas behind the steps, and a few even provide air paths through ducts that lead to the trailing vertical edge of the steps.

Planing Hull Dynamics

As we've discovered, a planing hull not only floats, but when traveling fast enough, it also skims along the surface of the water. When on plane, the bottom of a hull acts, to a limited degree, like an airplane wing. Water moving at high speed impinges on the hull, and since for every action there is an equal and opposite reaction, *dynamic lift* is created. A planing hull is unlike an airplane wing in that the latter mostly generates lift by creating a low pressure area along the top of the wing. This low pressure, and consequent pull upward, is due to the curvature, in cross section, of the top of the wing. This curvature causes the airflow to accelerate (and create lift from the resulting low pressure) along the top of the wing, since it has to travel a greater distance than the air on the bottom of the wing before it reaches the wing's trailing edge. See more below under Dynamic Instability.

Dynamic Lifting Surface

The *dynamic lifting surface* is the wetted surface of the hull that supports the vessel when on plane. It is bounded by an area termed the *stagnation zone* forward, by the spray rail or chines to the sides, and by the transom aft. On high-speed planing hulls, this surface is roughly triangular in shape and may be only 20 to 30 percent of the boat's length. The dynamic pressure on this small area equals the displacement of the boat. And ultrafast surface drive–powered boats may also be supported partially by the surface-piercing propeller's considerable vertical lift.

The stagnation zone is where the high-speed waterflow is tangent to the hull surface, with waterflow breaking off both ahead and astern. Since the waterflow impinges at a right angle to the hull, dynamic pressure is greatest here. This is called the *stagnation zone*, or *line*, since the water hitting the hull along this line, for the briefest moment, is not moving in relation to the hull. Dynamic pressure on the hull drops off both forward and aft of this region—rapidly forward, as water is deflected and turns to spray, and more gradually aft.

A Balanced Planing Hull

A planing hull's longitudinal center of buoyancy (LCB) is generally about 35 to 40 percent of the way forward of the transom at the waterline—farther aft than on a typical displacement hull. Why the difference? The planing hull's buttock lines aft must be nearly horizontal, or parallel to the waterline, so the hull can plane efficiently. On a displacement hull, the buttock lines normally sweep up aft to reduce drag and equalize fore-and-aft buoyancy at displacement speeds. Such a hull will lack the dynamic lift necessary to plane. The hull at the waterline must also be wide enough back aft to develop sufficient dynamic lift so the vessel can get up on plane. The planing hull also has its *longitudinal center of flotation* (LCF) farther aft, which reduces the impact of fuel level on trim when the fuel tanks are near the stern. The fullness of the planing hull's waterplane is reflected in its *prismatic coefficient* (see pages 36–37). Compared to its displacement and semidisplacement cousins, with their finer ends, the typical planing hull has a large C_p of about 0.70 or greater, which it needs to achieve dynamic lift.

The bow sections of planing hull must be full and buoyant enough so that when the stern is lifted by a following sea, the bow is not excessively immersed. If the bow roots, or digs too far into a following sea, yawing (or in extreme conditions, broaching) is introduced, with the bow turning into what is effectively a fixed rudder forward. The stern can't be so wide and buoyant that the bow tends to stuff when running downsea, and the bow shouldn't be so full (wide at the waterline forward) that it makes the boat pound upsea in a stiff chop.

Speed versus Deadrise

As increasingly powerful lightweight diesels boost a boat's speed capability, it's essential that the deadrise in modern designs increase proportionately to keep slamming loads down. A sharp entry for the first 20 percent of the waterline length isn't enough; the increased deadrise must continue aft to the hull's midbody, because that's where most of the wave impact is taking place at higher speeds. For most hulls, there must be at least 15 degrees of deadrise at the transom, and 25 to 35 degrees in the hull's midsection. There's no way around the need for deadrise here.

Over the years, many production boatbuilders like Tiara, Grady-White, and Viking have steadily increased deadrise forward as their boats have evolved from cruising at 16 to 20 knots in the 1970s to 32 knots (or faster) today. But these boats and yachts aren't lightweights, so there's a limit to how much deadrise is practical with a 30-knot cruising speed in demand. Bertram and Viking both opt for transom deadrise in the 15- to 18-degree range, delivering good lift at speed, but with enough deadrise for a smooth ride and improved course-keeping. The Bertram 46 (a stretched 43), as much as any other convertible of its size, is a smooth-as-silk marvel at speed in a chop.

Speed versus Weight

Since adding weight and deadrise reduces speed, all else being equal, a boat's speed can be increased by keeping the weight down. But two boats of similar size can vary in weight for a variety of reasons; the heavier boat isn't necessarily stronger or better built, but it may be. If Brand A's 36- by 12-foot express cruiser weighs significantly more than Brand B's, ask the builder to spell out specifically why that is. Is it because Brand A is heavily built with fiberglass-encapsulated plywood stringers and bulkheads, a solid glass hull, and plywood-cored decks, whereas Brand B benefits from advanced composite engineering with foam-cored stringers and bulkheads and a resin-infused, postcured, cored epoxy hull and deck laminate? Or are the two boats built pretty much the same, except for the thinner laminates and smaller scantlings in the hull grid system of the lighter one? Find out!

If two boats of similar dimensions weigh about the same and have similar drivetrains, and one is

Update Those Old Hull Designs!

The problem with some boats on the market today is that their hull designs originated thirty or more years ago. In the late 1960s, a 42-foot, low-deadrise sportfisherman might be fitted with a pair of 300 hp, 2,800-pound GM 671 diesels and would run along nicely at 16 to 20 knots. Nowadays you can fit 700 hp Yanmar or MAN diesels in about the same space as the old 671s, and suddenly a decent 16- to 20-knot fishing boat is transformed into a hard-riding, flat-bottom 32-knot race boat.

Some of the venerable New Jersey–built sportfishermen, like the Post 42—a well-engineered boat otherwise—and the Jersey 40, are prime examples. They're fast for their size and power precisely because of their relatively flat bottoms. But with their low-deadrise bottom sections forward, they pound noticeably in a stiff chop; there's no way to get around the laws of physics! With low or no deadrise aft, boats with similar hull shapes also tend to wander about their course with seas abaft the beam unless trimmed bow-up (which is possible only with plenty of fuel in the undercockpit fuel tank and trim tabs raised). If you value speed in calm water above all else, these boats may be right for you. But don't expect to comfortably keep up with the rest of the fleet when the wind picks up.

still significantly faster than the other, the reason is likely to be found in the deadrise. I'll take the deeper-deadrise, slower boat over the flatter, faster boat, since the first will deliver solid all-weather comfort and performance while the second will be a miserable ride in a chop.

The bottom line is that if a manufacturer claims that their boat is the fastest around with a given power plant, you should pull the string and find out why. If the boat isn't a whole lot lighter, it's probably because it has a flatter bottom than everyone else. You should care deeply about this if you plan on heading out past the jetties when the wind's blowing. Adding horsepower to an older hull, as we'll see, can also introduce dynamic instabilities if LCG isn't carefully managed during the repower.

Deadrise isn't everything, as this diagram by planing hull authority Dan Savitsky shows. The shape of the hull, in section view, has a significant impact (so to speak) on slamming, or pounding, which is measured as vertical accelerations. A bell-shaped hull section significantly reduces G-forces upon wave impact, when compared with a straight section. The downside is that more spray is generated.   DAN SAVITSKY

Ride Quality

As mentioned earlier, ride quality refers to the comfort of a boat's ride measured in vertical accelerations, or slamming loads. As a hull encounters waves at high speed, impacts of varying degrees occur repeatedly. These impacts are measured as accelerations using the force of gravity as a standard. A boat

This typical express cruiser is fully up on plane, but it's a harder-riding boat in a chop than, say, an Albemarle 26 or Formula 27, due to its also flatter, fuller forefoot. That makes a boat like this well suited to inshore waters, but not to running at speed in rougher water offshore.

high and dry in a parking lot subjects its cradle (and its occupants) to a G-force of 1. But if the same boat is slamming into a wave with sufficient impact to produce a G-force of 1.5, a 200-pound person standing in the bow of the boat will momentarily feel as if he weighs 300 pounds. Standing near the stern of the same boat, since the boat effectively moves vertically about a fulcrum just aft of amidships when pounding through small waves, the same man would experience less G-force and consider the ride more comfortable. Thus, where you happen to be standing in a high-speed boat is important to your morale. Remember if you are sitting farther aft than your passengers that they are being subjected to higher accelerations than you are, especially in a bowrider.

Course-Keeping and Handling

Course-keeping and boat handling have to do with the ability to control a boat at both high and low speeds. High-speed course-keeping is largely a function of hull form, which determines whether or not a boat will naturally tend to track in a straight line with minimal helm input. Here again, the deep-V has a distinct advantage over a boat with flatter sections aft, since a flat bottom tends to wander more about the desired heading, especially with seas abaft the beam. A full keel on a flat-bottom boat helps, but the added wetted surface increases drag and slows you down, and dynamic instability can occur at high cruising speeds. That's why a deep-V is so much better suited to waterjet propulsion (which has less directional stability than other drives) than a flat-bottom boat.

The LCG must not be too far forward, nor the VCG too high, to permit good seakeeping. In fact, if there is one other element in hull design that is most crucial to good performance, and this includes handling at speed and course-keeping, it's proper placement of the LCG. Put it too far forward and the boat rides bow down, making it directionally unstable and wet to boot. Too far aft, and the boat takes excessive power to propel through the water, decreasing range and wasting fuel, to say nothing of the bad effect on visibility from the lower helm station. A VCG that is too high will make the boat wallow and yaw excessively in a following sea, too.

The best test for course-keeping is a quartering sea some 20 to 40 degrees off the stern. If a boat tracks well in such a sea, then hats off to the designer and builder for getting weight distribution right. Most boats handle better running at a greater trim angle (bow up) in a following or quartering sea, while lowering the bow by depressing trim tabs makes for a smoother if wetter ride in a head sea.

Good *handling* characteristics presume rapid response to throttle and helm inputs and a hull that is not so directionally stable that it's hard to turn. For throttles to respond well, horsepower alone is only the beginning. Just as important, or more so, is how the power is delivered to the water. Larger reduction ratios with larger, slower turning propellers almost always respond better to low-speed clutch and throttle commands than smaller gear ratios with smaller, faster turning props. The volume *and* velocity of water being moved by the propeller is the key to responsiveness. Just try docking a typical 40-foot express cruiser with its shallow (1.64:1) gear ratio and too-small (22-inch) props; the boat hardly moves when you put an engine in gear at idle. While docking such a boat in Florida a few years ago, I backed the starboard engine only to have the bow fall off to port until I applied a strong burst of power. The same boat and engines with deeper gears and larger props would undoubtedly handle much more responsively and would likely reach the same cruising speed, though top speed (a mostly irrelevant and academic figure) might fall off slightly.

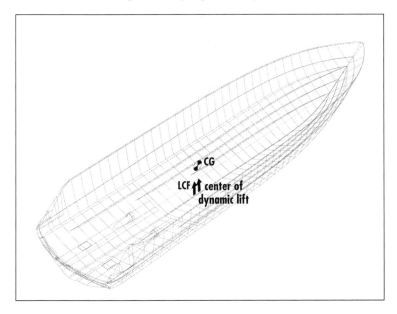

Another computer-generated 3-D wire drawing of the 65-foot Viking Sport Cruisers motor yacht shown in the figure on page 47. This is one of the best-running hull designs in the industry. Note the positions of CDL, CG, and LCF, the point about which the hull trims statically.

BERNARD OLESINSKI

Round-Bilge Planing Hulls

Though they are the most efficient at high speeds, not all planing hulls have hard chines. Some have round bilges (radiused chines), which have their own advantages, such as producing an easier, more comfortable motion in a seaway, and reducing resistance at slower speeds. Or a hull may have hard chines aft (to increase lift) and round bilges forward (to improve ride quality). A hard-chine planing hull creates more wavemaking resistance at displacement speeds and requires more power for a given displacement speed than a round-bilge craft. The round-bilge hull will tend to require less power to achieve a given speed up to S/L 2, whereas a hard-chine vessel will require less horsepower, and be more stable dynamically, above S/L 2.5. If the priority is low-speed efficiency and range, the round-bilge hull is the best choice. The larger waves created at slow speeds make the hard-chine planing hull a poor choice for operating extensively in no-wake zones such as canals and other protected waters. This is especially true of deep-V hulls, which leave a large wake and plane at higher speeds than flat-bottom boats.

There's no significant difference between round-bilge and hard-chine hulls of similar dimensions and displacement in pitch and heave at semi-displacement speeds. However, round-bilge vessels do have more comfortable motions at displacement speeds, and hard-chine planing hulls have superior ride quality at planing speeds. The hard-chine vessel rises significantly out of the water due to dynamic pressures, increasing the hull's effective freeboard, improving visibility from the helm station, and helping to keep spray and solid water off the deck. (As we've seen, length-to-beam ratio has a significant effect on crew comfort in a head sea, since vertical accelerations are greatly diminished in longer, narrower hulls of all persuasions.)

Compared to the round-bilge hull, the hard-chine vessel at planing speed will have better directional stability or course-keeping, especially with seas abaft the beam, and will be less prone to broach when operating near wave speed. The hard-chine craft will also have a stiffer, shallower roll and will tend to ship less water on deck in rough water. A hard-chine vessel running downsea at displacement speed will yaw more than a displacement hull, due to its flat buttock lines aft, wide transom, and buoyant stern. It will also squat less when coming up on plane, and once planing. And because of its superior course-keeping, a hard-chine, deep-V hull is generally better suited to waterjet propulsion than a round-bilge hull.

A round-bilge hull would need a full keel for acceptable directional stability, and possibly bilge keels or active stabilizers to reduce roll, all of which add drag to the hull. Naturally, there's a relation between course-keeping, yaw, and roll, since a single degree of yaw in a round-bilge hull can develop up to 5 degrees of roll. In fact, reducing roll angle in any vessel does wonders to improve course-keeping. And with a round-bilge hull's greater buttock lines curvature forward, as we'll see in the Dynamic Instability section below, bow diving becomes more likely.

This Four Winns 358 Vista is a good-running boat with its carefully engineered fore-and-aft weight distribution and Hunt bottom.

GENMAR HOLDINGS, INC.

Hybrid Hulls

One type of hybrid hull starts with a round bilge forward, the radius of which decreases gradually until a hard chine appears near the stern. The hard chine adds buoyancy and dynamic lift aft and reduces squatting at low planing speeds, helping to turn a semidisplacement hull into a planing hull.

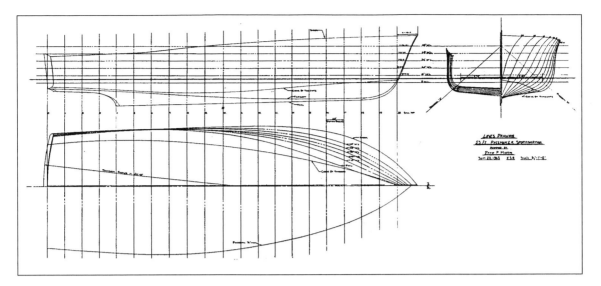

A 1960s-vintage Pacemaker designed by Dave Martin, who also has the Ocean Yachts line to his credit. This low-deadrise, round-bilge hull was well-suited to its day, when 16- to 18-knot speeds made for a fast boat. The entry is reasonably sharp forward where most wave impact takes place on a moderate-speed hull like this.
DAVE MARTIN

The hard chine aft also contributes to directional stability, improving course-keeping at higher speeds. Another hybrid design puts it the other way around, with the round bilge aft and the hard chine forward, a combination thought to improve course-keeping as well as transverse dynamic stability at semidisplacement speeds.

Other hard-chine design advantages include greater internal volume than a round-bilge craft of the same dimensions, improving load-carrying capacity and habitability. And since the hard-chine hull has greater form stability, it can carry more weight up high with greater impunity.

Large Planing Hulls

Large planing hulls, over about 75 feet, tend to run too flat in trim at high speeds, increasing frictional resistance and diminishing the vessel's handling. An easy way for the designer to drop the stern (and raise the bow relative to it) and improve matters is to put a little rocker in the buttocks aft. On many hulls, trim can be varied within a range of some 5 degrees in this manner. Savvy designers can also lock in optimum trim by shifting the LCG a bit farther aft than usual (remember that too-far-forward LCG is curtains for a planing hull) and then adding a little hook (concavity in the buttock lines) aft to raise the stern a whisker if needed. In fact, hook in the buttocks aft acts like a big set of trim tabs by shifting the center of dynamic lift aft. Hooked buttocks minimize drag at low speed (and are generally to be avoided on high-speed planing hulls), straight buttocks minimize it at intermediate speeds, and slightly convex buttocks (a little rocker) produce the least drag at high speeds.

A Refined Bottom

Besides waterline L/B ratio, the secret to efficiency and ride quality lies in refinements to the hull shape, including deadrise distribution from bow to stern; hull shape in station view (whether concave, straight, convex, or bell-shaped); the precise shape and size of the chine flats; the shape, size, and location of bottom strakes or spray rails; and the hull trim resulting from LCG and bottom hook or rocker. A padded keel, also known as a ski or delta pad, is a flattened keel section that adds lift, reduces tripping in a high-speed turn, and shifts buoyancy from the keel area to the chines, increasing stability. Chine flats (which improve form stability and add dynamic lift) can also improve a planing hull design. Expect most modern planing hulls, whether modified-Vs, warped-Vs, or deep-Vs, to sport a combination of these refinements.

Hull shape and refinements influence ride quality, handling characteristics, and optimum speed, and so do underwater appendages such as shafts, struts, strikes, fins, keels, and rudders. These appendages should be faired to minimize drag and to provide a smooth flow of water to the propellers and rudders.

Bottom Strakes and Spray Rails

Bottom or *running strakes* add dynamic lift and deflect spray, but their real purpose is to define the boundary of the hull's wetted surface when running on plane. The lift generated by bottom strakes can be significant forward, where water and spray direction is at an outward angle from the hull's centerline. Farther aft, waterflow lines up with the hulls' keel, or centerline, so dynamic lift from strakes is minimal or nonexistent, though they may still contribute to a small degree to tracking and roll attenuation.

Bottom strakes, like those we typically see on a deep-V hull, look great and, if properly designed,

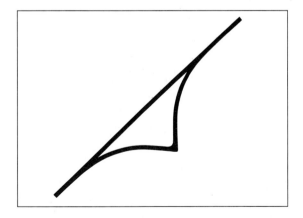

Spray rail detail from the 65 Viking Sport Cruisers. The soft inside corners have lots of advantages, including easier fabrication, greater strength, less frictional drag, focused spray deflection, and decreased slamming in a seaway at speed. The hard outside corner produces clean waterflow spearation   BERNARD OLESINSKI

can improve performance. It seems intuitively obvious that a soft radius in the inner corner of a bottom strake deflects spray most efficiently and effectively. Water tends to "crunch" up against strakes with hard inside corners, increasing slamming loads. It's also important that the edge away from the keel comes to a sharp point so waterflow breaks cleanly away, minimizing drag. Bottom strakes have to be carefully positioned, or they can create channels for air to flow to the propellers, struts, rudders, through-hull connections, waterjet inlets, and transducers farther aft, as we'll see in the Dynamic Instability section following.

Some boats—especially round-bilge, semidisplacement hulls—incorporate *spray rails* that deflect spray and add lift forward. These spray rails are something like oversized bottom strakes, and a single pair is usually fitted starting well above the waterline at the stem and gradually sloping down as you move aft. They may terminate just forward of amidships or continue to the transom. Overly large spray rails may increase slamming loads, and when improperly shaped and located on the hull may generate spray as well as deflect it. But all in all, they're indispensable when it comes to controlling spray forward, they generate lift forward, and they can encourage waterflow separation at the bilge aft.

Trim Tabs

Trim tabs are small flaps, usually made of thin stainless-steel plate, mounted to port and starboard on the transom just above the bottom of the boat. They're controlled from the helm station via a hydraulic piston that projects through the bottom of the boat or from the transom. In the Up position, they are on the same plane and at the same level as the hull bottom. When lowered, they generate lift by increasing their angle of attack. The effect of this lift, then, is to raise the stern and lower the bow.

Planing hulls can use trim tabs to advantage in order to run at optimum trim through any likely combination of speed, loading, and sea state. Trim tabs can be used to correct for heel (caused by wind)

A trim tab slightly depressed. Well offset from centerline, trim tabs, or flaps, acting in concert, can lower the bow by raising the stern, or individually correct for a small amount of heel. Adequate tab surface area is necessary to produce lift efficiently, and tab-angle indicators, which take the guesswork out of tab positioning, are great to have.   BENNETT

or list (caused by uneven weight distribution), to decrease time to plane, to help stay on plane at lower speeds, or to depress the bow in a head sea to re-duce slamming loads. Trim tabs will also increase a boat's speed range at low planing speeds.

Depressing the tabs might allow a planing ves-sel to slow down a couple more knots without falling off plane, a useful attribute in rough water since a hull on top (planing) at 13 knots is much more efficient than one that's fallen off plane. Tabs, then, can be used to "finesse" a boat's trim, meaning the skipper can tweak the angle of the hull so it op-erates at its most fuel-efficient, best-handling, smoothest-riding attitude.

Some boats need a lot of tab not only to get on plane in a reasonable time, but to correct for inap-propriate LCG (too stern-heavy) once *on* plane. With these boats, trim tabs are used to help com-pensate for poor design. Though there are excep-tions, if a boat needs tabs just to run well when nor-mally loaded in calm water, or to get on plane without aiming for the clouds, something was amiss in the design phase.

Tabs can be lowered and raised together or in-dependently. When both are lowered, the stern comes up and the bow drops, shifting the CDL aft.

Lowering the bow smoothes the ride in a head sea by immersing the sharper bow sections and shifting wave impact forward. Wetted surface and drag are also increased when depressing the bow, slowing the boat and increasing the amount of spray gen-erated forward. In a following sea, a depressed bow will often lead to bow steering and degraded direc-tional control.

When only one tab is lowered, that side of the stern is raised and the opposite bow is depressed. Using a single tab is a good way to correct for a small list caused by uneven weight distribution (say, with a 1,000-pound tuna to port), single-engine propeller torque, or a strong beam wind. Interest-ingly, a boat running on plane often tends to heel into the wind rather than away from it. That's be-cause a small amount of rudder is needed to coun-teract the wind and keep the boat going in a straight line, and this *steering effort* induces a lever arm that tends to heel the boat. So, depressing the starboard trim tab in a strong starboard beam wind will often return the boat to an even keel, using one trim tab to counteract that right-rudder lever arm.

Some larger boats are designed so the fuel tanks are centered over the LCF, which means that trim won't change noticeably as fuel is consumed. Such a boat needs trim tabs, then, only to adjust trim to suit the sea state and wind conditions. It's rare to see a sportfishing convertible with its fuel tanks over the LCF, though, since that's where the oversized diesels reside. A convertible's main fuel tank is usually under the cockpit, well aft of the LCF, so that as fuel is consumed the stern comes up sig-nificantly. Many convertibles, at least those over 50 feet, have a smaller fuel tank forward that they burn off first so they don't get into a bow-down at-titude offshore. Trim tabs can help compensate for a stern-heavy loading, but nothing can help when a boat is running bow-heavy other than a weight shift aft. The problem, then, is that trim tabs won't raise the bow if the LCG is too far forward to begin with; all they can do is raise the stern and depress the bow.

As discussed elsewhere, getting the LCG right during the design of a boat is crucial to proper

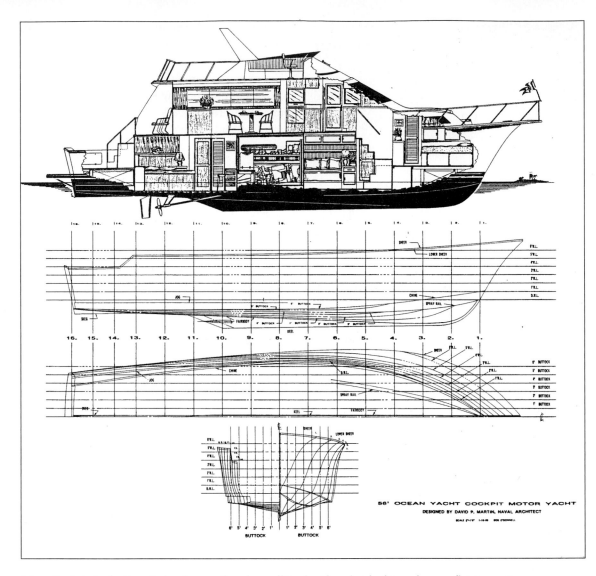

A Dave Martin design for Ocean Yachts planes easily and runs efficiently with modest deadrise and narrow, flat stern sections. DAVE MARTIN

performance and handling. If a boat runs excessively bow-high during all conditions of loading, the LCG is simply too far aft. Such a boat needs trim tabs at all times to achieve its best running trim, and having to rely on trim tabs can be a Band-Aid approach for ill-conceived boats. On the other hand, a few, usually well-designed planing boats (like the Hunt designs mentioned) don't even come with trim tabs, running naturally at their 2- to 5-degree trim angle, but you give up the

ability to offset list or depress the bow in a stiff chop. Length usually helps to minimize bow rise when accelerating up on plane, so a 70-footer will aim for the sky less than the 30-footer, all else being equal.

And tabs can help a boat get up on plane in less time while burning less fuel and with better visibility from a lower helm station, thanks to less bow rise. Certain dynamic instabilities can sometimes be corrected with trim tabs. For instance,

This mid-1990s 34-foot Egg Harbor convertible has lots of room and comfortable amenities on the inside, but its beamy hull and low deadrise produce a fairly bumpy ride in a chop. The ride quality, or smoothness of ride, is further diminished by the vessel's bow-high running trim, due to the linear relationship between trim and slamming loads. The laws of physics are intransigent; you just can't have both generous interior volume *and* superior ride quality.

porpoising can usually be controlled by dropping the tabs a bit, shifting the CDL aft.

It can be aggravating to run a boat that needs trim tabs to operate acceptably, only to find that the tabs are too small or that there are no trim-tab angle indicators. The tabs must be large enough to actually lift the stern at cruising speed. I tested a Chris Craft 300 (a nice-running and handling boat otherwise) fitted with tabs that managed only to slowly turn the boat when depressed individually. There was no noticeable difference in trim when depressing both tabs until the engines were running over 3,500 rpm, which is above their cruise rpm. So, if you don't see 3 to 5 degrees of change in trim from full-up to full-down tabs when running at a comfortable cruise rpm, they're probably too small for the weight and length of the boat.

Bennett Marine, the largest trim-tab manufacturer in the world, recommends an inch of tab width per side for each foot of boat length, but also takes boat weight and speed into account. So there would be 30 inches (called *span*) of trim tab width per side for a typical 30-footer. Their tabs are usually 9 inches long (fore-and-aft length referred to as *chord*) but are available up to 12 inches long for

heavier, slower boats, or if space for mounting the tabs on the transom is limited. Speed is an important issue when sizing tabs, since those that would be large enough to work well at slower speeds could cause the boat to get out of control at, say, 50 knots.

Trim-tab angle indicators are usually not included by the builder, but I wouldn't want to leave home without them. That's because it can be pretty tormenting fooling around with the tab rocker switches at the helm without having a clue as to their actual angle. These handy little tab angle indicators uses a series of LED lights to show the angle of each tab, which depress 20 degrees when fully lowered.

Trim Control with Outboards and Stern Drives

Outboard and stern-drive power offer a natural advantage with regard to trim: the ability to control the direction of propeller thrust vertically as well as horizontally. It's the ability to trim the lower unit up (raising the bow) that separates a stern drive or outboard from an inboard-, surface-drive-, or waterjet-powered boat. Raising the lower unit allows an operator to find the hull's sweet spot, where wetted hull area and drag are minimized but the boat is still not porpoising, or to select a bow-up attitude for better following-sea control. Even though you can trim the lower unit down to raise the stern, trim tabs get the job done more efficiently, allowing the propeller to run level and just push the boat.

Trimming a drive down will depress the bow as trim tabs do. The inefficiencies of a stern drive or outboard's smaller propeller and complex, energy-robbing hull-gear arrangement are more than offset by this ability to adjust propeller thrust to a more horizontal inclination, and by the lessened drag of the lower unit in comparison with an inboard's fixed gear (shafts, struts, rudders). It's also worth noting that in a small boat, three or four people moving from stern to bow or filling a fish box and livewell will alter trim significantly, and a lower unit's ability to compensate for a bow-heavy condition due to these variable loads is a welcome feature.

Though its ability to "dial in" optimum trim gives a lower-unit-powered boat with poor weight distribution a speed advantage, an inboard with optimum LCG shaft angle, gear ratio, and prop can perform nearly on a par with the stern drive or outboard, giving up at most 10 percent speed. The result is an inboard boat that will run at its sweet spot all day long without trim tabs, with the tabs still available to depress the bow in a chop, raise the stern when the fish box or livewell are filled, or correct for heel or list. Provided you don't need an outboard's light weight and you get the weight distribution right, the cheaper, simpler, more corrosion-resistant inboard just might be the ticket to your boating Nirvana.

Dynamic Instability

Predictability is favored by astronauts and boaters alike. No one appreciates the unexpected happening when traveling along at cruising speed. When things get out of control, it's invariably because of outside forces acting in an unanticipated way.

As we mentioned earlier, a planing hull bottom can develop low-pressure areas that destabilize handling and controllability. To understand how underwater hull shape produces positive and negative pressures, we return to our airfoil analogy. Note that the buttock lines on a planing hull describe a similar curve forward (seen in profile) to the top of an airplane wing (seen in section). The wing, more highly curved at the top than the bottom, develops lift not so much because of the high pressure on the bottom of the wing, but from the low pressure on the top. Low pressure develops on the wing's top surface because the air has to travel farther and therefore faster along its curved upper surface, creating a low-pressure region of aerodynamic lift.

Now here's where the bottom of a planing hull acts like the top of an airplane wing. Normally just the aft half of a planing vessel is in contact with the water, with the bow high and dry when on plane in calm water. But when the forward hull bottom is immersed—when the stern is lifted by a following

Fuel Tanks

While we're on the subject of LCG and trim, let's see where fuel tanks fit in—literally. From a performance perspective, the optimum location for tanks is about 5 percent of the waterline length ahead of the full-load LCG. Bow-up trim tends to increase as fuel is burned off and the LCG shifts aft, and tends to decrease as speed picks up with the loss of weight. The result of these opposing forces is a net trim change of zero. The problem is, it's just about impossible to get this balance just right on a marketable boat, since fuel tank location isn't as high on the average owner's priority list as, say, closet size and squeezing in that stackable washer-dryer unit.

Saddle tanks installed outboard of the engines is one way to get the tanks close to the LCG, but this also cramps the engine room and reduces maintenance accessibility. Saddle tanks usually force the engines closer to the hull centerline, and this of course reduces the boat's maneuverability at low speed, with the propellers and rudders being closer together. This tank location also places the tanks higher in the boat, raising the CG and decreasing ultimate stability.

The convertible's largest fuel tank must usually be placed under the cockpit, which is well aft of the LCB. As a result, most convertibles will change trim markedly as fuel is consumed, and fuel has to be pumped between forward and after tanks to compensate. In nonsportfishing layouts, V-drive configurations with the engines mounted well aft have a lot to commend them. This allows the large fixed weights (the engines) to be in the stern and moves the variable weight of fuel forward, nearer the LCG. But an aft engine room arrangement, which also isolates machinery noises and vibrations more effectively from living spaces, is not practical if the design calls for a cockpit or aft cabin.

sea, the hull is heavily loaded, trim is too low, or the boat is slowing down—low hydrodynamic pressures are created forward even if this area of the hull is at a positive angle of attack relative to the surrounding waterflow. Under these circumstances, the forward bottom sections may actually develop pressures that are less than atmospheric, pulling the bow down.

These negative, less-than-atmospheric pressures may be exacerbated when bow-down in a roll, since the roll presents the most negative pressure-inducing hull profile to the water. As a result of the loss of lift forward, the CDL shifts aft, the bow dives farther, and the boat becomes dynamically unstable. High pressures also develop at the bow, but the net change is a bow-down trim. You'll see the same effect if you dangle a spoon under a running faucet; it takes some effort to separate the spoon from the waterflow, even when the spoon surface seems to be at a positive angle of attack.

One type of dynamic instability called *bow diving* occurs when the bow pitches deeply into the water in the absence of a clear cause (waves acting on the hull), and it's compounded in a heavily loaded hull because the forward sections are already more deeply immersed at speed. The more highly curved the buttock lines forward are, the less lift is developed, so the bow of a poorly designed and overloaded planing hull can be drawn into the water by low pressure that's insufficient to support the hull's weight. One of the reasons a hard-chine hull makes a better planing boat than a round-bilge hull is that there's less curvature in the buttock lines forward, because the hard chines provide a natural place for the buttock lines to terminate. Low pressure can also develop locally due to depressions in a metal hull's plating or a fiberglass hull's imperfect tooling. The result can be chine walking, bow steering, and bow diving, which we discuss below.

In simple terms, a dynamically unstable vessel is one that, when up on plane and supported by the pressure of fast-moving waterflow, does not run like it's supposed to. This usually means the boat porpoises, chine-walks, runs bow-down, heels over to one side, yaws unpredictably, or is subject to some combination of these motions. The reason it runs at the wrong attitude (in trim, yaw, and heel) is usally due to inappropriate hull shape and weight distribution. The resulting distribution of dynamic pressures (or lack of pressures) acting on the hull, creates *dynamic* instabilities. (There may be other reasons, too, such as appendage problems, loose steering, and improper handling.)

As we've seen, the area of the hull bottom where the water pressure is greatest is called the *stagnation zone*. This is the forward area of the hull at the on-plane waterline where waterflow impacts with and is perpendicular to the hull bottom. Dynamic pressure drops off quickly aft of this point, but there should be some positive pressure all the way aft to the transom. Certain underwater areas of the hull are under normal pressure while others, due to inappropriate hull curvature or hull-skin irregularities, can in some case be under less-than-atmospheric pressure (slight vacuum). When you sum these pressures, their distribution and intensity don't combine to support the hull in its

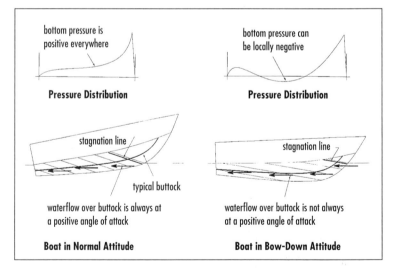

Naval architect Lou Codega, who designed such well-regarded boats as the Regulator and Carolina Classic, has long studied planing hull dynamic instabilities. These drawings show the relationship between hull trim, buttock lines, and dynamic lift. Excessive buttock curvature in the bow acts a little like a spoon held under a faucet, actually developing negative pressures forward that produce bow steering and other planing instabilities. LOU CODEGA

proper attitude. A normal, dynamically stable vessel, on the other hand, is suitably supported by the sum of hull pressures and will return to a state of equilibrium (usually an even keel) by restoring pressure or forces after being subjected to wave action. In displacement and semidisplacement craft, dynamic pressures rarely build to the point of causing instabilities, unless you count dynamic events like broaching, which is one reason designing a fine planing hull is such a complicated business.

So what factors are believed to cause a boat to be unstable dynamically? Speed is at the top of the list—the faster a boat can go, the more apt it is to become unstable. That's one reason why driving a semidisplacement hull to planing speeds can be a bad idea. Depending on hull length, dynamic lift generally starts to predominate over the static lift of buoyancy at about 25 knots. Instabilities resulting from dynamic forces alone are relatively uncommon below this speed. *Hull loading*, or the psi (static and dynamic) acting on the bottom of the hull, is another factor; the heavier the loading, the greater the chances of an instability developing. LCG is also critical: putting it too far forward will invariably result in a dynamic instability. It's worth noting that adding a cockpit extension effectively shifts LCG forward (as a percentage of waterline length), which can easily be a recipe for introducing dynamic instabilities, so this common hull-form alteration must be carefully engineered.

Too much buttock line curvature forward, excessive hook or rocker aft, and underwater hull appendages can also contribute to dynamic instabilities, as we'll see, and rudder and trim tab movement can upset the stability apple cart. Dynamic instabilities may also result when VCG, LCG, or displacement are wrong for the hull's shape and dimensions. So, a high-powered, heavy boat with a forward LCG, highly curved buttock lines forward, and ventilated appendages is likely to disappoint in terms of stability on plane. Sometimes the solution is simply to slow down a couple of knots.

Some dynamic instabilities result from putting too much power in an older design. Production builders are taking older hull designs, which behaved well with moderately sized engines and repowering with 75 to 100 percent more horsepower. Adding power usually necessitates shifting LCG aft (usually by moving the engines aft), but this requirement is all too often ignored. Now these boats are really operating in an altogether different performance regime, and their builders and owners seem to wonder why they're no longer well-behaved at speed.

Oscillating Instabilities

Instabilities can be either oscillatory (varying, moving back and forth) or constant. Oscillatory instabilities include *chine walking*: this is a roll oscillation in which the boat heels over on its chine, rights itself to an even keel, and then repeats the cycle. The cure for chine walking in outboard-powered boats may be as simple as tightening up the steering or shifting the LCF aft. Repowering with larger engines without moving the LCG aft can also result in chine walking.

Porpoising is an oscillation in pitch and heave, with the bow alternately rising and falling. The center of dynamic lift (CDL) changes as speed increases and trim and the area of the immersed hull change; porpoising results when the CDL constantly shifts forward and aft relative to a stationary LCG. Both chine walking and porpoising are associated with hard-chine hulls (chine walking is also sometimes found in certain boats with long length-to-beam ratios), and the intensity of these oscillations is often a function of hull speed. They can occur in calm or choppy water without any helm or throttle input from the operator, and they are often predictable.

Porpoising, in fact, like other oscillatory instabilities, can be anticipated by the operator once it's happened the first time, since it's based on a known combination of speed, trim (and trim-tab or drive position), and weight distribution. The operator may learn that her boat will never porpoise below a certain speed or engine trim setting. An owner may relocate her outboard from the transom to an aft bracket; this weight shift would tend to increase

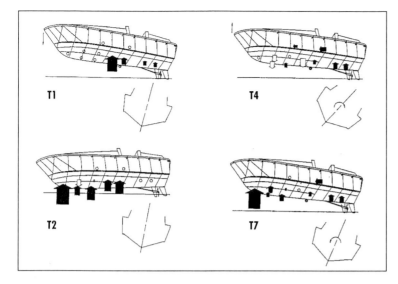

The relative pressures acting on a problematic planing hull's bottom set up dynamic instabilities at speed. At **T1** the boat is running normally, with positive pressure (black arrows) providing lift; at **T2** it slams downward, plowing into a wave; at **T4** it rolls, as negative pressure (white arrows) takes control of the hull; and at **T7**, it returns to normal operating trim. The "dots" depict atmospheric pressure, while the midsection views show rotation.

LOU CODEGA

action. A broach while traveling down the face of a wave is a dynamic instability in yaw and roll, for example. A broach can be initiated by a static instability if a hull is moving at the same speed as the wave supporting it, but the hull's inertia makes things worse. Sometimes, a one-in-a-thousand combination of wave impact, rudder angle, trim-tab setting, and LCG will cause a dynamic instability in an otherwise satisfactory boat.

While this discussion may give the impression that naval architects have a good handle on dynamic instabilities, this is not always the case. The interface between wave and hull, and the other elements that influence boat behavior in a seaway at speed, are complex. It may be easy to recognize a dynamic instability when it happens, but most of these phenomena are poorly understood even by those who make a living studying them.

the chances of the boat porpoising. Porpoising can be stable at a constant speed and trim, or it can be unstable, increasing while these conditions remain constant. A naval architect's ability to accurately predict the conditions in which a new boat design will porpoise, before it ever hits the water, is limited, but it's also one of the best understood planing instability phenomena.

Constant Instabilities

Constant dynamic instabilities usually occur on large, relatively fast-moving, heavily loaded craft with LCGs that are too far forward. These instabilities are potentially the worst kind, since they can occur rapidly and unexpectedly under pushing-the-envelope conditions of weight and speed, and the results, including broaching and erratic helm response, can be dangerous. Instabilities can be created entirely by internal influences such as a vessel's weight, weight distribution, and shape, or they can be triggered by external forces like wave

Low Speed Instabilities

Instabilities at semiplaning (semidisplacement) speeds are often caused by static as well as dynamic pressures, and can diminish both directional and transverse stability. Loss of transverse stability, for example, can result when gravity, acting on the bow wave, creates a deep trough alongside the midbody of the hull, diminishing form stability by exposing the turn of the bilge to the sea breeze (and low atmospheric pressure). In fact, positive and negative pressures distributed along the underwater portion of the hull affect planing and semidisplacement, and round-bilge and hard-chine hulls.

When round-bilge hulls are pushed to semidisplacement or planing speeds, the boat's GM (its metacentric height, the measure of initial stability derived primarily from hull shape), is decreased

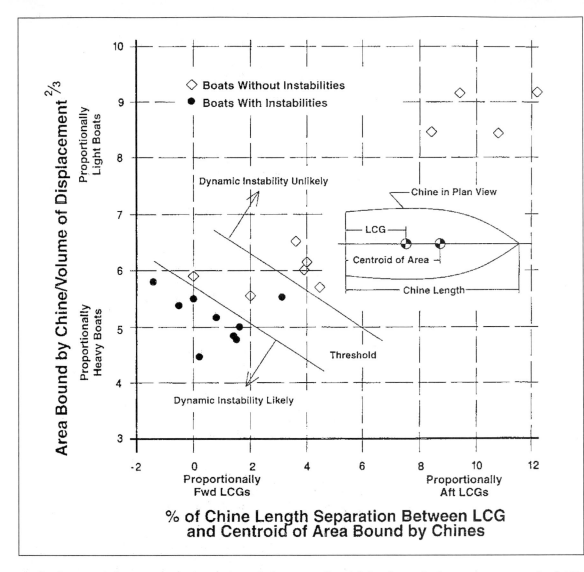

Naval architect Lou Codega's investigations into planing hull instabilities have resulted in this diagram showing the relationship between hull displacement and chine length relative to LCG placement, and the propensity for a hull to be dynamically unstable.

Hulls with lighter bottom loadings and proportionately aft LCGs in relation to the wetted chines are less likely to be dynamically unstable.

LOU CODEGA

because of the positive and negative pressures and changing waterlines that develop. In fact, some dynamic inclining experiments show a 20 to nearly 40 percent loss of GM at a speed-to-length (S/L) ratio of 1.7 and 3, respectively, resulting in a high degree of roll sensitivity. A reserve of static stability must be designed in to compensate.

Round-bilge boats that roll excessively at speed usually benefit from increasing bow-up trim, either by shifting the LCG aft, reshaping the hull by adding rocker aft, or adding wedges forward, just aft of the stagnation zone. Much as lowered trim tabs create lift at the transom, wedges forward provide lift at the bow, especially on the side more deeply immersed by heel and roll, thus countering excessive roll.

Ventilated Appendages

Hull spray strakes, which can as easily channel air as water, must be carefully positioned so they don't direct air to propellers, rudders, and underwater appendages. This may be counterintuitive, but if struts and rudders ventilate, they can cause dynamic instabilities, including roll moments and bow-down trim angles, by generating lift at the stern. An off-center ventilated strut or rudder will also cause the vessel to roll, potentially initiating a yaw or broach. The designer also has to make sure that cooling-water inlet through-hulls, depth sounder transducers, and waterjet inlets get a clean supply of solid water. Ventilation problems are best addressed by closing off air paths and reducing local disturbances with improved appendage fairing (streamlining).

Rudders can ventilate (and cause the stern to lift) when they're located too close to the transom. The low pressures created by the rudders can suck air in and cause the rudders to stall as well as generate lift. The best fixes are to move the rudders farther forward away from this ready air supply, to install horizontal cavitation plates above the rudders that project aft of the transom, or to notch out the rudders' upper trailing edges. Speaking of rudders, adding larger rudders or skegs to solve course-keeping problems will probably prove ineffective if the root cause is low-pressure regions forward in the hull.

A Viking 47 stays somewhat in the middle of the channel in the serpentine Bass River despite having the author at the wheel. There's no question about this boat being on plane. VIKING YACHTS

Solutions

Dynamic instability fixes that may work include shifting weight aft, building rocker into the hull to depress the stern, widening the chines or adding running strakes forward, fairing hull appendages, and adding wedges at the bow to introduce air to ventilate the wetted surface, eliminating the low pressure areas. Naval architects can conduct tests to determine the causes of dynamic instabilities, including a trim-speed test to look for low dynamic pressures forward that produce bow-down trim at speed, and dynamic inclining experiments to measure changes in transverse stability from dead in the water to full-speed. Older, overpowered hull forms need to be replaced with newer designs that can accommodate today's powerful diesels. The simplest fix, though, may be just to throttle back and enjoy the scenery.

CHAPTER 5

The Power
Catamaran

*Suppose you were an idiot, and suppose
you were a member of Congress; but I
repeat myself.*

—Mark Twain

Power cats have taken off in a big way over the last fifteen years in the United States, and with good reason. A proper cat offers an excellent ride, with a well-designed 25-footer purring along as smoothly in a 2- to 3-foot chop as a deep-V 5 to 10 feet longer. For many years, cats have been especially popular in countries—including Australia, New Zealand, and Norway—where fishing grounds can be a long way from safe harbor and where avoiding rough-water transits is not an option.

In the United States, small 20- to 30-foot outboard-powered cats are niche boats to a certain extent, often intended for the hard-charging offshore fisherman who requires a trailerable package. Many of these hardcore anglers would never consider going back to a monohull once they've lived with a cat for a while in rough water. Larger performance cats in the 30- to 40-foot range are also being produced for the offshore fishing crowd. Some cruising families, including former sailors, are even buying trawler cats for the extended voyages to which these craft may be well suited.

A cat's smooth ride is due to simple physics. Two narrow hulls are presented to a wave instead of one wide one, so vertical accelerations are minimized—as long as it's not so rough that the tunnel "roof" bottoms out. Cats have great form (initial) stability and, with their often-generous beam, offer a lot of open deck space for a given length.

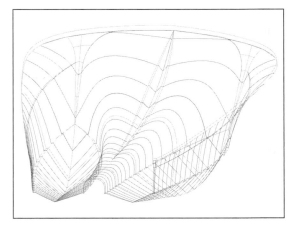

The lines to a John Kiley 40-foot cat show the hull shape nicely.
JOHN KILEY

Although cats are wonderful boats, they can't do everything—e.g., look good, according to a few pundits. Some cats are seriously homely, to be sure, but others, like the 36-foot Benchmark and 38-foot Hydratech, are as good looking (to these eyes) as they are smooth riding. As with any boat, there's no substitute for length when it comes to creating beautiful lines. The stylists are making improvements in the 22- to 30-foot outboard cats as well, and you sometimes hardly notice that these *are* cats at a casual glance.

Cats also have their quirks and limitations. Some of them have a tendency to "sneeze" when air compresses in the forward part of the tunnel and blows spray out over the bow. Though cats do indeed run very well in a light to moderate chop, they can't run at 30 knots in 15-foot seas like some builders would have you believe. They have to slow down when seas get short and steep enough, just like any other boat, though usually not as early.

Partly because they have a relatively high center of gravity, cats tend to lean *away* from a turn at speed, which can be disconcerting. The cat's two narrow hulls present more resistance to *lateral movement*, or sliding, in a turn than a monohull, which further works against any tendency to bank into a turn. Some cats stay on an even keel in a turn, or lean slightly into the turn, but they are the exceptions.

The Achilles' heel of any cat is its tendency for the tunnel to bottom out in certain conditions, usually involving overloading or just rough conditions. The whole boat, in fact, is designed around the tunnel's height requirements, though this is not as much of a problem with some asymmetrical cat-hull designs that have small tunnels. Let's look at some of the challenges a cat designer faces. Make sure to sea trial any cat you're considering because since tunnel height can be a real problem when the boat is not up on plane, with the tunnel clear of the water.

Design Considerations

While the main deck above the cat's tunnel is impressively roomy, it can't be any lower than the top of the tunnel. This means the hull freeboard has to be high enough to provide adequate cockpit freeboard, which further raises CG. The result, at least in a small cat (under 35 or 40 feet), is an ugly boat.

Most cats have a smaller waterplane area than monohulls of the same length, which means they'll settle deeper in the water with a weight addition. With their lower pounds-per-inch-immersion figure, the tunnel will settle closer to the waterline with just a moderate amount of weight, which can quickly add up in the form of fuel, passengers, and gear. With the tunnel closer to the waterline, and

closer to the tops of the passing waves, ride quality diminishes rapidly, and the added wetted hull surface slows the boat down. A monohull, on the other hand, just slows down and can actually ride more smoothly with added weight onboard.

This World Cat 270 is up on plane a full foot higher then when at rest. This extra height gives the tunnel the clearance it needs to eliminate bottoming out in a chop, and it results in a ride superior to any monohull of the same size and displacement.

A power cat is inherently heavier than a monohull of similar length, since its hull has much more surface area, and the tunnel especially has to be strongly built to absorb not only wave-slamming loads, but the wracking of the two hulls, which try hard to head off in different directions. A Glacier Bay 26, for instance, has seven structural bulkheads in the tunnel area to resist stresses and add stiffness. These bulkheads, which should cross over the tunnel "roof" from hull to hull for optimum strength, have to be securely tabbed in place to resist the significant stresses encountered in a seaway at speed. The challenge is to build a cat strong enough to resist these added stresses while keeping the boat light enough to perform properly. Some builders keep the weight down by using advanced composites and vacuum bagging or, better yet, resin infusion systems (see chapter 6).

So the trade-offs are starker with a cat. Add weight, and the tunnel bottoms out, increasing frictional drag and slamming loads. Make the tunnel higher, and the deck above it is raised just as much. Raise the deck, and the hull sides also have to be higher if interior (cockpit) freeboard is valued. The more things you raise, the higher the CG gets, the less stable the boat becomes (dynamic stability is especially affected), and the more awkward and homely it looks. An outboard-powered cat, especially, has a high center of gravity, and weight additions in the form of passengers, fish, and gear raise VCG higher still, since they will usually be concentrated on or above the main deck, which is already quite high atop the tunnel. Some owners may have a false sense of security about their boat's stability. Remember the difference between initial (form-derived) stability and ultimate stability. With its high CG, an outboard-powered cat may well capsize at a lower angle of heel than a conventional monohull.

Once you get up above 35 feet or so, the design possibilities start to open up. A longer cat doesn't

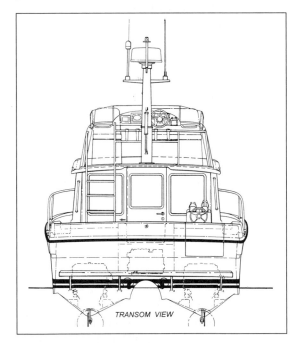

TRANSOM VIEW

The John Kiley–designed Sea Sport 32 as seen from astern in this drawing. Engines are low in the twin hulls, the cockpit deck is as low as possible over the tunnel top, and the slight asymmetry is noticeable aft.

JOHN KILEY

have to look disproportionately high, since the length-to-freeboard ratio becomes more pleasing. This is also the point at which inboards become the clear power of choice, and the hulls can each accommodate a small stateroom forward and individual engine rooms aft.

A small cat's cabin is often one of its weaknesses; there's precious little room to do anything with the tunnel running down the centerline. What you would expect to end up with on a boat like this is a very large berth forward over the tunnel, and on either side inside the twin hulls will be standing headroom areas, with the head to one side and the galley on the other. All in all, cat builders have gotten good at making the most of the breed's shape and putting the available room to good use. The boat's seakeeping and seakindliness more than make up for cabin design limitations for most owners.

Planing and Semidisplacement Cat Hulls

Recreational power catamarans come in both planing and semidisplacement versions. Some of these "displacement cats" are not so easy to categorize, though they tend to have round-bilge sections and very little flat lifting area on their bottoms. When the hulls narrow to a L/B ratio of 10:1 or more, as they do on many cats, all bets are off when it comes to traditional displacement speed limitations. Quite a few power cats with radiused hulls (in cross section) develop practically zero dynamic lift. That makes them displacement hulls by definition. But, thanks to their low wavemaking resistance, these narrow cats actually run at planing speeds.

At 25 knots, a cat with a 25-foot waterline length is running at a speed-to-length (S/L) ratio of 5, rather than the S/L ratio of 1.34 that displacement hulls are usually limited to. That's why a "slenderness" ratio is a valid component when discussing hull form and speed potential. The displacement cat becomes a semidisplacement cat, technically, if there is significant vertical rise at speed.

The ProKat 2360's hard-chine planing bottom shows radiused sections forward with V-shaped sections on centerline forward to reduce pounding; chines higher up pick up extra buoyancy.

The World Cat 270's rounded running surfaces make it a semidisplacement boat that's pushed to planing speeds; these narrow hulls produce a smooth ride.

The planing cat often has hard chines and moderate deadrise amidships and aft where the dynamic lift is produced. At least theoretically, the planing cat has to be built (to heavier scantlings) to withstand the higher G-forces that result from higher slamming loads at speed. The planing cat rises vertically at speed like any other planing hull, and this adds welcome clearance between the bottom of the tunnel and the water surface.

Some builders of high-performance cats use asymmetric hull sections, which provide both planing surface and the interior room needed for inboard diesel power. The wider, flatter inboard hull sections allow machinery to be easily mounted over the primary planing surface—essentially like a deep-V installation—while also making running gear installation more monohull-like and providing more planing surface. On the outboard sides of the hulls, which are more exposed to wave action (and this is the asymmetry), the deadrise is sharper. Some asymmetric designs actually bank slightly into a turn, a significant advantage from a human engineering perspective. This feature is due to the lift generated by the outboard hull's shape and the lesser lateral resistance produced by the inboard hull.

High-performance racing cats often have split-V hulls, which look a lot like a deep-V monohull sliced down the middle and separated by the tunnel. This design, while not as efficiently propelled as the asymmetric design, produces the smoothest possible ride at speeds that can exceed 100 mph.

The width of the tunnel varies markedly from cat to cat, and so does their sensitivity to added weight. Given the narrow tunnel and extra beam of some asymmetric designs, their pounds-per-inch-immersion values may actually be very similar to a mono of the same length, making them well suited to commercial applications requiring moderate load-carrying ability.

Many cats have a small, V-shaped nacelle, or pod (like a mini deep-V hull), located at the forward end of the tunnel, which helps prevent slamming below planing speeds while remaining well clear of the water at speed. The trailing edge of this pod may have an air channel built in to provide airflow in the tunnel even when the bow of the boat is immersed. World Cat, for one, gets around the sneezing problem by also raising the tunnel (and hull freeboard) forward.

Though most cats are trim-sensitive to weight changes, some planing cats with wide hulls forward actually have *more* waterplane area forward than a monohull, increasing resistance to trim changes. In a quartering sea, cats with narrow hulls are more susceptible to broaching since the lee hull, with its minimal buoyancy forward, will bury its nose deeply and tend to trip the boat in extreme conditions.

Cat Performance

Twin outboards are a natural power plant for a small cat, with each motor mounted on a hull, and a fuel tank for each motor inside its hull. The same goes for inboard power in larger cats; each hull is designed to be just the right size to hold a light-weight diesel engine. (In fact the width of a hull must be designed around this consideration.) A cat with outboard power will have a higher center of gravity than one that's inboard powered, all else being equal, since the engines sit higher on the boat.

Cats provide a great ride running into a stiff chop, but they also can do well running downsea, especially if LCG is far enough aft for the hull shape, and often don't slow down as much as a monohull when climbing the back of a wave. Many displacement cats also run well at 10 to 20 knots, speeds at which a monohull deep-V runs and handles sluggishly. This quality gives the operator more latitude in adjusting speed to match sea state. The better displacement cats, in fact, hardly notice the transition to plane, meaning you can operate easily at virtually any midrange speed. Some planing cats, depending on the make, also offer a degree of midrange versatility.

Cats are known for being efficiently driven, but this is not always true. Grady-White, for instance, made both monohull and (for a short time) cat 26-footers, and the mono was more efficiently driven in calm water. That's not surprising when you consider that the power cat has more windage (sail area) and more wetted surface than the monohull.

The 26-foot Glacier Bay is typical of the outboard-powered recreational cat; in a 1-foot chop, it slices through the waves like butter at any speed. With the waves running higher, say at 2 to 3 feet, 25 knots or so of speed definitely help improve ride quality, since the boat rises vertically, creating more clearance for the waves passing through the tunnel.

Seaworthiness

A catamaran's twin hulls can add passive protection against sinking if the hulls are separated from one another by a watertight longitudinal bulkhead on centerline. The chances of maintaining adequate reserve buoyancy, and staying afloat, increase if each hull further is subdivided with watertight transverse bulkheads, the more the better. If each hull has significant compartmentation or generous flotation

A computer rendering of a PDQ 41 with the hulls transitioning to skegs aft where the propeller shafts exit the hull. This design provides grounding protection for the running gear.　PDQ YACHTS

foam built in, the damaged angle of heel will be minimized and the boat's ability to survive single-compartment flooding greatly improved. Ask the builder if tests have been conducted to prove a boat's ability to stay afloat with one hull ruptured.

Since the small to midsize cat must be built high off the water, windage is higher than on most monohulls of the same length and absorbs a higher percentage of propulsion power as speed increases. On the other hand, the two narrow hulls create more resistance to lateral (sideways) movement through the water, so the cat may or may not be as susceptible to a crosswind.

Though variation in beam is more pronounced in sailing catamarans, a wide power cat (with the hulls set far apart) will have more deck space for its length, greater initial (form) stability, and less rolling. It will also be harder to turn, and finding a slip can be a problem.

Lessons Learned from Sailing Cats

The widest sailing cats are nearly as wide as they are long and are just as liable to pitchpole as to capsize in a strong wind. They must have their decks, or underwings, suspended higher off the water, since the hulls span a greater distance, making it easier for waves to build up between them. Narrower cats are much easier to maneuver and moor. The fastest sailing cats have narrow hulls (to minimize resistance) set far apart (to maximize form stability). A power cat isn't so concerned about the form stability as its sail-powered cousin, since there's no sail to support in a strong wind. But since cats don't have the *ultimate stability* of a full-displacement monohull, they arguably don't belong in extreme offshore conditions of strong winds and high seas, offshore racing trends notwithstanding. Once a sailing cat heels far enough to raise one hull out of the water, it can pass through the angle of maximum righting moment in an instant, and the crew must react quickly to prevent capsize from a sudden

gust of wind or rogue wave. The most seaworthy displacement and semidisplacement monohulls, on the other hand, can develop positive righting arm at over 120 degrees of heel, and in some cases even when fully inverted.

Nevertheless, the fastest sailboats used in round-the-world races are 100-foot-plus cats and trimarans. A cat or trimaran will beat a monohull every time, *if* it survives capsize, broaching, pitchpoling, and structural failure. To do so, these offshore cats rely on highly skilled crews, sound structural engineering, high-tech construction, and a good bit of luck—the latter augmented with escape hatches in the bottoms of the hulls and inverted living arrangements for use while awaiting rescue. Some of these high-performance, high-tech, light-displacement sailing cats are giving the breed a bad name, but only because they are pushing the speed envelope in extreme offshore conditions.

The *most seaworthy* (though not the *fastest*) cats have adequate tunnel clearance, moderate freeboard, and moderate beam. In chapter 2 we saw that any vessel (including a cat) with too much form stability is both uncomfortable and unsafe, since it is too eager to conform to the water surface (wave and swell) gradient, and it will also tend to have less ultimate stability.

Should You Own a Cat?

Cats are winners in many areas, and have developed a following accordingly. Part of the key to the cat's success in the U.S. market, certainly, is familiarity, or conditioning, on the part of the public. Builders of trailerable, outboard-powered cats are doing a lot to improve the cat's popularity. And who hasn't admired the incredibly smooth ride and thrilling speed of a 50-knot passenger ferry? If the cat's layout limitations, looks, and occasional handling quirks are of little concern, and ride quality is everything, a cat may be just the ticket for you. Whichever cat strikes your fancy, be careful about keeping extra gear, passengers, and fuel to a minimum, and add weight judiciously.

CHAPTER 6

Construction with Fiberglass and Cold-Molded Wood

I'm not offended by all the dumb blonde jokes because I know I'm not dumb. I also know that I'm not blonde.

—Dolly Parton

Fiberglass is the clear choice of material for most production boatbuilders, and it has been since the 1960s. It's strong, impact resistant, relatively immune to deterioration, easily shaped, easy to repair and maintain, and fairly inexpensive. Fiberglass production boats take their shape from female molds, which allow fast, high-volume output and ensure uniformity from one boat to the next.

This chapter explains the basics of production and custom fiberglass boatbuilding so that you're better equipped to ask the right questions and look in the right places when shopping for your next boat.

If you have the means to pay, and the time to wait for a custom boat, the world's your oyster. Custom builders can use "one-off" construction methods to build one-of-a-kind or semicustom yachts out of fiberglass or cold-molded wood epoxy. Most of these methods involve building a throwaway framework, or male mold, which gives the boat the desired shape and size, removing the hull from the form, and finishing it off. All these methods can produce excellent craft, and each has its distinct advantages.

One-off means that only one boat is built from a temporary mold, while *semicustom* (or *semiproduction*) refers to a product that is produced in smaller quantities and retains some potential for customization. For instance, a semicustom builder might use a single hull but completely customize

A Sea Ray cruiser plywood stringer system is precisely held in place with a steel jig. Next, the jig comes out and the plywood is completely encapsulated in fiberglass, thickening and strengthening the hull.

the interior arrangement and deck plan. It is also possible to produce hulls of different lengths from a stock mold: the hull mold is dammed off aft with a transom mold that can be positioned farther forward or aft according to the desired vessel length.

Whether building a production or one-off custom fiberglass vessel, though, certain fundamentals apply to ensure a well-found, long-lasting boat. A wide range of resins, fiberglass reinforcements, core materials, bottom-support structures, and manufacturing processes can be used. So, it's important when evaluating a boat to know how these elements interact to affect quality, strength, seaworthiness, and longevity.

The Basics of Fiberglass Construction

A fiberglass hull consists of a matrix of fiberglass reinforcements (see below), hardened resin, and, often, a core material. The fiberglass provides the strength and impact resistance; the resin keeps the fiberglass locked in the matrix and transmits loads within and between the layers of fiberglass. Without the hardened resin, the fiberglass would just flop around, lacking strength and rigidity in any direction but direct tension. Core materials, such as end-grain balsa wood and foam, are often added to increase the strength and stiffness of a fiberglass panel with minimal weight gain. A solid fiberglass panel, with no core material, is technically a composite—a combination of resin and fiberglass reinforcement—so we will use the term *sandwich* to mean a combination of fiberglass skins surrounding a structural, lightweight core. The term *fiberglass* can refer to the dry woven or knitted material still on the roll, or the finished lamination of the fiberglass reinforcement in a matrix of catalyzed resin. The more accurate term for the latter is GRP, or *glass-reinforced plastic*, also known as *fiberglass-reinforced plastic*, or FRP.

In any fiberglass panel, or laminate, the physical properties of the fiberglass reinforcement—including its ability to stretch, which is referred to as *elongation*—may differ greatly from the resin that binds it. If the resin can't elongate as much as the reinforcement before yielding, the resin will fail first when under high stress. If less expensive, and more brittle, polyester resins are used to build a boat—and these are the most commonly used—the designer has to add enough fiberglass reinforcement so that the overall laminate stress is kept within acceptable limits.

The adhesion between layers, or *plies*, of fiberglass reinforcement, called *interlaminar bonds*, must be very strong. As we'll see, the overall strength and integrity of the laminate, including the interlaminar bonds, varies widely depending on the materials and methods used in their construction.

Why use a core material? A single sheet of fiberglass is tough and resilient, but it's not especially stiff. But when two relatively thin skins of fiberglass are bonded to both sides of a thick, lightweight core material, the result is a sandwich panel that is far stiffer and stronger than the two skins alone would be, and one that's much lighter than a solid lamination of fiberglass achieving the same overall thickness. Sandwiches have wonderful advantages, but they have to be built carefully and with the right materials, as we shall see.

Fiberglass Reinforcements

Fiberglass is sold in a variety of weights and fiber orientations. Fiberglass gets its name because it's composed of molten glass extruded, or drawn, into filaments of 5 to 25 microns in thickness. These filaments are coated with a sizing that protects against abrasion and helps to bond the fibers together when they're wet out with resin. Then the filaments are combined to form strands, which become the basis of the many different types of fiberglass reinforcements. When a roll of fiberglass is made, strands can run with the roll in the *warp* direction, and across the roll in the *weft* direction. They can also run diagonally at a 45-degree angle.

Fiberglass comes in different grades. E-glass is relatively inexpensive and fairly strong, so it is most commonly used. S-glass, which costs a lot more, is more fatigue resistant and some 30 percent stronger. S-glass is sometimes used in high-tech applications when high strength is required, as are more exotic nonfiberglass reinforcements such as carbon fiber.

Chop and Mat
Chop and mat fiberglass are similar types of low-strength reinforcement consisting of short strands of fiberglass (1 or 2 inches long) oriented at random.

Mat comes in rolls, with the strands of fiberglass held together by a soluble binder that dissolves when it comes into contact with the styrene in polyester and vinylester resins. (Stitched mat must be used with epoxy resin, which has no styrene to dissolve the binder.) Chop is applied by a device called a *chopper gun* that chops up fiberglass strands, mixes them with catalyzed resin, and shoots them out under pressure. When the mixture hits the mold, it does so in a random pattern.

The end result is pretty much the same, though chop, lacking any binders to interfere with thorough saturation, can arguably be more thoroughly wet out, reducing the chances of osmosis (see sidebar, page 100) when used as a skin coat. On the other hand, if the chopper gun doesn't thoroughly mix the catalyst with the resin, and an incomplete cure results, blisters can occur. Mat typically results in a layup of more uniform thickness. Although chopper guns have gotten a bad reputation, there's nothing wrong with a boat laid up in part by a chopper gun controlled by a skilled operator, as long as it's not substituting for stronger fiberglass reinforcements. Though relatively weak in their own right, chop and mat are good for filling the valleys between layers of heavier fabrics, building thickness quickly and cheaply—while adding significant weight. Many boatbuilders also apply a layer of mat or chop immediately underneath the gelcoat as a skin coat to prevent "print-through" of woven fiberglass reinforcement. Boatbuilding resins shrink, both during the cure and afterward, allowing the underlying woven roving or other reinforcement to telegraph its impression to the gelcoat (this is called *print-through*). This is most noticeable when dark gelcoats are used. It also occurs more often when the resin is added under high pressure, as with the various vacuum techniques discussed below.

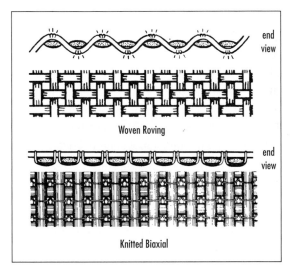

Woven Roving

Knitted Biaxial

In a woven roving the fibers are loaded out of plane, making the reinforcement less efficient, structurally, than a nonwoven, or knitted pattern. This type of weave pattern is weaker for much the same reason that a knot is weaker than the rope with which it is tied. A nonwoven reinforcement is therefore better able to absorb loads parallel to the fibers.   ERIC GREENE

Woven Roving

Woven roving, the most commonly used reinforcement, is made of flattened bundles of strands woven together in a coarse pattern, with slightly more fiberglass running in the warp than in the weft direction. The weave pattern makes woven roving thicker (of higher profile) and stiffer than unwoven reinforcements of the same weight. Woven roving generally affords good impact resistance, precisely because the fibers are woven together: under impact, individual fiber bundles have to be broken for an object to penetrate a woven laminate, while knitted reinforcement (see below) tends to split apart more readily. The woven reinforcement's higher profile means more resin must be used to fill the voids between layers of reinforcement, making for a more resin-rich and therefore brittle laminate. Resin is a lot cheaper than fiberglass, so it costs less to get a stiff panel with lots of resin than it does with more tightly compacted knitted reinforcements.

Because woven roving is made of interwoven fibers, which continuously change direction as they snake around crossing fiber bundles, its strength in the direction of the fibers is reduced compared with knitted reinforcements, which lie flat. High strain in tension (imagine pulling on a rope) will tend to straighten the fibers out, and high strain in compression (the 4-by-4s holding up your deck at home are under compression) will tend to make the fibers crimp further. In the real world, however, the

polyester resins used by most builders will give out long before these fiberglass fibers are fully stressed.

Knitted Reinforcements

Boatbuilders couldn't take full advantage of the potential of fiberglass until knitted reinforcements—also called stitched or unidirectional—were developed in the mid-1970s. Knitted reinforcements employ strands of the same thickness as woven roving but, instead of being woven together, the strands lie flat and run in a single orientation; a light stitching holds them in place. Knitted reinforcements allow the fiberglass strands to be fully loaded in tension; they are not crimped like the interlocking fibers of woven roving. For a given laminate thickness, knitted fabric is stronger than woven roving because the reinforcement fibers are already straightened out and the fiberglass is denser. And, since the voids between the layers of material are smaller, less resin is needed to wet out

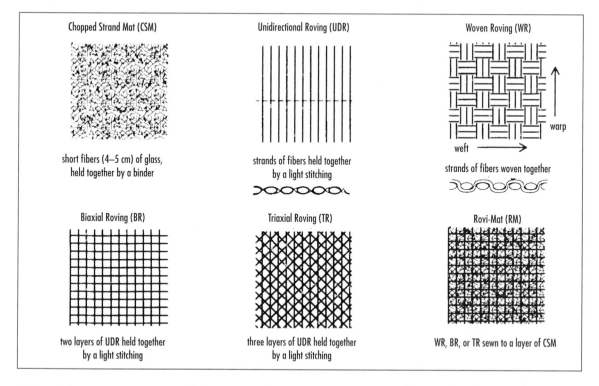

Various reinforcement weave patterns, including woven and non-woven, or stitched, materials. The closer the fibers align with the stresses in a structure, the more efficiently it can do its job.

LARSSON AND ELIASSON, *PRINCIPLES OF YACHT DESIGN*

A layer of gelcoat is sprayed on the open mold of a Sea Ray cruiser, followed by fiberglass chop or mat to prevent bottom blistering, a print-through blocker in the hull sides, and successive laminates of fiberglass that overlap for added strength at stress points including the keel and chines.

Formula's 350 SunSport starts with this male plug, framed and planked much like a wooden boat, which in turn is used to produce a steel-reinforced fiberglass female mold.

the reinforcement, improving the final glass-to-resin ratio.

Reinforcing fabrics are the structural backbone of a fiberglass boat, and they work by absorbing loads within the matrix. For this reason, the direction of the fiberglass strand orientation is very important. Reinforcements are selected based on the stresses anticipated in different areas of the boat. The simplest kind of knitted reinforcements is unidirectional, with the strand bundles running in a single direction. Unidirectional (0-degree) fiberglass has little strength in the weft direction, but is very strong in the warp direction. Unidirectional reinforcement is used where loads in a single orientation are expected, such as on the tops of hull stringers where tension and compression loads are absorbed, and for keel and stem strengthening.

When one layer of unidirectional reinforcement is stitched to another running in a different direction, a biaxial reinforcement is created. This allows a single roll of reinforcement to absorb stress in two directions simultaneously. Biaxial, triaxial, and even quadaxial knitted reinforcements, consisting of two, three, or four layers of strand bundles stitched together in 0-, 90-, or 45-degree directions, are commonly available to reduce production time and to

provide strength in the appropriate orientations. A 0/90 orientation means that a layer of fiberglass runs in both the warp and weft directions, while 45/45 indicates two fiberglass layers oriented with a 45-degree offset from the direction of the roll and at right angles to each other. A 45/45 reinforcement might be used in the sides of a long, narrow, low-profile offshore racing boat to better absorb the global loads present when running in a seaway at high speed. Fabrics defined as 45/45 also tend to conform to sharp corners, making them well suited for tabbing purposes (such as tabbing a bulkhead to a hull side). Knitted reinforcements are also available with fiberglass mat prebonded on one side to speed up production.

Cloth

Fiberglass cloth resembles a very fine woven roving. Because of its low profile, or smooth surface, cloth is usually used for finishing surfaces. Though very strong for its weight, it's not often used as a structural material because it can take as many as 50 layers to build up 1 inch of thickness. Cold-molded boats, which are built of wood bonded with epoxy resin, are often finished with layers of fiberglass cloth wet out with epoxy resin.

This Formula mold is nearing completion. Many layers of fiberglass are laid over the plug and supported by a network of steel pipes. The completed mold is lifted free from the plug and turned upright, ready to produce its first hull.

Bulking Materials

There's no substitute for thickness when it comes to making a panel of a given material stiff, so some boatbuilders try to save weight and money by using bulking mats. Used properly, bulker mats improve a hull's resistance to impact, fatigue, and blistering. Bulkers added to otherwise thin laminates, such as hull sides and center consoles on small boats, help prevent flexure or oil canning, reducing gelcoat cracking and crazing. Many builders also use bulking materials, along with a skin coat of mat or chop, to prevent gelcoat print-through. They cost

more per pound than fiberglass, but labor and resin savings offset the added expense. A syntactic foam called SprayCore, which contains resins and hollow glass microspheres, can be sprayed on and will block print-through like a bulking fabric, according to Omega Chemical, the manufacturer.

Exotic Reinforcements

Boatbuilders also have at their disposal expensive, high-strength reinforcements for special applications, such as aramid and carbon and graphite fiber. Generally such materials are used when great strength is required with minimal weight gain. The most often used aramid fiber is DuPont's Kevlar, which is lightweight and boasts significant resistance to fatigue and impact. It is not as strong in compression as fiberglass, though, and if left untreated, it will absorb water more readily than fiberglass. Aramid fibers can be wet out using either vinylester or epoxy resin, and since they deform significantly before ultimate failure, they can resist damage well.

Carbon fibers and graphite fibers are very stiff, strong, and temperature-resistant. Because of their stiffness, when these materials fail, they do so decisively. These fibers are expensive and must be wet out with epoxy or epoxy-based vinylester resins (which we discuss below), though carbon fiber may be wet out with vinylester resin if it's treated with the proper sizing. Their cost usually limits their use

Fiber	Density lb/in³	Tensile Strength psi x 10³	Tensile Modulus psi x 10⁶	Ultimate Elongation	Cost $/lb
E-Glass	.094	500	10.5	4.8%	.80-1.20
S-Glass	.090	665	12.6	5.7%	4
Aramid-Kevlar 49	.052	525	18.0	2.9%	16
Spectra 900	.035	375	17.0	3.5%	22
Polyester-COMPET	.049	150	1.4	22.0%	1.75
Carbon-PAN	.062-.065	350-700	33-57	0.38-2.0%	17-450

The relative physical properties of various reinforcements. Note the ultimate elongation of E-glass fiberglass, used most commonly in boats, compared to the resins in the chart on page 87. Vinylester and epoxy resins produce a far stronger matrix since they "stretch," or elongate, roughly the same as fiberglass.

ERIC GREENE

Construction with Fiberglass and Cold-Molded Wood   85

to high-stress areas and to parts where a combination of very high strength and low weight is needed. Both carbon and aramid fibers are stronger in tension than E-glass and S-glass, and carbon is nearly as strong in compression as tension, which gives it a significant advantage over Kevlar.

Another option for designers is Spectra, a high-density polyethylene reinforcement made by Allied Chemical. Its resistance to abrasion and its physical properties at room temperature are superior to Kevlar; in fact, it has the highest strength-to-weight ratio of any fiber. Resin adhesion is not good, however, so it's used mostly in sails, but seldom in boatbuilding.

The Laminate

The laminate "schedule" can combine these reinforcements with resin (as well as core materials) in a variety of ways. Some builders prefer woven roving since its higher profile, or more pronounced weave, builds up thickness and stiffness quickly. Woven roving also has excellent damage tolerance and impact resistance. Fiberglass boats were originally built with alternating layers of woven roving and mat or chop. The roving provides the strength and toughness, while the mat fills in the valleys in the roving's coarse weave patterns, improving the interlaminar (between the layers) bond between layers of roving. Without the mat, only the high spots of the layers of roving would come into contact, producing a weaker interlaminar bond. When building a boat, it is important to squeeze out excess resin in order to bring the layers of reinforcement in close contact; this is reflected in the *glass-to-resin ratio*. Mat or chop can generally be dispensed with if a laminate consisting only of woven roving is cured under pressure (with the use of a vacuum bag), compressing the layers of roving and ensuring good interlaminar bonds.

Other builders prefer knitted fiberglass for its lower profile and good interlaminar bond properties and for its higher glass-to-resin ratio. To save production time, combination reinforcements have also been developed that consist of a layer of mat bonded to the woven roving, allowing both to be applied and wet out at the same time. With four or more layers of woven fiberglass prebonded together, these "combination goods" can be applied quickly with relatively unskilled labor, and they cost less than knitted reinforcements. These fabrics are a good choice for building a solid fiberglass (nonsandwich) hull.

Resins

Resins are the glue that holds the laminate together; they bond the reinforcements together, fill the voids between the reinforcement strands and fibers, and create a solid composite matrix that allows the reinforcement fibers to absorb and distribute loads efficiently. Resins come in a variety of chemical compositions, including, in ascending order of overall quality and price, orthophthalic (general purpose) polyester, isophthalic polyester, vinylester, and epoxy. Since resins are intended to lock the fiberglass in a matrix, those that most closely match the physical properties of the fiberglass (in particular its tendency to stretch) and adhere best to other, cured fiberglass components result in the best product.

Polyesters

Orthophthalic polyester resins are the most widely used by boatbuilders, followed by isophthalic resins. These resins are cured—transformed from a liquid to a solid—by adding an accelerator and a catalyst. Cure times can be regulated by carefully controlling the amount of these additives used, and ambient temperature, humidity, and the thickness of the laminate are all factors affecting cure time.

Orthophthalic resins, which have been around longer, are relatively cheap and easy to use. They have the lowest tensile strength of the common boatbuilding resins: they break more easily when pulled under strain. They are also relatively brittle, so they won't stretch (elongate) very far before failing. A volatile chemical in the resin called *styrene* is released to the atmosphere during the building process, both through evaporation if the resin is sprayed and from the high heat generated during cure. When the styrene flashes off, microscopic voids are left in the resin. As a result, laminates

Resin	Tensile Strength psi x 10^3	Tensile Modulus psi x 10^5	Ultimate Elongation	2007 Bulk Cost $/lb
Orthophthalic Atlas P 2020	7.0	5.9	.91%	1.42
Dicyclopentadiene (DCPD) Atlas 80-6044	11.2	9.1	.86%	1.47
Isophthalic CoRezyn 9595	10.3	5.65	2.0%	1.72
Vinylester Derakane 411-45	11-12	4.9	5-6%	2.55
Epoxy Gougeon Pro Set 125/226	7.96	5.3	7.7%	5.60

This chart shows why the kind of resin used plays a crucial role in determining laminate strength and impact resistance. Vinylester comes the closest to matching the elongation of fiberglass rein-forcement, making it a much better choice, from a physical properties perspective, than ortho, iso, or DCPD resins.   ERIC GREENE

made of orthophthalic resin are the least solid and the least resistant to *osmosis* of the boatbuilding resins. Most production boats are built primarily or entirely with orthophthalic resin. This microscopic permeability can be addressed with proper quality control during the building process.

Compared with orthophthalic resins, isophthalic polyester resins generally have higher mechanical properties, which means they have greater tensile strength, over twice the elongation, and adhere better to previously cured fiberglass, resulting in superior secondary bonds. Isophthalic resins have better chemical resistance and, because they are more resistant to osmosis than orthophthalic resins, are sometimes used as a barrier coat under the gelcoat to help prevent osmotic blistering.

DCPD

A DCPD, or *poly dicyclopentadiene*, resin blend is sometimes used by boatbuilders because of its lower styrene levels. Too brittle in its pure form for boat-building use, DCPD is blended with orthophthalic (and sometimes isophthalic and vinylester) resin to allow builders to meet increasingly tough Environmental Protection Agency (EPA) styrene emission levels. Because there's less styrene (33 to 38 percent in a DCPD blend versus orthophthalic's 42 to 46 percent), there's also less shrinkage during cure. So, DCPD is often used in the first layer of fiberglass to minimize print-through of the underlying fiberglass reinforcement to the gelcoat. DCPD blends offer somewhat better osmotic blistering protection than pure orthophthalic resin, and cure faster, so a part doesn't have to stay in the mold as long.

Some builders use DCPD resin for the whole laminate since the time the part has to stay in the mold is reduced. The downside is that DCPD resins are the most brittle of all when cured, even more so than orthophthalic resin. DCPD-based laminates can also be hard to repair; chemical linkage in a secondary bond is impeded since the resin cross-links so completely and so quickly. The window for creating secondary bonds can be as little as 24 hours, and less if exposed to sunlight. (As a result, early DCPD laminates experienced problems with bulkhead and liner installations failing to adhere to the cured hull.)

This contrasts with orthophthalic and isophthalic resins, which, though the great majority of the cure occurs within a few hours, can take

Secondary Bonding

You get a secondary bond when you add a fresh layer of fiberglass to a previously cured fiberglass surface and rely on the adhesion of the resulting mechanical bond to glue the parts together. This wet-on-dry process is a weak link in fiberglass construction. In a perfect world, the whole hull laminate would be laid up and impregnated with resin at the same time, cross-linking the entire laminate with a primary, chemical bond at the molecular level. (This is, in fact, what SCRIMP and other resin-infusion processes do: all the resin is drawn through by vacuum in a single step, eliminating secondary bonds in the hull and, in some cases, in the supporting bulkhead landings and stringers as well. See pages 100–102.)

In conventional fiberglass construction, boatbuilders typically lay up one or two layers of fiberglass at a time, let it cure, sand it, and then apply another layer. Or peel ply, a layer of plastic that leaves a textured, bondable surface when removed, can be applied to the wet-out fiberglass. When the part cures, the peel ply is removed, the area lightly sanded, and follow-on laminates applied. To ensure that these secondary bonds are solid and secure, mechanically preparing the surface with sanding, grinding, or chemical preparation is essential. Some builders will apply a layer of mat to areas that are to be ground after curing in preparation for a secondary bond; this extra step protects the underlying layers of reinforcement, such as woven roving, from damage by heavy grinding. In reality, polyester resins take longer to harden completely, so a secondary bond applied 72 hours after the resin has cured to the touch may still establish some chemical as well as mechanical bonding.

Secondary Bond Joints

A secondary bond should include a tapered, or beveled, edge to maximize the bonding area, and provide an even transition for stresses being transferred from one part to the other.

ERIC GREENE

months to harden completely. Repairs to DCPD resin laminates thus call for large scarfs, or tapers, and correspondingly larger bonding surfaces when a damaged section is being prepared for a patch job. Using DCPD resin in the repair job is also thought by some to be a good idea since the patch's flex and expansion characteristics will then match that of the original DCPD part.

Vinylester

Vinylester resin, though applied in much the same way as polyester resin, is a far superior material with excellent fatigue and impact resistance. It will elongate 5 to 6 percent before failing, allowing the fiberglass reinforcement to absorb maximum loading, increasing its impact resistance and ultimate strength. Vinylester resins adhere very well to cured fiberglass, making them a good choice for many secondary bonds.

Most excess styrene in vinylester resin cross-links with itself during cure, rather than flashing off and leaving microscopic holes as in orthophthalic resin. So vinylester is more solid and has superior resistance to osmosis, which results in excellent, proven protection against osmotic blistering. For this reason, some builders use a skin coat of 3 ounces of chop or mat applied over the gelcoat in the mold (i.e., just under the gelcoat in the finished hull) and wet out with vinylester resin to prevent blistering. Many well-built, high-end boats are constructed using vinylester resin throughout the laminate, resulting in the best laminate you can get short of using epoxy.

Polyester and vinylester resins are usually air-inhibited, which means they won't cure when exposed to air. The resin remains chemically receptive for 12 hours to a week, allowing a small degree of primary bond cross-linking during this time.

Air-cured resin has paraffin wax mixed in, which rises to the surface during curing to form an air barrier, allowing the resin to cure completely. This paraffin film presents a secondary bonding (see below) problem when subsequent layers of fiberglass are applied to the cured laminate. The fiberglass must be sanded and washed with a solvent to remove the paraffin film so that freshly applied fiberglass will adhere to it. Polyester resins bought at the local hardware store or marina are usually air-cured and therefore air-inhibited.

Formula's FAS³Tech go-fasts are supported by a one-piece fiberglass grid laid up in its own mold and then bonded to the hull, effectively doubling hull thickness.

The ultimate elongation of E-glass—the amount it will stretch before failure—is about 4.8 percent, which is less than the ultimate elongation of vinylester and epoxy resins. That's a good thing, since the fiberglass is allowed to come under full strain without the weaker resin failing first, which is what would happen with far more brittle polyester resin. This is one of the reasons why a laminate of vinylester or epoxy resin and E-glass works so well structurally; the physical properties of the resins more nearly match that of the reinforcements.

Epoxy

Epoxies are the best resins used in the boatbuilding industry and, as you might expect, they're by far the most expensive. Although the various epoxies differ in their physical properties, as do the members of all resin families, they are all tough and strong, and elongate before failure more than other resins, resulting in the toughest, most impact-resistant and resilient fiberglass matrix. Epoxy is also the best possible glue, adhering tenaciously to a properly prepared, previously cured fiberglass

surface. It is often advisable to use epoxy to make repairs to damaged polyester or vinylester fiberglass components. Epoxy resin has no styrene, making it the most solid and blister-proof of all resins. Extremely resistant to osmosis, an epoxy hull can be expected to live a very long life blister-free. Epoxy resin is usually hand-applied with rollers or brushes, unlike polyesters and vinylesters, which can easily be sprayed.

Core Materials

People often equate stiffness with strength, but the two are not the same. A panel may have plenty of strength but inadequate stiffness. Walk on a limber deck and you think it's weak, when in fact it could easily hold your car. On a boat, however, it is very important that panels be designed to provide adequate stiffness. A panel may be strong enough to resist impacts with waves and underwater objects but, if it flexes excessively, fatigue will eventually set in,

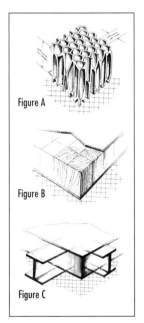

A close-up view of several sandwich panels, showing the relationship between the I-beam and the components (skins and structural core) of a composite sandwich. The integrity of the bond between the fiberglass skins and the core material is crucial. BALTEK CORP.

		core 2t	core 4t
relative stiffness	100	700	3,700
relative strength	100	350	925
relative weight	100	103	106

The relationship between thickness, strength, and stiffness in three different panels.

LARSSON AND ELIASSON, *PRINCIPLES OF YACHT DESIGN*

weakening the laminate over time. In addition, flexing in the skin of the hull will present an unfair surface to the passing water, adding drag and possibly creating dynamic instabilities.

Before composite sandwiches became commonplace, a boatbuilder just added more layers of fiberglass to get the necessary thickness for a strong and stiff structure. However, beam theory tells us that two relatively thin skins held fixed in relation to each other a small distance apart is a much more efficient use of materials. So boatbuilders began to use two relatively thin layers of fiberglass sandwiching a lightweight core material to create the same effect—strength and stiffness with light weight. The two thin skins of fiberglass, like the flanges of the I-beam, are separated by a core material, which acts like the web of the I-beam and holds the skins in place. In addition to reducing weight, cores add thermal and acoustic insulation, reducing condensation and noise levels, and help to attenuate vibrations. A cored hull also needs fewer support members, so more room is available for interior accommodations.

The I-Beam Effect

Let's look quickly at how beam theory works in this case. When a force pushes against an I-beam, the flanges (fiberglass skins) of the beam absorb tension and compression loads, and the web (the core material) keeps the flanges from separating in *shear* (one piece of paper sliding over another is movement in

shear). If the two I-beam flanges were able to move, or slide, in relation to each other, the I-beam would lose its strength and stiffness.

A core is used to form a "sandwich" consisting of two fiberglass skins bonded to a lightweight core, usually made of balsa, foam, or honeycomb. A sandwich of two ¼-inch layers of fiberglass separated by a 1-inch-thick core is far stiffer than a single layer of ½-inch-thick fiberglass. In a solid laminate, stiffness increases with the cube of the thickness; in a composite sandwich, the stiffness increase is somewhat less, but still significant, and depends on the core material used. Just as the web of an I-beam prevents its flanges from moving in relation to each other, the core material absorbs *shear stresses* between the two layers of fiberglass. Thickness also contributes to panel strength. Strength in a solid laminate is a function of thickness squared; strength in a sandwich is, again, somewhat less than that, depending on the core type.

Although we select core materials because of their light weight, the density of the core is also important. Strength and stiffness in a sandwich laminate are both directly proportional to the density of the core material, whether it's foam or balsa. A denser core is also more resistant to compression. So a dense, strong, and stiff core material can be thinner than one that's less so and still get the same job done. Put another way, a less-dense core must be thicker to achieve the same load-carrying capacity as a denser core. However, a thinner, denser core material will not deliver the dramatic gains in stiffness that a thicker sandwich will. So it's generally more practical to increase the panel's thickness, using a lightweight core, than to find a core material of high density. Dense cores are often used selectively in highly loaded areas, such as hull bottoms, where shear loads are higher.

Building a Sandwich Laminate

A stiff panel experiences high tension and compression stresses in its fiberglass skins, so selecting the right materials and resin is critical.

Knitted reinforcements are often preferred to roving woven because they permit lighter, thinner skins without sacrificing strength. As for the laminating resin, a vinylester or epoxy resin—with its greater ductility, elongation, and adhesion—will produce a better composite sandwich than is possible with orthophthalic polyester resin. If the resin that bonds the skin to the core is brittle, then the whole sandwich structure is brittle itself. Some isophthalic polyester resins have good elongation, and a hybrid orthovinylester resin can also produce an acceptably rugged, resilient sandwich at a lower cost than vinylester alone.

Although the fiberglass skins around a core could be thin and still absorb the loads generated by slamming into waves, the outer skin has other responsibilities, including resistance to collision impacts, so it must be made thicker. In fact, a sandwich bottom with two ½-inch fiberglass skins will have significantly higher impact resistance than a solid ½-inch laminate, especially if the core is one of the more plastic and ductile foams (see below). That's because the sandwich panel can absorb energy from the collision and bounce back, whereas the solid glass laminate is more brittle and more likely to shatter.

The bond between the skins and the core (the "skin-to-core" bond) has to be sound, and things get complicated because dissimilar materials with different physical properties are being joined together. When a sandwich hull or deck is built, the gelcoat is typically sprayed into the female mold first, followed by a skin coat and then the outer skin laminate. Then the core material is bedded to the outer laminate, either in a bed of resin-rich fiberglass or with a specially formulated core-bonding adhesive supplied by the core manufacturer.

If the core is to be bedded in fiberglass, the cured fiberglass outer-skin surface is ground smooth to minimize hills and valleys. Then, wet mat or chop is applied to the sanded fiberglass to fill in the remaining valleys. The core is primed with partially catalyzed resin and applied to the wet fiberglass. This priming resin seeps into the open pores of the foam or balsa core better than core bond adhesive can, providing a far better mechanical bond when it cures. If a core-bonding putty is used, the putty is troweled onto the partially or completely cured outer skin of fiberglass. The core is then squished into the adhesive and hand rolled to remove air bubbles or, preferably, vacuum bagged to ensure a sound bond. In general, the best results are often achieved with a combination of resin and bonding putty.

This Grady-White's hull stringers are bonded in place and the cavities filled with foam, producing an unsinkable boat. A hole almost anywhere in the bottom of the boat would be a non-event since water would have no way to flow to the bilge.

Any gaps in the core material itself or between sections of core must be filled to maintain structural integrity. In particular, the builder must be certain that there are no gaps or air voids in the hidden joint between the outer fiberglass skin and the core material. The best way to produce a solid skin-to-core bond is to use precoated core, a core-bonding adhesive, and a vacuum bag to apply great pressure evenly to the core while the bonding material is setting up. (Vacuum bagging is discussed on page 99.) Once the outer bond line has cured, the inner layer of fiberglass can be applied to the inside of the core, wet-on-dry. Vacuum bagging is not required here, as the builders can see what they're doing.

Core Material Evaluation Comparison Table

	Balsawood	Honeycomb Plastic	Linear PVC (Airex R63.80)	Cross-Linked PVC	SAN (Core-Cell)
Closed Cell Structure	3	1	10	10	10
Resistance to Fresh/Salt Water	3	6	10	10	10
Resistance to Water Vapor Transm.	2	-	9	9	8
Resistance to Rot/Deterioration	2	9	9	9	9
Resistance to Gasoline/Diesel Oil	7	6	9	9	10
Resistance to Styrene	10	6	4	8	7
Outgassing Tendency	8	-	10	1	10
Compression Strength	10	3	2	4	3
Flexural Modulus	6	4	4	6	8
Shear Strength	10	3	7	8	7
Impact Strength*	5	5	10	3	9
Fatigue Strength*	3	-	3	7	10
Resistance to Crack Propagation	8	5	10	2	9
Heat Distortion Temperature	10	4	3	6	5
Thermal Insulation	5	4	7	8	7
Damping Characteristics	4	3	8	4	7
Burning Characteristics	8	2	5	5	4
Smoke/Toxic Emission	8	6	3	3	4
Versatility in Boatbuilding	5	2	3	5	10
Weight (at common usage)	5	6	8	7	8
Economic Criteria/Price	9	10	5	7	6
Totals	134	85	139	127	161

Core materials are rated on a scale from 1–10, 10 being the most desirable, or best property. The ratings are our estimates, and are based on our general experience as well as data sheet values.

ATC's estimation of the relative merits of different core materials (ATC is the manufacturer of Core-Cell). Although other manufacturers would undoubtedly assign higher values to their own products, this chart is an excellent starting point for any discussion of core material suitability.

ATC CHEMICAL

The problems of skin-to-core bonds have discouraged many production manufacturers from building boats with cored bottoms, since a failed bond line here means a failed hull. That's too bad, because coring a bottom is a great way to keep weight down, increase bottom panel thickness, reduce framing requirements, and add insulation against water noise and condensation. And it's not that hard to do right using vacuum bagging and special skin-to-core bond adhesives. The problem is that some builders have insufficient quality controls in place to ensure a high-quality bond line during construction.

Although coring the bottom is a challenge, most builders do use coring on the hull sides, deck, and superstructure. It's a simple matter of saving weight and gaining stiffness at the same time, and a skin-to-core bond line failure likely won't have catastrophic consequences in these locations.

Balsa Cores

End-grain balsa is the most commonly used core material, offering excellent physical properties and low cost. The wood is cut from the tree like slices of bread from a loaf, so that the grain runs from fiberglass skin to skin. Balsa is resistant to compression along the direction of the grain, and it is excellent at absorbing the shear stress to which cores are subject. Balsa is available in a variety of densities from 4.5 to 15.5 pounds per cubic foot, from suppliers including DIAB and Baltek. It comes in rigid sheet form or in shapeable panels that are sliced into small squares and held together with a fiberglass mesh on one side, so that they can conform to curved surfaces. It's important that the gaps between the squares be filled with resin or bedding compound to maintain the structural integrity of the finished sandwich. This applies to both balsa and foam cores. Balsa should also be hot-coated, or coated with resin that is allowed to catalyze, before being fiberglassed in place. This prevents the lamination resin from being wicked out of the reinforcement and weakening the skin-to-core bond.

The Grady-White 360 Express's hull support structure has foam-cored fiberglass stringers and thwartships members tying the grid to the hull sides. The foam gives the structural members their shape, and fiberglass encapsulating the foam produces a moderate-weight hull.

Because it's commonly used in higher densities than foam, balsa typically has greater shear strength. (High-density foam is actually stronger than low-density balsa, but most balsa comes in a density of 10 to 12 pounds per cubic foot, versus 4 to 5 pounds for most structural foams.) The strength and stiffness of balsa make it a good candidate for decks and other rigid surfaces.

Due to its compressive strength and stiffness, however, balsa is not as good at absorbing impact energy as the more ductile foams. Under impact, say with an underwater piling, balsa will transfer the load directly to the inner fiberglass skin. This is why a resin that can stretch, like vinylester, will do a better job of holding the sandwich together at the skin-to-core bond than a more brittle polyester resin. Wave impact load attenuation with a balsa core is quite good, though, since the material's compressive properties transfer energy efficiently from one fiberglass skin to the other.

Like most organic materials, balsa is susceptible to rot in the presence of moisture, oxygen, and rot-causing spores. If the balsa core stays dry, it won't rot. If it becomes wet, it will rot and eventually delaminate from the fiberglass skins as the water migrates along the skin-to-core bond line. The cross-grain structure of the balsa coring slows down the permeation process, as do the resin- or putty-filled voids between the balsa scrims. Needless to say, the importance of keeping the balsa core dry is hard to overrate. That means you don't drill holes through deck, superstructure, or hull components cored with balsa without taking elaborate precautions.

Foam Cores

Structural foams are often used as core materials and are available in a wide range of densities to suit different applications. Compared with balsa, foam cores are generally lighter and more resistant to rot—or even rot-proof, depending on whom you believe. They are also more expensive.

The degree of molecular cross-linking (or interlocking of molecules) is a major factor in the behavior of foams and their desirability in different applications. Most structural foam cores are cross-linked to some extent. Foams with the most cross-linking, such as polyvinyl chloride (PVC) cross-linked foams, offer the greatest shear strength and stiffness, but they are also relatively brittle. Examples are Divinycell and Klegecell. As with balsa,

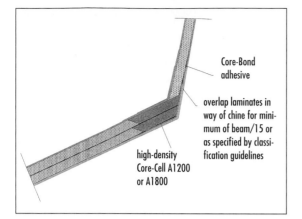

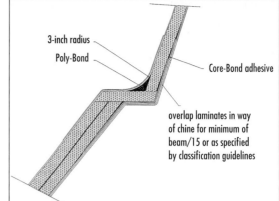

The double-core in this hull bottom allows the desired total core thickness to be achieved, even in the absence of a suitably thick material. Note the use of higher density foam at the chines, which, like the keel, will be subject to high localized loads from lifting straps. ATC CHEMICAL

Detail of a stepped chine showing how core materials can be used to negotiate complex shapes. The inside corner of the upper chine is radiused (in this case with a fillet of Poly-Bond) to spread out loads and to make sure the fiberglass reinforcement lays down smoothly and void free. ATC CHEMICAL

the stiffness of PVC foams makes them a good choice for decks and rigid surfaces.

Foams with the least cross-linking are commonly referred to as *linear*. Airex, for example, has the least cross-linking of the major boatbuilding foams. It has the least shear strength, but it is the most ductile. So although an Airex core gives less strength and stiffness to the panel than balsa or cross-linked PVC foam, it can yield and distort further—and absorb much more energy—before failing entirely. In a collision, a ductile core will absorb more energy than a brittle core, limiting damage to the fiberglass skins, the core itself, and the skin-core bond. And as long as the inner skin remains intact, the boat will not take on water. Airex is sold in 3.8- to 8.7-pound densities.

Blurring these categories is a linear foam called Core-Cell. Core-Cell has stiffness close to that of PVC cross-linked foam, but its ductility is close to that of Airex, giving Core-Cell some of the best qualities of each. Its physical properties make it suitable to use throughout a boat, from hull bottom to superstructure and decks. Core-Cell tends to stretch as it fails, helping to keep the hull intact after impact. In addition, its heat tolerance makes it well suited for

use in sunlit decks. Core-Cell is made by ATC Chemical and sold in densities from 3 to 12 pounds.

In general, the denser the foam, the higher the stiffness and weight, since there is more, or tighter, cross-linking with more core material and less air per unit volume, and the greater the cost. A very dense foam might be used in the transom of an outboard or stern-drive boat, where high compression loads are expected, while lighter foams could be used in the hull sides.

Not surprisingly, some boatbuilders use a combination of different core materials for different applications in the same boat. Out on the water you can find boats with solid fiberglass bottoms and balsa-cored topsides, boats with Airex-cored bottoms with Divinycell topsides, and boats made entirely with balsa, Core-Cell, and Divinycell sandwich panels.

Foams also respond differently to heat. The heat distortion temperature (HDT) of a foam—or any core material—is the temperature at which the core will lose its strength and shape and begin to deform. Balsa and cross-linked PVC have higher HDTs than linear foam, so they're a good choice for surfaces subject to heating from the sun, such as decks and the topsides of dark hulls. Linear foams such as Airex should be avoided in these surfaces, since the sandwich will more readily lose its stiffness when heated.

Foam cores are available in solid sheets and as flexible sheets of little blocks. Solid sheets are preferable, since there are no cuts to the core, but they can only be used on flat or very gently curved surfaces. With solid sheets, builders have to take great care that there are no gaps in the bond between the foam core and the fiberglass skin. Some solid-sheet foams can be thermoformed, or heated, to conform to a curved surface. The alternative is to use sheets of foam sliced or cut into little blocks and held together with a scrim on one side. The contour-cored core is used around curved areas, since the slits between the blocks will open up to allow the core to follow the shape of the mold. Again, these slits and voids have to be filled with resin or putty during construction to maintain the structural integrity of the core and prevent any water that gets into the core from migrating through the hull.

Honeycomb Cores

Honeycomb cores are extremely light, high-end materials derived from the aerospace industry. Marine applications have to be engineered carefully because of the potential for water absorption and because of the difficulties of bonding the surface of the honeycomb to the fiberglass skins. High-end boats, like some of the America's Cup contenders, use honeycomb cores because they deliver the lightest possible composite. At the top end is Nomex, a very expensive honeycomb made of aramid fibers, widely used in the aircraft industry. Sandwiches using paper or plastic honeycomb core are more affordable. Plastic honeycomb like Nida-Core has been used in decks, bulkheads, and even hulls. Tricel, a paper honeycomb, produces interior furniture, joinery, and nonstructural components at a fraction of the weight of solid plywood. Sandwiches with plastic or paper honeycombs have very good sound-dampening qualities, so they work well as saloon decks above engine rooms.

The Challenges of Cores

Sandwich composite laminates are marvelous creations when they are properly engineered and constructed. However, poor design or construction can have disastrous results. While it's relatively hard to screw up a laminate of solid fiberglass, which can be made stronger and stiffer just by adding more layers of reinforcement, sandwiches are complex and unforgiving. Premature failure will result if incompatible materials are used or if proper procedures are neglected during construction. As we have seen, the various core materials have different properties, so they must be carefully matched to the application.

Core materials, particularly those made of foam, are comparatively weak in compression, and the core must at all costs remain dry. High-density foam cores can be used in areas where compression loads are anticipated, but any areas that will be drilled for through-hull fittings should be solid fiberglass. Otherwise, the through-hull's bolts will compress the core and may crush the fiberglass, and the holes will become susceptible to water leaking into the core with disastrous results.

If a sandwich hull or deck section must be drilled through, the core must be removed in the immediate vicinity of the hole and the resultant void filled with a fiberglass filler, preferably using epoxy resin, which has superior bonding properties. Alternatively, the inner skin and the core can be cut back and a scarf created from the inside of the hull by grinding down the surrounding area to a

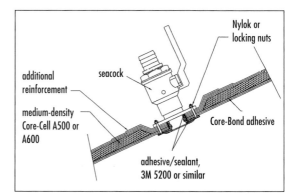

Section at a through-hull fitting, which should always be surrounded by solid fiberglass to resist compression when the mounting bolts are tightened and prevent water from leaking into the core. ATC CHEMICAL

gradual taper to the inside surface of the outer skin. This scalloped-out area is then laid up with solid fiberglass and the hole is drilled through the new fiberglass.

Going to all this trouble and proper planning should guarantee that water never gets into the core, an eventuality that would likely result in core delamination and water absorption over time.

The bigger the boat, the harder it is to keep the weight down. The balsa core in the bottom of this Viking convertible is being bonded to the outer fiberglass skin. Note that the hull is solid fiberglass wherever a through-hull fitting or penetration is to be located, such as cooling water seacocks and shaft strut pads. VIKING YACHTS

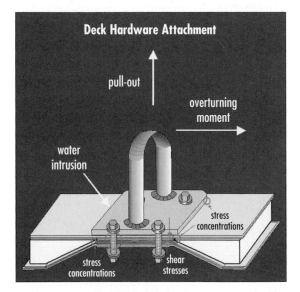

Proper deck hardware installation, with some of the stresses that are to be expected indicated. ERIC GREENE

The deck and superstructure of a balsa-cored boat is actually more likely to become water-soaked than a balsa-cored hull, if for no other reason than an owner is more likely to drill holes topside than elsewhere. Also, water can enter the core through both the inner *and* outer skins. All those little side-curtain fasteners, for instance, are a prime source of water intrusion, as are any other holes drilled into the skin. For this reason, most builders use marine plywood instead of balsa or foam as a core material around railings, cleats, and other areas of the deck where fixtures are likely, reasoning that the plywood will absorb the bolts' compression loads better and is more resistant to water penetration. While plywood is certainly more resistant to compression, the problem is that marine plywood will *also* delaminate and rot if it gets wet. And if a hole is drilled through a cored deck or hull section, it's almost guaranteed to leak during the boat's lifetime. Pressure-treated plywood is a better choice for this reason, though some experts report problems bonding permanently to pressure-treated plywood with polyester resins.

One alternative to plywood in this application may be a material called Xtreme Composites, made by Penske Plastics, which was originally developed for use in luggage frames and shipping containers. It's made of continuous-strand, nonwoven fiberglass in a matrix of foamed polyurethane resin. Fiberglass will stick to it, preventing water migration to the surrounding core material, and it's very compression resistant. As you might guess, it's more expensive than plywood. Whatever material is used to substitute around penetrations, a mistake sometimes made by builders is failing to carry the high-density core material and extra reinforcements far enough beyond the fitting to adequately spread out the loads to the surrounding hull or deck structure.

The challenge of weight reduction is not limited to hull structure. Interiors account for 25 to 30 percent of the average luxury yacht's gross weight, and can reach even higher percentages in very large yachts. A range of cored panels with excellent stiffness-to-weight ratios and good acoustic properties allows an architect and builder to achieve significant weight reductions. The use of these lightweight panels requires new techniques and a reevaluation of traditional carpentry skills.

Cores in Conclusion

Cores allow builders to produce lighter, stronger boats that go farther and faster on less fuel. As you dig into the engineering arcana of fiberglass sandwich construction, you quickly discover that there are differing opinions—firmly held and well-substantiated—among engineers about which core materials are best for a given application. There are a lot of different ways to build a good boat with core materials. However, none of these experts would disagree that, whichever materials are chosen, they must be properly matched and carefully constructed to be successful.

Building a Production Boat

Female molds are used to build all of the major components of a production fiberglass boat, including the hull, deck, superstructure, and countless hatches, doors, and other small components. Once the builder has created this mold (or *tooling*, as molds are called in the industry), it can be used repeatedly to build the pieces of the boat. That is what makes this method of boatbuilding fast and relatively cheap. The fewer parts that make up a completed boat, the better, too. For instance, many builders make their deck-superstructure-cockpit liners out of a single fiberglass part, eliminating a few leak- and squeak-prone joints and speeding up assembly time in the process.

Making the Mold

Fiberglass tooling is usually made by first building a male "plug" of the same shape and size as the desired component. Plugs can be built by hand, using wood or steel frames and usually wood or plywood planking. The wood surface is faired, and fiberglass cloth may be applied and the surface faired again.

Plugs can also be built using computer-aided design and computer-aided manufacturing (CAD-CAM). A special computer data file created from the naval architect's drawings is used to control a five-axis milling machine that carves the hull or other component shape out of a large block of foam. The foam plug is then coated with a thick layer of denser filler and milled again to very close tolerances, within thousandths of an inch.

Some builders use a combination of CAD-CAM and conventional methods, for example using CAM to cut out the hull plug's frames to within very close tolerances and then planking over the framework and fairing the plug manually.

Once the plug is finished to a mirror-smooth finish, it's time to build the female mold. The plug is waxed several times and a mold release agent may be applied, which creates a nonstick film on the finished surface. Next, layers of gelcoat specially formulated for mold building are applied to a combined 30- to 40-mil thickness (1 mil = 0.001 inch). Next follows a thick laminate of fiberglass chop or mat (which, being omnidirectional in reinforcement orientation, won't distort the mold surface) followed by layers of reinforcing fiberglass fabric. Molds are sometimes cored to add stiffness and strength, just like in the boat itself. A stiff supporting framework is then added to the outside of the mold to keep it from deforming, or changing shape, once it's lifted clear of the plug. Large hull molds often have "rocker" foundations that allow them to be rolled from one side to the other as alternating sides of the hull are laid up.

The completed mold is then lifted free from the plug and made ready to produce a fiberglass part, whether it's a hull, deck, or flybridge. The mold is waxed and, depending on the builder, coated with a special mold-release coating to help keep the part's outer layer, the gelcoat, from adhering to it. Some builders rely solely on the wax to assure the part lifts off easily, finding that the mold release agent leaves a visible pattern in the gelcoat surface.

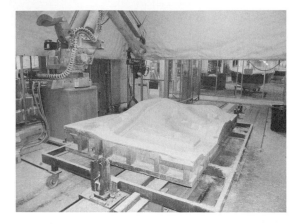

Sea Ray uses accurate robots to trim hulls and decks and to cut openings for various windows and other penetrations.

Grady-White uses high-pressure closed-molding to produce its hatches and doors, creating durable parts with tooled smooth surfaces.

Ranger took a perfectly good hull and cut it up to show the extent of its foam flotation, which makes the boats unsinkable.

GENMAR HOLDINGS, INC.

Laminating the Hull

Once the mold is prepared, a pigmented gelcoat is sprayed on to a thickness of 20 to 30 mils and allowed to gel and partially harden. The gelcoat is what you see on the finished, unpainted product, since the hull is laminated from the outside in. The gelcoat gives the hull its smooth, gleaming appearance and color and helps protect the underlying substrate of fiberglass.

Next comes a "skin" coat, usually made up of a couple of layers of chop (sprayed from a chopper gun) or hand-laid mat that forms a resin-rich barrier layer over the gelcoat. Chop or mat is used here because either cures uniformly, being random in fiber orientation. The resulting cure won't shrink the gelcoat, causing print-through once the hull is separated from the mold, as a heavy-weave roving might do. Low-profile DCPD resin is often used in the skin coat in topside areas. The mat layer and the following plies of reinforcements are wet out either with a spray gun or by using rollers and brushes with buckets of resin.

With either method, the resin must be carefully catalyzed so that adequate working time is provided and so the resin doesn't "kick" too quickly; the proper amount to use is largely a function of ambient air temperature. Using too much catalyst, or an overly thick laminate, will produce an excessive exothermic reaction, meaning that too much heat is given off by the chemical reaction of the curing process. The result may be reduced osmotic blistering resistance and distortion and print-through of the fiberglass reinforcement.

The layup process is straightforward. A fresh, thin layer of resin is applied to the mold or to the previous layer of cured reinforcement. The reinforcement is laid out dry over this wet coat of resin, positioned in place, and then wet out with spray- or roller-applied resin. Grooved metal rollers and squeegees are used to remove excess resin and air bubbles from the laminate. This process also ensures that the reinforcement is completely wet out.

Depending on the builder, and on which part is being laminated, the reinforcement material can be precut on a table in a cutting room, rolled back up, and delivered to the molding room. Then, when it's rolled out on the hull in the proper location, it'll fit perfectly as it's being wet out. Some fiberglass vendors even deliver the material precut in kits to reduce production time on the lamination floor.

Vacuum Bagging

Vacuum bagging is often used to hold core materials firmly in place when bonding a core to a cured fiberglass skin. The goal is to produce a consistent, high-quality secondary bond. The area to be bonded is covered with a plastic bag, the edges are sealed, and a strong vacuum is applied until the part sets up. Since the outer side of the core in contact with the vacuum bag is not wet out, this process is called *dry bagging*. A perfect vacuum of up to 14.7 psi would result in over 2,100 pounds per square foot of pressure applied uniformly to the entire surface being laminated, far more than can be applied using weights. In the real world, a vacuum of around 10 to 12 psi is more realistic in large molds.

Wet bagging applies the same procedure to wet laminates. However, in this case it is necessary to draw off excess resin before it gets to the pump that produces the vacuum, so a bleeder material that allows excess resin to drain off and a film that keeps the plumbing from sticking to the cured fiberglass are needed. Wet bagging results in a higher glass-to-resin ratio by removing excess resin, removes entrained air in the laminate, and eliminates interlaminar voids by compressing the layers of fiberglass against each other firmly, greatly improving the quality of the final product. Some builders lay up large parts like hulls and decks manually, but use vacuum bagging on cored saloon decks and bridge hardtops because they are easier to handle.

Impregnators and Prepregs

Keeping the glass-to-resin ratio consistent is a concern for boatbuilders, as is the speed with which large amounts of thick, multilayer fiberglass reinforcements can be wet out. Machines called "impregnators" address both of these points and are used by builders of very large fiberglass craft. An impregnator passes the dry fiberglass reinforcement, which comes in rolls up to 60 inches wide, through a pool of catalyzed resin and then through a pair of rollers that squeezes out the excess, precisely controlling the amount of resin saturating the material. Another pair of rollers controls the speed at which the fabric passes through. Glass content of 55 percent (relative to resin) can be attained using an impregnator. The impregnator is usually mounted on an overhead crane or gantry, which can be positioned directly over the part being laminated, accelerating production time significantly. Smaller, portable impregnators can also be used.

Preimpregnated reinforcements, or prepregs, are delivered to the boatbuilder wet out in partially cured, tacky epoxy resin, ready to be laid up in the mold. Prepregs, which are much more expensive than traditional reinforcement materials, require special handling; they must be stored in a freezer until they're used and then they must be postcured (allowed to harden) by putting the vessel, or part, in an oven set between 140° and 350°F, depending on the prepreg. Only a few custom boatbuilders use this method, but the advantages include a consistent glass-to-resin ratio, the ability to bond effectively to honeycomb cores, and a strong, lightweight structure. High-end boatbuilders like this method because of the material's easy handling, low styrene emissions (even when styrene-free epoxy isn't used), longer working times, and better quality and consistency. Many America's Cup sailboats, around-the-world race boats, high-end power- and sailboats, and high-performance hydroplanes are built using prepregs.

Resin Infusion and Other Specialized Techniques

If you're considering a boat that's built using one of the available resin-infusion processes, you'd be buying bragging rights to one of the best-built boats around.

Bottom blistering has been a recurring problem with fiberglass boats since the 1970s, supposedly when resin manufacturers changed their formulations with unfortunate results. Technically, osmosis is the migration under pressure of a solvent—in our case water—through a film, or barrier, that separates areas of varying salinity concentration. Blistering starts when moisture passes through the gelcoat and into the fiberglass substrate beneath by osmosis. Water finds its way into tiny air- or styrene-filled voids in the fiberglass, interacts with soluble chemicals left over from uncured resin and other vagaries of the construction process, and then expands under pressure, peeling off little—or not so little—bits of hull bottom.

It turns out that fiberglass hulls are surprisingly porous, especially when built using general-purpose orthophthalic resins. Water can migrate into the fiberglass hull structure at the microscopic level, or it can find resin-starved fiberglass strands and wick its way into the substrate. Water can also penetrate into the fiberglass from the inside, from the bilge. (Boats with water-soaked flotation foam have been known to develop osmotic blistering from the inside of the hull.) At the same time, a fiberglass hull can absorb moisture and *not* blister, provided there are no voids and no soluble chemicals for the water to react with.

There are a number of causes of osmotic blistering. An incompletely wet-out fiberglass skin coat will leave voids and dry glass fibers, which will carry water into the laminate by capillary action. The skin coat should be composed of mat or chop, thoroughly wet out to produce a resin-rich barrier against moisture. (The first few ounces of laminate is often called a *barrier* coat for this reason.) A low-quality gelcoat, or a gelcoat that is damaged or poorly applied, will not resist moisture penetration well. A poor bond between the gelcoat and the fiberglass beneath will allow water to pass through to the laminate more readily and cause the gelcoat to delaminate.

In the case of polyester resins, if too much catalyst is used in the resin, or the resin is not thoroughly mixed, unreacted chemicals may be left over in the laminate that will react with water. If the resin cures too quickly, microscopic (or larger) pathways can be left in the laminate that water will quickly find. Other causes include impurities or solvents in the fiberglass or the resin and damp, cold conditions during hull lamination. Left untreated, blistering can be counted on to worsen, with tiny blisters growing larger and larger and water wicking farther into the laminate until a resin-rich barrier is reached. In rare cases blistering can destroy the bottom of a boat structurally, or at least make it a very expensive proposition to repair.

Blistering can be prevented by using high-quality resins and careful quality control; in particular, builders must ensure complete saturation of the fiberglass and proper curing of the resin. Boats built of conventional, general-purpose orthophthalic resin are the most susceptible to blistering because this type of resin is less cross-linked at the molecular level, although with good quality control a hull built of orthophthalic resin can certainly be blister free. Some builders use isophthalic resin or vinylester resin in the barrier or skin coat because these resins are chemically more cross-linked at the molecular level and are significantly less porous. A vinylester skin coat is to be preferred over an isophthalic skin coat. Orthophthalic, general-purpose polyester resin is often used for the remainder of the laminate since it's cheaper. In terms of blister resistance, the ideal laminate would be all-epoxy, followed by all-vinylester.

Some dealers will tell you that their boats have a vinylester barrier coat, but that may just mean that a couple of coats of vinylester resin were sprayed over the gelcoat when the boat was laminated in the female mold. Unfortunately, such a thin layer can easily be ground off if bottom paint preparations are done carelessly. Or a builder may point to their premium gelcoat

Rather than adding hand-laid layers of fiberglass reinforcement to previously cured layers, resin infusion processes usually involve laying up all the reinforcement (except the skin coat) in one stack, including stringers and bulkhead landings, and infusing resin under vacuum pressure in one shot, eliminating the weaker secondary bonds.

SCRIMP

SCRIMP stands for Seemann Composites Resin Infusion Molding Process. SCRIMP uses either epoxy or vinylester resins to infuse the fiberglass hull, stringers, and bulkhead landings under very high vacuum all in one step, eliminating secondary bonds and carefully controlling the glass-to-resin

as their answer to blistering protection, but that 20- to 30-mil layer of gelcoat is susceptible to cracking, either from impact or from being applied incorrectly, or to being ground through during bottom paint preparation. Once the relatively brittle gelcoat is penetrated, the underlying fiberglass barrier coat better be built right, or watch out. A much better barrier coat consists of 3 ounces of mat or chop wet out with vinylester resin and applied over the gelcoat (i.e., "over" the gelcoat in the mold, and immediately under the gelcoat in the finished boat). Be sure to ask about blistering coverage in the warranty.

Osmotic blistering is mostly a problem with vessels that are kept in the water year-round, but some boats develop blisters after being left in the water for just a couple of months. The warmer the water, the greater the tendency to blister. Even after a boat has been hauled out of the water for months, water may still be present in voids and blisters and continue to permeate the hull laminate's glass fibers. If you discover blisters on the bottom of your boat, and try to fix things by just sanding it and applying a couple of coats of epoxy and bottom paint, you can actually make things worse by sealing the water *in*. The gelcoat and underlying fiberglass laminate have to be completely dried out before repairs are attempted, and this might take the application of hot air for a prolonged period.

Fixing a badly blistered bottom properly is a difficult undertaking. Doing the job right is an extensive, time-consuming process, usually involving the removal of the gelcoat and part of the fiberglass mat or chop substrate using a machine-mounted "peeler," or electric planer. Then the hull is thoroughly dried and several layers of specially formulated epoxy are applied (although some tests show that vinylester works even better over bare fiberglass). In no event should a hull be sandblasted, since this will leave the bottom more pocked than ever — and more susceptible to blisters later on.

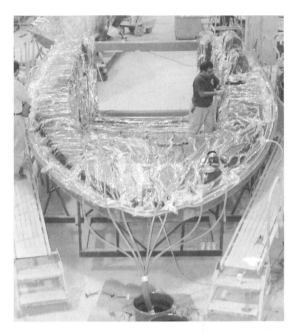

The True North 38 deck and superstructure being built using the SCRIMP resin infusion process. The reinforcements and sandwich core materials are stacked dry and covered with a plastic film bag. A vacuum is applied and catalyzed resin is drawn from the buckets in the foreground until the resin has completely saturated the fiberglass reinforcements. The bag is removed when the resin has cured, revealing the completed part.

ratio. It's an excellent way to build a boat, but it's expensive, licensed to users by patent-holder TPI, and limited to high-end builders, at least for now.

Here's how it works. The mold is prepared, coated with gelcoat, and a skin coat of mat or chop is applied and allowed to cure. Next, the dry reinforcements, core materials, stringers, and bulkhead landings are all carefully positioned in place. A plastic bag is placed over the whole affair, carefully sealed around the edges, and the stacked reinforcements can be leisurely checked for proper positioning before the resin starts to flow. Then, a vacuum is applied to the bag and a precisely measured amount of catalyzed resin is drawn by vacuum through the laminate until it's completely wet out.

The vacuum, which is significantly higher than that used for standard vacuum bagging, assures as-good-as-it-gets interlaminar bonds (between the layers of reinforcement) and skin-to-core bonds (between the fiberglass skins and the core material). The pressure also compacts the laminate, removing excess resin while achieving glass-to-resin ratios of 70:30 with woven roving and as high as 75:25 with unidirectional knitted reinforcements. Air is completely removed from the laminate, eliminating the tiny voids that otherwise reduce flexural strength by up to 10 percent. In a crucial step to ensure a thoroughly wet-out and air-free laminate, core materials are perforated to allow resin to flow to, and air to bleed off from, the outer skin.

The excellent interlaminar and skin-to-core bonds result in a stronger, lighter, and more durable laminate compared with conventional hand layup or even vacuum-bagged prepregs. A boat built using SCRIMP has twice the flexural (the ability to withstand flexing without structural failure), compressive, and tensile strength of hand-laid laminates. In addition the tensile strength and elongation properties of an epoxy-based laminate can be nearly doubled after the laminate has cured by heating in an oven at 140 to 250°F for three or more hours.

The J/125 high-performance sailboat built by TPI Composites, owner of the SCRIMP process, is an excellent example of a SCRIMP-built boat. Kevlar and fiberglass are used on the outer hull skin and two layers of carbon fiber are used on the inner skin; these materials provide lighter, thinner skins than would be possible using fiberglass alone. The hull is cored with thermoformed (heat shaped) Core-Cell, which is perforated to allow air pockets to bleed off from under the core and to provide a path for resin to flow from inner to outer skins. TPI turns out J/125 hulls that can vary less than 1 percent in weight, thanks to the control of resin use.

Another resin infusion process, now being used to build some of the larger composite sandwich vessels, is DRIP, or DIAB Resin Infusion Process. The foam core used in this process is scored only along the surface, and these grooves allow the resin to flow evenly through the entire part's inner and outer skins. DIAB offers this process free of charge to builders, making their money by selling the foam.

VIP

Another excellent resin-infusion process is VIP, for Vacuum Infusion Process, developed by Intermarine. This process was, quite generously, published by Intermarine, which means that it can't be patented and is therefore available to any builder to use without a license fee. The process involves scoring ⅛-by-⅛-inch grooves in both sides of the core material on 1-inch centers, and these grooves act as channels for the resin to flow through, completely wetting out the laminate. The core, then, acts as the resin transfer medium.

This process eliminates the need to perforate the core to wet out the inner skin, as is the case with SCRIMP. Vinylester is the resin of choice, since its chemistry can be adjusted to control the cure rate carefully, ensuring complete laminate wet-out. Intermarine has successfully resin-infused three 123-foot yachts with 2-inch coring using the VIP process, along with many smaller projects.

Intermarine's VIP (Vacuum Infusion Process) system sucks resin under high vacuum through a dry stack of fiberglass, using scored core material as the primary resin channel. The company generously "disclosed" the process so it couldn't be patented, making it available for all to use without a license fee.   INTERMARINE

Resin Transfer Molding

Some high-quality boatbuilders use a process called Resin Transfer Molding (RTM) to build small components like deck hatches and topside cabinet doors. The reinforcement and core are stacked dry inside a two-sided mold to which gelcoat may have been applied, which is closed and sealed tight with a pair of gaskets around the perimeter. A pump draws a carefully measured amount of resin (which may be tinted) into the closed mold, which completely

Glass-to-Resin Ratio

Glass-to-resin ratio, or *fiber-to-resin* if you prefer, refers to the ratio, by weight, of a cured fiberglass part's fiberglass reinforcement to its resin. The ratio common in conventional hand-layup construction is about 35 to 40 percent fiberglass to 65 to 60 percent resin—not very impressive when you see what's possible with SCRIMP and vacuum bagging. Measuring the same ratio of glass-to-resin by volume is a different kettle of fish—a 50:50 glass-to-resin ratio by weight amounts to a 34:66 ratio by volume.

By using knitted rather than woven reinforcements, and by vacuum bagging the laminate before it cures, this ratio can be improved markedly in favor of the glass. A greater glass-to-resin ratio makes for a more efficiently laid-up hull, less wasted resin, and a lighter boat for the same strength. With high-tech vacuum resin infusion methods like SCRIMP, the ratio can be reversed to as much as 80:20, but be careful! At extremely high ratios, there won't be enough resin to saturate the voids and bind the fibers together in the matrix. Since too little resin can be a bad thing, preventing the fiberglass from being completely wet out and adhering to the surrounding matrix, vacuum during construction has to be carefully controlled. Glass-to-resin ratio can be measured by a burn test, which involves taking a cured fiberglass sample, weighing it, burning away the flammable resin, and weighing the (inflammable) reinforcement that remains.

wets out the reinforcements and bonds them to the core. When the part has cured, the mold is opened, much like a waffle iron, the part removed, and the edges trimmed and polished smooth. The result is a high-quality, lightweight part that's tooled on both sides and around the edges, with the core completely sealed by the surrounding fiberglass.

VEC

Genmar Holdings, currently the world's largest boatbuilder, opened a new plant in 2000 that uses a patented closed molding process called VEC, which stands for Virtual Engineered Composites. VEC is an advance over the RTM process with a very high degree of automation. Dry fiberglass reinforcements

and core material are laid up in a two-piece mold that is closed and sealed before being placed in a vat of water. Both the pressure and temperature of the water can be controlled. Then resin is injected into the closed mold. Instead of a vacuum, water provides the pressure (some 50 psi) and the water temperature controls the rate of exotherm (resin curing). The process is managed by computers that monitor hundreds of variables such as resin temperature, viscosity, and flow rate. The molds themselves are fairly light; they get their structural rigidity from the surrounding water, much as an aluminum soda can is stiff while pressurized by carbonated water.

VEC produces high-quality components with excellent consistency and strength at less weight while using less labor. That's in part because, as with SCRIMP and RTM, the amount of resin is tightly controlled, resulting in a relatively low glass-to-resin ratio, and the interlaminar and skin-to-core bonds are tight and sound. VEC parts achieve 98 percent cure within 24 hours, much faster than with open-molded fiberglass components. The VEC plant runs around the clock to produce hulls four times faster than open molding could—it takes a little more than an hour to build a VEC hull. VEC also reduces volatile organic compounds (VOCs) by some 75 percent, and this figure may improve as the process is refined.

Genmar's up-front investment in the technology was considerable, but these may well prove to be the best-built boats (Glastrons and Larsons for starters) of their kind anywhere, since hulls and decks are molded in a single process, eliminating secondary bonds in a sealed hull-and-deck structure. All visible surfaces are tooled fiberglass thanks to the two-part molds, for a better looking, easily maintained boat.

Though not yet used in the pleasure boat industry, Picken's Plastics of Jefferson, Ohio, has developed a proprietary Closed Cavity Bag Molding (CCBM) process. A standard mold is used to lay up the fiberglass reinforcement, and a second, more flexible hard-body fiberglass mold, rather than a plastic film, is used to cover the reinforcement from

Volatile Organic Compounds

There is growing pressure to change dramatically the way boats are built. Wet layup in open molding, which presently accounts for the vast majority of boats built each year, is a simple and relatively cheap process, although it is labor-intensive. However, it also wreaks havoc on the environment in the form of volatile organic compounds (VOCs) that are released into the air by wet and curing resins. These fumes don't do the health of fiberglass workers any good, either. Styrene is the worst offender, and many countries are clamping down on VOC emissions in general.

There are solutions. One approach would be for chemical companies to invent new resins and gelcoats that don't produce VOCs. Another calls for a major tooling shift to closed molding, completely enclosing the part being fabricated and infusing resin within this contained system; SCRIMP, VEC, and RTM are examples of closed molding that can cut VOCs by 90 percent or more. Vacuum Infusion Process, or VIP, is another. Whichever solution boatbuilders choose in creating a VOC-less environment, it isn't going to be cheap, and some of them would likely go under as a result. One idea is to create a few super closed-molding centers that would mold hulls and major fiberglass components for smaller boatbuilders to finish off into completed boats. Or on a lesser scale, groups of boatbuilders could get together and invest in the closed-molding technology they need to stay in business. Subcontracting arrangements like this have been made to work in other industries, including automotive and electronics.

the inside. Resin is drawn through ports into the laminate and out through vents in the mold. This process results in a very smooth finish on both sides of the part, and it's probably the closest thing to the VEC process. Picken's has successfully laminated one-piece, 30-foot bus sides with this process. VEC and CCBM eliminate the need for bleeder materials and vacuum bags, which makes for less garbage to be disposed of after the lamination process is complete.

Thermoplastics

Small boats can be built of heat-formed plastics, or thermoplastics, most commonly polyethylene, nylon, and polypropylene. Very rugged and forgiving of impact, these boats have a definite place in the recreational marine marketplace. The molds are expensive to produce initially, but thermoplastic boats can be produced much more quickly and with less labor than those made of fiberglass.

ABS (acrylonitrile butadiene-styrene) plastic is a promising material for the small-boat industry. It can be thermoformed, shaped with a heat gun, glued, drilled, machined, welded, and bent. It's durable, impact resistant, abrasion resistant, light, and can be ordered with the color impregnated throughout the thickness of the material. Leisure Life Ltd., of Grand Rapids, Michigan, builds an electric-powered pontoon boat of Centrex/ABS plastic, for instance, while AB Inflatable builds a line of lightweight RIBs (rigid inflatable boats) using ABS plastic.

Genmar's Triumph boat line builds polyethylene plastic boats using a proprietary closed rotational-mold technology called Roplene. Triumph boats are durable and seamless, built much like a plastic gas tank and with the same compelling advantages of structural integrity, toughness, simplicity, and indefinite life. A polyethylene powder is poured into a high-temperature mold, which is rotated on two axes, horizontally and vertically, in a computer-controlled process. The powder melts, evenly covering the inner mold surfaces, and is soon

A MasterCraft wakeboard boat with a one-piece support grid installed and bonded to the hull, and white polyethylene ballast tanks placed within the grid. The result is a one-piece, rot-proof hull structure of great strength and stiffness.

transformed into a one-piece boat—with the release of little or no VOCs. The hull color is molded into the plastic, so there's no gelcoat to crack or chip, and the material is impervious to osmosis.

Triumph claims that their boats have five times the impact resistance of fiberglass (although that statement would have to define both materials to be very meaningful). In any event, the company says you can hit one of their boats with a sledgehammer and use a propane torch or other heat source to remove the dent. Triumph sounds like the perfect boat for the lousy boat handler. The company points out that although their boats aren't the only ones that can be sawn into parts and still float, they're the only ones that can be readily welded back together again. Triumph puts its money where its mouth is, too, backing their boats up with a structural hull and stringer warranty that's good for as long as the original purchaser owns the boat. We'd like to see other boatbuilders go as far out on the same limb.

Hull and Deck Support: Bulkheads, Frames, and Stringers

Even with core materials, every fiberglass hull still needs additional support, usually in the form of an interlocking network of bulkheads, frames, and stringers. Bulkheads are essentially solid walls that run transversely (from side to side) in a hull. They are usually made of plywood, which is tabbed to the hull on both sides and the bottom (see below). Bulkheads can also be made of cored fiberglass. Bulkheads are designated as watertight if they are solid and prevent water from flowing from one section of the hull to the next. "Intermediate" bulkheads give structural support to the hull but are not watertight, as they are not as high as the deck above. (Viking Yachts, for instance, uses intermediate bulkheads to support its engine beds.) Nonstructural bulkheads, which are not fiberglassed to the hull and therefore contribute little if any strength to it, are used to support furniture and other subassemblies.

Stringers are support members running fore and aft in the bottom of the hull. They can be made up of foam, wood, or plywood beams encapsulated in fiberglass, or they may be molded as a single grid work, or *grillage*, which includes landing spots for bulkhead and transverse frames, and then lowered into the hull and fiberglassed or bonded in place while the hull is still in the mold.

Transverse frames would be called *ribs* in a wooden boat. They stiffen the hull skin and, with the stringers, define the size of the bottom panels. While the bottom is essentially a continuous layer of fiberglass, in an engineer's mind it is also divided into panels defined by the spans between the interlocking network of bulkheads, frames, and stringers. The thickness of the bottom laminate and the sizes of these panels are engineered according to the anticipated weight and speed of the boat. For a given laminate thickness, a faster, heavier boat requires smaller panels (i.e., more support). On the other hand, the use of a core material permits larger panels to be used. The strength of the individual support members must also be carefully calculated to match the anticipated loads on the hull. And the support members must be securely and permanently bonded to the hull skin.

Bulkheads and stringers should be fiberglassed in place while the hull is still in the mold. Otherwise, the hull may deform and lose its shape before its structural supports are installed. The secondary bond between stringers and bulkheads and the hull skin is a weak link in the hull structure, and it's important that these members be ruggedly attached and that the inside corners where they meet are radiused to reduce high stress concentrations.

Engine beds are usually integral to the stringers. Twin-engine boats, for example, usually have four stringers that also serve as engine beds. Stringers should have either a wood or a dense foam as a core. A denser wood or foam core helps to absorb and dissipate engine vibrations and resists the compression loads of engine mounting bolts better than a less-dense foam core. If the engine beds are tall, they should be supported by gussets or knees to prevent racking.

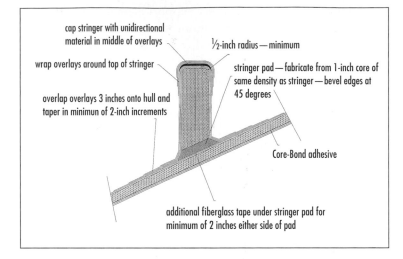

The engine beds must be strong enough to support the engines' weight and thrust and also rigid enough to prevent shaft movement, which could damage the drivetrain.

Bottom structural members, such as stringers, should be continuous in order to take advantage of their beam effect. If short stringer sections are butted against bulkheads rather than running continuously from bow to stern, the hull skin could be subject to greater flexing at the bulkheads, eventually leading to skin failure due to fatigue. Failing continuous runs, effective connections at the ends of short stringer sections and additional transverse frames can mitigate the hull-skin flexing problem. The worst case is an egg-crate plywood network of fiberglass-encapsulated stringers and frames without continuity in either direction.

A typical stringer done well, with mitered inside corners that distribute the stresses over a greater area. The unidirectional fiberglass used on top of the stringer runs in the direction of the stringer, and efficiently absorbs tension and compression loads caused by the hull hogging and sagging or just resisting local loading from wave impact in a seaway. This foam-cored stringer is strong, stiff, lightweight, and rot resistant. The foam pad between it and the hull skin (essential with a wood-cored stringer) spreads out wave impact loads.

ATC CHEMICAL

Securing Bulkheads and Stringers

Since a hull skin is relatively thin and subject to severe wave impact loads at high speed, it's important to avoid hard spots where bulkheads and stringers support the hull bottom. Plywood bulkheads should never actually come into contact with the skin; rather, the bulkhead is held a small standoff distance away from the hull skin and tabbed in place with fiberglass. Many good builders install a "landing strip" of foam or end-grain balsa along the hull around the bulkhead's perimeter, and radius all inside corners. The bulkhead tabbing (see below) then covers the

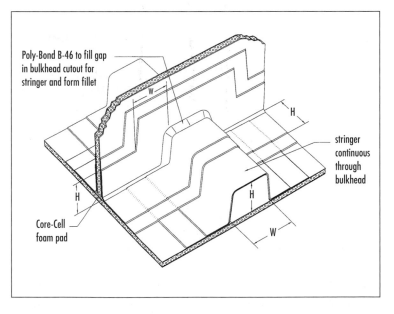

The way a hull should look with the continuous stringer passing through a slotted bulkhead. Note the foam pad landing between the bulkhead and the hull skin, the overlapping tabbing securing the bulkhead, and the radiused inside and outside corners.

ATC CHEMICAL

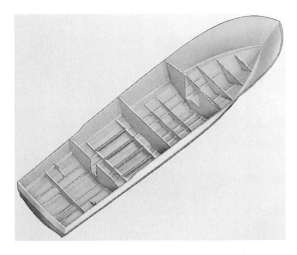

A typical bulkhead and stringer arrangement on a 74-foot Viking convertible. The steel engine beds are supported by low, intermediate bulkheads inside the engine room's main structural bulkheads. VIKING YACHTS

landing strip where it makes the turn from bulkhead to hull skin. This distributes the bulkhead-induced stresses much more evenly along the hull skin.

Wherever a bulkhead meets the fiberglass hull, a sharp corner is created. To secure the bulkhead, multiple layers of fiberglass reinforcement called *tabbing* are wet out and bonded both to the bulkhead and to the hull surface, over the seam. (The same technique can be used for stringers or anywhere else members need to be securely bonded at similar angles.) The corners should be radiused to spread out loads and to ensure that the fiberglass reinforcement can lay down without voids. Some builders use angled cant strips of wood ripped at a 45-degree angle, sandwiched in fiberglass and pushed into the inside corners, ensuring a more gradual transition from the bulkhead to the hull. Others use a putty to create a radius (called a *fillet*) at inside corners. When applied at the right radius, tests show that this results in a stronger joint than the cant strips. A foam or balsa landing strip accomplishes the same end while relieving the hard spot under the bulkhead edge.

Tabbing is typically cut from a roll of biaxial fiberglass in strips 4 to 8 inches wide. Opinions differ as to which orientation is best in the fiberglass. Although

A Century with its hull grid installed and the aluminum fuel tank held in position with a jig while it's fastened in place. The high stringers add strength and rigidity to the hull structure.

A large Boston Whaler getting fitted with its systems, including the fuel tank, plumbing, and cabinet modules forward in the cabin.

This upside-down Larson cruiser deck-superstructure includes pressure-treated wood strips in the cabin top — these provide a fair surface for attaching the cabin ceiling liner. The raised part aft is the bridge deck area at the helm.

some prefer 0/90, 45/45 knits will more easily conform to small radii, and both plies contribute strength to the tabbing. In any event, either reinforcement orientation works well enough if secondary bonding preparations to the cured fiberglass surfaces are done properly so good adhesion is assured.

Construction with Fiberglass and Cold-Molded Wood 107

Edgewater Powerboats' high-strength hull grid system includes a one-piece Permagrid part bonded to the hull and deck liner. It is bonded to the hull while it is still in the mold. In the bottom photo, the Permagrid has been bonded to the hull and is having foam injected in any remaining voids. The deck liner will then be bonded directly to the top of the Permagrid without relying on the low-density foam structurally, a good policy.   EDGEWATER

If a plywood bulkhead is to be tabbed to a fiberglass hull, the plywood should be coated with resin, which is then allowed to cure, at least partially, before the tabbing is applied. This ensures that the plywood doesn't wick the resin out of the tabbing as it cures. It is also important that the edges of the successive layers of tabbing don't terminate along the same edge, or a hard spot susceptible to delamination will result. The edges of the successive layers of tabbing should be staggered by one of a variety of methods to produce a tapered edge. In fact, *peel* is the most ready failure mode in a fiberglass laminate, and it's best prevented by eliminating reinforcement-edge hard spots, using higher-elongation resins (like vinylester), and by proper surface preparation, including liberal grinding of the surface to be bonded to.

Taking the time to do it right prevents the hull skin from being fatigued over millions of impact cycles by spreading impact loads more evenly and gradually over a wider area. This can be easily checked during a boat inspection with a little time crawling around in the bilges. Most importantly, if you find tabbing that, due to the absence of cant strips or fillets, actually buckles, or tucks, under the gap between the bulkhead and the hull, expect it to fail sooner rather than later. Find another boat.

Molded Bottom Grids

Some builders mold one-piece, bow-to-stern bottom-support grids that include the stringers, transverse frames, and bulkhead landings. The grid is then placed into the hull and bonded in place with adhesive or fiberglass tabbing. A bottom grid, or grillage, is usually the most complex and difficult-to-build part found in a boat, so it's expensive to produce. You don't necessarily save weight, and the builder probably doesn't save money, but what you gain, besides a very strong bottom, is a uniform and consistent foundation on which to support the engines and accommodations. And builders love consistency, since it speeds up production.

These grids are usually bonded by applying an adhesive to the bottom flanges of the structure

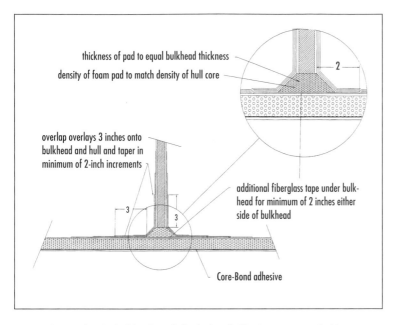

thickness of pad to equal bulkhead thickness

density of foam pad to match density of hull core

2

overlap overlays 3 inches onto bulkhead and hull and taper in minimum of 2-inch increments

3

3

additional fiberglass tape under bulkhead for minimum of 2 inches either side of bulkhead

Core-Bond adhesive

One good way to bond a bulkhead to a hull. The beveled landing strip or pad of foam serves as a hull-skin cushion. Note how the fiberglass tabbing edges are staggered to prevent stress concentration and weak spots. ATC CHEMICAL

and then pressing the whole assembly against the hull interior. Weight, or pressure, is applied until the adhesive cures. The potential downside is that, with some grids, the interior flanges can't be seen, so the builder is relying on a consistent fit between grid and hull to ensure a solid bond. Depending on their design, other grids are suspended an inch or so above the hull in a jig and tabbed in place with fiberglass rather than relying on an adhesive.

A preformed structural shape called Prisma is produced by Compsys, Inc., to be used as stock for prefabricated stringer and bulkhead landing systems of various shapes and sizes. They come ready to install with dry reinforcement material attached to the urethane foam-cored stringer. There's enough reinforcement extending beyond the stringer for tabbing them to the hull. The manufacturer claims time is saved in installation and that parts are more consistent and stronger, which is certainly plausible. Some boatbuilders using SCRIMP use these stringers and bulkhead landings,

eliminating secondary bonds in these crucial structural components. With their foam cores, these stringer and bulkhead landing systems are efficient from an engineering perspective, unlike a lot of plywood-cored structures, since the foam serves mostly as a form and a sandwich core, and the fiberglass is allowed to do the structural work.

Stick-Built Supports

Another way to support a fiberglass boat's bottom is by "stick building" foam or wood stringer and transverse frame cores, bonding them in position, and then encapsulating them in fiberglass. Foam-cored stringers and other support members are lighter than wood, and it's mostly the fiberglass that does the structural work anyway, so this makes good engineering sense for many applications.

A foam-cored, high-hat stringer (a tall stringer with a trapezoidal cross section) might have a thick

A small Sea Ray cruiser after the assembly of its engine, fuel tank, cabin furniture, and other systems. Here its one-piece deck-superstructure is lowered into place and bonded at the hull-to-deck joint.

layer of unidirectional fiberglass along the top to absorb tension and compression loads. This box-beam structure works like an I-beam, with the top of the high-hat and the bottom of the boat serving as the I-beam's flanges and doing the brunt of the structural work. Since the foam core is essentially a male mold on which to lay up the load-bearing fiberglass, eliminating wood is a great way to gain strength and stiffness at moderate weight.

Even though foam-cored stringers save weight, using a wood core where the stringers do double duty as engine beds is often a good idea and a common practice among boatbuilders. The added mass of the wood absorbs and attenuates engine vibrations before they reach the rest of the boat. Wood also resists the compression loads of engine mounting bolts better than medium-density foam could, though high-density foam could also be used here.

As mentioned, stringers (most boats have four) should be continuous from bow to stern, with slots cut out of the bulkheads to receive them. This continuous-stringer method provides maximum load distribution and helps prevent hull skin flexure where stringers meet bulkheads. Noncontinuous stringers are much weaker in way of their bulkhead joints than continuous stringers, and the bottom skin is consequently subject to greater stress and fatigue.

Limber Holes

Limber holes in stringers allow water to drain to the lowest part of the bilge where it's pumped overboard. How the limber holes are installed is important not only to ensure complete drainage but to ensure that water is unable to penetrate into the stringer core, whether it's wood or structural foam. In fact, the special bugaboo of wood-cored stringers, bulkheads, and transoms is the ingress of water and consequent rot.

If the tabbing joining the wood to the hull skin is continuous, and limber holes are thoroughly sealed against moisture penetration, then properly installed wood cores will last indefinitely. But that's a big "if," since water is tenacious when it comes to finding a way through cracks, screw and bolt holes, and other unnoticed openings. Pressure-treated plywood is becoming more widely used for this reason, as the wood itself is rot resistant. Even if the wood doesn't rot, though, water migrating into the fiberglass-wood interface can eventually delaminate the bond between the two.

Completely encapsulated foam-cored stringers, bulkheads, and high-density-foam-cored transoms are catching on for marketing as well as engineering reasons. But foam cores also have to be waterproofed, since water can soak into exposed, lower-density closed-cell foam given enough time.

Wood's bad rap is almost wholly due to shoddy quality control during construction or to inept attempts to seal water out. Some builders will drill a hole through a stringer and just paint the raw exposed wood with gelcoat or resin. This is a completely ineffective way to get the job done, since wood contracts and expands depending on ambient moisture content, even if it's completely encapsulated in fiberglass. Remember that fiberglass is porous at the molecular level. Once the wood changes dimension, even slightly, the less flexible gelcoat or resin cracks and allows water to enter. PVC pipes or half-rounds can be used to line limber holes. Polyurethane adhesives like 3M's 5200 adhere very well to PVC, but fiberglass doesn't, so glassing them in isn't the best solution.

A *good* way to get the job done is by cutting out the limber holes before the wood or foam part is installed in the boat, replacing the excised material with fiberglass, then fiberglass tabbing the stringer into position in the hull. This way, when the limber holes are cut, they're cut through solid fiberglass. Fiberglass tubes can also be used to line limber holes and then be sealed with the fiberglass tabbing.

Plywood

Plywood has been used as structural material in fiberglass boats for a long time. To form the core of stringers and egg-crate bottom support networks, plywood can be assembled and suspended from a jig while it is tabbed in place. The jig is removed after the tabbing cures, and the plywood is then completely encapsulated in fiberglass. In this case, the plywood is the primary structural material, with the fiberglass reinforcement serving primarily to bond the plywood to the hull and to seal the wood against moisture and rot. The inside corners where the plywood meets the hull, and outside corners along the tops of the stringers, must be radiused so the reinforcements can drape tight against the wood without air voids forming during the curing process.

Some boatbuilders use foam to core hull stringers except around the engines, where the added mass of plywood (or high-density foam) does a better job of absorbing engine vibrations and engine mounting bolt compression and shear loads. Even when fully encapsulated in fiberglass, the moisture content of the wood will change depending on the boat's environment, whether it's in the water or in dry storage on land. Though dimensionally stable, especially when compared with conventional timber, plywood will change thickness as its moisture content varies, making the fiberglass susceptible to cracking and moisture penetration. And plywood isn't the easiest surface to get polyester resin to stick to in the first place.

Plywood-cored transoms have been known to last decades when properly installed. They're probably better known for failing, though, sooner rather than later, due to water getting in through stern-drive and bolt openings. A cottage industry has grown around the need for new transoms in otherwise sound boats. This helps explain the increasing dominance of high-density foam core and other synthetic transoms.

Plywood is also commonly used to replace foam and end-grain balsa cores in way of bolt penetrations in decks, since the plywood is much more dense and therefore resistant to bolt compression loads. As discussed, since marine plywood will rot when exposed to moisture, penetrations must be completely sealed against leaking.

Component Installation

Once a hull structure is complete, the builder installs the propulsion and steering systems, generators, mechanical systems, fuel tanks, rough wiring and plumbing, cabin and furniture subassemblies, appliances and other large components, and the deck over the engine room. Better builders tab the subassemblies—such as enclosed heads, dinettes, and staterooms—to the hull and cabin sole; this fixes these large components securely, and can even add a bit of strength to the hull. Next comes the deck and superstructure, usually in one piece, molded just in time for installation as soon as the hull is ready.

Hull-to-Deck Joint

One critical area to ask about when shopping for a boat is how the hull-to-deck joint is fastened together. When a boat runs through a rough sea, the hull and deck are constantly doing their best to part company. They work hard at it. Viewed from a macro level, the boat's uppermost deck and hull bottom act as flanges of an I-beam, and the hull-to-deck joint has to be able to absorb significant shear stresses in a seaway as a result. So it's important that the hull and deck are firmly held together, and that the joint doesn't ever develop leaks.

The most common hull-to-deck joint is the shoebox type, which, you guessed it, looks like a lid covering a shoebox. Builders typically use a bonding putty or run a thick bead of death-grip adhesive—such as 3M's polyurethane 5200, methacrylate (Plexus), or epoxy—along the top edge of the hull (the gunwale) and also along the inside of the deck lip. It's important that the adhesive be applied liberally, since the mating surfaces might well have irregularities, so that the flanges actually make continuous contact evenly. The adhesive also acts as a sealant to keep the inside of the boat dry. A flanged joint, consisting of two flat surfaces, improves the chances of the adhesives making complete contact through the length of the joint.

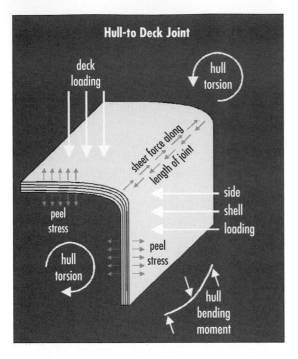

Hull-to Deck Joint

deck loading

hull torsion

sheer force along length of joint

side shell loading

peel stress

peel stress

hull torsion

hull bending moment

The significant stresses to which a hull-to-deck joint are subject.
ERIC GREENE

Once the adhesive is applied, the deck is lowered to mate with the hull. The next step, commonly, is to fasten self-tapping screws every 6 to 8 inches all around the boat. At this point the screws are clamping the adhesive between the two fiberglass parts to ensure it sets up with a good bond. Once the adhesive sets up, the screws become largely superfluous. That's because the structural adhesives should adhere so well that the fiberglass itself may well shred into little pieces before the adhesive lets go. In the absence of a significant backing pad for the screws to tap into, self-tapping screws in fiberglass can't be counted on to hold their grip for very long, so using such tenacious adhesives is a good thing.

For long-term security, many good builders also fiberglass the hull-to-deck joint from the inside, which further strengthens this critical area. Some builders add a row of closely spaced bolts, which, unlike self-tapping screws, should stay locked in position for the life of the boat. The next step is to fasten the rubrail in place, and this involves yet

another row of screws, or better yet, through-bolts. With the rubrail sealed with a silicone or similar sealant, the job is done. Perhaps the most practical rubrails are made of heavy PVC, which is strong and resilient and doesn't require maintenance. Stainless rounded stock, often used over wood rubrails, looks great, but it's hard to straighten out after an impact. Figure that a ding means replacement may be called for.

Flotation Foam

Urethane and polyurethane foams are commonly used in nonstructural small craft applications for positive flotation, either poured or blown in place or as blocks. Boats under 20 feet long are required by the coast guard to float level when swamped, although there is no analogous criterion for remaining afloat after a hull rupture. These foams have low strength and are not generally considered structural materials, although Boston Whaler, for one, relies on relatively low-density urethane foam to bond its hulls and deck liners together. Whaler also adds solid fiberglass shear-stress-absorbing supports between hull and liner to back up the foam. Whether a hull will stay afloat when ruptured depends on the weight of the boat and the buoyancy provided by the foam and any intact compartments.

Besides contributing positive flotation to a hull and a sense of security to its owner, poured or blown-in foam greatly reduces wave-slapping noises

Here's one of those great Boston Whaler marketing shots — a boat that's cut in two but keeps on truckin'. The two skins (hull and deck liner) are laid up in steel molds, clamped together, and foam is injected under pressure. What you give up in storage space you gain in peace of mind in your unsinkable Whaler. BOSTON WHALER

against the hull and adds weight, which tends to improve ride quality in a chop. When foam expands inside closed cavities, like those created by the hull and deck of a boat, significant pressure is applied as the foam begins to cure. This pressure also makes the deck feel stiffer underfoot and adds to the hull's impact resistance. In general, a boat should be designed without the stiffening effect of foam calculated in. Panels should be stiff and strong enough without the foam. (One exception is Boston Whaler, which has been using low-density foam for structural purposes for decades.)

If urethane foam is used, it must be kept dry. Urethane foam is referred to as *closed-cell*, but that doesn't mean that the foam won't absorb water. If foam is exposed to water for an extended period, it will become waterlogged—water will permeate right through all those little closed cells. The results of waterlogged foam can range from lost buoyancy and a gain of thousands of pounds in water weight, to a loss of structural integrity. Water-soaked foam can also cause osmotic blistering in the hull and the liner, from the inside, and well above the waterline. Leaking fuel tanks bedded in foam can also saturate the surrounding foam with gasoline, turning it into a thick, sticky paste that's a huge production to remove (see below). Unfortunately, the only fully effective cure for waterlogged foam is to remove it, reapply fresh foam, and seal up the original leaks.

As with soaked end-grain balsa core, the cause of waterlogged foam is usually holes drilled in the boat after delivery to its owner. In my experience, for instance, Boston Whaler dealers screw down a battery tray to the cockpit deck aft on their smaller, open-deck models, and if the screws aren't well bedded, the foam core in this area can gradually get soaked with water. Improperly bedded holes drilled in the decks and coamings for canvas side curtain snaps are a common water source affecting even the best boats. In addition to sealing off water entry points above, the builder should provide plenty of drainage below. Remember that limber holes used to drain foam-filled compartments can work both

ways, and a high bilge water level backflooding through limber holes into a foam-filled compartment over a period of time can cause saturation. If the edge of the poured foam is trimmed before the compartment is sealed, a face of open cells results, making the foam act like a sponge. Sealing the foam edges with thickened epoxy (polyester and vinylester resins will eat the foam) is one method of reducing water penetration. Some builders have tried coating exposed foam with latex house paint that serves to seal the foam surface while adding a measure of fire resistance (urethane foam is highly flammable and releases toxic gases when burning). C-Hawk, a North Carolina builder of rugged little fishing boats, has a novel solution: using planks of foam that, if water is poured on them, shed it readily into the bilge.

Fuel Tanks

Most tanks are made of aluminum, fiberglass, or plastic, with aluminum most prevalent. For reasons that will become clear, my preference is for plastic fuel tanks when the desired capacity is under about 100 gallons per tank. Water and holding tank materials and installation are less critical from a safety perspective. (Clean-tasting water is obviously important to the boatowner, as is keeping sewage contained in its proper place until discharge. Fiberglass and plastic tanks are well suited to these purposes.)

Aluminum fuel tanks dominate in the boatbuilding industry because they're relatively inexpensive, boatbuilders are familiar with them, and they're easy to buy in a wide range of shapes and sizes. But aluminum tanks are also susceptible to corrosion resulting from improper installation, with moisture getting trapped inside or especially outside the walls of the tank.

Aluminum tanks are better off left unpainted, since the metal naturally forms a protective oxide coating when it's left exposed to the air. This coating is not allowed to form when the tank is painted. Aluminum fuel tanks are usually built of 5052-grade plate in either 0.09- or 0.125-inch thickness; the coast guard holds that tanks made from material

Fire Resistance

We considered the relative fire resistances of steel, aluminum, and fiberglass in chapter 2, but let's take a look at what happens when fiberglass boats, with their varying construction methods and materials, burn.

Yachts over 500 net tons or 50 meters that carry more than twelve passengers and are built to the standards of the American Bureau of Shipping (ABS), the Maritime and Coast Guard Agency of Great Britain (MCA), and comparable regulatory bodies are required to meet *structural* fire protection standards. Structural standards ensure that the choice of building materials and the vessel's design are taken into consideration when deciding how resistant to fire a vessel must be for its intended service. A cruise ship that accommodates five hundred overnight passengers on offshore passages logically warrants a higher standard than an inshore, unoccupied barge, for instance. While yachts carrying fewer than twelve passengers, for instance, don't have to meet these regulations, those that do may be able to command a higher resale value, depending on the market. And the owner has the added peace of mind.

An MCA-classified yacht under 164 feet (50 m) would have gas-tight engine rooms designed to contain fire and smoke during a 60-minute burn test. (To pass a burn test, the structure must remain intact after being subject to high temperature for an hour.) Engine room ventilation and fuel supply lines must have remote shutdown capability. Accommodations spaces must have two means of escape. Fire detection and alarm systems are required in the machinery and galley spaces. U.S. Coast Guard Subchapter T regulations require the use of fire-retardant resins in certain passenger-carrying vessels.

The vast majority of recreational craft are not subject to any of these regulations, however; they only have to meet minimal coast guard standards and American Boat and Yacht Council (ABYC) recommendations regarding fire extinguishers, flammable gas tank shutoff valves, cooking stove design, smoke stacks, and so on. That's apparently because most unregulated pleasure boats are small, so fires are easier to detect and escape. Meeting the higher standards of rules-built vessels would also add to the builders' cost to manufacture boats. Few builders of fiberglass pleasure boats choose construction materials with fire resistance in mind. Unlike commercial vessels with their trained crews, most recreational craft are operated by people who have no knowledge or experience of firefighting. This fact should argue for a higher structural fire-resistant standard, and for better firefighting equipment standards, than are currently applied. This is especially true on fiberglass boats powered by gasoline. (Diesel fuel, of course, is inherently safer than gasoline, which gives off highly explosive vapors.)

The most fire-prone areas on a vessel are the machinery compartment (engine room) and galley area. The key points are: to have automatic fire suppression systems that work as intended; and to keep the fire contained. Even if a fire is contained, if it is not put out in short order, temperatures can quickly reach the point at which surrounding decks and bulkheads will collapse.

Since it's the resin that burns in a fiberglass composite, not the fiberglass reinforcement itself, the choice of laminating resin has more bearing on a fiberglass structure's ability to withstand the intense heat of a fire. The fiberglass reinforcement actually

of these thicknesses will last an average of 6.5 and 17.4 years, respectively, but these numbers vary widely in the real world. To put the issue into perspective, the coast guard requires inspected passenger-carrying vessels built under Subchapter T regulations to have their tanks built of at least 0.25-inch aluminum, which is twice the thickness used in most pleasure boats today.

Whatever the actual figure for a given boat, the point to keep in mind is that few aluminum tanks can be expected to last the life of the boat. A means for their removal must be provided, or the owner will be in for a costly fuel tank replacement process. Better builders of small craft provide a removal hatch directly above the fuel tank, and they don't foam the tanks in place. These hatches are bolted around their perimeter and caulked with a nonadhesive sealant. A less expensive approach is to mark a cutout perimeter with a nonskid-free 2-inch-wide swath around the tank. This makes it easier to cut out the right section of deck, replace the tank, and glass the deck back in place with a neat cosmetic finish.

Aluminum tanks weigh about a third as much as those of steel, are 20 to 30 percent lighter than

acts as a thermal insulator during a fire, unless we're dealing with thermoplastics, which can actually accelerate a fire's spread. Polyester resin is more flammable than vinylester or epoxy, but in the presence of an external fuel source such as gasoline or even diesel fuel in the bilge, the difference becomes academic. Very few builders use flame-retardant additives in their resins. Such additives add cost and can also degrade the strength and bonding properties of the resin, and can actually increase smoke production during a blaze. Core materials will generally impede the spread of fire, if only because they act as insulation to delay the time at which the far-side sandwich skin also heats up, softens, and fails structurally. Foam softens before balsa burns, but neither will burn until the fiberglass skin is burned through.

The best thermal protection comes in the form of insulation batts, including mineral wool and refractory materials, which are mechanically fastened to surrounding bulkheads and decks. These, in conjunction with special thermal-insulating treatments, can be designed to achieve a 60-minute fire rating in a fiberglass vessel. Other precautions against fire that will make any pleasure boat safer include: carrying plenty of working fire extinguishers; installing a fixed fire suppression system that shuts off ventilation and shuts down machinery before discharging; using high-pressure fuel lines instead of rubber hoses with hose clamps; holding regular fire drills; making sure engine room bulkheads are watertight so that smoke cannot spread and fire will spread to adjacent compartments less readily; and using the bilge blower every time before starting a gasoline engine.

fiberglass, and are reasonably priced. When properly installed, they will last many years. However, many aluminum tanks are installed in a way that guarantees they'll corrode through in just a few years. When water is allowed to stand against the aluminum, it deoxygenates and corrosion inexorably sets in. The tank must be able to breathe, with ample air circulation provided, and dry off if wetted. Tanks usually corrode from the outside, although it is possible for a tank to corrode from within (see below).

According to the coast guard and the ABYC, any material that comes into contact with an aluminum

tank must be nonabsorbing. Neoprene strips, which won't collect moisture and which also provide chafing resistance, are commonly used in lieu of carpet or wood strips under aluminum tanks both to cushion them and to admit air between the tank and the underlying structure. Tanks should be mounted so they don't flex as a boat moves through rough water. Mounting tabs or brackets can be welded to the tank, preventing water from collecting along the tank bottom and preventing chafing.

The life of an aluminum tank is often directly proportional to its thickness, so the thicker the better. High-quality aluminum fuel tanks start at 0.125-inch thickness, but many used in small boats are only 0.09 inch thick, since the thinner plate is cheaper for the builder. One high-quality aluminum boatbuilder, which builds aluminum components, including fuel tanks, as a sideline, is Winninghoff Boats of Rowley, Massachusetts. This company starts with 0.125-inch-thick stock on smaller tanks of up to 50 gallons, and increases to 0.16-inch plate for tanks in the 75- to 125-gallon range and 0.19 inch for larger tanks. (As mentioned, passenger-carrying vessels built to the USCG's Subchapter T regulations have tanks that are at least 0.25 inch thick.) Tanks should also be baffled at least every 30 inches.

When a new tank is installed in an older boat, and the capacity is changed, make sure you know what the effect on LCG and the static trim angle will be before proceeding. It could be that the tank will have to be relocated to avoid interfering with proper static and dynamic trim angles. On the other hand, if the original tank was improperly located, you may have a chance to fix the problem.

Aluminum tanks that are foamed in place have a couple of strikes against them from the outset. The coast guard requires that the bond between the foam and the tank be stronger than the foam itself. This is difficult to achieve in practice, and the result is that moisture can easily get trapped between the foam and the tank. The water is unable to drain off when the foam completely fills the fuel tank space, preventing the tank from drying. That's when corrosion starts, from the outside, and it's only a matter of time before the tank corrodes through and starts to leak.

Fuel tanks that are supported, as well as surrounded, by foam are especially vulnerable. The foam used to bed tanks can also compress and wear away over time, exposing the bare tank bottom to a hard fiberglass foundation that will probably eventually rub a hole in the tank. Foamed-in fuel tanks are also impossible to inspect, so you don't know what shape the tank is in short of removing it—and removing a foamed-in tank is a bear. If tanks are foamed in, the top of the tank should be higher than the surrounding foam so water is able to drain off the tank and, hopefully, into the bilge. Although welds are an aluminum fuel tanks' weak spots structurally, they rarely fail and cause leaks.

Some manufacturers mount the fuel tank on a flat shelf or platform, and water collects on the platform. Without proper drainage, the water stands against the bottom of the tank and you can bet corrosion will kick in.

Although corrosion from the outside is more common, if gasoline is allowed to stand for a long time while the boat is in storage, and water in the fuel settles to the bottom of the tank, then the tank can corrode from the inside, a problem that alcohol additives in the fuel can make worse. The newer reformulated oxygenated gasolines, especially those modified with ethanol, also increase the rate of corrosion in aluminum fuel tanks, because water precipitates out and settles to the bottom more readily.

Plastic fuel tanks, on the other hand, will never corrode, and if properly installed will last the life of the boat. Most plastic tanks are made of polyurethane or polyethylene in a seamless rotary molding process. The plastic actually absorbs minute amounts of the fuel, and the coast guard requires that the tank space be ventilated if the permeation rate is above a certain level. Plastic fuel tanks expand slightly when they are first filled with fuel, so the tank's installation must allow for this.

A vacuum-infused fiberglass fuel tank being installed in a Viking convertible. The rot- and rustproof tank, which conforms to the hull's shape, is bedded in bonding putty in the bilge and fiberglassed directly to the hull stringers. It's no lightweight, but it will last forever.

These tanks must also be protected from chafing, but this is easily accomplished with a little forethought.

All fuel tanks have to pass the same 2½-minute fire test for permanently installed tanks without leaking, and plastic tanks do just as well as aluminum tanks. Plastic tanks in the 25- to 55-gallon range weigh about the same as their aluminum counterparts, and many shapes and sizes are available up to about 100 gallons. Larger plastic tanks can be ordered on a custom basis from companies like Kracor, Inc., of Milwaukee, Wisconsin.

Fiberglass tanks are often used in high-end yachts, and they have the advantages of being corrosion proof and, if properly built, very rugged. A fiberglass fuel tank, then, should never need to be replaced. Well-built fiberglass tanks are usually fiberglassed to the hull stringers and may sit in a bed of fiberglass putty, adding impact resistance locally to the hull bottom. Chances are that a fiberglass tank will be heavier than one made of aluminum, so the boat's speed may be slightly reduced, but the trade-off is a worthwhile one.

Wrapping Things Up

Once the hull and superstructure are permanently mated together, the rest of the components,

An increasing number of builders are using frameless windows, and that's good for several reasons. Window frames are typically made of aluminum, which is a perennial source of corrosion, so eliminating them will save you a lot of aggravation. Window frames also tend to leak, so leaks become a thing of the past. Frameless windows are installed in rabbeted window openings after a strong adhesive has been applied (the rabbet is a groove cut along the window frame opening that allows the glass to sit flush with the outer fiberglass surface). Pressure is applied until the adhesive has cured. This is all very well, of course, until it comes time to replace a broken frameless window, which takes a lot of patience and time to remove. But with chemically strengthened laminated glass, a frameless window will probably never break, nor will it leak or corrode.

systems, and finishing touches are completed, including cabin liners, electrical fixtures, joinery, carpeting and exterior railings, hatches, windows, steering and engine controls, and davits. The bottom is painted, the name is painted on the transom, and the completed boat is rolled out of the final assembly building ready for its first dip into the water.

Once all the systems are checked out, the boat is launched, sea trials are conducted, and a detailed "punch" list of deficiencies needing correction before delivery is written up. The more trouble-free a boat is upon delivery, the lower the builder's warranty claims, the less the dealer has to do to fix the builder's oversights, and the happier the customer. When the process works, another boat is ready to provide many hours of enjoyment to a proud new owner.

By now you should be well on your way to being able to ask all the right questions and look in the right places to evaluate the quality of a fiberglass boat's construction. As we've seen, the methods, materials, and the level of quality control used to build your boat make all the difference in the world.

One-Off Custom Boats

Custom fiberglass boats, called *one-off* because they're one-of-a-kind, can be built by a variety of methods. Most of these involve building a temporary, upside-down male framework that defines the shape of the hull, fastening planks made of fiberglass or core materials to the frames, and laminating layers of reinforcement over the structure. The hull is then removed from the framework, turned right side up, and fiberglassed on the inside. Support structure is added to the hull, the interior finished, and machinery and other components installed. The downside of these one-off methods is the extra work that goes into building a boat from scratch. The hull has to be faired and painted, which takes many hours of painstaking and unpleasant labor. The decks, superstructure, and furniture all take longer to build and install since they are either stick-built on the spot, or molds have to be custom made for one-time use. The upside is that owners can have the exact boat they've always wanted, the boat of their dreams.

Seemann Fiberglass makes a fiberglass plank called C-Flex, consisting of fiberglass rods and fiberglass reinforcement. The rods allow the planks to assume a fair curve as they're attached to the mold framework, and the reinforcement forms the foundation of the fiberglass laminate that follows. These rods also have good rigidity and may require fewer mold frames and longitudinal supports.

Likewise, Baltek makes DuraKore planking material for one-off construction. It's composed of two layers of 1/16-inch hardwood veneer glued to an end-grain balsa core that's sealed with resin to minimize resin absorption from the reinforcements. The planks are 8 feet long by 12 inches wide and are finger-jointed at their ends to make it easier to join one plank to the next. These planks can be used in one-off construction using male molds as a framework, with epoxy gap-filling adhesive used to bond the edges of the planks together. Once planking is complete, fiberglass reinforcements are added to the outside, and then the inside of the hull is fiberglassed and faired to the desired finish. Du-raKore can also be used as hull stringer cores. ATC Chemical's bead-and-cove planking is also available for relatively easy one-off construction.

ATC Chemical's high-density foam-core planking system, called bead-and-cove. It's a tongue-and-groove plank arrangement in which plank edges fit together securely, making it easier to smooth the hull before fiberglassing inside and out.   ATC CHEMICAL

Cold-Molded Construction

Many high-end custom sportfishermen and other pleasure boats are made of wood encapsulated in epoxy. The wood delivers the strength, and the epoxy bonds all the wood pieces together, effectively forming a sealed, one-piece or *monocoque* hull. The process is often referred to as *cold-molded* since it's done without using heat or steam to bend the wood into shape. There are many variations on the cold-molded theme, but the usual procedure is to build a male mold consisting of station molds or frames (which define the hull's cross-sectional shapes), over which ribbands, or temporary wood straps, run fore and aft. The hull is built upside down, with the first layer of planking laid up over the ribbands or in some cases directly on the mold frames. Layers of overlapping plywood (whose width depends on the hull curvature) or wood strip

planks are bonded together with epoxy resin and then sheathed on the outside with fiberglass or other reinforcing cloth. The hull is then lifted off the mold, turned right side up, and finished off.

Wood-epoxy composite boatbuilding is a tried-and-true method of one-off custom construction. It produces a very strong, long-lasting hull of light to moderate weight that requires little maintenance. Wood has one of the highest ratios of stiffness and tensile strength to weight of any material, and the one problem that has always plagued wooden boats—rot—has been solved by epoxy resin saturation. Neither the spores that cause rot nor the water and air needed for the rot to spread can penetrate epoxy. Another problem with wooden hulls—poor abrasion resistance—is addressed by the epoxy sheathing on the outside of the hull. With a wood core, these boats are insulated naturally and don't sweat like a solid fiberglass hull. Wood boats are also quiet, with the wood acting as an acoustic insulator. The wood core (strip planks on laminated frames) also makes for high impact resistance when compared with some conventional sandwich layups.

Compared with a traditionally built wooden boat, the cold-molded process is superior for its durability, strength, low maintenance, and resistance to rot. A traditional wooden boat's planks are not bonded to each other (other than by their caulking), only to their frames. The planks, then, are on their own, structurally, in the event of impact. If the hull hits a log, the one plank impacted either has the strength to resist the impact or it doesn't; there's little load sharing with surrounding structure. The cold-molded hull is far stronger and also better able to handle the longitudinal stresses imposed by heavy seas and uneven weight distribution. This means that the wood-epoxy hull can be built lighter than a traditional wood boat for the same impact resistance and overall strength. Built to the same scantlings, or wood component size, the boat will be far stronger. Further, a traditional wooden hull is only as good as its fastenings, which can corrode, work loose, and fail over time. In a wood-epoxy hull, on the other hand, the fastenings are often superfluous once the epoxy has set up.

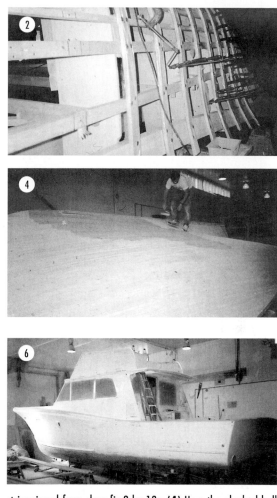

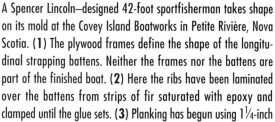

A Spencer Lincoln–designed 42-foot sportfisherman takes shape on its mold at the Covey Island Boatworks in Petite Rivière, Nova Scotia. (1) The plywood frames define the shape of the longitudinal strapping battens. Neither the frames nor the battens are part of the finished boat. (2) Here the ribs have been laminated over the battens from strips of fir saturated with epoxy and clamped until the glue sets. (3) Planking has begun using 1¼-inch strips ripped from clear fir 2-by-12s. (4) Here the planked hull has been sanded smooth and is getting its first coat of epoxy resin before the heavy, epoxy-saturated fiberglass cloth sheathing goes on. (5) Sheathing is complete and the frames and battens have been removed, but the hull is still upside down on the strongback. (6) The wood-epoxy Covey Island 42 sportfisherman is well on its way to completion.

After a conventionally built wooden boat is launched, the planking below the waterline soaks up water and swells, which tightens up the seams, reducing or stopping leaking. The problem here is that the wood planking gets heavier and weaker as it absorbs water. The constant stresses and strains imposed on the hull at sea eventually loosen its fasteners, which have to do their job while holding to this weaker wood. Over time, the boat's planking starts to loosen up and the hull strength diminishes as it loses rigidity. In a wood-epoxy boat, on the other hand, the 8 to 12 percent moisture content present in the wood during construction is largely maintained by epoxy encapsulation, allowing the wood to retain its original weight and strength.

CHAPTER 7

Aluminum
and Steel
Construction

It's no exaggeration to say that the undecideds could go one way or another.

—George H.W. Bush

Some of the finest yachts in the world are built of metal. Aluminum is the prime metal for yachts and small boats and has some distinct advantages over fiberglass. Steel is the only choice for large ships and many heavy-duty commercial vessels like fishing boats, tugs, and barges. But, steel also has its merits as a hull material for yachts and small craft.

A rendering of the Bruce Roberts–designed metal 16-meter (52-foot) Euro cruiser. STEVE DAVIS DRAWING, COURTESY BRUCE ROBERTS

Metal Basics

Steel weighs 490 pounds per cubic foot, costs about 35¢ a pound, and melts at 2,796°F. It has a yield strength (the force at which it starts to permanently deform or stretch) of 36,000 psi and an ultimate strength (the force required to make it separate or fracture) of 60,000 psi, so it has a relatively large "plastic" region of 24,000 psi, or 40 percent. In other words, steel is quite ductile. Its large "plastic" range means that it dents easily in relation to its ultimate strength, but this ability to stretch also allows it to absorb more impact energy before rupturing. Steel is relatively immune to fatigue resulting from the millions of stress cycles a vessel is exposed to over time. Steel welds are almost as strong as the members they join together, eliminating weak links in a steel vessel's construction. It's no secret that steel rusts when left unpainted; in fact, steel ships are built with thicker plating than a new ship actually needs, allowing for corrosion-related

strength loss over the life of the hull. Steel is very hard and therefore highly resistant to abrasion. This is an important attribute, especially for a commercial vessel that's subject to lots of abuse. Steel's hardness and abrasion resistance also make it harder to cut during the construction process.

Steel is the material of choice for the largest yachts—say, over 300 feet—and for commercial ships and small craft that are apt to take a beating. Steel has its limitations for small craft construction, however. A 35-footer is probably as small as you'll want to go with steel, but the thin steel plating (10 gauge, which is just over ⅛ inch) needed to allow such a small boat to actually float is difficult to weld without significant distortion. Thin plating also has little margin for corrosion built in, so it would have to be absolutely rust-free to last. A 45-footer, on the other hand, has enough displacement to allow heavier, and more easily welded, ³⁄₁₆-inch plate to be used. Smaller vessels have been built of steel, but they have to be squat, beamy little ducklings to float all that weight.

Depending on vessel design steel can be a great choice, especially for amateurs. It is the cheapest of all boatbuilding materials and is relatively easy to weld. For those new to welding, most high school adult education programs offer courses. Using a kit to build a steel boat is by far the best plan of attack; most useful is a kit that comes with all the pieces clearly labeled and computer cut so that all the parts fit together with precision. Steel construction is dirty work, but I haven't met many people who'd say that grinding fiberglass is a lot more fun. A steel hull is bulletproof once the boat is finally floating, and for some, that security alone justifies the effort. A steel hull is likely to win arguments with ice, logheads, or floating debris that a fiberglass hull might lose, and it will probably survive running aground on rock or coral quite nicely. This is especially true at the displacement speeds to which most steel hulls are limited. Guarding against rust through proper surface preparation, especially on the inside of the hull, is a tedious but essential step during the construction process. Many books are available to take the amateur through the building process and guide them through electrical work, joinery, insulation, mechanical installations, and other details. Steel and aluminum are sold by the pound, so estimating the cost of materials is relatively straightforward.

Derived from bauxite, aluminum is a silvery-white, ductile metal with excellent corrosion resistance. It is conductive and has thermal properties that make it a good choice for casting and welding. Aluminum has a melting point of 1,220°F. It weighs 170 pounds per cubic foot, just over a third as much as steel, and costs $1.90 per pound. Although aluminum's strength varies depending on the alloy selected, commonly used marine-grade 5083 H-32 aluminum plate has a yield strength of 34,000 psi and an ultimate strength of 45,000 psi, with a plastic region of 11,000 psi, or 25 percent. Since it is more brittle than steel, aluminum will start to yield at about the same loading as steel, but it fails before denting as deeply as steel and is more susceptible to fatigue. Aluminum welds are about 60 percent as strong as the members they join. Since aluminum welds are weak links, backing plates and longitudinal stiffeners to distribute loads beyond the welds are added to compensate. Aluminum hull plates are also butted in between, rather than at, the frames to minimize stress at these structural hard spots. Since aluminum is more susceptible to fatigue than steel, special care must be taken to increase

The bow sections of this aluminum Lyman Morse 62 include transverse and longitudinal framing. The radius in the transverse framing between the hull and deck greatly increases the vessel's strength.
LYMAN MORSE YACHTS

This 62-foot aluminum Lyman Morse cruising yacht is progressing nicely, with all hull and deck plating complete and the deckhouse welded in place.
LYMAN MORSE YACHTS

Aluminum and Steel Construction 121

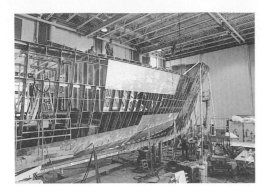

A Palmer Johnson 151-foot aluminum expedition yacht being plated.   PALMER JOHNSON

scantlings (the dimensions of hull plating and support structures) in areas subject to high loading and vibration, such as around machinery beds.

Aluminum vessels do not need to be painted above the waterline—since a corrosion-resistant layer, or film, of aluminum oxide forms naturally on the untreated surface. Although unpainted aluminum vessels are relatively low-maintenance, many owners prime and paint the gray aluminum, considering it well worth the added cost to pay for a glossy, hard-as-nails finish that looks good for years. Aluminum is also subject to crevice corrosion, so it must be painted anywhere moisture would naturally collect and stand.

Aluminum is not as abrasion resistant as steel, but lighter and tougher than fiberglass or wood. It is relatively easy to cut, even with ordinary hand

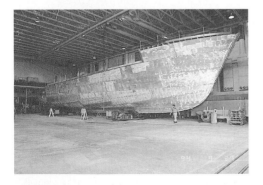

Designed to cross oceans, this 151-foot Palmer Johnson was doing just that a year or so after this photo was taken of the fully plated hull.   PALMER JOHNSON

tools and the right blades. Its light weight and builder-friendly qualities make this versatile metal the choice for thousands of bass boats, canoes, and other small craft every year.

Aluminum versus Steel

An aluminum vessel's scantlings need to be about 50 percent beefier to achieve the ultimate strength of a similar vessel built of steel, but the aluminum vessel will still be about 30 percent lighter. Consequently, aluminum, which pound for pound is stronger than steel, will provide a vessel with greater cargo and fuel capacity. The aluminum vessel will require less power to go the same speed as the steel craft, consuming less fuel in the process and increasing the vessel's range.

A 151-foot Palmer Johnson aluminum yacht's lower deck, showing the hull and main deck framing.   PALMER JOHNSON

Compared with an all-steel vessel, a steel-hulled yacht with an aluminum superstructure will be more stable due to its lower center of gravity, a result of less topside weight. A product called *triclad*, a strip of aluminum pressure-bonded to steel, is used to join the steel hull and the aluminum superstructure together.

An aluminum vessel may weigh considerably less than steel, but aluminum costs about twice as much. There are, however, trade-offs: carbide tools can be used for cutting, and welding goes quicker so labor costs will likely be less. When the added cost of a steel yacht's heavier propulsion machinery, ground tackle, bow thruster, and other equipment is considered, the scale starts to balance.

Over the years, an aluminum yacht will cost less to maintain and operate, and its resale will be higher. This is especially true if the hull is left unpainted. The inside of an aluminum boat can be left unpainted, like the outside, so the initial cost of preparing and painting can be avoided altogether, while a steel boat has to be sandblasted, primed, and painted inside and out.

Some builders say that once you add it all up a painted aluminum boat costs slightly more to build than steel whereas an unpainted aluminum vessel may actually cost less.

As we've seen in chapter 2, many factors contribute to a vessel's seaworthiness. The most seaworthy displacement hulls are heavy, of moderate beam, and deep; steel is a great material for building such a boat. A beamy boat with lots of form stability will benefit from a heavier steel hull to dampen the roll period. Also, the heavier a boat is for a given waterplane area, the gentler the vertical accelerations and the more comfortable the motion, at least to a point.

Metal versus Fiberglass

How does metal compare with fiberglass as a boatbuilding material? Since you can't lay up metal boats in a mold as you can with fiberglass, the hull and deck will take more time and often more money to build. But the cost of a yacht's hull, decks, and superstructure are only a fraction of the total price, so the difference in the drive-away price may be less than you think. This makes metal an excellent choice for custom, one-off boats, since the cost of a highly finished female mold is prohibitive for a single fiberglass boat, whereas a one-off fiberglass boat built over a male mold requires hundreds of hours of fairing before it's ready to paint. Properly welded and framed, an aluminum or steel boat requires minimal fairing or none at all, depending on the finish quality expected.

When it comes to fire resistance, steel, which as we've noted melts at 2,800°F, is superior. Aluminum is next at 1,220°F, while fiberglass burns at only 500°F. With their higher melting temperatures, aluminum and steel vessels easily meet IMO fire

Two Megayachts

Since the same design issues apply to all yachts regardless of size, let's consider a study done by naval architect Dick Boon, who has designed Palmer Johnson megayachts, among other multimillion-dollar pleasure ships. Boon compared a 164-foot, all-aluminum displacement yacht with a vessel of the same size having a steel hull and an aluminum superstructure (for more on yachts that mix metal with other materials, see below). Built to Lloyds rules, the aluminum hull weighs 86.8 tons compared with 206 tons for steel/aluminum. The steel hull's extra weight includes the larger engines, 2,665 hp versus 2,055 hp, needed to achieve the same speed. The steel bottom plating is 8.2 mm thick versus the aluminum at 10.4 mm, and the hull sides are 6.7 mm and 8.4 mm, respectively. When all is said and done, the strongly built aluminum version weighs 450 tons versus 584 tons for its steel-aluminum counterpart, a 23 percent weight savings, and draws 6 inches less water.

At hull speed (16.35 knots for both), the all-aluminum version has a range of 3,773 nautical miles compared with the heavier steel-aluminum yacht's 2,973 miles, due to the latter's greater displacement, increased wetted surface and frictional resistance, and larger power plant. At 12.2 knots, the aluminum yacht will use just 500 hp and achieve a range of 8,750 miles, whereas the steel-aluminum yacht would use 585 hp and have a range of 7,700 miles; these numbers reflect the heavier vessel's 29 percent higher propulsion resistance. In reality, such a light load at these speeds would damage the engines over time unless two smaller engines per shaft and controllable pitch propellers are fitted, but these illustrations make for a fascinating comparison nonetheless.

One of Boon's 151-foot Palmer-Johnson designs uses thicker aluminum plating still, and he notes that an underwater collision that would puncture 10 mm steel would just dent the 12.7 to 15.8 mm aluminum used in the bottom of this 151-footer.

containment standards, unlike fiberglass composites. And what's more conducive to peace of mind hundreds of miles at sea than built-in, passive fire and flooding protection?

Metal boats have other advantages. You can weld a cleat, towing eye, or chock directly to the

A bulbous bow in the making on a Bruce Roberts trawler.

BRUCE ROBERTS

deck, hull, or bulwark. Hull-to-deck joints are welded together, a structural improvement over the screwed-and-bonded joints normally seen on fiberglass boats. Welded decks don't leak, and there's no hull or deck core to rot and delaminate after becoming saturated with water. Also, metal boats don't get bottom blisters. A surveyor can inspect weld integrity using ultrasound and X-rays and determine plate thickness using an audio gauge. There's little guesswork involved in determining the structural integrity of a metal yacht; what you see is what you get, unlike fiberglass composites.

Modifying metal yachts is also simple—just weld on the new part (and any necessary supports), whether it's a davit or a cockpit extension. Whereas a secondary bond on a fiberglass structure will never be as strong as the original wet-on-wet laminate, a weld is there to stay.

Aluminum yachts are also more amenable to aft–engine room designs than those made of steel—and this layout offers distinct advantages. Because an aluminum hull weighs less, the aft sections can be made a little deeper and fuller, producing enough buoyancy in the stern to support the weight of propulsion machinery. An aft engine room isolates machinery noise in the stern and frees up the midships spaces for comfortable accommodations at sea, away from the propellers, where noise and vibration are minimized and the yacht's motion in a seaway is most comfortable. Propeller shafts and exhaust pipes can be shorter, lighter, and thus less expensive. An alternate means of engine room access (and emergency egress) may

be provided through the lazarette or transom. This arrangement also allows the fuel tanks, which represent the vessel's largest variable load, to be carried over the hull's longitudinal centers of buoyancy and flotation, so that little if any trim adjustment is needed as fuel is consumed. The midships area is also the deepest portion of the hull so any fuel tankage located there contributes more stability.

To summarize, both steel and aluminum offer excellent impact resistance. They are easily repaired as compared with boats built of fiberglass or cold-molded wood. Aluminum boats can essentially last forever if properly cared for, and they don't take a lot of work to keep in good condition. Metal boats face special threats from corrosion and electrolysis (corrosion specifically caused by the interaction of dissimilar metals), but with proper maintenance these are not insurmountable problems. Regardless of the material selected, construction costs rise more or less with the cube of a vessel's displacement, while the relative costs of hull, machinery, equipment, and furnishings vary depending on the quality of the components and the level of finish selected.

Framing Methods

Metal vessels are built in a variety of ways, but they generally fit into one of three categories. Vessels built with only transverse (side to side) framing are fairly common in Europe. In this approach, only the transverse frames, or ribs, support the plating, and no longitudinal (fore and aft) frames are used. As a side note, old wooden ships and boats are transversely framed, with the planking constituting the longitudinal support.

Transverse framing in combination with longitudinal stringers is the most common modern metal construction method. Usually, the longitudinals will be half the depth of the frames but have the same thickness. In fact, the American Bureau of Shipping (ABS) requires that transverse frames be twice the depth of the cutouts that allow the longitudinals to pass through uninterrupted. Longitudinal frames effectively absorb and distribute the great tension and compression stresses to which a hull is subjected in a seaway, and they also reduce the loads on the plating welds of an aluminum boat. They may permit the use of thinner plating, thus reducing weight overall.

Hull and deck frames of an aluminum Bruce Roberts—designed yacht.   BRUCE ROBERTS

The third approach incorporates web framing with longitudinal stringers. This is a system of webs (deep transverse frames, or semibulkheads) supporting fairly beefy longitudinal stringers. In some cases the large webs alternate with smaller intermediate frames that support the longitudinal stringers. Web framing is often used on lightweight vessels, including racing sailboats.

So-called frameless boats take their shape from the plating during construction and derive much of their strength from it when the vessel is completed. But *frameless* turns out to be a relative term; there are invariably frames, but there are fewer of them. This method can work without frames if the plating is thick enough, but only at a huge weight penalty, with the added skin thickness weighing more than the framing it replaces. There are certainly legitimate ways to reduce framing, including the use of bulkheads and carefully engineered internal furnishings that become structural members. A fair hull can be welded over a temporary jig, or framework, with framing inserted after the jig is removed. This method prevents prefixed, slightly misaligned frames from distorting the fair curve of the plating, but the result is still not a frameless boat.

Whatever method of framing is used, the design usually specifies a plating thickness based on the vessel's size and intended use, and that thickness in turn guides the frame spacing. Longitudinals, if used, are sized according to the size of the vessel, their spacing, and the distance they span between frames. Then frame size is determined by vessel size, frame spacing, their spans, and their need to be at least twice the height of the stringer cutouts. When longitudinals, or stringers, are used, the transverse frames support the longitudinals, which in turn support the hull plating. In the absence of longitudinals, the framing must be spaced more closely in order to adequately support the plating. When a longitudinal is large enough to become the dominant strength member locally, such as an engine bed support, it is called a *girder*.

Unlike fiberglass boats, metal boats have a real keel for a backbone, imparting longitudinal strength and impact resistance and providing a foundation for ballast in heavy displacement yachts and a landing for frames and hull plating. The keel can also help form integral fuel, potable (drinking) water, and ballast water tanks. Bilge keels can be easily attached to metal hulls, and ballast can be added to the keel and bilge keels, further increasing the vessel's roll moment of inertia, or inertial resistant to dynamic rolling influences.

When fuel and water tanks are built in as part of the hull structure, they can create a double bottom that strengthens the hull longitudinally and locally, adds significant watertight integrity in case of a holing, makes excellent use of internal space, and lowers the center of gravity with all that liquid as low in the hull as possible. On larger yachts, manhole covers in the top of each tank section allow complete access for hull inspection, maintenance, and tank cleaning.

Hull Plating and Design

Both aluminum and steel come in flat plates, which can be bent or twisted into simple or *developable* curves (around a single axis) with relative ease. Try to bend a plate into a *compound curve* (around two axes), however, and you will find the going much harder. Grab a sheet of plywood with someone else holding the other end, and you will find that you can twist the sheet or bend it in one direction, but you can't do both. Metal boat builders are subject to these same limitations unless they employ hydraulic presses and rollers. Because of the challenges and costs of bending plates into compound curves, the hulls of most commercial vessels, and many yachts, contain only developable curves.

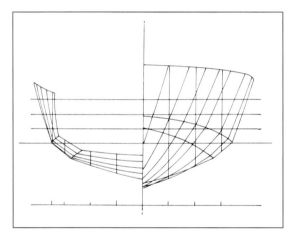

The developable curves on this multichine hull approximate a compound-curve hull while eliminating the need for heavy plate-forming presses.   STEWARD, *BOATBUILDING MANUAL*

Metal hulls come in several basic designs, including single-chine, multichine, radius-chine, and round-bilge. (Remember that a vessel's chine is the angle formed by the intersection of the topside and bottom hull plates.) Single-chine hulls are the simplest and cheapest to build since they essentially involve joining cut plates to each other along the chine while bending the plating to the framing. Because of its simplicity, single-chine construction is most often chosen for lightweight aluminum planing hulls,

but it also imposes the most limitations on hull form. Some appreciate the simplicity of the single-chine form, while others feel the absence of compound curves extracts too great an aesthetic price to be worth making. So what are the options?

Double-chine hulls, also drawn to plans incorporating developable curves, are one step up in complexity and expense. They involve an additional plate intersection to cut and weld on either side of the hull, providing the semblance of a round bilge. Add yet another angled strake (metal plank) at the turn of the bilge, and you've got a multichine hull. These are even more time-consuming and expensive to build, and may require a lot of fairing to achieve visually appealing curves. Some feel that multiple chines merely emphasize that a vessel is built from flat sheets of metal, but the hull shape is hydrodynamically improved.

Radius-chine hulls have rounded bilges surrounded by and joined to flat plates bent into developable curves on the hull's topsides and bottom. Imagine running a 2- or 3-foot-diameter pipe from stem to transom along the chine and welding the hull plating to its outside surface and you've got the idea. This combines something of the round-bilge boat's pleasing appearance with the hard-chine hull's ease and simplicity of construction. While this is not a true rounded hull, it is visually appealing and more closely resembles the real thing. Some designers even claim greater strength, lighter weight, and higher resale value. Since only the chine is rounded, or radiused, computer-aided design is needed to produce the right shapes to make all the pieces fit together while producing a fair surface. This is especially important forward, where the angle between the hull bottom and topsides gradually becomes less acute, a highly visible area where appearance is important.

Using the right equipment, designers and builders aren't limited to developable curves. Plates can be formed into compound curves by the application of pressure. Plates are often rolled or deformed into convex or concave shapes that actually stretch the metal. In this way, the hull can take on

A Broward motor yacht hull, having been framed and plated upside down, is ready to be rolled upright for finishing. BROWARD MARINE

curvature that creates less hydrodynamic resistance below the waterline and is more aesthetic above. When faired, the rounded hull looks like it might have come out of a fiberglass mold. It takes a lot of pressure to distort heavy steel or aluminum plates, and it takes a lot of skill to get it just right, but fortunately for the builder, even a rounded metal hull is mostly made up of developable areas.

Rounded metal hulls are more costly, but for many, the possibilities of real bow flare, tumblehome, and canoe and fantail sterns are well worth it. In addition to the obvious aesthetic advantages, this ability to shape the metal offers a seaworthiness payoff as well, creating a well-balanced, double-ended displacement hull with minimal drag aft and good following-sea characteristics.

In the absence of rollers and presses, a curved steel or aluminum hull can be built by running narrow metal plates, perhaps 1 to 2 feet in width (depending on hull size), along the length of the hull. The plating can also run diagonally to more readily adapt to a hull's three-dimensional curvature. Additionally, a builder might press and offset one edge of a sheet inward and lap the next plate over it much like a lapstrake wooden boat. This also adds stiffness and strength longitudinally, since the plate is twice as thick at the overlap.

Just as with fiberglass boatbuilding, there are plenty of strongly held opinions out there about these different metal boat designs and construction methods. Some designers favor a single chine and put the savings into a longer, roomier, more easily driven hull. A longer single-chine hull will have higher hull and cruising speeds and achieve the same speed with less power than a shorter rounded hull. Any measurable loss of propulsion efficiency caused by the hard chine's slightly greater drag will be more than made up for by simply building it longer.

While aluminum boats used to be limited, in practice, to single- or multiple-chine designs, CAD-CAM has made round-bilge aluminum hulls more feasible. With a computer figuring out the best plate shapes, life gets a lot easier for the builder. In general, CAD-CAM has greatly increased the speed and accuracy of cutting all the parts needed to build a boat. Cutting metal parts with computer-controlled equipment can now shave the hours needed to complete a hull in half. The cutting goes faster, the more precisely cut parts go together quicker, and the resultant plating surfaces are smoother and require less fairing. And once the computer files are saved in the computer, the same boat, or, say, a stretched version of it, can be built over and over with the same program.

The Challenges of Metal Boats

Coating Systems

Epoxy paint systems are preferred to prevent corrosion in metal boats, with six or more coats of primer and topcoats applied to build up a durable finish. The final coats are often a tough polyurethane paint that holds its luster for years. The metal is first cleaned with a solvent to remove oil and other contaminants from the surface. Steel vessels should be sandblasted to provide good adhesion for the first coat of primer, which is typically applied shortly after blasting. Plates are often ordered preprimed from the supplier to minimize surface preparation. Aluminum calls for gentler sandblasting in preparation for the primer coat, since the metal is much softer than steel. As mentioned, aluminum surfaces don't need to be coated for other than aesthetic reasons, notable exceptions including below-the-waterline surfaces of boats left in the water. Crevices should be filled in or faired where attachments have been welded on to prevent standing water from leading to crevice corrosion.

For ultimate protection against corrosion, steel hulls can be flame sprayed with molten aluminum or zinc as long as the surface is not subsequently abraded through to the steel. After a thorough "white metal" sandblasting, molten aluminum-zinc or aluminum is sprayed on the steel surfaces. This process seals the steel against moisture and oxygen penetration and is followed by an elaborate epoxy paint process. Regardless of the finish, it is essential that the integrity of the paint system be maintained.

Rust inside a steel hull is more of a concern than rust on the outside surfaces. There are so many hidden nooks and crannies where water can collect and accelerate corrosion. It's very important that the bilges be accessible for routine maintenance over the years. And of course, when steel starts to rust, it's obvious. Wood and fiberglass boats might look great, but have real rot or delamination problems lurking below the surface.

After primer coats are applied, two-part fillers are used to fill in the valleys to create a mirror-smooth finish above the waterline. The fairer the plates are to start with, the less filler (and extra weight) is needed to produce a smooth surface. That's where CAD-CAM technology can help, along with highly trained welders who know how to minimize plate distortion. A final coat of epoxy primer goes over the filler, followed by several polyurethane topcoats. Below the waterline, the builder is more concerned with sealing the metal against seawater than achieving an absolutely fair surface. Several barrier coats are applied, followed by primer coats and then topcoats of antifouling paint. Most builders stay away from copper-based antifouling paints, while some don't hesitate to use it on the premise that the barrier coat remains intact.

Corrosion

Corrosion, of course, is the archenemy of metal. Introduce a metal surface to an *electrolyte* through which ions can flow, and some degree of corrosion will result. (Corrosion is often confused with electrolysis, but to be strictly accurate the latter is what happens to the electrolyte, not to the metals involved.) Atmospheric moisture is itself an electrolyte, as any child who has lost a bicycle to rust can understand, but seawater is a far more powerful one, awash with loose ions to carry electrical currents. Expose a single pure or alloyed metal to an electrolyte and you get *electrochemical corrosion*, which proceeds extremely slowly. But the flow of electrons, or electrical current, that occurs when two dissimilar metals that are connected metallically—either by direct contact or by a conductor—are immersed in the same electrolyte is more problematic. Once this interaction is established, one of the metals—acting as the *anode*—will lose ions and corrode at an accelerated rate, while the other metal (the more "noble" in the galvanic series) will be unharmed. *Galvanic corrosion*, as it is known, can be combated effectively by the use of *sacrificial anodes*, which are usually made of zinc. Zinc falls at the very bottom of the galvanic series, so when a zinc anode, known simply as a *zinc*, is connected to another metal part, the zinc will always be the primary target for galvanic corrosion, leaving the other metal unharmed until the zinc is consumed.

If you introduce a stray electrical current or two from other sources into the electrolyte—say from an improperly grounded appliance on a boat, or abraded wiring insulation in bilge water, or a busy marina—you have the potential for *stray-current* or *electrolytic corrosion*, which can proceed hundreds of times as fast as galvanic corrosion.

Electrolysis is always a concern on boats, but it is an especially acute problem on metal boats. Builders strive to isolate every dissimilar metal fitting using plastic bushings and pads, thus preventing metal-to-metal contact. On a metal hull, sacrificial zincs should be placed at intervals from bow to stern to protect the bottom and running gear, and must be inspected regularly. Galvanic activity picks up significantly if bare metal is exposed to the water, so it's important to keep the bottom paint and underlying primer in sound condition. Aluminum is at the bottom of the galvanic-action food chain (only zinc and magnesium are lower), so it must be rigorously protected against galvanic corrosion.

Metal boat builders and owners have to be fanatical in preventing ground pathways for stray electrical current. Shore power should pass through an isolation transformer, and floating ground systems are recommended so that negative DC wires are not directly or indirectly (attached to the engine or through-hull, for instance) in contact with the hull.

Intriguing Hybrids

Hybrid steel boats with fiberglass or aluminum decks and superstructures make good use of both materials. They offer some excellent advantages, marrying a rugged hull with strong, lightweight, and low-maintenance topside structures.

A company called Safe Boats takes a novel approach to boatbuilding with their RIB-like aluminum hulls supported by tough, chemical- and water-resistant polyethylene foam collars. The aluminum hull makes the boats tough and durable, and the deflation-proof foam collars provide tremendous positive buoyancy and act as a built-in fendering system. The system is used by the U.S. Coast Guard and other law enforcement agencies on their vessels, a testimony to their beefy construction and ability to take abuse.

Another company, Hy-Lite, builds composite aluminum boats with a sandwich of 2-inch foam bonded to inner and outer sheets of aluminum skin. The foam acts as the flange of an I-beam, stiffening the hull, decks, and superstructure and adding acoustic and thermal insulation. The company claims that repairs are easily made in the event of damage. The boats are washed in a series of acid baths, primed with three coats of epoxy, and finished with three coats of polyurethane paint.

Home-Built on a Budget

Steel and aluminum hulls lend themselves well to home construction for the family on a budget, especially kit boats. Kits come with all the pieces precut and ready for assembly. Even when contracting with a professional boatbuilder, the welds do not have to be ground smooth, and you can skip fairing the hull and deck surfaces, saving a bundle. The result is a rugged, functional pleasure boat; it's just not a seamless yacht.

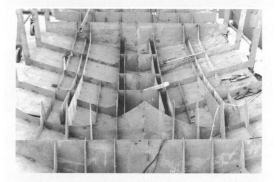

All the pieces of this Roberts hull kit, which are precut by CAM, fit together practically perfectly. BRUCE ROBERTS

Thanks to CAD-CAM technology, some companies are offering kit boats that can be built in either aluminum or steel; again the pieces are precut, marked, and ready for assembly. The computer-controlled cutters are so precise that the pieces fit together perfectly (within several thousandths of an inch), further reducing construction time and effort. Most of these kits involve setting up a framework to give the hull its shape during construction, but some take their shape from the plating itself.

Insulation

Any metal vessel must be insulated, both to eliminate condensation inside the hull and to provide thermal insulation against heat and cold. Blown-in polyurethane foam insulation works well as a thermal insulator and provides good acoustic insulation, but it's important that it adhere well to the primed metal, sealing it off completely. If applied to a properly prepared and primed surface, the foam can prevent corrosion; if not, it will just hide any corrosion that gained a foothold through faulty surface preparation.

Blown-in urethane foam is susceptible to absorbing water, so it must be kept dry. It also absorbs odors. Urethane foam is flammable, and when burning emits toxic vapors. A fire-retardant paint will help matters here. Closed-cell urethane is also available in panels and can be easily cut to fit. Urethane foam can be bought in a fire-retardant, non-toxic chemical formulation. It should be applied in a thickness of 1 to 2 inches, and coated with a surface skin that repels water.

Metal Boat References

A good resource for more detailed information on metal boatbuilding is yacht designer Michael Kasten's Web site www.kastenmarine.com.

Thomas E. Colvin, *Steel Boatbuilding: From Plans to Bare Hull,* 2 vols. (Camden, Maine: International Marine, 1985, 1986).

Glen-L Marine Designs, 9152 Rosecrans Ave., P.O. Box 1804WA, Bellflower, California 90706, 562-630-6258, info@glen-l.com, www.glen-l.com.

Gilbert C. Klingel, *Boatbuilding with Steel,* including *Boatbuilding with Aluminum* by Thomas Colvin, 2nd ed. (Camden, Maine: International Marine, 1991).

Stephen F. Pollard, *Boatbuilding with Aluminum.* 2nd ed. (Camden, Maine: International Marine, 2007).

Bruce Roberts-Goodson, *The Complete Guide to Metal Boats: Building, Maintenance, and Repair.* 3rd ed. (Camden, Maine: International Marine, 2006).

Robert M. Steward, *Boatbuilding Manual.* 4th ed. (Camden, Maine: International Marine, 1994).

The wiring on this Manitou pontoon boat is protected by the wiring chase design.

The aluminum deck framing on this Manitou pontoon boat supports the plywood deck.

This Manitou stern-drive well is big enough to provide plenty of maintenance room around the engine, and also to provide buoyancy to support the engine's weight.

Flat sheets of aluminum are rolled into aluminum tubes and welded at the seams with a series of interior circular bulkheads to produce compartmented pontoon logs.

CHAPTER 8

Propulsion Systems

A black cat crossing your path signifies that the animal is going somewhere.

—Groucho Marx

Anyone researching their next boat purchase may face what can be a bewildering choice of power plants: conventional inboards, stern drives, outboards, somewhat more exotic surface-piercing propellers and waterjets, and the new inboard steerable pod drives. In this chapter, we'll examine the particular strengths and weaknesses of each propulsion package, starting with a brief overview of the power plants and then move on to a more detailed look at each of them.

In the United States more boats under 21 feet are sold annually than all others combined, so it is no surprise that outboard-powered craft lead in number of units sold. The propulsion system best suited to *your* boat, however, depends on its hull design, size, and intended use. As with any choice, there are almost always trade-offs involved. For instance, outboard power on a center console sportfisherman might be a good choice for its light weight, ease of trailering, and speed, but having the motor sticking out 4 or 5 feet past the transom makes it hard to work a fish off the stern.

For many larger vessels above 30 feet or so, conventional inclined-shaft inboards with submerged propellers are a common choice. The drivetrain (propeller, propeller shaft, shaft log, seal, struts, and rudder) is relatively inexpensive, reliable, and efficient within its operating range, but all that underwater gear adds drag at higher speeds. The downward angle of thrust (shaft angle plus hull

trim) also results in a loss of efficiency. Compared with waterjets and surface drives, conventional submerged props are located well below the waterline, and consequently can be counted on to maintain thrust in all but the most severe conditions.

However, with the advent of the Volvo Penta inboard performance system (IPS) and the Cummins-MerCruiser (CMD) Zeus pod propulsion system, conventional inboard propulsion is certainly in the decline in boats from 30 to 100-plus feet. Pod propulsion is so much more efficient and maneuverable, quieter and smoother-running, lighter in weight and less bulky, while freeing up substantial space for accommodations, that I would not be surprised to see boatbuilders not offering it struggle to survive. This includes the sportfishing market, which stands to gain as much as any segment from pod propulsion's far superior maneuverability—especially when working a fish—to say nothing of 20 to 30 percent greater range and a much smaller engine room.

Waterjets, whose popularity in recreational boating was once driven at least in part by their sheer novelty, are now gaining acceptance based on actual merit. They function by drawing in water through an inlet grate in the hull bottom, accelerating it through an impeller, and shooting it out the stern through a steerable nozzle. Waterjets make sense when a lack of running gear, shallow draft, speed, swimmer safety, and maneuverability are primary concerns.

A surface-piercing propeller is, as the name suggests, only partially submerged. Excellent efficiency and performance at high speed are gained by eliminating much of the drag caused by underwater running gear and by the propeller itself. Waterjets and surface drives are significantly more complex and therefore more expensive than conventional propulsion packages. In terms of efficiency, conventional propellers are generally best for operating speeds below 25 knots, waterjets from 25 to 40 knots, and surface drives for sustained cruising speeds above 40 knots. Complexity, slow-speed maneuverability, and other issues also enter into the equation.

Real-World Speed

Though there's a big difference between the the speed a boat will do flat out with a light load and unpainted bottom, and how fast it can cruise loaded, top speed sells, so boatbuilders place great emphasis on it in their marketing. Just be aware of the ideal conditions under which the advertised speeds were probably achieved.

The advertised speed can depend a lot on the type of boat. Even a saltwater center console builder is likely going to talk about flat-out speed in miles per hour as opposed to knots, for the obvious reason that speed in miles per hour sounds more impressive. Plus, freshwater boats use statute miles to measure both distance and speed. A nautical mile, based on dividing the distance around the equator by 24,000, equals 6,076 feet. One knot equals 1.15 mph, and 1 mph equals 0.869 knot. On the other hand, a builder of luxury convertibles is likely to advertise fully loaded speeds in knots and usually knocks off a knot or two from the recorded sea trial speed to avoid disappointing the customer. As a result, the new owner who is told to expect 30 knots at 2,000 rpm is going to be pleasantly surprised when the boat makes 32 knots.

Many factors can influence speed. Just painting the shiny gelcoat bottom of a new boat can drop its speed by 2 knots due to the added frictional drag from a rougher surface finish. Imagine what happens when marine growth builds up over the season, not to mention the accumulation of provisions and extra gear. Even adding a tower on a big boat or a bimini with a full enclosure on a smaller one can slow a boat by 2 to 3 knots. Boatbuilders usually plan ahead by installing props that are slightly undersized originally so that additional weight and bottom fouling won't prevent the engines from achieving their full rated rpm.

Just use the top speed as a point of reference. When you hear "it'll run 60 mph" at your local boat dealership, consider that a sterndrive-powered Formula 240 bowrider with a 496 MerCruiser will top out at 59 mph and cruise at 31 mph (3,000 rpm) to

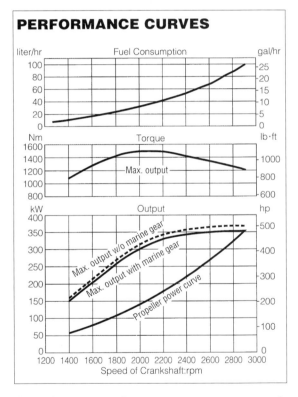

The 500 hp Yanmar's performance curves. Yanmar recommends running their engines at just 200 rpm off the top, maximizing available continuous power, in this case about 400 hp at 2,700 rpm. Note the fairly consistent 20 hp per gph fuel ratio in this curve. A 600 hp diesel typically burns about 31 gph wide open. Note that the marine gear (reduction gear) absorbs about 3 percent of the engine's power.   YANMAR

39 mph (3,500 rpm). An outboard will cruise a little faster as a percentage of its top speed; for instance a Century 2202 with a 250 hp Yamaha four-stroke will hit 53 mph wide open at 6,000 rpm, and can cruise all day at 35 to 41 mph turning 4,000 to 4,500 rpm, wave conditions permitting. With diesels the difference between full power and cruise is generally much less, since many can cruise at around 90 percent power. For instance, a Riviera 4700 with 715 hp Cat C12s will make 34 knots at full power, or 2,500 rpm, and 31 knots at a 2,200 rpm cruise. Of course, you can run an engine faster than in these examples, but you'll pay a penalty in noise levels, engine life, and fuel consumption. Bottom line—question advertised speeds, especially with smaller boats.

So what really matters is how fast a boat will go at its crusing speed under normal (for you) conditions. Compact, lightweight diesels have made it possible for cruising and sportfishing yachts to cruise in calm conditions in excess of 30 knots when fully loaded. In fact, boatbuilders design new models around the available power as the market continues to demand more speed. Hull forms have been refined accordingly to include finer entries, greater deadrise, and stronger construction in an effort to accommodate the higher horsepower available. But make sure that the power plant complements the hull. Unfortunately, some builders continue to produce flat-bottom hulls better suited to the 20-knot speeds of a decade ago than the 35 to 40 knots that these new powerhouses are capable of delivering.

As we saw in chapter 4, there's no substitute for deadrise to deliver a good ride. If you buy an older boat with the intention of repowering it, it's important that the hull shape and structure can support the extra speed, and that the center of gravity can be shifted farther aft to accommodate the extra speed.

With any planing hull, it's essential that the boat run easily on a plane when fully loaded, that the engines can turn up to their rated rpm, and that the desired speed can be sustained with the engines turning no faster than their continuous cruise rpm rating. Otherwise, the engines will burn excessive fuel, and

wear out prematurely. Beware of the price-point 35-footer sold with big-block V-8 gas engines. These boats are priced to get you on the water, but most are just too heavy for gas engines and, if you actually put out to sea on a regular basis, will only lead to a disappointing ownership experience. If the boat is over 18,000 pounds, consider paying the extra money for diesels, buy used, or get a smaller boat. Above all, sea trial the boat to find out how it performs!

Outboard Engines

Outboard engines are light, fast, easy to maintain, and can be changed out quickly. Compared with inboards of similar horsepower, outboards are more expensive, lighter, and possibly shorter-lived, with 800 to 1,200 operating hours being about average, though today's advanced two- and four-stroke outboards can be expected to last substantailly longer. But since the average boater puts well under 100 hours or less on their engine each season, and often as few as 40 or 50 hours, many outboards will last for decades, especially if used in fresh water. Most of the outboards sold today are electronically fuel-injected (EFI) four-strokes from Yamaha, Mercury, Honda, and Suzuki, or to a lesser extent, direct-injected (DI, or DFI) two-strokes including Mercury Optimax, Yamaha HPDI, and Evinrude ETEC. All of these motors are quieter, easier to start, more economical and reliable, and smoke a lot less than the old carbureted two-strokes.

A 250 hp gas outboard is faster than a 250 hp inboard since an outboard's lower unit is more streamlined than an inboard's running gear (shafts, struts, and rudders), creating less drag at high speeds. The engine's thrust is also closer to horizontal than an inboard's, resulting in better propulsion efficiency. On the downside, the outboard's smaller propeller with its oversized hub is inherently less efficient than an inboard's, especially when pushing heavier boats, and there is a 4 to 5 percent loss of engine power in the 90-degree turn from driveshaft to prop in the lower unit. But the engine's low drag, ability to lower the stern/raise the bow or vice versa (the Yamaha V-MAX trims from −3 to +16 degrees, for example), and its ability to operate continually at a higher percentage of its full power give it a big speed advantage over same-horsepower inboard engines. With rare exceptions, outboards run on gasoline, not diesel fuel.

The outboard's (and stern drive's) ability to adjust trim, or running angle, by pivoting the motor in or out is a big performance advantage. Trimming the motor out will depress the stern and lift the bow, and lowering it will accomplish the opposite. Raising the bow gets more hull out of the water, reducing frictional drag and increasing speed, and it can improve control in a following sea. Lowering the bow gets more hull in the water for a smoother (though slower and wetter) ride in a head sea, since the waves meet the hull farther forward where there's more deadrise. With an inboard engine, you can't raise the bow, though you can lower it by depressing the trim tabs. The center of gravity of an outboard-powered boat is also farther aft, which is part of the formula for a good-running high-speed boat (see discussion of center of gravity and speed in chapter 4). Outboards also offer excellent maneuverability because the propeller thrust is used to steer the boat as well as propel it. This makes an outboard more responsive to the helm at low speeds, especially in reverse.

Outboards come in different 15-, 20-, 25-, and 30-inch shaft lengths to accommodate varying transom heights; generally, the greater the transom height, the bigger the boat. The lower unit should be submerged enough to give the prop a good bite on solid water, preventing cavitation and ventilation, but not so much as to create excessive drag. For high-performance and shallow-water fishing boats, optional power mounts called jack plates allow a motor to be raised and lowered vertically to adjust prop immersion in real time. Unlike pivoting the motor up or down with its trim-tilt motor, moving the jack plate up and down does not alter the thrust angle, which is convenient for, say, flats boats that need to be able to get into very shallow water. Some outboard manufacturers have lowered the engine's cooling water intake location to accommodate the

This quiet-running four-stroke Yamaha slides up and down on its Flats Jack. A jack plate like this is a great way to adjust lower unit immersion (and overall draft) without having to tilt the drive up.

YAMAHA MOTOR CORPORATION

engines running higher out of the water when raised on a jack plate.

Outboards are mounted either directly on the boat's transom or on a bracket extending several feet aft. Transom-mounted outboards have less effect on the boat's static trim (since their weight is farther forward) and are less of an obstacle when fishing; they are also easier to reach for routine maintenance. Bracket-mounted outboards, on the other hand, can be faster, since they often balance the V-bottom hull's weight distribution more favorably by shifting the center of gravity aft, and they operate in a slightly cleaner waterflow. Because they are mounted farther aft, they also sound quieter from inside the boat and also minimize exhaust fumes in the cockpit. Since the motor is cantilevered farther aft of the hull's center of dynamic lift when planing, the boat can be trimmed higher by the bow, which can reduce wetted surface and increase speed. A bracket-mounted outboard eliminates the transom cutout, which makes for a higher transom that is less prone to taking on water over the stern.

This Dusky twin outboard is equipped with a B-Bracket motor mount, which adds buoyancy, but no dynamic lift at speed; the bottom of the bracket is above the hull's running surface. A ruggedly built transom is needed to hold nearly 1,000 pounds of engine and several hundred horsepower-worth of thrust.

An outboard on a bracket also moves a boat's center of gravity farther aft and therefore increases the speed needed for a hull to get up on plane, thus reducing midrange performance. Bracket-mounted outboards also submerge more readily, since a wave coming from astern will immerse the engine before lifting the boat. When backing, the bracket-mounted outboard's propeller wash also impinges on the transom, reducing backing power and control. In contrast, an inboard (with its more forward center of gravity) will tend to stay on plane at lower speeds and operate more efficiently in the 12- to 18-knot range.

Outboards have simple internal cooling systems that pump water through an intake grid in the lower unit, through the engine, and out the propeller hub. A small "telltale" stream of water is visible from the side of the lower unit to indicate that water is flowing freely through the engine and that the cooling system is working properly. All outboards are raw-water-cooled, which means that

they use the water the boat is floating in—as opposed to a closed, recirculating freshwater supply—to cool the engine directly. In salt water it's a good idea to flush your engine with freshwater after each use since salt water is so corrosive.

Two-Stroke Outboards

Far fewer two-stroke outboards are being sold today than just a few years ago. Due to new, more stringent emissions regulations, the old carbureted two-strokes are being largely phased out in the United States, leaving just a few electronically fuel-injected (EFI) models and mostly the high-tech, clean-running direct-injected versions. Two-stokes are so-called because they complete the intake and compression cycles in one stroke of the piston (the upward stroke), and power and exhaust in the downward stroke. What all two-strokes have in common is that the engine's lubricating oil is mixed in with the gas. With the old carb two-stroke, the oil is poured directly into the gas tank in a predetermined ratio. This ratio is worst case as far as the engine's actual

Yamaha's big 300 hp two-stroke HPDI direct-injected engine.

need for lubrication goes, meaning the engine gets more oil than it needs much of the time, making it smoky, rough-running, and harder to start.

The EFI and DI two-strokes, on the other hand, have a variable ratio oil (VRO) pump mounted on the motor that pumps oil from a small tank and injects it into the gas supply as it's being fed to the engine; this ratio is determined according to the engine's rpm, load, and other parameters. Since these pumps supply oil at the rate the engine actually needs, they run cleaner than carb engines using premixed fuel. The great advantage of the DI engine over the EFI (and especially the carb) is that it meters both gas and oil to the engine more precisely, and then injects the mix into the cylinders under tremendous pressure to atomize the fuel/oil mixture more completely, resulting in much better economy, less smoke, easier starting, lower noise levels, and smoother idling.

In the outboard market, the DI two-stroke is the four-stroke's only serious competiton in terms of quality and customer satisfaction, according to the annual J.D. Power and Associates Marine Engine Competitive Information Study (MECIS). They have comparable fuel economy, emissions, and noise levels. The DI two-stroke weighs less than a comparable four-stroke and has stronger acceleration, making it a good choice for bass boats with low transoms and those owners who put a premium on their 0-to-60 (or 70) times. While the four-stroke owner doesn't have to worry about mixing oil with the gas, the two-stroke owner doesn't have to change and dispose of the old oil.

Bombardier Recreational Products (BRP), which owns the Evinrude and Johnson brands, has staked its future on the success of its Evinrude E-TEC DI two-stroke. To date, BRP has made a solid case for its E-TEC line, in part because it has a

Mercury's largest two-stroke outboard, the 300 hp direct-injected Optimax high-performance motor delivers good economy, strong acceleration, and high top-end speed. MERCURY MARINE

Evinrude's largest model: a 250 hp E-TEC two-stroke direct-injected engine. BOMBARDIER RECREATION PRODUCTS

compelling product, and also because of an aggressive and equally compelling marketing campaign. Yamaha produces its HPDI series of DI two-strokes, and Mercury has its Optimax line, but both of these engine giants are focusing the majority of their efforts on four-strokes. Among two-stroke outboard owners, customer satisfaction ratings of DI outboards are higher than they are for EFIs, and much higher than carb two-strokes, according to the annual J.D. Power and Associates MECIS. In fact, owners with older carb two-strokes also tend to rate their boats lower, highlighting the negative impact these engine have on customer enjoyment.

Four-Stroke Outboards

Four-strokes are by far the most popular outboards sold in the United States today. Like car and inboard boat engines, four-stroke outboards have a four-step operating cycle: (1) intake/down, (2) compression/up, (3) power/down, and (4) exhaust/up. (As mentioned, two-strokes combine steps 1–2

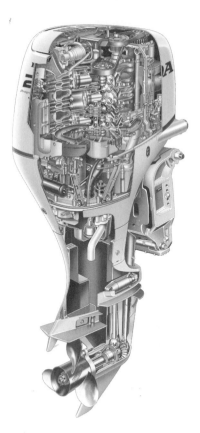

A cutaway of Honda's 225 hp four-stroke outboard. Honda produces 20 four-stroke outboards, including three with waterjet impellers instead of props. HONDA MARINE

and 3–4.) They are more expensive and heavier than two-strokes and don't deliver the same snappy acceleration, but they are quiet (especially at slow speed), fuel efficient, easy to start, almost fume-free (there's no oil mixed in with the gas), and reliable. Four-strokes can be either carbureted or fuel injected (EFI); the EFI engines score much higher in customer satifaction in the J.D. Power studies than carb models, and they are also reported to be more reliable. The major four-stroke outboard manufacturers are Yamaha, Mercury, Honda, and Suzuki, and all of these engines are highly rated. All deliver good service.

Environmental considerations alone make the EFI four-stroke an excellent choice for many boaters today, especially for boats operating on inland waters,

Honda's big, smooth, and quiet-running 225 hp four-stroke VTEC outboard. HONDA MARINE

Designed to take the place of triple 250s with twin engines, or twin 150s or 200s with a single outboard, Yamaha's new 350 hp four-stroke outboard, at the time of its introduction in 2007, was the most powerful outboard available. Designed from the start as a marine outboard, this V-8 has a whopping 5.3 liters of displacement (intended to produce long engine life) and weighs 804 pounds. The 350's power-to-weight (2.297 lbs/hp) is actually slightly better than the 592-pound Yamaha 250 four-stroke (2.368 lbs/hp).

YAMAHA MOTOR CORPORATION

rivers, and lakes. (Evinrude points out that its E-TEC two-stroke engines have also gained acceptance by regulatory agencies around the world.)

Whether DI two-stroke or EFI four-stroke, outboards are great for smaller boats because they can weigh 300 to 500 pounds less than stern drives or inboards producing similar performance, which, among other things, makes trailering significantly easier. But even outboard engine weights can vary considerably by horsepower. The accompanying table shows relative weights of 150 and 225 hp two- and four-stroke outboards, listed from lightest to heaviest in each horsepower category.

Diesel outboards are also available, and they're typically used in commercial applications where many hundreds of hours are put on an engine each year. Yachts and commercial ships sometimes carry tenders fitted with diesel outboards to avoid carrying gasoline onboard. Diesel outboards are durable, can be more economical to run long-term, and are much heavier than gas models. Yanmar's 27 and 36 hp models, for instance, weigh 207 and 256 pounds, respectively.

Whether you opt for a DI two-stroke or EFI four-stroke, all of these engines are light-years ahead of the old carbureted and EFI two-strokes that constituted most of the market just a few years ago. They start easier, run much quieter and cleaner (hardly any smoke and no more oil slick behind the boat), and are far more reliable. They're also getting more powerful: Suzuki's DF300 hp, Mercury's 300 hp Verado, and Yamaha's V-8 F350 allow boatbuilders to build bigger and faster boats. All of these improvements are the result of manufacturers responding to a stick

Comparative Weights of Two- and Four-Stroke Outboards

Manufacturer	Model	Technology	Dry Weight (lbs)
150 hp			
Evinrude	E-TEC	DI 2-stroke	419
Mercury	Optimax	DI 2-stroke	431
Yamaha	F-series	EFI 4-stroke	466
Yamaha	VMAX	HPDI DI 2-stroke	468
Suzuki	DF150	EFI 4-stroke	474
Honda	EFI	EFI 4-stroke	485
Mercury	Verado	EFI 4-stroke	510
225 hp			
Mercury	Opti 225	DI 2-stroke	505
Evinrude	E-TEC 225	DI 2-stroke	530
Suzuki	DF 225	EFI 4-stroke	580
Yamaha	F225	EFI 4-stroke	583
Honda	BF225	EFI 4-stroke	599
Mercury	Verado 225	EFI 4-stroke	635

Mercury Verado Outboard

Mercury recently came out with an all-new series of four-stroke Verado outboards. This high-tech engine is remarkable for a number of reasons, including its quietness, especially at low speed, smooth-running operation, and, for a four-stroke, strong mid-range acceleration, which it accomplishes with a mechanically driven supercharger. These engines burn substantially more gas than other engines when run hard, but, according to test results I've run myself, they are more competitive in terms of fuel flow at cruising speeds of 4,500 rpm and below. Mercury has also reported modifications to the Verado that improve fuel economy, though at the cost of increased emissions. Mercury's DTS throttle system makes the Verado a pleasure to operate.

Mercury's most powerful four-stroke outboard at the time of its introduction, the 300 Verado's race-car technology helps it deliver good power-to-weight and strong acceleration. This supercharged engine displaces just 2.6 liters and weighs just 635 pounds. MERCURY MARINE

(tightening emissions regulations from federal and state governments) and a carrot (a more demanding public willing to pay for a better outboard).

Electronic Monitoring and Engine Control Systems

Until recently, outboards and stern drives have been monitored with single or multifunction gauges and controlled with mechanical cables linking the controls at the helm to the engine at the transom. As good as any engine is, an owner's satisfaction with the drivetrain will be influenced, understandably, by the quality of these engine display and control systems. Many outboards still use mechanical cables for shift and throttle control, and these can often be real clunkers, in the literal sense, as you can read about in some of the boat reviews in part 2 of this book. The mechanical cable linkages are often stiff and difficult to operate: The engine "chunks" going into gear, the throttle setting falls off when you let go of it, twin throttles don't match up when the engines are in synch, the engines are hard to get into synch. Things get even worse with multiple stations, with controls in the tower and in the cockpit that make the controls even stiffer and more cantankerous.

Yamaha's popular 150 hp four-stroke F150 outboard.
YAMAHA MOTOR CORPORATION

The good news is that electronic monitoring and fly-by-wire control systems are becoming available in the outboard and stern-drive markets. These include Suzuki's fly-by-wire Precision Control and

Mercury has been in the vanguard of efforts to take much of the work out of running a boat with its SmartCraft CANBUS (controller area network-based system) linking the power plant, controls, and external sensors together. Based on CANBUS technology used in the automotive and aeronautical industries, SmartCraft puts a great deal of information at the operator's fingertips, and it can all be displayed on just one or two gauges.

Depending on the engine, readouts might include oil temperature and pressure, water pressure, engine temperature, voltage, fuel flow, engine hour meter, engine diagnostics, water in fuel, steering angle (on stern drives and inboards), engine drive trim, and engine rpm. External inputs to Smart-Craft include GPS, water depth and temperature, fuel used, fuel remaining, range with remaining fuel, gallons needed to reach next waypoint, water tank levels, temperature, and scheduled maintenance reminders. Besides making it easier to operate the boat and keep an eye on systems, SmartCraft is easy to hook up using plug-and-play connectors and a single wire harness.

SmartCraft includes an engine control system called DTS (digital throttle and shift), an electronic fly-by-wire system that makes running a boat sheer pleasure. DTS is available with Mercury four-stroke and Optimax outboards and MPI MerCruiser stern drives. Engines equipped with DTS shift as smooth as butter, with just enough detent at neutral to let you know when you're in or out of gear. Throttles also operate as smooth as silk, with just enough resistance dialed in so the throttles stay put when you let go of them. The engines start automatically with the brief push of a button, and the system won't try to start the engines when they're already running even when you push the button (which is a common problem with idling four-strokes since they're so quiet). A crash-back protection feature prevents transmission damage in a panic reversal, and even completes the maneuver faster than an operator could. All these elements make running any boat so equipped a pleasure; we hope to see the other engine manufacturers come out with similar engine control systems.

The triple-outboard DTS engine control binnacle has two levers controlling three engines, and it's the most intuitive control system we've seen of its type. The port control operates the port and centerline engines when maneuvering around the dock. For more information on triple-engine DTS operation, see the Triton 351 boat review in the market survey section of this book (page 335–339).

Mercury's engine control head for its SmartCraft system. Three engines can be operated by these two controls.

MERCURY MARINE

Mercury's SmartCraft display provides a wide range of selectable propulsion and environmental data. MERCURY MARINE

Yamaha's Command Link, which was introduced with its F350 outboard. (See the Mercury Smart-Craft sidebar opposite).

Stern Drives

Stern drives can be thought of as outboard lower units connected through the transom to inboard gas or diesel engines. MerCruiser and Volvo are the two leading stern-drive manufacturers. Although heavier than outboards, stern drives offer similar speed and trim advantages over inboards.

Stern drives are especially popular in fresh water, where it doesn't matter so much that the lower unit can't be raised clear of corrosive salt water when not in use. (This is a big advantage for outboards.) However, big advances have been made in stern-drive corrosion control. Volvo Penta also produces a composite-clad Ocean Series drive that is impervious to corrosion. A stern drive allows the operator to enjoy the maneuverability of an outboard combined with the quiet, efficient, out-of-sight operation, and lower price of an inboard. The engine can be shut off and the lower unit can be tilted so that, while not out of the water, it's higher than the bottom of the boat, making it possible to bring a boat into shallower water using a kicker or human power. To date, neither MerCruiser nor Volvo have come up with the equivaent of an outboard's jack plate.

Stern-drive engines, like outboards, are usually cooled by taking water in through a grill in the lower unit and circulating it through chambers in the engine block, as with other raw-water-cooled engines. A freshwater-cooled stern-drive or inboard engine, on the other hand, pumps raw sea or lake water through a heat exchanger mounted on top of the engine, which cools a closed-loop supply of coolant (water mixed with antifreeze), much like a car engine. The coolant is then circulated through the engine block, minimizing corrosion and prolonging

MerCruiser's Bravo 3 stern drive with counterrotating propellers is rated for up to 525 gas hp and 65 mph. Counterrotating prop stern drives deliver much higher customer satisfaction, according to the annual J.D. Power and Associates Boat Competitive Information Study (BCIS).   MERCURY MARINE

Comparing V-Drive Inboard and Stern Drive Performance

Maybe you're considering an express cruiser that's offered with both stern-drive and V-drive inboard power. If performance is your number one criterion, and especially if the boat will be in fresh water or in a storage rack, then the chart next page makes a strong case for stern drives. In this example, Regal tested two of its model 3260 express cruisers with MerCruiser 6.2-liter, 320 hp gas engines. One boat had Bravo 3 stern-drive power, the other V-drive inboard. The boats were within a few pounds of each other in displacement. The last two columns show the relative performance of the stern drive versus the V-drive.

(continued next page)

Comparing V–Drive Inboard and Stern Drive Performance (continued)

RPM	Stern Drive				U–Drive				Stern vs. V–Drive	
	MPH	GPH	MPG (sm)	Range (sm)	MPH	GPH	MPG (sm)	Range (sm)	MPH	MPG
1,000	5.5	2.8	2.0	338	6.1	3.4	1.8	309	90%	109%
1,500	7.8	4.4	1.8	305	8.2	7	1.2	201	95%	151%
2,000	8.9	8.8	1.0	174	9.2	9.8	0.9	161	97%	108%
2,500	17.2	13.4	1.3	221	11.1	16.6	0.7	115	155%	192%
3,000	26	16.4	1.6	273	19.4	20.6	0.9	162	134%	168%
3,500	33.1	20	1.7	285	28	26.2	1.1	184	118%	155%
4,000	39.7	28	1.4	244	33.7	34	1.0	170	118%	143%
4,500	44.2	35.2	1.3	216	35	39.8	0.9	151	126%	143%
5,000	52.1	50.4	1.0	178	39.4	49.8	0.8	136	132%	131%

Test boat: Regal 3260 Bravo 3 stern-drive vs. V-drive inboard. Power: MerCruiser 320 hp 6.2- liter gas engine. Range based on 172 gallons consumption (90 percent of tank capacity). All miles are statute miles (sm). MPH = miles per hour. GPH = gallons per hour. MPG (sm) = statute miles per gallon.

The results are pretty dramatic, with the stern-drive-powered crusier going 32 percent faster (52.1 mph vs. 39.4 mph) at wide-open throttle and 18 percent faster at a 3,500 rpm cruise. The stern-drive boat also had better fuel ecomomy and range, 55 percent better at 3,500 rpm and a whopping 68 percent better at a leisurely 3,000 rpm.

Volvo's Power Trim Assistant automatically adjusts stern-drive lower-unit trim angle based on engine rpm. You preselect the drive angle at various rpm settings. Typically, the drive would automatically drop down while the boat is coming up on plane, then come back up at high speed to minimize wetted surface and increase speed.

VOLVO PENTA

engine life. Raw water is returned to the sea through the propeller hub, a lower-unit exhaust line, a through-hull fitting, or some combination of these. Stern drives in boats that are trailered can be flushed using a water hose with Mickey Mouse ears placed over the cooling water intake grill on the

Yanmar's 260 hp 6BYZ diesel weighs just 899 pounds complete with the attached MerCruiser Bravo 3 stern drive. YANMAR

lower unit. Volvo has a system called Neutra-Salt that flushes salt water from the engine cooling system without hauling the boat or hooking up to a freshwater hose; the system leaves a corrosion inhibitor on all internal engine surfaces exposed to raw cooling water. MerCruiser has introduced similar corrosion prevention measures in its stern drives, including its SeaCore corrosion prevention system with closed-cooling and freshwater flushing.

Manufacturers, including Volvo and MerCruiser, make lower units of varying propeller size and reduction gear ratio to suit the application, and most stern drives have a single propeller, which is the cheapest, simplest design. Counterrotating propeller-drive systems (Volvo's DP and Merc's Bravo 3) have two props mounted one in front of the other that turn in opposite directions, thus canceling the side forces and eliminating the spiraling helix (which represents wasted energy) from the propeller wash. The result is improved propulsion efficiency, greater speed and acceleration at a given rpm, and better handling (and higher customer satisfaction according to J.D. Power's BCIS).

A counterrotating drive will also eliminate the tendency of a single-engine boat to heel at speed and to pull the steering wheel to one side. Finally, boats with counterrotating propellers turn and back exceptionally well. Twin diesel stern drives are also viable propulsion systems for cruisers over 40 feet, and a single diesel stern drive such as the 370 hp Volvo DPH would be adequate for a cruiser in the 30-foot range.

Volvo's Ocean Series stern drive has a composite-clad lower unit to eliminate any worries about exterior corrosion. The Ocean Series drives are available for 4.3- to 8.1-liter gas engines. Volvo says the drive is lighter as well as more hydrodynamic than the aluminum drive it replaces. It can be fitted with both stainless and composite DuoProps.

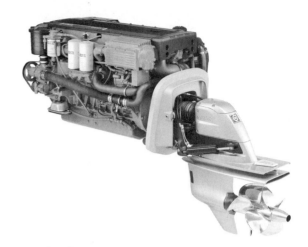

A 370 hp Volvo D6 common rail diesel, hooked up to a DPR DuoProp stern drive. The package, the most powerful diesel stern drive available at the time of its introduction, weighs just 1,698 pounds, and is rated for applications to over 50 knots. VOLVO PENTA

A stern-drive engine is usually installed in the stern. It's also possible to fit an intermediate jackshaft between the transmission and the lower unit using universal or CV joints, thus moving the engine farther forward to improve weight distribution, open up the cockpit for anglers, and in some cases eliminate the engine box. Of course, the reason for the outboard's popularity in the offshore saltwater fishing market is the outboard's greater speed and lighter weight, and it doesn't take up any

To allow a less obstructed transom and to move weight forward, this Volvo engine is connected via a jackshaft to an Ocean Series lower unit that is composite-clad to prevent saltwater corrosion. VOLVO PENTA

room in the cockpit. But when you look at a boat with between one and three 250 hp outboards projecting 4 or 5 feet aft of the transom, making it a lot harder to work a fish close to the boat, you may wonder why the stern drive/jackshaft combination isn't seen more often in center consoles, since the engine can be located under the console. Part of the reason concerns weight distribution, since high-speed deep V-bottom hulls run better with the center of gravity farther aft. Plus, with the corrosion problems inherent in a continually immersed aluminum lower unit, stern drives have a hard time gaining acceptance in saltwater fishing venues; this is in spite of big improvements in corrosion prevention by both Volvo and MerCruiser.

Single versus Twin Power

Larger cruising and racing boats often use twin stern drives when a single engine can't deliver sufficient power. However, twin engines—be they stern drives, outboards, or inboards—add cost, complexity, weight, and drag, and twin stern drives and inboards crowd the engine room and impede access. For instance, a single 300 hp engine would be significantly faster, cheaper to buy and operate, and more efficient than a pair of 150 hp engines. For these reasons,

Mercury's compact low-profile 100 hp Vazer stern drive is based on a 1.6-liter GM Vortec four-cylinder engine with closed-loop cooling to eliminate internal saltwater corrosion. This drive opens up new design possibilities for runabout, fish boat, and pontoon builders.
MERCURY MARINE

when a single engine can deliver sufficient power, it is often the better option.

On the other hand, twin engines offer both redundancy and superior maneuverability. The trick when maneuvering dockside with twin engines is to leave the helm amidships and let the engines do the turning. Both MerCruiser and Volvo are introducing stern-drive joystick control, making boathandling a walk in the park.

Inboard Engines

Inboard engines, whether driving IPS or Zeus pods, conventional submerged props, surface-piercing propellers, or waterjets, are the overwhelming choice for larger boats. Their weight is centered deeper in the hull, lowering the vessel's center of gravity and improving stability. They also tend to last longer (though the jury is still out on the durability of the latest high-tech outboards), a critical factor for larger boats that spend more time under way each season.

When well-designed inboard boats are running with optimum trim, efficiency, and drag, they can come close to matching the speed of same-horsepower stern-drive- and outboard-powered

MerCruiser's Bravo 1 XR stern drive has beefed up internal components, giving it a rating of up to 600 hp.   MERCURY MARINE

Pod Power

The latest propulsion news for boats 30 feet and over is pod power. Mounted under the bottom of the boat, pods turn and steer like an outboard, and they're streamlined, minimizing drag and delivering up to 30 percent better fuel economy and 15 percent greater speed. Counterrotating props take the twist out of the discharge race, producing more thrust, and blade loading goes down so the system gets more "traction" around the dock and on acceleration.

The forward-facing props of inboard performance systems (IPS) operate in clean, undisturbed water, pulling the boat through the water, which makes them even more efficient. Pod thrust is parallel to the boat's keel, unlike an inboard. Exhaust exits through the pod well below the waterline (except for Zeus when below planing speed), so they're much quieter with low emissions. The engines are soft-mounted (the pods take up the propeller thrust), so vibrations are hardly felt. There are no rudders, and engines are connected to the pods by a very short jackshaft, so they take up much less space inside the boat. This lets the builder make the engine room smaller, allowing more room for the people compartment.

Two brands are available: Volvo Penta IPS and Cummins-MerCruiser Diesel (CMD) Zeus. With either brand, there is only one vendor to deal with from helm to propeller. Both units are electronically controlled, including engine control and monitoring and fingertip steering control.

The Volvo IPS, on the market since 2004, is available with Volvo D4 (IPS 350 and 400) and D6 (IPS 450, 500, and 600) diesels and also a 375 hp, 8.1-liter gas IPS 500G, all using the same pod drive. Volvo D9 (IPS 750) and D11 (IPS 850) diesel units come with a larger pod. The IPS units are named according to the hp an inclined-shaft inboard would require to produce the same speed. For instance, the IPS 600, powered by a 435 hp diesel, does the work of a 600 hp diesel driving a conventional inclined shaft, while burning much less fuel. Zeus's models include a 3500, powered by a Cummins QSB5.9 diesel rated at between 330 and 480 hp, and a 3800 powered by a Cummins QSC8.3 rated at between 500 and 600 hp. CMD combines Cummins's diesels, ZF's expertise with underwater drives, and Mototron's acumen with SmartCraft electronic control and networking systems.

The concern some people have about pod power's susceptibility to grounding damage is largely unfounded; neither Zeus nor the Volvo IPS are any more exposed than conventional inboards. Unless you're in a single-engine full-keel lobster boat (or a waterjet boat), the props are going to be the first thing to hit bottom in any boat. Even if you hit so hard the pod shears off (which is what both IPS and Zeus are designed to do), the units are designed to maintain a watertight seal. And chances are very good that you'll have a new pod installed and be on your way long before the guy in the next repair yard has even gotten his new props, struts, rudders, shafts, and shaft seals delivered to the boatyard, let alone had it all put back together.

For many owners, pod power's fantastic maneuverability will clinch the deal. Zeus and IPS have joysticks that allow the boat to be walked sideways or obliquely or twisted in its own length, or any combination of these maneuvers, by merely moving the joystick in the desired direction. After a few hours practice, most people can handle a 60-footer like it's a baby buggy. The joystick reduces the stress for the operator, so everyone onboard is happier. No more skipper yelling at the mate because he screwed up the approach. It also removes the major impediment (besides being too poor) to moving up to a larger boat—fear of docking. Think of pod propulsion as putting the pleasure back in pleasure boating.

Pod power is so dramatically better than inboards that many builders have already designed new models entirely around pods. Tiara, for instance has basically designed its entire new Sovran cruiser series around IPS. You'd think that was a big risk for Tiara, building boats that can't be powered by any other vendor, but it's really a sure bet for the boatbuilder who gets to choose between three very positive options—keep the same size fuel tanks to increase range by 20 to 30 percent, decrease fuel capacity to lighten the boat up, or some mix of the two slightly smaller tanks with slightly more room and incremental speed and efficiency improvement.

I've run a dozen IPS boats from 37 to 75 feet, as well as a Zeus-powered 44-foot Sea Ray DA test boat and a Doral 45 Alegria; all handle superbly and work as advertised. I also got a chance to play with the Zeus Skyhook, which uses GPS to lock the boat into position—just push a button and the boat maintains its heading within 5 or 10 degrees and its position within a few yards. IPS has a similar system called GPS anchor.

(*continued next page*)

Volvo offers its IPS units in twin, triple, and quad installations. The Lazzara 75 LSX Quad (as in four IPS 600s) does well over 30 knots on a little over half the fuel it would take with conventional power. Lose an engine on the Lazzara, and you can still make over 25 knots; lose two engines, and the boat will still run at planing speeds close to 18 knots. Lose an engine with conventional twin inboards and you're going home at displacement speed (below 10 knots), and good luck docking the thing when you get back home. I don't see any reason quad IPS 850s couldn't be installed on a 100- or 110-footer with similar results.

In my view, boatbuilders who don't offer pods will no longer be competitive. If I owned an older inboard from 35 to 80 feet, I'd also be considering repowering with pods.

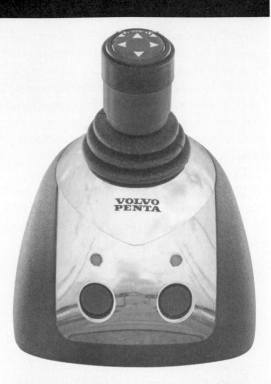

Volvo's IPS joystick control. VOLVO PENTA

Volvo's IPS 600 system. Powered by a 435 hp common rail diesel, the 600 in the name comes from the equivalent hp it would take to produce the same performance in an inboard application. VOLVO PENTA

The Cummins-MerCruiser Diesel (CMD) Zeus low-drag pod propulsion systems have electronically controlled drive units with aft-facing counterrotating propellers. CUMMINS-MERCRUISER

Part of the Cummins-MerCruiser Diesel (CMD) Zeus propulsion system, the Skyhook stationkeeping system uses position input from GPS and heading input from the vessel's sensors to maintain position and heading within close tolerances, even in adverse conditions. CUMMINS-MERCRUISER

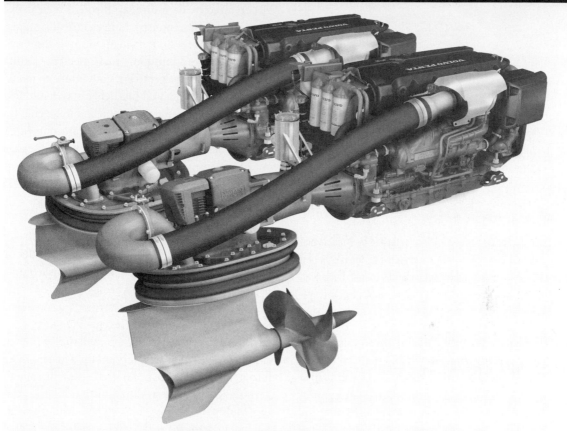

The Volvo IPS 850, which produces performance comparable to an 850 hp conventional inboard, is powered by the 670 hp Volvo D11 diesel. The IPS 850 burns less fuel, takes up less room, is lighter, quieter, and smoother running, and it is far more maneuverable than comparable conventional inclined-shaft power.

VOLVO PENTA

I would be surprised if pod power doesn't come to dominate the sportfishing market as well. One of Volvo's prototype IPS boats, a Tiara 3800 express, fit the 30-inch-high Volvo D6 common rail diesels under the cockpit, turning the engine room under the bridgedeck into a giant fender storage locker. Spencer Yachts also builds a 43-foot express sport-fishermen (see full-length review on pages 329–334) with the low-profile IPS 600 drivetrain completely under the cockpit; a large twin bed mid cabin takes the place of a conventional engine room. Volvo's intuitive sportfishing maneuvering mode also allows the boat to back on fish far more nimbly than conventional inboards ever could.

boats. But, since trim can change significantly with weight movement fore and aft, especially on smaller boats, the ability of outboards and stern drives to control trim usually gives them a speed advantage in the real world.

Gasoline Inboards

Gas inboards are efficient, quiet (with proper noise reduction material for the engine room and exhaust system), and less expensive than outboards. Largely because of their added weight, center of gravity

This Albin 32 had its running surface extended by 2 feet to add buoyancy and dynamic lift aft, necessitated by the weight of a V-drive diesel mounted in the stern under the cockpit. The built-in swim platform was a bonus. Note the full keel protecting the single-screw running gear.

farther forward, inability to trim the bow up, added running gear drag underwater, and shaft angle inefficiencies, the inboard is rarely as fast at cruise speed as an outboard of the same rated horsepower.

Gas inboards are marinized versions of automotive engines and are made mostly by the General Motors Corporation. They differ from their

Crusader's well-regarded durable 8.1-liter HO multiport fuel-injected gas inboard, based on a GM block, develops 425 hp.

car-bound brethren in that they're raw-water-cooled (either directly, or indirectly through a heat exchanger) and have nonsparking electrical systems. They come in three basic configurations: carbureted, fuel-injected, and multiport fuel-injected. Carbureted engines are cheaper to buy and simpler to maintain, but their mechanical fuel delivery system is less precise and therefore less efficient, and these engines can be hard to start. MerCruiser has come out with a Turn-Key Starting (TKS) system that makes life easier for carbureted engine owners, without the higher cost of an electronically fuel-injected (EFI) engine. TKS engines are easier to start, requiring no choking or throttle pumping on the part of the operator.

In an EFI engine, an electronically metered charge of fuel is sprayed under pressure into the cylinder or the intake manifold, increasing the percentage of fuel that is actually burned (versus being discharged in the exhaust). EFI systems lack points, rotor, cap, and condenser, and therefore require less maintenance. They are generally easier to start when cold, run smoother, and offer lower fuel consumption for a given power output. Spark advance is adjusted automatically to meet changes in air temperature and barometric pressure. Multiport fuel injection, which includes a separate fuel injector for each cylinder, helps meter fuel even more precisely for maximum horsepower output and cleaner emissions. On any of these gas engines, water pumps are preferably gear driven by the engine, not by a belt, eliminating a weak link in the system.

Though explosions are rare occurances, gas power plants are inherently more dangerous than diesel, since gasoline fumes are far more volatile. Whenever a gas tank or gas engine is installed in an enclosed compartment, the potential exists for a hose or fitting to come loose unobserved, allowing gas or gas fumes to flow into the bilge.

Any boat with belowdeck gasoline tanks should have a mechanical bilge blower installed with the suction hose reaching to the lowest point in the bilge. The blower should be allowed to run for several minutes before starting the engine and after refueling to exhaust the fumes and introduce fresh air. This points to the need for a well-engineered and properly installed fuel system that meets U.S. Coast Guard standards for hose and fittings and for proper grounding,

Gas engines certainly have their place in small planing boats, but the diesel's inherent safety provides a compelling argument in its favor. It's not that gasoline installations aren't safe—they are (and they're usually quite reliable), since thousands of these boats have been running around for years without incident. But why add an additional hazard to boating if you don't have to?

Gas engines require clean fuel (although they tolerate contaminants better than diesels), so there should be a fuel filter water separator between the tank and the engine. Water can condense in the tank (especially a partially empty one) or may be introduced during fueling. Sediment, a real risk from "dirty fuel," can find its way from the tank and clog fuel lines. The clear bowl on the bottom of a good filter-separator allows you to detect any water or sediment. These contaminants can then be drained off into a container for proper disposal ashore.

Ethanol

The use of ethanol as a fuel in gas-powered boats is wreaking havoc with some boatowners for a couple of reasons. In older boats with fiberglass fuel tanks made with general-purpose orthophthalic resin, the ethanol, which is a solvent, reacts with the resin and creates more sludge that can ruin engines; probably the best solution would be to replace the fiberglass tank with one made of aluminum or polypropylene, which is no easy job. In aluminum tanks, ethanol releases fine metallic particles that can clog carburetors and fuel injectors. Ethanol is also hygroscopic, so it attracts and attaches to any water that gets into the fuel, usually in the form of condensation when the tanks are not filled (the tanks vent to atmosphere) and creates another engine-stopping sludge that filters can't deal with. Draining the tank when winterizing the boat is reported to be a good idea since ethanol has a short shelf life. Mixing ethanol with the carcinogenic additive MTBE that it replaces also creates a sludge that clogs up the engine, so it's important not to mix the two kinds of gasoline. In short, don't carry around old ethanol, and carry extra filters and change them often.

Catalytic Converters

Catalytic Converters, which reduce harmful exhaust emissions, are now required on gas inboards. While mixing a very hot object with a potentially explosive bilge atmosphere would seem like a poor idea, Indmar, Volvo, Crusader, and others are installing special converters in the exhaust manifold that work at lower temperatures and actually improve fuel economy. Where there's a will, there's a way.

A Racor gas filter-separator with sediment bowl. Don't leave home without it.   RACOR

Electronic fuel injection and ignition systems are improving both inboard and outboard gasoline engine efficiency. Gas engines run cleaner and emit fewer pollutants than they used to. One well-known gas inboard brand, Crusader, is available carbureted or in two EFI configurations: TBI (throttle body injection), which has two fuel injectors and burns about 15 percent less fuel at cruise than the carbureted model, and MPI (multiport injection), which

This inboard's main, aft, and intermediate shaft strut pads are bolted onto, rather than being recessed into, the hull, adding drag and turbulence forward of the propellers. Flush pads would help here.

has eight injectors and is 17 to 18 percent more efficient at cruise. Both EFI models burn 40 percent less gas at trolling speeds. According to the manufacturer, there is little difference in engine life among these models. With GM stopping production of big-block gas engines, we may well see big outboards like the Yamaha 350 take over a portion of the runabout and small cruiser markets.

Note that the reduction ratios available for these gas engines run from 1.25:1 to 2.8:1 (for more on reduction ratios, see below). Depending on the boat, the steeper gear ratio will tend to produce better midrange performance and much better "traction" dockside, since it will drive a larger-diameter, slower-turning propeller. But larger propellers, shafts, struts, and other components cost the builder more, so they're rarely standard equipment and may not even be available as an option. A smaller, faster propeller generally gives less responsive performance overall and less speed at cruise, especially when a boat is fully loaded, so if you're repowering, the added cost of changing to a deeper-ratio gear may be well worthwhile.

Diesel Inboards

Diesels are often the best choice for boats over 35 feet and 18,000 pounds, as well as for boats that run more than 200 to 300 hours annually. Gas engines, lacking the midrange torque of a diesel of similar power, just aren't suited to pushing large,

heavy boats (though Volvo's gas IPS may well drive these figures up a few feet and a few thousand pounds). The potential life of a diesel is much longer than that of a similar-sized gas engine, and they burn considerably less fuel, so diesels pay for themselves with enough running time.

ACERT is Caterpillar's name for the emissions reduction technology used in its newer diesels. ACERT uses an ECM (electronic control module) to precisely control air and fuel injection and provide more cool air to the combustion chamber, improving fuel efficiency, and reducing vibrations and noise. The 32.1-liter 1,825 hp V-12 C32 ACERT weighs in at 5,617 pounds (3.1 lbs/hp). CATERPILLAR

Diesel engines are becoming more popular in small pleasure craft because of their shrinking size, superior fuel economy, and, as discussed, greater inherent safety. A diesel-powered boat is significantly more expensive to buy, but it will retain more value and may well be easier to sell later. It's also a lot more expensive to rebuild come overhaul time—up to three times that of a same-horsepower gas engine.

Compared with gas engines, diesels are often louder, since they rely on compression rather than spark to ignite the fuel. Thus they require more extensive noise reduction systems. Their exhaust odor is more objectionable than gas, though underwater exhaust systems do a good job of burying the fumes. The exception to the rule here is the new common rail diesel, a fuel-delivery technology being adapted by many diesel manufacturers. The common rail fuel system introduces

Twin Disc's MGX gears have a dual-stage piston that initially controls the clutch from 10 to 90 percent engagement until the second piston kicks in and locks up the clutch, making shifting smoother and allowing precise docking and trolling while decreasing wear and tear on the clutch, shaft seals, and engine mounts.

TWIN DISC

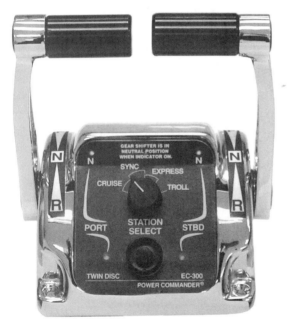

These Twin Disc engine controls work with any transmission, but have special capabilities with the manufacturer's MGX gear. Along with standard crash-back protection and engine synchronization, it controls shaft brakes to speed up crash backs and stabilizing fins. TWIN DISC

fuel sequentially in several injections near the top of the piston's power stroke, rather than all at once, resulting in more complete fuel combustion, very little, if any, fumes and smoke even when the engine is cold, far less noise and vibration, and much improved fuel economy. You can walk up to a boat at a dock with common rail diesels idling and hardly hear it running. Common rail is definitely one way to go if you value these qualities.

The popular MTU 16V2000 diesel, used in many 30-plus-knot, 60- to 75-foot sportfishermen, as well as motor yachts over 100 feet, is available in light-duty ratings to 2,400 hp at 2,450 rpm. This 35.7-liter V-16 diesel weighs 8,840 pounds (3.68 lbs/hp). MTU

Low-weight and emissions-efficient, and quiet, Cummins-MerCruiser's new QSD4.2 is a 350 hp common rail diesel weighing 1,014 pounds (2.9 lbs/hp). CUMMINS-MERCRUISER DIESEL

Diesels are the hands-down choice for displacement vessels, including heavier diesels, since weight isn't a critical factor. Diesel engines are durable, increasingly quiet, and becoming so light that they can produce more usable, continuous power than a gas engine of the same weight, making them well suited even to small, fast planing hulls. Some diesels from MAN, Isotta Fraschini, and Yanmar reach a pounds-per-horsepower ratio of 3:1 or less, an accomplishment unheard of just a few years ago.

A diesel engine can last anywhere from 800 to 20,000 hours between major overhauls. The exact figure depends on how well the engine was built and how much horsepower is squeezed out of each cubic inch of displacement. Fastidious maintenance and consistent running (the less downtime, the better) also add hours, as do clean fuel and oil. Some 1,200 to 3,000 hours may be a more realistic average life span for diesels that are run hard continuously at close to their rated power.

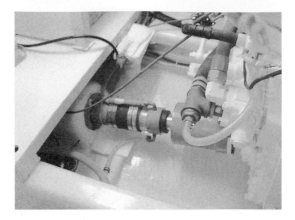

The dripless shaft seal on this Davis 58 keeps the salt content in the engine room to a minimum. Most modern yachts come with these dripless shaft seals, which lubricate the through-hull bearing supporting the shaft where it exits the hull.

MAN's new 550 hp in-line R6-550 weighs 1,980 pounds (3.6 lbs/hp).   MAN-MEC

Diesels may have a well-deserved reputation for lasting tens of thousands of hours in certain commercial applications, but on yachts and other pleasure craft they are often used infrequently. In yachts they may also be run at slow speeds under minimal loading for many hours, then run hard before being shut down for days on end. This sort of operation shortens the engine's life to an amazing degree (to as little as 1,000 hours on poorly maintained, infrequently or lightly used diesels) since diesels like to be run moderately hard and often.

Diesels are inherently more reliable than gas engines in part because they don't have electrical ignition systems, relying on compression rather than spark plugs to initiate combustion. But diesels are especially susceptible to being shut down by dirty fuel, largely because the clearances in their injectors are so small. Also, they can't tolerate water in the fuel as well as gas engines. So, high-quality, high-capacity fuel filter-separators are essential. A dual filter, with two units lined up in parallel, allows the engine to keep running while filters are shifted "on the fly."

A modern, high-speed, turbocharged, intercooled diesel can operate at as much as 90 percent of its rated rpm all day long, while a gas engine may wear out prematurely and burn lots of fuel in the process if run above 65 to 70 percent of its rated speed. Power potential is determined in part by how much fuel and air you can pump into a diesel. A turbocharger uses the engine's exhaust gases to drive a turbine that increases the amount of air

This dual Racor diesel fuel filter-separator has shift-on-the-fly capability, so an engine never has to be shut down to clean a filter. RACOR

forced into the cylinders. A supercharger does the same thing, but it's mechanically driven by the engine, so there's less lag time before you get a boost when the throttle is advanced, and the supercharger also increases fuel consumption since it becomes an added engine load. Some diesels have a turbocharger as well as a supercharger that only comes on in the mid rpm range when the extra boost is needed. An intercooler uses the engine cooling water to also cool the air being injected into the cylinders, and since cooler air is denser (i.e., more oxygen in the same volume of air delivered), the engine can develop more power.

When you put it all together, a 200 hp diesel will likely cruise your boat as fast as a 300 hp gas engine (since their continuous power ratings are similar), last a lot longer, and burn around 40 percent less fuel in the process. In any event, what's most important in any discussion of engine power is continuous horsepower output at the propeller.

Cooling system maintenance is crucial to any engine, especially diesels that are turbocharged,

How Slow Can It Go?

Whichever power plant is selected for a cruising boat, it's important that continuous engine loading and long-range cruise speed are considered. If a semidisplacement trawler capable of a 14-knot cruise is throttled back to produce an ocean-crossing, 6-knot cruise speed, it may be operating at 20 to 25 percent of its capacity, which will eventually result in damage to the engine. A better arrangement is to have smaller twin engines driving controllable pitch propellers, or perhaps two engines driving a single shaft with a controllable pitch propeller, so that the engine in use can be sufficiently loaded. For large yachts, an electric propulsion system offers several advantages: between two and four diesel generators can be used to drive two electric propulsion motors while at the same time providing the ship's electrical power. More generators can be fired up, depending on the ship's speed and the electrical demand for house services. An electrical power management system is necessary to provide overall monitoring and control.

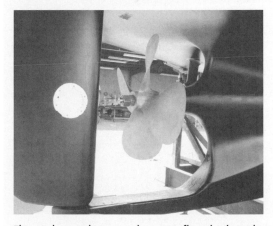

This trawler prop has a nice clean waterflow, thanks to the careful fairing in the aft end of the full keel. No chance this prop would be harmed in a grounding. NORDHAVN

aftercooled, or intercooled. In fact, cooling problems are directly responsible for many a premature engine overhaul. The complex wet cooling systems for modern diesels have to be kept working efficiently for adequate heat transfer, or you can kiss long engine life good-bye. Installing a temperature sensor with an alarm in the rubber exhaust line between the engine and the muffler is a good idea. That's because running the engine dry due to loss of coolant can quickly soften and melt the exhaust hose, and an exhaust fire and bilge flooding (if the exhaust outlet is partially below the waterline) could result.

An increasing number of diesel manufacturers offer electronically controlled (EC) and monitored engines. An EC diesel is designed to reduce emissions, though fuel economy may not improve in the process. They tend to run smoother, produce more power, and smoke less on cold startup and during normal operation. In fact, horsepower output can be controlled by tweaking the electronics, allowing diesel manufacturers to increase power output on newer engine models a little at a time once an engine has proven its durability at lower settings.

Volvo's advanced D11 670 hp diesel is controlled and monitored by its Electronic Vessel Control (EVC) system, based on plug-and-play CANBUS technology. Made of compact graphite for lighter weight and greater strength, and used in the IPS 850 propulsion system, as well as for inclined-shaft applications, the D11 weighs 2,408 pounds (3.7 lbs/hp).   VOLVO PENTA

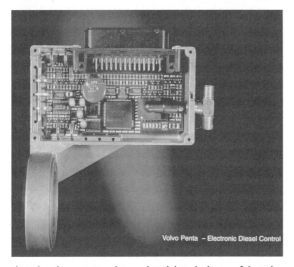

The Volvo Electronic Diesel Control Module is the brains of the Volvo propulsion system, which controls and monitors the engine.

VOLVO PENTA

The operating parameters of many EC diesels are recorded so the manufacturer can more readily troubleshoot, even via a computer modem. They can also tell if the operator has been running the engines at too high a power setting for too long, which has the ancillary effect of keeping owners from abusing their engines and voiding the warranty. Some electronically controlled diesels accelerate more quickly than their mechanically controlled stablemates, because their electronics are designed to limit smoke by regulating acceleration. EC diesels also depend on these sophisticated electronics to start and operate, adding yet another component with a potential for failure. Notwithstanding such drawbacks, however, EC diesels have many advantages and are clearly the wave of the future.

Many diesel (and gas) engines in recreational boats corrode internally before they wear out. This is especially true in the absence of freshwater cooling. A ten-year-old oceangoing boat's gas engine with 400 hours of running time may be near the end of its service life, whereas a gas engine that's used every day in commercial or charter service might easily run 1,200 hours or more.

Gas versus Diesel

Since diesels are preferred on most boats over 35 feet, the real sales contest is for boats in the 28- to 40-foot range. Both gas and diesel engines will get the job done, but each has specific advantages over the other.

When you consider that many people operate their boats between 50 and 150 hours each season, gas engines often make sense due to their lower initial cost. They won't last as long and they're less efficient, but you may be able to buy two or three gas engines in succession for the price of a single diesel. Gas engines also tend to fare better when standing unused for long periods of time. While diesels are more reliable, electronic fuel injection in gas engines has closed that gap. And some owners still prefer carbureted gas engines because they're cheaper and simpler to work on.

A gasoline inboard can't match a diesel for continuous cruise speeds. An inboard gas cruiser that makes 37 knots wide open (4,400 to 4,800 rpm) would cruise at around 24 knots at 3,000 to 3,200 rpm, while a 37-knot diesel-powered boat mighty cruise at 30 to 32 knots. The diesel can cruise at a higher percentage of its maximum rpm and deliver a lot more torque while doing so.

Yanmar's 6SY 720 hp, 11.7-liter, in-line 6SY engine weighs 2,536 pounds (3.52 lbs/hp). A 900 hp, 15.6-liter, V-8 Yanmar diesel weighs 3,650 pounds (4.05 lbs/hp).   YANMAR

Gas engines are a reasonable choice for boats that are used under 200 hours annually or that usually make short trips of an hour or less. Diesels win out when maximum range is needed, since they burn at least 40 percent less fuel for a given power output. Engines that develop high torque at lower rpm

(diesels) are better suited to heavier displacement and planing hulls, since they can develop enough power at intermediate speed settings to deliver good midrange performance. But, as mentioned, diesels not only cost more to buy, they cost much more to service, especially if an overhaul is needed.

Bear in mind that the greater the horsepower rating from a given displacement, the less time it will run between overhauls, and this goes for diesel as well as gas engines.

Inboard Cooling Systems

Inboard engines have either wet or dry exhausts and are almost always water- rather than air-cooled. A wet exhaust system discharges a mixture of cooling water and exhaust gases through a common muffler and horizontal hose that exits at or near the transom or though the bottom in case of an underwater exhaust. A dry exhaust system pumps the water over the side and discharges the hot exhaust gases through a muffler and out a vertical metal pipe high in the rigging.

A raw-water cooling system pipes water from outside the hull, usually through an internal filter, then the water pump, the engine block cooling passages, and back overboard. For a boat operating on the ocean, this means that the engine itself is constantly in contact with corrosive salt water. Any engine operating in salt water will last longer if it is freshwater cooled. In a freshwater-cooled inboard engine, the cooling water treated with antifreeze circulates through the engine block from an engine-mounted expansion tank and heat exchanger in a closed loop. This fresh water is in turn cooled by seawater pumped through the heat exchanger via a through-hull fitting and a strainer, then discharged overboard through the exhaust system. Because the seawater never comes in contact with the engine itself, a freshwater-cooled engine lasts longer. If you operate in salt water, don't be stingy when it comes to selecting freshwater cooling as an option.

Some gas engines come with 170°F thermostats when freshwater-cooled and 143°F thermostats if raw-water cooled. The lower setting minimizes scaling for boats used in salt water. Manufacturers of these engines recommend that owners using their boats exclusively in fresh water choose the 170°F unit even for a raw-water-cooled engine, since their gas engines run more efficiently at the higher temperature. They also recommend running their engines at 75 percent of maximum rpm, so an engine that turns up 4,400 rpm wide open can be cruised as high as 3,300 rpm continuously.

Seawater used to cool the engine combines with the engine exhaust at the exhaust riser before the hot gases reach the muffler and rubber exhaust hose. Without the seawater, the exhaust gases would quickly melt the rubber hose, so it's important to ensure a continuous stream of water all the way through the system. If cooling waterflow is lost, you can usually tell right away by the sound of the exhaust, which changes pitch and becomes throaty as it exits the transom.

A wet exhaust usually exits the hull aft and above the waterline, but underwater exhausts are not uncommon. These usually include a relief valve to vent the exhaust to the atmosphere should excessive back pressure threaten to harm the engine. When the boat is moving at speed, a venturi plate just forward of the exhaust outlet reduces the pressure at the outlet to below atmospheric pressure, helping to draw the exhaust out and greatly reducing engine back pressure. Underwater exhausts can be very quiet and generally do a good job of burying fumes below the surface long enough for the boat to pass them by. But the hot gases can damage a fiberglass hull under extreme conditions, and the exhausts must be located in such a way that they don't aerate and ventilate the props and rudders.

Although the cooling systems described above are inside the hull, slow vessels commonly employ an externally mounted heat exchanger—the so-called keel-cooler. This is nothing more than a series of pipes mounted on the outside of the hull, through which the engine's fresh cooling water circulates. Seawater passes around the pipes, cooling the water inside. Naturally, the system works better (with the improved heat transfer) when the boat is

moving, and the tubes must be kept clean inside and out for efficient cooling. Keel cooling adds drag, but it's negligible at displacement speeds. The system is simpler, since only one circulating pump—the one for the fresh water—is needed. Keel cooling systems are paired with dry exhaust systems, since there's no seawater to pipe through a wet exhaust hose.

Dry exhaust systems are popular with commercial vessels and some trawler yachts. Some commercial builders consider them safer than wet exhausts, since the exhaust gases only come into contact with metal pipes, not rubber hoses. Exhaust fumes are piped out a metal pipe (sometimes incorporated inside or attached to the mast) and into the atmosphere high above deck, while the cooling water is piped directly overboard. This minimizes or eliminates exhaust fumes and engine noise in the cockpit. Nothing's perfect, though; dry exhaust system piping also gets very hot, takes up interior space, and can interfere with accommodations above the engine room. These systems must be carefully designed, shielded from combustibles, and made of durable materials to prevent fire.

As with freshwater cooling, this is not a place to cut costs. When an exhaust manifold and risers fail due to corrosion, water can get into the cylinders, ruining an engine. If you end up with one of the manifolds leaking after a few years of use, replace them both, since the other won't be far behind.

Inboard Drivetrains

A conventional inboard drivetrain consists of an engine under the deck or engine box, a reduction or reversing gear to slow the prop down and allow it to operate in reverse, a propeller shaft and struts to support it, the propeller, and a rudder. The engine is fastened to mounts, which are usually soft or flexible to absorb vibration and are in turn bolted to rigid engine beds. This combination of soft mounts and rigid engine beds (themselves usually part of the hull's stringer system) works well to attenuate vibrations.

Whatever the power source, the propeller shaft angle should be no more than 12 degrees from horizontal, and less is better. The higher the angle of thrust, the less efficient the propeller becomes, especially as boat speed increases. A shaft angle of 13 to 14 degrees is not much concern to a boat that cruises below about 18 knots, but any boat capable of cruising above 30 knots wants a shaft angle below 12 degrees, and 8 to 10 degrees is needed for a 40-knot vessel.

Finally, consider that a 14-degree shaft angle, when combined with a hull trim angle of 8 degrees, will result in a propeller spinning through the water offset from the horizontal by 22 degrees! The result will be an inefficient drivetrain, to say the least, and excessive propeller vibration.

Drivetrains come in two main varieties: in-line drives and V-drives, with the former being the more common. In an in-line drivetrain, the engine, reduction gear, and propeller shaft are laid out in a straight line often spanning half the boat length. A V-drive greatly reduces this length requirement by turning the engine 180 degrees and putting the reduction gear at its forward end. The propeller shaft then runs back under the engine and out through the shaft seal. For hulls with sufficient buoyancy and lift in the stern to support the weight of the engine,

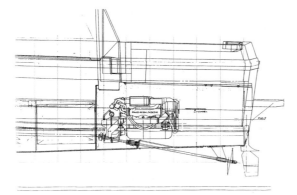

A typical V-drive installation, in this case in a planing catamaran designed by John Kiley. With the shaft exiting the other end of the engine, as in an in-line configuration, the engine would have to be moved forward an engine length. Of course, that's the whole idea behind the V-drive, which opens up room forward for accommodations or fuel. JOHN KILEY

the V-drive is a good way to make room for larger accommodations amidships, while still maintaining an acceptable prop shaft angle.

An argument against V-drives used to be that they were less efficient at transmitting engine power to the propeller shaft. However, modern designs have virtually eliminated this difference. Both transmissions operate at about 97 percent efficiency, which is largely a function of the number of pinions in the reduction gear.

Since the propeller shaft is usually at an angle of 8 or more degrees, a down-angle reduction gear is used in an in-line drivetrain to allow the engine to be mounted level, or close to it. The input shaft from the engine to the gear is horizontal—on a plane with the engine—while the output shaft, which bolts to the propeller shaft, angles down from 7 to as much as 10 degrees on larger engines. A horizontal engine has a lower profile and allows the deck above to be mounted lower. Gears with vertical and horizontal offsets are also available for special applications such as catamarans and quadruple-engine installations.

Most modern powerboats employ reduction gears to reduce the rpm of the propeller below the rpm of the engine. That's because a prop that turns as fast as the engine would have to be so small that it would be inefficient and produce very little thrust. A gear ratio of 1.5:1, in which 1,500 rpm from the engine delivers 1,000 rpm to the prop shaft, is considered "shallow." A ratio of 3:1, in which 1,500 rpm from the engine delivers 500 rpm to the shaft, is considered "deep," at least by small pleasure craft standards. In most cases, deep reduction gears and large, slow-turning propellers are preferable. Gear ratios up to 2.5:1 are commonly available with gasoline engines and smaller diesel engines, but builders usually select shallower gears, at least in part because engines with shallow reduction gears use smaller (and cheaper) props and shafts. In fact, the majority of pleasure boats on the market today would perform better with deeper gears and slower-turning propellers, especially when running fully loaded at cruising speed, and dockside engine responsiveness would be greatly improved.

Reduction gears come in three basic flavors: direct-mounted in-line or straight drive, direct-mounted V-drive, and remote V-drive. Direct-mounted means the gears are bolted directly to the back of the engine. Direct-mounted in-line drives are the most common, and they take up the most room since the shaft is attached to the gear at the aft end of the engine. Direct-mounted V-drives have the gear mounted at the same point on the engine, but the engine is turned 180 degrees, placing the gear forward as described above.

The third configuration, which offers significant advantages (and added cost and complexity), is the remote-mounted V-drive. The engine faces forward as in the direct-mounted V-drive, but the transmission is mounted several feet forward of the engine on its own foundation. A jackshaft connects the engine to the top of the remote gear, and the propeller shaft runs aft under the engine from the bottom of the gear. This allows the gear to absorb the propeller thrust, so the engine can be soft-mounted on its bed, reducing vibration. Placing the gear well forward also helps ensure a moderate shaft angle. Remote-mounted gears are identical internally to an engine-mounted gear, so they create the same 3 percent or so loss in propulsion efficiency.

The running gear of a conventional inboard-powered boat turning a submerged propeller adds significant hydrodynamic drag. In planing craft, more than 20 percent of the total hull resistance can be caused by these underwater appendages, and in vessels that cruise at over 60 knots, submerged appendage drag can be nearly as high as the drag from the entire hull. In addition, conventional underwater gear limits the size of the propeller: a clearance of 8 to 20 percent of the propeller's diameter is generally needed between the tips of the propeller blades and the bottom of the boat.

Propellers

The propellers familiar to most of us operate completely submerged in the water and are driven by outboards, stern drives, and conventional inboards.

Most boats in the 30- to 60-foot range use four-blade props, which deliver a good mix of performance and cost. Five-blade wheels are often used when vibrations need to be minimized or when there are prop tip clearance or draft constraints. In fact, five-blade propellers are usually used by larger yachts since they deliver an excellent combination of performance and low vibrations for high-horsepower, high-speed vessels.

Some boatbuilders, notably Hatteras, specify seven- or even eight-blade propellers, which actually improve efficiency by a few percentage points and also reduce vibrations. While there are certainly exceptions, a three-blade prop will deliver a higher top-end speed than a four-blade, but the latter will run smoother, perform better in the midrange, and accelerate more quickly thanks to its greater blade surface area.

The idea behind any well-designed propulsion system is to accelerate as much water as possible while keeping the speed increase (in relation to the surrounding water), or slip, as low as practical. That's why a relatively large, slow-turning propeller is more efficient than a small, fast-spinning one; it

Michigan Wheel's four-blade EQY propeller is used on many production inboards in the 30- to 60-foot range, providing both lower cost and high performance. MICHIGAN PROPELLER

Michigan Wheel's five-blade CY-5 is smoother running and more expensive than a four-blade prop. It is commonly used on 30- to 60-foot production yachts that cruise in the 25- to 30-knot range.
MICHIGAN PROPELLER

moves a greater volume of water at a lower velocity with less slip.

Prop Terms

Propellers are identified and classified by several characteristics, one of which is their rotation. Viewed from astern, a right-handed propeller turns clockwise when going forward; a left-handed prop turns counterclockwise.

Diameter is the overall dimension of the propeller from tip to tip. For a given vessel speed and available thrust, the bigger and slower-turning the propeller, the greater its efficiency.

Pitch, measured on the pressure face of the propeller, is the distance the propeller would travel, with no slip, through the water in a 360-degree rotation. Think of turning a wood screw a full turn; the distance it sinks into the wood is the pitch. In the real world, propellers slip from 10 to 20 percent or more due to the boat's drag and resistance.

Slip is simply the difference between the distance the boat actually advances through the water

with one propeller revolution, and the propeller's actual pitch; a propeller with 30 inches of pitch that moves a boat 24 inches forward with one revolution has a 20 percent slip.

A propeller will usually be stamped with its diameter and pitch on the hub. For example, a "26 × 28" prop has a diameter of 26 inches and a pitch of 28 inches. In a *square* propeller, the diameter equals the pitch—say 30 by 30. An *over-square* prop has more pitch than diameter, and is usually found on high-speed boats. A tugboat or displacement trawler prop would tend to have significantly more diameter than pitch.

Inboard propellers can be either fixed or controllable pitch. A *fixed* pitch prop is cast or machined from a single block of metal, and the blades are fixed relative to the hub and each other. A *controllable pitch* propeller (CPP) has articulated blades that are able to rotate on their hub, so pitch can be varied depending on the vessel's speed and engine load. Because CPPs have moving parts, they're more expensive, and they need larger hubs to accommodate the internal actuating gears; they are therefore less hydrodynamically efficient than fixed-pitch props. The propeller shaft must also be hollow to accommodate the pitch actuating linkage between engine room and propeller. CPPs work very well on vessels that have multiple engines driving the same shaft and on vessels, such as tugs, that have widely varying loads.

On some vessels, anywhere from one to four engines can drive the same propeller shaft fitted with a CPP, while that would be impossible with a fixed prop. Even on a single-engine application, more horsepower can be drawn out of the engine at mid-rpm settings just by varying (increasing) the CPP pitch. So, even though the CPP itself is less hydrodynamically efficient than a fixed propeller, this is more than offset by being able to optimize the efficiency of the engine(s).

A *highly loaded* prop has a great deal of pressure on each square inch of propeller blade. When a lot of power is delivered to a relatively small propeller, high *blade loading* results. Increasing the propeller size for a given horsepower lowers the blade loading and decreases cavitation, as we'll see below.

A propeller's *developed area ratio*, or DAR (also known as its *expanded area ratio*, or EAR), is the ratio between the total area of its blades when flattened out and a solid disk of the same diameter. A DAR of 0.7 means the area of the flattened blades would be 70 percent of the total disk area, as is common for a high-speed, highly loaded propeller. A tug or displacement fishing boat might have a DAR of 0.55. The higher the DAR for a given prop diameter, the less blade loading per horsepower, since there's more blade area to absorb the thrust. Thus, when propeller diameter is restricted by hull clearances, a prop with a higher DAR will deliver more horsepower before it cavitates.

Rake is the angle in degrees that propeller blades slant forward or aft relative to the hub. Props with more aft rake are often used in high-speed applications, in part because they tend to entrain water more effectively and therefore offer better resistance to ventilation when in a hard, high-speed turn or with the lower unit trimmed up. Especially with four- and five-blade props, aft rake tends to produce more downward force, raising the bow, which can further improve high-speed performance. Forward-raked props tend to produce more

backing power, and are more suited to heavier, slower applications.

A propeller's *bore* is the diameter of the tapered hole in the middle of the hub. The hole is tapered to match the taper at the shaft end, so that more force just drives the prop on tighter. A slot in the shaft lines up with a slot in the propeller hub, and a key is inserted in the aligned slots to prevent the prop from rotating independently of the shaft. Two nuts tightened on the shaft end hold the prop in place, and a cotter key is used to fix the second nut. Propellers are available in different classes. Class 1 is more precisely made than class 4. All else being equal, a class 1 prop will run smoother and more efficiently.

Ventilation and Cavitation

These are two often-misapplied terms that are actually quite simple to explain. *Ventilation* occurs when surface air is drawn in to the propeller, as in a sharp turn or with an outboard that is mounted or trimmed too high. It can also happen when spray strakes direct air into the propeller. The propeller loses its bite, and engine rpm shoots up very quickly. A high-speed boat can also ventilate its prop when jumping out of the water from wave to wave, and the rudder can ventilate if it is mounted too close to the transom.

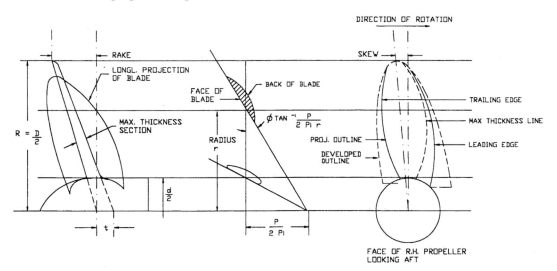

Propeller terminology.

TEIGNBRIDGE

A propeller *cavitates* when it is highly loaded. The suction (forward) side of the propeller blade is under very low pressure, and water vaporizes in this low-pressure region adjacent to the blade surface. The water is able to boil and vaporize at the relatively low temperature of the surrounding water because a liquid's boiling point decreases with atmospheric pressure. As the propeller cavitates, tiny steam bubbles are formed and then collapse upon reaching the higher-pressure region at the tips of the blades. These bubbles actually collapse in contact with the surface of the propeller, a little like a million tiny jackhammers banging away and gradually eroding the propeller. Excessive cavitation can also cause higher vibration levels and a loss of speed and efficiency. Some thrust is lost by moderate cavitation, but this is actually compensated for by the diminished power needed to turn the propeller spinning in a gas rather than a liquid.

Prop Materials

Most inboard propellers are made of bronze or a strong alloy such as nibral (*ni*ckel-*br*onze-*al*uminum) that's tough enough to hold its shape after absorbing tremendous water pressure but easy enough to manufacturer and repair so it's affordable. A bronze or nibral prop falls between aluminum and stainless steel in both cost and strength. Some very-high-performance propellers are made of stainless steel, but these are expensive and more difficult to repair.

Outboard and stern-drive propellers are commonly made of aluminum, stainless steel, or composites. Aluminum props are cheaper and lighter, and generally don't perform quite as well as stainless steel. But they also break and deform much more readily, reducing the chances of impact damage to the lower unit if you hit a rock. A stainless steel prop offers excellent performance because the blades are thinner yet remain stiff, deforming less under load than aluminum. Stainless also costs the most and is apt to cause damage to the lower unit gears upon impact. On the other hand, a stainless prop stands up much better to abrasion from contact with sand and pebbles.

Composite propellers for outboards and stern drives are usually made of fiber-reinforced plastic (FRP) or another synthetic material. Like aluminum props, they are cheaper and more forgiving on impact than stainless props. I've tested composite propellers made by Piranha Propellers and found that they offer distinct advantages over both stainless steel and aluminum. They performed nearly as well as a stainless prop and better than an aluminum prop on my 22-foot Grady-White powered by a 225 hp Yamaha. Each composite blade is detachable from the aluminum hub, so if you damage one it can easily (and cheaply, at about $25 per blade) be replaced. The blades are made of a composite fiberglass-nylon material called Verton that the manufacturer says has a tensile strength 10 to 15 percent greater than aluminum, and each blade comes from the same mold, helping to ensure that they're the exact same dimensions and shape to minimize vibration when running. I wouldn't hesitate to use one of these composite props on a stern drive or outboard.

Piranha's synthetic propeller blades are cheap and easy to replace one by one. In the author's experience, they perform at least as well as aluminum props and about as well as stainless steel.

PIRANHA PROPELLER

Side Forces

Propellers generate side force as well as thrust. That's because the blades get more bite, or meet more resistance, in the higher-pressure water at the bottom of their arc and because of the corkscrew effect caused by the angle of the blades as they rotate through the water; this refers to the tendency of the prop, free of its shaft, to follow the path of least resistance in the direction of its blade surface. A right-handed propeller going forward will want to pull the stern of the boat to starboard, giving the boat a slight tendency to veer to port. The same propeller will pull to port in reverse. This walking effect is why an outboard or a stern drive with a single prop will turn more easily (with manual steering) one way than the other; the propeller tends to pull the lower unit to one side or the other depending on its direction of rotation. A single-screw inboard with a right-handed prop will turn sharper to port when running ahead and will also back to port more readily for the same reason.

Side forces are canceled out in twin-screw boats with the props rotating in opposite directions and also with counterrotating props on a single shaft. On twin-engine boats with two propellers, the props nearly always turn in an outboard direction, with a left-handed prop to port and a right-handed prop to starboard. The combined walking effects of the twin props, when they're running opposed (both turning in the same direction of rotation) with one engine ahead and the other astern, increase the turning ability of a twin-screw boat, turning the vessel in its own length.

Since for every action there's a equal and opposite reaction, when a single-screw inboard's propeller rotates through the water, it transmits its torque to the hull, which tends to rotate in the opposite direction. That's why at high speed, some single-engine boats will heel to one side in the absence of a weight shift or wind and wave force. If the prop rotates to the right, the boat will tend to rotate (or heel) to the left, or port. This effect is more pronounced with larger propellers that develop more torque. In a twin-screw installation, the torque is canceled out.

With counterrotating propellers, two props are mounted on a single shaft, one directly behind the other, and they rotate in opposite directions to cancel out side forces. Counterrotating props also improve the efficiency of the engine by taking the twist out of its discharge race. They are used on single-engine stern drives from MerCruiser (Bravo 3) , Volvo (DuoProp), and on the new Zeus and IPS pod drives.

Propeller Efficiency

In all but very-high-performance boats, larger, slower-turning propellers are more efficient, faster, and more responsive than small, fast-turning props. Still, many builders use smaller props and run them faster to save weight, reduce draft, or just cut costs. Get the largest gear ratio and biggest propeller you can fit. Blade tip speed should be kept to a maximum of 150 feet per second to avoid blade tip cavitation. To find blade tip speed, multiply your propeller diameter (in inches) by pi (3.1416), divide by 12, multiply by shaft rpm at full throttle, and divide by 60.

The relationship between diameter and pitch is worth mentioning, too. In the average propeller, an inch of diameter will absorb about as much engine power and torque as 2 inches of pitch. For example, if your engine is under-revving at full throttle by 200 rpm, decreasing pitch by 2 inches would have about the same effect as shaving off an inch of diameter. Blades can also be *cupped* at their trailing (aft) edge, which increases the engine's load and therefore the boat's speed by increasing the velocity

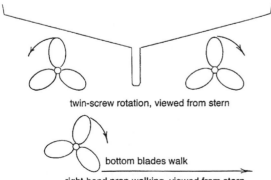

twin-screw rotation, viewed from stern

bottom blades walk

right-hand prop walking, viewed from stern

Here's how most twin-screw boats are set up. Outboard-turning props twist the boat more effectively. GERR, *PROPELLER HANDBOOK*

of the waterflow off the blade tip. Adding cup to a propeller is often a good way to improve performance without changing to a larger prop, assuming the engine has enough power to turn it.

Propeller Pockets

Propeller pockets are a poorly understood and sometimes poorly designed feature of modern inboard planing boats. Proper pocket design is critical to boat performance and handling but is often overlooked or misunderstood by both builder and owner.

Prop pockets should not be confused with propeller tunnels, which are deep recesses in the hull that more or less enclose a propeller, like on the old Penn Yan tunnel drives. A prop pocket, depending on the boat, might be a quarter to a third of the propeller diameter in depth. Properly shaped and matched to the propellers, prop pockets increase thrust, reduce propeller shaft angles, decrease draft, and allow engine placement farther aft. They can even increase propulsive efficiency, since a pocket will accommodate a larger, more efficient propeller even while permitting a reduction in draft.

In contrast, poorly designed prop pockets will decrease propulsive efficiency, detract from handling, increase vibration and, because they reduce buoyancy and dynamic lift, cause a boat to run with an excessive bow-high attitude.

The pad at the base of this Tiara's shaft strut is nicely contoured to match the propeller pocket radius, and it's flush with the hull to minimize drag and waterflow disturbance around the prop.

The differences between efficient and inefficient propeller pockets are functions of their shape, volume, and dimensions. A prop pocket has to be long enough to provide a smooth transition for water flowing into its forward end at high speed, but not so long as to compromise dynamic lift and buoyancy. The pocket's cross-sectional shape is also crucial to good performance, and should be properly radiused to conform to the arc of the blade tips. When pockets are properly shaped with the same radius as the prop, prop tip clearance requirements are reduced dramatically—in theory to zero, but in practice to just a few percent of the propeller diameter—allowing larger, more efficient propellers to be used while still decreasing overall draft.

This minimal clearance contrasts favorably with a pocketless design, which requires a 15 to 20 percent clearance between the tip of the blade at the top of its swing and the flat hull bottom above it. Without such clearance, vibration levels would be unacceptable. Put another way, propellers run smoother in a radiused pocket since the blades operate in a smoother, more even waterflow, and localized areas of high pressure (caused by flat bottom sections above the prop) are largely eliminated. Since propeller pockets reduce shaft angles, propulsion thrust is closer to horizontal and more efficient. And with the propeller closer to the hull bottom and the shaft exiting the hull at the forward end of the pocket, both the shaft and its supporting strut(s) can be shorter, reducing appendage weight and drag.

The tight blade tip clearances of a good pocket also reduces *tip loss*, which is the lost thrust of water flowing centrifugally outward rather than aft off a propeller. By focusing the discharge race aft, a pocket increases forward thrust and efficiency.

A planing hull with propeller pockets is a tricky thing to design properly. As we saw in chapter 4, planing boats have flat buttock lines aft and therefore run most efficiently at a trim angle of 2 degrees (for a warped-bottom design) to 5 degrees (for a constant-deadrise, deep-V design). The problem is that deep prop pockets detract from dynamic lift aft by forcing a large volume of water to flow up into the pocket rather than aft undisturbed along the flat buttocks. The resultant loss of dynamic lift causes the stern to squat and the bow to rise, increasing fuel consumption for a given speed or power setting.

Some boatbuilders produce prop pockets that are ill shaped for their purpose. Take a peek under the bottoms of some of these boats and you'll see propeller pockets that are excessively deep relative to the propeller diameter, with nearly vertical sides and flat tops. These deep slab-sided cross sections can detract from performance and handling, and their shape and excessive volume decrease buoyancy at rest and dynamic lift at planing speeds.

This frequently results in a boat that will "aim for the sky" when coming up on plane, and once over the hump will ride with an excessively bow-up attitude. The operator of such a boat will lose sight of the horizon at least some of the time, and may have to stand up to see over the bow even when trim tabs are lowered. Large pockets also add significantly to wetted surface, further increasing drag. Builders can decrease trim angle by reducing the "exit region" area of the tunnel aft of the propeller, thus accelerating the discharge race and deflecting it downward, but this too can be taken to extremes and will cause a dynamic instability with excessive bow-down attitude if carried too far.

The tops of deep prop pockets come closer to the waterline, and this too can be a problem. In extreme cases, backing down will introduce air into the pocket, and the resultant ventilation can cause the propeller and rudder to lose their bite.

Some of us have been on cruisers that responded bizarrely to steering and engine commands. Just fire up one of these shiny new propeller pocket–impaired beauties and head down the middle of the basin. When you back the starboard engine at idle, the bow falls off to port. Or, idling along with both engines in gear, put the rudders over full to port and observe as nothing discernible happens. Finally, throttle up and watch the boat head for the stars as the stern stalls underfoot as it struggles up on plane. The problem isn't with the

engines; it's in the way the engine power is transmitted to the water via gear ratio, propeller size, and prop pocket design.

So, to sum up, when prop pockets are reasonably shallow (no more than 40 percent of the propeller diameter) and radiused in cross section, and engines are mated to steeper gear ratios and larger propellers, we consistently see improved throttle and clutch responsiveness. Additional benefits include increased propulsion efficiency, faster cruising speeds, faster time to plane, lower vibration levels, less loss of buoyancy and dynamic lift aft, and better operator visibility. Steering is also improved without the excessive directional stability imparted by slab-sided prop pockets fighting the rudder's effort to turn the boat.

Waterjets

The popularity of waterjets in the boating industry was once driven at least in part by their sheer novelty, but they have since gained acceptance based on merit. Waterjets can be now be found on small craft such as personal watercraft (PWC), and also on larger vessels for which shallow draft, immunity from floating objects like lobster pot buoys, high-cruising speed, swimmer safety, and maneuverability are prime considerations. Waterjets draw water in through an inlet grate in the hull, accelerate it by means of an impeller, and shoot it out the transom in a small, high-velocity stream through a steerable nozzle. The nozzle is fitted with a reversing bucket—the deflector—that drops down and deflects water forward to stop or reverse the boat. This backing capability allows a waterjet-powered boat to stop quickly, since the engine need not be slowed and shifted into reverse. Waterjet-powered boats can be handled easily by setting the throttles and then using the steering and buckets to maneuver, providing essentially infinite thrust adjustment (unlike an inboard where you have a choice of either in or out of gear). Triple- or quadruple-engine waterjets usually eliminate the steering nozzles and reversing buckets on the inboard engines.

Because water is drawn up and into the waterjet housing, and the thrust is high relative to the vessel's center of gravity, the hull tends to run at a lower trim angle than with a conventional submerged propeller. This should be factored into the hull's design and weight distribution. Waterjets also take a lot of room (space is needed for both the engine and the waterjet) and hold a lot of entrained water, adding weight to the boat.

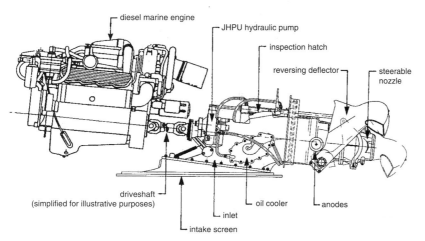

The components of a Hamilton waterjet.

HAMILTONJET

A waterjet impeller pulls less power from the engine than an inboard propeller at midrange throttle settings. For example, an UltraJet 376, rated at 700 hp at 2,200 rpm, would run at 1,920 rpm to absorb the same hp (470) as an inboard running at 1,850 rpm. The waterjet will get the same efficiency (miles per gallon) as the slower-turning inboard, but it will need to run 50 to 75 rpm faster than an inboard to produce the same thrust and hull speed. While an impeller's discharge velocity can be twice the vessel's speed through the water, a conventional inboard propeller moves the water just 10 to 20 percent faster than the hull is moving (this difference equates to the propeller's *slip*), but it moves a much larger *column* of water, too, and that's how it gets its midrange thrust or "traction."

While the *diameter* of both the waterjet impeller and the propeller are based on vessel displacement, *pitch* selection is different; impeller pitch is matched solely to engine power, while a propeller's pitch is selected according to hull speed (to control slip and to allow the engine to make its rated rpm).

A propeller also has to work harder due to its interaction with surrounding waterflow, which is at a different angle than the propeller shaft, subjecting the individual propeller blades to variable loading each time they swing though a revolution. But the waterjet impeller is enclosed in a pipe-like tunnel and receives an even flow of water, and working in a more benign environment—and since all of its discharge is also contained and directed aft rather than partially outward—it picks up more efficiencies. A waterjet's intake grate creates drag, but it's nothing like the inboard, which is dragging its running gear—struts, shafts, props, and rudders—through the water, especially as speed increases above 30 knots.

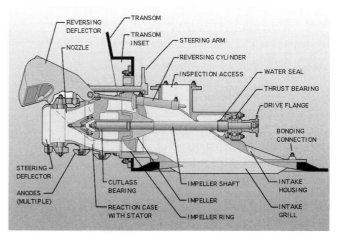

The UltraJet 305 waterjet, showing the location of the intake grill and the deflector buckets.

ULTRAJET

Matching Waterjet to Mission

Waterjets took a bum rap early on—through no fault of the product—when they were sold by vendors anxious to make a sale with the least expensive unit. This resulted in units that performed poorly, especially at lower power settings. What everyone learned is how important it is to match the waterjet to its usage. Whether it's a high-speed rescue boat or a heavier work boat, if the supplier knows how the boat is to be used, an appropriate unit can be optimized for the vessel's power-to-weight, speed range, sea conditions, displacement variation, and overall mission. There is a wide range of waterjets. Waterjets with low-volume, high-velocity impellers work well in high-speed, light-displacement vessels, but are relatively inefficient below 25 knots. On the other hand, waterjets that produce greater water volume (that's what produces low-end thrust) and lower velocity work well for heavier, slower boats operating at as low as 70 percent to 80 percent power, but are less efficient at high speeds.

If you're choosing between two waterjet models, the bigger of the two may well be the way to go just because of the midrange thrust issue; the biggest challenge for any marine propulsion system is getting the boat up on plane. That's because there is a lot of resistance (hull drag) while the boat is climbing over the hump and the engine is not yet at full power. In fact, if the propeller demand in an inboard exceeds the power the engine can develop while the boat is trying to get over the hump, it won't be able to plane. Making rpm is not a problem for the engine driving a waterjet impeller, but since the resistance for any boat getting up on plane remains high, it's easy to see why the waterjet's ability to achieve sufficient thrust in the midrange is so important. Another issue is the cavitation produced by a hull that's moving too slow for a too-small, high-turning impeller, and this in turn can cause erosion in the aluminum impeller housing and also in the impeller itself. The water moving through the intake grate and toward the impeller has to be moving fast enough in relation to the water being *discharged* from the impeller to prevent cavitation. And since many waterjets operate most efficiently at speeds above 25 knots, a boat must have enough continuous horsepower to *continuously cruise* at these speeds with a full load, painted bottom, canvas up, and when running into the wind. The point is to choose a waterjet that matches the power, hull, and mission of the boat, and undertake a sea trial with a full load to make sure the waterjet performs well at all speeds.

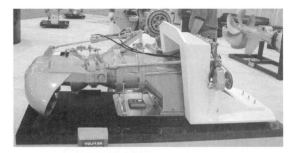

This Twin Disc waterjet is all shined up for presentation at a boat show. In clear view on top of the unit is the hydraulic cylinder used to control the backing bucket.

One of the great advantages of waterjets is that they don't have propellers or rudders projecting below the bottom of the hull so their draft is minimal. Vibration and noise levels are typically much lower than conventional inboards, too, with no propellers moving in choppy water flow. Plus, the engines don't absorb the impeller thrust (the thrust is transmitted via the intake housing to the hull), so they can be soft mounted and allowed to "dance" around freely.

Lacking propellers (or anything else) projecting outside the hull, a waterjet is the safest possible drivetrain, which is a big deal if your boat spends a lot of time around people swimming and diving. That's one of the reasons that jet-powered personal watercraft (PWC) are so popular: short of a direct hit by the hull of a PWC (which incidentally seems to happen often enough, which is not surprising considering that kids and more than a few idiots are driving these 60 to 70 mph, 800 lb missiles unsupervised) it's pretty hard to hurt someone with a one.

If a salesperson is taking you for a demo ride in a waterjet-powered boat, count on them showing off, doing donuts or maybe taking a spin

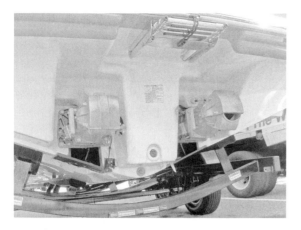
A Yamaha SX 230 waterjet runabout with the port reversing bucket lowered for reverse thrust and the starboard bucket partially lowered creating neutral thrust.

through the nearest string of lobster pots—and who can blame them. In fact that's what the venerable and otherwise grandfatherly Ted Hood used to do when sashaying off Newport, Rhode Island, in one of his gorgeous Little Harbor Whisperjets on a demo ride, as I seem to recall. The fact is, once you get the hang of it, it's hard not to show off when driving a twin waterjet. They're a kick to drive and, in the right hands, much more maneuverable than a twin-screw conventional inboard. And when they're integrated with a bow thruster and controllable by a single joystick, you can go in any direction you want around the dock. And waterjets are also easily maneuverable in a good stiff breeze, and for the same reason—there's so little underwater resistance.

Requirements for Waterjet Power

So why isn't every boat waterjet propelled? There are a number of reasons, including initial cost, hull form requirements, midrange performance, and rough-water capability. Waterjets are more expensive than inboards since relatively few are built each year, necessitating less automation and more labor during manufacture. (Some commercial operators are able to recoup the added expense within a relatively short period, however, due to lower operating costs.)

A waterjet needs a fairly deep-V hull, too, for a number of reasons. While an inboard has rudders with plenty of bite to control its heading, a waterjet relies a lot on the shape and weight distribution of its hull to run straight. It needs a buoyant entry—one that's not too deep and fine—to prevent the bow from digging in and steering the boat downsea. It also needs plenty of deadrise aft (at least 16 degrees, and 20 or 22 degrees is better) to keep it running straight (a deep-V creates more resistance to turning, acting like one long rudder, which is what makes it such a great downsea boat). Waterjets are also susceptible to fouling with weeds and plastic bags; sometimes back-flushing works, but if not cleanout ports are also provided in the waterjet housing near the impeller. On the other hand, you might have to go over the side to clear a line fouling a propeller that a waterjet would go right over, so each system has its advantages.

Some waterjet boatbuilders (e.g. Hinckley) even install hull fins aft to keep the stern from sliding out like a ski boat in a high-speed turn, which can aerate the impeller, causing it to stall, like slipping a clutch. On the other hand, turning in your own length at 35 knots in a 40-footer will really give your guests something to remember you by. It's also important to keep air from getting to the impellers, since air makes an impeller stall, and it's tough to control a boat absent thrust. This is another area where ample deadrise comes in, since a deep-V hull will encourage bow-generated bubbles to flow outward to the chines before they make it all the way back to the intakes. Hull strakes also have to be situated so they don't channel air to the intakes.

Waterjets must also be deeply enough submerged, at least to the centerline of the impeller shaft and preferably to the top of the tunnel (which is not always possible with twin waterjets in a deep-V hull) to keep them primed and to ensure a good, air-free bite on solid water in a chop. That's another reason a V-bottom planing hull with plenty of hull depth under the cockpit is a good waterjet design. The hull's buoyancy aft must also suffice to accommodate the added weight of waterjets (full of water) in the stern, and in some hulls this means shifting the engines a little farther forward to keep the boat from trimming too far by the stern and running bow high. All these requirements make some hulls poorly suited to waterjet propulsion; low-deadrise boats and traditional round-bilge semidisplacement hulls such as Maine-style lobster boats require modification to accommodate waterjet propulsion.

Sea State Limitations

Even with a good, deep-deadrise hull design, though, a waterjet has speed limitations in rough water, largely because of the constant-waterflow-to-the-impeller issue. It seems there's just no substitute for having propellers a couple of feet below the keel where there's (nearly always) plenty of the solid water needed for steady prop-generated thrust. On the other hand, waterjets are successfully being used in pilot boats routinely operating in rough water, so a combination of appropriate waterjets and hull form and not pushing the speed can produce good results. However, even with proper hull design and LCG (longitudinal center of gravity) a waterjet can be difficult to steer offshore running downsea for hours on end.

While no system is perfect, waterjet propulsion will be the closest thing for owners and applications placing a high premium on shoal draft, safety, maneuverability, smooth, quiet running, and boat-driving fun.

Surface-Piercing Propeller Drives

For cruising speeds above 40 knots, nothing beats a surface-piercing propeller. The faster it goes, the more efficient it becomes compared with other drives, since it creates so little drag. The surface drive (SD) concept goes back to the nineteenth century, but Howard Arneson is largely responsible for developing the idea into the best high-speed propulsion system, and one used by fast yachts and patrol boats around the world today. Surface drives are also the most expensive propulsion systems in use on recreational craft, in part because the specialized prop is so expensive.

With their low drag (only half of the prop is submerged, and there are no underwater shafts or struts) and high efficiency at high speeds, surface drives are an excellent choice for high-performance craft. Arneson drives are available from 290 to 2,400-plus diesel hp and to 10,000 jet turbine hp. TWIN DISC

With only half of the propeller submerged, the running gear and associated drag of a conventional inboard are eliminated. Some manufacturers and propulsion engineers claim that as much as a 50 percent reduction in drag is realized as a result. A surface-drive propeller can be much larger than a submerged propeller, since it's not buried below the hull, taking full advantage of a larger propeller's inherent efficiency. A deeper gear ratio and a larger, more lightly loaded, slower-turning propeller is the key to SD performance.

The thrust developed by a surface-piercing drive has both horizontal and vertical components. In fact, vertical lift from the spinning surface-piercing propeller is as much as 80 percent of the forward thrust. This huge vertical lift component raises the stern and contributes to the ease with which a SD-powered boat planes, the equivalent of a shift forward of longitudinal center of gravity (LCG). The vertical lift component is accentuated by the surface-piercing propeller's usual location 5 or 6 feet aft of the transom, creating a substantial lever arm. LCG should then be well aft, just 35 to 40 percent of waterline length forward of the transom, to help compensate for this significant dynamic lift at the propeller.

With this Sunseeker high-performance cruiser, the surface drives are incorporated into the hull overhang in the original design, a more satisfactory solution, perhaps, than bolting on an 8-foot swim platform.

Two pistons generally support the SD shaft and propeller; one controls side-to-side movement, and the other, vertical movement. The first is what allows the boat to be steered, while the second allows the height of the propeller—that is, its immersion depth—to be regulated. The deeper the propeller is in the water, the more thrust it produces. Consequently, the surface-piercing operator is effectively able to vary the diameter of the propeller and the load on the engine.

Since the engine can produce only so much power at a given rpm setting, propeller immersion is matched to the rpm setting, much like a controllable-pitch propeller. If the boat's trim or load changes, the propeller can be raised or lowered to compensate. When accelerating over the hump to get on plane, the propeller can be raised to decrease the load on the engine. This permits more rapid acceleration and eliminates the need for a two-speed transmission, a frequent requirement of submerged-propeller drives that are overloaded in their low to middle performance range.

Cavitation is a recurring problem in most high-speed applications with significant blade loading. If unchecked, it causes blade erosion, vibration, and loss of speed. The SD gets around this problem by using a super-ventilating propeller that introduces air bubbles into the low-pressure region on the leading (forward) edge of the blades where cavitation develops. Each time a blade slices down through the surface of the water, it takes along ventilating air bubbles with it that shroud the blade, cushioning the blade's surface and preventing the harmful effects of cavitation.

At low speeds, as with waterjets, surface-piercing drives steer less surely than conventional inboards. Backing can also be a problem, especially in some race boats that use highly raked cleaver props. A more rounded prop design takes a couple of knots off the top end, but time-to-plane, backing, and low-speed maneuverability improve.

The Twin Disc Arneson surface drive with (starting from the left) the transmission-reduction gear, short jackshaft with universal joint on either end (which makes alignment less exacting), the transom, and the exterior drive, which can be adjusted up and down to control thrust and engine loading, and from side-to-side for steering.

With the propellers churning partially out of the water 5 feet aft of the transom, safety is a definite concern. Stern projections or swim platforms cover the drives of most SD boats, helping to protect the boat's occupants as well as the propellers themselves.

Compared with conventional propellers, surface-piercing propellers endure far greater variation in blade loading as they rotate alternately through air and water. This generates high vibrations as well as creating higher stresses on drivetrain components and must be accounted for in the system's design. These propellers have high camber (curvature) and blade angle and essentially chop their way through the water, generating a reactive thrust from the pressure on the blades' trailing surfaces. (In comparison, a jet engine produces reactive thrust with its high-velocity gas discharge.)

Submerged propellers, on the other hand, have high- and low-pressure areas on the trailing and leading surfaces of their blades, respectively, that combine to provide thrust. Submerged propellers, in other words, act by pulling as well as pushing their way through the water.

Surface-drive propellers are very expensive. They can have from four to seven blades—five or six being most common—and the more blades, the more expensive and smoother running the system will be. Surface drive props from 15 to 30 inches in diameter are usually made of stainless steel, with larger propellers made of a bronze alloy.

Another view of an Arneson surface-piercing drive.

LCG is important to proper SD performance, and weight studies must be done to ascertain whether a vessel is suitable to be built or retrofitted with an SD system. Twin Disc Corporation, which owns the Arneson brand of surface-drive, also sells waterjets. They consult with their customers about speed, cost, and safety priorities, and then advise on propulsion system choice accordingly.

If you want high performance and like the idea of surface drives, but don't want the units projecting aft of the transom, the Power Vent may offer a solution. This surface-drive package fits into a tunnel system in the hull bottom, which makes the system well suited for new construction but very difficult to retrofit.

The Nava 38's Power Vent surface drive puts the middle of the prop at the waterline with the unit entirely under the boat for added safety. NAVA COMPOSITES

Power Vent's propellers are fixed, which requires that the tunnel design provide the proper water height to the props. This makes it imperative to get the initial installation right. The drive has been used in boats up to 51 feet long, and the manufacturer claims performance similar to that of conventional surface-piercing drives. The number of moving parts—including steering and trim

A novel setup, this PulseDrive surface-piercing unit is delivered ready to install, like a stern-drive package, with the platform above integral to the drivetrain.

cylinders, U-joints, and external seals—weight, and cost are all reduced by this system. Reliability should improve, but the ability to trim the unit is lost. The ideal candidate for Power Vent would seem to be a boat that does not vary excessively in weight (and thus, immersion and trim) from full to light load. The clear transom is a big bonus for fishing boats. As with any surface-piercing drive, excellent efficiency at high speeds and shoal draft are part of the package.

CHAPTER 9

Rudders
and Steering
Systems

There's nothing remarkable about it. All one has to do is hit the right keys at the right time and the instrument plays itself.

—J.S. Bach

O nce the hull form has been perfected and the most appropriate propulsion system and drivetrain selected, the next step is to make sure the steering system is up to snuff. A rudder's size and shape, maximum turning angle, and position beneath the boat, along with responsiveness to the wheel (turns lock-to-lock), are all important factors.

Rudders

To steer the boat, rudders generate lateral, or sideways lift, which creates a turning moment about the hull's pivot point. This point is usually about one-third of the waterline length aft of the bow, but depends on the fore-and-aft location of the rudders and the shape of the hull bottom. The pivot point also changes with speed, moving forward at higher speeds and aft as the boat slows and backs down. For instance, if you're backing with significant sternway and shift the engines into forward with a little power, the pivot point may momentarily be closer to the transom than the bow pulpit.

Shape

Not surprisingly, the shape of the rudder has a great deal to do with its performance. In cross section, the rudder of a low-speed boat might resemble the cross section of an airplane wing (airfoil) with a blunt leading edge trailing aft to a long, gentle taper. This is a shape that minimizes drag. However,

the thick leading edge of an airfoil creates turbulence and cavitation when turned at higher speeds, so rudders of this shape lose lift and stall at a fairly small angle. As a result, high-speed planing hulls usually have ax-head (wedge-shaped in cross section) or flat-plate rudders, which add a little drag when centered but create more lift at higher speeds and resist stalling at greater angles of attack.

Rudders must also be balanced, with the proper distribution of surface area forward and aft of the rudderpost to minimize strain on the steering gear. Generally speaking, about 16 to 17 percent

A Luhrs 40 Open's running gear. The flush shaft strut minimizes drag, and the ax-head rudder provides a stall-free, 70-degree range of motion. The cutaway aft-top corner of the rudder prevents air from being drawn in from aft of the transom and stalling the rudder. Prop tip clearance is well in excess of the 15 to 20 percent minimum standard.

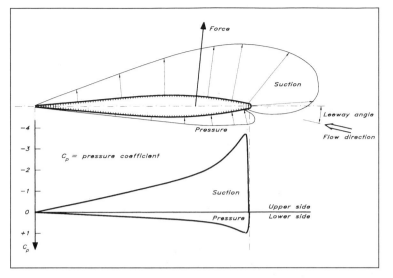

This illustration shows how lift is generated by pressure as well as suction on an airfoil-shaped rudder. The narrowing low-pressure area at the trailing (aft) edge of the rudder (when it's put over to one side) is the reason boatbuilders go to pains to prevent air from being introduced via the transom. They do this either by notching the top-aft rudder edge, by installing an anticavitation plate above the rudder, or by just locating the rudder farther forward under the hull bottom away from the transom.

LARSSON AND ELIASSON, *PRINCIPLES OF YACHT DESIGN*

of the rudder surface area should be forward of the stock. This reduces the effort required to put the rudder over at speed.

Size and Location

Rudder size is always a compromise between minimizing high-speed drag and maximizing low-speed responsiveness. If the rudders are too large, they will slow the boat at high speed. If too small (which is more often the case), helm response will be sluggish, especially at slower speeds, or outright hazardous when running at speed in a rough following sea. Generally speaking, larger rudders are more responsive, and greater rudder area confers greater low-speed maneuvering. When boats are equipped with flat-sided propeller tunnels, the rudders have to be large enough to overcome the resistance to turning created by the tunnel sides. In fact, that's another argument in favor of shallow, radiused prop pockets.

Since larger rudders add drag, slowing a boat at high speeds, some boatbuilders tend to minimize rudder size so their performance numbers look as good as possible. You may be willing to trade off a good deal of slow-speed handling ability for a higher speed potential, but you should be aware of what you're giving up.

In an effort to keep propeller shaft angles as near horizontal as possible, builders often place a propeller as far aft as possible. This naturally forces the rudder(s) aft as well, in order to preserve its proper location aft of the propeller, where propeller wash makes it most effective. Rudders placed nearer the transom can also be a little smaller than those placed farther forward, since they do their work farther from the pivot point and thus operate at the end of a longer lever arm. But rudders should be far enough from the transom not to ventilate (draw air in by vacuum) and stall in high-speed turns, or perhaps even cause

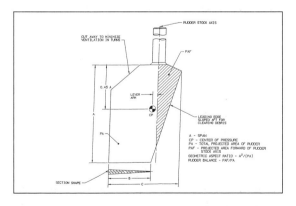

An ax-head or wedge-shaped rudder profile and cross section. CP is the center of pressure impinging on the rudders as a result of propeller discharge. The shaded area forward eases the strain on the steering gear by applying counteracting pressure *into* a turn.

DONALD L. BLOUNT ASSOCIATES

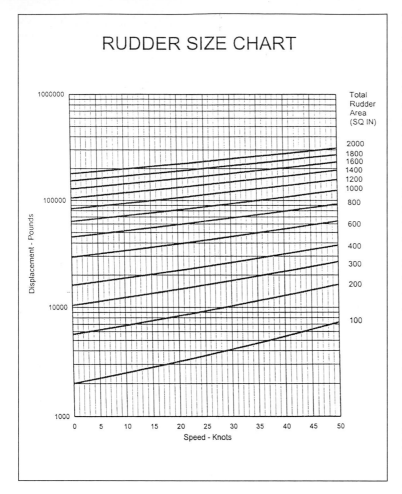

RUDDER SIZE CHART

Total Rudder Area (SQ IN)

2000
1800
1600
1400
1200
1000

800

600

400

300

200

100

Displacement - Pounds

Speed - Knots

The minimum rudder area needed for adequate steering responsiveness based on vessel speed and displacement. A bigger rudder adds drag at high speed but also adds responsiveness at slow speeds. DONALD L. BLOUNT ASSOCIATES

less drag and more lift than a shorter, wider one, the rudder's turning moment also has to be considered. If the center of the rudder's side force is excessively deep, an exaggerated heeling moment can be created causing the boat to lean sharply into a turn.

A slow boat can be overtaken by a strong following sea, which might throw the rudder full left or right and swing the boat into a broach in the opposite direction. To guard against this, a displacement hull needs a deep rudder that projects downward into undisturbed water, where it will be more effective. A deeper rudder also remains more effective as the stern rises or the boat heels, ensuring better control. Slow, heavy, deep-draft displacement vessels also require larger rudders and more powerful steering gear than lighter, faster boats of the same length because their greater draft and full keels produce greater directional stability and resistance to turning.

Dynamics

The best test of a rudder's effectiveness is a boat running downsea, especially if the boat is bow-heavy and its longitudinal center of gravity is a bit too far forward. An unusually deep forefoot also complicates matters, behaving like a rudder and causing the boat to bow steer. If such a forefoot is also fine, which it usually is, the bow won't develop enough buoyancy, or dynamic lift, to prevent it from being immersed even deeper when the stern is raised by a wave, making it harder still for the rudders to keep the boat on course.

The hull itself should provide a certain amount of directional stability when it's running at speed.

the stern to lift. If too close to the transom, they can be cropped at the top, trailing edge provided there is surface area to spare; alternatively, a horizontal plate can be installed on the hull bottom to extend its effective running surface aft of the transom.

Planing hulls bank into a turn in spite of the fact that the centrifugal force acting on their VCG (vertical center of gravity), which is well above the waterline, should make them bank away. This is a result of the dynamic pressures acting on the hull and the rudder(s). Thus, although a rudder of high aspect ratio (one that's deep and narrow) creates

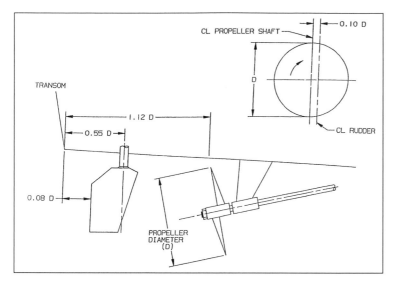

Rudder location guidelines. This rudder is placed optimally, well forward of the transom so ventilating isn't an issue, but far enough aft so that the rudders are still effective in turning the hull about its pivot point. A rudder that continues flush with the hull bottom is actually the most efficient, since waterflow or spillage off the top edge of the rudder is prevented. DONALD L. BLOUNT ASSOCIATES

with judicious use of throttles and gears. Running offshore in a heavy following sea at semidisplacement speeds, the engine speeds can also be varied or even opposed in direction to help the boat keep on course. When I was a coast guard coxswain on a 44-foot motor surfboat, our standard procedure was to put the most seasoned boat handler on the throttles and the less experienced seaman at the wheel when towing. Steering the boat is instinctive after you've spent a couple of hours at the helm, but backing an engine to kick the stern over with headway on and without stalling is trickier, especially when the shrimper you're towing is three times your size and you're trying to keep the hawser taut.

When twin engines are installed, a boat should also be fit with twin rudders. Though rarely seen

Too little, and the boat wanders; too much and the boat will require very large rudders to overcome the hull's tracking ability. The steering system must be selected with a hull's inherent directional stability in mind.

As we saw in chapter 8, a single right-handed propeller will tend to back to port and walk to starboard when running ahead. This effect is much more pronounced when the engine is first put in gear than at faster speeds, when waterflow around the rudder increases. Dynamic pressure builds up quickly as speed increases, and any walking effect is largely masked by the hull's inherent directional stability and by the effect of the rudder. Backing a single-screw boat will invariably result in the stern walking in the direction of the propeller's side force, and it takes a big, barn-door rudder to counteract this side force until the hull gains sternway. Very few single-screw boats will back downwind, though there are exceptions.

This is one time when twin engines come in handy: they will back in any direction you want

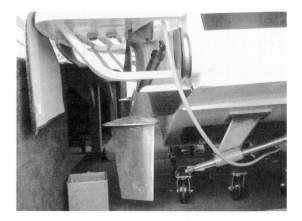

Here's a view of transom-mounted rudders on a Blackfin 29 sportfisherman. The engines are so far aft that, in the absence of V-drive transmissions, the props have to be situated practically right under the transom. Otherwise, shaft angles would be unacceptably high. These rudders have anticavitation plates built in, and the swim platform above obviates any obstruction otherwise presented by the projecting rudders to an angler playing a fish off the stern.

these days, a twin prop/single rudder setup is problematic for responsive steering, especially in a following sea. The single rudder receives little or no high-velocity prop wash to help it create lift. Rudders need to be placed in the propellers' slip stream, or discharge race, and offset just enough to allow shaft removal.

Rudders on twin-screw boats have to be sized for special circumstances, not simply to steer a vessel with both engines running ahead. They must be capable of steering the boat with only one engine, and be able to turn the boat quickly toward the running engine up- or downwind. By no means should this capability be taken for granted.

Twin rudders require special consideration when they're aligned. When a boat turns, the outboard rudder travels a greater distance. This means, for both rudders to be doing the same work, the inner rudder must be at a slightly greater angle to match the tighter circumference of its turn. This geometry requires that the rudder or tiller arms be offset so that the rudder inboard to a turn will always be at a greater angle than the outboard rudder.

Rudder and Hull Protection

The bigger a rudder and the greater the hull speed, the more heavily the rudder and its foundation in the hull bottom need to be built. The rudderpost, which passes through the hull inside a bearing with a watertight seal, must of course be able to withstand normal operating stresses, but that is not enough. Bad things happen to good boats, so rudders must be designed so as not to cause the sinking of a boat that runs aground or collides with an underwater object.

Rudderposts may be machined to accept an O-ring shaft seal. This necessitates a channel perhaps ½ inch deep around the post inside the hull, which then becomes the weak link in the rudderpost. If the post fails at this point, at least the inboard segment remains to keep the rudder bearing plugged.

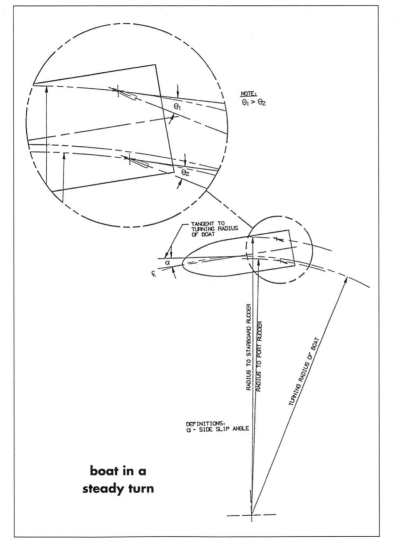

The different paths taken by twin rudders necessitate a sharper rudder angle for the inboard rudder. This angle variation is provided by the toed, or offset, tiller arm.

DONALD L. BLOUNT ASSOCIATES

The top of the rudderpost should be supported by a rudder shelf, or board, so that the entire force of a grounding or collision impact isn't absorbed by the hull alone. The effect of the rudder shelf is like holding a baseball bat at two points rather than just in the middle while someone pulls on one end. Lever arm advantage and strength are gained by supporting the rudderpost in the middle (at the hull) and at the top. This minimizes the chances of a hull rupture and flooding. See more on this subject in chapter 2.

A good way to protect a rudder in a single-engine installation is with a shoe projecting aft from the bottom of a full keel, into which the bottom of the rudderpost is secured. A full keel adds drag and slows a boat down, but the speed loss in a semidisplacement 16- to 20-knot boat is fairly insignificant. This protects the propeller is as well as the rudder, making the full keel an attractive feature for anyone who may bump bottom occasionally.

Some builders extend a rudder tube, similar to a shaft log, above the waterline inside the boat so that even if the rudder falls out the vessel won't flood. Yet another precautionary measure is to

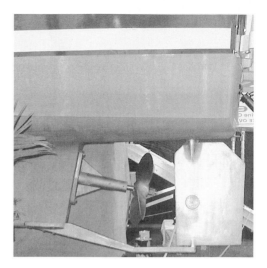

The flat-stock rudder on this Mainship 34 Pilot is supported at both ends, while the notch cut out of the upper trailing edge prevents air from being drawn in, when on plane, from the transom by the low-pressure side of the rudder and causing it to stall. The hull of this semidisplacement boat is heavily built up around the rudderpost, which must be able to absorb heavy impact loads from accidental grounding. With the skeg projecting below the bottom of the full keel, the rudder would absorb part of any grounding loads.

Built like the proverbial brick outhouse, this Viking convertible's fiberglass-encapsulated rudder board secures the top of the rudderposts. With the rudders held securely in two places, in the middle and on one end, the rudder should bend under impact rather than rupturing the hull and flooding the bilge compartment.

mount rudder stops inside the hull that prevent the rudders from swinging too far to one side or the other. Stops can be especially important with cable steering, since a rudder can otherwise travel to a point from which cable steering can't easily pull it back.

Steering Responsiveness

The faster a vessel can travel, the more responsive its steering needs to be, because evasive maneuvers have to be carried out more quickly as speed increases. The rudder angle induced by each 360-degree turn of the wheel is key. I've seen everything from 2½ to 10 turns lock-to-lock (i.e., full starboard to full port), with the former producing four times as much rudder angle from each turn of the wheel as the latter.

In the interest of helm responsiveness, four turns of the wheel from hard-left to hard-right

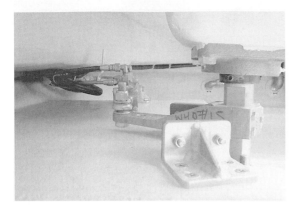

These hard rudder stops on a Nordhavn trawler prevent damage to the steering gear resulting from excessive rudder angle. (Rudders should swing through an arc of 70 degrees.) The recessed pocket above the rudderpost *(top right)* provides deck access for an emergency tiller. NORDHAVN

(based on a 70-degree rudder arc) is the most that should be accepted, especially on faster boats. Three or 3½ low-effort turns are even better. It simply takes too long to turn a wheel 5 or 6 turns. There's also a huge difference in driving ease when you only have to turn the wheel a quarter turn or less to make a small course correction.

There are plenty of 65-footers out there that handle much better than the average 35-foot inboard, and they do it with help from power steering. Power steering uses a small electric motor and pump, or the main engine-powered pump, to provide hydraulic pressure to turn the rudders. All the helmsman is doing at the wheel is indicating to the power steering unit and servo follow-up control valve which direction the rudder arm needs to move and how far. Typical power steering installations require just 3½ turns lock-to-lock and are truly a joy to behold.

When I take a boat on sea trials, one test includes timing a 360-degree turn to port and to starboard. (I test both directions in case the rudders turn farther in one direction than the other.) Using this method on a single-screw boat you can measure the effect of prop walk on the boat's ability to turn. For a typical inboard 45-footer, a

360-degree turn in 25 seconds is quite good, while 50 seconds or more is sluggish. It all has to do with the steering system design and underwater hull shape.

Some boats come with rudders that only swing 25 or 30 degrees when hard over. But according to the U.S. Navy, the U.S. Coast Guard, and the American Bureau of Shipping, rudders should swing an arc of 70 degrees, or a full 35 degrees to port and to starboard. Don't be told differently. After all, the same hydrodynamic lift and stall principles apply equally to ship and small-boat rudders. Major vendors like Teleflex design their steering systems to the 35-degree standard.

The reason for the standard is simple; the farther a rudder swings (up to a little beyond 35 degrees), the more sideways lift is generated and the shorter the boat's turning radius. Anything less than a 70-degree rudder arc cannot unlock the full potential of your steering system. I've seen some poorly engineered steering systems with maximum rudder angles of as little as 22 degrees. You can easily measure your rudder arc using a protractor against the rudder arm, or by measuring the angle between the rudder stops if installed.

I've seen rudders in workboats that swing as much as 40 degrees to either side, enabling single-engine boats to turn practically in their own length. Above 35 degrees, however, the lift component of the rudder force begins to diminish while the drag from the rudder will slow or even stop the boat.

Rudders need to be balanced to minimize steering effort, but even a well-balanced rudder will take considerable effort to turn, an effort that increases with boat speed, displacement, and rudder size. A smaller rudder naturally turns more easily, which may partly account for the undersized rudders we see on many cruisers and even a few sportfishermen. Of course, maneuvering requirements are higher for sportfishermen, since they spend a lot of time with their sterns pointed at a taut line. Power steering is at least part of the answer for responsive maneuvering.

Steering Systems

The several varieties of steering systems in common usage share a common task, of course: translating steering wheel movement into rudder action. The simplest of these is a tiller, which mounts directly on the rudderpost and dispenses with the steering wheel and intermediate control linkages altogether. Probably the next most basic is cable steering, in which the turning of a steering wheel actuates the rudder(s) via a wire cable or cables. In what is known as *pull-pull* cable steering, several turning blocks, or pulleys, provide a fair lead for the two ends of the cable (one to pull to port and the other to starboard) back to the rudder, where the ends attach to the corresponding corners of a curved quadrant mounted on the rudderpost. Pull-pull cable steering is cheap, simple, and reliable as long as the cables are protected from chafing. A disadvantage of this system is that every rudder vibration along with the propeller's side force is felt at the wheel.

Outboards and stern drives often have *push-pull* cable steering, which utilizes a semirigid cable in a sleeve, much like engine throttle and shift cables. This single cable both pushes and pulls to turn the lower unit, or rudder, as the case may be. It's important that the cable not be bent too tightly around corners between the helm and lower unit or rudder, because friction (and steering effort) build up quickly around sharp turns. All cables wear out quickly if not properly installed.

Many boats have manual hydraulic steering, in which turning the steering wheel actuates a pump that transmits fluid (and energy) back to a hydraulic cylinder attached to the rudder arm. The direction in which the wheel is turned determines on which side of the steering piston fluid is pumped, thus pushing the rudder arm to one side or the other, and the number of turns of the wheel determines piston and rudder arm travel along with the corresponding rudder angle. Twin rudders are rigidly connected, so that the same cylinder turns both simultaneously. The hydraulic fluid is usually carried by hoses made of high-strength plastic or copper, and an integral locking valve holds the rudder's position when the wheel is not being turned.

Whatever the steering system, the work of turning the rudders is done by the person spinning the wheel unless a power steering system is installed. The helmsman is the motor and the steering head is the pump. In contrast, the steering wheel in a power system merely sends a signal to the power steering unit, which works to match the actual rudder angle with what the helmsman ordered. The effort at the helm is much less.

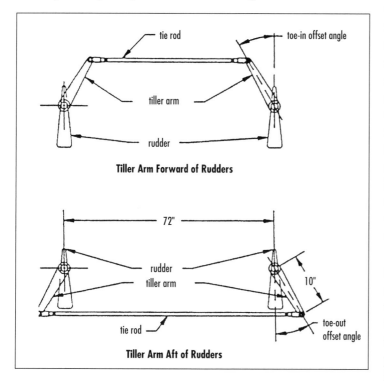

Tiller Arm Forward of Rudders

tie rod · toe-in offset angle · tiller arm · rudder

72" · rudder · tiller arm · 10" · tie rod · toe-out offset angle

Tiller Arm Aft of Rudders

In order for a twin-screw rudder installation to work properly, the tiller arms are toed in so that the rudder in the inside of the turn is at a greater angle than the other. This offset accounts for the rudders' traveling through the water at different angles in a turn.

DONALD L. BLOUNT ASSOCIATES

A manual steering system is cheaper, so manufacturers can save money by installing them on boats that are really too big for them. How big is too big? That depends on a boat's displacement and speed, but 35 feet might be a good average. Since manual systems require the helmsman to serve as the hydraulic pump, extra turns are needed on bigger boats to provide the necessary mechanical advantage to keep steering effort low. Power steering, which costs more to install, not only reduces the effort but, when properly matched to the boat, is able to put the rudder over more quickly.

On smaller cable-steered boats, a no-feedback steering option incorporates a clutch in the cable steering head that prevents the torque from a propeller's side force from having its way with the wheel. The clutch acts like the no-feedback valve in a hydraulic steering system by holding the rudder in place unless the wheel is moved. It's well worth the added expense if it is only offered as an option.

For a boat with multiple steering stations, hydraulic steering is often the way to go. Unlike with a mechanical system, the amount of work done at each helm station is virtually unchanged by the number of stations fitted.

Autopilots

Many boats, even some 20-foot outboards, are fitted with autopilots that tap into the steering system. These units sense the boat's heading, usually from an electronic compass or GPS input, and steer the selected course automatically. Their sensitivity can be adjusted to match the amount of rudder angle it takes to keep the boat on course, which in turn depends on rudder size, the hull's directional stability, displacement, trim, sea state, course, etc. Obviously, the less rudder movement needed to stay on course the better, since putting the rudder over adds drag. The downside of autopilots is that they encourage a lowered vigilance, tempting the helmsman to tend to other chores or simply daydream. Horror stories of resultant accidents abound. A reliable and properly set autopilot can keep a boat on course better than a human can, especially during open-ocean transits, but there is no substitute for a pair of human eyes to avoid collision.

Emergency Steering

It doesn't happen often, but when it does, loss of steering control offshore can ruin the best of days. The ensuing panic can be reduced, or even eliminated, if you have an alternative means of steering the boat home. Small boats might have a "kicker" (small outboard) bolted to the transom that can be used to steer, after a fashion. Larger inboards with hydraulic steering do well to carry a manual tiller that will fit on top of one of the rudderposts if needed. Just make sure there's an easy means of disconnecting the hydraulic lines from the rudder arm or bypassing the lock valve so the rudder is free to travel back and forth. A 6-inch-diameter access cover directly above the rudderpost permits mounting the emergency tiller while keeping the lazarette hatch closed—an important consideration when seas are running, which according to Murphy's Law will be the case when your steering fails. Also, be sure that the emergency tiller arm is long enough to give you leverage on the rudder, rather than the other way around. Finally, as long as the rudders are close to amidships (pointing straight ahead), twin engines can also be used to steer a boat home in a pinch.

Outboards and Stern-Drive Considerations

As mentioned above, no-feedback steering is especially important on outboard and stern-drive-powered boats. That's because the side force of the propeller tends to pull the lower unit to one side with significant force, and the operator ends up wrestling with the steering rather than enjoying the ride.

Inboards steer by deflecting prop wash off the rudders, whereas outboards and stern drives steer with their propeller's thrust as well as with the rudder effect of the submerged drive unit. As a result, steering response is more immediate and an outboard offers the further advantage of much better control while backing down. An outboard with a right-hand prop will still tend to back to port, like an inboard, but the stern can be jockeyed in the right direction by turning the lower unit if sternway and momentum are carefully controlled.

On the other hand, outboard and stern-drive-powered boats often heel more in a turn than inboards, especially if the propeller's center of effort is lower than the inboard's rudder. This tendency to bank sharply is especially pronounced in single-engine installations, which place the propeller lower in the water than with twin installations. The deeper propeller thrust depth adds lever arm and heeling moment.

Outboards and stern drives also tend to exhibit greater steering response because the steering force is aft of the transom, while inboard rudders are usually forward of the transom. Counterrotating dual-propeller stern drives, such as Volvo's Duo-Prop and MerCruiser's Bravo 3, have exceptional turning ability. Unlike single-propeller drives, they turn with equal facility to port and starboard, since the counterrotating props cancel out side forces.

Waterjets

Waterjet propulsion, like outboards and stern drives, offers an advantage in maneuverability over a propeller-driven inboard in that thrust is vectored from side to side through a steering nozzle. When the engine is shifted into reverse, a deflector scoop drops down over the waterjet discharge race, redirecting the flow forward. The steering effect is the opposite of what you'd expect; back down with the wheel to port and the stern pulls to starboard, and vice versa, due to the geometry of the reversing deflector. Once you get the hang of it, however, a waterjet-powered boat is more maneuverable than even an outboard. Single and twin waterjets have steerable nozzles and reversing deflectors, while triple and quadruple waterjets only include the steering and backing mechanisms on the outboard engines.

Surface Drives

Surface drives come in at least two basic flavors, steerable and fixed. Those that are free to rotate from side to side steer using propeller thrust. Fixed units have a rudder assembly mounted aft of the prop to deflect prop wash to one side or the other in the familiar fashion. Surface drives typically lack the low-speed finesse of other propulsion systems, but again, they're designed and intended to operate efficiently at very high speeds. Alas, you can't have it all.

CHAPTER 10

Engine Rooms and Onboard Systems

A lie can travel halfway around the world while the truth is still putting on its trousers.

—Mark Twain

Whether you're the owner of an outboard center console or a 140-foot megayacht, the systems that keep your vessel humming along are well worth your acquaintance. Murphy is alive and well, so anything man-made will eventually break. Understanding your vessel's systems, even just the basics, will put you ahead of the curve.

It's often amusing to observe new owners' reactions to their dreamboat's engine rooms. Some genuinely enjoy changing the oil, topping off the expansion tanks, and tinkering around—even cleaning the bilge. In fact, the engine room is the

The dry exhaust system on this trawler is well insulated to keep the engine room as cool as possible.   NORDHAVN

first place these owners want to show off to guests. Other owners couldn't care less about what goes on in the heart of the boat as long as all that mysterious machinery gets them from point A to point B. They're reluctant even to visit down there and wouldn't clean out a seawater strainer on a bet.

Modern pleasure craft, from small stern-drive-powered express cruisers to megayachts, can have surprisingly complex systems, but once you've spent a little time learning the various mechanical, electrical, and plumbing systems, things somehow don't seem quite so overwhelming.

Room to Maneuver

Builders cater to every market demand in order to sell their product, and as a result, emphasis on

The 8.1-liter Volvo stern drive in this Cobalt 272 bowrider is easily accessible, with the hatch (and sunpad) raised out of the way, leaving plenty of room around the engine.

systems engineering varies according to the market they're trying to reach. For instance, a builder's design philosophy, even within a class of boats, makes a big difference when it comes to allocating space for the engine room. If the priority is on accommodations, the forward engine room bulkhead may be pushed aft to make room for a bigger master stateroom, another head, or a big cedar-lined closet. But if priority is placed on engine room space, then there will be plenty of room to get around, even when options such as a watermaker or extra genset are included.

Being able to get around an engine room comfortably is important. In an emergency, you need to be able to get to the problem in a hurry. For routine maintenance, having more room means you or your mechanic is more likely to do the job right, and at manufacturer-specified intervals. Proper maintenance results in increased reliability and longevity, one area where single-engine vessels have a distinct advantage over their twin-screw counterparts.

The engine room on the Kadey-Krogen 58, looking aft, with a work table to starboard, fuel tanks with cleanout ports, shielded site gauges, port and starboard John Deere mains, and a watertight door leading aft to the next compartment. The space is well lit, finished white for good visibility, and plumbing and wiring runs are well protected. KADEY-KROGEN YACHTS

Entering the Kadey-Krogen 58's standup engine room involves walking down a set of stairs and through a watertight door.
KADEY-KROGEN YACHTS

Viking Yachts emphasizes space in their engine rooms, a fact appreciated by their engineering-savvy owners. And convertible sportfishermen owners are more likely to be involved in their yachts' mechanical system maintenance than their express or pilothouse motor yacht counterparts.

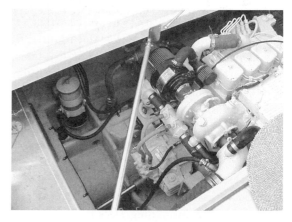

This express boat has reasonably good access to its aft-centerline maintenance points, but the fuel filter and raw-water seacock outboard to port are hard to reach.

Formula's 48-footer has access to the engine room from the swim platform (left). With the stern trunk wide open (right) there is easy access to oil dipsticks, expansion tanks, fuel filter-separators, and oil filters.

A single 600 hp diesel takes up a lot less space than a pair of 300 hp engines, leaving room to breathe for maintenance. But, many owners who are concerned about maneuverability and redundancy don't care to hear about the merits of single-screw propulsion.

Whether you have the typical convertible's roomy engine space or the more cramped variety found on many express cruisers, be sure to know where everything is and how the systems interrelate. You should also be clear about maintenance schedules and know what tools and spares will be necessary, and where they are stowed. Flat surfaces or catwalks along with sufficient overhead lighting all make for a more hospitable engine room environment. Other features bearing serious consideration are the size and location of hatches, bulkheads, and ladders.

If access hatches are exposed to the weather, be sure they're water- or at least weathertight. Any machinery or equipment mounted below the hatch perimeter will be susceptible to corrosion from leaks. Hatches and doors to machinery spaces should have gaskets to seal in as much noise as possible and to prevent rattling. Deck hatch openings should have deep gutters around their perimeters, with large (1-inch or greater) drain lines to keep things dry down below. Test for watertightness with

The twin MerCruiser gas inboards in this Sea Ray 310 express are readily accessible, with a deck that lifts high enough to get aft of the engines to the steering gear. Note the enclosed cableway (arrow) forward protecting the wiring runs.

a fully pressurized hose and a couple of buckets of water to be sure.

Engine start and stop switches and full instrumentation at the cockpit entrance for local control and monitoring are an advantage. Enclosing gensets further reduces noise levels when the main engines are shut down and electrical power is needed.

Well-planned twin-engine rooms allow you to do all routine engine maintenance, such as fluid level top-offs and filter checks, from centerline. All

Engine room vents on a Mochi Dolphin 74

The engine room on a Hatteras 80 motor yacht. There's standup headroom, lots of lighting, and surfaces are white to make it easier to spot engine or transmission oil leaks. The engines can be monitored locally, using the gauge panels overhead. Dual fuel filter-separators are visible inboard of the diesel propulsion engines, allowing shifting and cleaning of the filters without shutting down the engine. HATTERAS YACHTS

The V-drive gas PCM engine in this 22-foot MasterCraft X-Star is quite accessible. The main centerline hatch opens wide, the storage lockers are removable, and removing the aft cockpit seat allows access to the transmission forward of the engine.

auxiliary equipment such as air-conditioning units, generators, voltage isolators and transformers, inverters, batteries, watermakers, ice makers, and transfer pumps should be conveniently located. Systems and components should also be labeled to take the guesswork out of what you're looking at.

Fuel Systems

Designing an engine room, like the rest of the boat, involves a series of compromises. For instance, if the fuel tanks are placed outboard of the engines, where their effect on trim is minimized, it's often impossible to access the outboard sides of the engines. These saddle tanks are also higher up in the yacht than tanks mounted on centerline in the bilge, decreasing stability and increasing the vessel's roll amplitude.

If the main fuel tank is placed under the cockpit to make the engine room roomier, as on a convertible, trim varies significantly as fuel is consumed, impacting the boat's seakeeping ability. Builders of these yachts often rely on forward auxiliary fuel tanks and large trim tabs to help balance things out. If the battery banks are mounted in the bilge on the centerline, stability is improved but effective headroom between the engines is reduced. So, the best choice isn't always crystal clear.

Wherever the fuel tanks are located, fuel system integrity, redundancy, and reliability are all-important. Today's modern, high-speed diesels with their sophisticated electronic and mechanical control and monitoring systems are very reliable as long as clean fuel is supplied to the engines. A large fuel filter-separator should be provided for each engine and for each generator. The filter prevents contaminants from reaching the engine's injectors, which have very small openings and are easily clogged. Any water is separated from the diesel fuel and collects in a small, clear bowl at the bottom of the unit where, as the water level rises, it can be monitored visually and drained off as necessary.

Many of these units are available with alarms that let you know when they need maintenance. Some builders provide two fuel filter-separators in parallel so they can be shifted on the fly if one line becomes clogged. This allows the engine to stay running while the first filter-separator is cleaned. The filter-separators should be mounted high enough above the bilge to leave room under the clear sediment bowls for a bucket to collect the drainage. They should also be positioned so they're easy to see and access for maintenance—the closer to the engine room entrance, the better.

Look for high-pressure fuel line hoses with compression fittings connecting them to the engines, filter-separators, tanks, and fuel manifolds. Most small boats, and even some expensive yachts, have cheaper, less secure rubber hoses with clamps on their ends. These can give many years of good service, but a hose clamp is nowhere near as dependable as a compression fitting with a flare or O-ring seal. Also, the relatively soft rubber hoses are not as abrasion resistant as high-pressure hose. When hose clamps are used they should doubled up, and the nipple should be long enough that both clamps bear on it securely.

Abrasion resistance is an important consideration, especially if fuel lines are not routed out of harm's way and provided with protection from chafing. Builders sometimes use PVC pipes to route fuel lines and wiring from one part of the vessel to another. If this is done, make sure the hoses and wires are slack enough that they don't chafe against the pipe ends, which should be filed or sanded smooth to further guard against this.

Fuel supply and return lines valves ought to be capable of remote operation so that potential fuel sources to an engine room fire can be cut off.

There are two basic types of fuel fittings and hoses: rubber lines held to nipples with hose clamps, and high-pressure, aircraft-type compression fittings and hoses. The latter, seen here, is much to be preferred, since compression fittings are more secure than hose clamps will ever be, and the steel-jacketed high-pressure lines are far more abrasion resistant.

Remote operating gear in the cockpit (for both raw-water and fuel systems) is an excellent solution; don't leave home without it!

The fuel lines and fuel manifolds should be clearly labeled at their ends, so there's no question of where lines lead. If you have to disconnect a high-pressure fuel line from the engine, be careful not to overstress the fitting. Sometimes these are the weak links in fuel lines, so using a second wrench to relieve strain is essential. The worst combination is a rugged high-pressure line connected to ¼-inch copper tubing at the engine. A strong argument can be made for replacing any and all such copper tubing with high-pressure hoses all the way from the tanks to the engines and back. Diesel fuel supply lines are under slight vacuum since the engine-driven pump is drawing from the tank. Fuel return lines, on the other hand, are under pressure, which means a break in a return line will dump fuel to the bilge. Gas engines usually have a single fuel supply hose. Some diesels, including MTUs, cool the bypass fuel at the engine and send it directly to the injectors without returning to the tank.

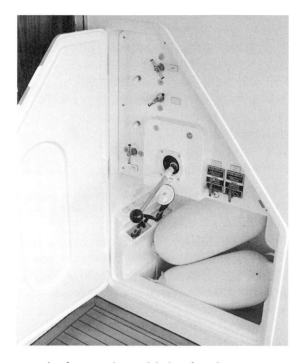

One cockpit feature on this British-built 65-foot Viking Sport Cruiser ought to be on every boat. Fuel lines supplying the engines can be remotely closed off, fire-suppressing gas can be dumped, and the bilge can be pumped manually.

A fuel tank sight glass is the most accurate means of knowing how much fuel you have left. The one on this Nordhavn trawler is well protected from breaking by a clear plastic screen. NORDHAVN

Electrical Systems

If you can't imagine going to sea without a CD player, microwave, or television, don't worry—there are amps aplenty, assuming your boat is properly outfitted. A simple electrical system starts with the typical outboard's battery, with or without a selector switch, to feed running lights, radio, and bilge pump. Small cruisers will usually have a 12-volt system fitted with shore power cables feeding a battery charger-inverter that also supplies power to a dual-voltage refrigerator. Larger yachts have sophisticated multivoltage AC-DC systems that provide power for everything from bunk lighting to engine starters, air-conditioning, and compressors.

Electrical systems on boats and yachts are usually divided into 12-volt DC and 120- to 240-volt AC sides, with a single electrical service panel divided into an AC and a DC side. In simple terms, an alternator on the main engine(s) charges the house and engine starting batteries. Separate battery banks are usually installed so that even if someone leaves an appliance on overnight and drains the house battery, the engine will still start using its dedicated battery. If the starting battery dies, a cross-connect or parallel switch may be provided to allow the house battery to start the engine. Many small outboards have a pair of batteries and a four-position battery switch from which you can select battery 1, battery 2, both, or off. This serves much the same purpose as more complicated systems by helping to ensure that one fully charged battery is always available to start the engine.

Unlike automotive batteries, which might use up just a small percentage of their charge in a short surge when the car is started, deep-cycle marine batteries are built to regularly discharge a significant percentage of their stored energy before being recharged, and to withstand many cycles of such use. Liquid electrolyte and deep-cycle gel cell batteries are commonly used. Even deep-cycle batteries last longer if they aren't discharged below 50 percent of their capacity, however. Batteries are very heavy, so they should be secured to prevent movement and placed low in the hull to improve stability. They should be protected with covers that provide plenty of ventilation. Lead acid batteries under charge give off hydrogen gas that's explosive, hence the need for ventilation. Batteries will sometimes continue to work when submerged, but a spare battery high in the boat (on the bridge, for example) to power a radio for an SOS call might be worth its weight in gold one day.

Direct current (DC) 12-volt systems need both a positive and a negative (ground) side to complete the electrical circuit. DC loads usually include lighting, electronics, engine starter, refrigerator (which may run off either 12 or 120 volts), bilge pumps, engine room blower, instrumentation, and so on. Bilge pumps, float switches, and alarms should be wired on the battery side of the selector switch so that they'll still operate when the latter is shut off.

Some boats carry an inverter, usually fed by a dedicated battery bank, to convert DC to AC electrical power for operating small appliances. An inverter can only be used as long as its batteries hold a charge, but they're great for smaller boats that don't have room or weight allowance for a generator, or for big-boat owners who want to restrict generator usage to a minimum. Inverters are inefficient, requiring a lot of 12-volt DC power to make a little 120-volt AC, but they're great for handling small loads intermittently.

Dual-function battery charger-inverters are also popular, since many of the electrical components required for charging a battery and converting DC to AC are shared. Like all electrical components, they should be mounted in a dry, well-ventilated area.

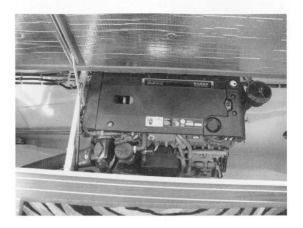

The single Volvo D4 common rail diesel in this Camano 34 sets down into the hull's hollow keel, lowering the saloon deck above, as well as the boat's center of gravity. The propeller shaft angle is less than 10 degrees, thanks to the low engine placement.

Many small 24- to 30-foot express cruisers and fishing boats and virtually all larger yachts have 120- to 240-volt systems fed either by shore power cables when dockside or the boat's generator when offshore. AC wiring should always be isolated from DC and differently color-coded to prevent confusion. Air-conditioning compressors, battery charger-inverters, water heaters, watermakers, ice makers, televisions, refrigerators, stoves and microwave ovens, built-in vacuum cleaner systems, and house lighting are just a few of the loads that can be served by an AC system.

Generators are the third source of AC power after inverters and shore power. A genset (generator set) consists of a prime mover, either a gas or diesel engine to conform with the vessel's main propulsion engine(s), and the generator itself. Gensets run as long as you want them to provided they're fed with fuel and air, and they're usually rated to carry a healthy percentage of the entire ship's load all at once. Modern wet exhaust systems make gensets very quiet indeed, so they're hardly noticed when running. An insulated enclosure makes them quieter still.

Overload Protection

Electrical circuits are protected against power surges by either fuses (that melt through) or circuit breakers (that trip, opening the circuit). They should be of the correct size (the same amperage rating or smaller) to match the wiring they protect (the smallest wire in the circuit) and located as near the power source as possible—the ABYC recommends within 7 inches. Without circuit protection, a fire could easily result from an overloaded or shorted circuit melting wire insulation and the copper wire itself. Electrical system failures are one of the most common causes of onboard fires. Engine starting circuits are wired separately and do not require surge protection.

Few boats have enough electrical generating capacity on board to run everything at once, and builders are usually clear about this. Depending on their number and amperage rating, shore power cables may not provide enough power to run everything in port, either.

Marine Wiring

The heavier the electrical cables—and thus the lower the AWG number—used between power sources and their loads, the less power and voltage loss there will be. Wiring strands should be tinned to protect against corrosion, and only marine-grade wiring should be used to withstand the salt air and potentially oily environment. Unlike house wiring, marine-grade wire also provides the flexibility needed to hold up in a dynamic environment. Other precautions against corrosion, including the use of heat-shrink tubing at connections, should also be used.

Wiring terminals are often the culprits when circuit failure occurs. If incorrectly assembled, terminals can increase resistance to current flow and the demand on the power sources. Common sense dictates that wires should be kept out of the bilge and that new loads not be spliced into existing circuits. If additional service is needed, run a new wire from the distribution panel. Each circuit should be grounded and connected to the vessel's common ground. Twisted-pair wiring, which cancels out the magnetic field created by current flow within a single wire, should be used near

This Canadian-built coastal trawler shows meticulous attention to detail throughout, including the electrical systems. The wiring behind the AC-DC breaker panel is neatly routed, color coded, and numbered.

compasses and other magnetically sensitive devices. In general, wiring ought to be supported every 18 inches unless it runs through a conduit.

Wiring throughout the vessel should be neatly bundled and routed through protective conduits to prevent chafing. It should also be color coded and labeled on either end to facilitate troubleshooting and future modifications. Wiring should be as continuous as possible from load to power source, with breaks only at panels and switchboards as needed. Under no circumstance should wires be spliced together where they will potentially come into contact with water. Breaker panels should be sited high in the vessel and at a height above the deck that makes their use comfortable and convenient. A voltage stabilizer-transformer to provide the correct shore power voltage to sensitive ship's electrical equipment is often provided on larger yachts.

Fire Prevention and Suppression

Among catastrophes at sea, fire ranks just behind flooding in vessels lost. Safe vessel design is essential, as are intrinsically safe fuel, mechanical, and electrical systems. Once a fire does break out, the speed at which it can be extinguished and remain extinguished is crucial to a vessel's survival.

Firefighting systems come in two basic forms: fixed and portable. Portable fire extinguishers should be plentiful, of the right type for the likely classes of fire, charged, and easily accessible. There's no substitute for running periodic drills with your crew so that all hands know where the nearest appropriate fire extinguisher is and how to use it. This goes for any onboard emergency, of course, whether it's a man overboard, flooding, or fire.

Fixed fire-extinguishing systems should be installed in any space that contains machinery or fuel: the engine room and lazarette or similar space in which a fuel tank is installed. Fixed systems automatically detect rises in temperature or the presence of smoke and discharge an extinguishing agent.

More sophisticated and effective fixed fire-extinguishing systems shut down machinery and close off ventilation before discharging. This might incorporate a delay of anywhere from 10 to 60 seconds while ventilation is shut down and air sources isolated, but the intermediate step prevents the discharged agent from diluting before the fire is completely out or before the space has cooled sufficiently to prevent a reflash. Most systems give audible and visual alarms, which give the captain time to manually override the discharge. The system might be overridden, say, if losing propulsion power would be more hazardous than immediately extinguishing the fire.

Once an agent, such as a gas equivalent to the now illegal Halon, is discharged, the space should not be entered for a period of time. Opening an engine room door too soon might introduce fresh oxygen into the space and cause the fire to reflash. Fire-suppressing gases don't cool the fire or the space as water or foam does; they just prevent combustion as long as their concentrations remain within a certain range. Waiting 30 minutes or more for the space to cool before entering is often recommended by fire-extinguishing system manufacturers and other experts.

Fixed fire-extinguishing systems should also have manual pump capabilities. The controls should be located on the bridge and outside the engine room or compartment. Engine room doors should be fitted with a small inspection window so that you can tell, once the smoke has cleared, if the fire has been extinguished before opening the door.

Keeping the Water Out

The engine room is often the largest, longest space at the waterline and is vulnerable to flooding. The seacocks necessary to provide cooling water to all that machinery present a particular risk. A sea chest, which is essentially a box fixed to the interior of the hull bottom, enables you to feed multiple seawater requirements from a single large through-hull fitting. The box serves as a manifold, feeding the various sources through secondary seacocks while minimizing hull penetrations.

As mentioned elsewhere, forward and aft bulkheads should be watertight to prevent flooding into surrounding spaces. Generous bilge pump capacity should be provided, along with high bilgewater level alarms should the electric bilge pumps fall behind the flooding or fail altogether. A manual backup bilge pump that can be operated from the deck should be installed for such contingencies.

Some builders provide Y-valves in the main engine raw-water intake line. This lets the suction be diverted from the through-hull fitting to a pick-up hose in the engine room bilge, so that the engine can serve as a pump in time of need. This Y-valve should close off one avenue as it opens the other, so that at no time does it establish a pathway from

Seacocks sprouting off this Davis convertible's sea chest mean there's only *one* hole in the bottom of the boat per side versus a half dozen. That's a good thing.

This Groco through-hull fitting can take a suction on the bilge by removing the plug in its side, as long as the through-hull water path is shut off first by closing the main valve. This either-or safety feature prevents a path for water to flow from sea to bilge, potentially sinking the boat. GROCO

the sea to the bilge. The type of Y-valve installed by many builders will open the bilge suction valve without closing the through-hull valve, which can quickly sink a boat. A main engine's pumping rate is an order of magnitude greater than an electric bilge pump's and can be measured in hundreds rather than tens of gallons per minute, provided the hoses and pipes are of adequate dimension. Bilge suction Y-valves should be located near the engine room entrance so they can be reached quickly, especially if the bilge is already flooded.

An engine power takeoff (PTO) high-capacity dewatering pump can be used to dewater a space or to provide firefighting water. A main drainage system, essentially a pipe with remotely controlled valves running fore and aft in the bilge, can also be fitted, so that another compartment, isolated from the engine room by watertight bulkheads can be pumped out remotely by opening the right valves.

Mechanical, hydraulic, or electric remote operating gear is available to allow engine room valves to be opened and closed from the main deck. The next best solution is to provide long handles that allow valves to be opened or closed from several feet above the valve. Many seacocks are mounted in out-of-the-way bilge areas, making it difficult to open or close them under the best of conditions; many are frozen. Seacock valves should

be regularly cycled and lubricated so they will actually work when needed. I prefer bronze over fiberglass-reinforced plastic seacocks. Bronze is stronger and more durable, and where any through-hull fitting is concerned you can't be too cautious.

My habit is always to close the engine cooling water seacocks at the end of each trip and reopen them just before starting the engines and heading out again. This practice will help to prevent a failed cooling water hose from sinking the boat and ensure that the seacocks open and close freely. The downside of this procedure is that if you forget to open the seacock before starting the engine, there is a good chance that you will burn out the seawater pump cooling impeller. Place a note or placard at the helm to remind you or your mechanic to open the valves before starting the engine.

Other Considerations
A No-Salt Diet Works Best

To minimize corrosion, keeping salt air out of the engine room is always a priority. This can be facilitated by installing demister pads in the combustion air intakes to help filter salt from the air, and by using dripless propeller shaft seals to reduce spray and bilgewater.

Machinery Overhaul and Replacement

Engines, gensets, and other major components will likely need to be replaced some day, so it pays to find out before buying a boat how involved that process may be. To facilitate removal, some builders provide patches or hatches on deck to make the process as easy as possible. Other boats will need to have holes cut in the side of the hull or in the deck above. In some hulls, even the fuel tanks might have to be removed before an engine can be replaced. If this kind of major surgery is needed, expect the job to cost more and take longer. The same accessibility issue applies to fuel tanks that are subject to corrosion or any kind of deterioration. Especially if they're made of aluminum, chances are they'll eventually need to be replaced. Fuel tanks need a way out, and a hatch directly above the tank is by far the best solution.

Fiberglass fuel tanks should last as long as the boat itself, but aluminum tanks have a limited life span: their longevity depends on the quality of the initial installation. Aluminum tanks tend to corrode from the outside where water is trapped against the tank by support members and allowed to deoxygenate. Supporting fuel tanks on neoprene strips or welded angle brackets and providing lots of breathing room for fresh air to circulate all around is a good way to prevent corrosion and increase tank life. Many experts recommend against installing aluminum fuel tanks in a bed of foam, since air cannot circulate around the sides and bottom of the tank.

Sound Reasoning

Some builders install one-piece, composite saloon decks above the engine room. This seamless process helps seal the engine space acoustically, containing most of the machinery noise. Different composite coring materials provide varying degrees of sound attenuation. Lead-and-foam foil-backed acoustic insulation helps attenuate machinery noise of different frequencies. Engine rooms with watertight bulkheads forward and aft further contain machinery noises. Since the proof of noise control effectiveness is in the pudding, take noise-level readings with a $50 RadioShack decibel meter throughout your boat at various engine speeds. Readings in the low 70 dBA range at all speeds indicate a successful noise attenuation effort on the builder's part. Continuous readings above 84 dBA at cruising speeds will necessitate the use of earplugs to prevent hearing loss from long-term exposure.

Auxiliary Equipment

Watermakers make it possible to stay at sea for extended periods. Seawater is converted to fresh water by condensing steam or by forcing seawater through microporous filters. An ability to make fresh water from seawater permits potable water tank capacity to be much smaller, increasing a vessel's speed and range.

Fin stabilizers are fitted on many round-bilge, displacement cruising vessels with minimal form stability. They're also used on a few hard-chine planing yachts whose owners want to keep rolling to an absolute minimum.

Bow thrusters are a great aid when it comes to maneuvering a yacht in tight quarters. Twin screws can walk the stern sideways while the bow thruster pushes the bow to either side on command. Essentially a propeller (or counterrotating propellers) in a fiberglass or metal tube mounted athwartships just below the waterline, a thruster is only effective when the boat is stopped or has very little way on. Some bow thrusters are powered by electric motors fed from a dedicated battery bank; others are driven by hydraulic pumps that are in turn powered by a power takeoff on one of the main engines.

Systems and Structure Accessibility

A vessel's systems and structure should be accessible throughout the length of the hull, not just in the engine room. When builders seal off portions of the bilge by putting a hatchless sole in the cabin, it's impossible to tell the condition of the wiring, plumbing, or hull structure in that area. It could be that water has gotten into that space and is rotting out structural members or causing other damage. In the event of a grounding or other impact that results in a hull puncture, it will be impossible to make temporary repairs if the bilges aren't completely accessible.

Deck hatches should allow you to see and access all of the bilge. Foam-filled compartments can trap water against wooden structural members such as bulkheads and stringers, causing the onset of rot. These concealed voids may well not have adequate ventilation or drainage, but you might not know the consequences of such poor design until you want to sell the boat and a surveyor discovers the damage. Access hatches are essential.

All machinery and equipment need adequate ventilation. AC compressors tucked under molded, nonopening bench seats, uninsulated AC ventilation ducts, cockpit washdown pumps sitting in puddles of salt water, water heater relief valves in

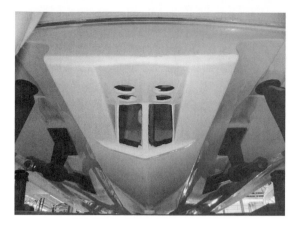

The Formula 48's underwater exhaust sets up a venturi when the hull is moving, drawing the exhaust gases out under partial vacuum. Note that the exhaust comes nowhere close to the propellers, clean waterflow to the props being essential to performance.

compartments without drainage, and battery chargers-inverters mounted under leaky cockpit hatches are all examples of corrosion-related problems. Ultimately, these problems will lead to premature equipment and component failure.

CHAPTER 11

Pilothouse and Bridge Design and Ergonomics

Pianists don't argue too much generally because we have such a hard time just getting things right; arguing is for string players.

—Emanuel Ax

If any area of a vessel can benefit from a little extra planning, it's got to be the helm station. Whether located on a flybridge, in a pilothouse, or on an express cruiser's raised bridge deck, the helm station is the heart and brain of a vessel. From here the craft is controlled and navigated, and all ships' systems monitored. The importance of visibility, comfort, and user-friendly helm console ergonomics can't be overemphasized. As we'll see, there are many practical and even legal issues to consider, and after reading this chapter you'll have a better idea of what to look for when evaluating a helm station.

Although there are many marine regulatory and advisory bodies around the world, we'll be making reference to the Maritime and Coast Guard Agency (MCA), a leading U.K. standards organization for commercial vessels and large charter yachts. MCA rules do not apply to most recreational craft built in the United States, but they spell out standards that abound with common sense and with which other agencies generally agree. Other vessel standards organizations, including some in the United States, are working closely with the MCA to develop clear, concise, sensible guidelines covering helm station visibility and other related issues.

Helm Station Ergonomics

Although some helm stations are carefully thought out, too often we find layouts that are more the province of stylists than ergonomics specialists. It's often a matter of form over function, which is too bad, since it's easy to design a helm station that works well and looks great. For instance, many builders achieve perfect symmetry of layout at the expense of practicality and utility. But if a toothbrush, vacuum cleaner, and an aircraft cockpit all are designed with ergonomics in mind, why not the helm station on a boat?

Ergonomics, by the way, is the science concerned with designing and arranging manufactured products to fit the human anatomy, and for maximum ease and efficiency of use. Physical movement, visibility, lighting, comfort, noise levels, and air quality are all ergonomic issues. Well-considered ergonomics result in greater comfort, efficiency, and safety, to say nothing of keeping your spirits up after hours at the helm.

Visibility

Many vessels are capable of great speed these days, and as a consequence the need for good visibility from the helm has never been greater. If inadequate visibility from the helm station prevents keeping a proper lookout, a requirement under rule 5 of the 1972 International Regulations for Preventing Collisions at Sea, best known as COLREGs, the odds of a collision or grounding increase, and any damage or injury could have legal consequences.

MCA rules and common sense dictate that the conning position should provide a good all-around

Radar Arches

In addition to making a boat look snazzy, radar arches support antennas, the radar, the deck, and running lights. In fact, an arch is often the best place to put running lights for maximum visibility from other vessels. On open cruisers, radar arches also provide a handy place to attach a canvas bimini top or awning, and they offer a handhold along the side deck. All too often, these arches are large, bulky, visibility-blocking fiberglass sculptures drawn by designers who've apparently never put to sea. They take a good-sized chunk out of the horizon for the operator, hampering visibility, especially to port, from the driver's perspective. Ocean Yachts has come up with a great solution to this problem by molding their bridge arches with a glass window slot down the middle. Another solution is to build arches out of aluminum pipe, which creates only minimal sight line obstruction.

This Albin 32 has my idea of the perfect radar arch: strong, functional, and good looking, and you can even see *through* it.

view of the horizon. This includes an unobstructed view of the sea surface two vessel lengths ahead and within 10 degrees of the vessel's heading. The exact length of the blind spot inside this range will depend on the operator's height of eye relative to the bow. When standing at the helm station, the operator must have a clear field of vision of at least 225 degrees, or from dead ahead to two points (22.5 degrees) abaft both beams. Visibility from a

This express cruiser's radar arch cuts a big swath out of the operator's sight lines to the horizon; it's a case of stylists winning the argument regarding form over function.

bridge wing must also extend at least 225 degrees, from 45 degrees on the opposite bow through dead astern on the same side. Blind spots created by obstructions cannot exceed 10 degrees, the clear sectors between blind sectors should be at least 5 degrees, and the total arc of blind sectors cannot exceed 20 degrees.

Window size and spacing are too often inadequately throught out by the boatbuilder, with many helm area windows too low to see through without ducking. As a practical matter, the upper window edge should accommodate an eye height of 5 feet, 11 inches (1.8 m) so that a 6-foot, 4-inch operator can see the horizon without ducking. The lower edge should be as low as possible, and in no case should it obstruct visibility ahead.

The mullions, or frames, between the windows should be kept to a minimum and should not be installed directly forward of the helm station. I see mullions as much as 6 or 7 inches wide, creating a significant blind zone for the operator. Well-engineered windshields or pilothouse windows have narrow frames, 2 to 3 inches wide, yet

The helm station on this 75-foot yacht boasts excellent sight lines. This U.K.-built Viking Sport Cruiser comes up on plane with minimal bow rise, so you never lose sight of the horizon when seated at the helm. Window mullions are narrow but plenty strong. A watertight door slides open for direct weather deck access. Controls and gauges are easy to reach and intuitively located.   VIKING SPORT CRUISER

still provide plenty of support to the surrounding structure. Don't be told by a salesperson that a 2- to 3-inch frame is inadequate to support the superstructure above—it's simply a matter of intelligent engineering. Many builders have been successfully constructing frames this way for years.

At least two of the forward-facing windows should provide a clear view in all weather conditions, a requirement that calls for windshield wipers and freshwater washers to remove glare-enhancing salt smear. It's also important that the operator's view not be blocked by the helm console, which is becoming more of a problem as consoles expand to accommodate burgeoning electronics suites. Wipers should cover the glass from at least 15 degrees left to 15 degrees right of the operator's line of sight and should sweep at a rate of two arcs per second. The blade should also be long enough to cover the majority of the glass pane from top to bottom.

The windows themselves should not be polarized or tinted, as this makes it hard to identify navigational aids and running lights correctly. Area lighting around the helm station should be of low intensity, and preferably red or blue. You'll never see a white light on the bridge of a navy or coast guard ship underway at night, and for good reason: night vision is impeded during and immediately after exposure to white light. On a related note, many flat-panel LCD displays are nearly impossible to see in direct sunlight, while monochrome displays are generally easier to read in daylight than color. Also of note is the positioning of running lights. Many builders put them in the bow, on either side of the pulpit. The problem is that they are directly in the operator's line of sight, and the backscatter from these lights can also interfere with visibility. A much better solution is to mount them high above the bridge where they're out of the captain's way, and their height makes them much easier to see from, and sooner seen by, another vessel.

The operator's external view outside the vessel should be glare- and reflection-free both day and night. To minimize window reflection off the instrument panels below, MCA dictates that forward-facing windows be inclined 10 to 25 degrees from the vertical, top forward. In the real world of recreational boating, however, styling constraints often prevent this forward-sloping design practice. What

In typical sportfish fashion, the large screen displays on this Bertram 670 stretch across the huge helm station. This is one of the better designs in this class regarding window frames as they are narrower, improving horizon visibility.   BERTRAM YACHTS

Tiara does a great job minimizing obstructions to visibility, providing excellent horizon sight lines. Prominence of place is given to the electronics displays in a heads-up orientation on this 4700 Sovran. The helm is set up with the bow thruster left and the engine controls right, which makes sense so you can keep one hand on each control while docking.   TIARA YACHTS

Windshields are another area where form is winning over function. The function of a windshield—which can be either freestanding, as on an open express boat, or built with an integral hardtop, as with a sedan cruiser—is to protect occupants from wind, spray, and rain. To do its job effectively, it needs to be high enough to see through when standing up. In fact, when standing and facing forward, the operator should be able to see the horizon, not the top frame of the windshield. This means that the bottom of the upper frame should be at least 5 feet, 11 inches above deck level.

Building a windshield to this height eliminates the need for forward plastic filler curtains; these plastic windows, especially when made of standard light-gauge material, are difficult to see through and invite trouble when underway. Since windshield wipers and washers can only be used on glass, filling a large gap between a windshield and the bimini or hardtop above with a plastic filler curtain almost guarantees an awkward and hazardous piloting arrangement. Pointing again to Tiara, we can see that it is possible to build a windshield that looks great and is also tall enough to keep you cozy.

Unfortunately, the side curtains offered as standard or optional equipment by most production builders can do is eliminate the gloss-white dashes that cause significant windshield glare and use a flat, darker color like tan or gray under the windshield.

Although it's a point of pride with many yacht builders to finish all pilothouse and flybridge surfaces with the brightest white gelcoat available, seamanlike pilothouses and bridges are painted a flat color throughout that prevents reflection and glare. Bright white overheads and helm consoles may look great with the boat tied up at the dock, but they impair visibility when running at night. In the sunlight, reflected glare makes running a boat with a bright white bridge impossible without sunglasses. I risk sounding strident, but bright-white surfaces around the helm area are anathema to the seasoned mariner.

Even small cruisers and runabouts are making room for electronics displays now, as shown by the large, flat area above the wheel for a GPS plotter-radar. Sometimes, however, the gauges are too far forward to read easily.

There are 10 inches between these windshield sections, making it hard to see what's in front of the boat. Many builders reduce this to 4 inches or less while providing plenty of strength (sometimes using aluminum) and stiffness for the superstructure. Compare this design to the Tiara, Viking Sport Cruiser, and Mochi windshields shown in this chapter.

From this helm, most of what you are looking through is plastic. This is unfortunate since plastic eventually clouds up, you can't keep it clear with a windshield wiper, and it takes a lot of work and aggravation to put up and take down. The biggest issue, though, is poor visibility in foul weather. For this reason more boatbuilders are shifting to designs that extend glass all the way to the hardtop, just like in a car.

boat manufacturers leave a lot to be desired. That's because the thin, crinkly plastic commonly used, although easy to roll up, markedly distorts vision. You'd be better off not ordering the standard-issue plastic, or deleting it from the standard equipment list for credit, and having a local canvas shop do the work for you using heavier-grade material. Examples of well-known, high-quality side curtain manufacturers are EZ2CY, Isinglass, and Strataglass. Generally speaking, the thicker the plastic, the less it will distort your vision.

Operator Position

On most small craft the operator is also the helmsman, lookout, navigator, and electronics operator. Not only must the skipper be able to see clearly outside the boat, but she must also have ready access and clear sight lines to all controls, switches, and instrumentation.

Most helm stations are designed for use by an operator who may be either standing or seated. If the helm station is to work effectively for an operator in either of these positions, her height of eye should be nearly the same whether seated or standing. That's because the location of the steering wheel, propulsion controls, gauges, switches, and electronics should remain constant relative to the

operator. For instance, a poorly positioned helm seat might put the operator lower and farther aft than when standing up, putting controls out of easy reach and hiding part of the electronics display behind the steering wheel.

Besides supporting you at the same height of eye as when standing, the helm seat should provide support side-to-side with contoured bolsters, especially in high-performance craft. Ideally it should adjust fore and aft and also vertically to accommodate different operators and to move back out of your way when standing up.

The helm seat foundation should be far enough aft to provide plenty of room to stand comfortably well back from the wheel. There's nothing more annoying than having your thighs jammed up against the steering wheel with your heels tight against the seat foundation. Every time the boat comes up on plane or rides over a big wave, you'll have to hang onto the wheel to keep your balance. The seat should be high enough to allow you to see over the bow even when coming up on plane. This is a tall order with boats that come up on plane or

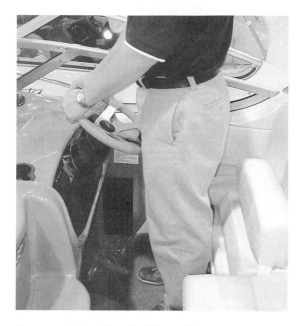

Things are a little tight at this helm. With the wheel all the way forward and the seat all the way aft, you should be able to move fore and aft a little. Otherwise, the first time you hit a wave while driving standing up, you'll be hanging onto the wheel instead of steering the boat. The seat base ought to be several inches farther aft.

run at excessive trim angles. You should never lose sight of the horizon above the bow pulpit from the helm of a well-designed boat, even when coming up on plane.

Controls and Instruments

It is important for a builder to prioritize the layout of the helm, since not everything can be right at your fingertips. The most important controls are the steering wheel and the engine controls, after which gauges and electronics get a high priority. Well-designed helm consoles are tiered, with flat sections arranged according to placement priority. It's also important that the most frequently used controls and instruments not take your attention from what's going on outside the boat, especially directly ahead. If a radar screen is mounted 3 feet to

Marinova's Jockey Seat

The Swedish company Marinova AB has produced a helm seat that allows high-speed operation in rough conditions. Resembling a saddle with a tall backrest, this unique design allows operators to support themselves partially with their feet, reducing the shock on the spine. The seat is fitted with a titanium shock-absorbing spring, further reducing G-forces, and is mounted higher than ordinary seats, improving visibility from the helm.

This is the Ullman seat and console, successfully used in Swedish rescue craft. A cross between riding a horse and a motorcycle, the Ullman helm station–seat has handlebars instead of a wheel, which makes a lot of sense if you need to hang on while driving in rough water. JOHAN ULLMAN

The result of this highly ergonomic design is a safe and secure operating position for the helmsman and an effective preventative for shock-related injuries. The Ullman cockpit, as it's known, also includes a motorcycle-style handlebar in place of a conventional steering wheel. This gives the operator a much better grip on the steering mechanism, which not only ensures continuous helm control but helps the operator stay put in extreme conditions. With the throttle mechanism integral to the handlebar, the operator always maintains full vessel control without having to let go. These Ullman cockpits, currently in use by the Swedish coast guard, are growing in popularity among recreational boaters in Europe.

The glass windshield on this Everglades Pilot 29 center console offers good protection from the elements, with a long wiper and washer to keep the glass clear.

starboard, for instance, the chances of seeing a hazard directly off the bow with your peripheral vision are much less than if the display were mounted right in front of you.

The compass is often poorly placed, despite its importance. When steering manually offshore you refer to the compass constantly. For that reason it should be on top of the helm console just below the horizon in relation to the operator's line of sight. The idea is to position the compass so that minimal eye movement is needed to shift between it and the horizon ahead. The height should be such that a shorter person can see it seated at the helm, and not so far away that it can't be easily read by someone with 20/20 vision. If the compass must be mounted 5 or 6 feet ahead of the operator, then it should be a more substantial model with numbers that are large enough for easy reading. The compass should be flat black so it doesn't reflect off the windshield above, and it should be lit with a red light for night use.

Since many helm stations are designed for both seated and standing operation, the location of the controls, gauges, switches, and electronics is often a compromise. The panels should face the average operator's line of sight as squarely as possible.

Otherwise, reflected glare will make the displays hard to see. If the seated and standing operator's height varies significantly, the panels should face either the middle ground or the line of sight from the more common position.

The movement of a control should be consistent with the direction of the desired response. When the throttles are moved forward, for example, the boat should move faster; when a gear shift is pulled back, the engine should shift to reverse, and so on. Knobs should turn clockwise for right turns or commands to the right, and counterclockwise for left turns or commands to the left. For switches on horizontal side consoles, forward is on, aft is off; on vertical panels, up means on and down is off.

All of the helm station's steering, engine, and maneuvering controls along with its switches and gauges should be grouped logically by purpose, significance, and frequency of use. Boat and yacht designers should also take into account temperature, vibration levels, adequate ventilation, and noise levels. Noise from machinery and other sources should not exceed 80 dBA continuously, a reasonable comfort level. Compare this with many diesel express cruisers that subject their owners to a hearing-damaging 85 dBA or greater for hours on end. When noise levels reach 85 dBA, expect a

This Cobalt has lots of standing room between the seat and the steering wheel, a quality missing on a few competitors' models.

The windshield on this Formula 45 offers all-around visibility for the operator, which makes running the boat safer and therefore more relaxing. FORMULA

decrease in cognitive performance to follow. And wear hearing protection above 84 dBA to prevent hearing loss.

Steering Wheel

The steering wheel should be high enough to reach easily when standing, without stooping over to spin the wheel from lock-to-lock. You should also be able to reach it comfortably while seated with your back against the seat, and without leaning forward. An angle of 15 to 30 degrees from horizontal is the most comfortable and convenient, especially when shifting the rudder from stop to stop. Steering with such a horizontally inclined wheel (seated or standing) minimizes body movement and allows the shoulders, triceps, and biceps to do the brunt of the work, rather than stressing the weaker forearms and wrists.

While certainly salty looking, a vertical wheel is not a great choice; in fact, it's probably the worst ergonomic arrangement available. It's more difficult to steer with one hand, as the hand's height relative to the shoulder varies so much more than it does with a horizontally inclined wheel. The larger the diameter the more difficult this becomes, with the operator having to stoop low with each rotation. Spinning a vertical wheel through four or five (or even seven or eight) turns is not a lot of fun, and is likely to divert the helmsman's attention from the view ahead.

Tilt wheels add a great deal of flexibility for people of different heights, and you may find that different angles work better whether seated or standing. Adding a telescoping capability to the wheel makes it easy to accommodate different drivers. In the interest of ergonomics, steering wheels that tilt and telescope should be standard equipment.

Some boatbuilders inexplicably use wheels with flat, sharp-edged spokes that dig into your fingers when you're spinning them. Common sense and ergonomics dictate that spokes should be rounded to prevent this discomfort.

Steering effort should be minimal, to allow palming of the wheel. To avoid the higher cost of power steering, however, most builders reduce steering effort by adding turns lock-to-lock or by increasing the diameter of the wheel. Both of these measures increase the mechanical advantage of the pump motor, which in the case of non-power steering is the operator. But the result, especially in a boat at high speed, is sluggish responsiveness. On smaller boats with well-balanced rudders, it's sometimes possible to find an acceptable combination

The electronics panel on the Grady-White 306 center console raises and lowers at the touch of a button, offering just the right angle, and protection from both the elements and prying fingers. Note all the piping to hang on to underway, and the easy-to-reach rocker switches up on top of the dash. GRADY-WHITE

of steering effort and responsiveness from manual hydraulic steering. But when you get above four turns from full left to full right rudder, your ability to respond rapidly in a collision avoidance situation is impaired. The faster the boat, the more responsive the steering should be. On any boat over 30 feet that's capable of 30 knots or more, I always recommend power steering to keep the steering both tight (around three turns lock-to-lock) and low effort.

Engine Controls

Like steering wheels, engine controls are at the top of the priority list for helm station placement. Since most people are right-handed, the controls should be to starboard of the wheel. They should also be located within easy reach whether seated or standing, at a convenient height, and mounted 10 to 20 degrees from horizontal. Vertically mounted engine controls are uncomfortable to operate and difficult to move with any precision, since the forearm is doing most of the work; this can result in hit-or-miss boat handling in tight quarters.

Caterpillar's Multi-Station Control System (MSCS) provides control for single- or twin-engine applications with up to eight control stations and quick control transfer between them. A backup system provides control in the event of MSCS failure, crash-back protection is built in, and a number of control heads are available. CATERPILLAR

With mechanical or hydraulic single-lever controls, you have to put the engine in gear, or at least start to, before throttling up, so damage to the reduction gears through a high-speed shift attempt is reduced. These controls use either cables within sleeves or hydraulic lines to transmit the movement of the throttle and clutch controls to the engine itself.

Locating single-lever controls together makes the most sense, but splitting them up, with port and starboard engine controls on their respective sides of the steering wheel, is favored by some sportfishermen captains. This arrangement lets the operator turn around to face the cockpit and, with a hand on each control, precisely maneuver the boat, whether backing on a fish or backing into a slip. The downside of this arrangement is that you can't advance the throttles when heading in the other direction and steer the boat at the same time, unless you were born with three hands, or you have electronic engine controls with an automatic synchronizer. Maybe the best idea is to put single-lever controls together to starboard, on the same binnacle, but also to duplicate the port engine control to port of the wheel, thereby meeting both objectives.

Despite my bias toward single-lever controls, I must acknowledge that dual-lever controls do have a couple of advantages. They let you run the engine up to a faster idle speed, so you can maneuver a boat dockside with just the clutches and still have plenty of power at your disposal. This is especially relevant with gas and high-speed diesels with small props and shallow gear ratios that need a shot of rpm to be noticed. In the mechanical cable versions, their throttles also have more throw, or travel distance, than single-lever controls, allowing for more precise adjustment.

Since it's important for an engine to shift into gear before adding power, some electronic single-lever controls have time-delay circuitry to prevent throttle linkage movement before the engine actually shifts. Electronic controls also accommodate up to a half dozen or more control stations, and some even feature remote units with steering and bow thruster controls included that can be carried around the boat. If you want to drive from the pulpit, or (if you're psychic) from your stateroom, the world's your oyster with one of these babies.

Another consideration is mounting the engine controls so they're well away from curious or careless fingers. This sometimes means placing them outboard of the wheel, away from the companionway where people tend to stand. You also want to make sure that the engine controls aren't placed so they serve as the first thing people grab onto in a sudden turn or when hitting an unexpected bump.

Switches and Auxiliary Controls

Although most larger boats have an extensive array of switches and auxiliary controls, only a few are used frequently, and these should have front-and-center accessibility. Controls for the trim tabs, horn (painted fluorescent orange), autopilot, bow thruster, windshield wiper-washer, and searchlight switches should be at your fingertips and easy to see. The same surface that's used for the throttles can be designed to accommodate the trim tab switches, their indicator gauges, and the wiper-washer switches.

I can't figure out why so many boatbuilders provide a long row of identical shiny black rocker switches in front of the wheel, while the switches that you really need are dispersed in the background among switches for lighting, bilge blowers,

Here's a row of rocker switches on a nicely sculpted helm. Problem is, you can't tell the horn from the bilge blower switch at a glance. The horn, wipers, washers, and trim tabs should be separated from the rest, clearly labeled, and at the operator's fingertips.

stereo system, and other incidentals. Engine shutdown and fire-suppressing gas discharge switches should be prominently displayed and unmistakably marked. In the interest of achieving an ultraclean Palm Beach look, an unfortunate trend being followed by some convertible boatbuilders is to hide the engine shutdowns and even the engine start-stop switches out of sight under the console! This is not a great location when panic sets in and the operator forgets where these vital controls are located. So much for these come-and-go styling trends, like the foot-high Palm Beach bow rails, followed dutifully even by builders and owners who know better.

Instruments and Gauges

Engine gauges or instruments are supposed to tell you at a glance what your engines are doing. This involves a couple of important design considerations. They should be angled so they're nearly perpendicular to your line of sight, using an average of a typical person's seated and standing height of eye. The most important gauges should get the most prominent position; for example, oil pressure and water temperature gauges are more critical than ammeters and voltmeters.

Engine gauges should be large enough to read without binoculars, but not so large as to take up a disproportionate amount of space; a 2-inch-diameter gauge is just about right. If you have twin engines, the gauges should be stacked in pairs by type, with like gauges for each engine side by side so you can spot any variance—of lube oil pressure, temperature, etc.—at a glance. Corresponding annunciators (warning light or audible alarms, each of which should have a sender that's independent of the gauge) should be right next to or even inside the gauges so your eyes are drawn to the relevant spot immediately. Positioning the throttles below their corresponding gauges makes for an intuitively obvious arrangement. High-priority alarms should be within 15 degrees of the operator's line of sight so they're readily identified. Audible alarms alert the operator regardless of head or eye position; spoken alerts are best, and audible alarms should be kept to a minimum.

The engine controls in the aft cockpit of this Mochi 74 allow improved maneuvering when backing into a slip, thanks to unrestricted visibility astern.

In any event, you're not very likely to find out about an errant engine from a gauge, since mechanical casualties often happen too quickly to be spotted with the occasional glance at the instruments. That's what alarms are for, so make sure your boat has them and that they're working. Instruments should also be mounted with sealant or gaskets so they don't allow water to get behind the helm console and corrode the wiring. We've seen a lot of expensive boats with gaps under their fancy gauges that you could push a gaff through.

Large tachometers and speedometers, some of which are a whopping 3 to 4 inches in diameter, are more a function of the overactive male ego than of any practical considerations. Builders may want the potential buyer to imagine himself cruising along with those tachs and speedometers pegged to the right, but they have no real merits. One of the most counterproductive arrangements is placing a large speedometer or synchrometer

between two equally oversized tachs. The intervening gauge makes it more difficult to read the tachometers. A synchrometer can be very small, placed above the tachs, and still be readable. Speedometers are for ski boats and are generally useless for the average boater. Most operators select a cruising speed based on rpm, fuel efficiency, or sea state, and the vessel's speed through the water follows. Who thinks, "I think I'll run the boat at 28.5 mph today" and sets the throttles accordingly? It seems unlikely unless you're running a log race or have to be at a destination at a given time, and for those purposes the speedometer doesn't need to be so large or prominently located, especially on a GPS-equipped boat. Save the dash space for the electronics.

Many engine manufacturers use proprietary digital or analog (or both) instrument and control panels, and although they serve up a lot more data than you'll ever really need to know about, these may present a couple of problems. First, they serve as advertisements for their providers, so they may well be bigger than necessary and take up a lot of real estate on the console. They are also generally provided in single-engine units, so the gauges can't

A much different yacht than the Viking Sport Cruiser and the Mochi, this Eastbay sedan has wider window mullions, but visibility is still good. The large radar and GPS chart plotter displays are positioned to create a heads-up display for the operator.

A good spot for a running light: up high in the clear, easy to see from another vessel, and out of the operator's line of sight so nighttime visibility isn't impacted.   NORDHAVN

Electronics

It's rare to find a 40-foot powerboat these days without an impressive array of electronics including a GPS and chart plotter, sonar or depth-sounder, radar, and a battery of VHF and SSB radios. Ideally, all these toys should be at arm's reach, and like the gauges, their displays should be perpendicular to your line of sight to improve readability. Many builders provide a concavely curved or angled electronics console situated at the best viewing angle. The radar and GPS chart plotter displays should be front-and-center, since they're most important to safe navigation and most frequently referred to and adjusted. Radios, depth-sounders, and other electronics should be arranged in sight and within easy reach.

be paired on a twin-engine boat. The best solution we've come across is to take them apart, if possible, and rearrange the component gauges and displays in a more sensible paired layout.

Engine-related gauges and alarms should include cooling water temperature, lube oil pressure, lube oil temperature, voltage, exhaust temperature, and the fuel filter-separator's water-in-fuel indicator. A ship's systems monitoring and alarm panel should include alarms for fire, smoke, high bilgewater levels, carbon monoxide, and bilge pump status displayed on a schematic of the boat's layout. Other indicators, depending on the systems onboard, might include refrigerator temperature, generator status, and low fuel level.

The Cabo 52 has three large-screen electronics displays. The wheel is nearly flat, and the Palm Beach—style engine controls are designed so the captain can back down on a fish while facing aft, with one hand securely on each lever.   FOREST JOHNSON/CABO YACHTS

CHAPTER 12

Topside Safety

No man will be a sailor who has contrivance enough to get himself into a jail; for being in a ship is being in a jail, with the chance of being drowned.

—Samuel Johnson

Small craft are called *pleasure boats* for a reason; you're supposed to be able to relax and enjoy yourself. But who can take pleasure and relax in an unsafe environment? Since boats should be as safe as they are fun, we'll look at the elements of topside safety that concern you and your family.

Marketing considerations aside, some customers have to be protected from themselves when it comes to topside design. The expanse of a shiny foredeck on a convertible may look great dockside, but it's a death trap at sea. And since boats can't choose their owners, they ought to be designed with a healthy margin of error built in for less experienced operators. Rather than catering to market demands, the best boatbuilders put safety ahead of fashion—and their astute marketing and sales departments capitalize on the results. In fact, many builders produce boats designed with safety foremost that look great at the same time.

Let's start with the basics. Recreational boats carry people of all ages, sizes, and levels of boating experience. It makes sense that safety-related features should be designed to the lowest common denominators: people with minimal strength, balance, and agility who need to get around a tossing and turning boat safely, and those lacking the experience with which to judge and anticipate naturally occurring hazards and vessel movements. Unfortunately not all boats measure up in the safety department. Instead we find slippery steps, low bow

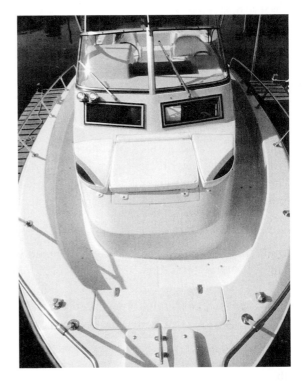

Here's why the walkaround can be such a great family boat. All the decks are recessed, flat, and safe to move around on, and the whole length is usable. You even get a cuddy cabin to get out of the weather, or for the occasional overnighter.

railings and 18-inch-high transom doors ready to cartwheel the unwary overboard, open transoms on outboards, foredecks that drop off like ski slopes, and other safety sins abounding.

When a boat has a safety problem, it's probably due to one of the following reasons: styling has won out over function and practicality, the designer has tried to squeeze too much into a given hull length, it costs more to do it right, or no one saw the problem coming. Foot-high bow railings, for example, may look stylish, and they certainly cost less.

The goal of topside safety is actually pretty uncomplicated. For the most part it involves keeping people from falling down or, what's worse, falling overboard. Falling overboard is the leading cause of boating deaths.

Nonskid

Most production boatbuilders mold the nonskid pattern into the part (foredeck, cockpit sole, etc.) using gelcoat. This minimizes the time it takes to produce the finished deck and results in a long-lasting finish; a nonskid finish can also be painted on an existing deck. If the nonskid is aggressive, it tears up boat shoes and pants knees in short order, and it can be harder to keep clean, but it also does a good job of gripping your feet. The best aggressive nonskid is not hard to clean, though, since its patterns allow scrub brush bristles to reach down into the valleys of the tread.

A finer pattern can also grip well and be easier to scrub off. Some builders use different nonskid patterns in different areas. For instance, a convertible's cockpit might appropriately get a coarser, more aggressive treatment on account of the fish slime and scales that tend to accumulate like a fine layer of motor oil underfoot. The foredeck and flybridge deck surfaces, which are usually just susceptible to getting wet, have a finer pattern.

The American Boat and Yacht Council (ABYC) is responsible for setting standards for the design of pleasure boats, with recommendations formulated by consensus among its industry members. The ABYC stipulates that nonskid surfaces should be used in exterior walkways and companionways, shower areas, weather decks, swim platforms, ladder steps and rungs, and on walkways adjacent to engines. The inclusion of weather decks suggests that

Safety rules on this Eastbay with its wide side decks, inboard-canted deckhouse for more shoulder room, and an unyielding, knee-braced 1¼-inch bow railing running from the cockpit to pulpit.

the whole foredeck should be covered with nonskid, not just a walkway strip down either side. It's a smart recommendation, since you'll eventually walk all over the foredeck for one reason or another. Nevertheless, partly in response to market demand, some manufacturers don't incorporate any nonskid forward, valuing a glossy finish over a safe working environment.

Cockpit nonskid should extend right up to the hull or hull liner and under the toe space, since that's where your toes typically are trying to dig in when leaning overboard to gaff a fish. Cockpit coamings, or washboards, should also have a nonskid finish. If foredeck access on an express cruiser is through an opening centerline windshield, the steps leading up from the bridge deck, the dash surface that gets walked on, and the centerline section of the foredeck, right up to and including the pulpit, should be covered with nonskid.

The bow of this railing-free convertible is a no-man's-land at sea. Curiously, this clean-and-uncluttered look takes precedence over safety offshore. It's too bad when a decent bow railing makes a boat uncool.

The term *aggressive nonskid* takes on a whole new meaning aboard coast guard ships. In the early 1970s, in the cutters I served on, we'd prime and paint the steel deck, roll out a fresh coat of paint, sprinkle on a layer of black beauty sandblasting

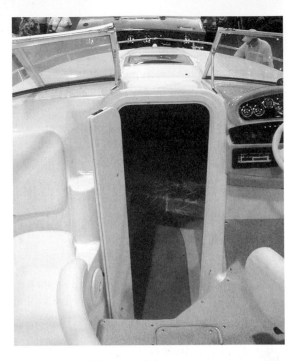

Steps are too small here for safe bow access on this personal injury lawyer's dream. Try climbing back down dockside, let alone when the boat's rocking in a chop.

grit, let the paint dry, sweep off the excess grit, and roll out another thin coat of paint. As a result, most of us wore out a pair of Boondocker boots every six months. In the yachting world, a two-part polyurethane paint such as Interlux's Interthane, into which a fine grit is premixed, is a better solution. It can be applied over a smooth or previously nonskid-surfaced deck.

Railings

Bow railings, side-deck grabrails, bridge railings, and cockpit coaming heights are common topside safety concerns on many boats and yachts. On numerous midrange, cruising-style boats, if the foredecks have railings at all, they're often less than 24 inches high, making them effective tripping hazards on your way overboard! Bridges frequently have low railings overlooking the cockpit and as often as not lack railings altogether around ladder wells.

This Four Winns has great centerline access to the bow on these large molded steps.

Cockpits on small outboard-powered boats typically have minimal coaming heights, no handrails of any kind, and little if anything in the way of protection aft to prevent the unwary passenger from somersaulting over the stern, even on boats capable of rapid acceleration. Transom doors on express cruisers are often as low as 18 inches, flimsily made of nonstructural plastic, and devoid of balance-enhancing toe kicks.

The Canadian Camano 31's cockpit is, like the rest of the boat, well-designed with a 39-inch-high railing atop the gunwale, making it a safe place at sea.

So, at the top of any list of deck safety requirements are rugged railings that are high enough to prevent falls overboard and strong enough to withstand the impact of someone falling hard against them. The question is, where should railings be fitted, and how high and strong should they be?

Where?

In a perfect world, railings, coamings, or bulwarks would surround all topside decks, making it tough to fall overboard anywhere on the vessel. If side decks are too narrow (as they often are) to permit extending bow railings all the way aft to the cockpit, chest-high grabrails should be provided wherever side railings aren't. Ideally, bow railings should extend from the cockpit to the pulpit. All too often there's a rail-less no-man's-land between the deckhouse grabrails forward and the beginning of the bow railing. I've

heard salesmen explain that there is no need to go forward at sea, so why bother with bow railings that are high enough to prevent falls overboard? One can only speculate that the boats they are selling will remain at anchor or tied to the dock.

The ABYC's (minimal) recommendations call for the perimeter of weather decks normally occupied when underway to be equipped with railings, lifelines, bulwarks, coamings, grabrails, or other enclosures. That's a good start, but unfortunately the ABYC makes an exception for open boats. They also exempt wide-open bridge ladder openings, which place the cockpit 8 feet below a single misstep away. Then there's the issue of rail height, which we'll address in a moment.

Common sense dictates that bow railings should be inboard of the rubrail at their tops as well as their bases so they aren't damaged by piling impact, an aspect of rail design that is overlooked by boatbuilders

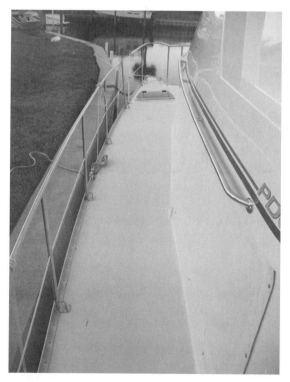

The side decks on the PDQ 34 power catamaran are 29 inches wide, enough room for two people to stroll past each other without giving way, and wraparound, 30-inch railings stretch from stem to stern.

This Eastbay 43 sedan has big molded steps leading up to wide side decks and a strong, high railing from pulpit to cockpit. Toe kick space all around the cockpit will keep passengers on their feet.

to a surprising degree. Mystifyingly, on many boats the tops of the bow railings flare several inches outboard of the rubrail. Such a design may increase the chances of a person falling overboard and further complicate the incident if the person strikes the rail while falling. The railings are also harder to reach when you're walking upright along the side decks, and they make it more difficult to stay balanced. In addition, many bow railings project well forward of the boat's stem or pulpit, further degrading their effectiveness. While poor bow rail positioning is in some cases part of the form-over-function syndrome, it seems just as likely that poor engineering is to blame.

The ABYC sensibly says that grabrails, or "handhold devices," are supposed to be provided on all weather decks intended for use underway. This includes side and foredecks, around topside seating, in companionways, and on ladders or stairways. Exceptions are made for the person at the helm, who presumably has the wheel to hold onto, and in areas already provided with railings. Grabrails should have a minimum clearance of 1¼ inches from adjacent surfaces to provide enough finger clearance.

How High?

What's a reasonable height for adequate safety in these areas? The American Bureau of Shipping

(ABS) maintains a standard railing height of 39 inches (1 m) for commercial vessels, and so does Britain's Maritime and Coast Guard Agency (MCA). ABS requirements for yachts state that railing height can be as low as 30 inches, although these requirements only apply to vessels over 79 feet.

U.S. Coast Guard regulations from 46 U.S. Code subchapter T for small inspected passenger vessels under 100 gross tons are also worth paying attention to, even if they don't legally apply to small pleasure boats. Aboard ferries and excursion vessels, these regulations call for 36- to 39.5-inch-high rails, or equivalent protection, around the perimeter of all decks accessible to passengers or crew. An exception for "big-game angling" is allowed under certain circumstances, with the railing height reduced in the immediate vicinity of the angler to 30 inches. When done fishing, the higher railing requirement is back in effect. To accommodate the regulation, the removable section of railing is replaced.

The ABYC, on the other hand, requires only a 24-inch height for railings, lifelines, bulwarks, and coamings. If the railing is higher than 24 inches, an intermediate railing must be provided. In my opinion, this is an inadequate height. Flybridges are an exception, with ABYC recommending a 30-inch railing or at least a 24-inch-high perimeter seat back.

With no railing aft, the sunpad on this 70 mph go-fast boat is unfit for human occupancy, unless perhaps the boat is tied to the dock.

A nice, wide, but railing-less side deck on the left, and a narrow side deck with a railing that's too low (14 in.) to do any good on the right.

Here's a bow railing begging for a redesign. This one's too short, and too far outboard, to be of much use to anyone, and it actually can create a false sense of security forward.

I am citing ABS and MCA standards as a point of reference—which is not to suggest that a 25-foot Chris Craft must be built to the same safety standards as an 800-foot container ship. But at what point below 39 inches does a railing become too low to be effective? If you're 4 feet tall, maybe a 2-foot railing is high enough. My own practical experience indicates that a 30-inch railing is the minimum height offering a tangible sense of security, and that's still 9 inches shorter than ship standards. The U.S. Coast Guard's relaxation to 30 inches for anglers seems to bear this out. Much lower than 30 inches, and the average person's center of gravity is just too high for such a low fulcrum point to be effective. If the fulcrum point, or point of contact with the leg, isn't well above the knee, a fall overboard is much more likely.

The 16- to 24-inch-high bow railings common to many small pleasure boats can actually be a greater safety hazard than none at all. A leg can easily get caught between the gunwale and the railing on one's

way overboard, breaking it cleanly between the knee and foot. It's a safe bet that you'll want full use of both legs while swimming back to the boarding platform. Low railings can also lend a false sense of security.

How Strong?

The ABYC says that any pulpit, bow railing, or coaming must be able to withstand a 400-pound static load in any direction at any point. In reality, many railings could not withstand such a load, at least not without significant deformation. Railing gates have to pass the 400-pound load test and are supposed to have sailorproof latches to prevent them from opening accidentally. Railings and grabrails, usually made of aluminum or stainless steel pipe, should be between ¾- and 1½-inch outside diameter so they're easy to grip. Naturally, the larger the diameter of the railings and stanchions for a given wall thickness, the stronger and stiffer the railing.

A decent railing has to be strong, stiff, and reasonably unyielding as well as adequately high. It needs strength to resist the high-impact load of an off-balance body slamming against it. Grand Banks's Eastbay-series planing yachts are excellent examples: their 1.25-inch stainless steel bow railings supported by stanchions just 3 feet apart feel stiff and secure. Perhaps another reason for the widespread use of 24-inch railings is that larger (more expensive) pipe stock is needed to support the extra lever arm created by a higher railing.

Going Overboard in Outboards

Boats with transom-mounted outboards are also a recurring safety problem. Most outboard-powered boats are capable of strong acceleration, so an adequate railing or coaming is needed, nowhere more than across the transom. Some of these boats don't even have motor wells, just a 1-foot-high transom for the center third of the boat. This configuration offers practically no protection against falling overboard. Then there are boats with motor wells and low, nonstructural plastic gates that flip up when the outboard motor is down. These hinged gates, often less than 24 inches high, offer little security during unexpected acceleration. Any solid water making its way over the stern would easily overcome the spring-loaded retaining clips that are sometimes used to hold the gates up.

The round or rectangular plastic inspection plates in the bottom of the motor well are often made of nonstructural material and are rarely leakproof. Anything made of metal below such an inspection plate will eventually corrode. The most seaworthy outboard boat is one with a full-height transom or a permanent, full-height, molded-fiberglass motor well. Both designs offer good passenger safety and improve seaworthiness to boot.

Transom doors come in two basic varieties, one-piece and two-piece, in the latter of which the coaming and door open separately. The door section can hinge either inboard or outboard; the inboard-swinging design is unlikely to come open when

A typical budget boat from hell. There are no toe kicks along the sides, so you'll be off balance every time you lean overboard to grab a line or gaff a fish. The motor well gate is about half the height it ought to be, and there's no toe kick there, either. The scuppers are too small, with 3/4-inch drain lines, so they'll drain slowly and clog readily. The stern cleats aren't recessed, so they'll attract line snags.

There is very little to keep a wave out, or you in, in this transom-free zone. No wonder it's for sale!

running offshore, since its weight will hold it shut against its frame even if the latch works loose, and is therefore safer. An inboard-swinging transom door is also less susceptible to damage when backing into a slip, and you don't have to worry about it interfering with crossed mooring lines.

A two-piece transom door with an upward-swinging coaming section offers excellent security,

This Correct Craft wakeboard boat has a large swim platform, which comes in handy when changing gear. The rubber nonskid material is grippy underfoot, yet comfortable to sit on in a bathing suit. The size of the platform keeps swimmers clear of the inboard prop under the boat.

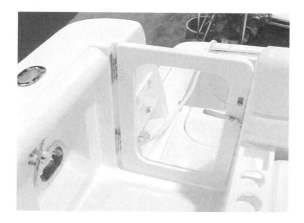

The transom door on the Tiara 50 is as high as the coaming. The stern line can be led from the cleat up to the washboard hawsehole or directly overboard through a hull-side hawsehole. Versatility is a great thing when it comes to mooring a boat. The window in the transom door gives a better view astern when backing into a slip.

since the coaming will provide passenger protection even if the door inadvertently comes unlatched. The strength and size of the hinges and latch should be sufficient to the task of holding the transom

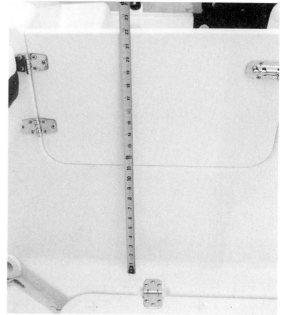

At 22 inches high, this transom door is 6 to 8 inches too low to do much good. Note the scupper at the end of the hatch drain gutter. Water will collect and turn the gutter a nice rust brown within a few weeks of delivery.

door securely open or closed. The transom door design ought to include a toe kick space, and the door should be as high as the surrounding cockpit coaming. It should be gasketed to admit little if any water when backing down.

Steps and Ladders

The ABYC tells us that a change in elevation greater than 12 inches to a flybridge, companionway, or walkway necessitates a step or ladder. Twelve inches is a pretty healthy step; an 8- to 9-inch rise is preferable. The same 400-pound load tolerance mentioned for railings applies to ladders, although a permanent deformation of $\frac{1}{4}$ inch is allowable. The clearance to adjacent structures is increased to 5 inches to provide adequate toe space. Step or rung spacing should be no more than 12 inches, and handholds or grabrails are to be provided.

A typical convertible ladder is seen on this Davis 58, with flat, level treads, a handrailing, and a slope of about 10 degrees from vertical. Its mounting design makes it easier to clean the deck below.

Silverton's unorthodox designs certainly make a boat safer to get around on. The stairs to the bridge on this Silverton 42 have a gentle rise and large steps, and there's a railing on either side for added safety. Big steps lead up to the wide side decks, where hand and side railings lead forward. The bridge has a high railing, too. The nonskid everywhere topside is grippy underfoot.

The Sailfish 30-06 has lots of interior depth, a full 30 inches high to the coaming, 4 to 6 inches more than some similar boats.

The wider and flatter a nonskid-treated tread is, the more comfortable and secure underfoot it will be. The most uncomfortable and least secure type is a pipe ladder, with no flat surface or nonskid at all. Fortunately, most builders who use pipe treads specify the oval-type, which has a more comfortable and secure stepping surface. Also important are the rise and run, the latter being the angle at which the ladder inclines from vertical. A vertical ladder is the most difficult to climb; inclining the ladder 20 degrees or so reduces the arm strength and effort required to hold on.

Although it's a long reach from the cockpit up to the side deck, many builders neglect to provide a step, either of the molded or folding variety. A molded step can't be moved, so it'll always be there when you expect it to be. A folding step, like the ones used on the Bertram 43, will stow out of the way when not in use but deploy easily when needed.

Speaking of steps, there's often a discrepancy of an inch or more in the height of two adjacent companionway steps. Uneven steps present a tripping hazard to the unwary. Just as in a house, a boat stairway or ladder's rise and run should be consistent from top to bottom.

Boarding

The ABYC calls for a means of unassisted boarding from the water to be provided on all boats. This means that the person in the water should be able to deploy the ladder from the water and climb up it unassisted. Another obvious call is to locate boarding ladders on boats with outboard or stern-drive power as far outboard as practical to minimize chances of propeller-induced injury. These boarding ladders, according to the ABYC, have to project at least 12 inches into the water, meaning only one step has to be submerged. I'd like to suggest that the standard-setters try climbing a ladder with the bottom rung

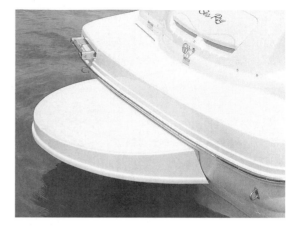

The cover over this Sea Ray's outdrive, if installed on all similar boats, would undoubtedly prevent a lot of diving and swimming accidents. SEA RAY

This ProKat boarding ladder is simple to deploy — just give it a shove to release it from its clip, and it's also wide and easy to climb. We'd just give it flat treads that are easier on the feet.

The teak steps on this aft-cabin yacht can't be climbed without hanging onto the ladder, a decided inconvenience considering this is the yacht's main access point.

The Dettling 51 has it all together in a lot of important areas. Note the waist-high wraparound railings and the water-deployable five-step swim ladder.

to be pulled from its normal stowed position leaning against the transom. This ladder projects several steps into the water, making it a relatively easy to ascend.

Express cruisers often have their stern cleats mounted externally outboard of the swim platform, thus creating a hazard to swimmers. The Eurostyled sloping transom puts the designer in a quandary as to where to mount the cleats, since there's no actual transom and the undersides of the washboards are inaccessible because of storage bins. An easy fix is to install pop-out cleats or to relocate them so they're out of the swimmers' way. Sportfishermen solve the problem with flush hawseholes leading to cleats mounted below the coaming. Either way, swimmers will be safer and anglers will appreciate the cleaner, snag-free surfaces.

just 12 inches below the surface, and nothing other than the ladder and a grab bar to hold onto!

Much less upper body strength is needed to use a ladder that projects two or more steps into the water. This is especially true when the swimmer is fully clothed and tired from swimming back to the boat. While we were waterskiing on a Cape Cod lake a few summers ago, we spotted three teenage girls who had been blown away from shore a quarter-mile or so. They'd been hanging on to their inflatable for 45 minutes and were unable to swim back to shore. We flipped the boarding ladder down on our 17-foot lake boat and invited them aboard. Two of the three girls couldn't get up the ladder, which sticks all of 12 inches below the surface, so my accommodating, teenage weight-lifter son promptly hoisted them up, thereby achieving something of a hero's status in their eyes.

Be aware of how difficult it may be to reach up and deploy the ladder from the water. Some boats have "concealed" hatches over the ladder, which would have to be flipped up out of the way to get to it.

One of the best examples of an ergonomic boarding ladder is on the Dettling 51; it merely has

Foredecks and Side Decks

In the interest of expanding interior volume, some builders have done away with side decks altogether, meaning you have to climb up on the dash and open the center windshield to get forward. These centerline-access designs can work pretty well if they include large, nonskid-covered, molded steps leading up to the dash, but a railing or handhold of some kind other than the windshield itself, which may be lightly built, is essential.

Sometimes the molded or folding steps become more of an afterthought, pushed off to one side because of the companionway opening, or there are no railings either at the windshield or along the foredeck centerline. This leads to a lurch-and-lunge routine as you try to make your way forward to the anchor in a chop—amusing to onlookers, maybe, but not to the performer. On heavily cambered foredecks,

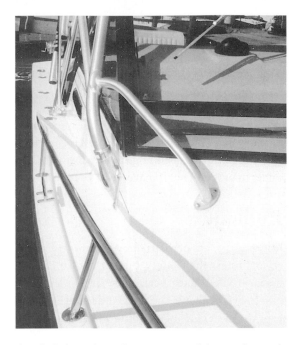

The side decks on this 27-foot express sportfish are wide enough, but obstructions like this poorly thought out half-tower leg make it hard to get by safely.

The Eastbay has a combination of handrails on the trunk cabin and 30-inch-high bow railings that carry aft for safety in a seaway. Excellent nonskid on wide side decks is another important safety feature. The dorades provide natural ventilation belowdecks, and two spring cleats a few feet from each other add docking versatility. This boat was obviously designed by fellow boaters.

Crew Overboard

Every boat should be outfitted and its crew prepared for the likelihood of a crew overboard. A life ring, life sling, or other throwable device should be mounted both in the cockpit and on the bridge for quick use. It's a good idea to have lifesaving equipment like a MOM8 crew-overboard kit that deploys in just a few seconds. These kits include a carbon dioxide (CO_2) cartridge-inflated flotation device with 40 pounds of buoyancy, an 8-hour steady-state light, a 16-inch sea anchor, and a recovery harness. Water-activated radio transmitters and strobe lights are also available. Some of these transmitters can even be rigged to turn on an alarm and shut down the engines. Direction-finding antennas are also available to help the crew locate beacon-equipped victims.

Don't leave home without one of these close at hand.

NORDHAVN

unless you are standing on the dock, it's also tough to reach the spring cleats when side decks are lacking. Not a pretty picture, but it's one that a plaintiff's lawyer would salivate over.

In the interest of expanding interior volume, especially on so-called express cruisers, functional side decks have just about been eliminated. To create more room inside, side decks are often just 3 to 5 inches wide, or are effectively reduced to the width of the railing stanchion mounts, leaving little space between the railing and the deckhouse. These boats typically have lots of pitch and camber in the foredeck to increase cabin headroom, so stepping from the cabintop down to the side deck can be hazardous.

A proper side deck is flat, covered in nonskid, and at least 10 to 12 inches wide. It should be clear of railing stanchions, antennas, and tuna-tower legs. The deckhouse sides and/or bimini top should slope inboard from the side deck so people aren't caught off balance if they should lose their grip. Handrails along the deckhouse should be continuous and mounted at a height that kids and grown-ups alike can grip securely. If the side decks are 14 inches wide or wider, extending the bow railing aft to the cockpit is a good idea. If the boat has a trunk cabin, it should also have a handrail to supplement the bow railing.

Toe Kicks

The need for toe kick space should be obvious, but it's often overlooked. As in a kitchen, toe kick space on a boat is provided so a person can stand right up against the countertop, or cockpit coaming, without feeling off balance. Good balance on a boat is even more important than in kitchens, which are generally stationary. Toe kicks can be created by carving out a space at deck level that's 3 or 4 inches deep and high, or by fitting wide coaming washboards that project farther inboard than the interior hull sides or cockpit liner.

Toe kicks allow your thighs to make contact before the toes do. Without it, you would be off balance. The balance problem only gets worse when leaning overboard to gaff a fish or grab a dockline. As mentioned on pages 207–8, nonskid should continue right up to the liner, since your toes are usually planted at the deck edge when leaning over the side.

Boats that lack cockpit toe kicks usually do so because of the added complexity and expense of the fiberglass tooling. On production fiberglass boats, the cockpit deck and hull-side liner are almost always molded as a single fiberglass part. If the coaming washboard is also part of that same mold, a toe kick cannot be provided unless expensive breakaway

tooling is used in the liner at deck level. Buyers should be aware of the trade-off here.

Better builders usually attach separately tooled washboards to the gunwale and cockpit liner. Sometimes this is a single, U-shaped fiberglass part that includes the washboard for both sides and the transom. The washboard, usually 8 inches or more wide, effectively creates a toe space at deck level. This extra unit is more time-consuming and expensive for the builder to produce, but it makes for a safer boat.

Drainage

Deck drainage has perhaps more to do with a boat's seaworthiness than safety, but it can also impact passenger safety since a clean, dry deck is less slippery. In everyday use, the cockpit drainage system keeps the deck clear of standing water that results from washdowns and rainwater. In extreme conditions, green water that makes its way aboard has to be shed quickly to preserve reserve buoyancy and stability. A deck drainage system must, then, work quickly and efficiently to direct water overboard and resist clogging by debris.

For a cockpit deck to be self-draining, it must be reasonably high above the waterline; that's because most scuppers work both ways, and would just as willingly let water in as out. With a full load of fuel, passengers, and provisions and a gaggle of anglers milling around at the transom, the deck should still be well above sea level to provide reserve buoyancy and prevent backflooding. The higher the deck, the greater the reserve buoyancy and the lower the likelihood of backflooding, but a balance has to be struck in the interest of keeping the angler close enough to the water to play her fish.

The deck must have enough pitch so that water runs aft to the scuppers, so the forward end of the cockpit deck needs to be higher than it is at the transom. Deck camber, which is the slight convex athwartships curvature, or crown, helps water drain outboard as it moves aft, making for a dryer deck. Gutters are sometimes molded in at the edges of the cockpit sole to channel water aft and to the corner-mounted aft scuppers.

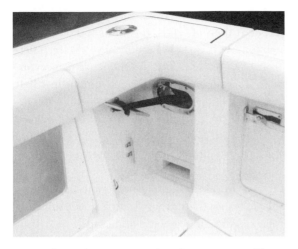

Here's a deep cockpit gutter—so deep that twisting an ankle is a distinct possibility. The rectangular scupper is not recessed below the gutter level, either, so an annoying and unsightly few ounces of standing water will remain onboard.

The hatch gutters in this cockpit drain directly to the scuppers and overboard. The stern scupper itself is not recessed below the gutter level, though, so standing water will remain. The hatch itself is flanged, and the gutter is deep, so the lazarette below should stay dry.

Sometimes these gutters are too deep, however, creating real ankle twisters.

Coast guard–inspected vessels operating more than 20 miles offshore are generally required to have their cockpit decks at least 10 inches above the full-load waterline, a standard that might be relaxed only if nonreturn devices are fitted. Guidelines for scupper size are also provided.

How fast the water makes it to the scuppers is one thing, but how fast it then drains overboard is another. The speed at which it drains is a function of the number of scuppers and hatch gutter drain lines, and how big they are. The cleanest, simplest, and most reliable scupper installation consists of a pair of rectangular holes in either corner of the transom, recessed slightly below deck level to collect that last half a pint of water. The bigger the scuppers, the faster the deck will drain, an important consideration when operating well offshore where seas can build faster than you can get back to port.

Scuppers should extend all the way to the cockpit corners, because that's where water naturally collects. Some builders install flaps on the outboard side of the scuppers to lessen the amount of water shipped when backing down. The large-hole-in-the-transom type of scupper is the simplest and my personal favorite; it won't clog like a hose and is easy to inspect and keep clear.

Nowadays, more builders are installing flush deck drains with hoses leading belowdecks and then overboard instead of transom scuppers. The reasons given for the shift range from reducing the water shipped aboard when backing or lying-to in a trough to aesthetic concerns. This is all well and good, but be aware that drainage is not complete unless the drain plate is recessed below deck level. The slots in the drain plate (if one is installed) also reduce drainage capacity and are subject to clogging. Drain lines are also susceptible to coming loose belowdeck where you can't see them, with the water ending up in the bilge instead of back in the ocean.

The other problem with drain lines, whether fed directly by deck drains or by hatch gutters, concerns the size of the hose used. Incredibly, some builders

Cockpits with gutter drain systems are all the rage, but make sure the cluster of hoses belowdecks doesn't come loose. This hose exits below the waterline, which is not a good design since it adds one more way for the boat to sink.

use hose as small is 0.5 to 0.75 inch, guaranteeing that the drain line will clog when presented with its first fistful of striper scales or pine needles. A 1.25-inch drain line, in my experience, is the absolute smallest diameter acceptable, both for its clogging resistance and for its drainage capacity. The U.S. Coast Guard seems to agree, with subchapter T regulations defining a scupper as a pipe or tube at least 30 mm (1.25 in.) in diameter leading down from a deck or sole and through the hull to drain water overboard. ABYC, on the other hand, only requires that "each scupper or freeing port shall have a cross-sectional area of at least that of a 1-inch diameter circle (0.785 sq. in.). The 1.25-inch scupper has an area of 1.23 square inches, more than half again as large as the 1-inch drain.

ABYC recommendations also say that, with a cockpit full to the brim (the fixed sill height), the scuppers should be large enough so that 75 percent of the water should drain off within 90 seconds. That's by no means a very stringent requirement, as 90 seconds is a very long time to have tons of water sloshing around on deck, decreasing stability significantly with its free-surface effect. If it took half that time to drain *completely*, I'd consider that a minimal drainage capacity. You'll feel the same way if you ever have a breaker dump 6 inches of seawater in your cockpit, let alone fill it up.

When gutters are used, of course, they must be deeper at their aft ends. It sounds too obvious to mention, yet it isn't always done. I've also seen networks of six or eight deck and gutter drain lines connected to a single pair of through-hull fittings that could not possibly manage the volume of water directed to them. Also, through-hull fittings should be well above the waterline to prevent backflooding, which can be a real problem if that maze of plumbing connections in the lazarette comes loose over time. But when a deck is close to the waterline—say, within 8 inches—there's little room left to provide sufficient slope for efficient overboard drainage.

A few convertible sportfishermen builders have taken to locating scuppers on the hull sides aft rather than the transom, reasoning that less water will be shipped when backing hard on a fish. Of course, this makes them susceptible to shipping more water when lying-to in a trough. The bottom line is that there's really no substitute for generous deck height above the waterline. I was once on a new 19-foot Boston Whaler Outrage that, with full fuel and two (big) guys onboard, floated with its cockpit deck scupper (located just aft of the console) right at the waterline. In this case, most of the reserve buoyancy (which Whaler prides itself on) comes from the watertight interior hull liner.

ABYC tells us that the minimum height of a cockpit deck, in inches, should be 0.22 times the boat's length in feet. That means our 19-foot Whaler should have a cockpit height, above the waterline, of 4.2 inches.

In summary, the elements of good cockpit drainage include adequate deck height above the waterline, a pitched and cambered deck, watertight hatches, large, clog-resistant scuppers and drain lines, and minimal belowdeck plumbing.

U.S. Coast Guard–Enforced Safety Regulations

Federal law weighs in, too, when it comes to the safety of small craft. The portion of the Code of

Federal Regulation identified as 33CFR 181–183 lists federal regulations for pleasure boats; the U.S. Coast Guard administers and enforces these codes. Many aspects of life afloat are addressed, including the use of and outfitting with life preservers and other lifesaving equipment, emergency position-indicating beacons (EPIRBs), and cooking, heating, and lighting systems.

Also covered is anything that is likely to cause a fire or explosion, including gasoline fumes and electrical sparks. On boats with permanently installed inboard gas engines, this is addressed by regulations concerning natural and forced ventilation, fire extinguishers, ignition protection, backfire prevention, battery installation, wiring, grounding, and overcurrent protection. Fuel system requirements for conventional inboards and stern drives over 16 feet are meant to eliminate or minimize the chances of fuel leaks causing explosion and fire. These address fuel tanks, pumps, hoses, carburetors, fittings, connectors, and fuel tank pressure testing.

Also included in 33CFR are regulations relating to preventing swampings and sinkings of boats less than 20 feet in length that require them to float when swamped (full of water) with a full passenger load onboard. Even when these boats are swamped or capsized, they should remain floating and level to give passengers safe haven until help arrives. Note that "level flotation" doesn't even necessarily keep the gunwales above the water. The occupants have to stay seated, and the test for compliance is done in calm water. In fact, the free-surface effect (the momentum of the water in the boat sloshing around) of a boat with level flotation would have a very good chance of capsizing the boat. But level flotation does keep the boat afloat, and will also keep the boat floating higher than less stringent flotation provisions would do.

Staying with the boat is almost always the smart thing to do, since it's easier for a rescuer to spot the boat than your head or life jacket. It's also smart because people often drown trying to swim for shore. 33CFR also requires that manufacturers of most boats under 20 feet display a boat's passenger and overall weight capacities as well as maximum allowed horsepower ratings.

Information on these regulations, and on boat recalls due to safety defects, can be found online at www.uscgboating.org. This is a good Web site for any boater to become familiar with.

CHAPTER 13

Accommodations

Boy, those French: they have a different word for everything.

—Steve Martin

People usually think of their boat as a home away from home, at least if it's big enough to have a cabin with a galley, head, and a couple of berths. Obviously the average boat doesn't have the room of the average house, but what the builder does with the room available can make a big difference in how eager you are to get back home after a weekend afloat.

Any boat has a finite amount of interior volume, defined by the space inside the hull, decks, and superstructure. The success with which that space is apportioned depends on the artfulness of the designer. A convertible sportfisherman will have a large cockpit, since anglers need plenty of space to move around aft. Cruising yachts have smaller cockpits and engine rooms (often at the expense of machinery accessibility), and commensurately larger saloons and cabins.

Some builders have taken to installing engines with V-drives or remote-mounted gears, which allows more flexibility in engine room location (see chapter 8). The engine room and its forward bulkhead can be shifted farther aft with these drivetrains, opening up more room for accommodations forward. An aft engine room makes a lot of sense for many cruising yachts, since the machinery noise is more easily isolated from the "people compartment," making for a quieter yacht.

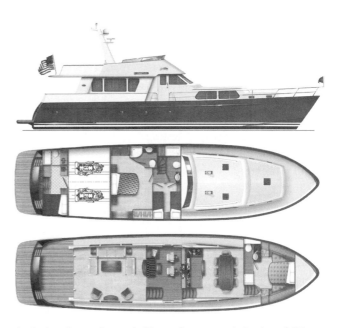

This high-end, Hunt-designed Alden 72 has a main deck saloon, full-beam owner's suite, aft engine room, and crew quarters; the lower deck includes galley, dining room, and guest suite. It also has a superb offshore hull form and high-strength epoxy resin–infused construction. ALDEN YACHTS

Obviously, the amount of space dedicated to accommodations, which we define as the interior living space of a boat, depends on the boat's intended use. A center console generally has *no* accommodations unless it's big enough to have a standup head inside the console (if you want to call that an accommodation!). A flush-deck or pilothouse motor yacht,

A Viking 54 saloon with L-shaped settee and cabinets aft, galley with granite countertops, a dinette opposite, and a large TV, all forward.　　　　　　　VIKING YACHTS

The Scout 262 from Abaco makes great use of space. A 6-foot, 3-inch single berth extends aft under the bridge deck and is open to the cabin, making it easy to get in and out of.

on the other hand, has tons of interior space thanks to its large, heavy superstructure, which of course also makes it less seaworthy than a lower-profile vessel.

Just be aware of the 30- or 40-footer that's advertised as having the largest master stateroom, or saloon, or whatever in its class. That space came from somewhere, and it was likely out of the engine room. Either that, or the boat is so beamy and so full in the bow that it will be a bucking bronco terror to ride offshore.

The Ocean 40 convertible is a great example of efficient space utilization. This boat has its master stateroom situated amidships, just forward of the engine room, instead of in the bow. This arrangement—rare or perhaps even unique in a convertible of this size—gives the owner a slightly better ride at speed in a seaway, with lower vertical accelerations. Ocean Yachts accomplished it by tucking the master stateroom partially under the saloon's raised dinette and galley countertop. The resulting layout, dominated by the centerline dinette, is a bit unconventional, but it's a trade-off that makes a lot of sense for many owners.

Companionways and Passageways

Just like at home, companionway stairs should ideally have a gentle rise and run to make descent safe

While most convertibles favor extra storage space instead of windows, Tiara compromises with a single window while still fitting in a large-screen TV and a storage cabinet. The galley-down design works well, putting the space below the windshield to good use.　　TIARA YACHTS

and easy, and the rise, or vertical separation between the steps, should be consistent from one step to the next, which is not something you can take for granted. A variation in stair or tread height is an invitation to stumbling. A step with a rise of over 10 inches is hard to climb, and may just indicate the designer's failure to think through the problem properly. Stairs or ladders on boats should always have handrails to grab on to in a seaway.

You should be able to navigate comfortably down a companionway and through a passageway without bumping into frames and bulkheads along the way. That calls for at least 22 inches, and preferably 24 inches, of unobstructed width. A few inches narrower may be acceptable on a smaller boat, leaving a little more room for adjacent staterooms and other compartments. Some boats have a 24-inch-wide companionway, but the sliding companionway door only opens to 19 or 20 inches, indicating a faulty design.

Saloon

The saloon, or *salon* for most of us (I happen to have an unusually highbrow editor who has appointed himself guardian of the language of the sea), is the yacht's living room. It's invariably in the middle of the boat. On a convertible, it's between the cockpit and the cabin and over the engine room. On an aft cabin motor yacht, it's between the aft cabin and the forward staterooms, and again over the engine room.

Saloons should have plenty of seating, generally on L- and U-shaped settees with either storage space or pull-out beds beneath. If a TV is installed, it should be viewable from the settees, or at least from one of them. On larger convertibles, the galley is often part of and on the same level as the saloon, separated at most by an island countertop. Many people like to cook with a bit of privacy, but while still remaining part of the social group, so this arrangement works well. Smaller yachts often have the galley down a few steps, under the glassed-in windshield.

Saloons usually have plenty of glass, at least on three sides, which lets in plenty of daylight while

This Bertram 510 saloon is divided into two conversation areas, one forward with the curved dinette opposite the galley, and one aft with the large settee. BERTRAM YACHTS

The upscale, offshore-bred Eastbay 47 saloon has big windows all around that permit a comfortable lower helm station. The open layout sports lots of teak and convertible settee to port. EASTBAY YACHTS

providing a good view of the great outdoors. Some trawlers and a few pilothouse motor yachts have either narrow side decks aft, outboard of the saloon, or do away with the side deck on one side altogether.

Head and Showers

Even some 26-foot walkaround models have an enclosed head these days, and that's a strong attraction for any family boat. Especially when the head doubles as a shower, with a pull-out spigot that serves as the

The asymmetrical deckhouse on this Nordhavn 57 opens up the saloon to port while providing weather deck access forward to starboard.

showerhead, this makes for a great use of interior space. On larger boats, the trend is for every stateroom to have its *own* head and shower, and builders try to meet consumer demand. But when you consider that space is at a premium on most boats, it's a questionable priority, considering how much time a head is actually occupied. Many three-bedroom homes only have one or two bathrooms, after all. While having a private head for each stateroom has its marketing appeal, and some owners insist on it, the trade-off is always less available space elsewhere. It means the staterooms, for starters, have to be smaller.

Any comfortable head needs to be at least 24 by 36 inches just to maneuver in, and a separate shower at least 24 inches square. As mentioned, many builders of smaller (26- to 40-foot) cruisers save space, making the shower part of the head by providing a bracket to hold the sink spigot so it can

This Chaparral 310's head has an electric toilet, sink with pull-out spigot for use as a shower head, opening portlight, toilet paper splash cover, mirrored vanity, and a seat over the toilet.

This trawler yacht's head includes a separate shower compartment with molded seat, a great feature to have when offshore.

NORDHAVN

do double-duty as a showerhead. With this design, make sure that the curtain provided completely encloses the person taking a shower to contain the water, and especially that it keeps water away from the head door's sill. Some of the European builders use circular shower units that are closed only when the shower is in use. These effectively contain the water and prevent the shower area from robbing head space. Inward-opening doors work better at containing shower water, since a drip flange can be fitted at the lower edge of the door, but they can be difficult to open from the outside if someone inside becomes injured or unconscious.

One variation on the head-and-shower theme that makes sense for many boats is separate toilet and shower compartments, allowing both to be used at the same time. Carver offers good examples of how to do this right, with the added nifty feature of a vanity between these two compartments in many of their models. Of course, the most economical use of space is to provide two staterooms private access to the same head, opening up deck space for a larger saloon or maybe larger closets. Or, two staterooms can have their own heads while sharing a single shower in between.

Toilets range from self-contained portable toilets that are carried off the boat and dumped manually, to fancy electric vacuum-flush units with holding tanks. Some toilets are supplied with Y-valves that direct the contents either to the holding tank or directly overboard when operating offshore, but there are restrictions on these Y-valves in some areas. Holding tanks are fitted with dockside pumpout connections that allow the tank to be emptied in suitably equipped marinas.

Larger yachts do very well with a day head near the companionway door, so that anglers covered with muck don't go traipsing through the cabin en route. An exhaust fan is always a welcome feature, of course—just make sure it vents somewhere it won't come back to haunt you. AC 120-volt outlets in any potentially wet area, like the head or galley, should be GFI (ground fault interrupted) protected to help prevent electrical shock.

Berths

The builder's brochure may tell you that a boat will sleep six, but that may be a qualified statement on some boats. A lot of midcabin cruisers, for instance, have a convertible dinette that's supposed to sleep two, but the occupants had better be under 5 feet, 8 inches if they want to stretch out! Measure all the berths before buying the boat, since you don't want to be unpleasantly surprised on your first overnighter with the whole family on board.

The minimum acceptable length for a berth is 6 feet, 4 inches, and that's really just long enough for a 6-footer to be comfortable; 6 feet, 6 inches long is better still. For a single berth, 6 feet, 6 inches long and 24 inches wide (which is 6 inches narrower than a single bed at home) is also just big enough to be comfortable. A 30-inch width is much more practical, though the foot area can be a little narrower (unless you have very large feet). Since boats are usually narrower in the bow, tapering the foot of the berth (with your head facing aft) to 16 inches or so wide can be both necessary and acceptable. For a double berth to sleep two comfortably, look for a minimum width of 46 inches (which

Century's 3200 Offshore fishing express model has a comfortable cabin. The forward berth is easy to get in and out of with the molded stairs, the galley is compact but functional, and the dinette opposite the galley converts to single berth that at 64 inches is long enough for a child. The boat also has a midcabin berth aft.

is 2 inches narrower than the standard double bed, and 14 inches narrower than a queen). Wider is always better, all things considered.

The midships (near the fore-and-aft middle of the boat) area experiences the least amount of motion at sea, and is generally susceptible to *surge* (vertical rise and fall), but not much *pitching* action that you can feel. Rolling motions will feel more pronounced as you move outboard and up in the boat. When you put all this together, the best spot for a berth is on the centerline amidships down low in the hull.

Notwithstanding the suggestion above that a forward berth works best with the foot end forward, in all other instances a berth with the head facing forward is the best plan. If it faces aft, your head will be downhill when the hull is up on plane, and an athwartships (across the boat, from side to side) berth is just not as comfortable for most people offshore in a seaway. At least that's what 10 years at sea in the coast guard and navy taught me. An island berth, one that you can climb in or out from either side, is also preferable when occupied by more than one person. It's the berth arrangement of choice for bow staterooms, especially when designed for two people to sleep in, since either can get out of bed without climbing over the other.

Putting midcabin berths below the raised bridge deck on express cruisers is a great way to add sleeping capacity. Ease of entrance and exit is important,

The midcabin entrance on this 24-footer is tight and hard to navigate, which the builder has since improved with a more open design. It's a challenge to include so much on a boat that is only 8 feet 6 inches wide.

Four Winns' well-designed 278 Vista cruiser with an easy-to-enter midcabin berth.

Formula's 280SS hybrid runabout-cruiser may lack standing headroom, but it has a comfortable convertible settee/berth forward and an enclosed head to starboard.

though, particularly in the event of an emergency. Having to crawl around companionway ladders, lockers, or stanchions in the dark to get up to the saloon is not a good plan. These are often the largest berths on a small cruiser, since they're essentially just filling an otherwise unoccupied void. Except for the berth being mounted athwartships, this is the most comfortable location from a motion perspective at sea.

Look for a four-person dinette table to be at least 30 by 40 inches, since a seated person needs over 24 inches of elbowroom to be comfortable. Table dimensions are often predetermined by its other function as a drop-down berth insert, though. Just how easy the conversion from dinette to berth is should be a matter of concern; on some boats it's fast and easy, while on others you have to wrestle the foolish thing into submission.

Headroom

Headroom has an outsize psychological impact on how big a space feels, and for that reason, the more the better. For smaller cruisers of 25 to 30 feet, 6 feet, 2 inches may acceptable, but 6 feet, 4 inches should be the standard on any cruising boat. With their sloping foredecks, many midcabin cruisers have 6 feet, 6 inches or more of headroom at the companionway but as little as 5 feet, 10 inches at the V-berth forward. A builder may, then, advertise, say, 6 feet, 10 inches of cabin headroom, but that will likely be only for the first couple of feet at the companionway entrance. The head, galley, and forward stateroom will likely have significantly less, depending on the design.

Seated headroom is also important, especially in the midcabins of these cruisers. Some builders provide a table to sit at during the day, but headroom is so tight only small children could actually use it. Look for at least 38 inches of seated headroom above the seat cushion.

Hatches and Portholes

There's nothing more claustrophobic than a cabin without hatches or portholes to let in sunlight and

fresh air. In the interest of meeting demand for an ultraclean look, many builders—especially of convertibles—have done away with portholes altogether. But that's unfortunate, at least in my view, since there's no substitute for being able to see the passing scenery, or at least to enjoy a little sunlight, from the galley or your berth. I can't imagine thinking, "Wow, the view is just too good through this big window. I think I'll paint half the window flat black to make it feel more like a cave."

Eliminating portholes also eliminates the possibility of leaks, which is another reason why you see so few of them, and it's also one of the reasons why convertible windshields were originally fiberglassed over. Builders then found they could put a lot of furniture, cabinets, microwaves, and large-screen TVs under where the windshield used to be, and that element soon caught on with boaters. Personally, I would take the sunlight and the view ahead over a standup refrigerator any day, but I might be the odd man out on this one.

From a safety perspective, hatches are essential as a means of emergency egress in the event of a fire or if the boat starts to sink. For that reason, having at least one 24-inch-square hatch forward in the cabin, with a ladder to climb through it with, is essential.

Regal's 2860 Window Express is so named for reasons that are obvious upon inspection — there's more sunlight down here than in the next two express cruisers put together. Bonded frameless glass (in those deck windows) prevents leaks, and opening hull portlights let in more light as well as fresh air.

Try climbing out a 15- or even 20-inch-square hatch, common on today's yachts, with or without a ladder, to see why I like bigger hatches. And when we speak of a hatch size, I mean the clear opening inside the frame that you actually crawl through. The average person just can't fit through these smaller hatches, and certainly doesn't have the upper body strength to pull him- or herself up without a ladder. After waking up to a saloon fire on a friend's cruiser a few years ago, the owners of a new Alden 56 I tested recently specified the installation of a 24-inch hatch and a folding ladder in their forward stateroom during the design phase. Good plan. Live and learn.

Galleys

Galleys range from being equipped with just the basics, with an icebox and a sink, to a veritable kitchen suite including stove, oven, trash compactor, dishwashers, freezer, and refrigerator. Even refrigerators on the smallest cruisers are usually dual voltage, so they can run on 12-volt DC battery power at sea and on 120-volt AC shore power when hooked up dockside.

The Four Winns' 258 small galley is functional and well proportioned. A sink, dual-voltage refrigerator, microwave oven, and storage cabinets are included. GENMAR HOLDINGS, INC.

A common view a few years ago was that alcohol stoves were least likely to cause fires. The theory was that alcohol is nonexplosive and that an alcohol fire is easy to put out with water, but while the former is true, the latter is not necessarily so. Indeed, dousing an alcohol fire with water may serve only to "float" the fire to nearby flammable materials. Some experts, and many cruising sailors, now feel that an LPG (liquefied petroleum gas) stove is safer provided the gas bottle feeding the stove is small enough not to produce explosive fume concentrations should it leak all its contents into the bilge. This means you have to change the bottle more often, of course, but the peace of mind is probably worth the extra trouble. Another benefit of a gas stove is that it burns hotter than alcohol and thus cooks faster. Sailboats always carry the gas bottle topside in a self-contained locker that vents overboard, and this arrangement is recommended for powerboats as well.

Most larger yachts with generators have all-electric appliances, including stoves and ovens, eliminating the issue of stove fuel. Of course, this means you have to fire up the genset to cook a burger. Whatever the stove type, though, make sure it has a solenoid switch to shut off the fuel source or the electricity when the stove lid is closed, to prevent a fire from starting.

Most boats come with a single sink, but having two, even on a smaller boat, can actually save fresh water, with one used for washing dishes and the other for food preparation. Having a covering board for one or both sinks will also increase counter space when it's needed most. A combination microwave-convection oven is a truly wonderful appliance to have on board any small boat; if you can install a kitchen-sized, 1.5-cubic-foot microwave instead of one of those shoebox-sized units that many small-boat builders include as standard equipment, so much the better.

Fiddle rails, those slats that line the perimeter of the counter to keep everything from falling onto the deck in a seaway, take many forms. The ones I like best fold down out of the way when in port. Drawers and cabinet doors should have push-to-open or other type of positive latches, or the drawers should

The Back Cove 29 includes a galley with a huge countertop. A one-piece cabin liner makes maintenance easy, and it's bonded to the stringers below, further strengthening the hull structure.

This Dettling 51 is guaranteed to have ample fresh air and daylight with all these opening deck hatches.

be of the lift-to-open variety, so they don't come open at sea without your direct involvement.

The inside corner of a countertop is often wasted, inaccessible space, except from above. But this area is perfect for a trash container (just open the lid and sweep those potato peelings right into the can) or even an insulated icebox, which works best with a top-opening lid rather than a side-opening door anyway, since much less cold air is lost upon opening. Or you can have a lazy Susan with cabinet door access just as in some kitchens at home.

Ventilation

You can't have too much natural ventilation in a boat. Just ask anyone who has woken to the sound of a carbon monoxide detector going off, or anyone who's cruised the Caribbean in the summer. Opening doors, hatches, and windows all let in light and fresh air, but they have to be closed when the boat is underway to prevent spray from getting inside. There are hatches that hinge on both sides, giving you a choice depending on conditions. Or some boats have two hatches, one facing forward and the other aft, serving the same purpose.

Dorades are used on high-end yachts for dry ventilation, and especially on sailboats. These are

essentially wind scoops that provide a path for air to enter the boat at one end of the cabin and exit it from the other. They're mounted on a baffled box that drains any water off before it has a chance to get inside the boat. Good natural ventilation will allow you to do a lot more cruising without the air conditioner turned on, saving wear and tear on the AC components and maybe allowing you to cruise without running the generator continuously.

Good natural ventilation throughout the vessel's interior is also essential for preventing mildew, condensation, and rot. Bilges, lockers, closets, and voids must all be provided with a continuous supply of fresh air to prevent these evils, to say nothing of musty odors.

Storage Space

Although it may not be readily apparent at a boat show or dockside, storage space on many cruising boats is sorely lacking. If the boat is advertised as a day boat and you plan on using it as such, then all is well. But if it's supposed to accommodate the whole family for a weekend or longer, make a mental note of how much food and gear you'll be taking along

Carbon Monoxide Poisoning

Besides comfort, your safety is another reason to have an effective natural ventilation system, with properly vented stoves, heaters, and engines, and plenty of carbon monoxide detectors. Carbon monoxide (CO) is the product of combustion of carbon-based fuels, such as natural gas, fuel oils, gasoline, and propane. Gas stoves and internal combustion engines on board boats are sources of this deadly tasteless, odorless, colorless gas. It weighs about the same as air, so it mixes with the air evenly in any enclosed compartment. When a person inhales CO, the lungs' oxygen-absorbing capacity is reduced, so sufficient exposure to the gas is eventually, and sometimes quickly, fatal. Depending on the CO concentrations in the air, death can come within minutes.

In a recent incident, two small boys on an anchored houseboat went for a swim, and paddled into a hull cavity where the generator exhaust was being vented. They lost consciousness and drowned, a tragic illustration of the potentially lethal effects of CO. Even if you don't have an engine or stove operating onboard, you can still be at risk for CO poisoning. For instance, CO from a boat moored alongside can have similar results if conditions are just right, and the "station-wagon effect," which is the vacuum created by a hull and large deckhouse moving along at speed, can suck CO from engine exhaust into a running boat's cockpit and interior.

Symptoms of CO poisoning, according to the ABYC pamphlet *Educational Information about Carbon Monoxide*, include the following sequence of symptoms: watery and itchy eyes, flush appearance, throbbing temples, inattentiveness, inability to think clearly, loss of physical coordination, ringing in the ears, tightness across the chest, headache, drowsiness, incoherence, slurred speech, nausea, dizziness, fatigue, vomiting, collapse, and convulsions. The solution is to make sure that your boat's ventilation, stove, heate, and engine exhaust systems are properly designed and that you have plenty of CO detectors on board, in every space capable of even temporary human occupancy.

Sea Ray's 310 Sundancer has an enclosed head, a galley, and a convertible lounge. Following the flare in the hull, the higher the forward berth, the larger it can be.

If you see that there are a lot of inaccessible voids behind lounges, cabinets, hull liners, and under the deck, the builder isn't taking the extra time to do the job right. A separate locker for wet foul-weather gear is a great idea, space permitting, and it should be well ventilated and near the companionway to keep dripping on that nice teak and holly sole (or carpet, as the case may be) to a minimum. Speaking of carpets, snap-in carpets on fiberglass liners are a great way to go. Unlike nailed-down carpet, which gets wet and eventually smells as bad as a barrel of pogies, they can be easily removed for cleaning and airing out, or for replacement when the time comes.

Not only is storage volume important, so is access to all that space. Many builders provide underberth storage that makes full use of that otherwise wasted space, and a few make it easy to get to by installing hydraulic lifts that make light work of lifting the berth, mattress and all.

and check out your next boat's available storage space to see if it's enough. You might be amazed at all the stuff a cruising family can accumulate over a couple of years.

CHAPTER 14

Finding Your Next Boat

Nobody goes there anymore. It's too crowded.

—Yogi Berra

In this chapter, we take a look at some of the ways people try to find the boat that's right for them. We also consider the broker and surveyor's role in your decisionmaking process, and give you some tips on what to look for on a dockside inspection and sea trial.

Where to Look

Advertisements

Boatbuilders spend a lot of money on advertising, and for good reason, since that's one way you're likely to learn about one of their new boats on the market. Advertising is almost always part hype, so when you read that some earth-shattering, mind-boggling new technique has magically produced a boat that is faster, better riding, more luxurious, better looking, easier to maintain, and roomier than anything else in its class, reading between the lines is definitely in order.

On the other hand, you can often learn a good deal about a boat from an ad. First, its dimensions and power options might be listed so you'll know whether it will fit in your slip or squeak under a local bridge. You may find out if it's available with diesel power. Exterior and interior photography will give you an idea as to whether a closer look is warranted. An accommodations plan, or *floor plan*, will show you how the interior and deck space is divvied up and whether it matches your priorities.

From a photo, you can also learn something about bridge accessibility, helm station visibility and ergonomics, foredeck access, ease of boarding, and other design elements. You can even learn something about how a boat will ride from a photo taken from the right angle to show bottom deadrise and the fineness (or fullness) of the bow.

When you read that a boat is the fastest around for its horsepower, chances are good that it has a flatter bottom than its competitors, which will mean a harsher ride in a chop. If it's a lot lighter than its stablemates, it could be very well built of an epoxy-infused composite sandwich, or it could just be lightly made with conventional materials at low cost and with low strength margins. Another ad will say a boat is the roomiest for its length, and then go on to say it has a great ride. Unfortunately, the laws of physics tell us you can't have both. As we saw in chapters 3 and 4, more beam at the waterline equals diminished ride quality, while greater length and less beam (but the same overall volume) translates into more speed and range for the power, and much greater comfort at speed in a seaway.

Ads in newspapers, weekly advertising publications, and boating magazines are great sources of information on both new and used boats. NADA used boat pricing guides offer their view of a fair price for your next boat, and another good source for larger boats are the *Boat Buyer's Guides* series by Ed McKnew. Such guides should offer a good

Two Ads You Can Believe

Few production boats stand out clearly from the crowd in their construction methods and materials, but a couple come to mind. The Tiara 58, certainly one of the most advanced and well-built production boats in its class, is constructed with vinylester—resin-infused, balsa-cored hull for a stiff, strong, and moderate-weight structure. The hull is considerably stronger, stiffer, and lighter than any open-molded boat, and you can forget about blistering or any other kind of water penetration to the balsa core. The joinery on this boat is not too far from what the best British and Italian boatbuilders are producing.

The VEC (Virtual Engineered Composites) boats produced by Genmar are also worth writing home about. As of 2007, Genmar builds many of its runabouts using this process. The hull and deck laminates are infused in one shot using a two-part mold immersed in water (to provide mold stability and rigidity and even heat transfer). The result is a tooled, mirror finish on all visible surfaces and the elimination of secondary bonds.

starting point for negotiations. The rubber-meets-the-road reality is that a boat is worth whatever a willing buyer will pay to a willing seller in a given geographical area. Yacht world.com and Boat-Trader.com are just two of the many boat classified Web sites available. More can be found using search engines.

Remember that there can be a huge disparity in depreciation from one brand to the next. A mass-produced express boat might lose 20 to 30 percent of its original value after just one year, while a high-end sportfisherman might be worth as much after two or three years as on the day it was launched. The high-end yacht's high resale price is due to many factors, but chief among them are high-quality construction, durable engineering, and perhaps most of all, strong consumer demand and a long waiting list for a new model. Buying an older boat that has spent its life in fresh water is a fine plan; the mechanical components (e.g., the lower unit in a stern drive) are likely to be in

superior condition in the absence of the corrosive effects of salt water.

Negotiating is a big part of the game. Dealers can make anywhere from 10 to 15 percent (on some high-end yachts) to 40 percent (on one or two mass-produced cruisers) markup on the sale of a new boat, with 25 to 33 percent being more the norm. The dealer's *ability* to discount depends on the difference between their wholesale cost and the retail sticker price. Their *willingness* to discount depends on supply and demand for their product.

While you'll want to bargain for a fair price, all dealers need to make a profit. A profitable dealer presumably has enough money to invest in service facilities. Their ability to fix your boat's widget on a Friday afternoon before the relatives arrive for a long weekend depends on staff size and competence, parts inventory, and maintenance equipment.

CSI (consumer satisfaction index) information, rigorously tracked during and after the sale, is a big part of the follow-up for companies like Tiara, Sea Ray, Cobalt, Grady-White, and others, and has helped make them successful.

Magazine Boat Reviews

What can you believe in a magazine boat test? Well, keep in mind that the same magazines that review boats also depend on revenue from boatbuilders'

Here's something you won't see often—a tender garage on a U.S.-built convertible, the Ocean 65 Odyssey. The trade-off is raising the cockpit to make room for the RIB. OCEAN YACHTS

This Moomba Outback ski boat has an in-line, inboard drivetrain, snappy acceleration, and tow options for skiing, wakeboarding, and tubing. SKIER'S CHOICE, INC.

advertising, which is a built-in conflict of interest. If there's no specific criticism in a review, and the overall tone is glowing, then read the article as though it were an extension of the builder's marketing efforts. Some publications do make an honest effort to separate their editorial and advertising departments, though, and try to provide useful and honest assessments.

Performance graphs (such as those in *Boating*) are always useful, since they tell you something about speed, propulsion efficiency, and noise levels. Read the review carefully, though, since many such tests are conducted with the boats under lighter conditions of loading than you'll ever see as an owner. A point-counterpoint format with two or more writers participating, as pioneered in automobile consumer magazines, opens the door to healthy disagreement and is always welcome.

Most magazines feel like they have to tell a story every time they write a review, so expect 20 or 30 percent of the story to be only loosely related to the boat at hand. Do expect to hear about how the boat being tested reminds the reviewer of his granddad's 1952 Mathews, or crossing Hatteras Inlet in the same brand's product 35 years ago. These may be good sea stories, but they detract from the space available for pure test-boat-related information. In fact, it is exceedingly difficult to write a thorough

and meaningful review in less than 2,000 words, especially when a third of the piece is scene-setting. But the average boat review is only 1,000 words long or less, and the trend is toward even shorter reviews, with a boat being given half a page including photos, specifications, and write-up. These "snapshots" let you know the boat exists, but don't expect any useful critical analysis.

No boat is perfect, and it ought to be evaluated in the context of its market, price, and advertised capabilities. In my own boat reviews, I'm always harder on a boat when a customer's reasonable expectations (based on the boat's size, cost, and the builder's claims) would not be met by the boat due to design, construction, or performance flaws. Some 50-foot-plus boats are wonderful in calm water, have top-drawer joinery, intelligent structural engineering, large frameless windows, and tons of room with full-beam saloons, but their flat-bottom sections also pound hard in a 1-foot chop. Such a big boat could reasonably be expected to offer acceptable performance offshore, only to disappoint when put to the test.

If you don't find any substantive criticisms in a boating magazine review—something more than the toilet paper dispenser being hard to reach or the taupe curtains clashing with the tan dinette—the magazine is probably not serious about reviewing boats. I've been on boats that had terrible visibility from the helm, or that pounded in a 1-foot chop at

Monterey's 290 express cruiser offers a comfortable weekend for a family of four, and you'll be able to bring along many of the comforts of home. MONTEREY BOATS

20 knots, or had fuel filter-separators or seawater strainers that you could hardly see, let alone reach, or 18-inch-high transom doors and ½-inch-diameter hatch gutter drain lines. Not a word about these issues appeared in reviews of the same boats in some of the major boating magazines.

The problem is compounded by the absence of clear standards for testing boats. For instance, almost no one measures ride quality with an accelerometer, which is the only objective way of distinguishing a smooth ride from a crab smasher. Or you will read that a 35-knot sportfisherman with six-turn lock-to-lock steering handles great, which is a self-contradictory statement. My hope is that this book, and in particular the boat reviews in the second half, will be a first step toward standardizing boat reviews.

Powerboat Reports, which accepts no advertising, just loves to print horror stories! I wrote *PBR*'s reviews for a couple of years and soon learned that I didn't have to worry about offending anyone if the criticism was justly deserved. My reviews were critical, to be sure, but I have long had a policy of sending the draft of the boat review to the manufacturer before publication for comments, corrections, or counterpoint out of fairness to them. And, like most boat reviewers, I'd rather review and report on a good boat than a poor one. In general, the major magazines won't print a review of a boat that's a real horror.

Of course, the reviewer must be competent. He or she must know what to look for, what strings to pull, what hunches to investigate, which questions to ask. Armed with that knowledge, the right equipment, and a thick skin, the reviewer is perhaps ready to write a useful review. I remember running a Bernard Olesinski–designed 65-foot Fairline for the first time in Miami five years ago; I hadn't known a boat that big could handle so responsively, track so well downsea, and ride so smoothly at 25 knots in a 4-foot head sea. I'd never been on an American-built express cruiser that handled and rode anywhere near that well. Since then, that Fairline, and other good-running boats like Eastbays, Aldens, and Viking Sport Cruisers (also British-built,

The Camano 41 is a well-engineered single-diesel cruiser designed for a couple. A pull-out sofa in the saloon accommodates visitors.

Olesinski-designed hulls), serve as my benchmarks for evaluating other boats.

One of my favorite sources of boat reviews is *Motor Boat and Yachting*, published in the United Kingdom. The reviewers seem to know what they're talking about, and they *say what they see*. Maybe that's what the chairman of Brunswick Corporation, one of the largest U.S. boatbuilders, meant when he said that European writers are "brutal" in their reporting on boats and equipment, but that U.S. writers defer to advertisers.

Some may wonder why Brunswick, which builds over 20 percent of the boats produced in the United States, would be looking for more hard-hitting journalism. So do I. But Brunswick's Bayliner, long a whipping boy in the industry press, has made significant strides in quality, such as using vinylester resin in 3-ounce skin coat to prevent blistering. They build boats that are better in some respects than their competitors' higher-priced offerings, though they still have a ways to go in component quality.

CAD-CAM (computer-aided design and manufacturing) is a great equalizer for boatbuilders. The fact is, many midprice boats are getting better (smoother surfaces, better-fitting components), and there aren't a whole lot of ways the best boats can get much better than they already are without pricing themselves out of the market. It's analogous to the auto industry; Japanese cars are still a little more reliable than their U.S.-built counterparts, but not by nearly as wide a margin as they were 30 years ago. (That's when, not coincidentally, J.D. Power and Associates started reporting on quality and customer satisfaction, an activity they extended into the marine industry. See part 2.)

Boat Shows

A boat show is a great place to investigate what's on the market and to do some quick comparisons between models. Bring along a tape measure, camera, and clipboard to take notes. Go to the end of this chapter and use the tips listed as a guideline. Then fill out the information for each boat so you'll be able to make some apples-to-apples comparisons. What boat shows are not good for is a deliberate, unhurried inspection. Salespeople are trying to move as many people through their product as possible, while culling the qualified buyers from the tire kickers.

A boat show can be a great place to get a good deal on a boat. How much you can expect to save off MSRP (manufacturer's suggested retail price) depends on supply and demand. But price isn't everything: buying a boat from a reputable dealer who takes care of their customers in the years following delivery can be worth a lot more than saving a few bucks up front.

Many boatbuilders have dealer networks with strict territories. If you're at a national show, like Miami or Fort Lauderdale, and you're in the market for a larger boat, manufacturers' representatives will almost always be present, and the boatbuilding company's owners and executives are usually available for the first few days of the show. You'll be asked where you live by the builder or one of their dealers, or where you do most of your boating, and then handed off to the dealer who covers your area. If you live in both Newport and Fort Lauderdale, both dealers for these areas may be involved in the sale of your boat and share the profits. At regional shows, such as Boston, Chicago, or New York, the builders may have reps at the show for the first day or so and after that local dealers may have things to themselves. You'll also be "qualified," or judged as to your ability to actually pay for the boat by the dealer if it's a bigger model.

The advantage of attending a show is that there are so many models to investigate, and prices may be favorable. The downside is that it can be a carnival, high-pressure atmosphere on a very busy (usually weekend) day, and you may feel like a herded Holstein at the more popular displays. Get there early or stay late, and attend on weekdays if possible and if you want to have a more leisurely look around. Collect all the information you can, take it home and spread everything out

This Hunt-designed Southport Boatworks center console is a great offshore fishing boat in a chop. SOUTHPORT BOATWORKS

on the kitchen table so that you can make detailed comparisons.

Brokers

You can also do well finding a used boat by working with a reputable yacht broker. Before selecting a broker, ask around and carefully check out their reputation for honesty and competence. Finding a broker whom you trust and can work with can be an advantage, since they should know the market, and after interviewing you, should have a clear understanding of what suits your needs, lifestyle, and budget. Internet-based brokerage services make it easy for the broker to find just the right used boat anywhere in the country.

You'll soon find out if the broker you've selected is really working for you when you see how close what you need matches up with the boats you're shown. If you need another boat in a few years, having already established a relationship with a broker will speed up the search and purchase process. Good brokers want you to be happy with your purchase, and they also want your repeat business.

Word of Mouth

Finding out what the owners in the next slip think about their boat is a good place to start if you're considering buying a vessel like theirs. Talk to everyone you know who owns a candidate boat to learn about its reliability, performance, quality, dealer and warranty service, and other issues. Both the satisfied and the disgruntled owner will have a story to tell, but especially the latter.

But even if an owner raves about their boat, that doesn't mean all is well. You sometimes have to take their praise for Brand X with a grain of salt. It is only human nature that people don't like admitting they've bought a lemon. On the practical side, the truth is many owners really don't know enough about boats in general to offer an informed opinion. They may be very happy with their boat, while the reality is that it's a terror to be aboard offshore and the bottom is blistering

away underneath them. I've evaluated boats whose owners were thrilled with their craft, only to come up with laundry lists of design, engineering, and performance flaws that, properly addressed, would make their boats the fine craft they had the potential to be.

It's rare that any owner will sing the praises of their dealer if they're getting poor service, so remarks about service can more often be taken at face value. Sometimes it may be a smart idea to buy the number two boat on your list from the number one dealer in your area. Even then, there will always be those with unrealistic expectations who make petty demands of dealers, who in their turn jump through hoops to try to satisfy these perpetually disgruntled owners.

Internet

Most boatbuilders have Web sites that duplicate the copy and photos in their brochures. You'll find the range of boats, the closest dealer, and sometimes the MSRP for each model. Some Web site names are obvious, like www.bertram.com and www.bay liner.com (no space). For the rest, try "www." plus the brand name, followed by "yachts.com" or "boattest.com," or use a search engine. Boats.com, www.motor boating.com, and yachtworld.com also have useful listing services. Be sure to check out www.jdpower.com, too.

Surveyors

When the time comes to buy that new or (especially) used boat, make sure to retain a competent surveyor. You may think that a new boat doesn't need a survey, but for many new larger models, paying a few hundred dollars to find out if any systems are improperly installed or if there are other problems is money well spent. The builder usually makes up a "punch list" of discrepancies to fix before it gets shipped to the dealer, and the dealer should also go through the boat to look for what are usually quality-control problem areas. The list tends to get longer as the boat gets bigger and more complex. The surveyor may find things on your new boat that the builder either didn't catch or didn't consider to be a problem.

A used boat of any size and complexity should always be surveyed, usually after signing the purchase and sale agreement and with the actual purchase contingent on the survey findings. After all, it may be on the market precisely because of some hidden flaw.

Competence and Accreditation

I emphasize the term *competence* because not all surveyors are created equal. The competent surveyor has developed an eye for discovering problem areas that would escape the amateur's eye. He or she can often find hidden structural problems based on surface abnormalities and nondestructive inspection. This sort of understanding is generally beyond the scope of even experienced boaters. Surveyors will look at your boat with a practiced eye. They know—or *ought* to know—precisely what they're looking for, and, unlike the eager buyer, they can put things into perspective dispassionately.

Choosing a surveyor belonging to an association such as NAMS (National Association of Marine Surveyors) or SAMS (Society of Accredited Marine Surveyors) is a good start. However, membership in one of these organizations alone doesn't guarantee your surveyor is the best choice, or even competent. Credentials from a professional surveyors' organization should mean that the surveyor has met at least minimum standards for technical competence. For example, NAMS members who've earned NAMS-CMS credentials must pass an extensive screening process, a day-long exam, and are held to clear ethical standards. Similarly, SAMS tests its members before awarding an AMS designation.

Naturally there's an incentive for surveyors to join an organization that conveys credibility on the part of the member, like the CMS or AMS designations following the surveyor's name. Some surveyor organizations allow the use of the term "Certified" though the surveyor may not have been screened or tested for competency. There are also associate

Regal's 2860 Window Express sleeps four and performs well in choppy conditions. REGAL MARINE

members of NAMS and SAMS who have not met the requirements for five years of professional experience and passed a test. Keep in mind that the most competent surveyor in your area may not be a member of any of these organizations at all. Talking to boatyards, managers, boatowners, and others involved in the industry will likely reveal a few names that come up more than once for your short list of competent surveyors.

A surveyor who does work regularly for the seller or his agents may have a conflict of interest; a surveyor (including honest, ethical surveyors), like any vendor, will tend to feel more loyalty to the repeat customer than the one-time client and it may influence their findings or the tone in which they're reported. On the other hand, the broker may be recommending someone who's a real professional. Just be wary of the broker who insists that you use one and not another.

Be sure the surveyor has experience in the type of boat you're considering; a crackerjack fiberglass boat surveyor may know little, if anything, about wooden or aluminum boats. A sailboat specialist will not be the best choice to survey a performance cruiser, and a specialist in large commercial vessels may not be who you're looking for to inspect your 30-foot walkaround. Best perhaps is the surveyor who is familiar with the builder's product line in general, and your model in particular, since design and construction problems tend to show up throughout a builder's product line. Ask the surveyor for a copy of their CV and references when you first talk to them. You'll want a list of previous clients whom you can contact as references.

Once you've selected your surveyor, make sure that their rates are understood up front. If you cancel without adequate warning, expect to pay for a day's work. It is better to pay for an expert surveyor than to get a bargain from an incompetent one. Surveyors' rates vary geographically and by the individual, but expect to pay a per-foot fee. This might range from $15 per foot for a 20-footer to $30 (or more) per foot for a 70-footer, plus expenses. Additional services, such as engine compression checks (often done by a mechanic), boat hauling, and lube oil analysis will cost extra but are well worth doing.

There are relevant standards. The National Fire Protection Association and American Boat and Yacht Council's Standards and Recommended Practices for Small Craft should be adhered to. These minimum standards may be considered voluntary guidelines for the builder, but adherence to them is often required by underwriters. Adherance to ABYC standards is also a recommendation now for NIMA members. The Code of Federal Regulations applies to the inspection of commercial and passenger-carrying vessels and not to pleasure boats, but serves as a sensible starting point for any boat. Meeting USCG requirements is also a start but by no means ensures that your boat is either well built or seaworthy.

Types of Surveys

Surveys come in several flavors. In general, the public deals with either prepurchase surveys or underwriting inspections called Condition and Value surveys. Both the prepurchase and the C&V surveys should check for the basics like proper wiring and systems installation.

Prepurchase Survey

The prepurchase survey is the whole ball of wax, involving a full inspection of the vessel as well as test running of equipment. A prepurchase survey is conducted to assess the structural condition of the vessel as well as the proper operation and installation of its systems. It is the surveyor's responsibility to comment on condition and to put these recommendations in a logical framework based upon her client's stated interests. Make sure that all systems will be tested, that the boat is sea trialed, and that all lights, machinery, equipment, and systems (main engines, generators, windlass, battery charger, inverters, toilets, tenders, and davits) are turned on and operated. Having a boat surveyed will give you leverage in negotiating the final price, though typically only structural repairs costing more than $500 are renegotiated during closing.

The surveyor may be asked for an opinion as to the market value of a used vessel for purposes of finance and underwriting. But the surveyor is not there to shed light on whether or not the buyer is

Bayliner has some of the more practical small cruiser designs on the market. The Discovery 246, with its airy cabin, raised main deck helm, and fishable cockpit, has a very livable layout.   BAYLINER

The Zodiac Pro Open 650 makes a great tender with its inflatable collar serving as a built-in fendering system.   ZODIAC MARINE

getting a good deal. Prudent buyers do their own research and shopping around before signing a purchase and sale agreement. Nor does the surveyor verify a vessel's seaworthiness. Obviously, this would entail a far more in-depth assessment of the vessel's stability and design (well beyond the scope of a simple prepurchase survey), as well as intangibles such as the vessel's outfitting and the competence of the captain and crew.

Condition and Value (C&V)

On the other hand, the underwriting C&V inspection is generally a quickie, and it's often what sellers are referring to when they say they have a "recent survey." It will rarely answer any substantial questions for the buyer. It's common for an insurance inspection report to paint a rosier than normal picture of the vessel. Under no conditions should a prospective buyer accept a recent C&V inspection as a basis for a purchase decision.

How Long Does a Survey Take?

A thorough inspection of virtually any boat is time-consuming—for most boats it's an all-day affair. In fact, the more experienced the surveyor, the more potential trouble areas she may know to ferret out. How much time it takes to get the job done properly, of course, depends on the condition, complexity, and age of a vessel. The accessibility of bilges, voids, fuel tanks, and other out-of-the-way areas are also factors.

A well-written, comprehensive survey report will take the better part of another day to write up. The surveyor should be able to get his client a list of items that require further investigation or negotiation in short order so that he'll have something to work with during negotiations with the broker or seller. However, it is not unusual to have to wait five working days for the final written survey. So, don't expect to close on a boat the day after the survey.

The survey report should include detailed recommendations. A properly worded recommendation should (a) state the problem or condition; (b) recommend repair in detail; and (c) state the possible hazards of leaving the condition uncorrected.

Make sure any boat you're considering buying is hauled for a thorough bottom and running gear inspection. You won't know for sure what you're getting otherwise. Blistering is a big problem with some fiberglass boats, even with some boats built in the last year or so (though their builders should know better), but you won't know until too late that your boat has a blistering problem if you don't have it hauled. Stern-drive-powered boats should have their transoms thoroughly checked for water penetration and rot in the plywood core, if so equipped, as should fiberglass-encapsulated wood stringers and bulkheads. Balsa-cored hulls, decks, and superstructures should also be checked for rot and water penetration through improperly bedded bolt and screw holes. And the list goes on.

Talking and Listening

While you're at it, tell the surveyor what you plan to do with the boat: where you plan to cruise; how many people will be with you; and whether you fish, ski, or dive. Ask what she thinks about the suitability of the boat for your intended purpose. You could also ask your surveyor up front what she thinks of the model generally—its design, construction, and performance—regardless of the actual physical condition of the boat you're considering.

It's natural for a prospective owner to want the surveyor to validate her own good taste; that's where the listening part comes in, so be willing to swallow the bitter pill if it's presented to you. It may save you a world of trouble to follow their advice up front and not get involved with a boat the surveyor knows to be problematic or unsuited to your needs. Don't waste your time and money: look for another boat before you get any more emotionally involved in a lemon.

Get your money's worth and be present for the survey and sea trial. You'll learn a lot from the surveyor about boats in general, and about your boat in particular. The surveyor will appreciate it if you arrange for the two of you to be alone, without the broker or seller's agent on board. This will allow him to speak freely without having everything he's saying refuted, and will prevent you from being distracted from what he's trying to tell you. Once you buy the boat, it's a good idea to have it surveyed periodically, maybe every two to three years. If water is getting into the balsa coring in the deck or hull, if aluminum fuel tanks are corroding, or if mechanical systems are getting ready to fail, the sooner you know about it, the better.

Surveyors can also act as owners' representatives on new boats during construction to make sure ABYC and other standards organizations' recommendations are being followed. A surveyor can be retained for acceptance inspections and sea trials and can provide litigation support and accident investigation or damage surveys on an owner's behalf.

The Dockside Inspection

Once you've narrowed your list of boat candidates, inspecting the boat is the next step. The checklists below are cross-referenced to the chapters where relevant in-depth discussions can be found.

SPECIFICATIONS *(see chapters 3, 4, 5, 6, 7)*

Type of boat (sportfisherman, express cruiser, trawler, etc.) _____

Hull design: planing __ full displacement __ semidisplacement __ catamaran __

Construction: wood __ fiberglass __ composite __ steel __ aluminum __

Dimensions: LOA ___ LOD ___ beam ___ draft ___ hull displacement _____

PROPULSION *(see chapter 8)*

Number of engines: primary __ auxiliary __

Type of propulsion: inboard __ stern drive __ outboard __ surface-piercing propeller __ waterjet __

Fuel type: gas __ diesel__

Horsepower: primary _____ auxiliary_____

Fuel capacity: _____

Tank type: aluminum __ fiberglass __

Propeller size: diameter __ pitch __ blade area __

Exhaust type: wet __ dry __

RUDDERS AND STEERING SYSTEMS *(see chapter 9)*

The steering is mechanical __ hydraulic __ power __

Number of turns lock-to-lock: _____

Is there an autopilot? Y/N

Number of steering stations: _____

Emergency tiller? Y/N

ENGINE ROOM AND ONBOARD SYSTEMS *(see chapter 10)*

Is there standing and sitting headroom in the engine room? Y/N

Is there room to move around and reach components? Y/N

Are walking surfaces flat, dry, and raised above the bilge? Y/N

Is lighting adequate? Y/N

Are engine start and stop switches with full instrumentation installed at the entrance? Y/N

Can the engine(s), generator(s), compressor(s), fuel tank(s), etc., be removed without deconstruction? Y/N

Can fuel filter–water separators be switched and changed "on the fly"? Y/N

Are all hose clamps stainless steel and backed up? Y/N

Are battery banks secure, covered, installed low in the hull, and properly vented? Y/N

Is there an inverter aboard? Y/N

Is there a generator? Y/N
    gas __ diesel __
    what is its rating? __ kW

How much electrical equipment can the generator power at one time? _____

Are surge protectors installed? Y/N

Is there a shore power hookup? Y/N

Is all wiring marine grade? Y/N
    numbered at both ends? Y/N
    protected by heat-shrink tubing (connections), grommets (bulkhead passages), and chases? Y/N

Is there an automatic fire-suppression system installed? Y/N

Does the automatic fire-suppression system shut down the engine before engaging? Y/N

Are there watertight bulkheads forward and aft to prevent progressive flooding? Y/N

Is there a raw-water suction Y-valve installed? Y/N
    does it have a valve interlock to prevent flooding the bilge? Y/N

Are the raw-water strainers accessible? Y/N

Is the bilge pumping system adequate, properly plumbed, and fitted with a bilge-level alarm? Y/N

Are seacocks accessible in the event of flooding? Y/N
    can they be operated easily? Y/N

Are the fuel tanks accessible for maintenance? Y/N

Are tank fittings and hoses the recommended high-pressure aircraft type (the common alternative being rubber hoses with hose clamps)? Y/N

Is the engine room easily accessed from the saloon or cockpit? Y/N

Is there adequate soundproofing (noise level of 83 dBA or less at cruise outside)? Y/N

Can fluid levels be checked from the centerline? Y/N

Can all machinery be accessed from either side and below for routine maintenance and inspection? Y/N

Is there a "day hatch" for quick equipment checks? Y/N

Are all plumbing, electrical, fuel lines, and components properly labeled and accessible? Y/N

Is there adequate ventilation and a blower system? Y/N

Is the bilge smoothly finished for ease of cleaning? Y/N

Are the shaft, transmission, and couplings accessible? Y/N

Is the shaft fitted with dripless seals or a spray guard? Y/N

Is there a work area or bench? Y/N

Is there adequate storage for tools, lubricants, and spare parts? Y/N

HELM *(see chapter 11)*

Does the helm give a clear and unobstructed view of the horizon? Y/N

Do the radar arch, hardtop supports, and other structures obstruct visibility in any way? Y/N

Are the windows large enough? Y/N

Do the window mullions noticeably obstruct vision? Y/N

Are there windshield wipers? Y/N
    do they sweep most of the glass surface? Y/N
    do they have a freshwater washer installed? Y/N

Is the windshield glass strong enough and clear? Y/N

Have precautions been taken to reduce glare such as minimizing glossy white surfaces under the windshield? Y/N

Is red or blue lighting installed for night operations? Y/N

Is there adequate headroom for the operator? Y/N

Can the vessel be operated safely and comfortably whether standing or seated? Y/N

Can all gauges be viewed easily whether standing or seated? Y/N

Does the helm seat have enough support? Y/N
is it adjustable? Y/N

Is there adequate seating for passengers/crew? Y/N

Are the steering and engine controls ergonomically positioned? Y/N

Are all switches and auxiliary controls conveniently located, easily reached, well labeled, and logically arranged? Y/N

Are the engine shutdown and fire suppression controls within reach? Y/N

Does the vessel have GPS? Y/N
VHF? Y/N
radar? Y/N
depth-sounder? Y/N
other _____

SAFETY AT SEA *(see chapter 12)*

Is the boat easy and safe to board? Y/N

Are the decks, walkways, ladder treads, stair treads, and swim platform covered with nonskid material? Y/N

Is the nonskid pattern easy to clean yet aggressive enough to grip? Y/N

If there is a swim platform, does it project past any running gear below? Y/N

Are there adequate railings? Y/N
are they strong and high enough? Y/N

Are adequate grabrails installed? Y/N

Are the cockpit coamings high enough? Y/N

Are there sufficient mooring cleats? Y/N
are they positioned usefully? Y/N
are they large enough? Y/N

On outboards, is the transom cut away with a motor well? Y/N
cut away without a motor well? Y/N
solid (not cut away)? Y/N

If equipped with a motor well, does it drain quickly? Y/N

Are the control cables in the motor well fitted with watertight boots? Y/N

Are all inspection ports or hatches watertight? Y/N

Are transom doors gasketed? Y/N

Are the transom door and hardware strong enough? Y/N

Is there a swim ladder? Y/N
does it extend at least two steps into the water when deployed? Y/N

Does the foredeck have excessive camber or pitch, making it difficult to walk on? Y/N

Are the side decks wide enough to walk on safely? Y/N

Are there enough PFDs and life rings? Y/N
are they readily accessible? Y/N

Are there toe kicks provided where needed? Y/N

Is the cockpit self-draining? Y/N

Is there sufficient deck camber to facilitate good drainage? Y/N

Are there gutters in the cockpit and around all hatches? Y/N

Are the scuppers or drain lines large enough to facilitate fast draining? Y/N

Are the scuppers high enough above the waterline when the vessel is fully loaded to prevent backflooding? Y/N

Do the scuppers have backwash flaps? Y/N

ACCOMMODATIONS *(see chapter 13)*

Is there enough overall space to suit your needs? Y/N

Does the layout accommodate your needs? Y/N

What is the number of staterooms? _____

Is there enough natural light in the saloon? Y/N

Is there enough electric lighting? Y/N

Does the saloon have adequate seating? Y/N

Is there a view out the saloon windows when seated? Y/N

Is there sufficient ventilation in the saloon? Y/N

What type of ventilation is there (hatches, opening portlights, fans, etc.)? _____

If there are windows in the saloon, do they open? Y/N
are they fitted with screens? Y/N

How many berths are there? _____

Are the berths long enough (at least 6′4″)? Y/N

Are double berths accessible from either side? Y/N

Are the berth cushions thick and dense enough to sleep on? Y/N

Is there an air-conditioning system? Y/N

Is there a heating system? Y/N
what type? _____

Is the standing headroom adequate (at least 6′4″)? Y/N

Is there an overhead hatch fitted with a ladder for emergency escape? Y/N

Is the hatch large enough in diameter to accommodate passengers exiting in an emergency (22″ or greater)? Y/N

Are the doors and companionways at least 6′4″ high and 22″ wide? Y/N

Is there adequate storage? Y/N

Galley

Is the dining table large enough? Y/N

Does the dining table easily convert to a berth? Y/N

Is the standing headroom adequate (at least 6′4″)? Y/N

Is there a refrigerator or icebox? Y/N
what is the volume? _____

What appliances are installed (microwave, trash compactor, etc.)? _____

What type of stove is installed? _____

How many sinks are there? _____

Do the counters have fiddle rails? Y/N
are they open at the corners for cleaning? Y/N

Do the drawers and cupboards have secure latches? Y/N

Is there adequate ventilation? Y/N

Is a carbon monoxide detector installed? Y/N

Is there adequate and secure storage? Y/N

Is there a hot water heater? Y/N
what type? _____

What is the freshwater tank capacity? _____

Is there a watermaker installed? Y/N
GPD (gallons per day) capacity? _____

Head

Is headroom adequate (at least 6′4″)? Y/N

Does the head door have a sill to prevent flooding from the shower? Y/N

Does the head door(s) open inward? Y/N

Is the toilet manual or electric? _____

Is there a holding tank and Y-valve? Y/N

Is there mechanical ventilation? Y/N

Is there an opening portlight? Y/N

Does the head have a shower? Y/N
   can the shower area be completely enclosed? Y/N

Is the shower sump adequate to prevent flooding? Y/N

Is there adequate and secure storage? Y/N

Is access to the head adequate? Y/N

Is there a seat in the shower or over the toilet? Y/N

Is all plumbing accessible and fitted with shutoffs? Y/N

CONSTRUCTION (see chapters 6 and 7)

What is the composition of the skin coat (a vinylester skin coat in the first 3 ounces of mat or chop is preferred)? _____

If wood is used in the hull structure, is it marine plywood (which is susceptible to rot) or, preferably, pressure-treated, rot-resistant plywood? _____

Is the wood core susceptible to getting wet in way of limber holes or other penetrations (even if otherwise fully encapsulated)? Y/N

Are the bilges smooth, painted with gelcoat, and easy to clean? Y/N

Is the hull divided into sections by watertight bulkheads to prevent progressive flooding? Y/N

Is there plenty of ventilation around aluminum fuel tanks? Y/N
   are they mounted on neoprene strips to prevent corrosion-inducing water from being trapped against the tank? Y/N

The Sea Trial

After the dockside inspection, take a sea trial. Don't forget to buy a sound-level meter at RadioShack to measure and compare noise levels in the saloon, staterooms, cockpit, and bridge. Also pack a stopwatch to time turns, and your handheld GPS so you'll know firsthand how fast your dreamboat really is at cruising rpm. Try to conduct your sea trial on a windy day in rough conditions. Otherwise, you may be disappointed in the vessel's rough-water capabilities after taking delivery. If the bottom is freshly cleaned and painted, the fuel tanks are less than full, and only a few people are on board for the ride, make sure to deduct an appropriate amount, possibly several knots, when calculating your own cruising speed and range at a given rpm. The engines should turn their full rated speed at full load, and a little over that with the bottom clean.

HELM (see chapter 11)

Are instruments and controls clearly visible both standing and seated? Y/N

Do the engine shift controls operate smoothly and have positive mechanical detents so you can feel the control shift? Y/N

Do the throttles move smoothly and stay set where you leave them? Y/N

Can you drive with one hand on the wheel, leaving the other on the engine controls? Y/N

Are trim tab controls within easy reach, and do they have tab angle indicators? Y/N

Is the noise level acceptable (low 80s dBA range or less) at cruise speed? Y/N

Is the steering easy and responsive, with no more than three or four turns lock-to-lock? Y/N

Can you move around comfortably with someone seated next to you? Y/N

Does the boat need trim tabs to get on plane quickly? Y/N

Do you lose sight of the horizon getting up on plane while seated or standing? Y/N

Does a radar arch restrict visibility abaft the beam? Y/N

How close aboard can you see your wake when seated and standing at the helm? ___ yd./m

Does the boat turn as quickly in both directions (use a stopwatch to time a 720-degree turn at cruise speed in both directions)? Y/N

What is the minimum planing speed with and without trim tabs? _____ mph

If the boat is fitted with a bow thruster, is it effective in a crosswind or crosscurrent? Y/N

When averaged over reciprocal runs with and into the current, using GPS, how fast is the boat at various rpm? _____ mph

Running into a sea (without using tabs) is the ride smooth and dry? Y/N

At what speed does the boat start to pound? _____ mph

At what speed does the motion become uncomfortable? _____ mph

If trim tabs are fitted, do they quickly produce a noticeable difference in trim and correct for list? Y/N

Does the boat track well in a following sea? Y/N

Does the boat slow down and speed up excessively in a seaway? Y/N

Is it seakindly in a trough and when the sea is broad on the bow? Y/N

Are vibrations around the cockpit or aft deck abnormally high (possibly indicating a need for prop repair or balancing before purchase)? Y/N

If a twin-engine, how fast will the boat run on one engine without overheating? _____ mph

Can you turn in the direction of the running engine? Y/N

Can you trail the inoperative shaft without damaging the gears (check with the dealer or your mechanic; if it needs to be locked up, it will increase drag)? Y/N

If a single-engine, is the steering responsive enough for safe maneuvering? Y/N

Whether twin- or single-engine, can you back down with control? Y/N

Are shifting and overall engine operation smooth? Y/N

In harbor, in a single-engine boat, can you back and make sternway in the intended direction, and will the boat turn sharply in both directions? Y/N

Will the engines shift smoothly at idle and the boat not run too fast when clutched in at idle speed (trolling valves may be needed on high-powered boats)? Y/N

Backing into a slip, is visibility from the helm acceptable and can you can see and communicate with your deckhands? Y/N

Can you read all the gauges in bright daylight (arranged in pairs next to each other by function is best), reach all the controls and switches, and see and reach the electronics seated and standing? Y/N

Is the vessel's systems monitoring console clearly visible? Y/N

Can the fire suppression system be easily monitored? Y/N

At night, do the helm station electronics, gauges, and switches interfere with night vision? Y/N

Is windshield glare from sunlight or night lighting a problem (glossy white helm areas are a problem, accentuating windshield reflection)? Y/N

TOPSIDE ON DECK (see chapter 12)

Can you walk forward and feel secure with the handrails; side deck width; bow railing height, solidity, and location; and nonskid provided? Y/N

Are bow railings 30″ high, unyielding to the touch, and inboard of the rubrail? Y/N

Are there sufficient cleats (two bow, two stern, and two spring cleats minimum), and are they large enough for your standard mooring lines and a couple of storm lines? Y/N
Can they accommodate a boat moored outboard? Y/N

Do cleats or chocks have sharp edges that could chafe the mooring lines? Y/N

Is the ground tackle (anchor, anchor line/chain, and windlass) sized adequately to hold the boat securely? Y/N

If fitted with an anchor locker, does it drain completely overboard? Y/N

Is there plenty of room for the anchor rode (line) and chain, and can the anchor be secured for sea? Y/N

Can the anchor be deployed from its chute/pulpit by gravity alone, without coaxing? Y/N

Is a washdown provided for the anchor and anchor line? Y/N

If centerline access to the foredeck is provided, are the steps large enough to negotiate safely, and are there railings to hang onto as you make your way forward? Y/N

COCKPIT (see chapter 12)

Do engine exhaust fumes get sucked into the cockpit by the "station wagon" effect? Y/N

Are exhaust noise levels acceptable (high 70s to low 80s dBA range)? Y/N

Does the cockpit feel safe for human occupancy at speed (nonskid effectiveness, coaming and railing height)? Y/N

Does the transom door stay securely latched? Y/N

Is there plenty to hang onto at speed? Y/N

Does the boat have a wet ride, rendering the cockpit unusable at speed? Y/N

Is access to the bridge safe and comfortable? Y/N

Is seating provided to meet your needs? Y/N

INTERIOR (see chapter 13)

At cruise speed, are noise levels satisfactory (mid-70 dBA levels throughout interior)? Y/N

Do cabinet doors and drawers stay closed in rough water and hard turns? Y/N

Do drawer and cabinet contents stay put offshore? Y/N

Do hatches, doors, and other components rattle? Y/N

Is the stereo usable at cruising speed? Y/N

Is at least one hatch 22″ square or round, and is a ladder to climb through it provided for emergency egress from the cabin? Y/N

Are there sufficient grab bars and overhead grabrails in the saloon and cabin? Y/N

Are there unusual noises coming from the engine room or drivetrain? Y/N

Do vibrations seem excessive? Y/N

Other Considerations
WARRANTY

New-boat warranties should cover all structural defects, including osmotic blistering. The better warranties are good for ten years or more and are transferable when the boat is sold.

Is the warranty transferable to the next owner? Y/N

What is covered by the hull-structural warranty and for how long? _____

Is osmotic blistering specifically covered and for how long? Y/N _____ yr.

When exactly does the warranty start: at purchase and sale signing, upon closing, or upon commissioning and delivery to the owner?

_____

Who warrants the vendor-supplied components like the generator, microwave, saltwater washdown pumps, and electronics? _____

Is there a dealer close by where you do most of your boating? Y/N

What is the builder's (and dealer's) local reputation for service? _____

Will the dealer or builder fix reasonable off-warranty items in a show of good faith? Y/N

Affordability and Suitability

If you have to ask, you can't afford it, right? Wrong! Make sure you ask a lot of questions about operating and maintenance expenses, especially if you are new to boating or to this class of boat. Be aware of the mileage you can expect when cruising and the price of fuel in your area. Naturally, your next boat must be *affordable* in every sense of the word, both to purchase, to operate, and to maintain (outfitting, fuel, insurance, slip fees, hauling, cleaning, storage, bottom painting, hull and exterior waxing and preservation, machinery and equipment maintenance, crew, etc). It must have the *range* to get you to your destination, and the seaworthiness and seakindliness to do so safely and comfortably. Its design must have a suitable layout to accommodate your lifestyle afloat, including sufficient sleeping accommodations and storage capacity. It must be safe for kids and seniors to move around, especially in a seaway offshore. Molded stairs to the bridge instead of a ladder might be a deal maker for you. To fish it must have a cockpit and, most likely, a flybridge and tower. If you plan to dive, a swim platform, tank storage locker, and air compressor locker will likely be needed.

Boat Buying Decisionmaking Guide
A Few Questions to Ask Yourself When Considering a Boat Purchase

You will use the boat for cruising _____% fishing _____% diving/skiing/watersports _____% other _____

_____

You need accommodations for _____ people in _____ staterooms and _____ heads.

Does the boat have enough sleeping capacity, living area, and privacy for the cruising you actually do? _____
_____

How many people do you cruise or fish with?
_____

How far offshore do you routinely travel?
_____
_____

Where will the boat be used primarily, and for what purpose?_____
_____

How many days at a time at the most will you spend on the boat? _____
_____

What price do you expect to pay? $_____
to $_____

What is more important to you: a smooth-riding, efficiently driven vessel, or one with great internal volume? _____
_____

How important to you are: styling/looks _____% and function/utility _____%

Approximate boat length desired: _____ feet
Is there a size restriction due to slip dimensions, nearby bridge, etc.? Y/N
draft _____ height _____ beam _____

Layout: convertible _____ pilothouse m/y _____
center console _____ walkaround _____
bass boat ____ ski ____ flush deck m/y _____
trawler _____ other _____

Propulsion: conventional inboard ____
stern drive ____ outboard ____
surface drives _____ waterjets ____

Cruising speed desired at full load: _____ knots

Range at full load: _____ nautical miles

Hull: planing _____ semidisplacement _____
full displacement _____ monohull_____
catamaran _____

If having this boat built, how long could you wait until delivery? 3 months ____ 6 months ____
12–24 months ____

Part 2 Boat Reviews

You're born. You suffer. You die. Fortunately, there's a loophole.

—Billy Graham

So Many Boats: A Market Survey

Having read through part 1, you should have an understanding of boat design and construction. Now we'll look at boats on the market, review a selection of those boats, and learn how marine market research from J.D. Power and Associates can help you chose your boat. As mentioned in the preface, new data gathered from the latest annual J.D. Power and Associates Boat Competitive Information Study (BCIS) is included here, and it represents a treasure trove of helpful information.

Here you will find a wide range of boat types. Most of the sections have at least one full-length boat review representing a typical real-world application of the insights gained from part 1. The boat reviews include how the boats are built and laid out, describe their propulsion systems, and discuss a sea trial including boat speed, how it rides, how loud it is, how it handles, and so on. All of the reviews in this book are positive, in the sense that if the boat is included, I can recommend it, though at times there are caveats.

For example, the Cabo 40, a ruggedly built convertible sportfishing boat (see pages 306–309), is neither efficient nor quiet compared to some other boats of the same size. While you might pass on this boat, its inefficiency and engine noise may mean less to you than craftsmanship, engineering, and a great ride. At least you'll buy the boat knowing what you're *not* getting.

All boats have capabilities and limitations, and that's the context in which you should read these reviews, and in which you should shop for a boat. All of the material discussed in the boat reviews is covered in part 1, so if a term comes up that you need a little brushing up on, like skin-to-core bond, vinylester resin, or chine walking, just look it up in the index.

I've met as a third-party adviser with clients shopping for a boat, and it was not unusual to start the conversation with, for instance, a few convertibles at the top of the their list, only to end up choosing a pilothouse motor yacht, given that design's unique, family-friendly attributes. Or maybe they started looking for a motor yacht only to end up with a convertible, attracted to the latter's seakeeping and speed capability.

The problem (and the opportunity) is that there are dozens of boat types, hundreds of brands, and thousands of models to pick from. Once you've gone through part 2 and have made a thorough investigation of all the options, you might find yourself leaning in a different direction. Maybe you've been looking at runabouts or deck boats and want to ski, fish, and sightsee, and take along twelve of your closest friends while you do it, and you discover that there are 45 mph triple-tube pontoon boats out there that can do all of those things. Or maybe you know you want an outboard-powered fishing boat between 22 and 24 feet, but want some help making a decision as to what layout and options to select, including choice of power.

Whatever your situation, maybe there's a boat type or brand out there you don't know about or for whatever reason just haven't seriously considered. Part 2 is intended to help you find the boat type and model that best suits your needs once boat capabilities and limitations are thoroughly understood.

J.D. Power and Associates Marine Market Research

As mentioned in the preface, I was a director of the marine practice at J.D. Power and Associates, a position I held for five years. The firm had recently launched its marine research and it was an interesting time to be involved. Though I have always been interested in how boats are designed and built and how they perform, this immersion in recreational marine market research helped me see how customer satisfaction studies can help manufacturers improve their products, and also help consumers chose a boat that will deliver a more satisfying boat ownership experience.

Every year J.D. Power and Associates conducts its Boat Competitive Information Study (BCIS), along with a derivative Marine Engine Study. (See page 475 for more on the study.) While data from the study is sold to boat and engine manufacturers on a subscription basis, I have been able to make some information available here that will help you select a boat with more insight. First, let's have a look at the study itself.

The study is based on a survey of thousands of people who have bought new boats in seven different segments:

- small runabouts (16- to 19-foot bowriders and cuddies)
- large runabouts (20 to 29 feet)
- express cruisers (24 to 33 feet)
- pontoon boats
- fiberglass bass boats
- ski and wakeboard boats
- coastal fishing boats (17- to 28-foot center consoles, dual consoles, and walkarounds)

The survey is comprehensive, running eight pages long with over 200 questions, and it generates a lot of data. Boat buyers are asked about their level of satisfaction with their boat, engine, and the dealer sales and service experience. Owners are also asked what problems they experienced with their boats and engines, and their replies form the basis of the study's quality ratings; the more problems reported, the lower the quality.

From these survey results, the industry has gained a good deal of insight into what really makes a boater satisfied or dissatisfied with a purchase. Since most people who buy similar boats use them for like purposes, the experiences of these survey respondents can be an extremely useful prism through which to view your own boat needs and decisions on basic equipment, options, and where to do business.

If you're wondering why your favorite boat brand isn't included, it's because there weren't enough boats built in the previous year to yield a sufficient number of survey returns. Every boat brand meeting the criteria is included automatically, whether or not the manufacturer subscribes to the reports.

If you are buying a boat in one of the seven segments covered in the study, the market survey sections on those boats will have additional information regarding customer concerns. These attributes will vary from one segment to another. For example, styling is more important to runabout owners, fishability to coastal fishing boat owners, and storage space to wakeboard boat owners. Even if you are shopping for a boat that is not in one of these seven segments, you can gain insight into what is important to boaters in general, and perhaps adjust your own boat selection priorities accordingly. Let's take a look at what the study has to offer you as a boat buyer.

Within the study, there are three fundamental categories of useful information for the boat buyer: product satisfaction, product quality, and dealer satisfaction.

Product Satisfaction

On a scale of 1 to 10 (with 10 being outstanding and 1 being unacceptable), customers are asked how satisfied they are with over 60 different attributes within various boat categories including: cabin, engine, ride and handling, helm and instrument panel, design and styling, sound system, maintenance, water sports and fishing. For example, questions in the design and styling category include exterior appearance, cleat functionality, fuel fill accessibility, fuel capacity, and ease of boarding boat from the water.

Satisfaction is a completely subjective rating, but it's surprising how consistently owners of certain boat brands rate their boats using the 1 to 10 scale from year-to-year. Therein lies the usefulness and actionability of the data.

Among all the boat segments, as an average, some are consistently rated higher than others. The

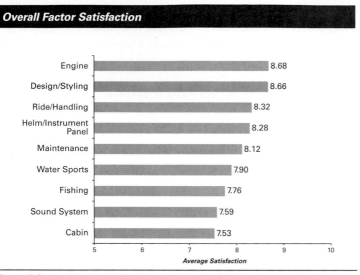

Overall Factor Satisfaction

Factor	Average Satisfaction
Engine	8.68
Design/Styling	8.66
Ride/Handling	8.32
Helm/Instrument Panel	8.28
Maintenance	8.12
Water Sports	7.90
Fishing	7.76
Sound System	7.59
Cabin	7.53

Source: J.D. Power and Associates 2007 Boat Competitive Information Study ℠

ski and wakeboard segment is rated the highest, as it has been for every year of the study, and it has also been the fastest growing. Small runabouts and express cruisers, in contrast, consistently appear near the bottom of the list. Chances are that if you buy an inboard-powered wakeboard boat that's included in the study, you will be satisfied with it.

Within this segment, in-line-drive competition ski boats make up a small part of the boats covered in the survey; most are V-drive wakeboard boats.

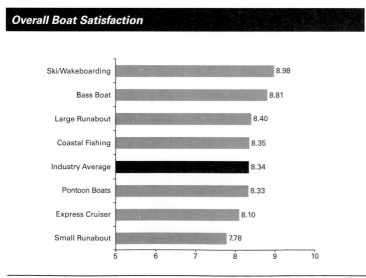

Overall Boat Satisfaction

Boat Type	Satisfaction
Ski/Wakeboarding	8.98
Bass Boat	8.81
Large Runabout	8.40
Coastal Fishing	8.35
Industry Average	8.34
Pontoon Boats	8.33
Express Cruiser	8.10
Small Runabout	7.78

Source: J.D. Power and Associates 2007 Boat Competitive Information Study ℠

Bass boats are also highly rated each year. Ski boats, wakeboard boats, and bass boats are also by no coincidence, rated high in quality. These are specialized boat types, wakeboard and bass, though wakeboard boats can also be considered as inboard-powered, open-bow runabouts in many cases.

At the other end of the scale, there are a number of likely reasons why owners rate their boats lower. Small runabouts, the lowest rated segment, have a greater tendency to be underpowered, since dealers are anxious to make a sale on these relatively low-priced boats. Once owners have had a chance to use their boats when they're loaded with passengers, gear, and fuel, they find they don't have enough power to tow skiers and boarders, and they don't cruise as fast as they had expected.

Small runabout owners tend to include more first-time boat buyers, who as a group rate their boats lower than experienced owners. Express cruisers, also a relatively low-rated segment, have more experienced owners, but these boats are more complex so there are more things that can go wrong, and they do go wrong, apparently to a greater extent than many owners expected.

There are two key elements driving owner satisfaction: the design and quality of the product, and the owner's expectations for the product. Therefore, it's important for the dealer to make clear to the customer, especially the inexperienced boater, the capabilities and limitations of the boat. Express cruisers are also more expensive boats, and it is natural for an owner to expect more from their bigger investment, but the boats frequently don't measure up to ski boats, wakeboard boats, and bass boats.

It's interesting that the highly rated, more expensive boat brands (like Cobalt, Grady-White, Correct Craft) are almost always rated much higher in value than the entry-level, budget-priced boats. In fact, many of the low-priced boats are rated very low in value (and in customer loyalty). This is just one of many truths that the data reveals, reminding all of us as boatowners that, to a large extent, you get what you pay for.

Even though you'd expect that anyone who pays a lot less for a boat of a given size would expect less performance, quality, and features, these entry-level boats are still only marginally satisfying. This is aggravated by very low satisfaction with dealer service after the sale. The net result is that owners are much less satisfied with the boat and the boating experience. The solution for an owner is to either dramatically lower their expectations, or spend more money for a boat.

Overall Boat Satisfaction by Boat Price

Source: J.D. Power and Associates 2007 Boat Competitive Information Study ℠

Product Quality

Owners are also asked to report any problems they've experienced with the boat, and the number of problems reported by owners determines the boat's quality. There are over 100 possible problems listed in each of five quality categories: engine and propulsion, ride and handling, exterior, cockpit and interior, and features. Ride and handling problems that might be reported would include stiff steering systems, boats pulling to the right, rides that are too rough, and the boat is underpowered. Five of the

ten most frequently reported problems are engine-related, and three of the ten are cosmetic, as shown in the graph. Because of its importance, we'll look more deeply at engine-related satisfaction below.

Overall Boat Quality

(Number of problems reported per 100 boats)

Source: J.D. Power and Associates 2007 Boat Competitive Information Study ℠

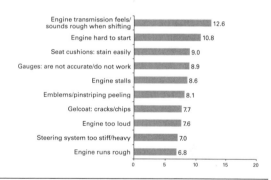

10 Most Frequently Reported Problems

Source: J.D. Power and Associates 2007 Boat Competitive Information Study ℠

It doesn't take a rocket scientist to figure out that quality impacts owner satisfaction; the more things on a boat that break, the less satisfied the owner will be with it. For example, 48 percent of the people who reported having no problems rated their boat a 10, while only 18 percent of people reporting three problems did so. People reporting more than three problems rated their boats even lower. This is revealing considering that across the segment the average boat had more than three problems reported. Most of the problems reported came from the engine, emphasizing why it's important to get a high-quality engine.

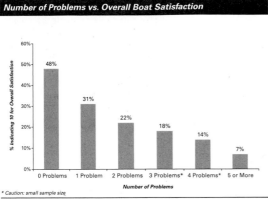

Number of Problems vs. Overall Boat Satisfaction

Caution: small sample size

Source: J.D. Power and Associates 2007 Boat Competitive Information Study ℠

Higher-quality boats tend to be ranked higher in satisfaction, and higher-quality boats tend to cost more, though that is not always the case. You usually get what you pay for; if you buy a budget-priced boat, you will likely not be as satisfied as someone who buys a more expensive boat, as shown in the graph. In fact, quality and reliability are the most frequently cited reasons customers give for buying a new boat. This leads us to the conclusion that it is almost always much better to initially pay more for a higher-quality boat with higher-quality components and power. You also may well be better off getting the smaller, higher-quality boat than the larger price point model, or by buying used. The corollary to this is that the bigger and more complex the boat, the more things there are to go wrong, and go wrong they do.

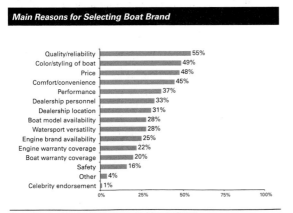

Main Reasons for Selecting Boat Brand

Source: J.D. Power and Associates 2007 Boat Competitive Information Study ℠

Dealer Satisfaction

The study has a long section on the dealer experience. Boatowners are asked to report on their experiences with their dealer in great detail, with this section generally divided into sales and service. The following are just a few of the attributes included in the report: dealership facility, working with your salesperson, how clearly the salesperson represented the boat's capabilities, the price worked out, and value received. The service questions include: quality of work performed, service representative, parts department, and promptness in having the boat ready when promised.

The study tells us repeatedly, in every boat segment and in every year that the study has been conducted, that the customer's treatment by the dealer is elemental to the overall boating experience. You might find the boat that does it all, but if the dealer is lacking, your overall boatownership experience will suffer. A good dealer will boost the manufacturer's satisfaction scores with the boat and engine, and a bad dealer will drive satisfaction with the boat and engine down. This may mean that you are better off picking the second or third boat on your list from the better dealer in your area.

The dealer section of the study drives home the point that successful businesses treat people well. Dealers who establish a personal relationship with the boat buyer and treat him or her honestly and fairly are highly rated. Unfortunately, dealer sales and especially service are consistently rated much lower than the boat and engine are.

Boat buyers place a lot of importance on the salesperson—how well they represented the boat's capabilities, as well as the handling of the paperwork and financing process. Owners put less importance on the price they pay for the boat (the dealer deserves to make a profit, and it's certainly in your interest that they do), or the facility, or the value received, believe it or not, and so should you.

My advice is to tell the salesperson up front that you want to have a clear understanding of what the boat can and cannot do, its capabilities and limitations. You don't want to take it for a test ride and hit 50 mph only to find out that with a full fuel tank

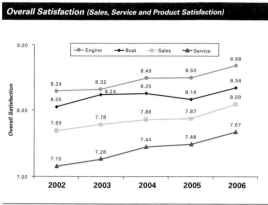

and the family and golden retriever on board it will barely get up on plane when towing a boarder. Make it clear you are making a big investment, and you'd like to establish a long, mutually beneficial relationship, both with the salesperson and with the dealership. You'd also like to be able to recommend the dealership to friends, of whom you have many in the surrounding area.

People who buy boats for the first time tend to rate dealers (and their boats) much lower than experienced buyers, and a big part of the reason has to be they overestimated what they'd be able to do with the boat. In other words, the dealer did not manage their expectations. On that note, it's important to keep two things in mind.

First, understand up front that you should not expect the same level of service at your local boat dealership as you do at your car dealership. There are exceptions, or course, but the average dealer does a poor job backing up the boat and the owner after the sale. Expect it, and if you actually get great service with a smile, be delighted.

Second, make sure to take the boat you're considering out on a prepurchase test ride. Once you've actually been out on the boat, you are no longer relying on the salesperson's word regarding how fast, how smooth, how dry, or how quiet it is. Allow a healthy performance margin between how well the boat performs with just you and the salesperson and a quarter tank of gas on board, and how it will run loaded to the washboards.

Better yet, take along as many people as you are likely to have on board once you buy the boat. Load her up. I've said it elsewhere, but it definitely bears repeating: make sure you've got a full load on board to see how the boat performs, especially when it comes to the issue of power to weight, or having enough horsepower, or in some cases, the right drivetrain, including gear ratio and prop size.

The reasons for the poor service across the boat industry are legion, ranging from simple apathy to the seasonal nature of the boat business in much of the country. This is why my position is to ask around and find out which dealer is the most highly regarded when it comes to service, and buy a boat from them, even if the dealer doesn't carry the brand you like best. That's how important service is to your happiness.

My brother's two-year-old (still under warranty) 26-foot express cruiser broke down on Labor Day weekend, leaving 20 people he'd ferried out to a local island stranded. The dealer (the guy who owned the business) pointed to a 16-foot aluminum skiff and told him to use it until the following week sometime when he'd get to the boat. I can't tell enough people that story, and I name the dealer, just like you would. Anyway, if it's close, or a toss up, when it comes to dealers in your area, go with the one who carries your favorite brand.

People tend to rate service lower than sales at the dealership, so be careful to get an accurate estimate as to how long the job will take and when you'll get the boat back. People are often misled here by the service rep, whether intentionally or otherwise, so make sure you're getting a realistic estimate on when you'll get the boat back. The best thing the dealer could do is overestimate the time it will take, and then you'll be delighted when you get the boat back sooner than expected.

On the other hand, don't rush the dealer. It's a lot better to give the service department time enough to diagnose and fix the problem on the first try. You will be mighty upset if you have to return the boat for repairs that should have been done right the first time. Mention that to the dealer.

Getting the best deal may not make a satisfied loyal customer of you. Be willing to spend more for a good boat and for good service, and be plain with the dealer as to your expectations and that you intend to reward good performance with your repeat business and advocacy.

Marine Engines

Choice of power is another of the most important boat buying decisions. Certainly one of the worst decisions you could make would be to save money by buying a boat with too little power. You might be tempted to buy a leftover model with standard power off the dealer's lot at a big discount, but it's just not worth it.

Getting the biggest engine available, or one of the biggest, is almost always a good idea. That's simply because there are so many things you can't do with a small engine—and this includes the standard power in many boats. Don't be fooled when the salesperson takes you out for a spin with a quarter tank of gas and two or three people on board. Especially with a small boat, under 30 feet, there will be a very big difference in the speed of the new, light boat, and one that has a painted bottom, full canvas, full fuel and water tanks, hundreds of pounds of gear, and a full load of passengers.

Keep in mind that dealers want to make the sale, and sometimes the only way they can be competitive is by making a certain price point. But the dealer's quarterly financial numbers are not your problem; being able to pull a boarder or skier up quickly, being able to plane easily with a full load of fuel, passengers, and gear, making it to the fishing grounds at the head of the pack, being able to get home quickly to beat the weather—these are the important things to the boatowner. Get the high-horsepower, optional power!

Besides having plenty of power in reserve, it's important not to skimp when selecting fuel delivery technology in a gas engine. There are basically three kinds—carbureted, found in outboards and inboards; electronically fuel-injected (EFI), also found in outboards and inboards; and direct-injected (DI), found in three outboard brands. While the carbureted outboard, gas inboard, or gas stern-drive engine may be initially cheaper, it will cause a lot of aggravation long-term. These engines are less reliable, harder to start, smoke more, and burn more fuel than an EFI or a DI engine.

My recommendation is to get the highest technology engine available. For inboards and stern drives (the engines are the same—just the drivetrain is different), this means getting the EFI and high-horsepower engine. For outboards, this means limiting your choice to either EFI four-strokes made by OEMs like Honda, Mercury, Yamaha, and Suzuki, or (DI or DFI) two-strokes—Evinrude E-TEC, Yamaha HPDI, and Mercury Optimax.

Again, if you want to be happy with your boat, power it with a big, high-tech engine (EFI four-stroke or DI two-stroke outboard, EFI stern drive or inboard). According to J.D. Power and Associates

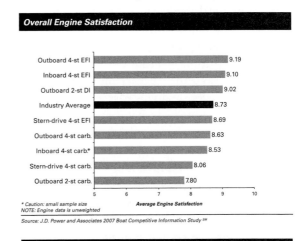

Overall Engine Satisfaction

Average Engine Satisfaction

Engine	Score
Outboard 4-st EFI	9.19
Inboard 4-st EFI	9.10
Outboard 2-st DI	9.02
Industry Average	8.73
Stern-drive 4-st EFI	8.69
Outboard 4-st carb.	8.63
Inboard 4-st carb.*	8.53
Stern-drive 4-st carb.	8.06
Outboard 2-st carb.	7.80

* Caution: small sample size
NOTE: Engine data is unweighted

Source: J.D. Power and Associates 2007 Boat Competitive Information Study ℠

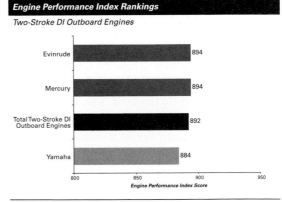

Engine Performance Index Rankings

Two-Stroke DI Outboard Engines

Engine Performance Index Score

Engine	Score
Evinrude	894
Mercury	894
Total Two-Stroke DI Outboard Engines	892
Yamaha	884

Source: J.D. Power and Associates 2007 Boat Competitive Information Study ℠

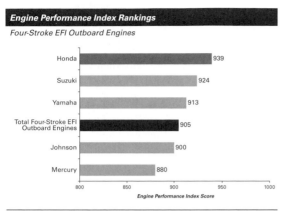

Engine Performance Index Rankings

Four-Stroke EFI Outboard Engines

data, most outboards being sold today are EFI four-strokes, which is a big change from just a few years ago when most were carbureted and EFI two-strokes. EFI four-strokes are also the highest-rated outboards (they all score well), followed by direct-injected two-strokes (Evinrude E-TEC, Mercury Optimax, and Yamaha HPDI), carbureted four-strokes and EFI two-strokes, and, in dead last position, carbureted two-strokes.

Another reason to buy the higher-tech engines is that they have fewer problems. Among coastal fishing boats, for example, four-stroke EFI outboards have about 0.6 reported problems per boat while carbureted two-strokes have 1.6 problems—about three times as many! Horsepower also makes a difference in quality, with larger engines having fewer reported problems. Bottom line, you'll be happier with your boat with the bigger, high-tech engine. You'll get more use out of the boat and have fewer problems with it.

In the stern-drive arena, the same thing applies, of course, that bigger EFI engines are the way to go. The other thing with stern drives is that dual-propeller drives, MerCruiser Bravo 3 and Volvo DP, deliver higher satisfaction than single propellers. We suspect the reason for this is that counterrotating propellers handle better, both around the dock (they'll back to either port or starboard since there is no side force, or walking effect) and at speed.

Boats with dual-propeller units tend to wander, or *yaw*, less at low no-wake speeds, and they accelerate strongly. They are also found more on bigger,

higher-quality, more highly rated boats, so there is likely some halo effect here—that is, the boat and the engine combining to get a better score than either would on their own. Of course, some boats are not suited to these dual-prop drives, such as most boats under 20 feet, heavy cruisers (they need larger-diameter, slower-turning props), and race boats that go over 70 mph or so.

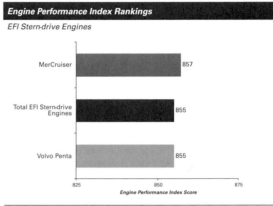

Engine Performance Index Rankings

EFI Stern-drive Engines

Only two EFI inboard engines garnered enough survey responses for inclusion in the study and, as shown, PCM outscored competitor Indmar.

If you have a feeling that a discounted boat in the dealer's yard is underpowered, it probably is. People who buy the boat with the engine they choose tend to be more satisfied than those who don't. This often includes having a choice of engine

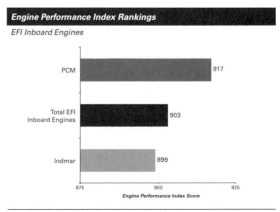

Engine Performance Index Rankings

EFI Inboard Engines

by brand, horsepower, and technology. Stick to your guns, in other words, and get the bigger power, with high-tech fuel injection, and, in a stern-drive application, with counterrotating props.

Power Circle Ratings

You can also learn about how each brand performs with regard to customer satisfaction by category by reviewing the Power Circle ratings that accompany each of the pertinent category write-ups. Boats are assigned between two and five circles in the major satisfaction categories and in overall satisfaction, depending on how their customers rated them.

You'll find that a good number of the brands are rated pretty much in line with their pricing. Some are rated higher or lower than you might expect, and this might be due in part to a dealer network that does a great or a lousy job selling and servicing the boats. But the most rewarding thing is using these power circles to find a boat brand that is clearly superior to its direct price point competitors in terms of customer satisfaction. Those are the jewels worth finding.

Saltwater Boats

Boston Whaler has been building offshore center console, walkaround, and dual console fishing and family boats for over forty years. This includes the brand's Dauntless series of inshore boats. The 190 Montauk, though not classified by Whaler as a bay boat, best fits into this category. This Montauk's hull is much improved over the original 13- and 16-foot versions, offering a better ride and features that include a built-in gas tank and a livewell. BOSTON WHALER

Bay Boats

Bay boats are designed for inshore use, with less deadrise and freeboard than offshore fishing craft. Less deadrise means less draft, and of course a bumpier ride, but the obvious priority is being able to fish comfortably in shallower water, with a flatter bottom that is more stable than a deep-V hull as anglers move from side to side of these relatively small boats. Interior freeboard, or coaming height, is also much lower than on offshore boats, and the decks tend to be closer to the waterline, making them less seaworthy (from a reserve buoyancy perspective), but still well suited for their intended use. This is a growing market segment, which is why so many of the offshore fishing boat builders also now build bay and flats boats. Many bay boats are offered with tunnels aft; the tunnel allows the boat to run with the engine raised higher out of the water on a jack plate while maintaining good waterflow to the prop.

Well-equipped bay boats generally have an insulated fish box, livewell, tackle storage locker and drawers, lockable rod stowage, depth- and fishfinders, rod holders, and a center console.

Built by Genmar's Champion Boats, a bass boat builder that like many others has branched out to serve similar markets, the 21 Bay is a good example of the genre, with its center console layout, low freeboard, and unrestricted fishability. GENMAR HOLDINGS, INC.

Built by Genmar's Hydra-Sports, which specializes in high-end offshore fishing boats, the Hydra-Sports 200 Bay is a well-built center console with fore and aft casting platforms, the layout favored by many in this class of boat. Fitted out with a bow-mounted trolling motor, this rig lets you sneak up on fish unannounced. GENMAR HOLDINGS, INC.

Key West, a builder of moderately priced but good-quality saltwater fishing boats, also builds inshore bay boats like this 186 Bayreef.

KEY WEST

Mako, part of Tracker Marine and a boatbuilder since the 1960s, has long specialized in saltwater center console fishing and cabin and dual console family boats. The 211, offered in a boat-motor-trailer package, is a good example of the builder's offerings in the bay boat arena, and it's offered in both conventional modified V-bottom and tunnel configurations. MAKO

Parker produces an extensive lineup of offshore saltwater fishing boats of all descriptions, but it is perhaps best known for its enclosed pilothouse models that are especially well suited to northern climes. Its bay boat lineup includes this ruggedly built 2100, with a layout ideally suited to unencumbered fishing. The center console is a little wider that usually seen, offering improved operator and passenger wind and spray protection. PARKER BOATS

Pathfinder builds conventional modified V-bottom and tunnel boats from 20 to 24 feet. This 2200 model is offered in both conventional modified V-bottom and tunnel hull configurations. Pathfinder is part of a small, high-end conglomerate building inshore and offshore outboard-powered saltwater fishing boats including Hewes, Maverick, and Cobia. PATHFINDER BOATS

Ranger, part of Genmar, is the world's largest bass boat builder, and certainly one of the best in terms of a quality product and customer loyalty. The 2400 Bay is Ranger's biggest model. GENMAR HOLDINGS, INC.

Sailfish, a relatively new (since 1986) private boatbuilding company, specializes in building good-running, well-built, and reasonably priced offshore sportfishing boats. The 1900 is the smaller of two bay boat models from Sailfish, and this boat sports a little more deadrise (18 degrees) than some others for a smoother ride, as well as a full 18 inches of interior coaming height, also a little higher than some other models. SAILFISH BOATS

Scout is another well regarded, relatively young, family-owned builder of high-end saltwater outboard-powered fishing and family-fishing boats. It also builds flats, bay, and fish-and-ski models. The upscale 221 Bay Scout is one of the builder's four bay boat offerings. SCOUT BOATS

Sea Pro, a high-volume, moderately priced saltwater fishing boat-builder founded in 1987, is now one of Brunswick Corporation's leading fishing brands. The 1900 Bay is one of four bay models. SEA PRO BOATS

Skeeter, part of Yamaha, builds high-end fiberglass bass boats, as well as fish-and-ski and inshore saltwater bay boats. The ZX 22 Bay is a low profile bay model with an optional tunnel hull for decreased engine draft. SKEETER BOATS

Triton, like many bay boat builders, specializes in saltwater fishing boats, but it also has a successful line of high-end fiberglass tournament bass boats as well as aluminum fishing, fish-and-ski, and pontoon boats. The 220 LTS (for light tackle series) bay boat benefits from the builder's long experience in other high-end fishing markets. TRITON BOATS

Trophy, a division of Brunswick Corporation specializing in the low-priced end of the market, builds solidly engineered, well-equipped offshore center consoles and family-oriented walkaround boats. The company also now builds bay boats, and the 1901 Bay Pro is the first in the series.   TROPHY SPORTFISHING BOATS

Wellcraft, part of Genmar, is another specialist in offshore saltwater fishing boats, and it has been at it for some 40 years. Wellcraft, which caters to the moderately priced end of the market, offers a pair of bay boats. The 195 is well-equipped and can be outfitted according to a buyer's wants.   GENMAR HOLDINGS, INC.

CENTURY 2202 INSHORE

Century 2202 Inshore Specifications

LOA:	22'
Beam:	8'6"
Deadrise:	14.5 deg.
Dry weight:	2,100 lb.
Draft (hull):	13"
Fuel capacity:	65 gal.

Century, a division of Yamaha, builds fiberglass inshore and offshore center console, dual console, walkaround, and express fishing boats from 17 to 32 feet. All are powered with Yamaha outboards (mostly four-stroke).

The Century 2202 Inshore is designed essentially as a bay boat with increased deadrise providing improved offshore capability. Our test boat ran over 50 mph, had a tower for spotting fish, was loaded with fishing features, and was fun to drive with its nimble handling. The boat has a capacity of six persons, or a total of 2,200 pounds including people, the motor, and gear. Our test boat had the maximum-rated 250 hp engine.

Construction

The Century starts with a 3-ounce skin coat of chop wet out in premium vinylester resin to help prevent osmotic blistering in the bottom and reduce print-through in the hull sides. The bottom strakes are filled with fiberglass and a matrix of resin mixed with angel hair fiber (for sharp bottom strake edges, which improves waterflow separation and reduces drag), and a syntactic print blocker is also sprayed on the hull sides to prevent print-through. The bottom is solid knit (versus woven) fiberglass, while the sides are cored with end-grain balsa for added stiffness.

The hull is supported by a one-piece flanged fiberglass grid that is bonded to the hull and supports the deck above. The transom is cored with 1½-inch-thick high-density foam sandwiched in fiberglass. The hull-to-deck joint is bonded with adhesive and fastened with self-tapping screws, which, structurally speaking, basically clamp the fiberglass together until the adhesive sets up. Decks are cored with Airlite foam of varying densities, depending on location, to add stiffness at lighter weight.

Hull Design

The Century 2202 Inshore has a moderate-deadrise hull that resembles the better bass boats below the chines. The entry is deceptively fine, resulting in a good ride in a light chop, while the flatter sections overall produce a good turn of speed. Spray strakes and reverse-angle chines add lift at speed and deflect spray down and out away from the boat.

The hull only draws some 11 inches of water (depending on loading and weight distribution, of course), so with the outboard mounted on a jack plate also drawing about a foot of water (Yamaha has recently lowered its cooling water intakes), this boat can get into very shallow water, though not quite as shallow as a flatter-bottom flats boat. The flats boat, on the other hand, typically lacks the inshore or bay boat's rougher water capability, as the latter has more deadrise and freeboard.

Walkthrough

Cockpit

At the bow is a raised casting platform with a large storage compartment below, accessed through a 45-inch-wide hatch, which, incidentally is very easy to lift with a well-balanced boost. The hatches on this boat are all closed-molded, so they look great and give the boat an upscale appearance, and they're gasketed to help eliminate vibrating and rattling. In the bow is a pair of 8-inch cleats, slightly recessed to minimize snags without resorting to pop-up cleats (we personally prefer this arrangement over the pop-ups). Also in the bow of the test boat was an electric Minn Kota trolling motor as well as a large anchor locker with a tie-off eye inside.

Built into the forward side of the center console is a seat with a 12-gallon livewell below, and outboard under the gunwales are rod storage lockers. The seat also has a pair of grab bars outboard of the seat cushion, and you'll also have the tow legs to hold onto at speed (you'll need them sitting in the bow at 40 mph).

The cockpit has low coamings, just 18 inches of interior height, which is typical of the genre and made necessary by the hull's low freeboard. It allows the angler to be that much closer to the water than on an offshore center console, which might have 26 to 30 inches of coaming height inside, and a deck that's a few inches higher off the waterline for additional reserve buoyancy. That low interior height makes having something to hang onto at the helm that much more important, especially on such a fast boat. Nonskid was very grippy underfoot, which helps from a safety perspective.

The tower, the platform of which stands 6 feet, 10 inches off the deck, is a welcome addition when spotting fish or just enjoying the view, which is much improved over the lower helm. Rolling and pitching motions are accentuated that high off the water, limiting use at high speed. The tower engine control is electronic, which makes shifting virtually effortless.

In the stern to starboard aft is a mechanical compartment with two starting batteries, the jack plate pump, battery switch, and fuel filter—all are easy to access. There's also a fiberglass catch pan or tray in the compartment, which makes the space easier to keep clean than if the bilge below was exposed. A pair of large livewells is also aft, to port and on centerline, along wih a removable transom seat with backrest on top of the centerline livewell. A rudimentary (two step) boarding ladder is provided at the stern—a longer one would be a lot easier to climb, but we do like the fact that this one is easily deployed from the water by a swimmer.

The deck drains overboard through four 1¾-inch drain lines, two per side. Access plates open to inspect the 60-gallon aluminum tank below the deck. Century feels aluminum tanks are the way to go, citing concern over a new E-10 gasoline additive's purported effect on plastic tanks. In the event the foamed-in tank ever needs to be replaced, there's a scribe line molded in the deck, but no removal hatch. We have reservations about foamed-in aluminum fuel tanks in general, since any water accumulating around the outside of the tank eventually deoxygenates and corrodes the tank from the outside, which makes leaving a ventilating air space around the tank a prudent measure. However, Century reports having no corrosion problems.

Helm

There are a lot of ways to design a good helm station, and this boat has one. The GPS chartplotter and fish-finder display is up high where it's easy to see, and easy to adjust with your right hand. The wheel and throttle are comfortably positioned for standup driving; our test boat did not have seats at the helm, though you could sit atop the leaning post. The windshield is just large enough to offer some wind and spray protection, but you'll want plastic side curtains to stay dry in the rain.

A portable cooler fits below the leaning post, and the seat flips up for access to a storage compartment inside. There's also a flip-down footrest below the helm seat, along with rocket launchers aft. Inside the console, accessed from the aft side under the helm, are three deep-cycle batteries for the trolling motor.

Engine

Our test boat had the maximum power, a 250 hp Yamaha four-stroke. It was mounted on a jack plate, which allows for vertical engine adjustment. This lets the boat get into shallow water without having to tilt the motor, and it also allows for the immersion of the outboard's lower unit to be adjusted for the conditions for minimal drag at high speed without ventilating. The jack plate also gets the engine away from the boat 10 inches or so, which provides slightly cleaner water-flow to the prop, and probably adds a mile or two per hour to the boat's minimum planing speed due to the shift aft in the boat's center of gravity.

Sea Trial

Our test ride took place with an unpainted bottom, a tower, three passengers, and a half tank of gas. With a single Yamaha 250 hp four-stroke, we reached 54 mph with the jack plate and trim tweaked just right, and recorded just over 40 mph at a 4,500 rpm cruise. This was with a 21-inch-pitch prop; Century reports reaching a few miles per hour faster with a 23-inch prop (along with slower acceleration), and also a couple more miles per hour without the tower. The single Yamaha four-stroke was one quiet engine (quieter than the numbers would indicate to our ears); about the only thing audibly discernable above 40 mph was wind noise, which is not the case with the same engines in twin installations.

The boat was easily on top at 3,000 rpm with full tabs and the engine trim tucked in, making about 22 mph. The engine was quiet at its 3,500 to 4,500 rpm cruising range. The ride was excellent in the light chop, and the boat handled well in all respects. In fact, we ran along twisting and turning through wakes and a 12-inch chop, with a lively but stable ride, and looked down to find we were going 45 to 50 mph. The boat had a dry ride, with hardly a drop making its way to the windshield. Don't expect it to keep up with a deep-V offshore boat like a Regulator or Sailfish in rough water, nor is it as inherently seaworthy with its lower cockpit deck and freeboard, but this boat does quite well in the lighter chop it's intended to fish in.

The Yamaha 704 single-lever engine control on our test boat was smooth-shifting, the smoothest of any of the Yamaha mechanical controls we've run, in fact. The mechanical steering was low effort, taking five turns of the wheel lock-to-lock (a little slower than the three to four turns we find optimal for responsiveness).

The Century 2202 Inshore has a lot going for it, including lots of storage space, three big livewells, great nonskid in the self-bailing cockpit, a good turn of speed, and an equally good ride in a modest chop. Plus, the tower is just a blast to drive from. Century has obviously put a lot of thought into the design, and we think they have been successful.

Options include dual batteries, seat upgrades, trolling motor system, bait well, hydraulic tilt steering, trim tab indicators, and bimini top.

CATAMARANS

Cats are king for some people. It's hard to beat the ride of a well-designed cat, with two narrow hulls slicing and dicing the waves with little fuss and bother. As long as the tunnel in between the hull sponsons doesn't bottom out from overloading, the cat's ride is something to write home about. It's a tough thing to make a cat look good, though some manufacturers have been doing a good job of addressing the aesthetics of a cat hull. Cats can have displacement, semidisplacement, or full planing hulls. The shape of the bottom, the weight distribution, and the height of the tunnel, rather than the hull design, determine how well the boat works.

Century 2202 Inshore Performance Results		
RPM	**Speed, mph**	**Noise Level, dBA**
600	2.5	59
1,000	3.9	68
1,500	6.2	69
2,000	7.2	72
2,500	9.3	79
3,000	20.6	82
3,500	30.5	84
4,000	35.1	85
4,500	40.8	wind
5,000	46.1	
5,500	51.4	
6,000	53.4	

Test conditions: Three passengers, half tank of fuel, with Yamaha 250 hp four-stroke outboard with 21-inch-pitch prop. Light chop.

Everything from deck boats to sportfishermen and cruising yachts have been built on cat hulls, all of which are most naturally suited to twin-engine propulsion, with an engine in or hanging from the back of each hull. Some cats, especially planing models, ride poorly at displacement speeds, since the tunnels are too close to the water when off plane and pound unmercifully. Make sure the boat you buy isn't objectionable when running slow in a chop.

Fountaine Pajot Boats is a French builder of sail and power trawler cats. The power models range from 35 to 75 feet, and include the Cumberland 44 shown. This cat is nearly as wide as it is long, with a 21-foot, 6-inch beam. Range at 7 knots is said to be 1,000 nautical miles. FOUNTAINE PAJOT BOATS

Glacier Bay Boats builds high-end cats from 22 to 34 feet in bowrider, deck boat, center console, walkaround, hardtop, and express layouts. The 3065 Canyon Runner is a big, beamy (10-foot, 8-inch) center console cat designed for fishing offshore. GLACIER BAY BOATS

Pro Sports Boats builds SeaQuest monohulls and ProKat cats. The company's extensive cat lineup runs from 20 to 36 feet, including this 36-foot center console.　　　PRO SPORTS BOATS

Twin Vee Boats builds power cat center consoles from 17 to 36 feet, including a 17-foot bay boat that draws just 8 inches when lightly loaded. Shown here is a new 29-foot center console. It offers a great ride, lots of room, and it's well-equipped to fish and has an economical four-stroke outboard power plant. Up to twin 250s are available.　　　TWIN VEE BOATS

Pro Sports Boats' other 36-footer is an express model.
PRO SPORTS BOATS

World Cat builds world-class power sportfishing and family cats from 23 to 33 feet. Models include center console, dual console, deck boat, and express cabin layouts. The good-running 250 DC is the builder's best-selling model, as it makes a good family boat (there's an enclosed head) and it's a natural to fish from as well.　　　WORLD CAT

Sea Cat Boats builds an interesting assortment of center console and dual console cats from 18 to 22 feet (Sea Cat 226 DC shown here). There's even a shoal-draft bay boat version, the 205, with a draft of 12 inches.　　　SEA CAT BOATS

PDQ YACHTS

PDQ YACHTS

PDQ 34 Specifications

LOA:	34'6"
LWL:	33'11"
Beam:	16'10"
Draft:	2'4"
Displacement:	15,000 lb.
Fuel:	184 gal.
Water:	80 gal.

hand-laid mat (the builder does not own a chopper gun) wet out in vinylester resin to prevent osmotic blistering; every hull also gets treated with a four-coat epoxy InterProtect anti-blistering system. The rest of the vessel—hull, deck, and superstructure—is wet out in isophthalic resin, which has better mechanical properties than standard general-purpose orthophthalic resin.

The bottom of the two hulls is solid fiberglass. Above the waterline, the sides are cored with ½-inch Core-Cell structural foam bedded in Core-Bond adhesive and vacuum bagged to the outer fiberglass skin—an excellent method of ensuring integrity in the skin-to-core bond line. Inner and outer fiberglass skins are 22-ounce nonwoven triaxial fiberglass reinforcements. The tunnel area, which is subjected to considerable wracking forces, has a double layer of fiberglass in the outer skin, as well as longitudinal stiffeners molded into the outer skin. The deck and deckhouse are also cored with Core-Cell, ¾-inch and ⅝-inch respectively.

The engines are supported by an all-fiberglass grid system; increasing the mass of the engine beds would be a simple way of reducing the vibration levels felt above the engines, especially at idle.

The hull-to-deck joint is a horizontal flange bonded with Sikiflex and bolted with ¼-inch bolts every 8 inches. A rugged aluminum rubrail is bolted through the hull-to-deck flange, and is designed to be replaced in the event of damage to a section. All deck hardware is through-bolted through solid, coreless sections of deck.

When it comes to space, ride, and economy, it's hard to beat a cat. Two narrow hulls push through the water with a lot less resistance than one wide one, and they cut through the waves with a lot less thrashing around—in certain sea conditions. And when you have a 34-foot cat with a 16-foot, 10-inch beam, like our PDQ 34, you can add space to the mix, with a combination of layout enhancements and limitations.

PDQ Yachts had this all figured out when they started building sailing cats over twenty years ago. Then they started getting approached by boaters asking them for a power version; some just wanted one of PDQ's sailing cats without the mast. PDQ quickly discovered there was strong interest in a power cat. It knew the sailing hull wasn't the right answer, and so it went to work perfecting and researching the boat that has become the PDQ 34. This involved investing in expensive hull design software as well as a regimen of tank testing before they were satisfied with the hull design.

Construction

The hull starts with a nearly ¾-inch layer of Cook CCP gelcoat, followed by a layer of 1-ounce

The 5052 aluminum fuel tanks are suspended by brackets welded to the upper sides of the tanks affixed to fiberglass composite bulkheads. This allows airflow completely around the tanks, preventing moisture from accumulating and corroding the outer tank surfaces. This is an excellent way to ensure long tank life.

The construction methods and materials were selected for their combination of structural integrity and light weight. For example, using Core-Bond instead of chop saves as much as 1,000 pounds in the hull laminate, while providing a better bond between the outer skin and the core.

The builder also addresses weight in furniture component choices. They are made of lightweight honeycomb-cored cherry veneer. Shaving weight is important in a cat for two reasons: The pounds-per-inch-immersion (PPI) figure is lower than it is for a monohull, so cats are more sensitive to weight changes. This matters because the deeper the hull, the greater the drag, and the more fuel it takes to go at a given speed. The other and probably more important reason is that as the cat gets heavier the tunnel roof gets closer to the waterline, and to passing wave crests, making tunnel impact more frequent and jarring.

Walkthrough

Cockpit and Topsides

One of the great advantages of the PDQ 34 is the ease and safety with which you can get around on deck. The sidedecks are 29 inches wide—about three times that of a 34-foot monohull, so two people can pass without bumping into each other. The deck is surrounded by a 30-inch stainless steel railing, which is high enough to offer a good handgrip in a seaway. The stainless is on the light side, though, at 1 inch in diameter. We'd like to see the builder increase it to 1¼-inches and also decrease the stanchion spacing to stiffen up the railing, since it will deflect as much as a couple of inches under moderate load (it may not meet ABS deflection standards).

The deckhouse is surrounded by a handrail which also gives something to hang onto when walking topside. There are breaks in the railing for access to the dock or another boat. (The test boat had stainless steel davits astern that did double-duty supporting a seat that was wide and strong enough for four or five people.) The batteries are under a cockpit hatch.

Up on the bridge, there are seats on either side, with storage below (a cooler fits in a nook to starboard), and a two-person seat is at the helm. There's more storage under the bridge front forward. The bridge railing is also 30 inches high, which is too low for a bridge (36 to 40 inches is more appropriate given the accentuated rolling motions higher up), but it's stiffer than the one on the main deck since the stanchion spacing is closer. The stairs leading from the cockpit to the bridge are wide and deep, and the rise and run makes them easily climbed while holding a drink in one hand and the railing in the other.

Another safety and convenience feature is the wide molded steps leading down to the water on either side, and there's a retractable boarding ladder and hot-and-cold shower to port. The grit nonskid is effective.

Cabin

Coming inside the saloon from the cockpit, a lounge seat with a fold-up table is immediately to port and the lower helm opposite to starboard. This area is raised above the main saloon, which improves helm station visibility and creates the headroom needed in the twin staterooms below. It's down two steps to the U-shaped dinette that converts by lowering the cherry table onto cleats to a queen-size bed, 80 inches wide and 70 inches long. It provides plenty of room for two adults or a couple of kids. Headroom is 80 inches in the forward part of the saloon, and the interior is a full 11 feet wide inside; this makes for a very large common room, which is what this space amounts to.

Outboard of the saloon, you step down several steps (3 feet) from the tunnel-top level into the hulls. To port is the galley, open to the saloon, with two large Corian countertops opposite each other, one 4 feet long facing outboard with a deep sink, cabinets, and drawers below, and the other, inboard-facing toward the saloon, with a two-burner propane gas stove and microwave oven. The refrigerator-freezer is forward at chest level, and there's a big storage locker below. In fact, there is storage everywhere one looks in this boat—under deck hatches and false floors, in passage-ways, under berths.

The port stateroom is aft of the galley, through a door. This stateroom has a queen-size mattress (80 inches by 60 inches) packed into the small space over the tunnel. Outboard are two large windows (34 inches by 22 inches overall), and aft at the transom is an opening hatch that's 19 inches by 14 inches, which is too small for emergency egress; we'd increase the hatch size to 24 inches square or larger so it can serve as an emergency egress route. Head-room in the staterooms is just over 6 feet. Over on the starboard side, the saloon stairs lead down to another stateroom, the mirror image of the other, and a passageway leads forward to the head with its separate roomy shower, molded sink, opening portlight, and Bemis electric toilet.

Concerning the few complaints we have about the boat, the builder is in general agreement with our observations regarding the windshield mullion width, fuel line connections, hatch size in the state-rooms, and the railing stiffness. PDQ is investigat-ing making changes to address these issues.

All told, we can recommend the PDQ 34 with-out hesitation. It's economical to operate, maneuver-able, carefully and strongly built, and makes intelligent use of the available interior space. It's easy and safe to get around inside and topside, pleasantly finished in cherry and molded fiberglass, bright and airy inside with all the big windows, and it's a good sea boat in moderate conditions. Workmanship everywhere is of high quality, from the stainless steel railings topside

(note the curved bridge railing stanchions to port) to the inlaid cherry soles and fiberglass tooling.

Engine

Placing inboard engines in a cat is easy for the designer, since the hulls are just the right size to hold the engines, and the very low shaft angle (2 degrees) makes for an efficient drivetrain. But for the person who installs the engines, and who maintains them afterward, the cat inboard becomes more problem-atic, since those narrow hulls restrict access out-board of the engines.

On the PDQ 34 the engines are below the state-room berths. A box opens up for access to the forward end of the engine, which is where all the maintenance checks (raw-water strainer, expansion tank, oil dipstick) are done. Hatches under the mat-tress also lift up for access to the aft end of the engine, and also to the battery and battery charger. Aft of the engine is a hot water heater and an engine starting battery, and all the way aft is the rudderpost; the rud-der board at the top of the rudderpost looks a little lightweight, but it is supported at the skeg at the other end so we suspect it would remain intact in a hard grounding. The fuel filter-separator is in a waist-high cabinet just forward of the engine compartment.

Getting to the engines for major maintenance takes some work, and removing an engine would involve a convoluted path up to the saloon and out to the cockpit, but the openings are just large enough for the engine to fit through with the removal of a few engine accessories. All in all, the builder has done an excellent job given the space constraints, and routine maintenance for the owner will prove straightfor-ward. Also to be mentioned is the wiring job through-out the boat. It is meticulously and neatly routed and protected from chafing throughout the boat.

Sea Trial

The PDQ 34 has twin semidisplacement hulls with radiused chines and flat sections aft that transition to an ax-head shape aft, which creates a vertical sur-face (think deadwood in a wooden boat) for the shaft

log to pass through. With 100 hp Yanmar inboard diesels, the boat reaches a planing speed (S/L of 3:1), though it was in semidisplacement mode (there is negligible hull rise), at 18 knots at full power, with an easy cruise speed of 15 knots. The propellers are fully protected by the hull, so a light grounding will just be a nuisance involving backing off, or getting towed back off into deep water; the running gear should emerge unscathed as it is completely protected by what is essentially a full keel and skeg aft.

Our test ride took place off Florida's St. Lucie inlet in a 1- to 2-foot chop on top of a 2- to 4-foot swell. The boat sliced through the chop like a knife through butter. In fact, the most noticeable motions were not pitching like it would have been in a monohull in these seas, but rather the boat's snap roll and the surge of the boat rising and falling vertically in the swells. The two hulls want to go up and down at slightly different times, too, so that results in some subsidiary hull motions and shuddering peculiar to catamarans.

The overall effect was not unpleasant. Although one could wish for a little easier roll period, this is the nature of a cat design with its tremendous form stability. Many people will forgive this trait considering there was no rolling past 8 or 10 degrees (compared to the 15- to 25-degree rolls a monohull would have sustained in the same seas) with the vessel following the angle of the wave fronts religiously. The hull only draws 2 feet, 4 inches, which is great, but it also means the tops of the props aren't far below the surface, and they tend to ventilate in heavy weather—though it only happened once or twice in the moderate seas we encountered.

The waves weren't rough enough on our sea trial, but count on the top of the tunnel bottoming out when the waves are high and close enough together and you're running right into them. Usually you can minimize or eliminate this by changing course so the seas are 20 or 30 degrees off the bow, or by slowing down. With full planing cats, the faster you run, the better, as the hull (including the tunnel roof) rise up with it, clearing all but the steepest wave peaks.

Any semidisplacement cat likes to go in a straight line more than it likes to turn. It took 45 seconds to do a 360-degree turn doing 15 knots at 3,000 rpm before putting the wheel over. This compares to 25 to 35 seconds for an inboard 34-foot

planing hull, but, then again, a full-keel Down East–style hull would also take a full 40 to 60 seconds. You can speed up the turn by almost 10 seconds, however, by stopping the inboard engine during the turn, which slows the boat a few knots, but it also tightens the turn considerably. The PDQ 34's natural course-keeping is a delight when not turning hard, though. Even when running downsea in those 3- to 4-footers, it took very little rudder input to head for the sea buoy on the way back in; an autopilot should never wear out on this boat.

Another nice thing about this cat is the get-home capability on one engine; with one engine running at an easy 3,000 rpm, we made 11-plus knots, and it took less than a half turn of the wheel toward the running engine to maintain a steady course. The Kobelt mechanical single-lever engine controls were as smooth and enjoyable to use as any we've seen, and much better than most.

Back at the dock, we couldn't think of a boat that's easier to handle than this one. The hulls are so far apart that the boat twists responsively with the engines staying at idle speed. In fact, we used no throttle at all when backing into and driving alongside a slip—we just let the transmissions do the work. The props provided plenty of traction dockside, and ran smoothly at cruise speed (15 knots) offshore. Our overall reaction is that this boat, as any cat does, has its ride-motion quirks (from a monohuller's perspective), but we would recommend it without hesitation for its stability, low amplitude in roll, natural course-keeping, smooth ride in a chop, and high propulsion efficiency. Just don't overestimate its heavy seas capabilities; it has its limitations like any other small boat.

The PDQ 34 has upper and lower helm stations. The lower is aft in the saloon, with a two-person seat and the wheel 10 feet aft of the windshield. With the minimal bow rise, and the large windows all around, visibility was quite good ahead and we always felt we had good situational awareness. We would like to see narrower windshield mullions; there's 10 inches between the windshield sections forward, and that's more horizon out of view than we'd prefer, though the impact on horizon sight lines was mitigated by the distance to the windshield from the helm. The center window opens, which directs a high-volume sea breeze right through the saloon, which is very pleasant. The spray rails kick up spray (they're supposed to knock it down, so we think they could be tweaked to good effect), so you'll be limited as to when you can have that window open under way. Noise levels were quite low at the lower helm up through the 3,000 rpm cruise speed.

Visibility on the bridge was excellent, and the wheel and engine controls were positioned just right in terms of height, angle, and distance from the helm seat to operate comfortably seated or standing. The forward-angled windscreen did a surprisingly good job of deflecting wind, and we never felt a drop of seawater on the bridge.

PDQ 34 Performance Results

RPM	Speed, knots	Noise Level, dBA (lower helm)
1,000	5.0	60
1,500	6.5	68
2,000	7.0	71
2,500	12.5	77
3,000	15.5	80
3,500	18.3	88
3,750	19.6	89

Test conditions: Two passengers, full fuel and water tanks, lightly loaded, with twin 100 hp Yanmar diesels driving 1¼-inch Aquamet 22 shafts and 17 × 15 three-blade props through 1:97:1 reduction gears. Moderate chop.

COASTAL FISHING BOATS

The coastal fishing category incorporates three different boat types: center consoles (CCs), dual consoles (DCs), and walkarounds (WAs). These boats are competent to handle rougher waters than bay boats, but are not intended to go so far offshore and stay so long as to justify a full cabin, like a convertible or sportsfisherman. Most manufacturers who compete in the coastal fishing category offer boats of two or all three types.

Results from the J.D. Power and Associates 2007 Boat Competitive Information Study (BCIS) show dominance for Grady-White, with the brand scoring 31 points ahead of the second place finisher. Grady-White's overall customer satisfaction superiority is underscored by the fact that it has been the top-ranked coastal fishing brand, by a large margin, every year since the study began in 2001. Grady's combination of a high-quality boat, four-stroke Yamaha outboard power, a high-performing dealer network, and a customer-focused management team lies behind the company's success.

Boston Whaler and Scout also stood out for their strong performance, as did Century. Trophy was ranked lowest, preceded by Sea Fox, Pro-Line, and Angler. It's interesting to note that the lowest ranked boat brands are also among the least expensive, and also that some of these price point boats also score lowest in value for the money. In fact, some of the most expensive boats often score highest in value, in part because the whole boat ownership experience—boat, engine, and after-sale customer care—are so much more satisfying. The coastal fishing segment average was right in the middle of the seven segments covered in the study at 822 index points. It's also one of the biggest segments with sixteen brands represented.

Grady-White also received five Power Circles in each individual category. (Recall that Power Circle Ratings are based on customer satisfaction measured from the study.) The only other brand with a five-circle rating in *any* category was Triton for fishing. Boston Whaler, Polar, Sailfish, and Scout received four Power

Boat Performance Index Ranking

Coastal Fishing

Company	Average Index Score
Grady-White	896
Boston Whaler	865
Scout	857
Century	840
Polar	828
Key West	825
Hydra-Sports	825
Segment Average	**822**
Sea Pro	820
Sea Hunt	819
Sailfish	816
Wellcraft	808
Seaswirl	802
Angler	789
Pro-Line	789
Sea Fox	779
Trophy	770

Included in the segment, but not ranked due to small sample size: Parker, Pursuit, Sea Boss, and Triumph

Source: J.D. Power and Associates 2007 Boat Competitive Information Study ℠

Power Circle Ratings ○○○○○ JDPower.com

J.D. Power and Associates 2007 Boat Competitive Information Study ℠

Coastal Fishing Boat Ratings

(Ratings shown as number of filled Power Circles out of 5.)

Company	Overall Rating	Quality & Reliability	Engine	Fishing	Design & Style	Ride & Handling
Grady-White Award Recipient	5	5	5	5	5	5
Angler	2	2	2	3	2	2
Boston Whaler	5	4	4	4	4	4
Century	5	4	4	3	4	4
Hydra-Sports	3	3	4	3	4	3
Key West	3	4	4	3	3	3
Polar	3	3	4	3	4	3
Pro-Line	2	2	2	2	2	2
Sailfish	3	3	3	3	3	2
Scout	4	4	5	4	4	4
Sea Fox	2	2	2	2	2	2
Sea Hunt	3	4	4	3	3	3
Sea Pro	3	3	3	3	3	4
Seaswirl	3	3	3	3	3	3
Trophy	2	2	2	2	2	2
Wellcraft	3	3	3	3	4	3

SCORING LEGEND:
5 ○○○○○ Among the best 4 ○○○○ Better than most 3 ○○○ About average 2 ○○ The rest

Circles in fishing. Pro-Line, Sea Fox, and Trophy each earned just two Power Circles in all of the categories, while Angler received two Power Circles in each category except its three-Power Circle Rating in fishing.

Center Consoles

Center consoles tend to be hard-core fishing machines, with the deck layout permitting a fish to be played all around the boat without interference from structure. The center console on many rigs, however, doesn't provide protection from the elements, particularly for guests hanging on to the leaning post or helm seat. Avoiding spray and rain can be difficult, if not impossible. With an obvious priority on clear fishing room, many center consoles have low cockpit sides. This means that your passengers will need plenty of grab bars to hold onto when operating at high speed. For children, older people, or others unused to a boat's motion, the center console may not be a great choice because of the lack of inherent cockpit safety and seating.

However, family-oriented versions of CCs with folding transom seats, enclosed heads, and forward seats molded in as part of the deck are available and becoming more common. Larger CCs also sometimes have a cuddy forward, or a sleeping compartment carved out below the forward deck, entered from the console-head compartment. CCs range from about 15 to 36 feet.

Boston Whaler builds high-end offshore outboard fishing boats — center consoles, dual consoles, and walkaround models — up to 34 feet. The 320 Outrage Cuddy is a hybrid CC with a cuddy cabin forward. This is a good-running boat with a bona fide offshore hull design (unlike Whalers from just a few years ago that were a hard ride). It is solidly built with Whaler's proprietary Unibond construction using foam as a structural component. An optional patented shock-absorbing deck is a big plus running at speed in a stiff chop.

BOSTON WHALER

Century builds all-fiberglass, Yamaha-powered center console, dual console, walkaround, and bay boats from 17 to 32 feet. Part of Yamaha, Century produces well-built, good-running boats that are designed by people who fish extensively themselves (which is not all that unusual in this business). The 2200 CC is a solid performer, and though it's one of the builder's smaller models, it's well-equipped to venture offshore in search of that trophy fish. CENTURY BOATS

Everglades is the second boatbuilding company (the first was Edgewater) founded by Bob Dougherty, for a long time the head engineer at Boston Whaler. Everglades boats are built using an innovative construction method that produces a rock-solid boat with an excellent running surface. There's more of that innovation topside where you can actually see it — the 290 Pilot has a unique console and windshield design that will appeal to anyone running regularly in inclement weather. EVERGLADES BOATS

Contender builds center consoles, and variations including cuddy and center cabin models, from 21 to 36 feet. These boats are substantially lighter than many other boats of the same size and run commensurately faster. True deep-V hulls with fine entries and 24.5 degrees of deadrise at the transom, Contenders run well offshore. The 33T shown here is a recent model that can take up to triple 300s, carries 400 gallons of gas (you'll need all of it with 900 hp), and has a 9-foot, 8-inch beam. CONTENDER BOATS

Grady-White has been in business since the 1950s, building well-engineered and good-running boats designed (from the chines down at least) by C. Raymond Hunt and Associates. The perennial recipient of the J.D. Power and Associates award for highest customer satisfaction in the coastal fishing segment (center consoles, dual consoles, and walkarounds from 17 to 28 feet), the Yamaha-powered Grady sets the pace when it comes to pleasing its customers. This savvy and individualistic company stands by its low-glare, eye-saving cream-colored gelcoat, one of many practical features setting them apart from the crowd. The unsinkable 306 is the builder's largest center console. GRADY-WHITE BOATS

Intrepid builds big high-end, vacuum-bagged, moderate-weight offshore fishing boats that, with their deep-V step-bottom hulls, will run with the best of them. Models run from a 30-foot center console to a quad-outboard 47-foot express; other models include center consoles with cuddies forward, and walkarounds. Bigger boats like those offered by Intrepid, including the 323 CC cuddy shown here, give offshore fishermen more range, on-station endurance, and comfort than smaller ones can deliver.   INTREPID BOATS

Regulator produces a lineup of high-end center consoles and 30-foot express model. Building on its original 23- and 26-footers, this North Carolina–based family-owned builder of offshore center consoles has expanded the line to 32 feet, filled it in with 24- and 29-footers, and added forward seating models designed to make these offshore fishing machines into nominal family boats. Running on deep-V bottoms, this 29-foot, Yamaha-powered Regulator runs very well in a stiff chop.   REGULATOR BOATS

Part of S2 Corporation (which also owns Tiara Yachts), Pursuit builds three series of quality outboard-powered fishing boats, including center consoles and express models. Pursuit dropped its larger inboard-powered fishing boats (leaving those to Tiara) to focus on outboards a couple of years ago. Good in a seaway, Pursuits have established an excellent reputation. The 310 CC is one of the newest models, and the second largest CC.   PURSUIT BOATS

Scout has firmly established itself in the upper tier of the saltwater fishing segment, running head-to-head with the likes of Grady-White, Boston Whaler, and Pursuit. Family-owned and operated, Scout produces well-engineered mostly Yamaha-powered center consoles, walkarounds, express fishing boats, and bay boats. The 242 SF serves as an excellent representative for the brand.   SCOUT BOATS

Sea Pro, one of the country's largest fiberglass fishing boat builders, was recently acquired by Brunswick Corporation to round out its line of center console, walkaround, and dual console offerings from 17 to 27 feet, and to provide more business for its Mercury engine division. Sea Pro also produces a few bay and fish-and-ski models. The 270 CC is the largest Sea Pro model, and it's a large-volume, seaworthy, good-running, and solidly built boat with high freeboard and a 9-foot, 2-inch beam.   SEA PRO BOATS

Triton produces a wide range of salt- and freshwater boats, both aluminum and fiberglass, and it enjoys an excellent reputation for its quality, high-end product in each of its markets, including bass and offshore fishing. Triton, which was recently bought by Brunswick Corporation to round out its high-end saltwater lineup, and also to help it enter the bass boat market, produces center consoles, walkarounds, dual consoles, and inshore bay boats from 19 to 35 feet. The 2690 CC is a well-built 26-footer.   TRITON BOATS

Trophy, also a division of Brunswick Corporation, builds center console, dual console, and walkaround fishing boats from 17 to 31 feet. The hull of the 1903 CC model shown is built with fiberglass-covered foam-filled stringers that won't rot.   TROPHY SPORTFISHING BOATS

Southport Boatworks is a new venture started by three young (at heart) and experienced marine management, engineering, and marketing veterans in North Carolina a few years ago. These good-running, well-built Hunt-designed hulls are designed to accommodate the added weight of four-stroke (mostly Yamaha) power. Southport is focusing on the market it knows well, with 26- and 28-foot center consoles and a new 28-foot express.   SOUTHPORT BOATWORKS

Wellcraft, a Genmar company, is a long-time builder of midrange (price-wise) saltwater fishing boats, including center console, dual console, walkaround, and bay boat models from 18 to 36 feet. Wellcraft also makes a high-performance lineup of center consoles from 30 to 35 feet under the Scarab name. The Wellcraft 212 is shown here.   GENMAR HOLDINGS, INC.

Saltwater Boats: Coastal Fishing Boats   277

KEY WEST

Key West 268 Bluewater Center Console Specifications

LOA:	26'8"
Beam:	9'8"
Deadrise:	21 deg.
Dry weight:	4,510 lb.
Cockpit depth:	25"
Draft (hull):	16"
Fuel capacity:	180 gal.

Key West builds a line of low-priced, well-equipped saltwater fishing and family boats from 15 to 28 feet. Included are center console, dual console, walk-around, bay boats, flats boats, and deck boat models.

The 268 Bluewater is an offshore fishing boat with unsinkable construction, high freeboard for increased seaworthiness, self-bailing cockpit, and, though its primary mission is clearly to fish, enough family-friendly features to make the boat of interest to buyers other than hard-core anglers.

Construction

The Key West is built to last with all-fiberglass composite construction. After the gelcoat goes on the mold, the hull bottom and the lower section of the hull sides are sprayed with a coat of vinylester resin-based SprayCore barrier coat to help prevent osmotic blistering. Coremat is used on the sides to help minimize print-through of the fiberglass reinforcement pattern. The hull bottoms are solid fiberglass while the hull sides are cored with Nidacore honeycomb for added stiffness and lighter weight. An iso-based DCPD blend resin, which does not

shrink as much during curing and therefore has better cosmetic properties, is used throughout the hull skin laminate. The hull is supported with a one-piece fiberglass stringer grid that's completely encapsulated in fiberglass. The transom is cored with a high-density Coosa urethane foam reinforced with fiberglass strands. The cockpit deck is cored with urethane foam for lightweight stiffness.

In addition to the stringers, the voids between the hull and the cockpit liner sides are filled with foam. This adds reserve buoyancy, making the boat unsinkable, and it also quiets the boat and stiffens and increases the impact resistance of the hull bottom and sides. The boat's polypropylene fuel tank will never corrode and, if properly installed, should last the life of the boat, as will the high-quality stainless steel fuel fill and vent hardware.

Hull Design

The Key West 268 Bluewater has a deep-V hull with a pair of spray strakes and reverse-chine flats to add lift and deflect spray. A fine entry transitions to 21 degrees of transom deadrise.

Walkthrough

Cockpit

The bow area is deep and provides a feeling of security, and there are wraparound gunwale handrails to hang onto. You really feel like you are down inside

rather than up on top of this boat. Of course the high freeboard also makes the boat more seaworthy in rougher water, as it helps prevent boarding seas. The seating forward, with seat cushions and backrests, offers a lot of dry storage space inside, and a table that mounts in a deck stanchion is an option. An in-deck, lockable insulated fish box doubles as an additional storage space as well.

The boat's hatches are all finished on both sides using a closed molding process, which makes the hatches lighter while giving the boat an upscale appearance. Forward is an extra rope locker along with a raw-water washdown, and an anchor windlass is mounted just aft of the anchor locker, which has its own tie-off cleat, close to the pop-up mooring cleats.

The boat has a unique head—it's entered from a lockable door on the front side of the console. This might make the occupant and the inside of the head a little more exposed to the elements when running at speed, but it sure makes it easier to get in and out of the head, which has a sink with fresh water (the spigot pulls out for use as a showerhead) as well as a toilet (a portable toilet is standard; a porcelain toilet is optional). Our test boat had five fishing rods stowed in the horizontal rod racks inside the head, which prevented the use of the toilet. Access is provided though a small door to the helm electronics and gauges.

Three rod racks are provided port and starboard below the coamings, and there's also tackle storage port and starboard below the gunwale next to the console. Our boat had an optional livewell (with a large-capacity pump and selectable tank levels, and a backup pump via cross-connect) built into the aft side of the leaning post; this option provides an extra, very large livewell that's essential for some anglers who often fish with live bait, the trade-off being the loss of deck space. The boat comes standard with a smaller livewell aft to starboard, as well as a second raw-water washdown hose.

In the stern is a large portable cooler that doubles as a seat. This cooler, which can be removed to open up the area for fishing aft, is one of the things that makes the 268 a bit of a family boat. Rod holders are practically everywhere—fourteen of them in the coamings, on the back of the leaning post, and on the back of the transom seat. The cockpit coaming is 25 inches high aft, increasing as you move forward. Side gutters drain deck water effectively to recessed scuppers aft, and the gutters give your toes a little extra grip when leaning overboard.

One thing we really like about all of the Key Wests is the cream-colored gelcoat used everywhere topsides; this non-white is very easy on the eyes in full daylight, and it also minimizes night glare off the instruments that interferes with night vision. The nonskid pattern is fairly grippy underfoot, though not as aggressive as a diamond tread pattern, and it should prove to be easy to clean with a bristle brush.

At the transom, a retractable boarding ladder pulls out of its hole in the transom, with the steps folding out flat once it's deployed. This design is deployable from the water, which might be the real story and the design's strongest selling point here since, this being an offshore fishing boat, it's certainly plausible that it would most likely be used by a man overboard.

Helm

Our test boat's helm console was wide and tall, offering good protection from wind and rain (as we found out on our test ride). The helm has a large flat space for flush-mounted electronics. There's plenty to hang onto at speed with the T-top piping close at hand, and a pair of cup holders are provided on the right side of the console. There is no windshield, and with the plastic side curtains removed, visibility is good, with only the T-top's piping obstructing vision ahead. The T-top was a canvas-covered pipe frame, which we like for its light weight. An integral electronics box adds room for radios and other equipment overhead.

The boat's driving position was comfortable, though we personally found the throttle to be on the low side. With the manual hydraulic steering system's five turns lock-to-lock, the suicide knob comes in handy when maneuvering dockside. The battery switch is easy to access, inside a door that hinges below the steering wheel, and inside the console are the batteries.

Engine

The 268 is rated for outboards of up to 450 hp, and can accommodate both single and twin installations.

Sea Trial

Our test ride took place in sheltered water with a 6-inch chop and a few wakes to cross. With a pair of 150 hp Yamaha four-strokes running full tilt at 6,000 rpm, we recorded 50 mph on GPS. At a continuous 4,500 rpm cruise, the 268 made 36 mph; figure on a cruise speed in the low 30s with a painted bottom, a full load of fuel, passengers, and gear. Noise levels were higher with the 150s than with either the 250 Yamaha twins (on other boats) or a single larger Yamaha, though at trolling speeds the engines are so quiet as to fade into the background wind and wave noise.

Acceleration with the twin 150s was impressive. Given the performance of this boat, we certainly don't feel that acceleration, or lack of it, is much of a reason for not choosing four-strokes, though some of the direct-injected two-strokes are certainly viable alternatives for some applications. The 268 showed a lot of sensitivity to trim—you have to get it right to optimize speed and efficiency, perhaps a little more so than with other boats. Coming up on plane while seated at the helm, the pulpit poked up above the horizon for a few seconds, but lowering the trim tabs first cured this transient loss of visibility ahead. The Yamaha 704 twin-engine throttles stay where you put them, which is great, but they clunk noticeably when shifting, especially into reverse. We only had a 6-inch chop and a few wakes to run through, but the boat showed a good deal of potential in the ride department, verified by an inspection of the hull out of the water.

Steering was manual hydraulic, five turns lock-to-lock, and it took a lot of effort to come out of a hard rudder turn at higher speeds. For this reason alone we'd opt for power steering. This boat turned more quickly than others in its class at lower speeds, essentially turning in about one-and-a-half boatlengths. The boat's heel angle (banking) in a turn was moderate and felt much under control all the time—we never felt like the boat heeled excessively as we've seen all too often with other outboard V-bottom boats. That earns this boat a big plus in the handling department. The propellers did ventilate in a hard turn more readily than other boats in its class, though, so the engines may need to be lowered a notch to cure this tendency.

One thing we'd opt for on this boat is a windshield; you can't see through the plastic, especially when it's raining, as it was on our test ride. We spent so much attention trying to see what was ahead, it was hard to focus on trimming the boat for optimum speed (the speed numbers below are Yamaha's). Definitely go with the glass, which you can keep clear with a windshield wiper.

Key West 268 Center Console Performance Results

RPM	Speed, mph	Noise Level, dBA
600	2.2	58
1,000	5.4	69
1,500	7.3	72
2,000	8.6	76
2,500	11.0	80
3,000	18.9	83
3,500	26.9	85
4,000	32.0	88
4,500	36.4	89
5,000	41.4	90
5,500	45.8	91
5,800	50.4	93

Test conditions: Two passengers, half tank of fuel, with twin 150 hp Yamaha four-stroke outboards.

This is a beefy, seaworthy boat ready to head offshore for serious fishing. The boat handles and rides well, it's thoughtfully designed, and it's well-built and should last indefinitely with minimal maintenance and reasonable care. It offers a few cruising amenities like the forward and aft seating and the enclosed head with fresh water, but it is first and foremost a hard-core fishing boat built for open ocean performance in moderate sea conditions.

There are a lot of practical features that make this boat a contender for consideration, first and foremost being its unsinkable design. With foam injected extensively between the hull and cockpit and deck liner, the boat is built to float upright even when holed and flooded, which is a step beyond U.S. Coast Guard requirements that only require boats below 20 feet to be so built. Then there's the builder's attention to detail— recessed sidelights that won't interfere with night vision, the cream-colored topsides, effective cockpit drainage, the retractable and water deployable ladder, two washdowns, and so on.

For a relatively low-priced boat, the Key West 268 is well-equipped: standard equipment includes trim tabs with angle indicators, cockpit bolsters, T-top with electronics box, rod holders and spreader lights, and popup cleats with drain lines, courtesy and cabin lights, dual batteries and battery switches, AM-FM-CD stereo system, forward fish box with macerator, Fortress anchor, pressurized freshwater system, two raw-water washdowns, and a battery charger.

SAILFISH 30-06 CC

SAILFISH

Founded in 1986 as a privately owned and operated boatbuilder, Sailfish has enjoyed remarkable success and today builds a wide range of good-running, well-built saltwater fishing boats. The Sailfish lineup ranges from 19-foot bay boats to 30-foot offshore center consoles, including walkarounds and dual consoles.

The largest model in Sailfish's lineup, the 30-06 Center Console, which has been in production since 2006, has a clear mission—offshore fishing. Not that it won't do other things well, like diving and day cruising, but this boat is designed to head far offshore, catch fish, and do it comfortably and safely.

Sailfish 30-06 Center Console Specifications

LOA:	30'6" (hull)
Beam:	10'
Deadrise:	24 deg.
Dry weight:	7,200 lb.
Cockpit depth:	30"
Draft:	23"
Fuel capacity:	300 gal.

Construction

The skin coat of chop in DCPD resin goes down over the gelcoat, then the solid hull laminate follows—knit fiberglass in the sides and woven roving in the bottom. The hull is supported by a fiberglass foam-cored Compsys stringer system, and the bulkheads are also foam-cored. The whole network is encapsulated in fiberglass and bonded to the hull. The transom is built of high-density poured foam core encapsulated in fiberglass.

The hull-to-deck joint is bonded with urethane adhesive and stainless self-tapping screws every foot. The rubrail and the stainless insert follows with two more rows of screws fastening the joint. The one-piece cockpit and liner is bonded to the stringers with urethane putty, becoming an integral part of the boat's structure. The cabin liner is also bonded to the hull and to the cockpit liner where they meet at the aft cabin bulkhead.

Hull Design

The 30-06 has a deep-V hull form with a sharp deep entry and 24 degrees of transom deadrise. Reverse running strakes (they turn up rather than down from garboard to chine), similar to the old Sea Craft hulls, run the length of the bottom. Its high freeboard increases seaworthiness, helping to prevent boarding seas, while providing high gunwale coamings inside the cockpit and a relatively high cockpit deck level above the waterline.

Walkthrough

Cockpit

Stepping onboard either through a low transom door or over the side, the cockpit immediately impresses with its full 30-inch coaming height. A portable cooler aft is held in place by rubber sockets against the transom. Depending on one's agenda, the cooler could be easily removed to open up more space for fishing, but on the other hand it also offers an insulated storage box for the catch. Below the cooler is a hatch leading to an in-deck storage locker, and just forward of the cooler is a door leading to the boat's mechanical compartment. The fuel filters are directly inside where they're easy to access, and all the wiring and plumbing is well secured inside.

The cockpit has plenty of toe kick space along the sides, thanks to a gunwale insert covered on its inboard surface by a comfortable padded bolster that runs along the cockpit perimeter. Eight rod holders in the gunwale, several cup holders, and six under-gunwale rod racks take care of business aft. The livewell is aft to starboard, integral to the deck liner. Corner-mounted scuppers clear washdown water overboard quickly, and flip-up slotted covers help keep large debris from clogging the overboard-leading drain lines. The large, 2-inch scupper drain lines, two per scupper, are recessed several inches below the deck, making for quick and easy water drainage from the cockpit.

The molded nonskid deck surface grips well, and is easy to clean with an aggressive but well-spaced pattern. Forward is a large unit on centerline that includes the helm and companion seats with flip-up bolsters on the forward side, a bait prep station with tackle drawers below on its aft side, and storage space below.

Bridge Deck

The helm station has room for a megayacht's electronics suite. As is appropriate for an offshore-capable boat like this, the navigation electronics, GPS chartplotter, fish-finder, and radar get priority in terms of sight-line placement. Engine gauges and accessory controls are down low, where they are still within sight and easy to reach as needed. Trim tab indicators, compass, Yamaha digital multifunction gauges, and tilt-wheel steering are all standard.

The wheel and engine dual binnacle are comfortably positioned. Flip-up bolsters provide plenty of standing room at the wheel, and seated and standing height-of-eye aren't that much different, thanks to the high seat. This arrangement also ensures good visibility to the horizon over the bow, even when coming up on plane. There's plenty to hang onto at speed offshore, with a grab bar running across the width of the console along with the hardtop supports at arm's length. On top of the console is a tackle organizer.

Foredeck

The builder leaves plenty of room to get forward past the console, and a flush gunwale-mounted handrail adds to the deep cockpit's sense of security in the bow. Here we find molded fiberglass V-shaped seats, all part of the deck liner, that offer plenty of storage space in three compartments inside. There's also a large in-deck storage locker with an overboard-draining gutter. The four cup holders and two rod holders provided ought to take care of everybody fishing forward. Forward of the console is a molded, cushioned seat with backrest and storage below.

In the forepeak is the anchor locker, with a hatch for access and rubber clips to hold the anchor stocks. Our test boat also had a windlass leading to the stainless anchor pulpit, which was bracketed by the bow-mounted sidelights. Inside the console, accessed through a portside door, is the head compartment, generously proportioned, and with clear access to the inside of the helm station instrument panel. There's a small window to let in light and storage space inside a locker and behind a couple of retaining nets for loose items. Aft is another door leading to the battery locker. The tooled fiberglass head compartment has a drain and should prove easy to clean.

Our overall impression of the Sailfish's forward and aft cockpit (and the rest of the boat, actually) is of an upscale boat with superb practicality and ergonomics, and extras you might not expect on a boat in this moderate price range, including the wraparound padded coaming bolster, the stainless railing around the gunwale forward, and the color-coordinated (matching the bolsters) seat cushions at the helm and in the bow area.

Engine

Our test boat had a pair of 250 hp Yamaha four-stroke outboards. Access to the mechanical compartment below the motor well is from the cockpit, while the batteries are in a compartment inside the center console and accessed from the head. A dual battery switch is standard. We found the twin Yamaha 250s to be a good fit for the boat's size, weight, and mission.

Sea Trial

Our sea trial took place in ideal test conditions—a 2- to 3-foot chop on top of a 3-foot swell off Gloucester, Massachusetts. These are the kind of waves the 30-06 was designed to handle easily, and it met our expectations on all counts. Running at 35 mph in these seas, the boat did not pound at all, but rather ran comfortably and smoothly into the waves because of the aggressive, deep-V entry. Running downsea, the boat tracked well, with no inclination to deviate more than a few degrees from course.

The hull banks moderately into a turn, with just enough heel to keep everyone on board on balance and securely situated. We always recommend power steering on an outboard of this size, to get the steering effort down and minimize the turns lock-to-lock, improving agility and maneuverability, both offshore and at the dock.

The Yamaha 250 hp four-stroke outboards were quiet and accelerated well throughout their rpm operating range. Most of the noise we recorded seemed to be coming from the spray, not from the engines. Fumes from the engines were essentially nonexistent. The trim tabs were very responsive, immediately raising the stern and dropping the bow. It's great to have the reserve lift in the event you bring on a lot of weight aft, or just want to keep the bow down for a good head sea ride in bigger waves.

Visibility to the horizon was good, with little interference to sight lines, thanks to an efficient T-top support and windshield design. The boat handled well when docking with the steering centered and using the engines to back the boat into

Sailfish 30-06 Center Console Performance Results

RPM	Speed, mph	Noise Level, dBA
700	3	56
1,000	5.9	64
1,500	8.3	68
2,000	9.7	70
2,500	12.3	78
3,000	15.4	79
3,500	22.3	81
4,000	31.3	82
4,500	36.3	83
5,000	41.5	84
5,500	45.3	87
6,000	48.7	88

Test conditions: Two passengers, fuel tank three quarters full, with twin Yamaha 250 hp four-stroke outboards.

its slip. This large center console is well suited for offshore use, providing a safe and comfortable platform for fishing, cruising, diving, or watersports.

We can recommend the Sailfish 30-06 without reservation. It has a good-riding offshore hull design, solid, quality construction methods and materials, high hull freeboard for enhanced seaworthiness and passenger safety inside, and good looks.

The boat comes well-equipped at its base price, including 12 stainless rod holders, leaning post with livewell and bait prep station, a 30-gallon transom livewell, insulated bow fish box, cockpit bolsters, freshwater shower aft, raw-water washdown, aft cooler seat, T-top with rod holders and spreader lights, compass, freshwater sink, hull color, and trim tab indicators.

A few of the options worth considering include the T-top, outriggers, anchor pulpit, transom sink and bait prep station, portable toilet, anchor windlass, and power steering. Up to twin 300 hp Yamaha two-strokes are available.

Dual Consoles

Dual consoles (DC), which are essentially bowriders with outboard instead of stern-drive power, and with self-bailing cockpits and no fixed upholstery, are excellent low-maintenance, easy-to-own, and versatile family day boats. There's a console to port and to starboard, and usually a folding windshield and door below that open for access forward. If the boat is 22 feet or longer, it should have a head compartment to port to be competitive; without the head, these boats are much less attractive for longer outings. The dual console's open bow is one of its strong points, since passengers can be accommodated along the whole length of the boat. Dual consoles are good for not only fishing but also other watersports, as well as towing, diving, and just cruising around. They range from about 18 to 28 feet.

The 1850 is Century's sole DC offering; it's rated for up to 150 hp and has a ski locker, bait well, and a 47-gallon fuel capacity.

CENTURY BOATS

Though Edgewater's 205 Express is not actually a dual console, think of it as a DC with a foredeck and cuddy. It's one of very few boats of its type, and it may be the only one, at least from a major boatbuilder. All the other cuddies are runabouts, basically bowriders with cabins. This boat actually reminds us of the old 20-foot Wellcraft cuddy that was such a good-running and useful boat in the 1970s. The 205 is a well-built boat that should find a ready market as a self-bailing, offshore-capable, and fishable cuddy with a great seating plan and a full 28-inch interior coaming height (think child safety). The cuddy has a portable toilet located out of the weather. Up to 200 hp and 10 passengers can be accommodated. EDGEWATER POWERBOATS

Whaler builds one DC model. The 21-foot Boston Whaler 210 has a capacity of up to 10 people, a 250 hp outboard, and a big 92-gallon fuel tank. BOSTON WHALER

The 202 is Hydra-Sports' one DC offering, and it has all the bells and whistles expected of a family fishing boat, including an enclosed head to port, which is unusual, and a pleasant surprise for a 20-footer. It's made possible by the 202's high freeboard (and wide beam at 8 feet, 8 inches), which also adds a degree of seaworthiness to the boat. The 202 is rated for up to 250 hp and has a full 22-degree transom deadrise. GENMAR HOLDINGS, INC.

Key West's series of inshore and offshore fishing boats includes this 17-footer, the 176 DC. With more deadrise than previous models, this boat has a smooth ride, is well-equipped for fishing or watersports, and is rated for up to 140 hp. KEY WEST BOATS

Mako produces a single DC, the 216 shown here. The boat features contemporary styling and lots of room in the bow—almost as much as a deckboat of the same length—which of course shortens the cockpit—but the upside is two separate and quite usable (and deep, with a high freeboard and low deck) deck areas. The 216 is rated for up to 250 hp and has a generous 93-gallon fuel capacity. MAKO

Robalo, sister company to Chaparral, has become a more upscale boatbuilder since its acquisition by Chaparral's parent a few years ago. The 227's profile is a little lower than some of its competitors, making it a hybrid bowrider of sorts, only with a better hull design and a self-bailing cockpit. Along with a livewell and stern washdown spigot, you can even get it with a wakeboard tower, an indication of this boat's wide-ranging intended market. Rated for up to 25 hp, and with an ample 112-gallon fuel tank, the 27 can hold up to 10 people (depending on their weight and the size of the engine). ROBALO

Scout is an upscale builder of a wide range of saltwater boats, including what they refer to as fish-and-skis, like this 205 Dorado and its 17-, 18-, and 22-foot sisters. No matter what you call it, this boat has a lot to like, including a distinctive Scout sheerline, an easily maintained interior, a cream-colored gelcoat that's easy on the eyes in direct sunlight, and plenty of fishing features. The 205 packs up to 225 hp (Scouts use mostly Yamaha power), and it has an 8-person maximum capacity. SCOUT BOATS

Saltwater Boats: Coastal Fishing Boats 285

Sea Boss builds a pair of modestly priced dual consoles—this 190 as well as a 180. More of an inshore boat than, say, the similar-sized Grady or Century, with less deadrise and lower freeboard, the 190 has a livewell, self-bailing cockpit (as do all dual consoles, or they'd be bowriders by our definition), all-fiberglass construction, and a 150 hp engine capacity. SEA BOSS BOATS

Sea Fox produces affordable boats that are well outfitted and attractively styled. The company has two lines, a moderately priced Pro series and a low-priced Sport series. The Sport series includes two dual consoles, an 18 and a 20, and the Pro Series has one, the 216 shown here. The 216 is an attractively styled and well-equipped boat with an enclosed head and a capacity of up to 200 hp and 8 people. SEA FOX BOATS

Triton's dual console offering is this 22-footer, an upscale, well-built boat that is also well-equipped to fish or pull boarders when fitted with its 250 hp option; the boat has up to an 8-person capacity and carries 79 gallons of fuel. TRITON BOATS

Triumph, the only builder that makes rugged, impact-resistant polyethylene boats, produces three dual consoles, one 17- and two 19-footers. One of the 19s is called a fish-and-ski, but it's also a bona fide dual console as far as we're concerned. The 195 is well-equipped to fish, and with enough power bolted to the transom to pull a boarder or skier. The 195 is rated for up to 150 hp and has a maximum capacity of 8 people. Fuel capacity is 60 gallons. GENMAR HOLDINGS, INC.

GRADY-WHITE 225 DUAL CONSOLE

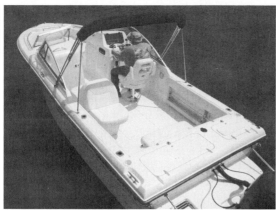

GRANDY-WHITE

Grady-White 225 Dual Console Specifications	
LOA:	22'2"
Beam:	8'
Deadrise:	20 deg.
Dry weight:	3,450 lb. (without engine)
Draft:	16" (hull)
Fuel capacity:	96 gal.

Grady-White is one of the oldest boatbuilders in the country, starting with wooden lapstrake fishing boats in the 1950s. Today Grady produces solidly built fiberglass saltwater fishing boats—both tournament and family oriented—from 18 to 36 feet, all outboard-powered (mostly Yamaha). These boats are the essence of practicality, from the cream-colored gel-coat hull and topsides that wears well and is easy on the eyes in bright sunlight, to the easy cleanup and low-maintenance exterior and cabin interior designs.

Grady's hulls are good-running boats in a stiff off-shore breeze. They're also unusually safe. All models (even those 20 feet and over) are unsinkable, thanks to the liberal use of foam between the hull and the deck liner. Gradys also have no fish or storage boxes below the deck, so all storage compartments and coolers drain directly overboard rather than relying on pumps for dewatering (all the space that would be taken up by in-deck storage boxes is full of foam, instead, which is what helps make the boats unsinkable).

Grady-White is also in the enviable position of having been ranked highest, by a wide margin, in the J.D. Power and Associates study within the marine customer satisfaction coastal fishing segment. It has achieved these high scores every year since the study was started in 2001. The combination of well-built, well-designed boats, high-quality, reliable outboard power, a top-notch dealer network and a customer-centric approach to doing business

on Grady-White's part has shown to be unbeatable in this market segment.

Grady-White builds a series of dual console models, including the 225. The versatile layout, enclosed head, as well as excellent ride and handling combine to make this a family-friendly day boat. The 225 is well suited to both fishing and day cruising, and compared to its near cousin, the bowrider, it offers low maintenance, fishability, and a self-bailing cockpit. The boat is easily trailerable behind a pickup or large SUV, with the whole rig weighing about 4,800 pounds, plus any gear and fuel in the boat.

Construction

The Grady-White has a solid fiberglass hull bottom and hull sides with a supporting stringer and bulkhead system of pressure-treated plywood encapsulated in fiberglass. Limber holes are cut through solid glass to prevent water absorption into the core. Plywood is also used to core the transom, which is supported by aluminum bracing, and the hull-to-deck joint is sealed with a gasket and sealant and fastened with a mix of stainless screws and rivets.

Hull Design

The Grady-White's hull is a C. Raymond Hunt and Associates design with a deep entry and high chines forward, producing a smooth headsea ride and transitioning to approximately 20 degrees of deadrise at the transom. A warped bottom, with deadrise decreasing gradually all the way to the transom (called SeaV2 by Grady-White), produces greater lift aft and a more level ride on plane, resulting in improved propulsion efficiency, compared to constant deadrise hulls, as well as improving sight lines from the helm. Chine flats add lift and deflect spray on plane and form stability at rest.

Walkthrough

Cockpit and Topsides

The 225 is an open boat, with the cockpit taking up the majority of the boat's length. The one-piece fiberglass deck-and-liner adds to the boat's structural integrity and makes for easy cleanup and maintenance. Aft, an optional full-beam swim platform bolted to the transom above the outboard bracket makes watersports that much more practical, and a water-deployable swim ladder is provided to port. Many similar outboards only have a small platform to one side.

The full-beam version in the 225 is made possible by the motor bracket, which also gets the engine out of the boat, reducing both noise and fumes (which are already low with the four-stroke Yamahas that Grady-White exclusively rigs their boats with). Stern cleats are recessed in pockets below deck level, making them less of a snagging hazard for fishing lines, while providing the convenience of fixed cleats.

The 25-inch-deep cockpit has deep toe kicks, toe rails just above deck level, and effective nonskid that combine to create a safe family boating environment. Padded coaming bolsters are optional. Rod racks under the gunwales and four rod holders in the washboards help make the cockpit well suited to fishing, as does a big 175-quart insulated fish box at the stern. Also available as an option is an insulated 22-gallon livewell to starboard with a light and 1,100 gpm pump, next to the fish box.

Grady also takes the extra step of putting a fuel tank removal hatch in the deck to make replacing the tank straightforward, fast, and relatively inexpensive. Many similar saltwater boats would require having the decks cut out for this job, which is an expensive, messy, and ultimately cosmetically challenging proposition.

With its fishing credentials firmly established, the 225 also serves as an able family day cruiser, starting with a comfortable, fold-away bench seat at the transom. This is also one of the easiest-to-operate seats we've yet encountered, since you can hinge it up and out for use, or fold it back down out of the way with little effort. Forward to port on our test boat was an optional back-to-back seat module that folds flat for use as a lounge; a pedestal seat is standard.

Inside the port console is the head, and that's the biggest change on this boat when it was updated in 2006. Having an enclosed sit-down head on a 22-foot day boat is a big bonus for any bowrider, and it greatly adds to the boat's appeal for day-long family use. A portable toilet is standard, and a head with pumpout and macerator is optional. The head door is also lockable, so it can be used for relatively secure storage when the boat is not being used.

Forward of the consoles are molded seats with storage plus an insulated 52-quart overboard-draining cooler or fish box below the starboard seat, as well as padded bolsters and grab rails along the gunwale. Also in the bow is an anchor locker under a flush deck hatch. The Danforth anchor hangs securely by its stocks in clips at the top of the locker, with the anchor chain and line stored below. The forward seating area expands total usable deck space by nearly a third, which makes this a roomy boat suitable for a large family. Besides sitting down and enjoying the view at speed, the bow is a great place to do a little casting, well clear of whoever's fishing in the cockpit.

Helm

One of the advantages of the dual console layout is that the helm is well aft in the boat—13 feet aft, in fact. That makes the motion felt at the helm much less pronounced, and therefore more comfortable, than a boat with the helm farther forward. Combined with Grady-White's excellent hull design, the effect is a boat with an exceptionally comfortable ride.

The helm includes a compass and a lockable electronics box, which adds an element of security and also keeps the electronics out of the weather. Trim tabs for correcting list and heel are also standard, as is a starboard windshield wiper. The center windshield opens up, as do large vents in the side windows. The relatively high windshield offers protection from the elements at speed.

Engine

The 225 is available with a single, bracket-mounted 225 hp outboard engine.

Sea Trial

One thing that was immediately clear was how quiet this bracket-mounted four-stroke outboard was. Even at a fairly high 4,500 rpm cruise, the dBA reading at the helm was only 83, very quiet for a boat of this size. Even when running at a high 5,000 rpm cruise, we could barely hear the engine above the noise of the wind. The center passage seals off with a centerline door and windshield, blocking off most of the wind and any spray that makes its way onboard.

We didn't record fuel flow, but this boat will certainly deliver a full day on the water under typical start-and-stop operating conditions, and a good range with its standard 96-gallon fuel capacity. Using figures from similar boats, fuel flow at 4,500 rpm (over 28 knots) would be in the vicinity of 13 gph, which would give this boat a range of 200 nautical miles or more, depending on the displacement, bottom condition, and so on. Range at 3,500 rpm would be even better. We recorded a top speed of nearly 38 knots (43.6 mph) with a light load and clean bottom; figure on dropping 2 or 3 knots when loaded up with fuel, passengers, and gear, and with the bottom painted.

The 225 handled well, turning easily and responsively with its standard hydraulic steering. The ride in the bay's 1- to 2-foot chop was smooth and dry. Putting the wheel over hard at 4,500 rpm, the boat tracked well, with no tendency to spin out or otherwise act unpredictably. It was a forgiving boat suitable for operators with relatively little boating experience.

There is a lot of standing room at the helm, which is often lacking on similar boats; this lets you stand right behind the wheel to drive. The steering wheel and throttle were also comfortably positioned and easy to reach whether standing up or sitting down.

Grady-White 225 Dual Console Performance Results			
RPM	Speed, mph	Speed, knots	Noise Level, dBA (at helm)
600	2.9	2.5	59
1,000	4.6	4	61
1,500	5.9	5.1	66
2,000	7.4	6.4	68
2,500	8.1	7	72
3,000	15.6	13.6	76
3,500	23.6	20.5	77
4,000	29.2	25.4	81
4,500	33.2	28.9	83
5,000	37.5	32.6	85
5,500	40.9	35.6	87
6,000	43.6	37.9	88

Test conditions: Two passengers, a quarter tank of fuel, with 250 hp Yamaha four-stroke outboard.

The Grady-White 225 is a good-riding and nimble-handling dual console. The combination of a comfortable sit-down head compartment and an open day boat deck plan makes this a versatile, family-friendly boat with excellent fishability. We feel strongly that the Grady's unsinkability alone makes it a strong contender, as nothing is more important than your family's safety when it comes to being out on the water.

HYDRA-SPORTS 2200 VECTOR DUAL CONSOLE

GENMAR HOLDINGS, INC.

Hydra-Sports 2200 Vector Dual Console Specifications	
LOA:	22'4"
Beam:	8'6"
Deadrise:	20 deg.
Dry weight:	3,400 lb.
Draft:	15" (hull)
Fuel capacity:	115 gal.

Part of boatbuilding giant Genmar's Saltwater Fishing Group, Sarasota, Florida–based Hydra-Sports is a highly regarded boatbuilder of strongly built, well-outfitted, and superb-riding offshore and inshore fishing machines. Hydra-Sports makes three lines of boats, all specializing in the saltwater fishing market: high-end Vector series center consoles and family fishing cabin boats; a Lightning series of mid-priced center consoles, dual consoles, and walkarounds; and, a Baybolt series of center console bay boats.

The dual console design is versatile. You can use it to fish, cruise, tow boarders, dive, or just about anything else a day on the water is likely to offer. Parents will like this boat, too, since it comes with an enclosed head that offers plenty of privacy.

In production since 2007, the 2200 Vector dual console is based on the smallest hull in the builder's Vector series. A beefy, high-freeboard, seaworthy boat with plenty of reserve buoyancy under the self-draining deck, the 2200 comes with all-fiberglass composite construction, generous fuel capacity, a smooth-riding deep-V hull, a family-friendly layout, and plenty of fishing amenities.

Construction

All-fiberglass composite construction includes a skin coat of 3-ounce chop wet out in premium vinylester resin to prevent osmotic blistering. Nonwoven fiberglass and Kevlar (used in the keel, transom, and stringers) reinforcements are used in the hull layup, and foam-cored fiberglass stringers support the hull bottom as well as the one-piece cockpit deck and liner above. The transom is a solid, rot-proof, high-density poured composite material. The hull-to-deck joint, which holds the two major structural components together, is bonded with a high-strength adhesive and clamped with self-tapping stainless steel screws. Decks are cored with PVC structural foam, making them stiff and light. The boat has a corrosion and rustproof 109-gallon polypropylene fuel tank, which we prefer over aluminum.

Hull Design

The Hydra-Sports 2200 Vector has a deep-V hull design with a sharp deep-deadrise entry for a smooth and dry ride in a chop. The hull flattens out to 20 degrees of transom deadrise with side chine flats adding stability at rest and lift at speed.

Walkthrough

Cockpit and Topsides

Laid out for cruising, fishing, or watersports, there's plenty of open space aft. The cockpit is 25 inches high, which is just enough to provide good balance, and the toe kicks are deep, which also is an important safety factor. The nonskid is grippy underfoot, but it's still easy to keep clean. The boat is ready to fish, with a livewell, a big in-deck insulated fish box, tackle drawers, and coaming rod holders and under-gunwale rod racks. The cockpit scuppers drain rapidly through four 2-inch hoses—this is about twice the drainage capacity seen on most offshore boats of this size, making the boat more seaworthy as well as easier to clean.

Aft to port and starboard are transom seats, and a filler section creates a one-piece transom lounge. There's also a hinged gate to keep you from falling into the motor well, and also most likely it's there to help keep waves outside of the boat. A hatch leads to the bilge aft where the fuel filter, bilge pump, and the livewell pump (that also supplies the wash-down hose) are located. The deep hatch gutter drains directly overboard, and keeps the bilge—which is smooth and bright white for great visibility and easy cleanup—and components dry below. Under the gunwales are bin-style storage lockers that hinge out.

Forward to port is a back-to-back seat that folds out flat for use as a lounge. This is an option that we'd opt for on a family day boat, unless you plan to do a lot of fishing; a pedestal seat is standard. The port console has a door that opens for access to the enclosed head that is roomy and easy to get in and out of, and there's even a sink and spigot. The other nice thing is the styling of the port console—it looks good, not big and bulky, thanks in part to the generous hull volume provided by the high freeboard.

Opposite to starboard and just aft of the helm seat is a console with a sink and counter-top lid, along with storage and tackle drawers below—perfect for a mixed-use boat like this one. There's also a shore power connector below the sink which is easy to access and a handy option when dockside and needing to keep the batteries charged.

Between the consoles are two deck hatches opening to a large locker measuring 87 inches long and 17 inches deep—plenty big enough for a wakeboard. Inside the locker is another pleasant surprise—rod racks that can hold six 7-foot rods, and that fold outboard when not in use, so they don't take up space if you're using it to store something besides rods. These gutters also drain overboard.

The bow area has a versatile seat design. There's a gap between the aft and forward seats in the bow, which practically lets you walk right up to the gunwale—perfect for fishing, or for handling lines dockside. Our only problem was the hatch latches were a little hard to reach with the cushions snapped in place.

This is also one of the safest bow seating areas we've seen—it feels very much like you sit down *in* it, not up *on* it. There's also a wraparound handrail—most boats just have a couple of short grab bars up here, so this is great. There's also storage below the seats. Our boat had an anchor pulpit and windlass, which are features not usually found on a 22-footer, and it's nice since you have a permanent home for the ground tackle.

Helm

The big, well-contoured helm seat has a flip-up bolster, which makes room for comfortable standup driving. There's room on the dash for a 9-inch GPS chartplotter, and the steering wheel and engine control are comfortably positioned and properly angled for both standing and seated operation.

The windshield is high enough to offer decent protection from the wind and spray, and in fact it's a lot higher than the windshields found on the average bowrider, which, along with the self-bailing cockpit and all-fiberglass interior, gives this dual console design a big advantage. The center windshield section closes to block off much of the airflow when running at speed.

Engine

The 2200 comes with single two- and four-stroke outboard power from Yamaha, Evinrude, and Mercury up to 300 hp.

Sea Trial

The 250 hp Evinrude pushed the boat to a little over 43 mph at full power. Note that we made just 5,200 rpm, which is about 600 rpm less than the maximum rated rpm for this engine. Barring a problem with the engine, that likely means that the prop was a little big for this boat, so expect a little more top-end with a smaller prop. We also were able to cruise comfortably at 31 mph at 4,000 rpm. The boat was quieter than the recorded noise levels might have you believe, since a lot of the noise was coming from the wind when running at high speed. Fumes were minimal, and only noticeable at all with the wind abaft the beam at slow speed.

Helm ergonomics were excellent, with the controls right at our fingertips and comfortably angled. There's enough room to stand and drive, thanks to the flip-up seat bolster, though moving the fiberglass seat base (not the seat itself), which is part of the deck liner, a couple of inches aft would add a little room where it's needed most, at your heels. Sitting down, visibility was good, and the big windshield lets you look through glass rather than right at the top of the frame.

The Evinrude mechanical shifter, we might add, is probably the best of its class, shifting smoothly and quietly with absolutely no clunking or gear grinding. The ride in the 1-foot chop was smooth and comfortable, and the boat heeled just right in a hard, high-speed turn, never slipping or sliding unpredictably. The manual hydraulic steering was not as nimble as we'd like at six turns lock-to-lock (we're a little spoiled—just drive a stern drive at three turns lock-to-lock, with power steering, to see why we feel this way), but the boat handled predictably both on the water and at the dock.

Well suited to fishing and cruising, it's hard to think of a dual console that has a more intelligent design, more thoughtful touches, or more versatility than the Hydra-Sports 2200 Vector. We like the seaworthy, high-freeboard hull design, the off-white interior that minimizes sunlight glare, the multifunction layout, roomy enclosed head, ample storage space, great ride, high-quality all-fiberglass construction, and the quality components used throughout this boat. Last but not least, we like the safety provided by the deep cockpit, nonskid, and plentiful handrails.

Hydra-Sports 2200 DC Vector Dual Console Performance Results

RPM	Speed, mph	Speed, knots	Fuel Use, gph	Nautical mpg	Range, nm	Noise Level, dBA (at helm)
600	2.7	2.3	0.4	5.87	792	58
1,000	5.5	4.8	0.8	5.97	806	67
1,500	7	6.1	2	3.04	411	70
2,000	8.2	7.1	5.1	1.40	189	71
2,500	9.1	7.9	7.3	1.08	146	78
3,000	13.8	12.0	9.6	1.25	169	82
3,500	24.9	21.6	9.9	2.19	295	84
4,000	31.3	27.2	12.4	2.19	296	83
4,500	38.2	33.2	17.4	1.91	258	88
5,000	43	37.4	21.3	1.75	237	91
5,200	43.7	38.0	21.4	1.77	240	91

Test conditions: Two passengers, fuel tank three quarters full, with a 250 hp Evinrude outboard. Light chop.

Walkarounds

The walkaround is an excellent cabin-fishing boat for families who fish, ski, swim, and cruise. They're perfectly competent fishing boats aft, with well-designed and well-equipped cockpits. In place of the center console or dual console's open bow, the walkaround adds accommodations forward, making these boats well suited not only for families but also for anglers spending the weekend (or longer, depending on the size of the boat) on the water. Recessed side decks take away some, but not much, of the interior space, since the sides of the cabin are not very accessible in most small boats, anyway.

The helm is generally well protected from the elements by a taller windshield and soft enclosure. The cabin is also a great place for small kids—they're safe and contained, as long as you're not going too fast for the conditions. Walkarounds range from 20 to 32 feet with both outboard (usually) and sterndrive power. In the larger sizes, they start to become indistinguishable from express fishing boats, especially when they lose their recessed side decks.

Grady-White has what is apparently the widest walkaround lineup in the industry, including 20 feet, 22 feet, 23 feet, 25 feet, this 28-footer, and a 30-footer. The 282 is an excellent sea boat, strongly built to fish hard as well as cruise. Twin Yamaha four-strokes to 600 total hp are available, and the boat carries 207 gallons of fuel. GRADY-WHITE BOATS

Whaler's saltwater lineup includes its Conquest series of walkarounds— 20 feet, 23 feet, 25 feet, 28 feet, and this 30-footer. Unsinkable and ruggedly built, the 305 has a 300-gallon fuel capacity, is rated for 600 hp, and is usually fitted with Mercury Verado engines. BOSTON WHALER

Cobia builds offshore and inshore fishing boats, including this 27-foot oceangoing, Yamaha-powered walkaround. COBIA BOATS

A superb boat for its size when it comes to running in rough water, the deck layout of the Harrier 25 from Hunt Yachts harks back to the 1960s and 1970s when there weren't any walkarounds, just big, seaworthy, low-slung, open cockpit, closed-bow bass boats (the saltwater variety) like this one. The Harrier 25 usually gets Volvo stern-drive power (gas or diesel) and can also be fitted with a waterjet or outboard. Putting the engine in the middle of the cockpit (with a jackshaft connected to the stern drive) opens up the stern for fishing. Hunt Yachts, an affiliate of the naval architecture and engineering group C. Raymond Hunt Associates, builds a range of good-running, traditionally styled, and well-proportioned boats up to 36 feet. HUNT YACHTS

Hydra-Sports builds a high-end line called its Vector series, which includes express-style 22-, 25-, 29-, and 33-footers (the line also includes center consoles). A well-proportioned and good-running offshore boat with overnight capability, the boat also successfully showcases Hydra-Sports' deep fishing roots. The 2500 is rated for up to 500 hp and holds 176 gallons of fuel. Hydra-Sports also builds a Lightning series of less expensive boats that includes 21- and 23-foot walkarounds.   GENMAR HOLDINGS, INC.

Mako produces three walkaround models, this 21-footer as well as 26- and 31-footers. The 31 is more of a center console with a cuddy.   MAKO

Key West builds moderately priced, well-equipped, and solidly built saltwater fishing boats, including this 2020 walkaround. The 2020 can take up to 200 hp (usually Yamaha with the Key West line) and has a good ride in a light chop.   KEY WEST BOATS

Parker's walkaround (the foredeck is not recessed, which increases cabin volume) models come in 23- and 25-foot versions, and the 2510 shown here is even available with two different hulls having either 16 or 21 degrees of deadrise at the stern (you get your choice of more speed with less power or a better ride). Parker may be the only boatbuilder in the industry that offers two hull variations, and we'd certainly recommend the better riding XLD version over the older XL. Up to 500 hp is available in the XLD version, with Yamaha being Parker's power of choice. The XLD has a 200-gallon fuel capacity.   PARKER BOATS

Parker also produces a series of eight sport cabin, or enclosed pilothouse, models, from 21 to 28 feet. The 25 shown here, like the 25 walkaround, comes with a choice of hulls, one 16 and the other 21 degrees deadrise at the stern. These boats make a great choice for northern climes, allowing extended season use in heated comfort.

PARKER BOATS

Pursuit builds upscale, nicely proportioned express models up to 34 feet, including the LS235 shown here. The helm is on centerline (instead of to starboard), the cabin provides overnight capability, and the cockpit is set up to fish. Pursuit is well regarded for its smooth- and dry-riding hull designs, and the 235 is no exception. The 235 can take up to 300 hp and holds 100 gallons of fuel.

PURSUIT BOATS

Pro-Line's 23 XP Pilot offers more protection than the average walkaround (the windshield attaches to the hardtop), making it well suited to northern climes where extra protection from the elements is much appreciated. The boat is well-equipped to fish and is rated for up to 250 hp.

PRO-LINE BOATS

Robalo offers four walkaround models from 22 to 30 feet. The 245 shown is built to fish, primarily, but it also has a little more cabin room than some of its competitors, and it's finished off upscale — a lot like a Chaparral express cruiser's cabin, which is no surprise considering they're sister companies. The 245 is rated for up to 400 hp and carries 150 gallons of gas.

ROBALO

Sailfish has three walkaround models up to 26 feet, including the smallest of the series, the 218, shown here. Well-built and good-running boats, Sailfish uses Yamaha power exclusively. There's room for a bunk, a small galley, and a portable toilet down below, and the boat is well rigged for fishing. Up to 250 hp is available and fuel capacity is 95 gallons.   SAILFISH BOATS

Trophy builds 10 relatively low-priced walkaround models from 18 to 29 feet. A number of Trophys are good-riding boats offshore, and all are set up for serious fishing. The 2302 has a berth and a portable toilet down below, and recessed side decks for easy access forward. The boat carries 125 gallons of gas and is rated for up to 250 hp from Mercury.   TROPHY SPORTFISHING BOATS

SeaQuest builds walkarounds from 20 to 30 feet, including the 25 shown here. Well-equipped for fishing, the cabin offers the potential for an occasional overnighter. The 2550 is rated for up to 300 hp and carries 121 gallons of gas.   SEAQUEST BOATS

Seaswirl builds five walkaround models from 18 to 33 feet, and all of them but the 33 are available with either stern-drive or outboard power. The enclosed pilothouse version shown with its optional heat and air conditioning is just the ticket for fishing in hot or cold weather. The 2901 carries 217 gallons of fuel and is rated for up to 600 stern-drive hp.   GENMAR HOLDINGS, INC.

Wellcraft's express fisherman Coastal lineup stretches from 23 to 36 feet, with the two largest (33 and 36 feet) models inboard-powered. The 232 is a good-running boat, ready to fish, and with enough room down below in the portable toilet- and galley-equipped cabin to spend the night. Up to 275 hp is available; fuel capacity is 115 gallons.   GENMAR HOLDINGS, INC.

GRADY-WHITE GULFSTREAM 232 WALKAROUND

GRADY-WHITE

The Grady-White 232 is a nicely proportioned family fishing boat, one of six walkaround models from the builder. Either twin (usually 150s) or single outboard power is available. The boat has a small but surprisingly accommodating cabin, a protected helm area with room for GPS and radar, and a large cockpit laid out and equipped for serious fishing.

The 232 will appeal to the family that likes to fish as well as spend an occasional overnight, and it will prove equally adept at pulling boarders and tubers or just cruising. The 232 is the smallest Grady model with a beam of over 8 feet, 6 inches, so a permit will be needed to trailer it in most states. The extra 15 inches of beam (compared to Grady's 8-foot-wide, 22-foot walkaround model) makes a big difference in terms of elbow room, though, especially in the helm area between the two seats.

Construction

The Grady-White has a solid fiberglass hull bottom and balsa coring on the sides with a supporting stringer and bulkhead system of pressure-treated plywood encapsulated in fiberglass. Limber holes are cut through solid fiberglass to prevent water absorption into the core. Plywood is also used to core the transom, which is also supported by aluminum bracing. The hull-to-deck joint is sealed with a gasket and sealant and fastened with a mix of stainless steel screws and rivets. Foam injected in the voids between the hull and deck liner makes the boat unsinkable.

Hull Design

The Grady-White's hull features a deep entry and high chines forward, producing a smooth headsea ride and transitioning to approximately 20 degrees of deadrise at the transom. The deadrise decreases gradually all the way to the transom (called SeaV2 by Grady-White), producing greater lift aft and a more level ride on plane, resulting in improved propulsion efficiency, compared to constant deadrise hulls, as well as improving sight lines ahead from the helm. Chine flats add lift and deflect spray on plane and form stability at rest.

Walkthrough

Cockpit and Topsides

Grady-White devotes the lion's share of 232's LOA to the topsides, and in particular the open cockpit. The 232 has bracket-mounted outboards, which puts them well aft of the transom; these four-stroke engines already produce very few fumes, so their location completely outside of the hull further improves on this score, and makes them quieter as well. Stretching across the transom is a roomy swim platform with a water-deployable boarding ladder to port, and this design will make boarders and tubers happy since there's plenty of room to walk from side-to-side aft.

Just inside the transom, a large fish box is up high and easy to access. A cutting board is built into the top of the RTM pressure-molded hatch (it's tooled and shiny smooth on both sides), and the insulated box, which has a recessed fitting to complete drainage, is big enough to hold a load of 40-pound stripers. To port, next to the fish box, is a smaller storage bin, which lifts out for access to the battery switches and mechanical space below. The seacocks, otherwise hard to reach down in the bilge, have remote operating gear, essentially stainless steel connecting rods with handles at the top end that allow the valves to be easily opened and closed.

The 28-inch-deep cockpit—deeper and safer than average for a boat of this size—is surrounded by a padded bolster for comfort. A deep toe kick and toe rails just above deck level along with a molded non-skid pattern provide excellent passenger security. Two 1¼-inch drain lines on either side aft drain overboard through flush scuppers and hoses.

One of the amenities that makes the Grady 232 a great cruising boat is the fold-out transom seat. This one lifts and folds into seating position nearly effortlessly—literally with one finger—and drops back down flush with the aft side of the cockpit just as easily. Many competitors' transom seats require that the owner be up on their wrestling moves to move the seat from one position to another; it's done right on this boat. There's easily room for two, and with a clean-running and quiet pair of Yamaha four-strokes well aft of the transom on a bracket, and a dry-running hull design, this transom seat should get a lot of use offshore.

The fixed stern cleats are recessed in molded pockets, out of the way of fishing lines. There is a pair of rod racks under the gunwales on each side, as well as a total of four rod holders in the washboards. Forward to port—behind the passenger seat—is a bait well with tackle drawers below, and opposite behind the helm seat is an insulated storage box or cooler.

The 232 has an access hatch above the fuel tank, so eventual fuel tank replacement will be a relatively simple job compared to boats without them; just remove the perimeter screws, use a utility knife to cut the sealant, and out the hatch comes. This is a significant feature we'd like to see on every boat with an aluminum fuel tank.

The recessed side decks make this layout appealing to families, since the side deck is a step closer to the cockpit. This boat is easy to walk forward on, with comfortably wide side decks; and there's enough flat deck space forward to cast or handle the anchor; and the trunk cabin makes a great seat when it's safe to be forward. The anchor pulpit design is simple and elegant, with the optional windlass on our test boat making light work of heaving an anchor.

Helm

The helm position is up high on the 232, and as mentioned, it feels quite roomy between the helm and port companion seats with the boat's generous beam. Ergonomics at the helm focus on the steering wheel and throttle positioning. Since they are comfortably reached whether seated or standing, the steering wheel and engine control are pretty much perfectly situated in terms of height, angle, and distance from the helm seat.

The big flat helm electronics display gets priority of place on the 232 boat (many other boatbuilders put the engine gauges up high, making the electronics hard to see and reach), up where it's easy to keep an eye on the GPS and radar while still watching where the boat is going. There's a lot of room here—enough for a pair of 10-inch electronics displays (chartplotter and radar). The panel comes right off for electronics installation or repair, which will cut down on the labor needed to do the job. Overhead, built into the hardtop, is more electronics space.

Our test boat had a hardtop with plastic filler curtains all around. The hardtop support stanchions and bracing interfere little with sight lines from the helm. The windshield has large opening vent windows outboard, which move a lot of air when the boat is cruising.

Cabin

The companionway is comfortably proportioned at 20 inches wide, especially for a 23-footer. The cabin is well-designed, with more features than are usually found in a 23-footer's cabin. There's a galley countertop to port and a V-berth/dinette seat forward and to starboard. With the table dropped down to hold the filler cushions, the berth is a full 84 inches long and plenty wide for a couple. The long seat back to starboard hinges up to do double-duty as a 6-foot, 4-inch-long bunk bed, partially suspended from the overhead by nylon straps.

In another space-saving design, a portable toilet is tucked below a hatch in the molded seat to starboard. Just above, a small access panel comes off for access to the helm station wiring. Overhead is a small hatch providing sunlight and fresh air when needed, and in the bow at the forward bulkhead is a small access door to the anchor line locker.

The 232's cabin will prove easy to maintain, with a full fiberglass pan, or liner below, and a tooled fiberglass headliner above that will just need an occasional sponging off. Eliminating the carpeting overhead, as Grady has done, is a good move in any small family fishing boat like this one.

Engine

The 232 is available with either single or twin outboard power to 400 total hp.

Sea Trial

Our test boat had twin 150 hp Yamaha four-strokes, which provided strong acceleration and a lively top speed of 37.3 knots, or 42.9 mph. With a full load of fuel and passengers and a painted bottom, you can probably figure on a cruise speed at 4,500 rpm of over 25 knots. Range with 150 gallons of fuel at 24 knots is 224 nautical miles.

At the helm, there was plenty of room while seated, and both the steering wheel and engine control were comfortably positioned for seated or standing operation. Seated visibility, including when coming up on plane, was good; you only stand if you want to, not because you have to, when driving this boat.

We had a stiff breeze on our test ride, and the boat ran smoothly with very little spray making its

Grady–White Gulfstream 232 Walkaround Performance Results

RPM	Speed, mph	Speed, knots	Fuel Use, gph	Nautical mpg	Range, nm
600	3.6	3.1	0.96	3.23	436
1,000	4.9	4.3	1.6	2.69	363
1,500	6.6	5.7	2.4	2.38	321
2,000	7.5	6.5	3.7	1.76	237
2,500	8.4	7.3	6.9	1.06	143
3,000	9.1	7.9	9.9	0.80	108
3,500	21.7	18.9	11.7	1.62	218
4,000	27.1	23.6	14.2	1.66	224
4,500	31.9	27.7	17.9	1.55	209
5,000	35.4	30.8	20.1	1.53	207
5,500	39.2	34.1	28.1	1.21	164
6,000	42.9	37.3	31.6	1.18	159

Test conditions: Two passengers, full fuel tank, with twin 150 hp Yamaha outboards. Moderate chop.

way on board in a strong crosswind in the 1- to 2-foot chop. In a hard, high-speed turn, the boat handled well, staying completely in control with very predictable handling, which is of course what to look for in any family boat.

The 232 is up comfortably on plane at about 13 knots, which means you'll have a wide operating range—from 13 to 37 knots on plane. At the dock, the 232 handled well, too, whether bringing the boat alongside or backing into a slip. Just put the rudder amidships and use the shifts to control the boat with complete predictability, even in the current and crosswind present during our sea trial.

Grady-White's 232 Gulfstream is a solidly built, nimble-handling offshore fishing machine that takes good care of the family. Attention to detail shows throughout, from the heavy transom tow eyes and easy maintenance to the versatile sleeping accommodations and the safe-and-secure foredeck. An excellent ride in an offshore sea, the practical and versatile Grady has a lot to offer.

WELLCRAFT 270 COASTAL

GENMAR HOLDINGS, INC.

Wellcraft 270 Coastal Specifications	
LOA:	28'1"
Beam:	9'9"
Deadrise:	21 deg.
Dry weight:	7,225 lb.
Draft:	34"
Fuel capacity:	188 gal.

Wellcraft has established a reputation for producing good-riding, solidly built boats aimed at serious fishermen who want to fish comfortably with their families. Part of Wellcraft's Coastal series of express-style fishing boats, the 270 is a sort of pocket battleship, with just about all the fishability and creature comforts you'd find in a big offshore boat, only scaled down to 27 feet. A good-sized fishing cockpit, raised helm station, and comfortable cabin combine to create a boat that's as well suited to family cruising as it is to offshore fishing.

Construction

The hull starts with a gelcoat followed by a 3-ounce vinylester skin coat in the bottom to prevent osmotic blistering, followed by a solid glass bottom laminate using orthophthalic resin. Layers of SprayCore, a skin coat, and then Coremat go on the hull sides to help prevent print-through, followed by a solid glass laminate wet out in orthophthalic resin. Transoms are cored with high-density structural foam for stiffness and compression resistance at moderate weight.

The hull is supported by a computer-cut, prefabricated fiberglass foam-cored stinger system that's tabbed to the hull and then fully encapsulated in fiberglass. The transom has a high-density composite core.

The shoebox-type hull-to-deck joint is bonded with Sikiflex adhesive and fastened and clamped with chrome-plated, epoxy-dipped self-tapping stainless steel screws. Decks are built using structural foam core for stiffness and lighter weight. Hulls have core kits that are cut to fit, ensuring the proper materials are used throughout the hull and deck, producing consistent quality from one boat to the next. All through-hull fittings are stainless steel.

Hull Design

The 270 Coastal has a deep-V bottom with a moderately sharp entry leading aft to 21 degrees of deadrise at the transom. Chine flats add lift and efficiency at speed, and improve stability at rest.

Walkthrough

Cockpit and Topsides

The cockpit has all the fishing features one could reasonably ask for. Two insulated in-deck fish boxes, a livewell and bait prep station with sink forward to starboard, raw-water washdown, and rod racks and holders are all included. The boat has LED cockpit courtesy lights. The switch is at the transom so you can turn it on when boarding the boat, and it's direct-wired to the battery (the amperage draw is very low) so the lights come on even when the battery switch is turned off.

Since this boat will likely double as a cruiser, it's good that it has seating everywhere. The transom seat in particular is a great feature, and it's also very well-designed—it just flips up or back down with a tug on a strap. Wellcraft uses a removable swim ladder that stows in the forward part of the motor well, against the transom. While there's something to be said for a fixed ladder that can be deployed from the water, this one is a step or two deeper than most hinged ladders, so it's easier to climb, and the open tread design makes it simple to climb with flippers on. It also floats, and it pops up on a hinge mechanism if you take off with it still in the water.

Wellcraft also pays attention to passenger safety topside, including a deep toe kick aft, handrails at the gunwale, plenty of cockpit depth, and great nonskid that grabs securely. Padded bolsters make leaning overboard easier on the thighs. The boat's generous freeboard and deck height make the boat more seaworthy, since there's more reserve buoyancy belowdecks. The cockpit deck drains quickly through two 2-inch drain liners per side—that's about double the drainage rate seen on some other boats of this size.

The door to the mechanical compartment aft in the cockpit leads to the batteries, battery switches, pumps, and seacocks (through-hulls).

The wiring runs and plumbing are neatly installed and labeled. As on many boats of this class, the through-hulls, being down in the bilge, are hard to reach. Rather than making it the owner's problem, though, Wellcraft added remote operating handles, right inside a portside door aft, with which to open and close the seacocks. These are usually found only on commercial and military vessels.

You can get the boat with a generator installed in the bilge under the forward end of the cockpit. It's accessed by a hatch, and the starboard seat hinges back as part of the hatch assembly.

You can get forward to the bow in two ways—via the opening centerline windshield and molded steps next to the cabin door, and up the flat side decks directly from the cockpit, also via molded steps. The 1-inch stainless steel bow railing is 22 inches, which is a little short, but with the centerline windshield access, and the modest slope in the cabin top, it's less of an issue than it would be with only side deck access and a ski-jump cabin top. There's a stainless steel anchor pulpit in the bow, and it's angled so the anchor seats readily. A windlass is an option, and there's also a hatch leading to the anchor line locker. As in the cockpit, the nonskid forward is excellent.

Helm

Both the portside passenger seat and the helm seat are up high, affording a good view all around the boat, and they're thickly padded and contoured for comfort. The helm electronics area includes plenty of room for a single 12-inch chartplotter, an 8-inch and a 12-inch, or a pair of 8-inch displays. The steering wheel and engine control are angled just right and mounted at a sensible height, so you can drive the boat comfortably standing up or sitting down.

The windshield is on the low side, which is what a lot of people want on a boat like this for the airflow. In colder climes, a higher Tiara-style windshield would be welcome for its added wind and rain protection. In any event, plastic filler curtains join the hardtop to the windshield frame when needed.

Cabin

A 19-inch-wide companionway leads down to the cabin where we find 6 feet of headroom at the entrance, which is not bad for a 27-footer. The cabin, finished in a mix of neutral upholstery, cherry veneer, and tooled white fiberglass, is built on a one-piece fiberglass liner. This liner, or pan, adds strength and stiffness to the hull structure, reduces or eliminates squeaking and rattling, and makes cleanup easy with the snap-in, removable carpet, which can be replaced inexpensively every couple of years to keep things fresh down below.

The layout is conventional, which means in this case that it works well. The dinette table lowers to double as a berth. There's a closet to hang clothes in, and the forward 72-inch V-berth and midcabin 6-foot berth, open to the rest of the cabin, provide plenty of choices of where to sleep.

The galley includes a sink, microwave, refrigerator (which runs on AC or DC power), an alcohol-electric stove, and a small countertop. The galley is right at the companionway, where it will be easy to prepare and serve meals. The enclosed head comes with a VacuFlush toilet (no smell, reliable) with holding tank, a sink, and a spigot that doubles as handheld shower.

Overhead is an opening hatch that lets in fresh air and daylight and doubles as an escape route. Opening side ports are also provided, and air conditioning is an option.

Engine

Up to twin 250 hp two- and four-stroke Yamaha, Evinrude, and Mercury outboards are available. We'd probably go with the 250s rather than the smaller 200 hp engines that are also available—the engines weigh about the same—just to have the extra few knots at cruise available. A 5 kW gas generator in a sound shield is also available.

Sea Trial

With a pair of 200 hp Yamaha four-strokes, we made just over 47 mph, or 41 knots. The most economical cruise was at 3,500 rpm, about 17 knots, which produced a range of 274 nautical miles at 90 percent fuel capacity. Many owners will want to cruise faster than that. Fortunately, this boat with the 200s can easily cruise at almost 32 knots at 4,500 rpm, though range drops off to 222 nautical miles, allowing for a 10 percent fuel reserve. With more passengers, gear, and fuel in the boat, and with a painted bottom, cruise speed will likely be a few knots slower. Noise levels from the 200 Yamaha four-strokes was modest, just 83 dBA at the helm at 4,500 rpm.

We didn't get out in rough water, but the 270 delivered a smooth, solid ride in the 1-foot chop we encountered at 30 knots. Handling was excellent, with the boat responding well to a hard, high-speed turn, heeling over just right. As on any manual-steering boat of this size and power, it took a lot of effort to straighten the wheel when coming out of the hard turn at speed, and it's six full turns lock-to-lock; this puts power-assist steering at the top of our desired options list.

Visibility over the bow, even when seated and without using the trim tabs, was good, thanks to a high seat and modest bow rise. The steering wheel and engine controls were just at the right height and angle, and there's plenty of room to stand at the helm and drive, with the other options being sitting on the seat or leaning against the flipped-up bolster. All these driving positions work well.

The 270 Coastal is well worth considering if you're in the market for a boat that can cruise with the whole family as well as fish competitively offshore. It's well-built, intelligently designed, and extensively outfitted with all the necessities for serious fishing.

Wellcraft 270 Coastal Performance Results

RPM	Speed, mph	Speed, knots	Fuel Use, gph	Nautical mpg	Range, nm	Noise Level, dBA (at helm)
600	3.8	3.3	1.1	3.00	508	55
1,000	5.9	5.1	2.1	2.44	413	62
1,500	7.2	6.3	3.5	1.79	302	64
2,000	8.9	7.7	5.4	1.43	242	71
2,500	10.2	8.9	10.4	0.85	144	77
3,000	19.3	16.8	13	1.29	218	80
3,500	26.3	22.9	14.1	1.62	274	80
4,000	31.6	27.5	18.4	1.49	252	81
4,500	36.5	31.7	24.2	1.31	222	83
5,000	40.8	35.5	27.2	1.30	221	87
5,500	44.1	38.3	31.8	1.20	204	87
6,000	47.3	41.1	36.9	1.11	188	88

Test conditions: Three passengers, fuel tank one-third full, with twin 200 hp Yamaha outboards. Light chop.

The boat doesn't have any of the quirky handling characteristics we see in some cabin boats. The hull form is just right for this style of boat, with a bow that's sharp enough to smooth out a head sea running at a decent clip, but full enough to resist yawing and bow steering downsea. The helm design provides plenty of room for electronics, and the helm station is high enough to provide a great all-around horizon view.

As a cruiser, there's room to sleep four down below, the galley and head are as good as can be found on a similar-size express cruiser, there's a lot of light and ventilation and what should be plenty of headroom, and the four-stroke Yamaha power delivers excellent range and economy.

Convertibles

Convertibles have been around as long as the cuddy cabin, and with good reason. This design allows a two-deck design in a relatively small boat, providing a large interior for cruising, a flying bridge for good visibility, and a big cockpit for fishing. The early convertibles had an uncovered flying bridge as the secondary control station (the main station was below in the pilothouse), with steering and engine controls, compass, and depth-finder. Now it's rare to find a convertible with a windshield and lower control station; instead the windshield is made of leakproof fiberglass and the space below

filled with large TVs, full-height refrigerators, and microwave ovens.

The species has evolved to the point where the flybridge is the main operating station, with full electronics, seating for six or more, and a hardtop with full plastic enclosure. The bigger cruising convertibles are also available with a two-deck superstructure, creating an enclosed, climate-controlled flying bridge reached from both internal and weather deck stairs. But the pure fishing convertibles stick with the aft console arrangement on the bridge so the skipper can keep an eye on the cockpit action. An aluminum tower 30 feet or more off the water is de rigueur for spotting fish. Plus, it's just cool to run a boat from the tower. The downside is that all the air drag from a big tower can slow a sportfisherman by 2 to 3 knots and absorb 10 percent of the propulsion power.

The business end of the convertible is the cockpit, which is outfitted by the builder with every imaginable fishing amenity, from gaff storage lockers to saltwater icemakers for chilling the catch. While a 12-foot-long cockpit on a 60-footer only represents a fifth of the boat's LOA, a smaller percentage than on the older, smaller boats, they're still bigger than ever, thanks to the bigger boats' greater beam. A transom door allows 1,000-pound tuna or marlin to be pulled aboard, and cleats are mounted below hawseholes in the washboards to reduce snag potential when playing a fish. A coaming height of 29 to 30 inches is ideal.

A tournament-ready sportfisherman must be able to maneuver quickly on agile gamefish, and the freeboard aft and cockpit deck must be relatively low to the water to handle big fish alongside. These boats also must be fast to have any chance at winning a modern, big-money tournament. Some sportfishermen can cruise in the high 30-knot range with a full load of fuel and supplies, sea state permitting. The same seakeeping qualities that allow a convertible to make it over a hundred miles offshore in a little over 3 hours, fish all day in sloppy conditions, and race home for the weigh-in make them excellent offshore cruising boats as well.

With many production and custom convertibles being built in the 55- to 80-foot range, these are true liveaboard cruising yachts as well as fishing boats. A 60-foot convertible has less interior volume than a 60-foot motor yacht, but it's also a better, faster sea boat. The saloon is just forward of the cockpit, and it's the yacht's living room, with a lounge (convertible to a pullout bed), TV, stereo, galley, and dining area. The cabin forward on a big 65- to 75-foot convertible might have three or four staterooms and as many heads, all luxuriously appointed. The engine room on a convertible is usually generously proportioned compared to strict cruising yachts, first because the engines tend to be so big, and perhaps because their owners do some of their own maintenance and appreciate being able to get around all that machinery.

Part of the Italian Ferretti Group, Bertram builds high-end sportfishing convertibles from 39 to 67 feet, as well as a 36-foot express boat. The 630 has recently been introduced with an enclosed flying bridge — a real improvement for all but the hard-core tournament fishermen who'd rather be out in the open and farther aft where they have a better view of the cockpit. Bertram has a reputation for building seaworthy rough-water boats, and the 630 is no exception. Three- or four-stateroom layouts, interior access to the bridge, and up to twin 2,000 hp MTUs (33 to 36 knots) are available. BERTAM YACHTS

Hatteras builds convertibles from 50 to 90 feet, and every time you go to a Florida boat show these days it seems like another Hatteras model is coming out (practically as often as Viking). This is a big change from the '80s and '90s when word of a bona fide all-new model from Hatteras was relatively rare. Now owned by Brunswick Corporation and with brand-new hull designs, these luxuriously appointed convertibles are designed for the speeds to which modern common rail diesels can push them (around 40 knots). Deep gear ratios and seven- or even eight-blade props give these heavy planing hulls the brute force needed to keep moving in a seaway. The 100,000-pound, three-stateroom, three-head 64 shown, with up to 3,600 hp available, is one of the new tournament fishermen from Hatteras. Its seaworthiness makes it a good offshore cruiser as well. HATTERAS YACHTS

Luhrs builds moderately priced diesel-powered express, sedan, and convertible yacht-fishing boats from 28 to 41 feet. There are three convertibles, the others beside this 38 being 36 and 41 feet. Luhrs has earned a reputation for producing solidly built boats well-equipped with standard features, nicely outfitted but not high-end. It's a formula that many owners appreciate and that has worked well for the Luhrs-Silverton-Mainship-Hunter group over the years. They are beamy boats (the 38 is 14 feet, 11 inches wide), so don't expect them to keep up with a moderate-beam deep-V hull in short steep seas, but they offer a lot of living space and run well enough. The 38 convertible has a galley-up arrangement; it sleeps six with a two-stateroom, one-head cabin and a roomy saloon. It can take up to twin 500 hp Yanmar or Cummins diesel power.   LUHRS CORPORATION

Silverton's yacht series includes commodious motor yachts as well as convertibles well suited for fishing or cruising. The convertibles run from 33 to 50 feet, including this 45-footer. Three staterooms and two heads accommodate up to six people (maybe two couples and two kids). This model features another welcome anomaly in the U.S. convertible market — a windshield in the saloon to brighten things up inside. One upscale feature is the helm console that has a power lift that can hide all the expensive electronics at night. Twin diesel power goes up to Volvo D12s rated at 715 hp.   SILVERTON YACHTS

Ocean has a pair of unique cruising convertibles it calls its Odyssey series, 57- and 65-footers (the 65 is shown here). These yachts are designed with more emphasis on interior accommodations and a much longer saloon, rather than on fishing. Under the raised cockpit is a garage for the PWC, just like on the high-end European express yachts. The shorter enclosed bridge (there is interior access directly from the saloon) keeps topside weight down and improves seaworthiness while providing climate-controlled comfort at the helm.   OCEAN YACHTS

Tiara builds well-appointed cruising and fishing express yachts up to 58 feet. This 39 is Tiara's sole convertible offering. The 39 has a galley-down floor plan, the one that usually makes the most sense in a boat this size, and the cabin has two staterooms and a single head. The saloon has a forward-facing window, not a bad compromise between the cave effect of most convertibles and a storage cabinet—eating full windshield. Up to twin 575 hp diesels from Volvo, Cummins, or Cat are available.   TIARA YACHTS

CABO 40 FLYBRIDGE

Cabo 40 Flybridge Specifications	
LOA:	40'2"
Beam:	15'9"
Draft:	3'5"
Weight:	32,000 lb.
Fuel:	550 gal.
Water:	95 gal.
Deadrise:	17 deg.

Cabo is a respected builder of luxury express and convertible sportfishing boats from 32 to 52 feet. Founded in 1991, California-based Cabo wasted no time establishing a reputation for producing well-engineered and solidly built boats, and for fastidious attention to detail. Recently purchased by Brunswick Corporation, Cabo has turned to naval architect Michael Peters to design its hulls from the keel up, and their ride quality, handling, and seakeeping is superb (unlike early Cabos), as we'll see in this review of the Peters-designed 40 Flybridge convertible.

The 40 is a 35-knot, two-stateroom, two-head (the cabin layout is quite innovative and makes clever use of space, reminding us of Ocean's equally innovative discontinued 40-footer) convertible designed for the tournament fishing circuit. Of course, some of the same attributes that make this boat suited to offshore sportfishing make it a good cruising yacht: speed, a great ride with seakindly motion, and a comfortable interior.

Construction

The Cabo is well-built, starting with a standard 1-inch layer of gelcoat against the mold. The hull is certain to be blister-proof with vinylester resin used throughout the solid bottom and cored hull side laminate. Vinylester resin is far more impervious to water migration at the molecular level, since it cross-links more completely, preventing osmosis. Plus, its elongation neatly matches that of the fiberglass substrate, resulting in a much stronger and more impact-resistant laminate. It's also better glue, so secondary bonds are stronger. Cabo even paints two coats of epoxy on the bottom of the boat, which is certainly not needed to prevent blistering on this boat.

Nonwoven fiberglass reinforcements are used throughout the hull laminate. The bottom is solid while the sides are cored with Core-Cell. Cabo has a laminating crew that does nothing but work with the core materials, using bonding putty and vacuum bags to ensure a sound skin-to-core bond line throughout the hull structure. Controlling the temperature while building helps regulate exotherm so the laminate hardens when it's expected to.

A female-molded hull grid is bonded to and supports the bottom of the hull and doubles as engine beds amidships. Its tooled finish results in an easily cleaned engine room bilge area. The flange-style hull-to-deck joint is bonded with 3M 5200 polyurethane adhesive, bolted every 4 inches, and glassed from the inside from bow to stern, making this critical joint permanently bulletproof.

The fuel tanks are fiberglass, laminated with fire-retardant resin and glassed to the hull, so they should last essentially forever with no rust, corrosion, or other trouble. The fuel supply lines have large pickup fittings in the bottom of the tanks with strainers to keep any sediment out of the filter-separators downstream. All stainless steel is 316-grade, and all topside hardware (most of it made in-house by Cabo) is through-bolted.

Walkthrough

Cockpit

The Cabo 40's 12-foot, 6-inch by 8-foot cockpit is laid out for open-ocean fishing. There's good deck drainage with plenty of pitch aft and large corner scuppers, and 27-inch-high coamings with toe kicks all around (except, unfortunately, around the transom livewell). Grippy, easy-to-clean nonskid makes for a safe and efficient fishing platform. Stern lines lead unobstructed either forward or crossing at the stern from large, 12-inch cleats through nicely radiused transom-corner hawseholes.

A livewell is built into the transom coaming (a clear side window is an option), as is a two-part, outboard-opening transom door, and large insulated in-deck fish boxes straddle the fuel tank below. Coaming rod holders and under-gunwale rod racks are provided, and a bait prep station and tackle center are forward on either side of the engine room entry.

A single cockpit hatch opens to the lazarette below. Fuel line shut-off valves are in easy reach atop the fuel tank. Livewell pumps and strainers are neatly plumbed and labeled on centerline. Heavily built rudder boards support the top of the rudderposts as well as the power steering cylinders. Fit and finish inside the lazarette, sanded smooth and gelcoated, is as impressive as it is in the engine room.

Foredeck

Side decks varying from 6 inches to 10 inches wide lead forward to the foredeck. They're too narrow to traverse without hanging on, but you pick up a foot or so of saloon width inside, which is well worth it. Cabo provides a handrail along the base of the bridge, though this would be too high for a shorter person to reach comfortably. Since a handhold is a necessity with the modest side deck width, a lower handrail would be a help here.

Our test boat had a 1¼-inch aluminum East Coast bow railing, 25 inches high and leading partway back to the deckhouse. A higher, and safer, West Coast railing that extends farther aft is also available, as is a very short and low Palm Beach version; all three are available in stainless steel or aluminum. A 25-inch cabin hatch opens to the cabin below—a large hatch like this is a most welcome feature, as it provides an emergency egress route (often omitted by other builders) from the cabin. At the bow, the ground tackle is cleanly laid out with a flush-mounted vertical windlass and an integral pulpit with stainless steel chafe plate housing the boat's Danforth anchor.

Bridge

A sloping portside ladder with handrails leads to the bridge; at the base, it's mounted to the deckhouse to make deck cleanup easier. A helm seat on centerline and a companion seat to starboard are provided. A high triple railing with integral rod holders provides good security aft, and a railing is also provided inboard of the ladder well.

The Palm Beach–style helm is conventionally laid out, with a helm pod supporting the wheel and separate engine controls to either side. Digital engine displays are forward and below the wheel, and partially obscured by it, depending on your position. The rest of the dash is given over to two large-screen displays front and center, as well as miscellaneous radios and control pads to starboard. Seated and standing visibility are good in all directions, with a tall pedestal helm seat that adjusts up and down as well as fore and aft. The helm is designed for stand-up driving, though you can steer and operate the engines in synch mode while leaning forward in the seat.

A seating area is just forward of the helm console, accessed from the port side. The Isinglas plastic side curtains are as easy to see through as clean glass.

Cabin

The inside of the 40 belies this boat's reputation as a hard-core fisherman. Accommodations are plush, featuring teak and holly soles, teak cabinetry, and other amenities. In the saloon, the generous 6-foot, 4-inch headroom makes the area inviting. The electrical panel is handy right inside the cockpit door, and it's at eye level so it's easy to read and operate. Two L-shaped settees, aft to port and forward to starboard, provide two socializing areas. A 27-inch flat-screen TV built into the forward bulkhead can be seen from the aft settee and from part of the other one. The large side and aft windows let in plenty of daylight, and the powerful air conditioning is well diffused, minimizing cold spots.

Down a step from the saloon, the galley is forward to port, below where a windshield would be, putting this space to excellent use. The roomy, U-shaped Corian countertop is well-designed, providing lots of meal prep space and hosting a deep sink and two-burner cooktop (a covering lid allows this area to be used as a countertop when not cooking), along with a side-by-side refrigerator below. Storage cabinets are situated above and below the counter.

Down three more steps from the galley, a companionway leads to the starboard bunk bed stateroom. Well, nominally a bunk bed—this 45-inch-wide berth could sleep two people. The novel feature here is the upper bunk, which slides out for sleeping and partially disappears when not in use. There's private access to the head with stall shower just forward. Opposite to port off the companionway is a day head.

In the bow is the master stateroom—which has nearly 6-foot, 2-inch headroom, not bad for a 40-footer—with an island berth measuring 6 feet, 3 inches by 5 feet. There are drawers and a storage locker below, and more storage room is accessible by hinging the bed up—it lifts effortlessly on air shocks.

Below a deck hatch, the clean, well-lit bilge area is used for auxiliary equipment, including a pair of air-conditioning units and the sewage system.

Engine

Cabo has always been well regarded for its systems engineering. A look through the engine room on this boat shows this opinion to be well founded; Cabo's engineers have obviously put a lot of thought—and priority—into this intelligently designed space. The engine room is easy to get into, especially for a 40-footer, with a 24-inch-wide companionway and a series of entry steps. It's hard to believe these compact engines put out 800 hp each. The main engine raw-water cooling seacocks and strainers are at your feet as you enter, where they're easy to get to and service (we're of the old school that says the seacocks should be cycled every day so they'll work when you need them), and the dual shift-on-the-fly fuel filter-separators are also on centerline and easily accessed. The slightly raised, flat centerline walkway is comfortable to stand on, and should stay dry even with a few cups of water in the bilge.

Those same bilges are shiny, tooled fiberglass, thanks to a molded grid system that doubles as an engine bed. Along with the all-white machinery and generous fluorescent lighting, this engine room is a mechanic's dream. Plumbing and wiring runs are neat and securely installed and labeled. Compression fittings and high-pressure hoses are used in the fuel system, and the fiberglass fuel tank will never have a corrosion issue. There's even room to work outboard of the engines, and part of the reason is the auxiliary equipment space below the deck forward in the cabin, which frees up space around the engines. Cabo showcases its wiring acumen with a display case attached to the forward bulkhead. The genset is hidden aft under the engine access stairs. Cabo also installs a bilge suction pickup line plumbed to the starboard seacock.

Sea Trial

This was the first Peters-designed Cabo we'd run, and we're glad to be able to report that our test boat delivered a superb ride, certainly as good as any we've seen on a convertible of this size, and much better than most. Among boats of similar size and displacement, you'd look to an Eastbay or Bertram to find the equivalent in ride quality.

Turning two full 360-degree circles at full rudder and full power took under 28 seconds, a very respectable turning rate for an inboard of this size and displacement. Steering was also very responsive, at four turns lock-to-lock, and effortless with the power assist. The boat heels instantly and comfortably when you put the rudders over. MAN's Rexroth electronic engine controls worked well.

The hull runs smoothly in a head sea, tracks well with minimal yaw downsea, and runs dry in all directions. Weight distribution, both longitudinal and vertical, has to be bang-on to deliver both downsea tracking and low-speed planing capability.

The Cabo danced around the dock just clutching in those 800 hp MANs, and all-around close-in visibility was good. The boat does 7 knots at idle and over 5 knots with just one engine in gear; running on one engine, it only takes about a quarter turn of the wheel to keep going straight.

The Cabo 40 is as well-engineered and as capable in a seaway as any boat on the market that I've tested. High points for the Cabo 40 include a smooth and dry ride, and crisp, responsive handling, an accommodating saloon and cabin layout and appointments that make excellent use of space, textbook systems engineering throughout, rugged all-vinylester laminate construction, and excellent engine room layout and equipment accessibility. On the other hand, the Cabo is too heavy (any 40-footer that needs 1,600 hp to make 35 kts needs re-engineering) and it's very loud.

Options include Cat and MAN diesels to 800 hp, a 12.6 kW generator, colored hull, bow rails, leather sofa in the saloon, cockpit freezer and refrigeration plate, and a swim platform.

Cabo 40 Flybridge Performance Results

RPM	Speed, knots	Fuel Use, gph	Nautical mpg	Range, nm	Noise Level, dBA (at helm)
600	6.8	4	1.70	842	78
900	9.3	8	1.16	575	82
1,200	12.3	22	0.56	277	85
1,500	18.7	34	0.55	272	90
1,800	27.1	46	0.59	292	91
2,100	32.8	69	0.48	235	92
2,260–2,280	35.3	82	0.43	213	92

Test conditions: Fuel tank one-third full, with twin 800 hp MANs. Range assumes 90 percent burnable fuel.

Express Cruisers

Express cruisers, or open-style yachts, are a popular style for people who like the convenience of the helm station within a few steps of the lower-deck accommodations and the cockpit. About half the length of the boat is dedicated to the cabin on the lower deck; the rest is open topside space, including a bridge deck protected by a windshield and a cockpit aft. Either a canvas bimini top or hardtop provides protection from wind and rain. The express cruiser's raised bridge deck typically includes the helm station, usually to starboard, and a lounge or pilot chair opposite.

The deck is raised for two reasons: to improve the skipper's visibility and to add headroom for a midcabin stateroom below. The engine room is either below the bridge deck or below the cockpit. If the engines are below the bridge deck, then the cockpit can be low enough to easily fish from. If they are shifted aft, below the cockpit, then the accommodations can also be pushed aft, providing room for a midcabin below the raised bridge deck above. Express cruisers with aft engine rooms make excellent use of space, with either stern drives or V-drives providing propulsion power. Plus, putting the engines in the stern creates a quieter interior. Express cruisers start at 24 feet and run up to 100 feet.

An exotic example of the express cruiser taken to its limit is the Sunseeker Predator 80, which has a garage in the stern to stow a tender. The cockpit is down a step or two from the bridge deck, and usually features convertible lounge seating and a sunpad, an icemaker or wet bar, a transom door leading to a swim platform, a handheld shower, and a swim ladder.

Lacking the topside weight of a big superstructure and flybridge, the express cruiser rolls and weighs less than a convertible of the same size. However, the express gives up the convertible's enclosed saloon and superior flybridge sight lines. The cockpit on some express-style cruisers is rigged to fish with rod holders, bait prep stations, fish boxes, livewells, and other amenities. Sea Ray's Amberjack series and Tiara's line of cruising yachts are good examples. There's only one helm station on most of these boats; if the boat isn't properly designed, visibility ahead can be a problem if the bow rises excessively when climbing on plane and cruising.

The annual J.D. Power and Associates boating study measures customer satisfaction with express cruisers between 24 and 33 feet. Boats in this segment are defined as cruisers with standing headroom, berths, an enclosed head, and galley facilities. Only brands with over 100 survey returns are included in the published results, which limits the number of brands reported on to just four. But since most express cruiser manufacturers in this size range also build runabouts, some insight into product quality and customer satisfaction can be gained by studying those results.

Regal placed at the top of the 2007 rankings by a substantial margin of 39 points over Sea Ray, which took second place. Regal also ranked highest in the small runabout segment, so the brand is obviously doing something right. Bayliner ranked lowest, also by a large margin, at 38 points below Rinker. The express cruiser segment average is the second-lowest of the seven covered in the study.

Regal scored highest in every Power Circle Ratings category, a measurement of customer satisfaction. Sea Ray received five Power Circles in quality and reliability, and four in every other category except helm and instrument panel. As the lowest-ranked express cruiser brand overall, Bayliner received just two Power Circles in every category.

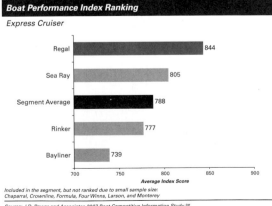

Boat Performance Index Ranking

Express Cruiser

Brand	Average Index Score
Regal	844
Sea Ray	805
Segment Average	788
Rinker	777
Bayliner	739

Included in the segment, but not ranked due to small sample size:
Chaparral, Crownline, Formula, Four Winns, Larson, and Monterey

Source: J.D. Power and Associates 2007 Boat Competitive Information Study ℠

Express Cruiser Ratings

Company	Overall Rating	Quality & Reliability	Engine	Design & Style	Helm & Instrument	Cabin
Regal *Award Recipient*	⚫⚫⚫⚫⚫	⚫⚫⚫⚫⚫	⚫⚫⚫⚫⚫	⚫⚫⚫⚫⚫	⚫⚫⚫⚫⚫	⚫⚫⚫⚫⚫
Bayliner	⚫⚫○○○	⚫⚫○○○	⚫⚫○○○	⚫⚫○○○	⚫⚫○○○	⚫⚫○○○
Rinker	⚫⚫⚫○○	⚫⚫○○○	⚫⚫⚫○○	⚫⚫⚫○○	⚫⚫○○○	⚫⚫⚫⚫○
Sea Ray	⚫⚫⚫⚫○	⚫⚫⚫⚫⚫	⚫⚫⚫⚫○	⚫⚫⚫⚫○	⚫⚫⚫⚫⚫	⚫⚫⚫⚫○

SCORING LEGEND:

⚫⚫⚫⚫⚫	⚫⚫⚫⚫○	⚫⚫⚫○○	⚫⚫○○○
Among the best	Better than most	About average	The rest

The 40 Brenton Reef is built using a vacuum-bagged laminate of epoxy resin, E-glass, and Kevlar (it doesn't get any better than that). Joinery and appointments are top-drawer, as good as anything on the market. These yachts are all designed and engineered (including laminate schedules and weight distribution) by C. Raymond Hunt and Associates, making them superb open-ocean sea boats.   ALDEN YACHTS

Nearly one of a kind, the Bayliner Discovery 246 is a restyled and upgraded Bayliner classic sedan-type cruiser. This very practical lay-out makes me wonder why more of these boats aren't built and sold by Bayliner's competitors. The 246, and its bigger brother, the 289, feature a big and bright cabin, and a high helm station, affording great visibility through big windows (no plastic to fool around with), and a small but useful cockpit over the single stern drive. MerCruiser power to 300 hp is available, which makes this boat move right along.   BAYLINER

Chaparral's Signature express cruisers start at 24 feet and end with this top-of-the-line 35-footer. The 350 is available with either stern-drive or V-drive inboard, gas or diesel propulsion. The upscale cabin includes sleeping capacity for six; Chaparral places a design focus on roomy interiors and sumptuous accommodations, with offshore ride getting less priority. There's a companion seat next to the helm, creating a portside companionway to the cabin. One of the largest builders of its type (after Sea Ray), Chaparrals are positioned at the top of the production cruiser market, competing directly with brands including Sea Ray, Formula, Regal, and Four Winns.   CHAPARRAL BOATS

Cruisers Yachts builds express, aft-cabin, and flybridge motor yachts from 28 to 56 feet. Cruisers does a good job building boats that look stylish in a Euro sort of way, while not straying from the elements that make a boat practical to maintain, use, and move around on at sea. The 300 is one of the smallest models, introducing buyers to Cruisers' boats and allowing them to keep moving up with larger Cruisers for years to come (it's sure worked for Sea Ray). The midcabin is wide open to the rest of the interior — which sleeps up to six — and the boat has a salty feel to it, thanks to pleasant but not overdone joinery and furnishings. Cruisers are roomy inside, but also run well offshore. Volvo twin gas and diesel stern-drive power is available.   CRUISERS YACHTS

Cobalt Yachts is a new company founded by the owners of highly regarded Cobalt Boats (see Runabouts), which ranked highest in the J.D. Power and Associates study award for highest customer satisfaction with runabouts to 29 feet. Cobalt Yachts' first two models of express cruisers are 36- and 45-footers (the 45 is shown here), and the company's stated intentions are to build world-class yachts to 60 feet, directly targeting the best European and American express brands. These Donald Blount—designed yachts, some of which will feature CMD Zeus and Volvo IPS pod drives, promise to be excellent in offshore waters.   COBALT YACHTS

Doral is a Canadian builder of Euro-style runabouts and cruisers to 45 feet. The Mediterra is one of the company's newest models, a 40-footer with accommodations for up to four with two private suites. Volvo IPS and stern-drive and MerCruiser stern-drive power are available.   DORAL BOATS

Fairline is an English builder of high-end, good-running Bernard Olesinski–designed yachts to 74 feet. The Targa series is Fairline's moderate-beam, performance-oriented line (competing against Princess's Vee-Class, for one), and includes the Targa 47 shown here, one of their newest models. The 47 has the line's signature retractable hardtop, just in case you're in the mood for some fresh air, and an aft garage for the requisite RIB tender. Volvo and Cat V-drive inboard diesels to 575 hp (35 knots at the top end) are available. Precious few American express cruisers run as well as a Fairline in rough water. FAIRLINE YACHTS

Four Winns retained C. Raymond Hunt to design its three largest express cruiser models, and it was a smart move, producing what are several of the best-running U.S.-made offshore cruisers of their type on the market. Four Winns has publicly targeted Sea Ray for market share, and appears to be hard at work upgrading cabin interiors and feature content (as well as improving hull designs and weight distribution, as mentioned). It is certainly on the right track with this 35-footer. MerCruiser, Crusader, and Volvo stern-drive and IPS pod power are available. GENMAR HOLDINGS, INC.

Formula is a top-drawer builder of bowriders, FAS³Tech muscle boats, express cruisers, and yachts from 24 to 48 feet. Formula cruisers, including this 31 PC, are good-running and nicely appointed boats, all with a hint of the builder's racing heritage. Formulas are among the few American express cruisers that can hope to keep up with a Fairline or Princess in big waves, and they still manage to fit it with comfortable and upscale accommodations. MerCruiser and Volvo stern drives are available. FORMULA BOATS

Hunt Yachts is part of Hunt Design, one of the leading naval architecture and engineering firms in the world. You'd think their boats (they build 25- to 36-footers) would run well, and you'd be right. The Hunt Harrier 36 is a great-running boat in rough water, one of the best with its deep-V bottom and moderate beam. These boats offer either Volvo or Yanmar diesel power to 480 hp (that's 480 each, making this boat a pocket-rocket), driving either inboards or Hamilton waterjets. They are traditionally styled, resale value is high, and these boats are built so well they'll likely look and run as well 30 years from now. HUNT YACHTS

The 322 sits near the top of Monterey's express cruiser lineup from 25 to 35 feet. A boat with a contemporary profile, there's a sunpad forward, an airy cabin, three-person helm seat, and power options to twin 320 hp stern drives.   MONTEREY BOATS

Sea Ray's Sundancer express cruisers run from 24 to 60 feet, the most comprehensive lineup in the business. The 60 shown here is the company's flagship, and like many of its competitors, Sea Ray has been going upscale to a degree unimagined just 15 years ago. That includes features like power roofs, power gangways, the use of frameless glass, and high-quality cabinetry and upholsteries. It's not all glitz, either; the visibility and view from the helm on the 60 is among the best seen on any boat of that size. Cabin natural light is better than ever with large, inset hull windows. MAN 1,050 hp diesel inboards are standard.   SEA RAY BOATS

Rinker is another builder of runabouts, deck boats, and cruisers, in this case to 42 feet, as shown. This flagship is a big step up for Rinker, recently acquired from its founder by an investment firm, and apparently thereby the recipient of fresh capitalization allowing it to produce this new model and others like it. Interior fit and finish has also improved in recent years. The fiberglass hardtop side supports take a big chunk out of the operator's sight lines, detracting from all-around helm visibility, but it certainly gives the boat a yachty look. Volvo IPS and Volvo and MerCruiser stern-drive power is available.   RINKER BOATS

Tiara produces upscale, well-built cruising and fishing yachts to 58 feet. The Sovran class is their cruising series, and it includes this 3900, which was specifically designed to accommodate Volvo's IPS propulsion system. This boat takes full advantage of the IPS's space-saving design, placing all the propulsion machinery well aft, allowing for larger accommodations amidships and making for a quiet, smoke-free, and low-vibration living environment. The 3900 has a welcome single-stateroom cabin layout, which doesn't try to squeeze too much into a 39-foot sock, as it were. The result is a livable boat for a couple cruising for several weeks, including the benefits of a large saloon living area. Volvo IPS power options include the 400 and 500 series drives using common rail D6 diesels.   TIARA YACHTS

Viking Yachts established a relationship with Princess Yachts of the United Kingdom, creating an Americanized version (open layouts, U.S.-made and -serviced appliances and systems, etc.) of these high-end yachts and distributing them in the U.S. Viking Sport Cruisers come in three lines: express yachts (like this V53), flybridge yachts, and motor yachts. These are superb rough-water yachts. VIKING YACHTS

CHAPARRAL 310 SIGNATURE

Chaparral 310 Signature Specifications

LOA:	33'4"
Beam:	10'7"
Deadrise:	18 deg.
Dry weight:	11,395 lb.
Cockpit depth:	30"
Draft:	33" (drive down)
Fuel capacity:	147 gal.

Chaparral is one of the world's largest manufacturers of runabouts, deck boats, express cruisers, and under the Robalo brand name, saltwater fishing boats. Solidly positioned at the upper end of the market with its stylish bowriders and plush cruisers, and backed up by a well-established dealer sales and service network, Chaparral has been under the same management since 1965. Chaparral, an affiliate of Marine Products Corp., builds a high-quality, well-regarded product.

In production since 2004, Chaparral's 310 Signature cruiser provides all the comforts of home for a weekend, or longer, on the water. Spaciously proportioned and well outfitted, this cruiser packs a lot of liveaboard comfort in its 31-foot length.

Construction

The Chaparral 310 starts with gelcoat and then a coat of $1\frac{1}{5}$-inch-thick vinylester to prevent osmotic blistering. The bottom laminate is solid fiberglass, starting with chop and then fiberglass reinforcements. In the hull

sides, next comes a $3\frac{3}{5}$-inch layer of SprayCore; this spray-on bulking agent helps prevent print-through of the follow-on fiberglass reinforcement to the gelcoat surfaces, which is especially important with colored hulls. The hull sides are built with inner and outer fiberglass laminates sandwiching a $\frac{1}{2}$-inch Nida-Core material for added stiffness at moderate weight. The transom is a solid sandwich composite of fiberglass- and pressure-treated plywood. Chaparral takes care to prevent bulkhead-edge hard spots in the hull skin by padding the plywood edges with strips of $\frac{1}{2}$-inch Nida-Core, and then tabbing the bulkheads to the hull.

The bottom of the hull is supported with a pressure-treated plywood stringer grid network tabbed to the bottom, then fully encapsulated in fiberglass. Forward, the one-piece fiberglass pan or foundation for the cabin is in turn bonded to the structural grid, making for a solidly constructed hull. Aft, the one-piece deck and cockpit liner is also bonded to the hull. The hull-to-deck joint is fastened mechanically using self-tapping screws through the shoebox joint, which is backed up by a strip of pressure-treated plywood for improved screw grip and retention. Structural bulkheads at the anchor locker and forward of the engine room are also fiberglassed to the hull-to-deck joint area. The outer edge of the joint is then sealed with a caulking compound. No balsa coring is used anywhere in the boat.

Hull Design

The 310 Signature has a modified-V bottom with hard chines and spray strakes.

Walkthrough

Cockpit

Starting our tour at the stern, the attached swim platform is large, with a three-step swim ladder under a hatch and grab bar across the aft end. A small transom trunk with its tooled fiberglass liner holds fenders and lines, as well as dockside connectors. A pair of stern cleats is affixed at the sloped stern quarters.

Coming on board from the swim platform, the transom door is 30 inches high, adding a measure of passenger safety missing on many similar boats with lower doors. It also has a simple but effective design, lifting to open and close, with detents holding it in both positions. The battery switches are just inside the door, a handy location that increases the odds that they'll be used, and that the batteries will consequently be fully charged when you need them.

The cockpit has a big U-shaped lounge to starboard, with a flip-up seat section providing access to a cooler below. The table drops down to create a big sunpad with filler cushions. The aft lounge seat can be lowered to open up more cockpit space aft for fishing or tubing. Opposite the lounge area to port is a small cockpit entertainment center with sink, storage compartment, and refrigerator, along with a grab bar along the countertop. Molded steps lead to the side decks, in case you want to board the boat from a dock alongside, but the preferred route is through the opening centerline windshield. Forward to port, and opposite the helm, is a lounge seat, with storage below for the cockpit table that forms a second conversation area forward.

Helm

The helm, up a step from the cockpit on starboard, is neatly laid out. We liked the big 12-inch-square electronics area reserved at the helm for a chartplotter, and its priority placement right in front of the wheel. The compass, up high and in front, is directly in the operator's field of vision.

We're glad to see that Chaparral is using red lighting at the helm station, preserving night vision for safer night running. The same goes for the tan-colored dash area that minimizes windshield glare in bright sunlight.

Standing room at the helm is excellent, thanks in part to the flip-up seat bolsters that rise out of the way. The seat is padded, contoured, and comfortable. The upholstery is top-drawer throughout the boat.

Foredeck

Access to the bow is by way of molded steps at the centerline-opening windshield. As in the cockpit, the nonskid pattern is excellent, gripping securely, while the surface is easy to keep clean with a bristle brush. There is also little slope in the deck leading forward, which makes things more secure underfoot. A hatch in the bow opens for access to the anchor windlass, anchor rode, and tie-off cleat.

Cabin

The cabin is huge for a 31-footer, and the feeling of space is accentuated by the generous 6-foot, 5-inch headroom at the cabin entrance. The Chaparral's excellent construction is plain to see, with a full fiberglass pan bonded to the stringer system serving as a strong and consistent foundation for the cabin's head, galley, and furniture. The tooled fiberglass is also easy to keep clean, and it's easy on the eye. The maple laminate furniture, the wood laminate sole, and the thickly upholstered seats give the cabin an upscale appearance.

The midcabin under the helm is wide open to the main cabin, and its 4-foot, 4-inch headroom is ample when sitting. The open stair treads, supported by a single pipe, add to the midcabin's wide-open feeling. The 6-foot, 3-inch berth is well-padded and comfortable. A cedar-lined hanging locker is next to the berth.

The enclosed head is roomy and comes standard with a stainless steel sink, storage below, mirrored vanity above, opening portlight, and a VacuFlush toilet with holding tank. The fiberglass liner has a sculpted look that pleases the eye and will prove easy to clean.

The galley to port and forward of the head is well-equipped and has plenty of cabinet storage space and a large Corian countertop. A two-burner electric stove, oversized refrigerator with a stainless steel door, sink, and microwave complete the kitchen. A flat-screen TV above and forward swivels so it can be seen from practically anywhere in the cabin. Opposite the galley is a C-shaped lounge with table; the design creates a functional floor plan, not too crowded, but with plenty of room to sit and relax.

The cabin on our test boat had a rubber-backed wood laminate floor that's durable and easy to keep clean. Below a hatch in the cabin sole is a smoothly finished bilge locker that, at least with some owners, sees duty as a wine cellar.

Sea Trial

Our sea trial took place on the Richelieu River near Montreal. The river was calm with a slight current. Coming up on plane with a good deal of bow rise, the hull started to level off at 25 mph and ran well at 3,500 rpm, about 29 mph. With the test boat's 260 hp 5-liter MPI MerCruiser gas engines driving Bravo 3 stern drives, 3,500 rpm—no less—is the boat's sweet spot as a cruising speed.

Seated at the helm when accelerating to cruising speed, using full trim tabs momentarily keeps visibility ahead unobstructed while coming up on plane. Steering was sensitive at 2¼ turns lock-to-lock, with fingertip control possible thanks to the power assist,

The large berth forward, 6 feet, 6 inches long, and 4 feet, 1 inch wide, has a lot of storage space below, including drawers and bin storage for the bow sunpads and cabin table. The storage space is also easy to access, with the mattress lifting easily on strong boosts. Over the forward berth is a 21-inch hatch that lets in ample light and fresh air, and is large enough to serve as a second way out of the cabin if needed, an indispensable safety feature. The hatch also has a combined sliding screen and light-blocking panel. Next to the berth is a cedar-lined hanging closet.

Engine

A large deck hatch comprising most of the cockpit raises high on an electric lift, taking the cockpit table (which lightly brushes against the upholstered transom seat back) up with it, providing open access to the twin engines.

Chaparral provides extra room forward of the engines, which makes maintenance a snap. The bilges are ground smooth and gelcoated for good visibility (it's easy to spot an oil leak in a white bilge) and easy cleanup. Wiring and plumbing are neatly run and securely fastened with chafe-resistant clamps. Chaparral's Web site lists 30 available Volvo Penta and MerCruiser engine packages, ranging from twin 190 hp to twin 320 hp engines with single or counterrotating (our preference) prop stern drives.

and the 310 Signature handled well in a turn. If you lose an engine, figure on an easy 9 to 10 mph get-home speed at 2,500 rpm on one engine.

Standing room at the helm is good, with plenty of room between the wheel and the seat. The fixed double helm seat is comfortable and easily accommodates two people. Dockside, the 310 handled well with the twin Bravo 3s providing responsive control. Visibility close aboard from the helm is good; it really helps to be able to see the swim platform when backing into a slip.

This boat is an excellent representative of the high-end express cruiser genre. The Chaparral

310 Signature fulfills its mission handily, providing a beautifully appointed, comfortable environment for family cruising and vacationing on the water. The boat is solidly built, using proven construction methods and materials, and quality components and accessories. The layout, from cockpit to cabin, has stood the test of time, and its innovations show that Chaparral produces boats that meet customer expectations.

We especially like the livability added by the cockpit's folding transom seat and the midcabin's accessibility and open feeling. Two conversation areas in the cabin and two more topside in the cockpit make this a livable boat for extended cruising. For a family of six, there's room to spread out and kick back. The appointments down below are upscale and pleasing aesthetically, while the finished surfaces should prove to be durable and easy to maintain. Chaparral is without question a master at delivering what its owners want.

Chaparral 310 Signature Performance Results

RPM	Speed, mph	Noise Level, dBA
650	4.1	64
1,000	5.6	72
1,500	8	77
2,000	9.4	81
2,500	10.9	84
3,000	18.4	84
3,500	28.9	85
4,000	36.1	88
4,500	41.3	90
4,750	44.7	91

Test conditions: Two passengers, fuel tank full, lightly loaded. Calm water.

FOUR WINNS 378 VISTA

GENMAR HOLDINGS, INC.

Four Winns 378 Vista Specifications

LOA:	41'3"
Beam:	12'9"
Deadrise:	19 deg.
Dry weight:	20,000 lb.
Cockpit depth:	28"
Draft:	42" (drive down)
Fuel capacity:	300 gal.

Part of Genmar, Four Winns builds bowriders, cuddies, deck boats, and express cruisers from 17 to 45 feet. Four Winns retained C. Raymond Hunt to design its three largest (as of this writing) express cruiser models, and it was a smart move, producing some of the best-running U.S.-made offshore cruisers in the industry. Four Winns also seems to be improving lately in product quality and eye appeal. The 378 (in production since 2002) benefits from Four Winns's competent styling and interior functionality, including the boat's ergonomic bridge deck and helm, intelligent use of space, great foredeck access, and elegant accommodations. And then there's the 378's solid value proposition.

Construction

The 378 is conventionally and solidly built. The fiberglass hull begins with a skin coat of vinylester resin sprayed on the gelcoat, followed by a 3-ounce layer of chopped strand mat (CSM) to ward off blistering. A DCPD blend follows in the rest of the laminate of CSM and 24-ounce woven roving. Hull sides and decks are cored with end-grain balsa for added stiffness at lighter weight. Stringers and bulkheads are pressure-treated plywood encapsulated in knitted fiberglass. The hull-to-deck joint is secured with self-tapping screws driven into a plywood backing strip and sealed with caulking.

Hull Design

The 378 has a modified-V hull. These hulls have proven themselves in many commercial and pleasure applications, and they are plainly superior to other express boats in headsea ride quality and dryness, seakindliness, low-speed planing ability,

and downsea tracking. A fine entry with high chines in the bow transitions to a modest 19 degrees of deadrise at the transom, producing a boat that is not only smooth-riding, but it stays on plane at 12 knots and has very little bow rise transitioning to planing speed. This makes for excellent visibility from the helm at all speeds, and it increases the cruising speed options available to the skipper; since the boat planes at such low speed, the engines can be throttled back in rough water without the boat digging a hole in the water all the way home.

Walkthrough

Cockpit

Getting around the 378 Vista is hassle-free. Boarding from the dock to the extra-large, full-beam swim platform, it's a small step up onto the cockpit. The transom door is 29 inches, which is a safe height with the toe kick under the door. Many of the 378s we've seen have the faux-teak (the look without the work) Flexiteek decking option aft, and it really sharpens up the boat's first impressions by giving it the look and feel of a high-end British or Italian cruiser. It's an option from the swim platform to the cockpit, and it gives the boat a little extra soul. A four-step ladder folds out of a storage pocket in the swim platform, projecting far enough underwater to make boarding easy on the arms. A separate swim platform locker provides wet storage.

A transom storage compartment provides plenty of room for line and fender storage, though it needs drains and vents added. To starboard in the transom a separate hatch raises to reveal twin shore power hookups, a freshwater connector, freshwater washdown, and TV and Internet connections. Large stern cleats leave plenty of docking options aft.

Through the transom door on port, the cockpit has an L-shaped lounge to starboard with a table that drops to form a base for a large sunpad. To port and opposite the lounge is a refreshment center with refrigerator, sink, garbage receptacle, and icemaker.

Helm

The helm station is forward and up a step on the bridge deck to starboard; the step improves visibility from the helm, and creates extra headroom in the midcabin directly below. At the helm, Four Winns provides room for chartplotters and radar to port on large console flats. There's also plenty of room for digital engine gauges in the event electronically controlled (EC) diesels are chosen to power the boat. The angled wheel and digital engine controls are comfortably positioned for seated or standing operation. An optional Raymarine navigation package includes a GPS plotter, radar, VHF radio, and autopilot. Outboard of the helm seat is a large storage bin, with additional storage found in lockers below the helm seat.

Foredeck

This boat has possibly the easiest and safest access forward of any boat in its class. It's up a few large molded steps and through the centerline-opening windshield to a nonskid-covered foredeck. Using the side decks, the walking surface at the gunwale is flat and 8 inches or more wide all the way from the cockpit to the bow. The 25-inch bow railing starts well aft, so there's something to lean against all the way forward.

In the bow, the anchor windlass is mounted in a recessed overboard-draining tub that gives the foredeck a clean look, providing a clear working surface for line handlers dockside, and protecting the ground tackle from the elements. The anchor pulpit is integral to the hull, also contributing to the clean lines forward. There are a pair of 10-inch bow cleats and an 8-inch anchor cleat inside a recessed windlass compartment. A second set of 10-inch spring cleats is farther aft.

Cabin

After the hull design and rough-water ride, the cabin may be the crowning glory of the 378. It's beautifully finished in synthetic cherry veneer and real wood trim, it's wide open from anchor locker to engine room bulkhead, and it's comfortably livable with a family-friendly layout. There's storage everywhere, from large bins and lockers in the mid-cabin aft, to the hanging locker and under-berth storage in the forward stateroom.

The cabin gets its decidedly upscale look from that cherry finish, as well as the thick upholstery and sculpted headliners throughout. A 16,000 Btu air-conditioning system is standard, as is a central vacuum system, and a convertible couch in the mid-cabin. Structurally, the cabin is built on a one-piece liner bonded to the hull stringer system, which makes for a more consistent structure and better-fitting components than a stick-built cabin would offer, and it contributes substantially to hull strength and rigidity. Note that the 378 is a big boat to have the single-piece cabin liner (not many builders do it because the mold takes up so much floor space), but it's certainly to the owner's advantage.

There are two staterooms and one head. The forward stateroom with its hanging locker, under-berth storage, and private head access can either be enclosed with a solid bulkhead as an option, or it can be left open to the saloon with a soft partition for privacy. The head with its separate shower and VacuFlush toilet is forward to port; the separate shower bears expanding on: its folding Lexan door is easy to open and close, and it provides a splash-proof seal between it and the head compartment. There's even a molded shower seat with adjustable height and a pulsating showerhead.

The galley is to port near the companionway. It includes a pair of refrigerators (one of them can be replaced by an icemaker), coffeemaker, microwave, two-burner stove, and an L-shaped countertop with lots of storage space for extended cruises. Opposite the galley is a lounge with easily accessible storage space below. Aft, under the bridge deck and helm area, is a second lounge area, with hanging locker and central vacuum system, that converts to a second stateroom with a pullout berth for two. The settee converts to a double bed with the touch of a button, with the seat back lowering and flattening to double the width of the settee.

Three 19-inch-diameter translucent hatches overhead in the cabin provide light and fresh air, as do hull side ports. The forward-opening hatch also doubles as an emergency exit route, since it's an easy step up and out from the forward berth.

Engine

There are a variety of power options on the Four Winns, including gas or diesel V-drive inboards and Volvo's IPS system. Whatever power is selected, Four Winns makes it easy to do daily maintenance checks with a centerline power hatch providing access to the engine room. In the event engine change out is needed, the whole cockpit deck lifts clear; this is a feature we'd definitely look for on any inboard boat, as having to cut out decks or even hull sides to change out the engines is expensive and time-consuming.

With gas power, a 7.3 kW genset is standard, while diesel power includes an 8 kW unit. Four batteries, two bilge pumps, a fixed fire-extinguishing system, and remote engine oil filters for easy accessibility are included. Fuel capacity totals 300 gallons in two aluminum saddle tanks. Dripless shaft seals keep the bilge dry and corrosive salt air to a minimum.

Four Winns' battery management system is also worth mentioning: it features separate ship's systems and engine start circuits. Just turn on the three switches and go boating, and then turn them off when you leave the boat. The system ensures the boat always has DC power.

Sea Trial

Our test boat was powered by twin Volvo Penta 8.1-liter, big-block gas engines. Handling dockside was crisp and precise, with the 2.5:1 ZF gears and 21 by 24 three-blade Acme props providing plenty of bite maneuvering around the marina. Shaft angle is modest, and for this boat, appropriate at 12 degrees; shallower shaft angles like this produce thrust more efficiently.

The boat's Teleflex electronic engine controls worked smoothly, including a synchronization feature that shifts and throttles the engines simultaneously using a single lever. Neutral detents provide plenty of sensory indication of when the engines are shifting.

When accelerating briskly, the bow rose slightly and quickly settled in at a modest running angle of 4 degrees. Using full tabs speeds up the on-plane time by a second or two, and also lessens engine load (and improves hull speed) when running at low planing speeds of 14 to 15 knots at 2,800 rpm (at which speed the 378 is getting about 0.8 nmpg). The boat actually gets better fuel economy at 3,500 rpm, 0.9 nmpg, so consider this to be a 21-knot cruise boat with the gas Volvos.

Visibility all around the helm was excellent, and the horizon was in sight even while coming up on plane. For this 15- to 21-knot cruise boat, the manual hydraulic steering's responsiveness was quite acceptable at a low-effort 4.7 turns lock-to-lock. The low steering effort at this ratio indicates well-balanced rudders. With the rudders hard over, a full 360-degree turn took just 30 seconds with the engines running at 2,800 rpm before starting the turn; this seems to be evidence that rudders are properly sized for the boat, and that they probably turn as hard over as they should, about 35 degrees to either side. In get-home mode with one engine running at 2,000 rpm, the boat made 7.6 knots with one full turn of the wheel into the running engine holding our course, so the boat could be turned in the direction of the running engine very easily, which is of course essential.

The standard trim tabs did a good job dropping the bow and compensating for list and heel. At the marina, the boat backed predictably and under complete control into its slip, with visibility close-aboard as good astern and abeam as it was ahead from the helm.

Four Winns 378 Vista Performance Results

RPM	Speed, knots	Noise Level, dBA (at helm)
1,000	4.9	69
1,500	6.7	73
2,000	8.7	77
2,500	11.5	81
3,000	15.4	84
3,500	21.2	88
4,000	25.1	90
4,400	26.3	92

Test conditions: Three passengers, a dog, fuel tank three quarters full, water tank half full, with twin 375 hp Volvo 8.1-liter inboard V-drives with 2.5:1 ZF gears driving 21 by 24 pitch props. Lightly loaded.

The Four Winns 378 is arguably (and demonstrably) one of the best sea boats in its class. It rides and handles exceptionally well and has a comfortable motion. It also has a livable layout with intelligently arranged accommodations, and it represents uncommon value. If you are stretching financially to buy the boat, and don't put hundreds of hours on the boat every year, the gas V-drive engines may be the way to go.

Just keep in mind that this is a lot of boat (over 20,000 pounds) for a pair of gas engines to handle. The diesel V-drives will cruise the 378 at 25 knots while burning a lot less fuel than the gas engines. Though you'll pay $50,000 to $70,000 more for the diesel option, you'll also get much of that back when you sell the boat. We'd very much like to see the Volvo IPS or Cummins-MerCruiser Diesel (CMD) Zeus drives in this boat, as continuous cruise speed, economy, noise levels, and maneuverability would also improve substantially.

Options include a bow thruster (not needed with IPS with joystick controls), colored hull, satellite TV, a solid bulkhead providing privacy for the forward stateroom, a freezer replacing one of the galley fridges, a cockpit cover, Flexiteek swim platform, and cockpit covering. Though it reportedly gets pretty warm underfoot in the sun, the Flexiteek looks a lot like the real thing, and it is easy to keep up (unlike real teak). Power options include MerCruiser and Volvo gas V-drives, Cat and Volvo diesel V-drives, and Volvo diesel IPS.

REGAL 2860 WINDOW EXPRESS

REGAL

Regal builds a wide range of well-regarded, well-built, and good-riding open- and closed-bow runabouts, express cruisers, and flybridge yachts from below 20 to over 50 feet. A large Orlando, Florida–based, family-owned, high-volume production boatbuilder, Regal has also developed a dealer network that is a big part of the brand's success, and perhaps part of the reason for its being the only manufacturer to receive two different J.D. Power and Associates awards for highest customer satisfaction in the same year (2007, small runabouts and express cruisers). A second generation of the Kuck family now runs the company, which is steadily expanding its offerings in the large yacht category.

Regal knows its market well, and has been a leader in the welcome trend to add more light and fresh air inside its boats. Put a circle around a picture of a cave with a slash through it, and that could be Regal's motto, given the way it has been developing its Window Express series of cruisers.

This sort of highly visible innovation is present in its smaller boats as well, though sometimes in some not-so-visible ways, as we'll discuss in this review.

One of Regal's newest express cruisers, the 2860 Window Express, in production since 2005, signals Regal's focus on creating airy and bright cabins. Most express cruiser cabins have only a few small windows since it's faster and therefore cheaper to build a boat with little glass, and older-style windows can leak. One look through the 2860 will convince any buyer that Regal's approach, using fixed zero-maintenance, leak-free frameless glass is preferred, as it results in a much cheerier and hospitable cabin that's a pleasure to live in.

Construction

Those of you who enjoy fiberglass construction tech-speak will appreciate this construction section, which is more technical than most. Regal puts a lot of extra effort into getting it right and we want to share the news with you.

The Regal 2860's construction starts off with gelcoat and a 1-inch coat of specially formulated epoxy blister barrier on the bottom and up to 6 inches above the waterline. A skin coat of 2-ounce fiberglass chop wet out in a low profile (which means there's very little shrinkage from the exotherm and curing process) isophthalic polyester resin follows as print-through prevention.

Next comes a layer of 1708 45/45 biaxial in the strakes, a poly filler to round out the strakes' corners, and then three layers of 2415 fiberglass reinforcement in the hull bottom, with an extra layer at the bottom steps and under the engine beds.

The hull sides get a 1⅕-inch coat of ceramic print barrier, 3 ounces of chop, and a layer of 24-ounce woven roving. The transom is cored with a 20-pound high-density, 1½-inch-thick PVC composite that includes glass fibers for added strength, with Trevera stop-print used to bed the coring to the outer skin, with a final inner layer of 2415 reinforcement completing the composite sandwich. The result is a transom that can't rot (unlike plywood-cored construction), resists the outboard or stern-drive bolt compression loads, and is strong and stiff. Bulkheads are ¾-inch pressure-treated plywood with balsa cant strips along the hull sides to spread out the load, preventing point loading and hull skin distortion.

The 2860 has a one-piece fiberglass stringer grid that's tabbed to the hull with two layers of 2415. The cabin has a full liner that is bonded to the grid below with polyester putty and that is fiberglassed to the hull sides along its top perimeter. The cabin subassemblies follow, including the head and galley units, which are fiberglassed to the hull and become part of the load-transmitting structure of the boat.

The cockpit is made of a one-piece fiberglass liner, with Nida-Core used to core the deck. Nida-Core is expensive, a lot more so than balsa, but it can't rot, water won't migrate through the core, has superior sound-dampening qualities, and it's lighter than other cores. Hatches are all made using Coosa coring and a closed-molded resin transfer molding (RTM) process, which produces parts that are finished on both sides with smooth tooled surfaces.

Hull Design

The Regal has a modified-V bottom with reverse chines, spray rails, and a fine entry (for a cruiser) that delivers a smooth, dry ride in a chop. The hull's running surface extends aft on either side of the lower units, which is almost certainly an advantage, helping with acceleration (by adding dynamic lift and buoyancy aft where you need it when climbing on plane) and minimizing bow rise on plane with all that iron (and weight) aft in the engine room.

Walkthrough

Cockpit and Topsides

Passengers board the Regal 2860 from the large swim platform with its built-in boarding ladder leading over the side instead of over the stern—this adds a welcome element of safety, as it puts the swimmer a bit farther away from the four stainless steel props below.

There are two sets of stern cleats, aft on the platform and up on the hull gunwales, so there's plenty of flexibility when it comes to docking. A large transom door hinges up for access to a fender and line storage locker, and a hot-and-cold transom

shower is provided. From the platform, it's up two steps and through the pipe-framed transom door to the cockpit.

The convertible cockpit has a foldaway seat aft at the transom, as well as a table that seats four. The foldaway seat is a great feature as it lets circumstances drive how the cockpit will be used, rather than letting a fixed furniture layout limit a family's options. With the transom seat tucked out of sight, this could be a staging area for boarding or tubing, or it'll even serve as a fishing cockpit in a pinch. Facing the transom seat and forward of the removable table is another seat with a reversible seat back, so you can face aft seated in the cockpit or forward from the bridge deck. To starboard is a wet bar with sink, optional refrigerator, and portable cooler, and the battery switch is easy to access, facing aft below the bridge deck's reversible seat. The fiberglass radar arch holds the stereo speakers for optimal sound quality under way.

Helm

Just forward in the cockpit, or bridge deck, is an L-shaped lounge to port. What's clever about this seat is the reversing seat back, which lets you face aft or forward. Opposite is the pedestal helm seat, thickly padded and upholstered, with a flip-up bolster for added standing room at the wheel. The helm's steering wheel and engine controls are perfectly positioned for seated or standing operation, placed at just the right height and angle.

In addition to the instrumentation, the nonglare dash with its light brown gelcoat finish makes things easy on the eyes in bright sunlight. Nice touches include the stereo controls built into the steering wheel, the spotlight remote control, and tilt steering. There's also an electronics flat to port with room for a chartplotter-radar unit. Full canvas is standard, including a bimini top, cockpit camper canvas with bimini extension, and bimini plastic side filler windows.

Foredeck

Molded steps lead up to the foredeck through the opening windshield. The great thing about this foredeck design, incorporating as it does a trunk cabin, is the complete lack of a ski slope effect. You pretty much walk forward on a terraced deck to the pulpit, which makes for a much safer environment than usually found on an express cruiser of this size.

Our test boat had three bow cleats, including one for tying off the anchor line. A triangular hatch leads to the anchor locker, and the anchor windlass in flush-mounted on deck.

There are a number of noteworthy cabin features on the 2860. First is the openness of the midcabin stateroom—it's wide open to the main

cabin, making it much more inviting. No need to worry about feeling confined or cramped.

Next is the cabin's floor plan—it includes a U-shaped lounge forward with a drop-down table that converts the seating area to a berth. This design, which lacks a dinette with facing seats, is commonly seen on trailerable (8-foot, 6-inch beam) boats. The effect in this cabin, with its additional full foot of beam, is to create a roomy, uncrowded, and open feel with more deck space. This space is further enhanced by all the sunlight that streams in through the large forward-facing windows at the bow end of the trunk cabin above, as well as the long side windows. The boat also has the conventional opening ports in the hull seen in many similar cruisers. But it's the overhead glass that makes the difference. Last but not least is the cherry laminate that gives the boat an attractively upscale look and feel.

The enclosed head is at the foot of the companionway stairs; it has an opening port window, full-length mirror on the door, sink with storage below, and a VacuFlush toilet on a raised platform. The molded fiberglass head unit will prove easy to keep clean. The galley is opposite to starboard, equipped with a Corian countertop for good looks and easy cleanup, microwave, stainless steel sink, electric stove, concealed trash can, and a refrigerator. The AC-DC electrical panel is easy to reach and read, positioned fairly high off the deck next to the galley. An AM-FM-CD stereo is standard.

The forward dinette converts to a berth, while the midcabin aft has a queen-size mattress. Cedar-lined lockers provide hanging storage for a weekend on the water.

Engine

Engine accessibility is good on the 2860; the entire aft cockpit deck, including the transom and aft seat, rises high on a single boost for excellent access from the swim platform. You can still get on the boat along the starboard side with the hatch raised, and this arrangement, with the hinge forward, allows engine work to be done from the swim platform, rather than from inside the boat. It's nice to be able to keep things clean inside the boat. Deep gutters surround the deck hatch, directing any water overboard through drain lines, and a thick gasket around the hatch perimeter helps seal in engine noise. Twin stern drives power the Regal 2860, with Volvo Penta and MerCruiser gas options to 225 hp and Volvo D3 160 hp diesels also available.

Sea Trial

The light Lake George chop wasn't much of a challenge for the 2860, but the few waves and wakes we crossed of any significance hinted at a very smooth-riding hull design. Coming up on plane, even when sitting down and not using the trim tabs, we didn't lose sight of the horizon. Visibility all around was excellent and handling was nimble with the MerCruiser's quick-acting power steering.

With the helm seat's flip-up bolster, there's plenty of room to stand at the helm. This is important, and yet it's often overlooked, in spite of the need to stand to dock the boat and see what's going on in close proximity. The throttle, as mentioned, is very well positioned for comfortable operation, both by height and fore-and-aft position, and also by the angle from horizontal. The wiper switch, one of the controls most likely to be used underway, is well positioned to the right.

The boat was on plane at 15 mph, and running bow-down and comfortably on top at a moderate 2,800 rpm for just over 20 mph. Engine noise was exceptionally low; we registered just 79 dBA at 3,000 rpm, and 80 dBA at a fast 3,500 rpm cruise, which makes for a much more pleasant and relaxing cruising environment than a louder boat. Worth noting is that the radar arch, while made out of fiberglass and not metal pipe, is fairly narrow and therefore not much of an impediment to visibility aft to port, as is the case with many similar boats. The standard

There is a lot of equipment in the engine room, but it still does not seem crowded, with plenty of room for maintenance forward of the engines. Wiring is neatly loomed for protection and color-coded for easier tracing, and plumbing is likewise neatly installed.

trim tabs are responsive, adjusting trim decisively as well as correcting easily for list and heel.

Regal 2860 Window Express Performance Results

RPM	Speed, mph	Noise Level, dBA
600	3.6	66
1,000	5.3	68
1,500	7.8	72
2,000	9.3	77
2,500	14.6	78
2,800	21.4	78
3,000	25.2	79
3,500	30.6	80
4,000	37.1	82
4,600	43.4	86

Test conditions: Two passengers, fuel tank half full, with 220 hp 4.3L MerCruiser.

The Regal 2860 is a well-built cruiser and one of my personal favorites. A welcoming, bright, and cheery cabin; a versatile family-friendly cockpit; an accessible foredeck; and a great ride are all pluses in its favor. With its excellent manners in a chop, and its many other strengths, we can recommend it without hesitation.

Express Sportfishermen

These are mostly open sportfishing boats that look a lot like express cruisers at first glance, but the emphasis is on cockpit size, outfitting, and overall fishability. Since the cockpit must be within a foot or so of the water for landing gamefish, the engine room is situated below the bridge deck, which reduces the amount of room available for accommodations. While they do have a raised bridge deck and tall windshield (taller than on the average styling-driven express cruiser), most of these boats also have hardtops, full plastic enclosures, and at least half-towers, so they're not so open after all.

The layout typical of express sportfishermen has found favor with the cruising couple weary of hiring a crew for their bigger yacht, and with owners of large outboards moving up. The captain is just a few steps from the cockpit, can see well enough form the elevated bridge deck to catch fish, and there's always the tower when visibility isn't quite good enough from the main helm station. Older couples can easily handle the open layout, with no bridge stairs to climb. Some open sportfishermen are based on manufacturers' existing convertible models (Viking, Ocean, and Bertram, for instance), only with the deck house and flybridge removed. Removing this topside weight, as with the express cruiser, makes the boat faster and more seaworthy. The bigger open sportfishermen are anything but day boats. Some of the 50-footers sport two-stateroom, two-head cabins, complete with a saloon and fully equipped galley.

Bertram started it all in the offshore racing world in the early 1960s, with Dick Bertram winning the Miami-to-Nassau race in a Ray Hunt deep-V hull. Today Bertram is part of the Italian conglomerate Ferretti, and builds mostly convertibles from 41 to 67 feet. The 360 Express is a good-riding offshore boat available with up to twin 600 hp Cummins diesels (that's a lot of power for a 36). Both Open and Express models are available, with the Open being the fishing version and the Express for cruising. Bertram's interior appointments have come a long way from the early days, with fine cherry woodwork and upscale upholstery below.   BERTRAM YACHTS

A relatively new company started in 1991, Cabo quickly established a reputation for solid engineering and showcase engine rooms, but its early 31- and 35-foot express boats were as hard-riding in a head sea as they were well-built, with full, flat forefoots. The company, recently purchased by Brunswick, has brought in Michael Peters to design its new models, and the results have been dramatic, steadily transforming the Cabo lineup (like the 52 shown) into great-running boats whose ride matches their top-shelf engineering. Today the Cabo lineup includes express and flybridge convertible models from 31 to 52 feet. The 52 has a two-stateroom, one-and-a-half head cabin. Power options up to twin 1,550 hp include MAN, MTU, and Cat.   CABO YACHTS

Century builds Yamaha-powered center consoles, walkarounds, dual consoles, bay boats, and the 3200 Offshore. A good-running boat in a chop with comfortable overnight accommodations in a pleasant cabin, and a highly fishable cockpit, the 3200, shown here with a pair of Yamaha 350s, is based on the same hull form as Century's 32-foot walkaround and center console models, with the express marketed as a family boat that fishes. CENTURY BOATS

Grady-White builds a range of hard-core (center console) and family (walkaround, dual console, and express) fishing boats from 20 to 36 feet. These Yamaha-powered, C. Raymond Hunt–designed boats have an excellent ride and they're ruggedly built. Grady is regularly ranked highest in customer satisfaction in the annual J.D. Power and Associates study within the coastal fishing segment. The 330 Express takes up to 600 hp, sleeps four in a roomy upscale cabin, and has a centerline helm for a good all-around view.

GRADY-WHITE BOATS

Fountain is well-known for its 100 mph plus offshore racing boats, but it also puts out a series of fishing boats, presumably aimed at the guy who wants to get there (whether that's to the fish or back to the dock) first. The fish boats range from 23 to 38 feet, and in fact Fountain offers five different 38-footers, including one twin 425 hp MerCruiser stern-drive-powered model (the rest are outboards, all powered with triple Mercury Verado 275s). The 38 Sportfish Cruiser Outboard shown here is one of those 38s, running to over 65 mph (or 52 mph on two engines), according to the builder. There are sleeping accommodations for four in the lacquered cherry cabin, the helm is on centerline so the captain will always have someone to talk to, and the cockpit is fully outfitted for tournament fishing. FOUNTAIN POWERBOATS

Luhrs builds express, hardtop, and flybridge sportfishing boats from 28 to 41 feet. Solidly engineered and moderately priced, these boats deliver when it comes to taking their passengers offshore for a day's fishing. The 28 Hardtop has an express boat windshield with a freestanding hardtop, with plastic side curtains used to fill in the gaps as needed; a tower is optional. The cabin sleeps up to four, and has a full galley and enclosed head. A sharp entry helps produce a good ride in a seaway, and twin gas or diesel inboard power is available. LUHRS CORPORATION

Pursuit builds high-end, smooth-riding Yamaha outboard–powered center console and express family fishing boats from 23 to 34 feet. A well-proportioned boat, the 345 Drummond Runner has comfortable accommodations that sleep a couple on a V-berth forward, along with a full galley and enclosed head with shower. Visibility from the centerline helm through the large full-height windshield is excellent. Standard power is twin 250 hp Yamaha four-stroke outboards that push the boat to about 42 knots at wide-open throttle.   PURSUIT BOATS

Tiara builds a single 29-foot Coronet model (shown), which has a smaller cabin and a larger cockpit for the LOA compared to Tiara's Open models. The cabin is suitable for an occasional overnight, but this is primarily a big day boat with a little added versatility built in. Three Crusader gas inboard packages are offered.   TIARA YACHTS

Sea Ray builds a wide range of family cruisers, but they also put out a limited number of 25-, 27-, and 29-foot express cruisers that fish called the Amberjack series. These boats basically have the accommodations of a Sea Ray Sundancer, but the cockpit is set up for fishing. Fishing gear includes rocket launchers on the aluminum arch, rod holders in the gunwales, bait prep station, livewell, and a raw-water washdown in the cockpit. This stern-drive-powered 290 Amberjack makes fishing over the stern a lot easier than it is on an outboard. A good compromise between a hard-core fishing boat and a family cruiser, the Amberjack is worth investigating if a wide range of activities afloat is on your agenda.   SEA RAY BOATS

Viking is a leader in large high-end sportfishing and cruising yachts to 82 feet, and it has secured its position and reputation through over forty years of consistent family ownership and management. Most of its boats are well-engineered tournament fishing convertibles, but its few open express models include this 52-footer. Based on the 52 convertible's hull, the cockpit includes a mezzanine, or raised seating area just forward of the cockpit, a lot like the 70- and 80-footers have. The cabin has two staterooms and heads while the bridge deck has three tall pedestal chairs for a great view of the proceedings. MAN common rail inboard diesel power to 1,360 hp is available.   VIKING YACHTS

Wellcraft builds a wide range of outboard-powered hard-core and family fishing boats. It also has a line of Coastal express fishing boats, the largest ones having inboard power. The 360 is the largest Wellcraft, and it has a C. Raymond Hunt hull that delivers an exceptionally smooth and dry ride in the rough weather these boats are likely to encounter offshore. The cabin takes Wellcraft to new levels of fit and finish, with a yacht interior that sleeps four. Several diesel inboard options are available. GENMAR HOLDINGS, INC.

SPENCER 43 EXPRESS

SPENCER YACHTS

Spencer 43 Express Specifications

LOA:	43'0" (hull)
Beam:	14'6"
Deadrise:	12 deg.
Dry weight:	25,000 lb.
Cockpit depth:	26"
Draft:	not available
Fuel capacity:	660 gal.
Water capacity:	100 gal.

Spencer Yachts is a large, custom builder of fast, high-end sportfishing boats based in Wanchese, North Carolina. The builder specializes in one-off cold-molded boats, known for their lighter weight and great strength, as well as structural Core-Cell hulls like the 43 Express.

Spencer built 50 boats in its first ten years and is now launching 6 to 9 boats a year. In production since 2006, the Spencer 43 Express is the builder's smallest boat. The next biggest one is a 54-footer, and the largest model is a 76. The company's bread and butter is its 60- and 66-footers, and as of this writing Spencer has an 84-footer on the drawing board.

The Spencer 43 Express is a conventional low-profile express-style sportfish layout, with the boat divided into three areas—a cabin forward, a bridge deck amidships, and a large cockpit in the stern. Compared to a convertible, the express is lighter (and faster) since it doesn't carry several thousand pounds of deckhouse and flybridge. It also has a lower center of gravity, which makes it more seaworthy, though it lacks the added climate-controlled accommodations of the convertible's saloon.

The 43 was a venture into something new and different for the builder, initiated when Volvo Penta approached Paul Spencer about his potential interest in the new Volvo Penta IPS propulsion system. The more Spencer learned about the idea, the more Volvo Penta IPS power intrigued him. The tournament sportfishing market is very conservative, so no matter the strengths or the merits, the only obstacle remaining is market acceptance.

Once Spencer had the Volvo Penta IPS drawings and knew that it would fit under a cockpit, he knew he could make the IPS work. Moving the engines aft moves the boat's center of gravity aft too, and the faster a boat can go, the farther aft CG should be for both optimum ride quality and open-ocean handling.

With the engines aft, room was opened forward for the fuel tanks, where the engine room would ordinarily go. This allowed the variable liquid load (the fuel tanks) to be placed just forward of the hull's center of buoyancy, which lets the boat rise slightly bow-first as fuel is burned, which is also ideal for ride and handling. Spencer also quickly saw that it could put this amidships space to good use as a midcabin, adding a comfortable two-berth stateroom to the boat's accommodations. In fact, each of the midcabin's beds is built around a 330-gallon fiberglass fuel tank.

With no weight-and-balance downside to Volvo Penta IPS, and with several positive design improvements, the final element was low-speed handling. Sportfishing boats have to maneuver and back down on a fish, reacting quickly while stripping a reel or suddenly heading off in a different direction. Volvo Penta IPS already had its joystick-maneuvering mode, designed to allow a boat to be handled precisely and easily dockside. But the joystick mode couldn't maneuver the boat quickly enough for tournament fishing, so working with Spencer, Volvo Penta came up with a maneuvering mode specifically for sportfishing boats, discussed below.

Construction

Spencer was a good choice for Volvo Penta since it's one of the few production boat companies that builds boats of modest displacement; many production boats of this size are 5,000 to 10,000 pounds heavier. The Spencer 43 is built using 1-inch high-density Core-Cell foam that's laid up over an inverted male mold, and then fiberglassed with two layers of 3408 on the outside. Epoxy resin is used exclusively throughout the boat's construction, including the hull and all deck parts. The hull is lifted off the mold, turned right-side-up, and then fiberglassed with two more layers of 3408 on the inside. Hull stringers of Core-Cell foam encapsulated in fiberglass and Core-Cell-cored bulkheads are installed, followed by the engines and auxiliary machinery and equipment.

Large flat cored-composite panels such as the bulkheads are laid up on a vacuum table (the vacuum bagging ensures a high-integrity bond between the core and the outer skin of fiberglass, an interface that's subject to high sheer stress loading) and cut to shape, resulting in an efficiently produced and strong lightweight part. The hull-to-deck joint is fiberglassed together for the length of the boat, producing, in effect, a monocoque load-sharing hull-deck structure. The all-foam-core hull construction, along with the use of high-strength epoxy resin, explains why Spencer can build a 43-footer that only weighs 25,000 pounds dry.

Foredeck and deck carlines are built like a wooden boat, with laminated fir plywood athwartship deck beams supporting the deck. The deck is ½-inch okoume plywood with an epoxy-saturated skin of fiberglass on the outside. The cabin's composite sole is bonded to the hull stringers, the cabin components built and installed, and the bridge deck, cockpit, and foredeck constructed. The bridge part, which includes the deckhouse, helm console, and forward seating area, is resin-infused, using a mold from a larger Spencer flybridge boat. This construction process produces a strong and lightweight part, and the same process is used to construct the fish box.

Hull Design

The Spencer 43 has a modified-V, hard-chine planing hull with reverse chines and 12 degrees of deadrise at the transom. The hull has a fine entry for a smooth headsea ride and a moderate chine beam of 12 feet, 5 inches, which further contributes to good ride quality and propulsion efficiency. Paul Spencer's hull design philosophy has always been to make the boat longer if more room is needed, not just wider, and this approach—staying with a moderate beam-to-length ratio—is what accounts for his boats' superior ride. The Spencer 43 prototype was designed for conventional power, and with the IPS weight centered farther aft, the hull will run better (at a flatter trim angle) with less rocker (upswept buttocks) aft, which is how the next hull will be designed.

Walkthrough

Cockpit

The Spencer's roomy teak cockpit, 8 feet, 5 inches long, 10 feet, 5 inches wide, and 28 inches high on centerline with deep toe kick space, is cleanly laid out and well-equipped for tournament fishing. Standard equipment includes a Release Marine fighting chair and an Eskimo icemaker. There's a big transom storage area or fish box, as well as a pair of insulated fish or storage boxes.

Four rod holders are provided in the teak covering boards, which create a good toe kick around the cockpit perimeter. Plugs for the two 24-volt teaser reels are easily accessible under the covering boards. Fresh- and saltwater washdowns help keep the area clean, and large corner-mounted scuppers rapidly drain water overboard. A connection is provided for dockside fresh water, along with a house pressure valve. Stern cleats lead through corner-mounted hawsepipes in the covering boards.

Considering the importance of working a fish close to the boat, one of the design criteria for any serious sportfishing boat is cockpit deck height and hull freeboard at the stern. The Spencer 43's freeboard at the stern measures 42 inches off the water, which with an interior cockpit height of 26 inches puts the deck 16 inches off the water. Paul Spencer finds that putting the deck any closer to the waterline results in wet feet when fishing, and in fact the 43's freeboard and deck height were drawn into the boat before he decided to use IPS power.

This is worth mentioning since although the Spencer 43's engine room is beneath the cockpit, the builder did not have to raise the deck to accommodate the D6 Volvos. This is due to the adequate depth of a 12-degree deadrise hull of this beam, and the low profile of these compact, 31-inch-high 435 hp diesels that are 7 to 8 inches lower in profile than the 600 hp traditional (non-IPS) diesels it would take to produce the same performance. For a boat buyer who wants a cockpit lower to the water, there is the option of locating the engines farther forward below the bridge deck or saloon, and connecting them via jackshaft to the IPS pods. You lose the midcabin, but keep the efficiency and smooth, quiet running of IPS.

Foredeck

The foredeck is tournament fisherman minimalist in design, with a pair of side cleats at the forward end of the deckhouse, a single Bomar hatch providing sunlight and fresh air to the cabin below, and an anchor locker and a pair of bow cleats forward. There is no bow railing, as is the custom with most southern-waters sportfishing boats, though you could order one as an option. The anchor locker includes a freshwater washdown.

Bridge Deck

The open bridge deck, up three steps from the cockpit, affords a good all-around view of the horizon. The centerline helm is laid out in standard sportfisherman style, with Palm Beach single-lever engine controls (one on either side of the helm pod) designed for intuitive backing control when working a fish while facing aft. Two large-screen electronics displays are positioned on either side of the engine monitoring and control panels, and a compass is perched atop the console where it's easy to read.

We'd like to see another foot or so of room between the aft railing and the helm seat to make it easier to move around and get to the port pedestal companion seat. This is one of the areas that Spencer is looking at before developing final tooling for this model. Plastic side curtains are clear as glass and easy to see through. Forward of the helm is a separate seating area, and there's storage space below the molded lounge seating. The boat's optional Pipe Welders tower with its center outrigger is a good addition.

Cabin

Through the sliding companionway door to starboard, a curved, six-step varnished teak staircase leading down to the cabin creates a positive first impression of Spencer's woodworking craftsmanship. In addition to the open companionway, there's a single overhead hatch to let in daylight, since, like most hard-core sportfishing boats, there are no hull portlights. The neutral colors down below help brighten things up and make the attractively finished space seem large and accommodating.

A dinette sofa along the hull with storage below is immediately to starboard, and at 6 feet long it doubles as a small single bed. A highlight here is a beautifully finished teak and holly–inlaid table by the sofa. The galley is opposite to port and it's well-equipped with countertop lighting for good visibility, a 5-foot Corian countertop, a big deep sink, refrigerator, microwave, two-burner cooktop, and ample storage provided in drawers and cabinets.

Now we come to another area that Volvo Penta IPS makes possible in this layout—a midcabin right where you'd ordinarily expect to find a pair of hulking diesels. A centerline door in the cabin's aft bulkhead leads to a stateroom with high, amply proportioned berths to port and starboard measuring 6 feet, 5 inches in length and 3 feet, 5 inches in width. These berths are perched atop the two 330-gallon fuel tanks, placed just forward of the hull's center of buoyancy, so the bow rises very slightly as fuel is consumed, which is every naval architect's goal with a high-performance planing hull.

Since the stateroom is below the bridge deck, headroom is only 5 feet, 5 inches, but that hardly matters given the advantage of having this bonus room in the first place, which doubles the yacht's sleeping accommodations. Cedar-lined lockers are provided, and there's rod storage above the berths along the hull. Spencer includes a pass-through door for the rods directly from the cockpit.

A hatch opens to a large dry storage compartment in the bilge, and the surfaces are ground smooth and painted white for good visibility and easy cleanup. A 12,000 Btu air conditioner keeps things cool down below in the tropical climes this boat was built for.

Engine

With the engine room beneath the cockpit, the whole cockpit deck lifts electrically and hinges up to provide good access to the machinery below. The twin low-profile Volvo Penta D6 diesels and Volvo Penta IPS pod drives fit neatly in the engine room, leaving plenty of room to get around the engines for maintenance. There is just a short jackshaft connecting the engines to the pods, so space requirements for this propulsion system are minimized.

Since the engines don't absorb any of the propeller thrust, they can be soft-mounted to further reduce vibration throughout the vessel. This is on top of the fact that the engines are smooth-running to begin with since their sequential fuel injection common rail design minimizes noise and vibration. The engine room is uncluttered, in fact, and the smooth bilges, finished in white gelcoat, present an attractive and easily maintained working surface. Wiring and plumbing runs are neatly installed and carefully labeled.

Sea Trial

We had a 1- to 2-foot chop on top of a 3-foot swell on our test ride off Miami's Government Cut. The conditions were not much of a challenge for this 43-footer, but enough of a sea was running to confirm the boat's excellent hull design and handling capabilities. Paul Spencer has designed a hull that runs smoothly up sea and tracks well, with little helm correction downsea.

This was hull number one for the 43-foot Express series, and we had to use tabs to keep the bow down at cruise speed. This is a common issue with Volvo Penta IPS. That's because the horizontal thrust (compared to the conventional inboard's 8 to 12 degrees of shaft angle) is not only more efficient, it also tends to increase the vessel's running angle, as does shifting the weight of the engines aft in the hull, particularly when the boat is accelerating up on plane. The builder has since modified the bottom and the trim is now dialed in.

Tricks like adding a little hook in the buttocks aft, or keeping some warp in the bottom (with the chines essentially running slightly downhill all the way aft) to increase lift at the stern, are commonly used to good effect. With tabs down, the boat ran fine, but Spencer will have the next hull running at a flatter trim without using tabs, just as other builders using this new propulsion system have done and are doing.

The big story with this boat is its performance with Volvo Penta IPS, and that includes efficiency on plane at cruise, a good turn of speed with modest horsepower and fuel burn, and superb handling while working a fish. Regarding efficiency and range, just consider for a moment that this is a 43-foot boat that will cruise all day long at over 30 knots and hit nearly 36 knots with a pair of 435 hp diesels. We've seen similar-sized express fishing boats with 600 hp diesels that don't go this fast, and can point to at least one twin 800 hp 40-footer that actually burns twice the fuel (over 80 gph) and goes half a knot slower.

Volvo Penta already had two basic underway modes for its Volvo Penta IPS system. The first is the conventional mode using the steering wheel and the electronic engine controls to shift the transmissions and vary engine rpm. The second is joystick mode, which uses a single lever (the joystick) to steer and control the thrust of the pod drives independently of each other. The joystick allows the operator to move the boat sideways by pushing the stick sideways, twist the boat by twisting the joystick,

go astern by nudging the joystick aft, and so on, with some tweaking required depending on wind and sea conditions. Using joystick mode, the boat twisted 360 degrees in 20 seconds, which is about the same amount of time it takes a conventional inboard to twist using opposed engines and hard rudder. (See more on the Volvo Penta IPS on page 146.)

The third maneuvering mode, developed specifically for the Spencer 43, is a fishing mode. The Palm Beach engine controls are used as on any other boat, but with very different results. First of all the boat responds more quickly when backing, going from astern to port to astern to starboard in just a second or two. Also, the boat does not slow substantially (as a conventional inboard does) when backing, say, first to port and then over to starboard, so you don't lose momentum when backing and twisting on a frantic fish. A fish can be stripping a reel in one direction, then take off in another, but the boat will be ready to react quickly, crisply, and smoothly.

On our test ride, the boat backed and twisted at 6 or 7 knots, and walked sideways at 3 knots, with no fumes detectable in the cockpit. The Volvo Penta IPS steering responsiveness is preset (limited) by the boatbuilder, since allowing the pods to turn their full arc at high speed would have it skidding sideways like a ski boat. The Spencer was set so it did a 360-degree, 30-knot turn in 32 seconds, which is about average for an inboard of this size.

The final noteworthy element in our sea trial involved fuel consumption. At an easy 29-knot cruise, the boat got 0.9 nautical mile per gallon, which is more typical of a 34- or 35-foot twin diesel sportfisherman. Even at full power, nearly 36 knots, the boat got well above 0.8 nmpg, which is the best we've ever recorded on a boat of this size, by a wide margin.

Most inboard diesel boats in this size get closer to 0.45 to 0.5 nmpg at full power. A typical 40-foot express gets about 0.5 nmpg by comparison, and a 35-footer gets 0.7 to 0.8 nmpg. All this efficiency in the 43 Express is the result of the joint effort between Spencer, which knows how to build a strong boat

Spencer 43 Express Performance Results

RPM	Speed, knots	Fuel Use, gph	Nautical mpg	Range, nm	Noise Level, dBA (at helm)
600	3.7	0.86	4.30	2,581	68
900	5.9	1.85	3.19	1,914	72
1,200	7.8	3.78	2.06	1,238	77
1,500	9.1	6.95	1.31	786	78
1,800	11.2	10.8	1.04	622	78
2,100	15.6	16.7	0.93	560	84
2,400	19.1	20.1	0.95	570	87
2,700	24.5	26	0.94	565	88
3,000	29.3	32.6	0.90	539	88
3,300	32.9	41.2	0.80	479	89
3,470	35.8	42.9	0.83	501	90

Test conditions: Four passengers, with twin Volvo Penta IPS 600. Moderate chop and swell.

that's still light, and Volvo Penta, which knows how to build low-drag, high-thrust Volvo Penta IPS units.

While engine exhaust noise levels were low, radiated noise through the cockpit deck were on the high side, compared to other IPS boats we've run. The builder is in the process of adding sound-deadening material to this prototype's engine room hatch and cockpit deck, and future boats will have this improvement. Dockside, the boat handled well and would be easy to maneuver even in challenging conditions.

The Spencer 43 Express is an exceptionally well-built sportfishing boat with an excellent hull design. The added space in the midcabin stateroom transforms this 43 into an express with a 50-footer's accommodations, adding private sleeping accommodations for two below the bridge deck. Hull trim is optimized throughout the day as fuel is consumed with the fuel tanks forward near the hull's center of buoyancy. And the handling with IPS fishing mode

has to be experienced to be believed, particularly when working a powerful, escape-minded gamefish. The exceptional fuel economy and range (well over 500 nautical miles at 29 knots), like the midcabin, is one more factor exponentially increasing the Spencer 43's overall functionality and delight quotient.

The tournament fishing crowd may be tradition-bound, but it will be difficult to imagine Volvo Penta's IPS system not taking off quickly in this market given the unprecedented, real, quantifiable advantages in range, maneuvering responsiveness, and extra cabin space it gives the captain, angler, and boatowner.

Most of the equipment on our test boat was standard, the only exceptions being the Pipe Welders tower, Eskimo icemaker, the pearl paint job, and the electronics. Spencer designed the 43 around Volvo Penta IPS power and has no plans to use any other propulsion packages, feeling such a move would be a step backward for the company.

TRITON 351 EXPRESS

TRITON

Triton 351 Express Specifications	
LOA:	34'10"
Beam:	10'
Deadrise:	24 deg.
Dry weight:	9,432 lb.
Cockpit depth:	28.5"
Draft:	25" (hull)
Fuel capacity:	355 gal.
Maximum capacity:	12 people

Triton launched the 351 Express in 2007 to provide a solid fishing platform along with more than a few creature comforts for long days offshore and weekends on the water. This boat is a good offshore family day boat for some of the same reasons it's a good offshore fishing boat. Its deep-V hull delivers a comfortable ride, it has a generous fuel capacity for long trips, it is solidly built and intelligently designed for long and dependable use, and it has plenty of freeboard and sole height above the waterline for seaworthiness and safety.

Construction

The Triton has a solid fiberglass hull, starting with 2 ounces of mat over the gelcoat wet out in premium vinylester resin to prevent osmotic blistering and to prevent cosmetic print-through of the fiberglass reinforcements to the gelcoat. A one-piece structural fiberglass grid is fiberglassed to the hull and pumped full of foam; this grid supports and strengthens the hull and also carries the cockpit

deck liner (one piece from the transom to the cabin's aft bulkhead) and cabin pan above.

The transom is a composite of high-density foam and fiberglass, a full 4½ inches thick. This unusually strong and thick transom (most are closer to 2⅜ inches thick) was specifically designed to carry the weight and torque of the three big Verado outboards cantilevered over the stern. The hull-to-deck joint is a shoebox design, bonded with 3M 5200 adhesive and bolted and screwed every 6 inches, producing an extremely strong joint between these two structural components. The cabin is built on a one-piece fiberglass pan, with a one-piece overhead liner and inner and outer head compartment liners as well.

Hull Design

The Triton 351 Express has a deep-V hull with a full 24 degrees of transom deadrise, and a fine entry for a smooth and dry headsea ride. The hull's design makes it well suited to open-ocean use.

Walkthrough

Cockpit

Entered from a transom door to port, the cockpit, like the rest of the boat, comes with a nonskid pattern that is easy to clean, and it grips boat shoes securely underfoot. The scuppers are a novel design, with a starboard cover that flips up for access to the

slotted stainless steel grating covering the drain lines. The whole affair is recessed to the level of the bottom of the gutter surrounding the cockpit aft, which should ensure nearly complete drainage.

Three rod racks are provided per side under the gunwales, as are three rod holders in the coaming on either side, and another six rod holders are in the forward side of the motor well, right on the other side of the fish box and livewell built into the transom. A freshwater washdown is aft. One of this boat's most attractive features is the transom seat. Most of these seats are a real hassle to operate, but this one pops up and down with little trouble. It adds a lot of versatility to the boat, with its obvious function of making the boat more attractive as a cruiser. But it's so easy to fold up and down, we wouldn't be surprised to see it used offshore when trolling between strikes.

The interior freeboard is 28½ inches, a little above average for a boat of this type, and most welcome given the added security it provides when working fish in rough water. Along those lines, we'd like to see the transom door moved to the cockpit side of the walkthrough so there's something more substantial to lean against aft to port.

Triton offers an optional larger livewell that's built into the leaning post in case the transom livewell isn't big enough. The livewell comes equipped with both fill and recirculating pumps, and tuna tubes keep the bait fresh above the recirculating inlet. The fish box has a macerator drain, and insulated in-deck boxes forward outboard of the leaning post could be used to provide extra fish box capacity.

What's really nice about this boat, besides the big cabin, is the conversation area forward of the helm console. It's a pleasant and quiet place to socialize, with an L-shaped lounge nicely sheltered by a surrounding windshield and optional plastic side curtains. There's a cooler below the seat, along with drawers for storage, and it's close to the cabin. This seating area and the cabin make this a candidate as a family boat as well as a hard-core fisherman.

Inside the center console, accessed from a port side door (which we found to be a bit tight getting in and out of), are four batteries, a Fischer Panda 4 kW diesel genset inside an enclosure (you can hardly hear it running), and copious wiring supplying current to the electronics and accessories installed in this surprisingly complex (electrically) boat. Having a diesel genset is a great idea, since it will run so

much longer on a tank of fuel, and the sound shield keeps noise levels unobjectionable.

Bridge Deck

The helm console is large, and intelligently laid out. There's plenty of room for the electronics typically installed on a boat like this, and indeed the electronics flats get priority placement—high and directly in front of the driver. The wheel and engine controls are situated at a comfortable height and angle. The suicide knob on the wheel is a hint that it takes lots of wheel revolutions to turn the engines. If it was our boat, as we found out on our test ride, we'd add a few handrails at the console so there's something to hang onto. The battery switches are handily located to port of the console.

Foredeck

There are two options for getting forward—either step up from the cockpit and walk down the flat but narrow side decks, or climb up the molded fiberglass stairs in the forward seating area and step over the low centerline windshield. The foredeck is covered with nonskid, and the ground tackle—anchor, windlass, and anchor rode—is completely out of sight below a flush deck hatch for a clean appearance forward. The railing is too low to offer much to hold onto forward. The close-molded anchor locker hatch is built just like all the other ones on this boat, with tooled fiberglass surfaces on both top and bottom, a sign of a well-built boat.

Cabin

For a fishing boat, this Triton does well in the creature comforts department. The cabin, entered through a companionway that's a full 20 inches wide, is roomy, and headroom is over 6 feet at the companionway door.

The convertible V-berth forward is also well-proportioned, a full 6 feet, 6 inches long measured along the hull. We see many boats that claim to have sleeping accommodations for four, but that's on 5-foot, 10-inch berths, which are pretty much useless for most people. The berth also converts to a dinette by removing the filler cushions and raising the table. There's another berth in the midcabin, but this one is on the small side at just 6 feet long and just under 3 feet wide. Another 6 inches of length would make it a real bed.

The cabin is nicely finished off, with a tooled fiberglass liner, Corian countertop at the galley, and attractively upholstered cushions. The fiberglass liner has a sculpted look above near the overhead hatch, giving the cabin an upscale feel, and it should prove easy to keep clean.

The galley, right at the cabin entrance, comes standard with a sink, microwave, and refrigerator.

The head includes a sink and a porcelain toilet with holding tank and pumpout as standard equipment. Air conditioning is also standard.

For an overnight, or even a weekend on the water, the 351's cabin has all the basics for a couple, and room for a small person or child in the mid-cabin berth.

Engine

The Triton 351 is rated for up to 900 hp, while our 50-knot test boat had 750 total hp with its three 250 hp four-stroke Mercury Verados. The boat's single aluminum fuel tank holds 355 gallons.

Sea Trial

Standing at the dock getting ready to cast off, we measured very low sound levels of just 67 dBA 2 feet from the three idling 250 hp Verado outboards. Standing aft in the cockpit, vibrations from the three engines were hardly discernible. We did our speed run in the Intracoastal Waterway between Dania and Ft. Lauderdale and then headed offshore.

It was an unusually good day for a sea trial of an offshore fishing boat, with a steady southeast breeze kicking up 3- to 5-footers and occasional 7-footers. These conditions are perfect for a boat this size—much rougher, and most people wouldn't want to go any distance to fish, and much calmer wouldn't be much of a challenge for a 35-foot deep-V hull. Coming slowly up to speed, all that weight bolted to the transom produced a fair amount of bow rise, obscuring visibility ahead while coming up on plane, with the aft end of the foredeck proving to be the highest point forward looking from the helm. At 3,500 rpm, making about 23 knots, we had to stand up to see over the bow.

Running right into the waves, we could comfortably cruise at 18 to 20 knots, and 28 to 30 knots was not entirely uncomfortable, though you are apt to pay much closer attention to what's going on directly ahead of the boat at that speed. At 20 knots the ride was pretty wet, while at 28 to 30 knots it was mostly dry, with the hull driving the spray farther aft.

The boat heels just right in a turn, allowing passengers to keep their feet firmly planted on the deck while turning at a brisk rate—there was no discernible centrifugal force other than that transmitted straight down to the feet, so the heel angle was perfectly matched to the turning rate.

The Mercury SmartCraft Shadow units have two engine levers to control the three engines. The port and centerline engines are controlled by the port lever, and the starboard engine by the starboard lever. All three engines can be trimmed by a single rocker switch built into the port control. The control mode is selected by a touch pad built into the binnacle. These are by far the best triple-outboard engine controls we've run, and a lot of thought has gone into the design and operation to make it as easy as possible to control three engines.

If you back both controls, all three engines go into reverse. If you back just the port control, only the port engine backs, and if you oppose the shifters (one forward, one reverse) only the outboard engines shift—the center engine stays in neutral. If you start off backing the port engine, then move the starboard control into reverse, all three engines back down. And another thing: if you turn the ignition key to "start" on a running engine, the engine shuts down. Just turn it again to restart the engine.

Get-home speed on one engine, with two engines stopped and tilted clear of the water, was about 8 knots at 3,000 rpm. While dodging breaking waves offshore we did a little experimenting with the Shadow controls. For instance, if for whatever reason you wanted to run on just the center engine, you'd turn the port engine ignition key to "on" (without actually starting it), which allows the port throttle to control the center engine. Standing aft in the cockpit, with the engines all running at 2,000 rpm, we could carry on a conversation with the driver without raising our voices, pointing out how quiet this rig was. Fumes were essentially nonexistent. We didn't record sound levels at high speeds since the wind and spray made so much more noise than the engines.

While the engine controls worked well, the same can't be said for the steering. At 8.8 turns lock-to-lock, this is the slowest-acting steering we have ever encountered on any boat, and that includes a couple of dozen displacement trawlers. We have no idea why it's set up this slow, and it's completely unnecessary considering that the boat has power steering.

The 351's hull is well-designed, running superbly in those big waves, and it also seemed solidly built, taking the occasional hard slamming (falling off a wave at 30 knots heeled over 20 degrees to one side will do it every time) without complaint. It was also predictable and controllable in any direction to the sea. The Triton ran with little course correction downsea, and was wet, though steady, with the seas broad on the bow in the 20- to 25-knot range. We would expect this boat to keep up with anything its size in this market in rough water, the only exceptions being an 8-foot-wide racing deep-V or a power cat.

With triple Verado power, this boat is clearly going to perform best in the 30- to 36-knot range, at least if fuel consumption is a consideration. Our test boat recorded just over 1 nautical mile per gallon at 4,000 to 4,500 rpm, and fuel economy falls off rapidly above these speeds. If range and economy are important, consider this a solid 32- to 34-knot boat by the time you load it up and head offshore with bottom paint and full canvas up.

We like this boat for its excellent hull design, its performance in rough water, and its strong and durable construction. The boat's layout provides options for both families and anglers, it has a sensible diesel genset, and the boat's topside safety features—generous cockpit height, toe kicks, and grippy nonskid—are other bonuses.

Triton 351 Express Peformance Results

RPM	Speed, mph	Speed, knots	Fuel Use, gph engine	Fuel Use, gph total	Statute mpg	Range, statue miles	Range, nm	Noise Level, dBA
1,000	5.1	4.4	0.7	2.1	2.43	776	674	67
1,500	7	6.1	1.4	4.2	1.67	533	463	69
2,000	8.8	7.6	2.8	8.4	1.05	335	291	73
2,500	9.7	8.4	4.4	13.2	0.73	235	204	76
3,000	17.4	15.1	6	18	0.97	309	268	79
3,500	26.8	23.3	7.7	23.1	1.16	371	322	84
4,000	33.3	28.9	9.1	27.3	1.22	390	339	86
4,500	41.4	36.0	11.2	33.6	1.23	394	342	88
5,000	46.3	40.2	14.6	43.8	1.06	338	293	
5,500	51.7	44.9	21.6	64.8	0.80	255	222	
6,000	57.5	50.0	28.9	86.7	0.66	212	184	

Test conditions: Three passengers, fuel tank three quarters full, with triple 350 hp Verado outboards. Calm in the Intracoastal, then moderate to heavy seas. Note: Range in this table was calculated at 90 percent of fuel capacity. Noise levels were measured at the dock.

We highly recommend the Triton for anyone in the market for an offshore sportfisherman–weekend cruiser.

Standard equipment includes a battery switch, china toilet, anchor windlass with a stainless steel plow anchor and 315 feet of chain and nylon line, shore power hookup with battery charger, water heater, cabin A/C, K-Plane trim tabs, cockpit hardtop with rod holders and spreader lights, transom shower, aft fold-down seat, raw-water washdown, removable cockpit bolsters, leaning post with livewell, and stereo with remote control.

Flats Boats

Similar in many ways to bay boats, flats boats are designed for even shallower water, using outboard jack plates and tunnels to reduce draft. Drafts of 7 to 14 inches and good form stability at rest are prerequisites. Lightweight construction helps, and some high-end builders use a weight-saving combination of Kevlar, carbon fiber, foam cores, and vinylester resin. Once the flats boat is in really skinny water where "sight fishing" is possible, the engine is trimmed up and the boat is poled from an aft raised platform with a 21-foot pole, which can also be stuck in the bottom and tied to the poling platform to anchor the boat temporarily. An electric trolling motor can also be fitted in the bow, as on a bass boat. Like bay boats, flats boats have insulated fish boxes, livewells, lockable tackle and rod stowage, depth- and fish-finders, and center consoles.

Part of the upscale Maverick fish boat group, Maverick builds flats boats from 15 to 21 feet. Designed for skinny water, these boats will run and pole with the best of them. Shown here is the Maverick 17 Master Angler.

MAVERICK BOATS

Part of the Pathfinder group of high-end inshore fishing boats, Hewes builds shallow-water, high-end skiffs in two series — Redfishers and Tailfishers. Three Redfishers, described as lightweight (but strong) backcountry boats by the builder, are offered from 16 to 21 feet, including this 16-footer.

HEWES BOATS

Ranger specializes in freshwater bass boats (which also do fine in sheltered salt water), but also draws on its deep fishing roots to produce a series of purpose-built saltwater flats boats. The 183 Ghost is one such model with a shallow draft, poling platform aft, fore and aft casting deck, an electric trolling motor forward, and a single center console layout for all-around fishability. The 183, a light boat at 1,050 pounds without the engine, is rated for up to 150 hp.

GENMAR HOLDINGS, INC.

Scout makes a pair of high-end flats boats as part of its Costa series. The 170 shown here is the smaller of the two. (See below for a review of the 190.) It comes well-equipped for fishing, and includes wide side decks connecting the fore and aft fishing platforms and aft poling platform. Yamaha power to 115 hp is available, and the hull draws just 8 inches with a light load. The boat looks like a custom one-off with its optional teak cockpit deck.   SCOUT BOATS

Like Scout and Ranger, Triton builds a wide range of upscale fishing boats. Well suited for shallow water fishing, with minimal deadrise and fore and aft casting platforms, the 191 is built strong and light, weighing 400 pounds less than its 19-foot sister, the 190 LTS. With a 15-degree deadrise, the hull still draws just 13 inches. Outboard power to 150 hp is available.   TRITON BOATS

SCOUT 190 COSTA FLATS

SCOUT

Scout 190 Costa Flats Specifications	
LOA:	19'5"
Beam:	8'6"
Deadrise:	10 deg.
Dry weight:	1,200 lb.
Draft:	10" (hull)
Fuel capacity:	45 gal.
Maximum capacity:	6 people
Total capacity:	2,000 lb.

Scout builds a wide range of high-end outboard-powered (mostly Yamaha) fishing boats from 17 to over 30 feet. These include offshore center consoles, walkarounds, and fish-and-skis as well as flats and bay boats.

In production since 2007, the Scout 190 Costa Flats is a pure flats boat, with a retractable casting platform in the bow (a little extra height helps put the lure where you want it) and a second, higher casting platform in the stern. It has a capacity of six passengers (or 1,100 pounds), a 2,000-pound total capacity, and a rating of 225 maximum hp.

Construction
Scouts are well-built, as good as any we've seen in the saltwater fishing industry. They are built entirely

of rot-proof fiberglass and composite coring materials—no balsa or any other kind of wood is used. Each Scout starts with a 3-ounce skin coat of mat wet out in general-purpose resin over the gelcoat, followed by fiberglass reinforcements. Many manufacturers use a premium vinylester resin for the skin coat, since it is inherently more resistant to osmotic blistering, but Scout says they have never had a problem with blistering, being careful to completely wet out the mat with properly catalyzed resin. We prefer the vinylester route, but we also take Scout's word for it that blistering has never been a problem.

Divinycell coring is used to stiffen the hull sides, while the bottom is solid fiberglass. A one-piece flanged fiberglass hull support grid is bonded to the hull skin with methacrylate adhesive. One unique characteristic of Scout's design is that the hull stringers continue past the transom to the outboard bracket, so the main hull structure directly absorbs the engine's weight, torque, and thrust. Another unique feature is the hull-to-deck joint, which is a sort of reverse shoebox joint: the deck fits inside the hull part, and the joint is continuously bonded together using methacrylate adhesive.

Through-hull fittings are drilled through high-density composite Whale board that resists bolt compression loads and reliably holds fasteners. All Scouts up to 30 feet are built with level flotation, which means they will not sink if holed and will float level at their damaged waterline. Transom edges are hand-finished at the hull-to-deck joint rather than using the more common metal or plastic cap cover to hide an unfinished joint.

Hull Design

The hull is a low-deadrise design with a radiused, convex hull forward transitioning aft to a fairly flat (for extra form stability) transom deadrise of 10 degrees. The convexity, Scout feels, helps rduce wave-slapping noise, and this is plausible. The rounded shape is also used by designers to reduce slamming, though at least theoretically it also increases wetness (though we saw no evidence of a wet ride on our sea trial). The keel has a wide pad that extends from the stern nearly to the bow, which, as we'll see, positively affected the boat's handling at speed. Spray strakes and chines forward add lift and help keep the boat dry in a chop. The boat is beamy and extra stable for its length at 8 feet, 6 inches wide overall. Hull draft is around 10 inches, depending on the boat's overall displacement and fore-and-aft weight distribution.

Walkthrough

Cockpit

The cockpit has fishing platforms fore and aft, about 12 inches and 41 inches high off the deck, respectively. Wide side decks make moving from bow to stern easier than stepping down to the recessed cockpit. In addition to five pop-up mooring cleats, Scout also provides flip-up poling pole holders. Recessed scuppers aft fed by side gutters do a good job of draining the deck completely, and the scuppers are covered with serrated caps that unscrew for cleaning with a standard gas cap key, a clever feature. Inside the scupper drain line, a floating ball helps prevent backflow of water into the cockpit, a feature long seen in U.S. Coast Guard motor whaleboats, though this also serves as a reminder of how close the deck is to the waterline. Access to the fuel filter is through a hatch just forward of the engine.

More fishing features include two livewells and a large centerline release well aft. Five rods stow on either side of the boat in compartments below the coaming. Sand texture nonskid is grippy underfoot, while easy to keep clean with a scrub brush. Our boat did not have a boarding ladder; we would urge buyers to have one installed, as there are no railings and the boat's sides are low, and this combined with the raised fishing platforms makes the occasional fall overboard possible.

Helm

The low-profile center console contains a simple helm station with a comfortably positioned steering wheel and engine control. The engine gauges take up most of the available space, so there is little room for flush electronics. To drive you sit on the aft deck atop a large storage box hatch, just forward of the release well; our boat didn't have one, but you can order a backrest, which we would recommend for long rides. Handrails are provided on either side of the console.

The center console itself has a low profile, making it easy to fish around. Don't expect much in the way of protection from the elements, but this will likely be fine with any self-respecting flats boatowner. A forward seat with an insulated storage box below is built into the console. The batteries are inside the console, and the battery switch is positioned below the steering wheel.

Engine

The Scout 190 Costa is rated for up to 225 hp, though our 150 hp Yamaha four-stroke pushed us to over 50 mph. We recorded just under 38 mph at 4,500 rpm, so you can figure on an approximate 35 mph cruise with a painted bottom and a light load. An electric trolling motor provides shallow water access with the main engine raised.

Sea Trial

Our test ride took place in water that ranged from flat to a 6-inch chop. The boat had a pleasantly smooth and dry ride in the chop, though the dry part was not put to the test by strong winds. The hull's smooth and rounded section forward is responsible for the smooth ride, and it also makes the boat less directionally stable, meaning that when you put the wheel over a quarter turn or so, the boat initially turns robustly, then the turning rate decreases as the hull slides sideways. A boat with a sharp edge or angle at the keel would definitively establish a pivot point to turn on. Each successive turn of the wheel produces the same result—a sharp initial reaction, followed by a diminished turning rate. With the wheel over hard in a high-speed turn, the boat handled well, with relatively little heel in a turn since the low-deadrise stern was free to slide sideways, and without the excessive heel (banking) seen in many deep-V hulls.

We recorded a top speed of 51 mph with our 150 hp Yamaha four-stroke, which ran quietly and shifted smoothly (the Yamaha single-engine controls shift a lot smoother than the dual-engine controls). Figure on a cruise speed of 35 knots or so with a normal load of two or three people, light gear, and a painted bottom. If you need to cruise all day at 45 knots or so, get a bigger engine, though we found the 150 to be perfectly adequate and plenty strong when accelerating.

Scout 190 Costa Flats Performance Results

RPM	Speed, mph	Noise Level, dBA
1,000	4.3	61
1,500	5.8	67
2,000	7.1	74
2,500	10.8	78
3,000	22.4	wind
3,500	27.7	
4,000	33.2	
4,500	37.6	
5,000	42.1	
5,500	47.4	
6,000	51.3	

Test conditions: Two passengers, fuel tank half full, with 150 hp Yamaha four-stroke outboard.

The Scout 190 Costa Flats is a well-built, intelligently designed flats boat with a serious fishing layout. Three livewells, storage lockers, lots of rod storage in racks and holders, quality hardware and components, and the cream-colored gelcoat all add up to a practical fishing machine that we can recommend without reservation. Don't use it in the open ocean, as its low deck limits the reserve buoyancy needed to shed water quickly and the freeboard is low to accommodate flats fishing.

We'd recommend the optional jack plate for improved shallow water capability. The Stu Apte (Apte is a well-known pro on the fishing circuit) package gets you the pole holders, poling platform aft and fishing platform forward, trim tabs, and a recirculating livewell. Options include hull colors, hydraulic steering, pole holders, jack plate, trim tabs, helm seat backrest, transom-mounted trolling motor, and a retractable bow casting platform.

Go-Fasts

High-performance boats, whether used for racing or recreation, are often referred to as go-fasts, which is apt for a boat that is meant to do just one thing: go fast! Long and narrow, these hulls are strongly built to take wave impacts at speeds of 60 to over 100 mph. Deadrise on a go-fast monohull hovers right around 24 degrees all the way to the transom. Deep-V deadrise at the transom is an important ingredient for a very fast hull, since the boat comes clear out of the water on a regular basis, and rides on a narrow, V-shaped section of hull within a few feet of the transom.

Go-fasts are usually monohulls, but catamarans are also popular, especially at the high-end, fast segment of the market. No one in this go-fast world talks about knots as a unit of speed, even though these are saltwater boats, since 80 mph sounds more impressive than 69 knots. Go-fasts have little functional purpose; most of the hull's length is given over to the engines aft and a long, low sloping foredeck.

What's left, maybe 30 percent of the hull's length, becomes the cockpit and helm area. If there is a cabin at all, it probably has little headroom, since the bow deck is kept low to reduce air drag, and to help with the sleek look. You don't want to be riding forward in one of these boats at high speed, anyway, since the vertical accelerations forward would be hard to tolerate.

One unfortunate consequence of the go-fast culture is noise pollution. Even though mufflers could be added, or switched on, that would drop exhaust noise levels on these high-horsepower (usually gas) engines considerably without sacrificing significant horsepower, many owners think

it's fine to run around with exhausts blaring, audible from literally miles away.

If you get a kick out of pure speed, a go-fast may be just the thing for you. They're not for amateurs, by any stretch. Because their speed makes them inherently dangerous, they take a lot of skill and experience to operate safely.

Baja's Outlaw series of high-performance boats goes from 20 to 40 feet (see full-length 35 Outlaw review on pages 345–348). The 26 shown here is a true deep-V with 24 degrees of deadrise at the transom. Tall bolster seats offer the lateral security needed in a hard turn. A 375 hp MerCruiser is standard, while up to a 600 hp SCI MerCruiser is available. BAJA MARINE

Checkmate builds performance boats, including runabouts and race boats from 16 to 33 feet. CHECKMATE

Cigarette builds high-performance race boats from 30 to 46 feet. One of the oldest names (along with Formula) in the business, Cigarette's output includes this high-end, race-derived 45-foot Maximus Center, which is available with a pair of whopping 1,075 hp MerCruiser SCI racing engines.　CIGARETTE RACING

The 343 is luxury cruiser and runabout builder Cobalt Boats' (not Cobalt Yachts) largest model, and its fastest. A step bottom with pad keel speeds up the boat, and the futuristic helm is part of the package. Standard power is twin 375 hp MerCruisers, while up to twin 500s are available, as are twin Volvo 337 hp diesel stern drives.　COBALT BOATS

Donzi's offshore high-performance series ranging from 28 to 38 feet includes this top-of-the-line 38ZX. Wider and therefore more commodious than a race boat with its 9-foot, 3-inch beam, the 38 sleeps two and has an enclosed head and a deep-V step-bottom hull design. With twin 600 SCI Mercs and Bravo XR ITS, the 38ZX has been clocked at 85 mph.　DONZI MARINE

Donzi's largest offshore racing boat, the Flagship 43ZR shown here has an 8-foot, 10-inch beam. With twin staggered T-1075 hp Mercury racing stern drives, this model has been clocked at 114 mph.　DONZI MARINE

Luxury yacht builder Ferretti Group now includes the Itama line of high-performance offshore boats, including the 55 shown here.　FERRETTI

Formula builds runabouts, yachts, and cruisers as well as a series of high-performance FAS³Tech boats from 27 to 31 feet. In fact, racing has been in the company's DNA since it was founded 40 years ago. The 382 shown here is the largest in the series. Double steps in the bottom reduce frictional drag and increase speed. Hulls are painted with long-lasting Imron paint. MerCruiser power options range from twin 375 hp 496s to 700 hp racing engines.　FORMULA BOATS

Fountain may be one of the newer high-performance boatbuilders, but they build indisputably fast boats. Fountain's lightning series of high-performance race boats includes this 35-foot ICBM.

FOUNTAIN POWERBOATS

Nor-Tech builds high-performance 39-, 43-, and 50-foot V-bottoms and 36-, 43-, and 50-foot cats. The 3600 Supercat shown, with twin 850 hp Mercury SSM VI stern drives, will reach nearly 140 mph.

NOR-TECH BOATS

BAJA 35 OUTLAW

BAJA MARINE

Baja 35 Outlaw Specifications	
LOA:	35'
Beam:	8'6"
Deadrise:	24 deg.
Dry weight:	8,100 lb.
Draft:	40" (drive down)
Fuel capacity:	185 gal.
Maximum capacity:	8 people

Building boats since 1971, Baja Marine produces 100 mph plus offshore race boats, high-performance family runabouts, and fast fishing boats. Part of Brunswick Corporation, Baja has been turning increasingly to high-tech closed-molded construction methods to build its high-performance models.

In production since 2006, the Baja 35 Outlaw is a boat built for speed with good control. In fact, at 90 mph, the feeling of safety, stability, and control the 35 Outlaw provides is remarkable.

Construction

Baja's 35 Outlaw is built using the SCRIMP closed-molded construction technology. After the gelcoat and a skin coat are applied to the mold, the fiberglass and carbon reinforcements and balsa coring are placed in the mold, a plastic bag covers the whole affair, and high vacuum pressure is used to draw the vinylester resin through the dry-stacked structure in one shot. This results in a precise glass-to-resin ratio (by weight, there's more fiberglass than resin with closed molding, unlike open molding).

It eliminates secondary bonds since the whole structure, including stringers and other hull-support members, sets up at once.

The result is a lighter hull with increased strength and stiffness compared to an open-molded hull of similar size, and lighter means faster for any given horsepower. A one-piece fiberglass stringer-grid system is bonded to the hull with adhesive, screws, and through-bolts, and the cockpit in turn mates to and rests on the stringer system.

Hull Design

The Baja's hull is a deep-V with the low beam-to-length ratio necessary for high speed. The aggressive deadrise, 24 degrees at the transom, allows the hull to produce a comparatively comfortable ride offshore in rough water at high speed. Less deadrise, and more beam, would slash the boat's speed potential in anything but calm water. The chines have low profiles, which means they are not as wide as on slower boats, hinting at the extreme water velocities and slamming loads these hulls are subjected to.

We usually just talk about hull design in this section, but aerodynamics plays such a big role in influencing a very fast boat's top speed, we'll just point out that the Baja discusses using wind-tunnel testing in an effort to minimize drag. They also use tank testing to fine-tune hull design, to minimize drag, and to improve ride quality and controllability.

Walkthrough

Cockpit

The cockpit is small and functional, meant to keep you in the boat when rocketing from one locale to the next. It's a full 38 inches deep, a big improvement over slower-paced runabouts that are typically 26 to 28 inches high (from deck to gunwale) inside. Like elsewhere on the boat, the fiberglass cabin pan and overhead liner are tooled fiberglass, producing a cabin with reasonably (with the headroom limitations) comfortable accommodations out of the weather. Aft against the engine compartment bulkhead is a three-person seat with head bolsters.

Helm

The 35 Outlaw's helm is functionally laid out. A large pair of tachometers take center stage, with an equally large GPS-driven speedometer in the middle. Using GPS for speedometer input is clearly the way to get the most accurate readings at 80 to 90 mph. The Livorsi shifts are to port and the throttles to starboard of the wheel, which is a better setup than grouping them all together on the starboard side, since the wheel is often left amidships for dockside handling, anyway.

The trim tab and drive trim controls are just ahead of the throttles, within easy reach when the throttles are advanced. The Livorsi tab and drive angle indicators are above the controls, creating a practical and sensible continuum of controls and indicators.

The helm and companion seats are well-designed. When running at speed the preferred position is standing, settling deeply into the confining three-sided embrace of the seat back and bolsters. A push of a rocker switch raises the seat bottom into position should you want to sit. The windscreen is quite low—you have to duck way down to get out of the wind, which is just the way these boatowners like it, according to the builder.

Foredeck

Unless absolutely necessary, you'll want to stay off the foredeck on this boat, as there are no bow railings and there's no nonskid surface—just a shiny, white long-nosed catwalk that leads to the bow cleats and ground tackle.

Cabin

A cabin on a boat like this is not the main priority of the designer; speed is. Headroom is just 4 feet, 8 inches, a necessity driven by the boat's low profile. Baja does a good job with the interior considering the height and volume in the forward third of the hull. A galley has all the basics: sink, microwave, refrigerator, and enough counter space for preparing simple meals. The enclosed head is cramped, but it too has the basics: a toilet on a small platform. There is no sink in the head.

The big berth forward is actually an improvement on those found in other 35-footers. It's 7 feet long, longer than we usually see on cruisers of this size. There's also a table for use when the berth is converted to a U-shaped settee. There's another small berth in the forepeak, easily long enough for a child to sleep on. A Clarion CD-AM-FM stereo system is included.

Engine

A push of a button raises the engine hatch, which hinges aft at the transom, on a single ram. The hatch is built using tooled fiberglass parts, both above and below. The big blue MerCruiser 600 SCI gas engines look like something out of a meticulously restored roadster, with bright cobalt-blue paint, topped by huge belt-driven superchargers and shiny chrome exhaust risers.

The tooled fiberglass bilges were spotlessly clean, and cableways were neatly routed and secured at close intervals. All engine components are high-quality in appearance and installation in this sparsely populated, purpose-driven space. Things are decidedly tight between these big-block engines on this 8-foot, 6-inch-wide boat, but the builder leaves plenty of room to maneuver forward of the engines.

Below the aluminum pipe swim platform aft, a pair of MerCruiser Bravo 1 XR drives, gleaming black and stainless steel with their five-blade 17-by 32-inch stainless props, are poised for action.

Sea Trial

Our test ride took place on the Richelieu River in Iberville, Quebec, between Lake Champlain and the St. Lawrence Seaway. Going nearly 90 mph on a river that's only a couple of hundred yards wide does a lot to amplify the perception of speed. The houses and docks fly by with startling alacrity, to say the least. On the other hand, it was calm on the river, so we can't report on the boat's offshore ride attributes.

Our sea trial revealed other attributes. The boat's performance picked up once over the hump and fully on plane: we saw our hull speed double from 2,000 to 2,500 rpm. There was also strong acceleration between 4,000 rpm (62 mph) and wide-open throttle (88 mph). In this rpm range, the engines are working at the top of their torque curve, and the amount of acceleration remaining above 60 mph was substantial. Finally, we have to comment on the feeling of control produced by this boat and engine combination. Even running at over 80 mph, the boat felt like it was on tracks, rock-solid with no hint whatsoever of instability.

When we asked owners how hard they ran their boats, some indicated they ran them wide open when they had access to open water and appropriate conditions. When inquiring how long the engines lasted at these speeds, we were told that the drives typically give out before the engines, and part of the reason is the high temperatures that the drives operate at due to the high gear loading (nearly 600 hp is being transmitted to each propeller in a compact package). While it may seem counterintuitive that a lower unit submerged in rapidly flowing water would get hot, keep in mind the tremendous torque being absorbed at high rpm. One solution to minimize gear oil temperatures is to use the highest-grade lube oils.

For a pair of stern drives that are mounted so close together, and given the length and narrow beam of the boat, it was surprising how easily the boat twisted in its length at the dock. Just oppose the shifts and give it a little gas, and it comes around quite nicely.

The Baja 35 is a well-built (in the boatbuilding world, it doesn't get any better than what SCRIMP produces), high-performance boat quite capable of holding its own in this specialized, demanding market. It promises speed, controllability, and safe, predictable handling, and it delivers.

Baja 35 Outlaw Performance Results

RPM	Speed, mph	Noise Level, dBA
650	5.8	
1,000	8	
1,500	13	
2,000	16.5	
2,500	34	
3,000	45	
3,500	53	
4,000	62	90
4,500	74	
5,200	88	

Test conditions: Conducted with twin 600 hp SCI MerCruiser high-performance stern drives.

The degree of control and steadiness at the wheel was surprising for such a fast boat. All of the details speak of high quality and meticulous attention to detail. The Baja is certainly worth a close look if a high-performance offshore machine is on your shopping list.

Options include air conditioning, cockpit cover, K-Plane trim tabs, GPS speedometer, aluminum swim platform with ladder, electric drop-down seat bolsters, cabin table, VacuFlush toilet, hull graphics (built into the gelcoat, not decals), fixed fire-extinguishing system, and an electrical package for the galley.

Maine-Style Boats

Maine- or Down East–style boats have been around for many years, and the class was at least originally inspired by Maine lobster boats, with a small cabin forward and large open cockpit aft, with either a windshield and bimini top or a hardtop. The genre has grown to include high-end, hard-chine planing yachts from builders like Lyman Morse and Alden, as well as other builders, including Hunt, Legacy, and Eastbay. These are all hard-chine planing hulls, so they are not true Maine boats, which traditionally have round-bilge, full-keel semidisplacement hulls.

"Maine-style" has become an umbrella term that includes faster planing yachts as well as gussied-up lobster boats. The smaller boats are often intended for overnights and weekends afloat, so the cabin and amenities are basic. These traditional-looking boats relinquish interior volume for a sweet sheerline and a low center of gravity, improving their seaworthiness.

Alden Yachts is a Rhode Island builder of semicustom power (and sail) yachts from 40 to 68 feet (the 49 is shown here). Alden serves the upper end of the market, with joinery, appointments, and general attention to detail at the highest level of craftsmanship. Aldens have Hunt hull designs, making them superb sea boats. They are constructed using vacuum bagging, Kevlar, and post-cured epoxy resin, which produces exceptionally strong and durable, as well as moderate-weight yachts. ALDEN YACHTS

The Atlantic 42 is a Spencer Lincoln design with a Down East–style, full-keel, round-bilge semidisplacement hull. A comfortable ride in rough water and an excellent fishing boat offshore because of its easier motion (compared to a hard-chine boat), the Atlantic 42, and boats like it, are well worth considering for cruising and fishing. Atlantic will be glad to finish off one of these hulls as anything from a no-frills lobster boat to an upscale lobster yacht. These boats can be powered to run 30 knots, but they burn a lot of fuel doing so with all the drag from the full keel and the moderate lift from the round-bilge bottom. They're really best suited for a cruise speed in the 16- to 22-knot range.   ATLANTIC BOAT COMPANY

Eastbay Yachts is part of Grand Banks, which is a long-time builder of upscale trawler-style yachts. Built in the Far East, Eastbays are high-speed, hard-chine planing yachts produced in sedan and convertible configurations from 39 to 58 feet, like this 47-footer. Hunt hull forms deliver excellent seakeeping and ride characteristics. Traditionally styled and sumptuously finished with lots of interior teak, Eastbays are built for people who are experienced boaters and know what they're looking for.   EASTBAY YACHTS

Dyer has been building their 29 since 1958, making it what is possibly the oldest model in continuous production in this country. Hardtop sedans, windshield express, and flush-deck saltwater bass boats have all been produced on this hull, and now they're even building a center console version. Whichever layout you choose, this is hands-down one of the most comfortable, seakindly boats in its size range to be found anywhere. The Dyer 29 shown here, like other round-bilge, full-keel Maine-style hulls, is a comfortable sea boat, but don't succumb to the temptation to put too much power in it. A 250–300 hp Yanmar, Volvo, or Cummins, for instance (whichever diesel brand you pick, get a quiet, low-smoke, low-vibe common rail design), will push the boat to its design speed of 16 to 20 knots.   DYER BOATS

Ellis is another builder that uses real lobster-boat hulls for its yachts. These built-down, semidisplacement hulls run great at 12 to 20 knots, and you can't beat the seakindly motion of a Down East hull at these speeds. The boats, like the 36 shown here, are built using fiberglass tooling for the hulls and topsides, with the rest of the interior layout finished off on a custom basis. Even the headroom in the cabin and pilothouse can be adjusted to suit the owner. All are single diesel inboard-powered, with the exception of one twin waterjet 36 built a few years ago.   ELLIS YACHTS

Hunt Yachts, affiliated with Hunt Design, builds a series of express and sedan yachts from 25 to 36 feet, like this 33. All are excellent sea boats, solidly constructed and nicely finished, offered with inboard or waterjet power. They're designed with the operator in mind, and have a traditional well-proportioned look that will never grow old.

HUNT YACHTS

Legacy Yachts, based in Rhode Island, builds express and sedan-style cruising yachts from 28 to 52 feet. This is the 32-footer.

LEGACY YACHTS

Island Packet, a boatbuilding company with a naval architect for a CEO (would there were more) has been building sailboats since 1977 and powerboats since 2001. The good thing about having a sailboat heritage can be an increased awareness of ergonomics and old-fashioned attention to detail lacking in more than a few powerboats, and these IPY powerboats seem to incorporate the best of both worlds when it comes to their design. The company builds two powerboats, the 41-foot Packet Craft Express (shown here) and the 41-foot PY Cruiser, an intriguing self-righting displacement cruiser. The Express has twin 370 hp Yanmar inboard diesel power, a salty interior, good sight lines from the helm, and good helm ergonomics.   ISLAND PACKET YACHTS

Lyman Morse builds everything from SCRIMP fiberglass 120-footers (sail and power, monohull and catamaran) costing enough to make Bill Gates blink (but you get what you pay for in this case), to research and workboats in the 40- to 50-foot range. All their boats are custom-built — great examples of American craftsmanship. Shown here is a top-shelf 62-foot custom convertible built in the Maine tradition.

LYMAN MORSE YACHTS

In a perfect world, all boats would be constructed like the MJM 34, built at Boston Boatworks. Epoxy resin is used throughout the laminate, and a resin-to-glass ratio of 6:4 is achieved using resin infusion. The result is an extremely strong, stiff, and lightweight boat that goes fast with little power (1.8 mpg at 28 knots compared to 1.0 to 1.3 on the best conventionally built planing hulls of the same length) and planes at 10 knots with such light bottom loading. A moderate 11-foot beam along with a fine entry creates a great ride in a seaway.

MJM YACHTS

True North came out with the innovative 38 (shown here) a number of years ago, and has since added 33- and 45-foot sister ships. Sold factory-direct (which helps improve their margins and decrease your purchase price), these boats are as good as it gets in construction quality, using the SCRIMP resin infusion process. There's nothing Down East about the hard-chine planing hull, but the boat has a classically quirky look. With its plumb bow it has the waterline length of a typical 43- or 44-footer, so you're getting more boat underwater than you bargained for. The True North 38 is efficiently driven with single diesel power (the prop is not exposed in case you run aground). The most innovative feature is the tailgate at the transom which allows a tender to be brought right into the cockpit.

PEARSON YACHTS

Sabre builds classically styled well-engineered and practical express, sedan, and aft-cabin cruising yachts from 34 to 52 feet. Priced below high-end yachts like Hinckley or Alden, these boats offer excellent value. The 47 shown sports an aft cabin that adds an extra degree of privacy for the owners, and allows the saloon to buffer the two staterooms. An aft-cabin layout is a good design to own if you want to still be friends with your guests after a week on board. Two- and three-stateroom layouts are available. This Sabre, like its sister ships, rides on a good-running, hard-chine planing hull.

SABRE YACHTS

Maine-based Wilbur Yachts builds genuine Down East semidisplacement yachts, and has been at it for over 30 years. Offered in models ranging from 31 to 61 feet, these are solid sea boats with full keels and round bilges for easy motion in a seaway, and well suited for the 14- to 20-knot cruise speeds they can achieve with big single diesels. Shown is the Wilbur 31 Hardtop Express.

WILBUR YACHTS

BACK COVE

LOA:	29'6"
Beam:	10'5"
Deadrise:	18 deg.
Dry weight:	10,000 lb.
Cockpit depth:	28"
Draft:	30" (drive down)
Fuel capacity:	150 gal.

A new brand and an affiliate of Sabre Yachts of Casco, Maine, Back Cove is an expanding line of midsize (mid 20s to mid 30s as of this writing) Maine-style cruising boats. Good-riding and efficient hard-chine planing hulls, traditional looks, high-quality construction, and livable, practical layouts with roomy cockpits and wide side decks make these boats highly appealing, perhaps especially appreciated by the experienced boater who has learned what doesn't work so well on other boats.

The Down East–style boat is a floating catalogue of fundamentals. Based on the traditional round-bilge, full-keel lobster boat populating every cove and harbor in Maine, the Down East–style boat is first and foremost practical and utilitarian; its classic proportions and simple beauty follow its function. In production since 2004, the Back Cove 29 is built with modern fiberglass construction methods and materials, and a hard-chine planing hull with its greater speed potential substituting for the lobster boat's semidisplacement, round-bilge bottom.

Construction

The hull starts with an ISO NPG gelcoat. The hull laminate is wet out with a premium vinylester resin with structural E-glass. The hull bottom is solid glass, and the hull topsides are vacuum bagged Divinycell PVC foam core. Back Cove uses a smooth-surfaced biased E-glass in the first layer below the gelcoat in order to provide the best possible gelcoat finish on the topsides.

The transom is E-glass with Divinycell PVC foam core bagged in place to ensure a structurally solid skin-to-core bond line. Stringers are PVC foam core covered with structural E-glass. Aluminum angles are through-bolted and engine mounts are mounted on the flat surfaces of the aluminum "L." Bulkheads are tabbed to the inner hull skin using strips of PVC foam to prevent hard points.

Bulkheads are marine-grade plywood tabbed to the inner skin of the hull. The hull-to-deck joint is a shoebox-style with 3M 5200 adhesive bonding the parts together. Bolts are then tapped into aluminum plates in the hull flange. The joint is covered with a PVC rubrail, which is also screwed to the deck flange and covered with a stainless steel rubrail. The cabin liner is a single structural fiberglass part bonded to the stringers, as is the headliner in the accommodations section.

The hatches are tooled on both sides using double-sided molds, resulting in a durable and attractive part, and they're gasketed to seal out noise and prevent rattling.

Hull Design

The Back Cove's hull is a modified-V with lifting strakes and spray rails and reverse chines for added dynamic lift and form stability. It also has a propeller pocket to reduce draft and shaft angles.

Walkthrough

Cockpit

The Back Cove 29 has a traditional cockpit, open and with 28-inch-high coamings (or washboards as they were once called), toe kick space all around, and good nonskid underfoot, all conspiring to keep you on your feet and in the boat. A swim platform is about the only nod to modernity back aft. Measuring 5 feet, 8 inches long and stretching 9 feet wide, there's plenty of room to cast for stripers, or to have a seat on the full-width transom seat and enjoy the view. A single hatch, well guttered to keep the bilge components dry below, provides access to the steering gear and the aft end of the aluminum fuel tank below. Pop-up stern cleats lie flush so they don't snag fishing lines.

Bridge Deck

A single step leads to the bridge deck, or saloon as it might be called in a larger enclosed boat. An L-shaped settee is to port and the helm seat is forward on starboard, right where you'd expect it. There's plenty of room up here for a small crowd: 7 feet, 6 inches from cockpit step to cabin bulkhead. Headroom under the hardtop is quite acceptable at 6 feet, 3 inches (and good for a 29-footer).

If you look closely at the pilothouse construction, you'll notice the sides are tooled fiberglass on both inside and outside surfaces, producing a sculpture of sorts, with flanges molded in. This constitutes an exceptional fiberglass tooling job by Sabre, resulting in a strong and stiff structure that's also a pleasure to look at. You'll get plenty of fresh air when you want it, with the center windshield and both side windows opening to let in a sea breeze.

Foredeck

Unlike most boats in this size, which have you walking through the opening windshield on centerline, on the Back Cove 29 you access the foredeck from the cockpit, up molded steps along 11-inch-wide unobstructed side decks. There's a railing along the hardtop to hang onto as you go forward, and the most obvious sign of the boat's high-bred origins, the 1¼-inch diameter stainless steel bow railing, leads forward from there. A close look tells you the builder even takes the time to grind the welds, as on a megayacht. The railing is 26 to 27 inches high, which affords a measure of safety in a seaway, and is about a foot higher than many style-driven express cruisers of the same size.

More attention to detail shows in the two pairs of spring cleats. The ground tackle is laid out in business-like fashion, and three 10-inch bow cleats give plenty of options whether dockside or on the hook.

Cabin

Down three steps through a wide companionway is the uncluttered, roomy cabin with its teak and holly sole, varnished ash plank hull-side liner, and solid teak cabinetry. Anyone who appreciates fine woodworking in particular and classic yachts in general would feel at home down below on this boat. The galley is to port, an enclosed head to starboard, and a large dinette or berth forward, depending on what position the high-low table and cushions are in. Headroom is 6 feet, not bad for a 29-footer. A 17-inch opening overhead hatch lets in light and fresh air.

The cabin's overhead liner is tooled off-white fiberglass, presenting a clean and crisp look, as well as a surface that's easy to maintain. It also sets the teak woodwork off nicely, the old Herreshoff look for the traditionalist. The whole cabin has as its foundation a single molded fiberglass pan, to which all the components, such as the galley, berth, and head units are mounted. This has several advantages over stick-built cabins, including its contribution to the hull structure, its consistent shape providing a fair surface to mount the cabin modules on, and ease of maintenance.

The galley's countertop is exceptionally large, which is great since it serves as both a meal preparation area and a storage place. An alcohol-electric stove lets you cook with or without AC power. There's also a microwave, stainless steel sink, and refrigerator. The drawers all have dovetail joints to keep them in one piece over many years of steady use.

The head is large and accommodating, with a meandering countertop, sink, and marine toilet on a raised platform. An opening side port provides daylight and fresh air. Tooled fiberglass throughout the head interior makes cleanup straightforward.

The forward settee converts to a berth that is 7 feet, 3 inches from one end to the other. The table is solid cherry with maple inlays.

Engine

A large hatch lifts easily on boosts to provide excellent access to the single Yanmar diesel. The fiberglass work in the bilge is beautifully wrought; no need for the builder to grind, sand, and cover with gelcoat. Every strand of nonwoven fiberglass can be seen and appreciated, and it's smooth enough, thanks to having been compressed by a vacuum bag during construction, to run your hand over without fear of fiberglass shards nicking the skin. Cableways are expertly routed and neatly fastened at close intervals, out of the way of wayward feet. The cable is heavy and color-coded, and looks like it belongs on an 80-foot yacht.

Sea Trial

Compared to an outboard or stern drive, the Back Cove's inboard shifts the center of gravity forward. This makes it easier for the boat to get on plane; in this case, the boat was comfortably semi-planing, without using the trim tabs, at just 12 mph, or 10.4 knots, evidenced by the clean waterflow from the transom and low rooster tail well astern. Planing at such a low speed opens the boat's effective operating range, so rather than digging a hole in the water and aiming for the sky at 12 to 15 mph, you can comfortably and efficiently cruise at these speeds, which incidentally makes slogging home in rough water that much more tolerable, or even enjoyable.

Backing out of the slip, the right-hand prop backs to port, and like any backing boat, the stern seeks the wind. By backing and filling, the operator has decent control over direction astern, and the standard bow thruster is available to help out as needed.

The hydraulic steering takes five turns lock-to-lock, which is certainly adequately responsive for a boat that can comfortably cruise at 28 mph (24 knots). The boat also turned adroitly—a full 360-degree turn to port took 19 seconds, and to starboard 23 seconds, the slight difference attributable to the walking effect of a single propeller.

The 315 hp Yanmar started with a puff of smoke from the side exhaust aft and it accelerated strongly; this engine will be plenty of power for this boat.

Course-keeping was good, with the boat tending to go in a straight line even at low speed. The waves were only 6 to 12 inches high, so we were not able to evaluate the boat's seakeeping or ride quality. With a low profile and low center of gravity, and a seakindly hull form, we would expect the Back Cove 29 to ride well in a 3- to 4-foot sea at moderate cruise speed. Visibility from the helm, as on most Maine-style boats, was excellent. Maneuvering around the dock, shifting with the engine mostly at idle, produced plenty of thrust with little throttle needed.

Back Cove 29 Performance Results

RPM	Speed, mph	Speed, knots	Noise Level, dBA
750	4.6	4.0	66
1,000	6.8	5.9	69
1,500	8.8	7.6	77
2,000	11.5	10.0	82
2,500	17.3	15.0	83
2,800	20.2	17.6	84
3,000	22.5	19.6	84
3,200	25.6	22.2	87
3,500	28.7	24.9	88
3,830	32.6	28.3	89

Test conditions: Two passengers, fuel tank three quarters full, with a 350 hp Yanmar diesel inboard. Bottom was lightly covered with two months' worth of freshwater slime.

The Back Cove 29 is a good-looking, practical, easy-to-own, well-built, and intelligently designed boat that seasoned sailors and powerboaters will best appreciate. You won't find 5-foot, 10-inch berths and 16-inch-high bowrails on this boat. There's really no substitute for the propulsion economy, simplicity, accessibility, and reliability of a single diesel inboard. If you need to sleep six and can't live without the extra interior volume, then the express cruiser is the boat for you. If your needs are simpler, and you value traditional styling and practicality, seaworthiness, and safe bow-to-stern accessibility, then the Back Cove 29 is well worth your consideration.

Options include a generator, air conditioning, hardtop, anchor windlass, a 315 hp Yanmar (a 260 hp Yanmar is standard), a Volvo 310 hp D6 common rail diesel, inverter, and cockpit seating.

Motor Yachts

A number of layouts are available for large yachts, including pilothouse motor yachts and variations on this layout. These yachts have a pilothouse or bridge deck forward that's raised above the saloon level, from one to a half-dozen steps. These motor yacht layouts typically have the master stateroom below the pilothouse, and in the bow are anywhere from one to four staterooms, depending on the size of the vessel. If the boat is above 50 feet, the two decks in the bridge area permits a lot of interior living space. The most space is available when the master stateroom deck is as low as possible in the bilge so the pilothouse isn't too high for the boat's beam. The saloon is down a few steps and aft, and a flybridge tucks neatly above the saloon and just behind the raised pilothouse.

These yachts not only have ample space, they also look like little ships. The pilothouse is usually the primary helm station (though on some yachts it may be the bridge above), and it's high enough to afford a good all-around view. Aft-facing windows should be fitted so you can see what's going on behind you and to make backing into a slip less stressful. Doors leading out to the weather decks make it easy for a couple to handle a big pilothouse motor yacht alone.

Because the pilothouse is only a few steps from the cabin, flybridge, and saloon, it's the heart of the ship, and it makes a good family boat. Everyone is close enough, yet privacy is afforded by the multi-level layout. Seaworthiness is improved since the saloon is relatively low, directly over the engine room, which reduces topside weight. A main deck–level cockpit is usually included with a transom, and perhaps a pair of side-bulwark doors, leading to the swim platform and dock.

For the cruising family, the aft-cabin motor yacht makes a lot of sense. The master suite, including the stateroom and head, are separated from the rest of the staterooms by the saloon, offering privacy. The guest staterooms are forward and the saloon amidships, with the engine room below the saloon. This layout is ideal for two couples or for a couple with kids. What you give up is a cockpit with all its conveniences and utility, though some manufacturers offer aft-cabin yachts with cockpits, too, since cockpits make boarding so much easier.

More than a few builders have produced aft cabins initially and then added cockpit extensions in response to market demand. Convertibles have also been modified to produce aft-cabin models, with the master suite replacing the cockpit. Some of the more successful such designs include exterior exhaust lines with the exhaust exiting the hull at the engine room and ducted aft via fiberglass tubes incorporated in the hull side at the waterline, or the lines are routed for underwater exhaust systems. This frees up space in the master suite, the sole of which is placed as low as possible in the hull to minimize the height of the cabintop.

Rhode Island–based Alden Yachts builds high-end, semicustom yachts from 40 to 70 feet, like the 53-foot aft-cabin model shown here. Built using epoxy resins and vacuum bagged, and post-cured, Aldens are considered to be among the finest yachts of their type in the world. C. Raymond Hunt planing hull designs make these among the most seaworthy and seakindly boats of their size available.   ALDEN YACHTS

Carver began this new high-end line of cruising motor yachts from scratch. Donald Blount and Associates and the Italian yacht design firm Nuvolari-Leonard were both involved in product design and engineering. Joinery and accommodations and fishing are world-class. Models from 55 to 65 feet are available.   GENMAR HOLDINGS, INC.

Carver builds cruising yachts from 36 to 52 feet in three styles, including aft-cabin and cockpit motor yachts, futuristic sedans, and a Voyager series of pilothouse motor yacht hybrids. Carvers are designed around their accommodations, and they are among the roomiest boats for a given LOA on the market. You pay a price in seakeeping ability, but these boats shine for their space. Carver makes good use of structural aluminum and frameless glass to produce the Euro-plus styling effects that have come to define the brand. The Carver 43 shown here is part of their aft-cabin series. It has a small cockpit and a twin suite layout with two staterooms, heads fore and aft, and a large, full-beam saloon in the middle.

GENMAR HOLDINGS, INC.

Originally an express cruiser builder, Cruisers Yachts has recently expanded into aft-cabin and flybridge sedan boats. The builder does a good job of combining interior volume with decent offshore performance, and the Euro-styling doesn't get in the way of practicality. Models range from 28 to 56 feet, and include the 455 Express Motoryacht aft-cabin shown here. This three-stateroom yacht has suites forward and aft with an airy, well-lit saloon and galley up in the middle. A third twin-bunk stateroom is tucked under the saloon dinette.   CRUISERS YACHTS

British yacht builder Fairline builds high-end cruising yachts in three series — Squadron motor yachts, Phantom flybridge yachts, and Targa performance yachts. Fairline has been increasing its presence in the U.S.; the Squadron line should help in this regard, as these yachts are fitted with luxurious accommodations, go fast on less power than many of their American competitors, and have some of the best rough-water hull designs in the business. The 68-footer is shown here. FAIRLINE YACHTS

Grand Banks is an established builder of high-end trawler and pilot-house motor yachts, as well as its Eastbay series of fast express sedan and flybridge yachts. Grand Banks has been updating its hulls with flatter buttocks aft for greater speed, and they've also been building bigger boats, including a 25-knot, 3,100 hp 72-foot Aleutian. The Grand Banks 59 is shown here. GRAND BANKS YACHTS

Italian boat and yacht conglomerate Ferretti is Europe's version of Brunswick, comprised of nine high-end yacht brands. The Ferretti Yacht brand includes cruising boats in the 50 to 90 foot range, like the 630 shown here. FERRETTI YACHTS

Hatteras is well-known (and equally well regarded) for two series of yachts — convertible sportfishermen and yachts. The yacht series has had a major overhaul recently, with new models coming out regularly, and they have Don Blount hulls for improved seakeeping and performance. The 64 shown here is the smallest of the motor yacht series, and it's one the new models with gracefully flowing Euro-styling. These heavily built yachts (the 64 weighs 116,700 pounds) have drivetrains to match — deep gear ratios and seven- or even eight-blade propellers make them smooth-running in heavy weather. HATTERAS YACHTS

Krogen builds a single model, the 52 Express shown here. It is a heavily built, offshore-capable semidisplacement yacht with proportions to make it seakindly in the open ocean in rough conditions. Visibility from the raised bridge pilothouse is good, and the yacht sleeps two couples in two staterooms with room for overflow in the cherry saloon. (Krogen Express is no longer affiliated with Kadey-Krogen Yachts, builders of displacement trawler yachts.)

KROGEN EXPRESS YACHTS

Meridian was created by Brunswick Corporation a few years ago to take over the Bayliner yacht brand, substantially improving the lineup in quality and prestige, with Meridian revamping old models and introducing new ones at a rapid pace. The line consists of sedan, aft-cabin, and pilothouse motor yachts from 34 to 58 feet. The 368 shown here is the smallest of the aft-cabin models, and like the rest of the line (and most of its direct competitors), it sports Euro-styling and lots of interior volume for the length. Molded stairs from the swim platform lead to the aft deck and down to a two-suite (each with island berth) cabin and an optional sleeping cubby. A lower helm is optional.

MERIDIAN YACHTS

Lyman Morse is a custom builder of high-end power and sail cruising yachts. Designed by Ward Setzer, the 80-foot Wombat is as easy on the eyes inside as it is out. Wombat's inlaid woodwork is as good as it gets. Twin 1,000 hp Cats deliver a top speed of 25 knots for this 105,000-pound beauty.

LYMAN MORSE YACHTS

Maine-based Sabre builds sail and power boats that will appeal to anyone looking for an upscale, traditionally styled boat that still offers good value. The powerboat line runs from 34 to 52 feet, and includes express and sedan models as well as this 47-foot aft-cabin-with-cockpit offering. Basically a sedan with an owner's suite taking up most of the cockpit, this design offers greater seaworthiness than most other aft-cabin models (lower CG), a good turn of speed, and Maine-style looks. Two-stateroom galley-down and three-stateroom galley-up layouts are available, as is exterior teak trim and a dinghy davit. A 43-foot, cockpit-free version of this boat is also available.

SABRE YACHTS

As the world's biggest boatbuilder, Sea Ray produces not only more hulls annually, it also offers more models than any other company: open- and closed-bow runabouts, deck boats, express boats from 24 to 68 feet, express fishermen, sedans to 58 feet, and this 40-foot aft-cabin yacht. Visibility from the helm in this inshore yacht is good (you're up high, and the windshield is top-drawer). The cabin has fore and aft suites (with a handy split head in the aft master) and a large, bright saloon in the middle. Gentle-sloping molded stairs to the aft deck make boarding safe and easy.

SEA RAY BOATS

Silverton offers a wide range of offshore convertibles and inshore motor yachts at prices that make these roomy, well-appointed boats affordable for more families. The builder's yacht series includes aft-cabin motor yacht models from 35 to 43 feet. The 43 shown here comes with a single helm on the bridge, a family-friendly layout with privacy for two couples in fore and aft suites, safe and easy access from the swim platform, a roomy, well-lit interior, and a large covered aft deck.

SILVERTON YACHTS

Viking Sport Cruisers imports Princess Yachts built in England and distributes them via its U.S. dealer network. Viking specifies design features and components that will make them suited to, and competitive in, the U.S. market. The yachts are available three styles: express yachts, flybridge yachts, and motor yachts like the 70 shown here.

VIKING SPORT CRUISERS

LAZZARA LSX QUAD 75

Lazzara LSX Quad 75 Specifications	
LOA:	76'9"
LWL:	62'1"
Beam:	18'2"
Deadrise:	12.2 deg.
Displacement:	78,000 lb. (half-load)
Draft:	42"
Fuel capacity:	830 gal.

The Lazzara LSX Quad is the result of a simple proposal Volvo Penta made to the boatbuilder: build a new boat around a quadruple Volvo Penta Inboard Performance System (IPS). Just as an increasing number of twin IPS boats in the 35- to 45-foot range have been benefiting for several years from twin IPS power, there was no reason that the same economies and space savings wouldn't apply to a larger boat with double the power (50- to 60-footers are also available with triple IPS power).

That Volvo Penta chose Lazzara for this venture was no accident. The builder has advanced the science of building yachts that are strong and lightweight, and nothing has as much impact on speed in a planing vessel as weight. IPS has an impressive power-to-weight ratio, better than any inclined-shaft inboard. The LSX Quad 75 displaces about 86,000 pounds, compared with competitors' similar-size models that weigh as much as 125,000 to 135,000 pounds. Lazzara's 80-footer cruises at 29 knots while competitors' models with the same power make 20 knots, at most, at cruise.

In production since 2007, the Lazzara LSX Quad 75 is the firm's entry-level model, which puts the builder in perspective considering this is a multimillion-dollar, 40-ton, 75-foot high-end oceangoing yacht. The styling is as graceful and flowing as any of the Italians' or Brits', but Lazzara doesn't let aesthetics overpower practical considerations

elemental to any well-found oceangoing yacht. The deckhouse side windows are a good example—there's not a straight line anywhere in their profile, but they're long and tall, providing excellent visibility from the lower helm station.

Construction

The Lazzara LSX Quad 75 is 20 to 30 percent lighter in displacement than its competitors, and this weight savings is achieved through the extensive use of composites and by treating the hull and superstructure as a monocoque (one-piece, load-absorbing skin) structure so that loads the hull is subjected to at speed in a seaway are transmitted and absorbed evenly and efficiently throughout the hull, deck, and superstructure.

The ability of the yacht's skin to absorb these tension and compression loads is a result of the builder's extensive use of hand-laid nonwoven composite fiberglass inner and outer laminates with a structural core of high-density end-grain balsa. Further, the entire hull, deck, and superstructure are laid up exclusively with premium vinylester resin that produces a stronger, lighter, more resilient, osmosis-proof, print-through-resistant, and more durable structure than standard general-purpose resins.

After the gelcoat is applied, two layers of hand-laid ½-ounce mat are rolled out the length of the hull as a print-through and anti-osmosis barrier. This is followed by two layers of triaxial fiberglass reinforcement, with each roll running seamlessly the length of the hull. Next comes 1-inch balsa AL600 coring in the bottom and ¾-inch in the hull sides. The balsa is vacuum bagged into a layer of ¾-ounce mat to ensure skin-to-core bind integrity against the outer hull skin. Two more layers of triaxial reinforcement follow on the inside of the hull over the balsa. The hull is solid fiberglass, with up to 20 layers of reinforcements at the keel, chines, and hull penetrations.

Six fiberglass composite stringers run the length of the hull, providing stiffness for the bottom and a continuous foundation for the yacht's interior and propulsion system. These stringers are completely encapsulated in three layers of fiberglass reinforcement running the length of the hull and from chine to chine. Cross members, much like ribs in a wooden boat, run between the stringers every 24 inches from bow to stern, locking the stringers together and defining the hull skin panel size. One-inch balsa-cored Lauan-skinned bulkheads notched to receive the continuous stringers are tabbed to the hull.

Main decks, molded in one piece from bow to stern, are cored with 2-inch high-density balsa. All hull and deck penetrations are through solid fiberglass. The shoebox hull-to-deck joint is as bulletproof as possible, bonded with a high-strength adhesive, fastened and clamped with stainless steel screws every 6 inches, and then fiberglassed with two layers of fiberglass from the inside the length of the hull. Wiring and plumbing chases of PVC pipe are built into the yacht's hull and deck structure, making it easy to add or remove systems throughout the yacht's life without disturbing the surrounding structure.

Walkthrough

Topsides

The LSX Quad 75 is unique right from the start of our walkthrough. At the swim platform is a tender garage, and outboard of it are windows looking down into the engine room. The name of the boat includes Quad, which alludes to the four Volvo Penta IPS engines, and they're prominently on display.

The superstructure, which has minimal mass in its supports, can be thought of as a seagoing version of a Nascar race car's roll cage. The mullion frames between windows are made of steel encapsulated in carbon fiber, which minimizes their cross section and maximizes window area. These structural members tie together in the top of the superstructure, and also to cross members in the cabintop below the windshield.

The deckhouse, which was subjected to dynamic loading analysis during the design phase, is cored with high-density structural foam, further reducing weight above the yacht's center of gravity. Frameless glass windows are bonded to rabbets molded into in the deckhouse, creating a smooth, uncluttered appearance topside. The overall effect is a light and airy saloon and minimal weight topside.

The yacht's one-piece interior is completed on the production line floor and then lifted as a unit into the hull. It is placed on ¼-inch rubber discs that help absorb high-frequency vibrations, and then bonded to the hull structure. This lack of direct hard contact decouples the yacht's interior from the hull structure, creating a quieter living environment.

Hull Design

The Lazzara LSX Quad 75 has a hard-chine planing hull with a fine entry tapering to a modest 12.2 degrees of transom deadrise. Bottom sections are slightly radiused in section view, improving ride quality by reducing slamming, and increasing the strength and stiffness of the hull. A moderate beam-to-length ratio produces an efficiently propelled, seakindly hull with a smooth ride and favorable seakeeping properties.

Port and starboard stairs lead to the aft deck from the swim platform. A big sunpad is on centerline, and it's interesting to consider the design of the main deck area aft: the superstructure stops well forward, which gives the boat a lower profile as is appropriate for a hardtop express layout. It also reduces weight and top-hamper aft, which contributes to the yacht's flat running angle at cruise speed, and makes it less susceptible to crosswind dockside. Our test boat had a seat forward of the sunpad along with a table and deck chairs.

Wide side decks lead forward with a bulwark topped by a teak and stainless steel railing. At the bow atop the trunk cabin is a second sunpad. The deck forward is flat and convenient to walk on. The megayacht-class quality and scantlings of the ground tackle, cleats, and chocks is impressive. These oversized chrome-plated fittings hint at the construction quality found throughout the yacht. The teak decks topside are beautifully fitted and finished, providing an effective nonskid surface underfoot while looking good.

Saloon

Stainless steel framed sliding doors open from the aft deck to the main deck saloon. Large all-around windows and 6-foot, 8-inch headroom make this an inviting open living area. Woodwork throughout the yacht is of okoume, a dark African wood with a beautiful grain pattern, finished with Lazzara's durable, high-gloss polyethylene finishing process. The okoume cabinetry and joinery stacks up head-to-head with the finest yacht woodworking in the world. It was also our first exposure to the proprietary polyethylene coating process Lazzara acquired from a Korean piano company that was vacating a manufacturing facility in South Carolina a few years ago.

The saloon has a day head aft, along with a central seating area with leather stuffed chairs to port and an L-shaped settee opposite to starboard. Forward to port is the stairway to the lower-deck atrium and to starboard is the helm. The single interior design innovation most evident on the LSX is the atrium forward below the windshield that makes the main deck saloon open to the dining and galley area below. Lazzara first used this basic layout on its Gulfstar trawlers in the 1970s, and it works equally well on this 75-footer. Stairs lead down from the main deck saloon to the atrium, which has a dining area with settee and table to port, and the generously equipped and proportioned galley

opposite to starboard. This is a pleasant living space, bathed in light and with what is effectively a two-story ceiling.

Helm

The helm station, with its high seats presenting a commanding view all around, is open to the rest of the saloon, as well as to the atrium below. The electronics panel swivels on demand to suit the driver's height and position, whether seated or standing. When standing, the wheel and engine controls, including the IPS joystick, are at your fingertips; you can also run the yacht while sitting on the comfortable, well-padded, and nicely contoured adjustable helm seat. Gauges and switches are ergonomically laid out and easy to reach and see. We'd like the corner posts supporting the superstructure narrowed to show more horizon, but otherwise visibility ahead is good.

With the atrium directly below the windshield, the first concern is interior lights reflecting off the glass and hampering night visibility. To prevent this, Lazzara engaged an automotive glass manufacturer to develop windshield sections that have both heat-reflective and antiglare properties.

Cabin

The LSX Quad 75 has a four-stateroom accommodations plan. A guest suite forward is finished with the same attention to detail as the rest of the yacht's interior, offering guests 6 feet, 5 inches of headroom, along with a 6-foot, 4-inch double bed, a hanging closet, and private head with separate shower. A pair of guest staterooms is off the central passageway just aft of the galley. Each has a 6-foot, 3-inch double bed, hanging closet, and private head with a large separate shower. Each also has a large hull side window, which really enhances the welcoming appeal of these staterooms.

The master stateroom is aft on the lower deck where the ride and motion at sea are most comfortable. This is one of the most pleasant staterooms we've seen. This exceptional full-beam bedroom has big windows—almost 9 feet long and 16 inches high—in the hull sides, which had us wondering why boatbuilders haven't been doing this all along, as it makes the area so much more appealing and enjoyable. A king-size bed, 6 feet, 5 inches long, is on centerline, with drawers and storage space below. Dressers and seats are along either side of the stateroom, with a glass table to starboard. The master head is aft to port, finished in a beautiful marble (cored with honeycomb to reduce weight) on the decks and bulkheads. His-and-her sinks, an open linen locker, and a large closet are included, as is a megayacht-style two-person walk-in shower.

Aft and accessible from the engine room is the crew stateroom with bunk beds and private head.

Engine

The starboard stairs leading from the swim platform hinge up for walk-in access to the well-lit, cleanly laid out engine room. The four D6 Volvo diesels line up athwartship, one next to the other, and there's plenty of room to work around them. The engines sit on soft mounts, transmitting little vibration to the hull, since the IPS pods absorb the propeller thrust.

The engine room bilge is cleanly finished, ground smooth, and painted white for easy visibility and cleanup. Plumbing is minimized around the engines, with the cooling water taken in through the pods below the hull and sent directly to the engines' heat exchangers. Engine maintenance points, including oil dipsticks and freshwater expansion tanks, as well as the engine-mounted raw-water strainers, are easily accessible. The high-pressure fuel lines leading to and from the fuel filter-separators, conveniently lined up along the forward catwalk, are jacketed in stainless steel shielding for extra strength and chafe protection.

Lazzara estimates that in addition to the propulsion efficiencies provided by the quad Volvo Penta IPS power plant, there is a weight savings of 5,500 pounds over the conventional inclined-shaft, twin 1,050 hp inboard diesels it would take to produce similar performance. The quad system costs considerably less for the builder to purchase than a conventional power plant with all its inboard running gear, and takes far less time—9 hours versus 5 days—to install. The builder estimates that operating costs for a quad Volvo Penta IPS boat will be 30 percent less than with conventional diesel inboards.

In the event an engine needs to be replaced, the tender garage floor unbolts and lifts out, providing unrestricted access from the stern to the engine room interior.

Sea Trial

We had ideal conditions for our sea trial off Ft. Lauderdale, with 5- to 7-footers kicked up by a strong easterly wind. With an 11-foot, 4-inch height of eye, the distance to the horizon is about 4 nautical miles, and we never lost sight of that horizon coming up on plane. The Lazzara runs at an impressively flat 2.8 degrees once it reaches 18 knots, which for this hull optimizes both efficiency and ride smoothness in big head seas. This low trim angle and the convexity in the bottom made the boat a little on the wet side in these seas and strong wind, as would be expected, with the bow slicing the waves well forward. But it was great being able to maintain 22 to 24 knots, which was made possible by the trim and the slightly radiused hull form, along with a moderately fine entry and ample deadrise in the forward sections.

Turning to put the seas on the quarter, the boat tracked with hands off the wheel, running downsea as well as any we've experienced, and much better than most. Acceleration was strong, with the boat reaching 25 knots in 22 seconds.

In addition to the superior handling characteristics provided by IPS, noise levels were the quietest we've seen in fourteen years of evaluating yachts of all descriptions. We recorded 68 dBA at the helm at 2,700 rpm and 57 dBA at idle. At these levels, there was essentially no discernible engine sound, just ambient wave and wind noise. Likewise, propulsion plant–related vibrations were barely discernible at the helm. Down in the master stateroom, noise levels at full power were a very low 71 dBA, the result of extensive sound-deadening materials and a complete second bulkhead between the engine room and the yacht's accommodations.

The boat managed to stay comfortably on plane with a solid wake astern at just 12.5 knots, an indication of a well-considered center of gravity and efficient hull form. This low-speed planing capability also broadens the yacht's range of efficient operation at sea. Lying-to in the trough, the roll period was comfortable and easy, with none of the uncomfortable snap roll experienced on more than a few other express-style planing yachts. The builder reports speeds as high as 32 knots with the quad propulsion in optimum conditions. In our rough seas, we saw 29 knots in a beam sea, but didn't expect to set any speed records in those conditions. We also ran for a while with the sunroof open, creating an open-air effect in the saloon.

The great advantage of four engines is the propulsion versatility in the event one of them breaks down. With a twin-screw boat, you'd be reduced to a get-home capability at displacement speed running on one engine. With just three Volvo IPS units running, the LSX is capable of 27 knots at full power, and a comfortable 20 to 22 knots at cruise.

In fact, in our 5- to 7-footers, we recorded 19.5 knots at 2,750 rpm with stable temperature and pressure parameters for the three running engines. Forgetting the efficiency and maneuverability benefits for a moment, just this one advantage makes a compelling case for specifying the quad IPS power in a larger yacht. A quad installation also permits low-speed cruising capability by moderately loading up two engines, which is how diesels are designed

to run, and shutting down the other two. This assumes that the IPS drives are fitted with reciprocating oilers that lubricate the offline trailing props, allowing them to freewheel indefinitely without damage.

Back at the marina, we thought we'd use the aft-deck control station to dock the boat, but visibility all around the boat is so good from the main helm station we ran the boat from there. IPS gave us complete control in the 2-knot current, and this combination of great helm visibility and such complete control will make a few owners think twice about hiring someone to run the boat for them.

From an interior appointments, woodwork craftsmanship, and fit-and-finish perspective, the Lazzara LSX Quad is as fine a yacht as is built today anywhere in the world. This Lazzara is also an uncommonly successful homogenization of form and function; the builder has produced in its LSX Quad 75 a beautifully styled, yet eminently operator-friendly yacht that will appeal to the experienced boat operator.

In terms of its structural and propulsion engineering, the LSX Quad 75 is superior to anything we have tested to date; the boat is arguably even better below the surface than it is in plain view. Our only quibble is with the width of the forward deckhouse corner posts, which interfere with sight lines from the helm—more so than is the case with some of the best British and American yachts. On the other hand, it interferes less than on many other yachts. Since this is the yacht's only helm station, it remains the one area impacting vessel operation that we would recommend modifying. The Lazzara LSX Quad 75 is an exceptional vessel that has earned our highest recommendation.

Rigid Inflatable Boats

Rigid inflatable boats (RIBs) have soared in popularity, mostly due to their seaworthiness and built-in fendering system. Their air-filled (and sometimes foam-filled) collars give them positive buoyancy galore. Unless the collars are punctured in several different places, the boat will remain afloat in the worst sea conditions. This makes them especially popular for surf-rescue work.

Although most RIBs have fiberglass (the rigid part) bottoms, aluminum is also popular, especially for commercial and military duty where boats tend to take a beating. RIBs with foam collars (foam with small air bladders) are puncture proof; however, they also have less buoyancy because they weigh more, and are not as popular among rescue workers for that reason.

The critical thing in any RIB is the quality of the collar and the bond holding it to the hull. The base cloth of polyester or nylon is impregnated with PVC, polyurethane, or Hypalon for durability and abrasion resistance. PVC is the best value, and earlier problems with longevity have been solved by the chemists. Hypalon is the longest lasting and has great abrasion resistance; its downside is its cost, and it has to be hand-glued, as opposed to PVC, which can be welded. Hypalon is used on professional boats used by outfits like the navy and coast guard, which are more concerned with the end result than cost. More expensive than PVC or Hypalon, polyurethane coatings can be welded like PVC and may even be more durable than Hypalon (the jury's still out).

Achilles makes a full line of commercial and recreational RIBs and inflatables. The HB-DX shown here is a new model with a deep-V bottom and is available in 9- and 10-foot sizes.   ACHILLES INFLATABLES

Achilles' LSI series is comprised of soft-bottom inflatable tenders with inflatable floors, like the one shown here. These boats are lightweight and designed for easy deployment.   ACHILLES INFLATABLES

Avon makes a full line of commercial, military, and recreational RIBs and inflatables, powered by outboard, waterjet, or stern drive. This 19-foot SeaSport 580 Deluxe has a deep-V fiberglass hull, a center console, and ample seating. AVON INFLATABLES

Custom made by Almar of Tacoma, Washington, these rescue boats are built to towing and salvage company SafeSea's specifications and used for rescue work in Rhode Island. This boat is 35 by 12 feet and has twin Yanmar 370 hp diesels driving Hamilton 274 waterjets. Top speed is 43 knots and fuel capacity is 200 gallons. Foam fills all voids between the aluminum hull and deck. The collar is air-filled and has seven individual chambers, which, as with any RIB, gives the vessel tremendous form stability. The coxswain has to stay on his or her toes when working around breaking waves, though, since all that form stability applies when the boat is inverted as well, so it is not self-righting. ALMAR BOATS

Mercury's largest RIB, the 27-foot, 9-inch PT-850 is capable of carrying up to 10,538 pounds or 26 people, and can handle up to twin 250 hp outboards; a stern-drive version is also available. MERCURY MARINE

Apex builds a wide range of RIBs used for everything from tending yachts to rescue work in the open ocean. Apex's lineup includes this A-20 tender, which looks like a little yacht with all the hardware up high. This RIB can carry up to 12 people or a 3,250-pound payload, and it is rated for outboards up to 180 hp. APEX INFLATABLES

Nautica makes a wide range of RIBs, including jets, diesels, outboards, and stern drives. This 16 jet is a racy little model with a 165 hp four-stroke Yamaha waterjet power plant (like the one used in Yamaha's own jet boats), and the engine box doubling as a helm seat. The boat has a shoal draft and can pull a skier, who will be safer with no prop to worry about. The profile is low so the boat can easily fit inside a yacht garage. Toe kicks inside the cockpit make getting around easy and safe. NAUTICA INTERNATIONAL

Zodiac's RIBs range from small yacht tenders to all-weather offshore rescue and military craft. This Cadet Fastroller 260 is designed as a versatile tender with quick setup capability. ZODIAC MARINE

While not actually a RIB, in the sense that it does not have inflatable collars (though it is rigid, and it is a boat), the Triumph 120 CC is nevertheless a RIB at heart. It is constructed with rigid polyethylene and its collars are filled with foam instead of air, rendering it unsinkable and hard to damage. GENMAR HOLDINGS, INC.

Sedans

The sedan is a close cousin of the convertible. It's not too often you hear the term on the waterfront these days (probably because it sounds more pedstrian than "hardtop express" or "coupe"), but it used to refer to a boat that was basically a convertible with a small cockpit and big saloon. Whether this is the in-vogue label or not, it works for me. These boats usually have a flybridge, like the convertible, but the cockpit is sparsely equipped, if at all, for fishing. The saloon may well have a windshield instead of a fiberglass deckhouse up front, which is great for those who like to see where they're going as well as where they've been, from down below. Sedans may or may not have the seakeeping and sustained speed capability of a convertible. It all depends in their hull form, and (as on any boat) whether ride quality or acreage triumphed in the design phase.

Part of the high-end Ferretti Group, Apreamare builds upscale express cruiser sedans with an obvious Mediterranean pedigree. Available in sizes from 25 to 53 feet, these boats are distinctive for their teak-covered topsides, radiused sterns (the running surface continues aft below the swim platform, well past the visible transom), cherry or mahogany interiors, and oversized teak swim platforms. The 60 shown here, is certified for ocean service 100 miles offshore. The 60 has three staterooms and 900 hp inboard diesels capable of 31 knots at full throttle. FERRETTI GROUP

The 49 Sedan is quintessential Alden, a bridgeless sedan (you can also get it with a bridge, and in different pilothouse designs). There's a choice of layouts, including one with two suites, and galley-up and galley-down plans are available. This is a very high-end, semi-custom, Hunt design that is at home in the open ocean. Hull design and construction are world class. ALDEN YACHTS

Carver Yachts, builders of sedan and aft-cabin cruising yachts from 31 to 56 feet, has long stressed internal volume over offshore seakindliness, so these yachts are not suitable for anyone looking to operate regularly in moderately rough conditions. That said, you won't find a roomier, more accommodating calm-water yacht anywhere. The 35 Super Sport shown here is an entry-level model, with a roomy, well-lit (thanks to lots of glass) interior, including a full-beam saloon. There is a roomy bridge with forward seating, molded stairs to the cockpit below, nicely crafted cherry cabinetry inside, a single owner's suite with private head, and even double recliners in the saloon. Gas power is standard and diesels are optional. GENMAR HOLDINGS, INC.

Cruisers builds express, flybridge, and aft-cabin cruising yachts from 28 to 56 feet. The 447 Sport Sedan shown here has a livable layout with a master suite with private head forward, and a second stateroom below the raised saloon sole—which is a great way to use that interior volume. The large saloon takes up much of the yacht's LOA, and the bridge deck extends partially over the cockpit below, providing extra protection from the elements. Twin gas engines are available (at 29,000 pounds, this is much too heavy a boat for gas engines), as are Volvo and Yanmar diesels to 480 hp.

CRUISERS YACHTS

Luhrs, like its sister companies Mainship and Silverton, packs a lot of boat into a given budget. It's well-known for its line of offshore convertibles and express fishing boats. Recently added to the mix is the 41 hardtop sedan shown here, a boat that cruises as well as it fishes. Great for people who don't like climbing ladders, or just like being with the rest of the family and guests, this layout has a lot to offer. Two sliding skylights brighten up the saloon. Visibility from the lower, raised helm station is excellent, with little to obscure the horizon from the operator's line of sight. The boat sleeps up to six in two staterooms and the saloon. Twin Cummins or Yanmar inboard diesel power to 645 hp is available.

LUHRS CORPORATION

Grand Banks builds upscale sedan and convertible cruising yachts from 39 to 58 feet. The 39 shown here is their entry-level model, and it serves as an excellent introduction to the lineup. Traditionally styled and designed and engineered by C. Raymond Hunt, the 39 has good manners offshore with a pair of 500 hp inboard diesels producing a top speed of around 30 knots. The cabin has a master stateroom forward and a large dinette that converts to a double berth. Visibility from the lower helm is excellent, as are ergonomics at the helm.

GRAND BANKS YACHTS

Mainship builds well-equipped, relatively low cost trawlers (34 to 43 feet) and a Pilot series of express and sedan cruisers from 34 to 43 feet. The 43 Pilot shown here has Down East styling, with traditionally appealing lines, an enclosed pilothouse, and an extended hardtop providing sun and rain protection in the big cockpit. A forward master stateroom and a second stateroom tucked under the saloon provide sleeping accommodations, with overflow for two to sleep in the saloon. The big windows in the saloon give it a cheery feel lacking in some express cruisers. Twin diesel inboard power to 540 hp is available.

MAINSHIP TRAWLERS

Mochi is part of the Ferretti Group specializing in a line of Dolphin high-end sedans that are an interpretation of the Down East lobster boat with curves in every direction and a clean, sweeping sheerline. Three Mochi Dolphins are available: 44-, 51-, and 74-footers. The 51 shown here has a hidden garage for the tender aft and three staterooms, including crew quarters amidships. Standard power is a pair of V-drive inboard 800 hp MANs that deliver a 35-knot top speed. FERRETTI GROUP

Riviera is an Australian builder of upscale convertibles from 33 to 60 feet (it also builds sport and express yachts), and is making steady inroads in the U.S. market. The 4700 shown here is one of the brand's newer models, built on a good-running hull and featuring a stern garage for the tender, underwater exhaust, hydraulic swim platform, a two- or three-stateroom and two-head layout, main deck galley, and aft saloon windows that open to the cockpit. Twin Cat 575 hp diesels are standard. The 4700 I ran was one of the quietest boats I've ever tested. RIVIERA YACHTS

Regal builds a wide range of runabouts, flybridge, and express cruisers to 52 feet. The 4080 shown here is a solidly built, well-appointed yacht with lots of Euro-style looks and features, including a big molded stairway up to the bridge, a roof over the cockpit, and all-glass contoured sliding doors from the cockpit to the saloon. The master stateroom is forward, and a midcabin is below the saloon dinette, all of which combine for a six-person sleeping capacity. REGAL MARINE

Sabre builds well-built, good-running express, sedan, and aft-cabin yachts from 34 to 52 feet. The sedan lineup includes this 36-footer, which is offered with an extended hardtop and with and without a bridge. Yanmar diesels to 370 hp are available, which deliver a 30-knot top end. Cherry is used extensively in the light-and-bright interior, which includes a private owner's stateroom forward. A very practical design, the 36's wide side decks make getting around topside safe and easy. SABRE YACHTS

Sea Ray is best known for its runabouts and express-style Sundancer cruiser. Sea Ray also builds a line of Sedan Bridges, including this 58-footer, the largest in the series. The 58 has a full-beam master suite, molded stairs to the bridge, three staterooms and two heads with separate showers, and up to twin 862 hp MAN inboard diesels.

SEA RAY BOATS

Norwegian boatbuilder Windy builds runabouts and cruising yachts from 25 to 58 feet. Pictured is the queen of the fleet, the 58-foot Zephyros. Featured are a retractable sunroof, triple helm seats, a good-riding deep-V hull, Volvo or MAN inboards delivering up to 40 knots, and twin suites.

WINDY YACHTS

Pearson Composites builds three True North models—this 33, the original 38, and a new 45. A plumb stem delivers more running surface, and a commensurately better ride, than the typical 33. Sold factory-direct, single diesel power provides economical operation. These seagoing SUVs have big multi-function cockpits, galley-up layouts with airy pilothouses, and small but functional cabins.

PEARSON YACHTS

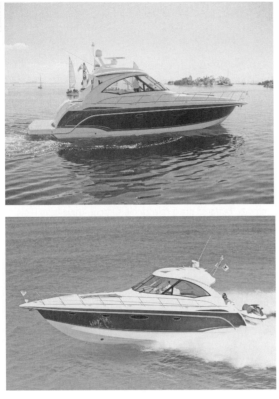

Formula 45 Yacht Specifications	
LOA:	45' (hull)
Beam:	13'11"
Deadrise:	18 deg.
Dry weight:	31,800 lb.
Draft:	3'3"
Fuel capacity:	350 gal.
Water capacity:	100 gal.

Formula has been increasing the size of its boats, with the Formula 45 Yacht now the second-largest model in their lineup. In production since 2006, the Formula 45 has a cabin that's large and accommodating for a 45-footer. A large well-designed and -engineered windshield that eliminates the need for canvas and plastic filler curtains provides excellent visibility from the helm. The Formula 45 also has excellent engine room accessibility thanks to an entire cockpit-transom hatch that hinges well clear. It also has Volvo Penta IPS propulsion, which presents many benefits regarding performance and accommodations.

Construction

The Formula 45 starts off as a layer of gelcoat followed by a coat of vinylester resin and then a coat of chop, also wet out in vinylester resin. This skin coat with its premium-resin foundation protects against osmotic blistering on the hull bottom and print-through on the hull sides. The bottom is a solid fiberglass laminate, while the sides are cored with Divinycell for added lightweight stiffness (Formula has never used balsa coring in its hulls).

The hull bottom is supported by a one-piece molded and flanged fiberglass grid that's bonded in place with Plexus adhesive. A fiberglass-encapsulated stringer grid built using Coosa board composite supports the cabin, and structural bulkheads are composite fiberglass and Coosa board. The shoebox hull-to-deck joint is also bonded with Plexus and through-bolted every 18 inches. Areas that can't be reached from inside the boat have aluminum backing strips that are tapped to serve as nuts for the through-bolts, which means no lag bolts are used, which is good. Decks are cored with Divinycell, and all through-hull and through-deck penetrations are drilled through solid, coreless sections.

Hull Design

The Formula 45 has a modified-V, hard-chine planing hull with reverse chines and 18 degrees of deadrise at the transom.

Walkthrough

Cockpit

You board the 45 from its big optional hydraulic swim platform; the whole affair lowers to 20 inches below the surface to launch and retrieve the tender. A transom trunk provides storage for fenders and lines, and a pair of steps lead up to the cockpit. Formula includes two pairs of stern cleats, one pair at deck level on the platform and a second set up near the gunwale. The stern door, which is to starboard, is only 25 inches; that's about 5 inches lower than we like to see for safety, especially considering how strongly this boat accelerates.

The boat has two topside conversation areas, the aft cockpit and the bridge deck. The aft cockpit has a U-shaped lounge settee and table mounts on a pair of recessed deck sockets. The whole transom and cockpit hinges up for access to the engine room below, and a day hatch in the middle of the settee provides quick engine access as needed.

Forward to starboard, behind the helm seat, is a refreshment center with sink, refrigerator, and optional grill. Unlike many yachts of this size, the cockpit is actually habitable under way, given the virtual absence of fumes and the quietness of the Volvo Penta IPS system. All the cockpit canvas fits inside a single purpose-built locker to port.

Engine

Engine room accessibility is excellent. The one-piece cockpit and transom lifts at the touch of a button, which opens up the engine room completely. Large steps lead down from the swim platform, and the engine room is large and uncluttered, with plenty of space to access the compact Volvo Penta IPS engine and pod installation. Wiring and plumbing runs are neatly installed and well labeled. Both Volvo and Cummins V-drive diesel inboard and Volvo Penta IPS 600 power are available, though Volvo Penta IPS with its increased efficiency will be the preferred choice for many people.

Foredeck

The side decks leading forward from the cockpit are narrow—just 5 inches wide, so you have to shuffle along and hang on tight when walking on them. On the other hand, the builder has provided a path through the opening centerline windshield, complete with molded steps up to the dash, and the narrow side decks open up another foot or so of internal room, which is a reasonable trade-off well suited to the intended use of this boat. What looks to be a pair of fiberglass panels just forward of the windshield are actually translucent windows that let sunlight into the cabin below; the color of these windows matches the surrounding trunk cabin gelcoat so well it's by no means evident at first glance what they are.

The foredeck has aggressive nonskid. We'd like to see Formula raise the 26-inch bow railing by about 4 inches for better security forward. The windlass and integral anchor hawsepipe (there is no need for a separate anchor pulpit on this boat) are hidden below a deck hatch in the bow. Formula also provides a pair of sunpads on the cabin top.

Helm

Forward on the elevated bridge deck is a portside lounge opposite the helm. All the seating on the bridge deck of our test boat had real leather upholstery. There's an air-conditioning outlet at the helm in case all that glass heats things up in the tropics, but the natural ventilation provided by the opening centerline windshield and side vent windows kept things quite comfortable on the 78° day of our sea trial.

The helm is ergonomically laid out, with a pair of large-screen electronics displays positioned directly in front of the operator. The steering wheel and engine controls are comfortably positioned for either standing or seated driving. The helm's bench seat fits two, with each seat having a flip-up bolster, and there's plenty of room between the seat and the steering wheel to stand and drive comfortably.

Visibility from the helm is exceptionally good, and it's one of the main reasons this boat is such a delight to operate. When you have a clear view of the horizon in all directions, spatial awareness is much improved over the standard helm with thick windshield frames, radar arches, canvas, and other obstructions interfering with your ability to see.

Those high glass windows eliminate the need for canvas of any kind, which greatly simplifies life afloat. Industrial-size, 48-inch windshield wipers with washers and defrosters are provided, and a dark dash treatment minimizes glare. Wide molded stairs lead forward through the opening center windshield, which doubles as a door and has a sliding window for ventilation with four open positions.

Cabin

The companionway stairs down to the cabin have a gentle rise and run, so they're easy to navigate. The cabin's 6-foot, 9-inch headroom adds to the commodious feel, as does the natural light from the hatches and side windows; in fact those hull side windows, measuring 40 by 9 inches, are really picture windows when compared to similar-style boats. Our test boat's combination of natural wood decking and cherry cabinetry combined with off-white bulkheads for a salty-yet-contemporary look, with enough woodwork to remind you you're on a yacht, but not so much as to be overpowering.

Immediately to starboard is a big C-shaped dinette-settee that converts to an amply proportioned 6-foot, 5-inch by 3-foot, 6-inch berth. Flat-screen TVs are all the rage on yachts these days, and this boat obliges with its 37-inch model above the dinette. Opposite is the big L-shaped Corian-topped galley, with lots of counter space,

a deep double sink, large refrigerator and cook-top, and another of those picture windows behind the sink.

Just aft of the galley is the entrance to the private midcabin where, just as on most European yachts of the same size, a pair of single berths are found. These convert easily to a single 6-foot, 3-inch by 5-foot, 6-inch king-size bed, with the filler piece cleverly hinging out from below the right-hand berth. There's a generous amount of headroom—6 feet, 4 inches at the entrance to the midcabin, and 5 feet, 6 inches by the beds (which are below the helm station). The midcabin has its own head with a sink spigot that doubles as a showerhead; in another utilitarian touch, the sink is conveniently situated in the companionway between the saloon and the head.

Forward is the master stateroom with its 6-foot, 3-inch by 5-foot, 6-inch island berth (in our view, any 45-footer really ought to have berths 6 feet, 5 inches long or better, just like at home). Formula pays attention to the details, installing a full-length mirror on the back of the stateroom door, and there's also an optional electronic safe in the closet. Access to the saloon's TV is inside the head. The master head has a fold-down seat over the VacuFlush toilet and a separate shower stall. Our test boat had the optional Ralph Lauren interior, which gives it an upscale look that will be identifiable to many. You can expect to stay cool on this boat, with three air conditioners provided; 7,000 Btu forward in the master stateroom, 18,000 Btu in the saloon area, and 30,000 Btu on the bridge deck by the helm.

Sea Trial

The helm is high off the water, which, combined with the minimal obstructions to visibility caused by windshield and deckhouse structure, made driving this boat a pleasure. If you have to quantify what makes driving a boat pleasurable, you would include visibility, helm and propulsion responsiveness, helm

station ergonomics and, for us at least, machinery quietness—each of these elements satisfies on this boat.

Volvo Penta's QL trim system uses interceptor plates instead of trim tabs for stern lift; these plates drop vertically at the transom to create a high-pressure area, just like trim tabs. Tests have shown (perhaps counterintuitively) that interceptor plates provide more lift and less drag than standard trim tabs, while reacting more quickly (which actually can be a problem on high-speed boats). We tested the boat's speed and fuel flow at 2,700, 3,000, and 3,300 rpm. At each rpm setting, we picked up about 0.5 knot with the interceptor plates lowered, while fuel flow decreased 1 gph at 2,700 rpm and 0.5 gph at 3,000 rpm, remaining essentially unchanged at 3,300 rpm.

Even with the weight of the Volvo Penta IPS system in the stern, we had good visibility ahead while coming up on plane, with the pulpit just nudging the horizon (from our seated height of eye). With the QL plates lowered, the pulpit stayed below the horizon throughout the maneuver, which means you can always see the water in front of the boat while coming up to cruising speed, a critical safety consideration. Running at 18 knots without the QL system, the horizon was visible above the pulpit from our seated height of eye.

The IPS system produced superb handling; it takes just 3.5 turns from lock-to-lock, and it was fingertip-easy to spin the wheel at any speed. Boatbuilders can limit the steering angle of the IPS pods to prevent the boat from turning too fast and heeling over too far at high speed. On the 45, they're set at 24 degrees at low speed, and 12 degrees at full power. Since the propeller thrust changes direction as the pods turn, the boat does not tend to slow down in a turn as is the case with inboards with rudders. In any event, the electronically controlled engines maintain their rpm setting throughout the turn, regardless of speed and load.

Course-keeping was also good. The boat stayed right on course with no tendency to yaw or wander about our heading at any speed or direction to the seas. Using the IPS joystick mode, it took 35 seconds to twist 360 degrees in high-speed mode (engines turning 1,400–1,800 rpm), and 46 seconds in low-speed mode (1,100–1,250 rpm).

The side window vents blast a sea breeze into the helm and bridge deck area, so any greenhouse effect from all the glass should not be a problem, especially if the AC is also up and running. The center windshield also opens, as does the power sunroof; the latter comfortably adds to the airflow but it doesn't blast passengers in their seats. The dark-colored dash eliminates glare from the windshield, and the defrosters would take care of any fogging on the inside of the windshield.

While back on the dock we lowered the hydraulic swim platform using the remote control, showing how easy it would be to launch and recover the tender.

As mentioned, the 45 is available with both inboard and Volvo IPS power. The 435 hp IPS units produce the same top speed as a pair of 575 hp inboard diesels—32.2 knots—but the inboards burn 30 percent more fuel (58.2 versus 44.5 gph). At 25 knots, the IPS units get 16 percent better efficiency (0.77 versus 0.66 nmpg). Our view is that their superior economy, along with the lower noise and fume levels and joystick maneuverability, make IPS the clear choice. They are also no more vulnerable to object-strike or grounding damage than inboards, and could take a lot less time to repair. They certainly take a lot less time for the builder to install.

The 45 is a delight to drive, thanks to two elements—IPS and the superb helm visibility. IPS makes low- and high-speed boat handling pleasurable, and maneuverability dockside is child's play with the IPS joystick. This 45-footer is much more controllable and predictable in a crowded marina than a 25-foot outboard or stern drive. IPS, and some sound-deadening know-how from the builder, also makes this a quiet boat. The cabin is well thought out and offers two couples privacy and comfortable environs.

Our list of recommended changes for the 45 is short: increase length of berths to at least 6 feet, 5 inches, and increase height of topside railings and transom door to 30 inches to provide an added measure of safety in the open ocean.

Options include the hydraulic tender platform, hull color, Ultraleather seating, cherry cabin sole, cockpit grill, electronics, and Ralph Lauren décor.

Formula 45 Yacht Performance Results

RPM	Speed, knots	Fuel Use, gph	Nautical mpg	Range, nm	Noise Level, dBA (at helm)
650	4.9	0.77	6.36	2,005	66
900	6	1.53	3.92	1,235	68
1,200	7.4	2.3	3.22	1,013	69
1,500	8.6	5.9	1.46	459	71
1,800	9.3	9.7	0.96	302	74
2,100	10	16.4	0.61	192	77
2,400	14.5	20.4	0.71	224	78
2,700	18.7	26.6	0.70	221	80
3,000	22.4	29.1	0.77	242	80
3,300	27.6	35.2	0.78	247	80
3,630	32.2	44.5	0.72	228	82

Test conditions: With twin Volvo IPS 600.

TIARA 3900 SOVRAN

TIARA

Tiara 3900 Sovran Specifications

LOA:	39'3" (hull)
Beam:	13'11"
Deadrise:	14.5 deg.
Dry weight:	23,000 lb.
Cockpit depth:	26"
Draft:	3'5" (drive down)
Fuel capacity:	300 gal.
Water capacity:	102 gal.
Sleeping capacity:	5 people

In production since 2006, the 3900 Sovran is a Euro-styled family cruiser with a single-stateroom cabin. It has a raised bridge deck and windshield extending to the hardtop, eliminating plastic side windows. Tiara's practicality and emphasis on seamanship (the practical nonskid, wide side decks, navigable foredeck, high-sided cockpit, and superb helm visibility) are all evident on this boat, though somewhat camouflaged by all those Euro-style curves.

The 3900 Sovran was designed around Volvo Penta's inboard performance system (IPS), which frees up interior space usually given over to an engine room,

creating roomier accommodations. That's important, apart from the performance benefits of IPS, since the boat's single stateroom was specifically designed for a cruising couple. Rather than squeezing two staterooms into the layout, Tiara opted to make this boat appeal specifically to couples that seldom bring along guests, maximizing the comforts and amenities.

The builder opened up the saloon, placing the forward engine room bulkhead well aft of where it would usually be in an inboard of this size, increasing living space, enlarging the head to include a separate stall shower, and adding a step-down lounge or "home theater" area aft where the engine room would ordinarily be. For the young couple with small children, this is actually an ideal layout, as the aft lounge is perfect for kids.

Construction

The 3900 Sovran is built strong and light using a closed-mold resin-infusion process. Resin infusion has a number of advantages over traditional hand-layup, open-molded boatbuilding. The skin-to-core bond, essential to structural integrity, is virtually guaranteed to be sound using this method. The resin-to-fiberglass ratio, usually 60 percent or more resin in hard layup, has a much higher percentage of fiberglass and correspondingly less resin, creating a stronger, lighter structure.

Hull thickness is uniform, with the vacuum pressure pulling the resin through the laminate consistently and predictably. The balsa core is more resistant to water intrusion or migration, with the voids between skin and core, and within the core, filled in by resin during the infusion process. Finally, the consistency of the part is far more uniform in composition, thickness, and weight, which translates into a higher-quality structure.

Tiara starts out conventionally by gelcoating the hull, then spraying on a coat of vinylester resin (this premium resin is used throughout the laminate) over the cured gelcoat (to ensure a resin-rich skin coat), followed immediately by a 3-ounce layer of fiberglass chop, which acts as an anti-osmosis blister coat in the bottom and helps prevent print-through in the hull sides. Next, the outer fiberglass skin, end-grain balsa coring, and inner skin are dry-stacked in place, and then covered with a plastic bag. The edges of the bag around the perimeter of the mold are sealed, then a vacuum is applied, and resin is drawn through the dry stack of fiberglass skins and balsa core (the low-viscosity resin, specifically formulated for infusion processes, flows through kerfs and grooves cut into the balsa) until it is completely wet out and saturated to the specified resin content.

Once the hull sets up, the plastic infusion bag is removed, and the fiberglass surfaces to be bonded are roughened up with grinders. Four full-length, fiberglass-encapsulated foam-cored stringers and bulkheads are set in place on jigs to assure precise alignment and then fiberglassed to the hull. Installing the stringers and bulkheads takes place quickly, before the infused resin completely sets up, providing a chemical as well as a mechanical bond.

The stringers are continuous from bow to stern, and the bulkheads are notched to receive them, which makes the hull bottom stiff and strong. Thanks to precise jig alignment, the bulkhead edges are not in contact with the hull skin prior to being tabbed in place, which prevents hard spots that can both fatigue and mar the appearance of the hull. The cabin is built outside of the boat, with all the furniture modules attached to the balsa-cored floor before the whole unit is lifted into the boat and secured. This saves the builder time, and helps make for precise component alignment.

The hull-to-deck joint is bonded with a structural adhesive and then fastened with self-tapping screws to clamp the joint during cure, and also to contribute to the joint's strength. Decks are also cored with balsa; Tiara goes to great lengths to make sure holes in the bottom are only drilled through solid fiberglass to prevent water from getting into the core.

Hull Design

The Tiara 3900 Sovran has a modified-V, hard-chine planing hull with 14 degrees of deadrise at the transom. The hull of any Volvo Penta IPS–powered boat has to be modified to accommodate both the shift in weight aft as well as the horizontal thrust from the props. Both of these elements call for added buoyancy and lift at the stern.

Walkthrough

Cockpit

It's easy boarding this boat, with a big, full-beam swim platform leading through the starboard side transom door (it's about 4 inches too low at 26 inches, especially given this boat's strong acceleration) to the cockpit. A large trunk opens at the transom, with plenty of room inside for line and fender storage. Tiara put a pair of stern cleats inboard below the transom trunk near deck level, which is a good spot for crossing stern lines, since the lines tied off at that height are easy to step over. There's another pair of stern cleats on the gunwales just forward.

The cockpit has a U-shaped seating and conversation area, and a deck socket supports a table stanchion between the seats. There's more storage space below the settee, along with a refreshment center with sink and refrigerator to starboard aft of the helm. This area is welcoming when the boat is underway with IPS power since it's so quiet and fume-free.

A deck hatch leads to the engine room below (the cockpit table is kept secured to the underside of the hatch), and the whole cockpit deck lifts up for engine room access. The hatches have gaskets that seal in engine noise and eliminate rattling, and the all-tooled closed-molded hatches are a class act on the part of the builder with shiny surfaces on both sides. The nonskid is trademark Tiara—safe and aggressive underfoot, yet not too rough on the knees, and easy to clean.

Helm

A couple of steps up from the cockpit, the bridge deck has a raised L-shaped lounge to port. Tiara raised this guest seat so passengers can see as well as the captain, which many builders neglect to do. This raised seat also carves out headroom in the head directly below.

The helm is on starboard, and this station is a departure for Tiara with its smaller tilt wheel being much more comfortable and ergonomically designed than the large vertical ships' wheels used previously. It's a comfortable boat to drive standing up, with plenty of room between the helm seat and the wheel, and the wheel, throttles, and joystick are at a good height and well positioned. The dash gives prominence to a pair of large-screen electronics displays, and the compass is perched high where it's easy to see.

Visibility from the helm on the 3900 is exceptional thanks to the windshield design, which supports the hardtop without heavy mullions between the windshield sections. Visibility to the corners is especially good, thanks to curved glass sections in this area. Once you've run a boat with sight lines like this you won't want to go back to inferior layouts. The 31-inch windshield wipers are long enough (and clearly of high quality and made to last) to keep lots of glass cleared.

A centerline window opens with a power lift for ventilation. Tiara has long treated the dash area on its yachts with a dark-colored finish to reduce or even eliminate glare, another nod to the requirements of good seamanship on the builder's part. You won't be roughing it, either, with an air-conditioning duct right below the helm seat keeping things cool all around.

Foredeck

Flat 10- to 12-inch-wide side decks with nonskid lead to the bow, with a 1-inch stainless steel bow railing that's 27 inches high. We'd like to see Tiara extend the hardtop handrail another 3 feet forward to where the bow railing starts, avoiding this short no-man's land where there's nothing to hang onto. The bow railings are certainly adequate, but the safest foredecks we see, such as on Eastbays, have 30-inch railings made of 1½-inch stainless steel that are noticeably stiffer and stronger; the extra 3 inches makes a big difference in balance and the overall feeling of security when the boat's rocking and rolling.

Tiara provides a sunpad on top of the truck cabin, which is commonly seen on Euro cruisers. Just make sure this area is clear when underway so the skipper can see where he or she is going. In the bow is the ground tackle, with an integral pulpit housing the anchor, a flush-mounted vertical windlass, and a hatch to the anchor line locker. Three cleats are provided, including one for tying off the anchor.

Cabin

Like all Tiaras, the 3900's cabin has a traditional appearance, with teak paneling and a teak and holly sole providing a salty look. The size of the cabin on this boat is one of its strong suits. It's not only big in square footage, it's laid out for comfortable living rather than trying to cram a lot of berths or heads or whatever else into too little space. The 6-foot, 5-inch headroom adds to the spacious feeling, as do the big, 22- by 8-inch opening portlights in the hull sides. The effect created is an open, airy, and bright living space that's welcoming and cheery.

The lower cabin, or saloon, has a sofa immediately down the companionway and to port along the hull. There's lots of teak and holly (all-teak is also available) decking between it and the galley opposite to starboard. Like everything else in this cabin, the galley is larger than you'd expect on a 39-footer, with a countertop that measures over 7 feet long. A big side-by-side refrigerator-freezer and an oversized microwave-convection oven are below the counter.

Aft of the galley is what Tiara calls the "theater" lounge area, so-called because of its surround-sound stereo system. Basically, it's a midcabin with 4 feet, 3 inches of headroom that's open to the saloon, and this openness is helped by the open stairs design. This midcabin area, and the aft head, use the bonus room made possible by IPS power. There's a pair of facing sofas along with a flat-screen TV. The sofas also convert to a king-size 6-foot, 5-inch by 5-foot, 6-inch berth for any guests along for the ride. To port is a large head with a separate shower stall, which you don't always see on a boat below 40 feet.

In the bow, a solid bulkhead with a large doorway sets the stateroom apart from the saloon and adds a good dose of privacy. The curved stateroom doors are cleverly designed—they slide outboard, disappearing into the bulkhead on either side. These doors also give Tiara's craftsmen a chance to showcase their cabinetry skills, with the doors finished as book-matched quarter panels. The stateroom has a raised queen-size island bed, and plenty of storage in lockers, drawers, and below the berth. Above is a 16- by 20-inch hatch that lets in sunlight and a little sea breeze, and it's also available for emergency egress if needed, though those dimensions are certainly tight for a large adult. The only thing the stateroom does not have is private access to the boat's single head, which is aft in the cabin; this may or may not be an issue for the owner, but the cabin's other attributes may win you over in any event.

Engine

Access to the twin 370 hp Volvo D6 common rail diesels driving the IPS pods is excellent. There's a day hatch for quick inspections, and the whole cockpit deck rises on power boosts to create unimpeded access. The engine room holds a lot of machinery and systems, including batteries, the Cablemaster, electrical panels, seacocks, and fuel filter-separators, but everything is accessible, and there's a surprising amount of clear floor space outboard of the engines. All the wiring and plumbing runs are textbook examples of systems engineering.

Sea Trial

We had a 2- to 3-foot chop on a slight swell on our test ride. The boat rode well, better than many competitors in its size range, though the wide, 13-foot, 11-inch beam gives the boat some limitations in a head sea. The IPS handled well, with the boat turning quickly upon putting the rudder (OK, pod drives) over. Steering is fingertip-easy, and tight and responsive at just 3.8 turns lock-to-lock.

The other nice thing about IPS is that the boat heels just the right amount for its turn rate, which makes the boat stable underfoot and contributes to the high rate of turn available. The boats comes up on plane easily, with the horizon still visible, leaving a clean, reasonably flat wake astern at just 12 knots; this is remarkable given the boat's aft CG with the IPS units in the stern.

Walking back to the cockpit, no smoke or fumes were discernible, even with the stern pointed into the wind at low speed. Vibrations were also very low, and noise levels when running along at idle were just 72 dBA.

A look at the performance chart below is instructive. The first thing to note is how quiet these common rail Volvos are. Even at full power, we only measured 81 dBA at the helm, and at cruise speed, the noise levels were in the 79 to 80 range, which is good for any inboard with a helm station open to the cockpit. The next thing to look at is the nmpg (nautical miles per gallon) column. Getting 1 nautical mile to the gallon in a 25,000-pound 39-footer is impressive; 0.7 to 0.8 nmpg is pretty

typical of conventional inboards in a boat of this size at 30 knots, which speaks to the efficiency of IPS.

Handling the boat at the dock was a cakewalk. Some would say that it's too easy, that it takes the challenge and fun out of boat handling, but most like it just fine.

The Tiara Sovran 3900 is an excellent family cruiser. The cabin layout is commodious, comfortable, and well designed. The IPS propulsion adds several advantages, from more space to better and more economical performance—buying a boat of this type with pod propulsion should be a given. The helm ergonomics and visibility are good, which along with the IPS, makes this boat a low-stress pleasure to operate.

The change list we'd recommend is quite short: we'd increase the height of the railings forward and the transom door to 30 inches, extend the hardtop rail forward a few feet, and increase the size of the bow hatch to at least 24 by 24 inches to provide emergency egress for large adults.

Tiara 3900 Sovran Performance Results

RPM	Speed, knots	Fuel Use, gph	Nautical mpg	Range, nm	Noise Level, dBA (at helm)
1,000	6.4	2.1	3.05	823	71
1,500	8.9	5.5	1.62	437	72
2,000	11.6	13.3	0.87	235	77
2,500	18.9	19	0.99	269	79
2,800	23.6	23.2	1.02	275	79
3,000	26.7	26	1.03	277	80
3,200	29.7	31.1	0.95	258	80
3,450	32.4	40	0.81	219	81

Test conditions: Seven passengers, fuel tank half full, with twin Volvo IPS 500. Moderate chop.

Trawlers

The redoubtable trawler conjures up images of a stout displacement hull powered by a single diesel traveling at jogging speed for thousands of miles. These yachts usually have a forward pilothouse, accommodations forward on the lower deck, a saloon aft of the pilothouse, and a small cockpit in the stern. Some include a flybridge above the saloon, and those over 50 feet might have a full-beam master suite directly below the pilothouse, as in the pilothouse motor yacht design. Other trawlers have been built with aft-cabin designs.

Although trawlers used to be based exclusively on heavy displacement hulls (the originals were mostly converted trawlers, hence the name), a couple of trends have developed to address owners' need for speed. On some designs the displacement hulls have been lightened and lengthened, allowing them to achieve cruising speeds above a speed-to-length (S/L) ratio of 1:4. Their lighter weight decreases resistance, and their longer length increases their hull speed.

Another variation is to build the trawler on a semidisplacement hull, which gets on plane and achieves an S/L ratio of around 2:5. Of course, the slower the hull moves through the water, the more efficiently it can be driven. But many owners want to be able to have the option of running at 18 knots occasionally to meet a cruising schedule, so a hard-chine or Maine-style semidisplacement hull works well for these applications.

When a boat has a semidisplacement hull and a conventional pilothouse or aft-cabin motor yacht design, the builder may still call it a trawler, even though the lines are blurred at this point. Some trawler aficionados, in fact, protest that only displacement hulls qualify a vessel for the label, and that range must be measured in the thousands rather than hundreds of miles. If it does have a displacement hull, it will also need a means of stabilization, since this hull type's slack bilges have little form stability (though great weight stability). Paravanes or flopper-stoppers suspended from outriggers do the trick, as do active, gyroscope-guided fin stabilizers mounted at the turn of the bilge.

Although the fishing vessels on which "true" trawlers are based have relatively low decks and small superstructures, trawler yachts often have large, boxy deckhouses that enhance interior space but also amplify roll, and increase the need for stabilization. So, if you're not in a great hurry to get there, you appreciate a seaworthy vessel underfoot, and you enjoy the process of cruising as much as reaching your destination, the comfortable, economically propelled trawler may be the boat for you.

American Tug builds rugged 34- and 41-foot pilothouse trawler models with hard-chine semidisplacement hulls and full keels providing grounding protection for the single-diesel running gear. The 41 shown has a two-stateroom, two-head layout forward. AMERICAN TUG

The French boatbuilder Beneteau, best-known for its sailboats, produces an ever-expanding line of power cruisers as well. The Swift Trawler 42 shown here, with a two-stateroom, two-head layout, can cruise at up to 18 knots with a pair of 370 hp inboard diesels.

BENETEAU USA

The Fathom 40 combines a contemporary look—sort of a mini expedition yacht—with innovative features, like a tailgate at the transom that lets you walk right from the cockpit onto a tender or the dock. The pilothouse top extends aft over the cockpit for added protection from the elements. A single 425 hp common rail diesel will push the 40 to the 17- to 19-knot range, while letting you throttle back to displacement speeds to save fuel. Fairly beamy at 14 feet, 6 inches, there are two staterooms, an engine room with near-standing headroom, and a full-beam saloon that's roomy for a 40-footer. The hull is built using a high-tech (vinylester) resin infusion process.   FATHOM YACHTS

Island Packet Yachts is a sailboat manufacturer that has recently gotten into the powerboat business with a 41-foot express yacht and this 41-foot self-righting PY Cruiser. Originally a motorsailer, this version eliminates the mast (improving stability by lowering the center of gravity), turning the boat into a bona fide trawler. The 5,000 pounds of ballast in the hollow keel turns the PY into a self-righting vessel. Maximum speed for this full-displacement hull is 8.9 knots with the standard 110 hp diesel. Five people can be accommodated in three cabins.   ISLAND PACKET YACHTS

Grand Banks builds trawler yachts from 46 to 72 feet. The 47 Heritage EU shown is classic Grand Banks, with a large pilothouse extended well back in the stern and twin staterooms below; the second stateroom can be replaced by an office or a double in place of twin berths. Teak woodwork is everywhere inside, another Grand Banks trademark. Twin diesels to 567 hp are available. GRAND BANKS

Kadey-Krogen's flagship 58-footer is quite a little ship. The deckhouse extends flush with the port side, making more room inside the saloon and leaving the starboard side deck as the only way forward. The master suite is full beam and amidships, with a guest suite (stateroom and private head) forward and a separate office.   KADEY-KROGEN YACHTS

Kadey-Krogen's well-built 39 shown here is a mini ship able to cross oceans at the displacement hull's top economical cruise speed of 6 knots. A true full-displacement hull and single economical diesel provides great range: 4,100 miles at 6 knots, or 1,600 miles at 8 knots. Krogen builds very seaworthy offshore yachts up to 58 feet, including an impressive new 55-foot expeditions trawler.

KADEY-KROGEN YACHTS

Nordhavn builds 14 different ocean-crossing displacement yachts from 35 to 86 feet. The shiplike 55 shown incorporates Nordhavn's trademark design features including generous freeboard forward and a western-style windshield for improved visibility from the bridge. The deckhouse extends to the port side, opening things up considerably inside. Range with a single 330 hp John Deere diesel turning a 40-inch propeller is 3,000 nautical miles at 8 knots.

PACIFIC ASIAN ENTERPRISES

Mainship builds moderately priced semidisplacement trawlers from 34 to 43 feet, including an aft-cabin model. The 34 Trawler shown here is a popular model containing a large saloon with large windows, upper and lower helm stations, and a master stateroom forward with a private head. A similar version of this yacht without the bridge but with an electric sunroof is also available.

MAINSHIP TRAWLERS

Nordic Tugs builds pilothouse trawlers from 32 to 52 feet. The 42 shown has two staterooms and heads, and a hard-chine, semidisplacement hull with a single 540 hp diesel for power and a full keel to protect the hull and running gear.

NORDIC TUGS

CAMANO 31 FAST TRAWLER

Camano 31 Fast Trawler Specifications

LOA:	31'
LOD:	28'
LWL:	26'
Beam:	10'6"
Draft:	3'3"
Displacement:	12,000 lb.
Fuel capacity:	133 gal.
Water capacity:	77 gal.

The Camano 31 is a rugged semidisplacement trawler yacht with more than a little western-rig influence in its deckhouse and a good deal of commercial fisherman influence below the waterline. The 31 is designed for a couple who wants to spend extended periods of time aboard. It makes no attempt to provide sleeping accommodations for the extended family as most owners cruise by themselves; a pull-out berth in the saloon takes care of occasional overnight guests. This boat is built to go to sea (in moderate conditions) just like its commercial fishing brethren, and to treat its owners with seakindly motion and a 12- to 15-knot cruising speed provided by its single, economical diesel.

The boat comes equipped with everything needed to cruise; however, there is a wide range of factory options available (e.g., our test boat's fancy oven), and the dealers take it from there with add-ons such as canvas, flat-screen TV, dinghy, electronics, and seating on the flybridge.

Construction

The Camano 31 starts with a (Ashland) gelcoat sprayed just over an inch thick. A skin coat of 1-ounce mat wet out with vinylester resin followed by a DCPD blend resin in the rest of the laminate, which consists of a mix of woven and nonwoven reinforcements, is added. The hull sides get further print-through protection in the form of a follow-on layer of 1½-ounce mat before the reinforcement goes on.

The bottom is supported by an all-fiberglass structural grid laid up in a female mold and bonded to the hull skin with a polyester structural putty; this is an extra step most builders do not take, and it's indicative of the care and attention to detail that has gone into this boat's engineering. The bottom is reinforced with carbon fiber in the keel. Hull sides are cored with ⅜-inch Divinycell closed-cell structural foam bedded in Core-Bond and using a vibrating roller to ensure a good skin-to-core bond.

Hull side fiberglass-reinforced plastic through-hull penetrations are drilled through the resin-coated foam-cored hull skin; we feel any through-hull should be clamped down on a solid coring, whether solid fiberglass or a dense core material. Engine room bulkheads are composite (¾-inch) foam-cored, and the forward bulkhead separating the galley from the stateroom is pressure-treated plywood. Hard spots in the hull skin are prevented by two means: by foam fillets separating the bulkhead edges from the hull skin and by jigs that hold the bulkhead edge away from hull skin during tabbing.

Decks are cored with $^1/_2$-inch balsa core. Water absorption into the hull side balsa core is prevented by coring the area around the penetration with foam core material that won't wick. The shoebox hull-to-deck joint is screwed together and then fiberglassed together from the inside for the entire length of the rubrail, creating a rugged joint. SoundDown acoustic foam with a barium-loaded layer of vinyl is used to insulate the saloon deck from the engine room below. Windshield glass thickness is $^1/_4$-inch laminated shatterproof safety glass.

The fuel tanks are made of 5052 aluminum. They sit atop neoprene strips, and there is plenty of air circulation to prevent standing water from accumulating. The tanks are held in place with nylon cinch straps; we'd like to see the builder use a more permanent lag-bolted system like they use on the new 41. Hardware is 316-grade stainless steel, and it is through-bolted to the deck.

The Camano 31 builder goes beyond the call with the extra impact resistance and rigidity provided by the inner hull liner and grid system. The builder's goal was to build the boat with hull scantlings that can withstand hitting a 4-foot-diameter log at 15 knots without damage, and we wouldn't be too surprised if they've achieved this objective. Each boat undergoes sea trials for 2½ hours or so before delivery, undergoing a thorough a six-page punch list of about 250 items.

Hull Design

The Camano 31 has a unique running surface. Essentially, it's a semidisplacement hull with a modified hollow keel (or high-volume keel, as the builder calls it); the modified part means the hollow keel is a lot wider (and V-shaped in section view) at the garboard than is the case with Down East–style keel hulls. This design provides more

room inside the boat low in the hull, which allows the engine to be installed lower in the bilge. It also adds buoyancy low in the hull, which in itself decreases the metacentric height and reduces stability. But things balance out in terms of righting arm with the lower center of buoyancy compensated for by lowering the engine a full foot, which also lowers the saloon deck above the engine room, and therefore lowers the boat's overall profile. This further lowers the center of gravity and also happily reduces the boat's profile, which in turn improves seakeeping and seakindliness as well as weight stability.

The fine, deep-displacement hull entry transitions from no chines forward to a planing hull's hard chines amidships and flat buttocks aft. This tremendous warp in the hull's running surface works fine for a 15-knot-maximum boat, and in fact it makes the Camano a good 12- to 15-knot sea boat; it would, however, add a good deal of hydrodynamic drag at higher speeds. All that additional hull surface area from the full keel also adds frictional drag, which is another reason this is a 15-knot and not a 30-knot boat.

The hard chines also add drag at displacement speeds, but that is likely to be fine with Camano owners who would have had the option of buying a real displacement hull if they only wanted to go 7 knots (based on a 28-foot waterline length and S/L of 1.4). The hard chines works well when running at 12 to 15 knots, since they produce a more efficient planing surface than round bilges.

Another advantage of this hull is the full keel. It has a skeg projecting aft under the propeller and supporting the bottom of the barn-door rudder, which lets the boat turns on a dime. This means the prop and rudder are well protected against grounding damage, unlike 98 percent of the planing cruisers available today. Bottom line: This hull does not run at displacement speeds as well as a round-bilge displacement hull, nor as well as a conventional hard-chine hull at planing speeds (say, above 18 knots), but it does run well in and is appropriate for its 10- to 15-knot cruising speed range.

Walkthrough

Cockpit

Coming on board the boat from the swim platform, the 4-foot, 5-inch long by 8-foot, 4-inch wide cockpit is small but functional. It's big enough for two portable chairs, and with the railing atop the 34-inch-high coaming, it's a full 39 inches deep, which makes it fit standards for a 10,000-ton liner! We would suggest making the transom door just as high to complete the safe feeling aft. We'd like to see a more aggressive nonskid pattern on board—the current one counts on the boater wearing shoes with good tread, and no soapy water or fish slime underfoot. To port are a handheld hot-and-cold shower, a washdown hose, and a compartment for the propane tank.

Molded stairs port and starboard lead to the side decks, which are fairly narrow, but appropriate for the extra room opened up in the saloon. Deckhouse-mounted handrails and 30-inch-high bow railings lead forward to the simple-but-effective anchor pulpit and ground tackle. All the walking surfaces forward are flat and easy to traverse. Below the cockpit a lazarette hatch opens easily, providing a 24-inch by 33-inch access to this watertight space (both fore and aft engine room bulkheads are watertight). Most of the bilge surfaces are tooled fiberglass, thanks to the molded grid support system.

There's a lot of deck space on the bridge, with a helm and two companion pedestal seats forward. We'd definitely like to see a higher bridge railing—at 25 inches this is at least 5 inches too short, and our comments concerning the nonskid also apply to here and to the bow area.

Lower Helm

The starboard side lower helm is laid out with a large angled flat area leaving plenty of room for custom layout of electronics and engine gauges. The compass is up where it's easy to read, and the vertical steering wheel, which we usually criticize, worked well since we drove our test boat standing up. The Volvo digital engine control is comfortably positioned atop the helm station. While we were surrounded by 360 degrees of glass, we'd still like to the see the frames, or mullions, between the forward windows narrower than their present 7 inches.

Bridge Helm

The upper helm could use a little more attention to its layout. The chartplotter and all the engine gauges and controls are laid out across a single flat dash panel. The helm would benefit from a couple of raised and angled flat panels to bring the chartplotter closer and at right angles to the driver's line of sight.

Cabin

The use of interior space is ideal for the boat's mission. With the short foredeck and small cockpit, the saloon gets the lion's share of the main deck space. The sheer size—10 feet long and 8 feet, 5 inches wide, with 6-foot, 3-inch headroom—is what makes this bright and airy space so welcoming, along with all the glass that lets in light.

Immediately inside the cockpit door, an L-shaped lounge with a beautifully fashioned mahogany table to port converts to a double berth. The helm is forward to starboard, and the galley is down two steps to port below the windshield. Wide open to the saloon, the galley offers a good deal of counter and storage space, a large sink, a three-burner stove with oven and microwave plus a generously proportioned refrigerator-freezer.

Opposite the galley to starboard is the head with a VacuFlush toilet. The toilet sits on a raised platform, making it comfortable to use, and the molded fiberglass sink projects out a few inches from the countertop, so less water drips on deck when shaving. An opening portlight, a curtain to contain shower water, and storage compartments are all provided in this amply proportioned space.

Forward of the galley through a clever half-door (it's a closet door that folds open to seal off most of the stateroom entrance for a modicum of privacy) is the boat's stateroom with a V-berth. The berth is just 5 feet, 8 inches long measured on centerline, though if you lie along the hull side you can find 6 feet, 4 inches. We'd recommend that the filler cushion on centerline extend aft another 6 inches or so to give a 6-foot adult another sleeping position—the builder agrees and will make this change. Overhead is a 19-inch hatch (we like 24-inch hatches as they offer better emergency egress from the stateroom) and 6 feet, 3 inches of headroom, which is fine for any 31-footer.

Engine

The engine hatch in the saloon lifts easily on an articulated boost mechanism; it probably takes no more than 10 pounds of pull to lift it. When fully raised, the hinge support locks into place, preventing the hatch from falling inadvertently. Our test boat had a 210 hp Volvo D4 common rail diesel and, as you'd expect, it can be removed through the 81-inch by 27-inch hatch without any cutting. All daily maintenance checks can be done from the forward end of the engine, where the engine seawater seacock and filter, expansion tank, and oil dipstick are located. The oversized dual Racor fuel filter-separators are outboard to port, also within easy reach.

The ingenuity of the hollow keel design again becomes apparent here since the engine would be mounted a full foot higher without it. The structural grid supporting the hull is also prominent, with this female-molded part providing a shiny surface and compartmented battery and tool storage trays in the upper sections of the bilge.

The 66-gallon aluminum fuel tanks are all the way outboard, nestled in fitted fiberglass bins that are part of the hull grid structure, as are the freshwater and sewage holding tanks. There is a cross-connect hose aft, so the tanks are self-leveling when the valve at the bottom of either tank is open. The bilge in the bottom of the hollow keel is dry, thanks to a dripless shaft seal that lives up to its name. All the wiring cables are neatly bundled and secured every 7 inches.

Sea Trial

We picked a good day for our Florida sea trial, with seas in the 4- to 6-foot range that were nice and steep and close together. We were running at 15 knots when we left the bay and entered St. Lucie Inlet, and we never touched the throttle plowing right through the seas. We took a few buckets of spray over the bow, but the boat handled the seas nonchalantly, maintaining its heading and not coming close to pounding. (There is constant curvature in the forward chineless sections, so there's nothing to pound with.)

When you're used to wide, hard-chine hulls, it's easy to forget how nice it is to be in a seakindly semi-displacement hull in sloppy weather. You can quantify seakindliness by measuring accelerations in heave, pitch, and roll, and a boat that has light bottom loading and a lot of beam with a flat bottom will snap roll and react to every wave. The Camano's bottom loading (the psi of water pressure on the bottom of the hull, based on the vessel's weight and the bottom surface area), gyradius, and metacentric height all make for very comfortable motion.

Visibility over the bow was good while coming up on plane when operating the boat from the pilothouse, with the pulpit never coming close to poking above the horizon. The wraparound windshield offered good visibility all around the boat (though narrower windshield frames would improve things); we never felt like we'd lost sight of what was going on around us with buoys and other boats, and that's quite a statement considering what it's like to run many similar pilothouse boats from down below. The lack of ventilation was noticeable, though, since there are no opening windows forward. We'd like to see the builder install dorade vents, or a ventilation system such as on the Dettling 51, which lets lots of fresh air, but no water, inside.

Dropping the tabs to 30 or 40 percent helped the boat pick up speed between 0.5 and 1 knot, but you'll want to keep them raised all the way when running downsea to prevent yawing.

Steering was a full six turns lock-to-lock, which is two more than you want for responsive handling. However, once the rudder was hard over at 35 degrees (like it ought to be, but rarely is on other inboards), and with the throttle at 3,200 rpm, the boat consistently turned 360 degrees in 19 to 20 seconds, both to port and starboard. This is an excellent turn rate, compliments of a rudder that both turns far enough and is big enough to create substantial lateral lift.

The downsea ride in a full-keel hull is rarely something to write home about—you want to be in a deep-V for that. But the Camano showed little tendency to yaw running with the seas on the quarter, compared with similar hulls, and part of the reason is that we were running at pretty much the same speed as the similar-length waves.

Back at the dock the boat turned in a little over its own length. The bow thruster Camano installs on the 31 is quite responsive (it's the one used on the Nordhavn 40), with an 8-inch propeller and 5 hp motor. The Volvo turned a 2.43:1 gear driving

a 1.5-inch Aquamet 22 shaft (set on a very low 8-degree angle, thanks to the hollow keel) and a 20- by 17-inch, four-blade left-hand prop that always offered plenty of grip when maneuvering dockside without using much throttle.

The Volvo electronic controls were a pure pleasure to operate, and it would be great to have controls like this on every boat we run. They shift as smooth as can be, with just a slight detent at neutral to let you know when you're going into gear. When you set the throttle, the engine stays at that rpm no matter whether you put the rudder hard over or are laboring in heavy quartering seas.

With the engine idling, we measured engine noise level with the engine hatch closed and open, and got 62 dBA and 87 dBA, respectively, which is a big difference and indicates how well-engineered the deck structure and hatch are.

The Camano marketing literature is a bit optimistic in places, claiming that at 14 knots the boat only burns about 4.5 gallons per hour. A look at the results of our sea trial shows the Volvo D4 (25 hp more than the original engine used in this boat) burned just about twice that amount, or 8.25 gph. Any diesel will put out 20 hp for each gallon per hour of fuel flow, give or take 5 percent

Camano 31 Fast Trawler Performance Results

RPM	Speed, knots	Fuel Use, gph	Nautical mpg	Range, nm	Noise Level, dBA
1,000	5	0.4	12.50	1,500.0	68
1,500	6.8	1	6.80	816.0	69
2,000	7.7	2.46	3.13	375.6	74
2,500	9.2	4.61	2.00	239.5	79
3,000	13.1	6.84	1.92	229.8	80
3,500	15.1	9.66	1.56	187.6	84
3,700	17.3	11.25	1.54	184.5	84

Test conditions: Two passengers, fuel and water tanks full, with single Volvo D4 common rail 210 hp diesel. Lightly loaded. Clean bottom.

(10 gph = 200 hp). That means 4.5 gph will produce 90 hp at any given moment, and no 12,000-pound semidisplacement hull that we know of will go 14 knots on 90 hp. Nine or maybe 10 knots is more like it.

Our list of criticisms is short: more aggressive nonskid topside, ventilation in the saloon forward should be added, the bridge railing height should be increased, and the forward-facing windows should be wider and the spaces between them made narrower.

The Camano 31 is an easy boat to like. Handsome styling and proportions driven by functionality, a livable and thoughtful layout ideally suited to a couple, a safe and secure cockpit, intelligent engineering and top-drawer construction throughout, and a seaworthy and seakindly hull design make this boat worthy of a close look. It's easy to maintain, with an all-fiberglass exterior, and it handles well, thanks to a big rudder, big enough prop, and a strong bow thruster.

We can give the Camano 31 a wholehearted recommendation based on its many intelligent attributes and its thoroughly delightful livability.

Freshwater Boats

Aluminum Fishing Boats

Aluminum fishing boats range from low-profile bass boats to modified-V, high-freeboard walleye boats. The bass boats are designed for calmer water with casting platforms fore and aft. Walleye boats, a growing market with people venturing farther offshore in pursuit of bigger fish, have more freeboard for added seaworthiness. Deeper-V bottoms provide a decent ride in the chop that these boats often encounter on large lakes, including the Great Lakes.

The transom is designed to take a 9.9 to 25 hp kicker, since these boats often troll at 1.5 to 5 mph for hours on end. The boats are rigged for trolling aft and casting forward. Up to four aerated bait wells for different kinds of live bait, and two livewells to keep the catch fresh and healthy until weigh-in and subsequent release, may be included. Walleye boats are commonly available in lengths from 16 to 23 feet with a 50 to 225 hp outboard. Layouts include dual and center consoles, though some of the smaller models may have tiller steering.

Crestliner is a leading U.S. manufacturer of a wide range of aluminum fishing, sport, utility, and pontoon boats. Part of Brunswick Corporation, Crestliner's fishing boat lineup includes the Fish Hawk series ranging from tiller-steered 16-footers to 18-foot windshield boats with fixed helm stations. The 1700 shown here was new in 2007, and includes a livewell, rod locker, prewiring for a trolling motor, and a welded hull. CRESTLINER BOATS

The 1850 Crestliner Sportfish has a welded aluminum hull along with dry storage lockers, built-in tackle storage, and a tall windshield that does a good job protecting from wind and spray.

CRESTLINER BOATS

The Crestliner CJX utility boat series runs from 16 to 20 feet, and includes side and center console layouts. Dry storage compartments, an aluminum floor, provisions for an electric trolling motor forward, livewell, shallow draft, and welded aluminum construction are featured. The 1870 shown here takes up to 90 hp.

CRESTLINER BOATS

Part of giant Tracker Marine, Fisher produces aluminum modified-V fishing and deep-V fishing boats, family sport boats, pontoons, deck boats, jonboats, and utility boats. The 16 Pro Avenger shown here is part of the builder's deep-V series. The welded 16 comes with aerated livewell, bait well, locking rod storage, a fish-finder, and an electric trolling motor. A fore and aft casting deck with chair mounts is included.

TRACKER MARINE

G3, a division of Yamaha, manufactures Yamaha-powered aluminum fishing, utility, fish-and-ski, and pontoon boats. The Angler V185 FS shown here is part of G3's deep-V series of big-lake fishing boats. High freeboard and generous deadrise make the boat well suited to larger lakes and inland waters. The riveted hull is double-plated in the bow and bottom, and the boat includes large lighted livewells, lockable rod storage, and plenty of dry storage space. Its dual console layout and large windshield makes it suitable for family activities such as watersports and cruising. The boat is rated for 200 hp, plenty of power for towing a pair of tubers or boarders, along with an 8 hp kicker.

G3 BOATS

Part of G3's high-performance series of aluminum bass boats, the HP 200 shown here is a 20-footer with lots of casting room on the raised fore and aft platforms, in-deck storage, and a pram bow for easy planing. The HP 200 is rated for up to 200 hp, which offers strong acceleration and top speed in this 1,420-pound riveted aluminum boat. Available in either side or dual console arrangements, the HP 200 has a Hot Foot throttle, a 6-inch jack plate for improved shallow-water capability, an insulated cooler, a 32-gallon fuel tank, and two livewells.   G3 BOATS

Princecraft, a Canadian division of Brunswick Corporation, builds aluminum pontoon boats and deck boats, and a series of aluminum deep-V, bass, utility, and jonboats. The 207 SE shown is part of a series from 17 to 20 feet intended for serious fishing as well as family activities with its dual console design. Raised casting platforms fore and aft with storage below, high windshields and generous freeboard, hydraulic steering, stereo, anchor locker, insulated cooler, aerated livewells, fish-finder, lockable rod storage, and trolling motor setup are included. The boat is rated for up to 225 hp and ten people.   PRINCECRAFT BOATS

Lowe Boats, part of Brunswick Corporation, builds aluminum pontoon and deck boats and a wide range of fishing boats including bass, deep-V, modified-V, and welded and riveted jonboats. The riveted jonboat shown here is part of a rugged and utilitarian series of workboats from 10 to 18 feet used to fish, hunt, and otherwise work on the water.   LOWE BOATS

Tracker's top-of-the-line formed-aluminum bass boat is the Avalanche, finished so well with its compound curves that it looks pretty much like a fiberglass boat.   TRACKER MARINE

The Tracker series of Mercury-powered aluminum boats includes modified-V, deep-V, riveted utility boats, and jonboats. The 2072 welded jonboat shown is one of Tracker's Grizzly series from 14 to 20 feet. A side console provides remote steering and engine control, and features include an aerated livewell and a structural floor. The 2072 is rated for up to 1,890 pounds total capacity and 125 hp, and is commonly sold as a boat-motor-trailer package.

TRACKER MARINE

Triton, a division of Brunswick Corporation, builds a wide range of fishing boats including offshore fiberglass center consoles, high-performance fiberglass bass boats, fish-and-ski boats, and aluminum fishing boats, deck boats, and pontoon boats. Aluminum fishing boats include fast bass boats, crappie boats, deep-V hunting boats, jonboats, and utility boats. The 186 shown is a dual console bass boat with rod and gear storage lockers, a pram bow for easy planing, and fore and aft raised casting platforms. Options include a larger trolling motor, bow-mounted depth-finder, battery charger, and Hot Foot throttle.

TRITON BOATS

G3 EAGLE 175 PF

G3/YAMAHA MOTORS

G3 Eagle 175 PF Specifications	
LOA:	17'5"
Beam:	6'
Deadrise:	12 deg.
Dry weight:	920 lb.
Fuel capacity:	13 gal.
Maximum capacity:	4 people
Total capacity:	1,000 lb.

G3, the aluminum boat manufacturing division of Yamaha Motors, produces a wide range of welded and riveted aluminum boats, all with Yamaha (mostly four-stroke) outboards. Serving the value-priced and midrange ends of the market, the builder manufactures two- and three-hull pontoon boats, modified-V fishing boats, jonboats, and high-performance bass boats. We have found their offerings to be ruggedly built and designed with a refreshing emphasis on value, practicality, and functionality. G3 applies the same attention to quality and customer service that the engine division is noted for.

In production since 2003, the G3 Eagle 175 Panfish jonboat is positioned in the middle of G3's 15- to 19-foot Eagle modified-V series of fishing boats. Specifically designed for the crappie fisherman, the boat includes a bait well, two livewells, and lockable rod storage and tackle storage forward. The deck is low in the boat compared to similar fishing boats with their raised casting platforms fore and aft, making this 175 PF an especially good choice as a small family boat, or one that can be used by passengers of all ages.

Construction

The Eagle 175 PF's hull is built of welded 0.1-inch aluminum with a stamped-in keel and full-length aluminum longitudinals for added hull stiffness, and running strakes in the bottom for improved tracking. The hull is supported by extruded aluminum ribs and frames with reinforced transom and corner bracing. The pressure-treated plywood deck is covered with 18-ounce marine-grade carpeting.

Walkthrough

Cockpit

In the bow is a large, slightly elevated (nearly a foot lower than the gunwale) carpeted casting deck, with a dry storage locker all the way forward on centerline. Also forward are nonskid strips in the painted bow deck and a pair of functional 6-inch bow cleats, along with a bow light pole that clips alongside the port gunwale. A standard Minn Kota electric trolling motor is mounted in the bow, and foot pedal controls, as well as a trim control switch for the main engine aft, are included. Below the raised platform's aluminum hatches are dry storage compartments, including six tackle trays, and a socket receptacle for the forward pedestal seat.

Lockable, carpeted rod storage sized to hold 7-foot rods is provided under the gunwale to port. A pair of livewells with 13- and 19-gallon capacities

Foam is injected between the hull and the deck to provide upright flotation in the event the boat is swamped. A transom hole with plug helps drain the boat when on the trailer. The boat has a built-in 13-gallon gas tank and comes with a 12-volt trolling motor in the bow.

The hull is painted with a baked-on, two-part urethane metallic finish resistant to scratching and fading from exposure to sunlight. Color options are firemetal red or gunmetal blue; graphics are also available.

Hull Design

The G3 Eagle 175 PF's hull is a skiff design with modest deadrise, extruded running strakes for added directional stability, a pram bow, and low freeboard for easy reach to the water when landing or releasing fish. This low-deadrise design makes the boat easy to plane and relatively stable compared to a deep-V of the same size. Since the boat is designed for protected waters like small lakes and rivers, the design is appropriate for the boat's intended purpose and works well with the hull's inherent form stability.

are located forward of the console to starboard and also aft below the port passenger seat. Both come standard with aerating pump timers and insulated livewell lids to keep the water inside cool.

The aft cockpit, or casting area (recessed at the same level as the helm console cockpit) has a socket for the pedestal seat stanchion, along with a mechanical compartment for the L-shaped 13-gallon polypropylene fuel tank, batteries, and a 800 gpm bilge pump. There's also a small compartment under the deck hatch for a pair of tackle bins. A small motor well helps prevent waves from boarding the boat aft.

Helm

At the fiberglass helm console, and just forward of the aft casting platform, helm and passenger seats fold down out of the way when not in use. The helm console, sensibly finished in a flat tan color to minimize glare, comes with a Plexiglas windscreen, full instrumentation (speedometer, tachometer, trim gauge, and fuel gauge), toggle switches for accessories such as the livewell pumps and running lights on an angled panel to the right of the steering wheel, and Yamaha side-mounted single-lever engine controls. A Garmin fish-finder is standard equipment. The boat comes standard with full-fledged breakers (not cheap throwaway fuses) in the electrical system.

The test boat's owner says the 175 PF is perfect for live bait fishing, equipped with two livewells. He also pointed out that you can do all your fishing without leaving the bow area, with the trolling motor, tackle storage, rod storage, and a livewell all at arm's length forward. Typically, the bait goes in one livewell, the catch in the other. Also, the cockpit is recessed, which a lot of older owners seem to appreciate, as walking around a raised casting platform on a 17-footer can seem like a balancing act in windy conditions. This boat lets you have it both ways. As such, it also makes a good family boat, suitable for watersports or a little day cruising.

Engine

The boat is rated for up to 75 hp, which includes Yamaha four-stroke outboards to 75 hp and two-strokes to 70 hp. The boat comes with a transom saver, which is basically an aluminum prop used between the trailer and the lower unit of the motor to reduce strain on the transom when trailering the boat.

Sea Trial

Our test ride took place on Missouri's Table Rock Lake with a steady breeze blowing. In spite of the relatively flat hull shape, the boat rode quite well in the 6-inch chop at 20 to 25 mph. Our seating position near the stern, where wave impact is felt much less than in the bow, was a big help, as were the well-padded seats. The helm (and passenger) seat was nicely contoured and comfortable (and attractively detailed), and there was plenty of legroom at the helm.

Our test boat had a 60 hp Yamaha four-stroke engine, and it was hard to hear it above the wind at speeds of more than 20 mph. We made more than 32 mph, and up to 5,000 rpm (26 mph) the engine noise was essentially obscured by wind noise. Steering was responsive at just two and three quarter turns lock-to-lock, giving the 175 commendable agility.

The wheel's height was just right for seated operation, which is the only way to drive this low-freeboard boat. The control shifts easily into forward, but was a little clunky going into reverse (shift decisively). The boat got up and planed nicely at 3,500 rpm, and heeling (banking) in a turn was minimal, thanks to the hull's low deadrise. The boat performed every bit as well as we expected it to.

G3 Eagle 175 Panfish Jonboat Performance Results

RPM	Speed, mph	Noise Level, dBA
800	2.1	58
1,000	2.8	58
1,500	3.8	64
2,000	5.4	67
2,500	6.5	67
3,000	7.4	70
3,500	12.9	70
4,000	17.5	78
4,500	22.9	82
5,000	26.4	82
5,500	29.5	86
6,000	32.4	90

Test conditions: Two passengers, fuel tank full, with a 60 hp Yamaha four-stroke outboard.

The G3 Eagle 175 PF is a practical, well-built, and an attractively finished all-purpose boat. Designed first and foremost for fishing, the multipurpose 175 PF should prove easy and economical to own and operate with very little required maintenance or special care.

Bass Boats

A low profile, shallow draft, and huge outboard characterize the typical 18- to 22-foot 130 to 300 hp bass boat. Bass boats are used for inland fishing, and the market segment is growing steadily. Designed for serious fishing, these craft also double as occasional high-performance race boats capable of reaching speeds of 60 to 70 mph, and considerably faster in some cases. Due to a beamy, low-deadrise hull, these boats are stable at rest, accommodating anglers walking from side to side; they must have clear sides all around for unobstructed fishing.

Typical accessories include swivel seats, a livewell, dry in-deck storage, all-fiberglass construction, and fish- and depth-finders. Even the low-end bass boats are well-built, but some of the components among the price point brands aren't of the highest quality. Most bass boats are built of fiberglass, though tough aluminum construction is also popular.

The J.D. Power and Associates rankings are for fiberglass bass boats only; the study excludes aluminum bass boats. The results of the 2007 study in the bass boat segment show that Bass Cat, a small Arkansas boatbuilder, was ranked highest in customer satisfaction. In fact, Bass Cat's index score of 936 makes it the highest-scoring brand in the entire marine industry. Triton was the next highest-scoring bass brand, followed closely by Ranger and Skeeter. Nitro was rated lowest by its owners, and by a wide margin. The bass boat segment was rated very highly as a whole with an average of all the brands of 875. Only the ski and wakeboard segment, with an average score of 885, was rated higher by owners than the bass segment. To put it in perspective, even the lowest-scoring bass boat brand, Nitro, was rated higher than the average brand in the coastal fishing segment.

Bass Cat also received five Power Circles (a measure of customer satisfaction in the study) in each of the six performance categories, while last-place finisher Nitro received two Power Circles in every category. In fact, no manufacturer received a single performance category score that differed by more than one Power Circle from any other performance category score. Ranger and Triton were the only brands to earn four Power Circles in the fishing category.

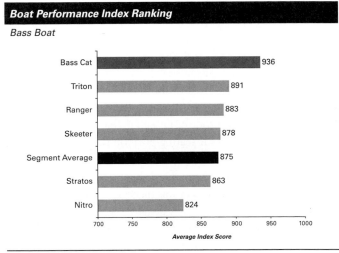

Boat Performance Index Ranking

Bass Boat

Brand	Average Index Score
Bass Cat	936
Triton	891
Ranger	883
Skeeter	878
Segment Average	875
Stratos	863
Nitro	824

Average Index Score

Source: J.D. Power and Associates 2007 Boat Competitive Information Study ℠

Power Circle Ratings™ ●●●●●
JDPower.com

J.D. Power and Associates 2007 Boat Competitive Information Study℠

Bass Boat Ratings

Company	Overall Rating	Quality & Reliability	Engine	Ride & Handling	Design & Style	Fishing
Bass Cat *Award Recipient*	●●●●●	●●●●●	●●●●●	●●●●●	●●●●●	●●●●●
Nitro	●●○○○	●●○○○	●●○○○	●●○○○	●●○○○	●●○○○
Ranger	●●●○○	●●●●○	●●●○○	●●●○○	●●●●○	●●●●●
Skeeter	●●●○○	●●●●○	●●●●●	●●●●○	●●●●○	●●●●○
Stratos	●●●○○	●●●○○	●●●○○	●●●○○	●●●○○	●●●●○
Triton	●●●●○	●●●●○	●●●●○	●●●○○	●●●●○	●●●●○

SCORING LEGEND:	●●●●● Among the best	●●●●○ Better than most	●●●○○ About average	●●○○○ The rest

The well-built Pantera II shown here is Bass Cat's best-selling model. It's a 19-footer with an 8-foot beam and a 200 hp capacity. Dual rod lockers and storage boxes, trolling motor, insulated cooler, fore and aft raised casting platforms, dual livewells, and helm console are included (a port side console is an option).   BASS CAT BOATS

Part of Tracker Marine, Nitro produces value-priced fiberglass bass boats and fish-and-ski boats. The 898 shown here is a 20-footer, Tracker's biggest bass boat. It comes well-equipped and is rated for four persons and 225 hp. Like most bass boats, it has all-fiberglass composite construction. Features include a built-in battery charger for the trolling and starting batteries, a fish-finder, in-deck dry storage, locking rod lockers, raised fore and aft casting decks, aluminum deck hatches, and a large recirculating livewell.   TRACKER MARINE

Champion Boats, a division of Genmar, builds competition bass, saltwater, and fish-and-ski boats. Its bass boat lineup includes its flagship Elite series from 18 to 21 feet, including the 210 Elite shown. Introduced in 2007, the 210 features room to flush-mount electronics at the helm console, plenty of in-deck rod and gear storage, trolling motor, jack plate, a divided livewell, and interior lighting. The 210 is rated for up to 300 hp and five people.

GENMAR HOLDINGS, INC.

ProCraft is part of Tracker Marine, and produces fiberglass bass and fish-and-ski models from 16 to 20 feet. The 200 Super Pro shown is the builder's top-of-the-line model, sporting a single helm console, hydraulic steering, fixed jack plate, fish-finder, trolling motor, onboard battery charger, insulated cooler, lighted livewell, and lockable rod storage lockers. The boat is sold as a package with motor and matching trailer. The 200 is rated for up to 200 hp and five people.   PROCRAFT

Ranger Boats, part of Genmar, is the world's largest bass boat builder (and one of the largest boatbuilders of any kind), and has either ranked highest or performed well in the annual J.D. Power and Associates study each year. Well-equipped and built as solidly as the brand's top-line models, the Ranger 188VS shown here is part of the boatbuilder's lower-priced VS series, and it was selected as best in its class by *Popular Mechanics* magazine. GENMAR HOLDINGS, INC.

Skeeter, a division of Yamaha, produces excellent fiberglass bass, saltwater, and multipurpose fishing boats. Skeeter's three classes of bass boats include the well-built, good-riding 20i (see full-length review on pages 408–411). The ZX190 shown here is one of Skeeter's entry-level bass boats. It's rated for four people and 175 hp. SKEETER BOATS

The well-designed Skeeter SX200 shown is the largest of the builder's SX "value" series of bass boats. The SX200 is a dual console model with large windscreens and lots of in-deck storage space. It's rated for up to 200 hp and can carry up to five passengers. SKEETER BOATS

An entry-level model designed in part to convert aluminum bass boat anglers to Stratos owners, the 176XT shown offers solid all-fiberglass construction, lots of dry storage space, a good ride, no-feedback steering, plenty of fishing room forward and aft, and a long standard equipment list including a trolling motor, fish-finder, divided aerated livewell with timer, and pedestal seats. The 175 is rated for up to 1,000 pounds, accounting for passengers, the motor (up to 75 hp), and gear. GENMAR HOLDINGS, INC.

Triton builds high-end saltwater and freshwater fishing boats (like the 21-footer shown), both aluminum and fiberglass, as well as pontoon and fish-and-ski boats. Part of Brunswick Corporation, Triton's fiberglass bass boats range from 16 to 21 feet. A variety of engine brands are offered. TRITON BOATS

BASS CAT PUMA 20

Bass Cat Puma 20 Specifications

LOA:	20'4"
Beam:	7'10"
Dry weight:	1,685 lb.
Draft:	36" (drive down)
Fuel capacity:	52 gal.

Bass Cat is a small, family-owned and -operated builder of high-end bass boats located in rural Arkansas, right down the road from bass boat builder powerhouse Ranger. The highest-ranking brand in the bass boat segment of the J.D. Power and Associates 2007 study, Bass Cat has a lot to be proud of, including some extremely satisfied customers. A hard-core, single-mission tournament bass boat in production since 2006, the Puma was built specifically to take the weight of a large V-6 outboard, with a little more beam than previous models, and give the boat some Euro-styling for good measure.

Construction

The Bass Cat Puma starts with high-quality construction methods and materials. Probably most significantly, the complete hull laminate is wet out using a premium vinylester resin, which has physical properties close to that of the fiberglass reinforcements. This makes an all-vinylester laminate superior (it's stronger, more impact-resistant, has better cosmetics, and is far more resistant to osmotic blistering) to one using orthophthalic or isophthalic resins.

The solid fiberglass hull layup is supported by a one-piece fiberglass flanged stringer gridwork bonded with fiberglass between the hull skin and the grid's flanges, then vacuum bagged in place while the fiberglass sets up. Vacuum bagging is the best possible means of clamping two surfaces under great pressure, and it does so uniformly to all the surfaces covered by the bag. When the fiberglass is cured, the bag is removed and the voids within the grid (and elsewhere in the hull) are pumped full of foam, adding positive flotation and substantial sound deadening.

The transom is built of solid fiberglass and microsphere fiberglass composite laid up between inner and outer molds. No wood is used in the boat, structurally or otherwise. The hull-to-deck joint is riveted together to hold it in place, and then fiberglassed together and also to the hull grillage and transom.

Hull Design

The Bass Cat has a modified-V bottom with a sharp entry tapering to moderate transom deadrise. The boat has a good ride, especially considering how shallow the hull deadrise is on bass boats in general. The Puma's hull adds a pair of what are essentially molded-in trim tabs, which tend to reduce or eliminate porpoising and help get the boat up on plane a bit faster. Our boat was also fitted with a keel chafe pad forward that offers protection for the gelcoat against abrasion from grounding.

Walkthrough

Cockpit and Topsides

The Puma is conventionally laid out (the generic bass boat layout is pretty standard, with slight variations in features like storage locker and livewell location) with fore and aft carpeted casting areas atop a deck comprised largely of hatches leading to various lockers and livewells.

Starting our walkthrough forward, we find rod storage lockers outboard, and net, tool, and incidental storage inboard on centerline, including tackle storage and even a plastic box inside one of the lockers especially for the registration and other papers to keep them dry and out of harm's way. There's also a deck compartment for a net and measuring stick forward, as well as an insulated cooler just forward of the cockpit along with a day storage box. A pair of Velcro-fastened straps hold rods securely when they're not in the rod storage boxes below the deck.

The electric trolling motor is in the bow. Like most units, it stows strapped down horizontally on the deck when not in use. A pull on a line releases a mechanism that allows the motor to be raised up and lowered into trolling position. Connected to two deep-cycle batteries aft, the motor is controlled by a foot pedal that uses heel-and-toe action to turn it left and right, and a second pedal to control the on-off switch. A third control adjusts current flow to the motor, which regulates propeller speed and thrust. The model on our test boat had more than enough thrust to move the boat along, even into a 10 mph wind.

We liked the fixed cleats in the bow and stern; they're recessed to prevent snagging, and you don't have to go to the trouble of popping them up and down every time you need them.

In the center of the boat in the recessed cockpit the helm and companion seats are well-padded and contoured, and even have adjustable spring-loaded lumbar supports. The padded bolsters help restrict lateral movement in a tight, high-speed turn. In a little touch of class, the plastic handrails outboard of the two cockpit seats light up with the company logo. There's also a bonus pair of pop-up cleats that are handy for tying off. Between the two cockpit seats is a flip-up deck panel that holds a throw cushion— a clever design feature.

Our boat had a pair of side consoles, with the one to port affording wind and spray protection for the passenger, as well as a glove box for dry storage of small articles. To starboard is the helm console, ergonomically laid out with the steering wheel, engine control binnacle, gauges, and electronics intelligently situated for comfortable operation. Our boat had a padded steering wheel that afforded a good, comfortable grip. The Lowrance GPS plotter took up a big chunk of the helm console to starboard, and it's an important piece of equipment, helping anglers get back to their favorite spots without involving any guesswork.

Below the side-mounted engine control at the helm console is a master switch for the electrical system, including the helm console, engine starting, and trolling motor. There is plenty of legroom at the helm console, and the steering wheel and throttle double as handholds for the driver when running at the 60 to 70 mph speeds this boat is capable of. The passenger has a strap to hold onto under the seat, along with the gunwale-mounted acrylic handrail.

Aft is a second casting platform with more storage compartments, along with the boat's two-compartment livewell below. On the Puma, all of the deck hatches, or lids, are equipped with micro switches that turn on lighting inside the boxes when opened, and there's also cockpit courtesy lighting around the deck perimeter. Back at the stern, the discharge fittings for the livewell pumpout and the two bilge pumps are near the boarding ladder, up where you can see them, and higher off the waterline than hull-mounted fittings could be located. The idea is to add more insurance against taking on water through these fittings if the hoses popped loose.

At the transom, a Detwiler hydraulic jack plate supported the engine. Being able to vertically adjust the engine height was a plus. The jack plate allows the engine to be raised in shallow water to reduce draft; it also minimizes risk to the prop when putting the boat back on the trailer, and it also lets you fine-tune engine height to optimize high-speed performance.

Engine

Our test boat came with a Mercury Optimax 225 hp Pro XS mounted on a hydraulic jack plate. The mechanical compartment is under a hatch just forward of the engine. Inside are two deep-cycle trolling motor batteries, a starting battery, the outboard's VRO tank, and a charger that feeds all three batteries. There's a pair of bilge pumps (one manual and one automatic), as well as livewell recirculating and aerator pumps with pump bodies that, incidentally, are interchangeable with the bilge pumps if need be.

The Puma comes with three fuel tanks: one on centerline forward, and two aft on either side outboard of the mechanical compartment. Two valves control suction from the tanks, either drawing from the center tank or the two aft tanks together.

Sea Trial

Our test ride on Lake Champlain offered a bracing few hours on the water. With temperatures in the low 40s, and a steady 20 mph southeast wind, conditions were perfect for putting our Bass Cat Puma through its paces.

Our first order of business was the speed run. Our test boat's big 225 hp Optimax XS made short work of getting on plane and up to speed. The engine not only offered strong acceleration from any mid- to high-range throttle setting, it also ran clean, with few noticeable fumes, even at low speed with the wind coming from abaft the beam. These direct-injected two-strokes have come a long way from the days of carbureted engines—cleaning up their act and burning a lot less fuel in the process.

The Puma topped out at 71.8 mph with two passengers who rarely miss a meal (about 500 pounds total) and the fuel tank about two-thirds full. Having run three bass boats within a two-week period, a Ranger Comanche Z20 (250 Yamaha HPDI), a Skeeter 20i (250 Yamaha HPDI), and this Bass Cat Puma 20 (Mercury 225 Optimax XS), it gave me a good opportunity to make some direct comparisons.

The Optimax's trim limiter stopped the engine from tilting up so far that the prop would ventilate, but far enough so the hull was clear of the water with the exception of the last foot or so of running surface. Running at 65 to 70 mph in this condition, the boat had a tendency to chine walk, but that could be controlled by slowing down, trimming the engine in, or moving weight forward. This is a great deal of power for a small boat, so if you're not experienced at driving a small high-powered light boat, be sure to spend time with your dealer or a knowledgeable bass boat owner before taking delivery.

As mentioned, I was also testing a Ranger Z20 with a 250 hp Yamaha HPDI VMAX and a Skeeter 20i with a 250 hp Yamaha HPDI VMAX at the same time I tested the Bass Cat. Both the Ranger and the Skeeter felt more stable to me at high speed than the Puma, which needed more attention on the part of the operator to control. While the Puma was a thrill to drive at 70 mph, with this much power it is not well suited to inexperienced owners or for families that intend to let kids run the boat.

I was also able to record sound levels with the Yamaha HPDI–powered Skeeter and the Mercury Optimax–powered Bass Cat running at the same time. The difference in noise levels was surprising, to Yamaha's advantage. Standing on the dock by the engine, the Optimax recorded 78 dBA and the Yamaha 72 dBA—a big and noticeable difference. At the helm with the engine idling, the Opticemax registered 69 dBA and the Yamaha 67 dBA. Seated in the bow, the Mercury registered 67 dBA and the Yamaha just 60.5 dBA. And while standing 15 feet from the Merc and 6 feet from the Yamaha, their noise levels sounded about the same. I only mention this because this was the first time I had Yamaha and Mercury direct-injected outboards at the same dock at the same time, and the difference was noticeable walking around the dock from boat to boat.

The Bass Cat did not have any tendency to porpoise at any throttle or trim setting, likely due to the small hull extensions aft and outboard that limit bow rise and increase dynamic lift at the stern.

Helm ergonomics worked well, with the controls nicely positioned for seated driving. There's also ample legroom at the wheel, and plenty to hold onto at speed.

The hydraulic jack plate lets the boat get into shallow water with the motor level, rather than having to tilt it up to clear the bottom. It comes in handy when adjusting the depth of the lower unit at high speed. In calm water, you can raise the motor to reduce drag, and in rougher water, lower it just enough to keep the prop from ventilating. It's also great to use at the launch ramp, where raising the motor makes powering onto the trailer a lot less hazardous.

It is worth noting how easy it is to drive the Bass Cat onto the trailer at the ramp. The carpeted trailer

Bass Cat Puma Performance Specifications

RPM	Speed, mph	Noise Level, dBA
600	3.3	69.0
1,000	5.3	71.0
1,500	7	76.0
2,000	8.4	78.0
2,500	18.5	83.0
3,000	28.6	84.0
3,500	34.2	86.0
4,000	42.7	
4,500	47.6	
5,000	56.3	
5,500	68.5	
5,800	71.8	

Test conditions: Mercury Optimax 225 hp, Pro XS engine, two passengers, two-thirds of a tank of fuel.

wheel well liners serve as natural guides keeping the boat centered over the rollers and bunks.

This Bass Cat Puma is a high-performance boat that clearly takes experience to operate safely with a 225 hp outboard. Like the 100 mph plus, open-ocean race boat, the high-performance 70 mph bass boat is not for the novice, and should be driven at high speed only after mastering its handling. Once you've mastered driving techniques, and fully understand the performance dynamics, and how to control them, it'll be a blast to own.

Options include rigging for Yamaha or Evinrude outboards, the port console, boarding ladder, a ski tow bar, GPS and fish-finder, trolling motors from either Minn Kota or MotorGuide, hydraulic jack plate, lighted livewell, windshield, stereo, keel protector cladding forward, foot-pedal throttle, and center fold-down seat.

RANGER Z20 COMANCHE

GENMAR HOLDINGS, INC.

Ranger Z20 Comanche Specifications	
LOA:	20'5"
Beam:	7'11"
Deadrise:	16 deg.
Dry weight:	2,800 lb.
Draft:	22"
Fuel capacity:	48 gal.
Max. horsepower:	225

One of four high-end, tournament-level, high-performance bass boats in Ranger's Comanche series, the Ranger Z20 is an able performer, with sure handling and speeds to 70 mph. It began production in 2005 and is designed for two anglers to fish at the same time on fore and aft casting decks. The Z20 is loaded with both storage space and fishing amenities, including a two-compartment livewell, lockable rod storage, and a high-capacity electric trolling motor with generous battery capacity.

Construction

The Z20 hull starts off as a layer of gelcoat sprayed over a female mold. This is followed by a 3-ounce resin-rich layer of fiberglass chop that helps to prevent osmotic blistering on the bottom and cosmetic print-through of the fiberglass weave pattern on the hull sides. A series of fiberglass laminates follows to complete the hull skin. The hull is supported by a one-piece fiberglass longitudinal grid held precisely in place with a jig and fiberglassed to the hull.

Holes are drilled and the hollow stringer system is filled with foam and sealed off. The closed-cell foam used throughout the hull, including inside the hollow stringers, deadens sound, stiffens the structure, and makes the boat unsinkable. In fact, all Rangers are unsinkable, with foam used throughout the structure to fill voids and create positive buoyancy even if the hull is damaged. The foam also adds stiffness to the hull skin, and makes

the boat quieter, reducing wave noise transmitted through the hull. The transom is made of multiple layers of fiberglass pultrusions bonded together and stiffened with heavy aluminum structural members.

A series of fiberglass boxes are glassed in place between the hull and the deck, and these are also injected full of foam to provide additional reserve buoyancy. A floor of pultruded fiberglass then goes down over the top of the stringers and is bedded to them with bonding putty and fiberglassed to the hull sides. The hull-to-deck joint is fiberglassed from the inside and sealed on the outside as the rubrail is fastened in place, and the entire area below the gunwale is injected with foam.

Decks get a coat of SprayCore applied over the gelcoat to prevent print-through, and this is part of the reason for the mirror-smooth clear-coat gelcoat finish seen in the topsides of each Ranger. The deck hatches are cored with Klegecell, a medium-density structural foam that's vacuum bagged in place to ensure a solid skin-to-core bond. These open-molded "lids" are built finish-side-down (the top is carpeted) for a classy look.

Even the fish and storage boxes in the Z20 are made of fiberglass, rather than the extruded, nonstructural plastic used by other boatbuilders, which makes them very strong and damage resistant; Ranger's well-nourished yet remarkably fit 270-pound regional service representative made this point convincingly, jumping up and down inside one of the storage boxes during our walkthrough.

It's unusual for large boatbuilders (Ranger built close to 6,000 boats last year) to do so, but Ranger uses a premium vinylester resin throughout the laminate. This resin is superior to the isophthalic and general-purpose orthophthalic resins used by most boatbuilders. A laminate using vinylester resin is much stronger, since the vinylester will elongate, or stretch, nearly as far as the fiberglass reinforcement itself (the other resins are relatively brittle). It's much better glue, so subsequent layers of fiberglass stick to each other more tenaciously. It's also closely cross-linked at a molecular level, which makes it practically impervious to osmotic blistering. The result is a much superior hull in every respect—stronger, more impact resistant and durable, and also better looking (especially on a dark hull) since vinylester shrinks less on curing.

Ranger uses several quality-control measures to manage the fiberglass-to-resin ratio, including metering the resin flow from the spray head and controlling the chopper gun's elapsed time building each component. These and other steps ensure the boats aren't resin rich and don't weigh any more than necessary, which improves performance and economy. In another step to ensure a high-quality finish, Ranger leaves each hull and deck (the two major structural parts of each boat) in their respective molds for three days, which produces a higher-quality finish and a uniform and stable part. And while most fiberglass production boat hulls and decks are engineered as a single unit once bonded together, Ranger engineers its boats to be both stiff and strong enough, even with the largest engine permitted, without the deck installed!

Ranger's involvement with safety goes back a long way. In the 1970s the company helped the U.S. Coast Guard establish the original standards and write the formulas used today for calculating maximum horsepower ratings for small boats. Ranger also helped establish the level flotation standards mandated for all boats under 20 feet—and applies these same standards to all its boats, even those 20 feet and longer.

Hull Design

The Z20 has a modified-V bottom with concave sections forward producing a fine entry at the keel. The bottom transitions to 16 degrees of deadrise at the transom. The hull bottom cuts off well short of the transom. This reduces buoyancy aft, but it also reduces wetted surface, which makes the boat go faster with less frictional drag, and along with the fixed jack plate, it allows the engine to influence trim more (either bow up or bow down)—the trim lever arm in this case being a function of the distance from the prop to the aft end of the running surface. The transom is also designed to pick up buoyancy gradually, either when stopping suddenly or fishing stern-to the waves, and to prevent swamping the motor well.

Walkthrough

Cockpit and Helm

There are three seats in the Ranger's cockpit: one is to port for a passenger, who also gets his or her own console with a big glove box, space for flush-mounted electronics, footrests, and lots of legroom below. In the middle is another passenger seat, more like a jump seat for the occasional third passenger, with less padding and support, and the backrest folds down to serve as a hard step to the aft deck, so there's no need to walk on upholstery on this boat.

Ranger includes what it calls Soft-Ride seats in the Z20—both of the outboard cockpit seats as well as the portable, fold-down pedestal seat that can be plugged into a deck socket either forward or aft. These seats have a coil-spring suspension system built right in, so you're not just relying on foam to absorb impact. Along with the hull's very smooth ride, these seats really make for a comfortable day on the water.

The Z20's helm is ergonomically designed. The steering wheel is car-like in its position, angle, and height, making it comfortable and familiar to drive this boat. Likewise, the side-mounted Evinrude engine control is ergonomically located and comfortable to operate. It shifts in and out of gear with little resistance, and the throttle stays where you leave it when released. The helm instruments are intelligently arranged and easy to see when seated. The low-profile windscreen is mostly cosmetic and does very little to deflect wind or spray.

The Ranger's waterproof touch-pad control panel, which can be used with any brand of outboard engine offered by the builder, was a real treat to use. You enter a four-digit code to activate the helm's electrical components, including the engine monitoring system and electronics, and enter it again to start the engine. The system shuts down automatically after 8 hours, or when you re-enter the code sequence. There's room on either side of the wheel for flush-mounted electronics, though our test boat was set up for a pedestal-mounted GPS plotter/fish-finder combo unit on a flat to starboard of the helm console. Just aft of the throttle are controls for the livewell pump (recirculation, auto-fill, or empty), as well as a fuel-suction selector switch for the twin gas tanks; you don't even have to get up to switch fuel tanks.

The driving seat is comfortable, well-padded, and nicely contoured (you really notice the springs when running at 50 or 60 mph in a chop). There's also lots of legroom, as well as a pair of nearly vertical boot-shaped footrests to plant your feet against at high speed, keeping you securely in position. Also down on the inboard side of each cockpit seat is an "oh-shoot" (though that's not actually what they call it) retractable handle to hang onto at high speed, otherwise known as "Nina straps" after Ranger's founder's wife, who reportedly requested them one day after moving from one fishing spot to another with her husband. Also below the center seat is a receptacle for a fishing net handle, as well as a deck drain leading to the bilge.

Foredeck

Our Z20 test boat had a cockpit amidships with port and starboard side consoles, and fore and aft carpeted casting decks, under which are a variety of fish and storage boxes and livewells. Starting at the bow, the area forward where you do most of your fishing has extra-thick padding under the carpet, which makes a real difference to your feet.

The Minn Kota 101 Max Pro electric trolling motor is strapped down forward to port. It's connected via heavy cables to a series of deep-cycle batteries that typically provide 8 hours of intermittent use—good enough for a full day on the water. The trolling motor on our boat puts out up to 101 pounds of thrust, as the name hints, and comes with a clever Lift-Assist boost that makes swinging it up and over into position a casual, low-effort undertaking. The motor has a 42-inch shaft, so it projects well underwater, which is helpful when operating in choppy water to prevent it from ventilating and losing thrust.

The motor is operated using foot controls, whether flush-mounted or recessed into the deck. The amount and the direction of thrust can be precisely controlled once you get used to the pedals. The thrust is infinitely variable up to full power, which pulls the boat along at about 4 mph. The Minn Kota also serves as convenient get-home power in the event you lose the big motor. Also in the bow is a flat spot for a combination GPS plotter/fish-finder and controls for the navigation lights.

The boat comes with what is known in the trade as a pro pole, which is actually a lot like a bike seat. It has an adjustable-height stanchion, and you can use it either as a seat or a leaning post. Apparently, the pros don't use either seat very much, preferring to stand, or at least preferring to be seen standing.

All the deck hatches, or lids, on the Ranger are made of vacuum-bagged, foam-cored fiberglass, which makes them stiff and also insulates them, keeping things inside (including live fish) a lot cooler than standard, single-skin aluminum lids would. Up forward to port is a large carpet-lined fiberglass storage box that holds ten 7½-foot rods, with an intelligently designed rod butt rack at the aft end. The carpeting is easier on those expensive rods than a bare-fiberglass box would be.

Opposite to starboard is a same-size carpet-lined storage box for more general storage, as well as containing the stern light stanchion and a fire extinguisher. In between, on centerline, is a fiberglass box, with drain, designed to hold a tackle storage system (there's room for ten Plano storage boxes aft in the compartment) along with life jackets and other gear.

Aft Deck

More in-deck compartments can be found aft, including a centerline fiberglass storage box with a drain just behind the cockpit. Just aft of that is a livewell with a perforated bulkhead down the middle and two lids for access. Outboard to port and starboard is another pair of fiberglass storage boxes. All of the fiberglass lids close tightly, taking a little pressure to latch, which helps keep each compartment insulated and eliminates rattling. They also are fitted with small boosts that lift the hatch an inch or so once the latch is released so the hatch edge is easy to grip and pull open.

At the transom are three hatches providing access to the boat's mechanical systems, including the engine starting, house, and deep-cycle trolling batteries, engine VRO tank, and pumps for the bilge and the livewells. A shallow motor well in the stern provides a gentle radius for the engine control and fuel lines leading from a sealed hull tube to starboard out to the engine.

Under one of the hatches is a female receptacle blank to plug the battery charger cord into when it's not plugged in for recharging. This keeps it from getting wet or damaged and makes it easy to find when needed. Below another aft hatch is a complete wiring schematic that will come in handy for equipment replacement or troubleshooting, and it will always be there if you need it.

Engine

Ranger offers a wide range of two- and four-stroke outboard power options from Evinrude, Yamaha, and Mercury. In the case of the Z20 Comanche, up to 225 hp outboard power is available. All Rangers over 150 hp come standard with Teleflex's Sea Star Pro hydraulic steering, which eliminates feedback at the wheel.

Trailer

We don't usually report on trailers, but the one that comes with the Ranger has a number of features that are hard not to appreciate. The trailer is not a one-size-fits-all model—it's specifically built for this boat. The basic design, with its sloping, padded, and carpeted fenders inside the trailer wheels, guides the boat right onto the trailer, making it easy to recover the boat in a strong crosswind (like the day of our boat test).

The trailer wheels are lubricated by an oil bath, the level of which can be seen through a clean sight glass lens. Racheting tie-down straps are provided at the aft end of the trailer to secure it to the boat transom. The trailer tongue folds back out of the way (and locks in that position), making it a couple of feet shorter than when the boat is being towed, which makes it easier to fit the boat in a garage. The trailer jack is also built in just aft of the winch, which allows the trailer to be lifted higher than a standard forward-mounted jack of the same length.

The trailer framing is built using open C-section steel, so there is no tubing or box channel to collect water and rust out from the inside. Finally, the whole trailer is coated with a rubberized material called Road Armor that retains some flexibility and therefore won't chip upon impact with a rock or other hard object. This bodes well for long trailer life, and for keeping the trailer, which incidentally is nicely painted to match the boat, looking good for many years.

Sea Trial

Our test ride took place with a 15 to 20 mph wind blowing up Lake Champlain, so we had a good chance to check out the boat's rough-water capability. In a word, the Z20's ride was superb, and much better than one would think possible given the bottom's moderate deadrise and shallow hull draft. Ranger's sharp entry, produced by concave hull sections forward, sliced through the chop and delivered impressive tracking control as well. We could let go of the steering at 40 mph with the 1- to 2-foot waves on our quarter and the boat stayed right on course without any tendency to wander.

The balance between hull form and weight distribution was just right, and with this combination of a smooth headsea ride and hands-off tracking downsea, the Z20's ride and handling is matched by few boats on the market. Often we see a fine-entry boat that runs well into the waves but bow-steers running in the other direction, and another boat with full sections forward that runs well downsea but pounds mercilessly up sea. Riding on a boat that runs in any direction so comfortably and competently was a real pleasure.

Running our speed trials in calmer water in Valcour Island's lee, we managed 68.6 mph at 5,200 rpm, and this might have improved a mile per hour or so if we'd had a longer course to run in a lee. Particularly impressive was the hull's low drag, combined with a very smooth and comfortable ride. For each 500 engine rpm increase above 3,500 rpm, the boat picked up 10 mph or more in speed. When away from the lee and running at 3,500 rpm for 37 mph in the rough Lake Champlain chop, the boat was a delight to drive in any direction to the seas.

Our test boat had a fixed jack plate, which extends the engine about 10 inches aft of the transom. With the engine trimmed down, the extra lever arm helps get the stern out of the water quicker on initial acceleration, producing a faster hole shot (if that's important to you). The builder also feels it will produce a slightly higher top end, with a little cleaner waterflow to the prop.

The steering took four turns lock-to-lock, which offers a reasonable degree of agility for a boat as fast as this one. However, with the effort required to manually steer any big outboard motor our preference would be for power steering with three-fingertip control turns lock-to-lock (just like stern drives have), which we feel would be more appropriate for a high-performance boat like this one.

Another comment on this boat's handling: bass boats (like our Ranger Z20) tend to be high-powered, with a very high power-to-weight ratio. We've been on a number of bass boats that, when running flat out, felt like they were at the outer limits of controllability, with chine walking (rolling sharply from side to side with just a couple of feet of the bottom aft in the water) and porpoising (bow rising and falling in the absence of corresponding waves) coming into play. While the pros that spend hundreds of hours running these less stable boats know how to handle them, a boat like the Ranger Z20 is inherently more stable (we could not make the boat chine walk or porpoise at any boat speed or engine trim) and therefore safer to operate. With 225 hp on a boat that weighs about 1,800 pounds before the motor is installed, we would make the Ranger's high degree of dynamic stability a condition of purchase for any bass boat, whether a Ranger or another brand. Accepting anything less on a 70 mph boat is courting trouble, in our view.

We also had a chance to run the same Ranger with a Yamaha 225 VMAX two-stroke, and it's interesting to compare it to the 225 hp Evinrude E-TEC. The Yamaha, with the same advertised horsepower, ran about 3 mph faster (we might have hit 70 mph in ideal conditions with the Evinrude-powered boat), and sound levels were a little higher than the Evinrude's at the lower rpm range (when running above 35 or 40 mph in an open boat like this bass boat, the wind makes a lot more noise than the engine, making noise level readings less useful and sometimes misleading).

On the Evinrude boat, the engine alarm went off, which restricted engine speed to 1,200 rpm until

Ranger Z20 Comanche Performance Results

RPM	Speed, mph	Speed, knots	Noise Level, dBA	RPM	Speed, mph	Speed, knots	Noise Level, dBA
500	2.8	2.4	58	1,000	5.3	4.6	68
1,000	5.7	5.0	66	1,500	6.6	5.7	68
1,500	7.5	6.5	69	2,000	7.5	6.5	72
2,000	8.7	7.6	74	2,500	11.6	10.1	79
2,500	25.4	22.1	78	3,000	32.5	28.2	83
3,000	31.9	27.7	81	3,500	39.3	34.2	
3,500	36.9	32.1		4,000	46.6	40.5	
4,000	46.4	40.3		4,500	52.5	45.6	
4,500	56.6	49.2		5,000	59.1	51.4	
5,000	66.2	57.5		5,500	68.4	59.4	
5,200	68.6	59.6		6,000	72	62.6	

Test conditions: Two passengers, fuel tank three-eighths full, with 225 hp Evinrude E-TEC.

Test conditions: Two passengers, fuel tank full, with 225 hp Yamaha VMAX.

the fault was cleared (shut it off, wait 30 seconds, and then restart). This is a two-stroke motor, which relies on oil mixed with the gas for lubrication, but you can run it without oil—in an emergency—for up to 5 hours, according to Evinrude.

Ranger's Z20 is at the top of its game in this demanding market. We have never operated a boat of this size and speed that offered a greater feeling of security at the top of its operating range; all-around controllability is remarkable. Designed primarily for practical tournament-level fishing, the Ranger Z20 Comanche is built to last for generations, and it's unsinkable. Intelligent design is evident throughout the boat, from the superb hull design and rough-water ride to the extra padding and recessed foot-control option built in at the bow, and the spring-supported seats and cored insulating deck lids. We can recommend this boat unreservedly.

SKEETER 20i

Skeeter 20i Specifications

LOA:	20'2"
Beam:	7'10.5"
Deadrise:	0 deg.
Dry Weight:	1,850 lb.
Fuel capacity:	48 gal.
Maximum capacity:	5 people
Total capacity:	1,484 lb.

Skeeter, a division of Yamaha, produces high-quality fiberglass bass, saltwater, and multi-purpose fishing boats that score well in the J.D. Power and Associates study. Skeeter's three lines of bass boats include the 20i, a high-performance, high-end model used on the tournament circuit that can hit 70 mph with a 250 hp Yamaha HPDI. The 20i went into production in 2006.

Construction

Skeeter's construction uses an isophthalic DCPD blend resin, which has good cosmetic properties as well as osmotic blistering resistance, throughout the laminate. The hull bottom and sides are solid fiberglass using a mix of woven and nonwoven reinforcements. Running strakes are solid fiberglass, not filled with putty. The one-piece fiberglass stringer grid is flanged and bonded to the hull skin using a two-part adhesive. It supports and stiffens the hull, and carries the deck above. The stringers meet at the bow, a design that helps to minimize hull wracking in this low-freeboard hull. Outboard of the full-length molded stringers is another pair of hull supports running forward 8 feet from the transom; these additional stringers reduce hull bottom skin panel sizes.

The transom is a composite of fiberglass skins and 2-inch Divinycell foam core. This in turn is supported by aluminum knees through-bolted to the transom and to ½-inch-thick aluminum plates through-bolted to the side of the main stringers. This aluminum structure absorbs and transmits engine thrust and weight loads (which are magnified by the lever arm created by the jack plate hanging off the transom) directly and reliably to the primary hull structure. The great thing about aluminum is that what you see is what you get. There's no wondering if secondary bonds are going to hold under high peel loads where the knee meets the transom.

The boat's deck (or floor) is made of a single sheet of CNC-cut, black-powder-coated aluminum plate supported by welded aluminum supports. The many deck hatches are also aluminum, so this is a good choice of material since it provides a consistent assembly of fixed deck and movable hatches. The deck design also permits easy fuel tank change-out in the unlikely event the fuel tank needs replacing (it's unlikely because it's a polypropylene tank, which can't corrode and will, if properly supported and protected from chafe, last as long as the boat).

The carpeting is glued to the aluminum deck. Carpeting is preferred by the bass fishing market since it is comfortable underfoot, provides a good nonskid walking surface, is easy to clean with a hose, and when the time comes, is reasonably easy to replace. The shoebox hull-to-deck joint has a two-part adhesive applied around the perimeter, then it is clamped with self-tapping screws on 3-inch centers. These screws are nylon-coated, which prevents them from backing out over time; since the adhesive is used to bond the hull and deck, their presence becomes somewhat superfluous.

Hull Design

The Skeeter 20i has a modified-V hull, with a deep forefoot (it extends below the boat's baseline), radius chines, and spray strakes all contributing to an extremely smooth and solid ride. This boat's ride in a light chop compares favorably to many saltwater center consoles. This is a substantial achievement for such a low-deadrise hull. Stern sponsons outboard add buoyancy at rest, helping to support the weight of the engine cantilevered past the stern, improving astern performance by adding buoyancy early as waves and wake approach the transom, and adding form stability to reduce list when people walk from one side of the boat to the other. The sponsons' added lift and buoyancy also improve acceleration by reducing bow rise coming on plane, letting the engine focus more on forward thrust and less on vertical lift.

Walkthrough

Cockpit and Topsides

Like all bass boats, the Skeeter 20i's design includes flat casting areas forward and aft with a recessed cockpit with helm console and seating in the middle. At the bow is the electric trolling motor, which raises and lowers on an aluminum frame, as well as a pedestal fishing seat from which the motor can be controlled. You can also raise and lower the Yamaha in the stern, and there's a handy fish-finder at your feet.

Just aft are four large storage compartments (rod boxes, day box, and lockable storage lockers) under deck hatches; these aluminum deck hatches comprise the majority of the forward deck area, which tells us something about the sheer volume of storage space in this boat.

The cockpit has three seats, with a cooler under the center seat. The seats are thickly cushioned and contoured to offer lateral support as well as comfort. The port console has a large glove box and a small windscreen. To starboard is the helm console with its tilt wheel and mechanical engine control. A fish-finder has prominence on the dash surrounded by engine gauges. Skeeter's Digital Multifunction System acts as a control center for the boat's systems, including livewell controls. The single on-off switch acts as a battery switch.

Aft of the cockpit are the livewells and a mechanical compartment with batteries, bilge pump, and engine VRO tank. A 12-inch fixed jack plate is standard, as are four 6-inch pop-up cleats.

Sea Trial

The test ride took place in a light 4- to 8-inch chop on Lake Champlain. As might be expected of a 1,850-pound boat with a 250 hp two-stroke outboard, acceleration is quick and strong from 4,000 rpm to full throttle, which tops out at 5,700 rpm.

The Skeeter 20i had an excellent ride in the light chop, slicing through those little waves without a hint of pounding. The boat also felt solid, as if it were a lot heavier than its actual weight. We made it to just above 70 mph, and the feeling was one of complete control; there was no indication that the boat was on the edge of controllability. It tracks as if it is on rails, and when a wave throws it a few degrees the boat finds its way back to its original heading with little helm input. We don't often get excited about ride quality, but this Skeeter, like the Ranger Z20, is truly exceptional.

We're not bass experts, so the foot throttle took getting used to. However, by the time we were done with the boat (it was on loan to us for several weeks) it seemed like a perfectly sensible way to run this kind of boat, since you can keep both hands on the wheel, with the foot-pedal accelerator providing faster throttle response in rough water.

With the engine trimmed up almost all the way to tilt mode, the boat ran best. The same trim had the boat porpoising a bit at 35 to 40 mph (just drop the trim to solve that problem); however, it was steady as a rock at 45 mph plus. Hanging the 539-pound Yamaha 12 inches aft of the transom obviously pays off in terms of weight distribution; boats need their center of gravity farther aft as speed increases.

Keep in mind that the speeds registered on our test ride were with a light load, with one 250-pound driver and half a tank of gas. You can easily add another passenger weighing around 250 pounds, another 150 pounds of gas, 30 gallons of water in the livewells at 240 pounds, and assorted fishing tackle and food at about 100 pounds; however, loading the boat another 750 or so pounds will slow the boat down commensurately.

Since our official test ride took place in a driving rain, the lack of a windshield was noticed. This boat is clearly designed to be driven sitting down, due to the boat's low profile and low cockpit height.

The wheel and throttle are right where they should be for comfortable reach and feel, and the foot throttle is also well positioned.

The Minn Kota Max 80F electric trolling motor gets the job done, pulling the boat from the bow soundlessly. We found the foot pedal uncomfortable when turning to port, since pushing your heel down turns the motor to port, and pushing the toe down turns the motor to starboard. The port turn requires the heel down, and at the same time you need to keep pressure on the toe where the on-off switch is located to keep the propeller turning.

The Skeeter 20i is well-built and designed for its purpose, catching freshwater fish, and should provide many years of reliable service. Its ride in a chop is superb. It has all the bells and whistles needed to catch bass, and it offers all the comforts and conveniences to make a full day on the water enjoyable.

Skeeter 20i Performance Results

RPM	Speed, mph	Noise Level, dBA
1,000	5.6	70
1,500	7.1	73
2,000	8.1	74
2,500	16.9	82
3,000	33.5	83
3,500	38.1	84
4,000	46.7	85
4,500	54.2	86
5,000	59.6	92
5,700	71.6	93

Test conditions: One passenger, fuel tank half full, with a 250 hp Yamaha HPDI VMAX. Six-inch chop.

DECK BOATS

The deck boat typically has a low, wide monohull supporting an equally wide deck that's open from bow to stern. The helm console is usually near amidships to starboard. Lounge seating is often provided around the perimeter of the deck, so there's room for a large group of family or friends. Some of these deck boats have bow and stern boarding ladders, and side gates as well as a transom door, making getting on and off the boat easier.

A wide range of amenities is usually included or available as options. Some examples are a refrigerator, wet bar, head with toilet and sink, rod holders, livewell, and fish box.

Deck boats have planing hulls, so they're also capable of pulling skiers or tubers, assuming that enough power is available. If you plan to ski from any of these boats, getting the biggest motor permitted is a good idea. Usually wide for their length to maximize deck space, and with minimal deadrise to provide a good turn of speed with a crowd on board, a deck boat's hull may not deliver as smooth a ride as a similar LOA runabout.

Deck boats are not covered in the annual J.D. Power and Associates study. However, most of the manufacturers producing deck boats also build runabouts, so some legitimate conclusions about deck boats may perhaps be drawn from studying the runabout data (see page 432).

Bayliner's deck boats run from 19 to 23 feet. The 237 shown has MerCruiser stern-drive power options to 300 hp, what looks to be a race boat's helm station, and an accommodating seating plan with a big convertible sunpad forward.   BAYLINER

Chaparral's upscale Sunesta deck boats run from 21 to 27 feet. The 27-footer shown here has an enclosed head (that looks like it belongs on a yacht), lots of seating and sunpad room, and a big swim platform for staging watersports. Volvo and MerCruiser stern-drive options range up to 375 hp.   CHAPARRAL BOATS

Crownline's deck boats run from 22 to 26 feet. The 252 EX shown is a sleek (looks more like a bowrider) model with an enclosed head, and a convertible lounge-sunpad and big recliners in the bow for the ultimate in over-the-top pampering. It's rated for up to 300 stern-drive hp.   CROWNLINE BOATS

Four Winns makes a nicely styled Funship series of deck boats from 20 to 27 feet. The 244 shown has dual consoles with a center windshield that closes (offering protection on those off days), and an enclosed head compartment that makes a full day on the water more appealing. Volvo and MerCruiser stern-drive options to 320 hp are available.   GENMAR HOLDINGS, INC.

Glastron's modestly priced deck boats run from 20 to 23 feet. The DS 205 shown, its entry-level offering, is ready to go fishing, wakeboarding, or cruising. The deck plan is open, leaving lots of room for whatever you want to do on the water. Power options from MerCruiser and Volvo range up to 270 hp.   GENMAR HOLDINGS, INC.

Godfrey's Hurricane deck boats range from 17 to 26 feet in three lines—Sundeck, Fundeck GS, and Fundeck. The 195 Sundeck is shown here. Both stern-drive and outboard models are available.
GODFREY MARINE

Mariah makes three moderately priced deck boat models from 21 to 25 feet. The DX 213 shown has a ten-person capacity and is rated for up to 260 stern-drive hp.   MARIAH BOATS

Regal's 2120 Destiny deck boats are built a lot like the rest of the line — solidly with a good-riding (especially for a deck boat) hull design. The boat comes well-equipped, and there's also an enclosed head and even a changing room. The 2120 is rated to carry up to 12 people.   REGAL MARINE

Princecraft, based in Quebec, builds aluminum deck boats, including this 250V LPW. The hull is painted with urethane for a durable, high-gloss finish. There's a portable changing room (there's a little cross pollination going on here . . . Princecraft also builds pontoon boats), seating is thickly padded and contoured, and there's a big swim platform aft of the engine compartment. MerCruiser stern-drive power options to 300 hp are available.   PRINCECRAFT BOATS

Rinker builds a pair of deck boats, 24- and 26-footers. The 240 Captiva shown is rated for up to 12 people, has lots of storage space, and is available with a number of MerCruiser stern-drive options. The bigger the engine, the better able you'll be to tow a skier or wakeboarder.   RINKER BOATS

Sea Ray's high-end Sundeck series starts at 20 feet and runs to 27 feet. The 270 Sundeck shown, the builder's largest deck model, is luxuriously fitted out. It has an enclosed head to port and a berth down below to starboard under the console — not bad for a deck boat. MerCruiser stern-drive power to 375 hp is available.   SEA RAY BOATS

Southwind is a new fiberglass brand started up by pontoon builder Bennington. The company builds both deck boats — like the 229 shown — and deck boat hybrids (pontoon boat decks on fiberglass monohulls).   SOUTHWIND BOATS

Vectra, part of aluminum boatbuilder Smoker Craft, builds fiberglass runabouts and deck boats. The 2040 shown here, part of a lineup from 19 to 25 feet, both stern-drive- and outboard-powered, is an outboard-powered model with a 12-person capacity and a rating of up to 200 hp.   VECTRA BOATS

Tahoe builds deck boats from 19 to 26 feet. The 265 shown, the top of the line model from Tahoe, is finished in upscale style, with a changing room, enclosed head, and refreshment center included. MerCruiser power to 320 hp is available. The 265 is rated to carry up to 14 people.   TAHOE

SEA RAY 240 SUNDECK

Sea Ray 240 Sundeck Specifications

LOA:	26'4"
Beam:	8'6"
Deadrise:	21 deg.
Dry weight:	4,680 lb.
Cockpit depth:	30"
Draft:	41" (drive down)
Fuel capacity:	65 gal.
Maximum capacity:	12 people
Total capacity:	2,100 lb.

Of all Sea Ray's sport boat lineup, which includes bowriders, cuddies, and deck boats up to 29 feet, the 240 Sundeck is in some ways the most family-friendly, with a deep cockpit adding a tangible sense of security for small children, and the excellent hull design providing an enjoyable ride in a chop. Like most deck boats, the biggest difference between this model and a standard bowrider is the position of the consoles—the deck boat's is farther aft, which opens up more space in the bow, creating two more equally proportioned seating areas. The 240 went into production in 2006.

Construction

The Sea Ray 240 Sundeck starts with a gelcoat applied to the mold, followed by a layer of chop wet out with resin, followed by a solid glass laminate (no coring) in the hull. Preformed foam stringers are encapsulated and tabbed to the bottom with fiberglass, an excellent structural means of reinforcing the hull. The one-piece cockpit and deck is bonded to the stringers using an adhesive. A shoebox hull-to-deck joint is fastened with self-tapping screws drilled into a composite backing strip. A caulking compound seals the joint.

The transom is cored with plywood. The important thing here for the manufacturer is to make sure the stern-drive cutout through the plywood is sealed and kept dry to prevent plywood end-grain water absorption and eventual rot. Sea Ray makes the point that the dense plywood absorbs vibrations better than foam, which is true, and it also saves the builder money; we'd rather see a high-density wood-free transom. The 240 SD deck also has end-grain coring. Sea Ray notes that it goes to lengths to make sure the balsa is not drilled through or penetrated in any way—this helps prevent water intrusion and migration.

Hull Design

The 240's hull has 21 degrees of deadrise at the transom and a sharp entry with high chines forward, all combining to deliver a smooth and dry ride in a chop.

Walkthrough

Cockpit

The bolt-on swim platform is huge, extending well over the stern drive below for an added measure of safety. It also includes a three-step boarding ladder (four steps would be better, making it easier to climb from deep water) under a flush deck hatch and grab handle. A walkthrough is provided on the starboard side of the engine hatch to the cockpit.

The cockpit has an L-shaped lounge aft to port with storage and a cooler below, and an entertainment center is opposite with a sink, freshwater spigot, and storage space inside.

This boat feels especially secure inside with a 30-inch coaming height and grippy nonskid underfoot. A cockpit table that's supported by a stanchion in a deck socket at the aft end of the L-shaped lounge is standard. The in-deck locker near the helm is 22 inches from deck to bilge, which provides a lot of storage space for wakeboards and skis. A bimini top and a snap-in carpet are standard.

Forward to port, the passenger pedestal seat is fully contoured to provide a comfortable ride. The flip-up bolster adds standing room, and a grab bar and cup holders are installed at the port console. The console glove box contains all the toys—a Clarion CD-AM-FM stereo, an MP3 port, and a Sirius radio, all included with the boat's base price. Inside the console is a surprisingly roomy head compartment with a portable toilet and opening portlight. The one-piece liner, which includes a sink with removable spigot, should prove easy to keep clean.

The bow seating area is huge on the 240. It takes up a good percentage of the boat's overall length, and Sea Ray also carries the hull's beam well forward to expand the usable space. There's room for four to sit comfortably, grab bars are provided forward and at the gunwales, and there's a cup holder for each person and an insulated cooler forward. Forward is an anchor locker and a second three-step boarding ladder that can be used to get on board the boat from the beach, but it's too short

to use easily from the water. Another in-deck storage locker is below, with a socket for the bow table built into the hatch.

Helm

The helm station is cleanly laid out, with multifunction engine gauge, tachometer, and speedometer high on the dash area. The helm's pedestal seat has a flip-up bolster, and it's heavily padded and contoured to provide generous lateral support, which is especially welcome in a hard turn out on the water. The wheel, comfortable to the grip with no sharp-edged spokes, is comfortably positioned for seating or standing, as is the side-mounted, single-lever engine control. Legroom is generous, and the dark dash treatment under the windshield minimizes glare in full sunlight.

At the helm, a compass, horn, power-tilt steering, and SmartCraft engine monitoring system are standard. The SmartCraft system reads out such data as boat speed and fuel flow and fuel consumption as well as engine operating conditions, so it's a great feature to have.

Engine

The engine hatch, comprised of the centerline section of the cockpit L-shaped lounge and the sunpad aft, lifts easily on boosts, providing excellent access to our test boat's 350 MAG MPI MerCruiser stern drive. There's room to comfortably get to all the maintenance points on the engine, and a gutter surrounding the deck perimeter keeps things dry inside.

Sea Trial

Our test boat had a 350 MAG MerCruiser rated at 300 hp. A 320 hp 6.2-liter engine is an option. We recorded just under 45 mph in calm water at wide-open throttle. At a continuous 3,500 rpm cruise speed, with a load of passengers and gear onboard, figure on about 27 mph. We made 30.4 mph at that rpm with a light load and a clean, unpainted bottom.

The boat handled very well, with the power steering registering just 2.5 turns lock-to-lock, providing good responsiveness. With the drive tucked in, there was no loss of the horizon momentarily when coming up on plane. The ride in the light Lake George chop was surprisingly smooth and solid feeling, more so than a number of similar size runabouts we've tested. In a hard, high-speed turn, the 240 handled well, with no tendency to skip or slide unpredictably in a turn. The MerCruiser ran well and was quite quiet in the cruising rpm range.

Sea Ray 240 Sundeck Performance Results

RPM	Speed, mph	Noise Level, dBA
600	3.3	66
1,000	6	69
1,500	7.6	71
2,000	9.7	76
2,500	18.6	78
3,000	23	79
3,500	30.4	82
4,000	34.9	84
4,500	42.1	88
4,800	44.8	92

Test conditions: Three passengers, fuel tank full, with a 300 hp MAG MPI. Six-inch chop.

This boat has a great deal to commend it, such as the intelligent layout with good use of space for people and storage for gear. The head compartment makes this an especially family-friendly platform for a full day on the water. It also includes a high level of versatility with the fore and aft tables available, the large forward seating creating a separate area for the kids or adults, a well-designed helm station, and a great ride in a light chop. In fact, this deck boat rides better than more than a few bowriders we've been out on. With the wakeboard tower, the 240 would make a decent towboat, creating a big wake with adequate acceleration for wakeboarding or even skiing.

Sea Ray is at the head of its class with many of its offerings. Quality construction, impressive fit and finish, and a responsive dealer network bode well for the Sea Ray owner.

Fish-and-Ski Boats

Fish-and-ski boats are often fishing versions of small bowriders. The manufacturer adds a livewell or bait well, an insulated fish box, rod holder, space on the dash for a fish-finder and maybe a small GPS, and fore and aft fishing seat pedestals, and you have a fish-and-ski. Sometimes they're more like bass boats, but with storage space for skis, or slightly higher freeboard. Look for basic fishing amenities, as well as enough power to pull a skier or wakeboarder with a full load of fuel, passengers, and gear.

The 185 is Bayliner's second-smallest bowrider model (they run from 17 to 24 feet). Adding a fishing package turns this competent family bowrider into a fish-and-ski, including an electric bow-mounted trolling motor, fore and aft casting platforms, casting seats, fish-finder, pre-wiring for dual batteries (for the trolling motor), a livewell, and rod racks. Capacity is up to 8 people, and standard power is a four-cylinder, 135 hp MerCruiser stern drive. We strongly recommend getting the 190 or 220 hp V-6 as the four-cylinder is just too little power for most owners. BAYLINER

Champion is well-known for its good-running competition bass boats, and they also make a fish-and-ski series, including this 21SX. In fact, it's hard to tell the 21SX from a bass boat, with its low sides and dual console cockpit. A trolling motor, livewell, and fish-finder are included, as is a bimini top, boarding ladder, stereo, and ski storage compartment. Up to 300 hp is available, which, incidentally, is way too much power for a family-oriented boat that weighs 1,650 pounds. GENMAR HOLDINGS, INC.

Glastron, like many other bowrider builders, offers a number of stern-drive- and outboard-powered fish-and-ski versions, including this GXL 185. Built with Genmar's high-tech VEC resin infusion process (Glaston is part of Genmar), this boat should last for generations. Standard equipment includes a livewell, tackle trays, rod holders, casting decks, pedestal seats fore and aft, a ski locker, and a ski tow eye. A trolling motor forward and a fish-finder are options. Stern-drive power options from Volvo and MerCruiser to 225 hp are available. GENMAR HOLDINGS, INC.

Four Winns makes a wide range of well-built cruisers and runabouts, and the 183 shown has been modified to attract occasional anglers with the addition of a depth-finder, forward casting platform filler cushion, livewell, trolling motor forward, and an aft pedestal seat. The boat even has removable windshield side sections to open up fishing room off the beam. Volvo and MerCruiser stern-drive power to 225 hp (go for one of the bigger engine options) is available. GENMAR HOLDINGS, INC.

Nitro, which is part of Tracker Marine and is perhaps best known for its tournament bass boats, builds a series of fish-and-skis as well, including this 288. Affordably priced and well-equipped, the 288 comes with a trolling motor, ski pylon, swim platform with ladder, CD stereo, two trolling batteries, in-deck ski and wakeboard storage, trolling motor storage, and two livewells. This 20-footer (the name may be a little confusing) is rated for up to 225 Mercury outboard hp and can carry up to seven people. NITRO BOATS

Best-known and well regarded (and highly rated by owners each year in the annual J.D. Power and Associates study) for its tournament bass boats, Ranger also builds an outboard-powered Reata fish-and-play series from 17 to 21 feet. This is more of a utilitarian and practical fish boat that's also able to pull a skier or wakeboarder, rather than a stern-drive-powered bowrider that can also fish, so this is a good type of boat to consider if you mostly fish. Well outfitted for fishing, the 1850 comes with a trolling motor in the bow or stern. The 1850 shown here is rated for up to 175 outboard hp from a variety of engine brands. GENMAR HOLDINGS, INC.

Besides its well-regarded series of bass and inshore saltwater boats, Skeeter builds fish-and-skis like this SL210. Its bass boat pedigree shows through with its low freeboard, extensive fishing features, and fore and aft casting platforms. But otherwise it's a genuine family boat with plenty of seats (including pedestal casting seats), in-deck ski and wakeboard storage, and a dual console toward the bow. The 210 can carry up to six people and 200 Yamaha hp (Skeeter is owned by Yamaha). SKEETER BOATS

Scout builds high-end, well-built saltwater fishing boats, as well as this series of dual console family boats that are well-qualified for a day's fishing, skiing, wakeboarding, and otherwise messing around on the water. Well-equipped to fish and pull skiers with all the expected features, the Dorado is easy to maintain with its self-bailing cockpit and all-fiberglass construction and finish. The cream gelcoat is easier on the eyes in bright sunlight than a white gelcoat. A good ride in a light chop, the 175 shown is rated for up to six people and 130 hp from Yamaha. SCOUT BOATS

Part of the Smoker Craft group, Vectra manufactures a series of fiberglass runabouts, deck boats, and pontoon hybrids (pontoon from the deck up, with fiberglass monohulls below). This 172 Fish is a stern-drive fish-and-ski bowrider that can handle up to eight people and 220 hp. VECTRA BOATS

Tahoe builds budget-priced family bowriders and deck boats as well as a few outboard- and stern-drive-powered fish-and-skis like this 20-foot Q6 stern drive. Fishing features include a trolling motor in the bow, livewell, fore and aft pedestal seats, and a dedicated trolling battery. Hull colors are standard. The Q6 is rated for up to 6 people and as much as 300 MerCruiser hp. TAHOE

Triumph's line of polyethylene saltwater fishing boats has been expanded to include this 19-foot fish-and-ski. Like Ranger and Triton, this is primarily a utilitarian fish boat, easy to maintain and keep clean. It's also well-equipped to both fish (livewell, kicker motor option, lockable rod storage, convertible aft casting platform, self-bailing cockpit) and tow wakeboarders and skiers (in-deck storage locker, ski pylon). The rugged, practically bulletproof 191 shown is rated for up to 150 outboard hp from a number of engine brands and can handle up to eight people. GENMAR HOLDINGS, INC.

Triton's extensive fish boat lineup includes a few fish-and-skis, like the 21-footer shown here. (Triton is well-known for its high-quality bass and saltwater fishing boats.) These are genuine fish boats that can also make the whole family happy, and therefore these boats work especially well for families that put a lot of stock in fishability. There's room for skis under the deck, a livewell, rod storage lockers, casting decks fore and aft, and so on. A variety of engine brands are available. TRITON BOATS

PONTOON BOATS

Few vessels are more versatile than the pontoon boat. Pontoon boats are stable and easily driven through the water, due to their twin (or nowadays often triple) narrow aluminum hulls. A lot of clear topside space is provided, a result of the deck being attached atop the hulls. Great for partying afloat, pontoon boats are also easily beached for picnics and swimming ashore, and their aluminum pontoon hulls are quite durable, which is a great feature since many are dragged over pebble-strewn beaches hundreds of times in their lifetime.

With enough power, and especially with a third, centerline pontoon and spray rails for extra buoyancy and dynamic lift, pontoon boats can also plane, hit speeds of 45 mph or more, and pull skiers and water toys. Builders including Manitou and Bennington are getting their triple pontoons to heel in a turn, which makes the boat a lot safer at speed. One advantage of skiing behind a pontoon is the low wake these boats generate, though these boats will turn nothing like a real towboat. Twin-hull boats without running strakes to provide lift often start to yaw above 20 mph since the hulls don't generate lift, being round on the bottom (unless they have strakes), so don't plan to save money by buying a basic twin-hull without lifting strakes and just put a big motor on it; get the triple-hull version with the strakes.

A wide variety of seating options are available, and it may be surprising just how many people a pontoon boat will comfortably and safely accommodate. Most manufacturers offer stern-drive as well as outboard models, though outboards predominate. Biminis or hardtops provide protection from sun and rain, head compartments may be included, and a wet bar and refrigerator may also be part of the package.

The annual J.D. Power and Associates study measures customer satisfaction with pontoon boats, both twin and triple hulls, of any length, and with outboard (the great majority of the boats in the study) and stern-drive power. Harris FloteBote was ranked highest with an index score of 857 points, followed closely by Bennington. Premiere, G3, and Godfrey's Parti Kraft brand followed in close succession. Starcraft, relative newcomer Bentley, and Odyssey were rated lowest by their owners.

While some segments in the study have had fairly consistent award recipients from year to year (including Grady-White, Cobalt, Correct Craft, and Regal), the pontoon segment is more fluid, with Bennington, Harris Kayot, and Manitou all having been ranked highest in past years. The pontoon segment is rated below average overall (below small runabouts and express cruisers) by its owners, with an average index rating of 813 points, and it's the largest in terms of brands in the study, with 18 brands included.

Harris FloteBote received the most Power Circles—five in three categories, four in two categories, and three in maintenance. Parti Kraft ranked highest in maintenance, Bennington ranked highest in ride and handling, and Parti Kraft ranked highest in quality and reliability. Bentley and Starcraft received just two Power Circles in all of the categories.

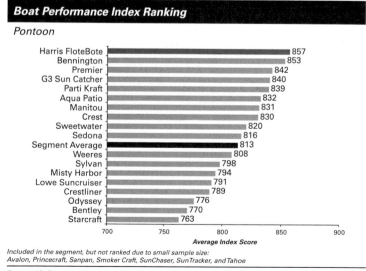

Boat Performance Index Ranking

Pontoon

Brand	Average Index Score
Harris FloteBote	857
Bennington	853
Premier	842
G3 Sun Catcher	840
Parti Kraft	839
Aqua Patio	832
Manitou	831
Crest	830
Sweetwater	820
Sedona	816
Segment Average	813
Weeres	808
Sylvan	798
Misty Harbor	794
Lowe Suncruiser	791
Crestliner	789
Odyssey	776
Bentley	770
Starcraft	763

Included in the segment, but not ranked due to small sample size:
Avalon, Princecraft, Sanpan, Smoker Craft, SunChaser, SunTracker, and Tahoe

Source: J.D. Power and Associates 2007 Boat Competitive Information Study ℠

J.D. Power and Associates 2007 Boat Competitive Information Study℠

Pontoon Boat Ratings

Company	Overall Rating	Quality & Reliability	Engine	Design & Style	Ride & Handling	Maintenance
Harris FloteBote *Award Recipient*	●●●●●	●●●●○	●●●●●	●●●●●	●●●●○	●●●○○
Aqua Patio	●●●●○	●●●●○	●●●●○	●●●●●	●●●●○	●●●●○
Bennington	●●●●●	●●●●○	●●●●●	●●●●●	●●●●○	●●●●○
Bentley	●●○○○	●●●○○	●●○○○	●●●○○	●●●○○	●●●○○
Crest	●●●●●	●●●○○	●●●○○	●●●○○	●●●○○	●●●○○
Crestliner	●●○○○	●●●○○	●●●○○	●●○○○	●●●○○	●●●●○
G3 Sun Catcher	●●●●○	●●●○○	●●●●●	●●●○○	●●●●○	●●●●○
Lowe Suncruiser	●●○○○	●●●○○	●●○○○	●●●○○	●●●○○	●●●●○
Manitou	●●●●●	●●●●●	●●●○○	●●●○○	●●●○○	●●●○○
Misty Harbor	●●●○○	●●●○○	●●●○○	●●●○○	●●●○○	●●●○○
Odyssey	●●○○○	●●●○○	●●○○○	●●●○○	●●●○○	●●●○○
Parti Kraft	●●●●●	●●●○○	●●●●●	●●●○○	●●●●●	●●●●●
Premier	●●●●●	●●●●●	●●●○○	●●●●●	●●●○○	●●●○○
Sedona	●●●○○	●●●●○	●●●●○	●●●○○	●●●●○	●●●●○
Starcraft	●●○○○	●●●○○	●●●○○	●●●○○	●●○○○	●●○○○
Sweetwater	●●●○○	●●●○○	●●●○○	●●●○○	●●●●○	●●●●●
Sylvan	●●●○○	●●●○○	●●●○○	●●●○○	●●●○○	●●○○○
Weeres	●●●○○	●●●○○	●●●●●	●●●○○	●●●○○	●●●○○

SCORING LEGEND:
●●●●● Among the best ●●●●○ Better than most ●●●○○ About average ●●○○○ The rest

Bennington builds five different series of high-quality twin- and triple-hull pontoon boats, outboard- and stern-drive-powered, including luxury, entry-level, and fishing models, to 28 feet. The 2275 GL shown comes in twin- or triple-hull versions and several layouts, including a fishing version. A new company founded in the mid-1990s, Bennington also produces a well-built and low-priced Sedona pontoon boat brand as well as fiberglass Azure open and cuddy runabouts and express cruisers, and the Southwind line of deck boats and hybrid pontoon boats with fiberglass hulls.   BENNINGTON MARINE

Fisher manufactures a wide range of low-priced aluminum fishing, utility, and pontoon boats, including the Freedom 221 DLX pontoon shown here. This Mercury stern-drive-powered boat is available with up to a 135 hp four-cylinder engine and can carry up to 12 people. A range of Mercury outboard- and stern-drive-powered family cruising and fishing models from 18 to 24 feet and with twin or triple hulls is available.   FISHER BOATS

Yamaha Motor division G3 builds a range of moderately priced Sun Catcher pontoons, in both twin- and triple-hull versions. These boats are laid out for fishing, cruising, or both, and range from 18 to 25 feet. The U-shaped (rather than circular) logs are foam-filled to guarantee positive buoyancy even if punctured. Shown is the LX 22 FC (fish and cruise) that takes up to 115 or 200 Yamaha hp, depending on whether the twin or triple version is selected.   G3 BOATS

Sun Tracker builds a wide range of twin- and triple-hull pontoon boats from 18 to 36 feet. The 36-foot Megahut (appropriately named, in this case) shown here is 10 feet wide, has two decks, and can handle up to 14 passengers and a 150 hp Mercury motor. This is the biggest production pontoon boat we know of.   SUN TRACKER

Premiere builds upscale pontoons in triple- and twin-hull configurations, and with stern-drive or outboard power. The 22-foot Sunsation 225 shown here is available with two or three hulls, and can take up to 200 hp and carry up to 12 people with the triple-hull option.   PREMIERE MARINE

Triton builds an extensive range of boats in fiberglass and aluminum, including a series of pontoons from 18 to 28 feet. The 240 Gold pontoon shown can carry up to 13 people and is rated for 135 hp.   TRITON BOATS

The Vectra line, made by Smoker Craft, includes hybrid pontoon boats with fiberglass hulls. The Vectra 1900 shown is rated for 10 people and 200 hp.   VECTRA BOATS

Quality pontoon builder Weeres builds a number of lines of fishing and cruising boats from 16 to 24 feet, including the 20-foot Cadet twin-hull model shown here, which can handle up to 11 people and 90 hp.   WEERES INDUSTRIES

BENNINGTON 2577

Bennington 2577 Specifications	
LOA:	28' w/platform
Beam:	8'6"
Dry weight:	3,223 lb.
Cockpit depth:	26" at rails, 30" at furniture
Fuel capacity:	62 gal.
Maximum capacity:	14 people
Total capacity:	2,400 lb.

Although the Bennington 2577 triple-hull has been in production since 2002, it was not until recently that we had the boat for a long-term test period. We got to know the boat well, operating it in a wide range of conditions and though my background is almost exclusively on open-ocean boats, I grew to be a big fan of this deceivingly capable vessel. It quickly became a family favorite. The Bennington is a high-end boat. It has a functional and luxurious layout with thick upholstery and carpeting, classy graphics, a solidly constructed bimini top, and a fully appointed helm station.

This day boat has a rated capacity and seating for 14 passengers, or a total of 2,400 pounds including gear. This is a fast pontoon boat; we reached 42 mph with our quiet and smooth-running Volvo Penta stern drive, and the ride was much smoother upsea and the boat tracked much better downsea than the typical monohull of the same size.

Construction

The Bennington has three 25-inch-diameter pontoons made of 0.09-inch 5052 series (marine-grade) welded aluminum. The round shape of the pontoons makes them strong, stiff, and impact-resistant for their weight. They're divided into watertight sections so the boat will stay afloat with any one section punctured, which is a beneficial seaworthiness consideration.

The aft section of the center hull is not a round tube at all, but essentially a hard-chine planing hull about 3 feet wide, bolted to the deck above, and supporting the engine and the fuel tank. This hull section is wider than the pontoons, adding the extra flotation needed for the stern drive's 1,000-pound-plus weight. The hard-chine planing bottom adds dynamic lift at speed, allowing the boat to plane easily and run efficiently. The forward half of the centerline hull is actually a 25-inch-diameter pontoon, like those outboard. It mates to the forward end of the engine and fuel tank section.

The deck has aluminum frames attached to the pontoons, and these frames in turn support a carpet-covered, pressure-treated plywood deck. The deck is surrounded by an aluminum railing, and the furniture modules and fiberglass helm console are screwed to the deck. This is a high-performance model, so the underside of the deck, which is exposed to the occasional wave top, is finished off with aluminum sheeting for a smooth, low-drag surface.

Hull Design

The hull design is simple, as mentioned above; three hulls, creating a trimaran, consisting of 25-inch-diameter pontoons, with the aft section of the center hull transitioning to a planing hull module designed to contain and support the engine and fuel tank. Spray rails, or chines, are welded to the pontoons to add lift, which allows the boat to plane easily; the round shape of the pontoon by itself is better suited to slow displacement speeds. The length and relatively light weight of the hull gives it the ability to go from 0 to 42 mph with little change in trim or bow rise; this also allows it to cruise efficiently at any speed in between.

Walkthrough

Topsides

The Bennington is surrounded by a 26-inch railing, with three gates allowing access to and from the dock aft to starboard from the swim platform, amidships to port, and forward on centerline. The doors are held closed by deck-mounted receptacles; just lift the door up half an inch, move it over the receiver, and drop it into the clips. The all-around railing makes for a safe and secure environment for passengers, and the boat's full 8-foot, 6-inch beam is carried all the way to the bow. This makes a 25-foot pontoon a lot bigger, as far as deck space is concerned, than a monohull of the same length.

The Bennington's seating arrangement is ideal for cruising around the lake, with two conversation areas. There's an L-shaped lounge seat opposite the helm to port, so the skipper can have three or four people to talk to. And forward are lounges to port and starboard, and a pair of reclining pedestal seats in the bow.

One of the advantages of the triple pontoon hull is the ability carry more weight, including in the ends of the boat, compared to a twin-tube model. On the 2577, the whole deck is usable by passengers underway, with the railing even with the forward end of the deck. While any pontoon is essentially a day boat, with full camper canvas, which involves a second bimini top and all-around side curtains with plastic windows and screens, the boat is capable of hosting a sleepover. You could even tow it around to campsites and use it as an overgrown camper. Another welcome feature is the full-beam swim platform with retractable swim ladder over the stern drive's single-prop lower unit.

Helm

The Bennington's helm is sensibly laid out, with a tilt wheel accommodating seated or standing operation. A large tachometer and two multifunction gauges make good use of the console's limited space. In addition to the horn, and docking and navigation lights, Bennington provides three accessory switches for additional options and the standard Garmin depth-finder. The Alpine AM-FM-CD stereo fills the area with clear sound, driving one pair of speakers in the helm area and another pair in the bow.

Engine Access

Access to the Volvo 5.0-liter GXI stern drive is excellent. Just tilt the back of the L-shaped lounge's seat forward and then tilt the engine box aft. You can get to all the engine's maintenance points with ease. The battery switch is also easy to get to, and the 62-gallon polypropylene fuel tank is in plain sight just forward of the engine.

Bennington has done a great job engineering the stern-drive power in this boat, designing a centerline aluminum hull to accommodate the engine and fuel tank aft, and a conventional aluminum pontoon forward of that. The shape of the engine pod creates plenty of room to get around the engine,

and it adds lift and buoyancy aft where it's needed most.

Engine

The 270 hp, 5.0-liter electronically fuel-injected (EFI) Volvo Penta gasoline stern drive provides easy starts and improved fuel economy over the carbureted versions. Engine exhaust exits underwater through the propeller hub, which accounts in part for the quiet operation; you can barely hear the engine over the wind noise at cruise speed. Power steering is standard, and the resulting fingertip control is precise and a pleasure to operate. The weight of the stern-drive engine and lower unit, 1,034 pounds, is nearly twice as much as a 250 hp outboard. As a result, the engine sponson is considerably wider than the 25-inch pontoon logs used elsewhere, so it provides plenty of buoyancy for all that weight. The Bennington is rated for 425 hp maximum (an 8.1-liter big-block stern drive) and can also be ordered with outboard power.

Sea Trial

Maneuvering around the dock, the triple-tube Bennington resists sideways movement a lot better than a typical planing monohull of the same size with its added submerged hull surface area. The three tubes actually improve handling dockside, with the boat behaving very predictably, and under positive control, in a stiff crosswind. It doesn't turn quite as tightly as a similar-size monohull, but you can quickly learn to compensate in close quarters. Once out on the water in a 1- to 2-foot chop, the boat ran exceptionally smoothly, slicing through the waves at 20 to 30 mph very comfortably.

A big cruising advantage of this pontoon design is the speed range. You can run the boat efficiently and comfortably from 8 to 15 mph, speeds at which monohulls are using a lot of power to climb over their bow wave and up on plane. With a triple-hull like the Bennington 2577, there is no

"hump" speed. It just gradually and easily goes faster and faster. The reason for the improved performance is that the pontoon boat has a much smaller bow wave to climb over. You can cruise the boat efficiently and comfortably with little bow rise at any intermediate speed you want, and forward visibility is never a problem thanks to minimal bow rise. You can also pick just about any speed to tow an inflatable or a wakeboarder.

Though the boat's turning rate at low speeds is less than a monohull's, turning time while running at cruising speed was impressive—a 360-degree turn to starboard took just 18 seconds at 3,000 rpm. Sound levels were in the low 80 dBA range at 4,000 rpm—the Volvo stern drive was barely noticeable over the wind and spray noise. These boats are frequently for beaching and partying ashore, so the bow and stern doors come in handy.

Bennington 2577 Performance Results

RPM	Speed, mph	Noise Level, dBA (at helm)
650	2.3	57
1,000	4.3	63
1,500	6.5	67
2,000	9.4	72
2,500	15.7	78 (on plane)
3,000	21.8	79
3,500	27.4	81
4,000	32.5	82
4,500	38.3	84
4,850	42	89

Test conditions: One passenger, fuel tank two-thirds full. Six-inch chop.

Well-built using the finest materials and components, our Bennington 2577 test boat offers a number of compelling reasons to consider buying one. It's a lot of boat for the money, with a deck plan that's open and accommodating for a variety of functions. The ride is mooth, dry, and comfortable, and the boat is efficiently propelled with either stern-drive or outboard power. The Bennington 2577 offers a stable, safe, and secure environment for the whole family, as well as multifunction utility with the ability to fish, cruise, ski, or wakeboard. There's also the 2577's speed—well over 40 mph—when you want it. And don't forget the overnight capability with full camper canvas. High-quality components and simplicity of construction bode well for long-term enjoyment. Based on our long-term (six-week) test of and close familiarity with the Bennington 2577, we can say without qualification that it has earned our highest recommendation.

MANITOU 22 OASIS

MANITOU

Manitou 22 Oasis Specifications

LOA:	22'
Beam:	8'6"
Dry weight:	2,405 lb.
Fuel capacity:	35 gal.

Like all of its models, the Manitou 22 Oasis SHP is offered with the company's triple-log Sport Handling Package (SHP), which basically means it has a large centerline pontoon and two smaller outer pontoons. The increased volume, buoyancy, and dynamic lift of the center tube, and the fact that it's mounted a little lower than the other tubes, helps the boat heel in a hard turn, rather than remaining on an even keel as most multihulls do.

The transverse framing on the bottom side of the plywood deck is covered with aluminum sheeting (under skinning), which decreases drag and turbulence from water and spray under the boat. SHP models also get power-assist steering, which is appropriate for their large engines. SHP models are available with both stern-drive and outboard power. The SHP innovation has a patent pending on the design. The Manitou 22 went into production in 2006.

One of several Manitou pontoon lines, the Oasis series features upscale models with fiberglass helm consoles, stainless steel steering wheels, and four-speaker AM-FM-CD stereos. The 22 Oasis is available in four deck plans, including a full sunpad aft, aft entry, and various forward seating configurations. The 22 Oasis is also available without the SHP package, with twin or triple tubes, in both 8-foot and 8-foot, 6-inch beams, and with a capacity of up to 10 people and 1,605 to 1,740 pounds.

Construction

The Manitou is built on three aluminum tubes that support a framework of aluminum cross members. The tubes are 0.01 gauge aluminum, with slightly heavier aluminum in the bow nose cones, which strengthens them to better withstand beaching and impacts. The tubes are placed in five separate compartments for improved seaworthiness in the event one is punctured. The deck is supported by extruded aluminum transverse cross-member frames bolted to the tube channels.

The outboard motor pod, made of 0.16-inch aluminum, is attached to the cross members with 20 stainless steel bolts. The deck is $3/4$-inch-thick, seven-ply pressure-treated plywood. Heavy marine-quality carpeting is glued to the plywood flooring. All of the seats have double-wall roto-molded plastic bases, which are rot-proof and won't retain moisture. All fasteners are stainless steel, and the railings in the deck walls are all made of anodized aluminum. The overall effect of Manitou's construction methods and materials is to create a high-quality, long-lasting, low-maintenance, and rugged structure.

Hull Design

The Oasis 22 SHP hull has a 27-inch-diameter center tube and 23-inch outboard tubes (25-inch outboard tubes in heavier stern-drive models). Running strakes on the outboard sides of the three tubes, or hulls, add lift at speed and deflect spray for a drier ride. The outboard motor pod on centerline in the stern is also designed to add buoyancy at rest and lift at speed.

The SHP hull, and its ability to make the boat heel in a turn, is worth a little background information. Most catamarans and trimarans (two- and three-hulled vessels, which is what pontoon boats are) heel *away* from a turn because of the lateral forces acting on the multiple hulls and because of the considerable form stability inherent in the design. This level ride is disconcerting for anyone used to planing monohulls (at least those without keels), which bank *into* the turn. That's because turning flat, or worse, banking *away* from the turn tends to make passengers and other objects go flying across the deck.

Think of a car on a racetrack. Banking the track in the turns transfers much of the centrifugal force *downward* rather than *outward*, allowing the cars to go much faster. Imagine what would happen if the track was flat, or even banked in the other direction—that's what you get with most pontoons. So when the boat is heeling into a turn, passengers feel more comfortable and safer. All you feel in a flat turn is centrifugal force throwing you outboard; when the boat is heeling, much or all of the centrifugal force is directed downward to the deck so it's easier to stay on your feet or in your seat. The more the boat heels (up to a point, which is not reached by these pontoon boats), the less you feel the centrifugal force as outward, and the more it is felt as downward force. With 40 and 50 mph pontoon boats becoming common, this ability to heel is increasingly important, not only for comfort but also for safety. As a result of this design, the SHP pontoon handles more like a standard, hard-chine monohull planing hull, which is a wonderful thing indeed.

Cockpit and Topsides

Our test boat had a pair of lounges forward, the one to port being a little shorter to accommodate a boarding gate in the side of the boat. There was another boarding gate in the bow on centerline. The helm console on these boats is to starboard, just aft of the long lounge seat. Opposite is an L-shaped lounge to port, with a stanchion socket in the deck for the portable table. All of the lounge seats have storage below, and the plastic storage bin liners and the seats' wood-free construction will eliminate many of the mildew problems experienced on older pontoon models. The seat cushions also have dual-density foam for added comfort. Our boat's deck plan made it feel roomy and accommodating, with plenty of seating for a crowd, but we didn't feel crowded by the furniture.

Aft of the lounge was a sunpad with engine access and a fuel compartment below. The pad lifts up easily on boosts for access to the outboard motor and battery on centerline and the fuel compartment to port. Our boat had an optional 35-gallon, built-in polypropylene fuel tank with fill and vent accessible from the outside of the side railings. Aft to starboard is a third gate leading to the boarding ladder. The ladder is well-designed, with big, wide steps and an extension (as on a swimming pool ladder) at its top end to make it comfortable to climb. Our test boat also had an optional ski tow bar, a rugged and nicely finished component made of heavy polished stainless steel piping.

All the door latches on this boat worked very well—nothing should be coming loose out on the water, which is especially important for these family boats. Railings are 27 inches tall all around the boat, so little ones will be kept safe and secure given prudent boat operation. The bimini top, with a well-designed square-stock frame, was easy to set up and take down. Cleats were readily accessible and large enough for their purpose.

Helm

On the SHP version of the Oasis 22, the fiberglass helm console comes with power steering (which is certainly welcome with any 200-plus hp outboard), basic engine instrumentation, a lockable glove box, standard JBL stereo, a courtesy light, and a thickly upholstered helm seat. A fish-finder, reclining helm seat, double helm seat, engine trim gauge (which we recommend on any high-performance boat), and burl wood steering wheel are optional.

The console had a low profile and a small windscreen, which make it suitable for use in weather, and it's ergonomically designed with a comfortably angled steering wheel and throttle. There's also storage room below accessed through a side door.

Engine

The 22 Oasis SHP is available with Evinrude, Honda, Mercury, Suzuki, and Yamaha outboards up to 225 hp. MerCruiser stern drives to 300 hp are available on 24- and 26-foot Legacy models. Our test boat had a 225 hp Evinrude E-TEC HO outboard.

Sea Trial

Our test ride took place on a small Michigan lake with a single 225 hp Evinrude E-TEC outboard. The Evinrude two-stroke rocketed the boat up on plane, and even from 3,500 rpm up to full throttle the acceleration was strong. These triple pontoon hulls create little drag when coming up on plane, with modest bow rise and a flat wake at all speeds. It's a big advantage being able to operate efficiently and comfortably throughout the speed envelope, including the 8 to 16 mph range where we find deep-V monohulls hard at work digging a hole in the water. This boat planed nicely at just 2,500 rpm, which is just 13 mph, so you can run slowly and efficiently if you have the urge, or if it's a little rough and you want to take it easy coming home.

On our 22-foot test boat, the engine trim was effective at adjusting hull running attitude, or bow rise. Tucking it in while starting kept the bow well down while coming up on plane, while trimming it out to just short of ventilation maximized speed quite predictably.

The SHP triple-tube design was intended to add buoyancy and dynamic lift on centerline, lessening buoyancy and lift outboard, thereby coaxing the hull to heel into a turn. On our test ride, our SHP performed as advertised, heeling (*banking* is the aeronautical term) into a turn, especially when the wheel was hard over, making it a delight to drive. While the SHP does not heel as much as a monohull in a hard turn, the sense of balance and security is much better than in a conventional pontoon. Starting out at 3,600 rpm, we put the wheel hard over, with engine rpm slowing to 3,000, and the boat took just 13 seconds to turn 360 degrees, which is quite respectable for any boat of this size and power, even compared to a monohull.

We had to create our own waves to ride through on our small test lake, but all indications are that the Manitou triple-hull delivers a smooth ride. This is the nature of most needle-hulled trimarans and cats. The upturned strakes minimize slamming on wave impact and also allow the stern to slide sideways in a turn, which is needed to bank properly. Running in a straight line, the right-hand propeller torque induced a degree or two of port heel, so the boat heels slightly more in a port turn than when turning to starboard. This torque, of course, would be cancelled out by a stern drive with counterrotating propellers.

We recorded a top speed of 49.8 mph on GPS (just over 43 knots) at 6,000 rpm. At a leisurely 3,000 rpm we could hardly hear the engine at just 73 dBA at the helm. Even at 4,000 rpm and almost 32 mph, the engine was barely discernible above the wind noise; this Evinrude was a pleasantly quiet engine. Keep in mind that the speeds we recorded were with a clean bottom and a light load, including just two passengers, so figure on going a few mph slower with a typical passenger and gear load on board.

The tilt wheel was comfortably positioned for seated or standing, and the power-assist steering was easy to operate and responsive at four turns lock-to-lock. You can drive this boat with your fingertips, which is how we'd like to see every outboard boat perform. The flip-up helm seat bolster provides more room for driving while standing.

Back at the dock, with 1,500 rpm in reverse, the engine provided plenty of backing power, and the three hulls with their hull strakes tended to keep the boat from blowing around as much as older twin-tube pontoon boats.

Manitou 22 Oasis Performance Results

RPM	Speed, mph	Speed, knots	Noise Level, dBA
600	2.1	1.8	57
1,000	4.5	3.9	61
1,500	6.2	5.4	67
2,000	7.9	6.9	71
2,500	13.1	11.4	72
3,000	19.7	17.1	73
3,500	26.6	23.1	78
4,000	31.8	27.7	84
4,500	36.4	31.7	85
5,000	40.7	35.4	86
5,500	45.8	39.8	89
6,000	49.8	43.3	92

Test conditions: Two passengers, fuel tank full, with a 225 hp Evinrude outboard.

The Manitou 22 Oasis SHP is a well-built, family-friendly design that we would expect to give many years of reliable, enjoyable service. It's a great cruising boat, can easily tow skiers, wakeboarders, or tubers, is ideal for beaching for a picnic, and can even be used for fishing. (If you like to fish, consider one of the builder's fishing models with seats, livewell, and other features designed for the angler.)

The SHP hull design is a bonus for anyone looking for a high-speed (30 mph plus) pontoon boat, as it provides comfort and security in hard, high-speed turns. The 225 hp Evinrude provides superb performance—strong acceleration, low noise levels, and economical, reliable operation. The pontoon design in general has a number of benefits compared to a monohull, assuming you boat in calm, protected waters; pontoons are not rough-water boats. For lakes, rivers, and even in inshore, protected salt water, it's hard to beat a pontoon for its efficiency, huge deck space, stability, safety, versatility, and economy of ownership.

The Oasis can be set up for cruising, fishing, and watersports, with options that include full canvas, a barbeque grill, filler bed, galley with sink and storage, ski tow bar, livewell, trolling motor, and a 35-gallon built-in gas tank.

Runabouts (Bowriders and Cuddies)

Runabouts are generally considered to encompass two boat types: bowriders and cuddy models. Both designs are basically family-fun boats, used for days on the lake or river, noncompetitive watersports (skiing and tubing), and just tooling around. Although most are designed primarily for freshwater use, many larger models with self-bailing cockpits can handle the somewhat more exposed conditions of saltwater bays and coastal areas.

The bowrider is a close cousin to the dual console, usually stern-drive-powered and with an open bow instead of a small cabin. It's a popular family day boat. There are exceptions, of course, but bowriders usually have cockpits that drain to the bilge rather than overboard. As a result, the inboard freeboard is often higher than on a typical dual console.

The full length of the bowrider can be used underway, and the added bow seating is welcome when the entire family tries to spread out on a relatively small boat. Plus, the bow area is a great place to sit when the boat is running along at cruise speed: the view is splendid, the engine noise is (or should be) practically nonexistent, and the breeze keeps you cool. There should be railings and grab bars to hang onto because the last place you'll want to fall overboard from on a moving boat is the bow, and that's where the vertical pitching is most accentuated. Larger bowriders (22 feet and over) usually have small head compartments under the port console, adding to the boat's popularity with families. Bowriders are also usually powerful enough (or should be) to pull a skier or wakeboarder out of the water quickly with a full load of passengers, gear, and fuel in the boat.

The cuddy layout has been around for decades. The bow is covered over with a short foredeck, leaving the aft two thirds or so of the boat open for passengers. This is the tried-and-true family cruiser layout among small boats. The foredeck includes a small (hence the name cuddy) cabin with maybe enough room to sit on the V-berth below. A full-width windshield protects the helm area and passengers forward in the cockpit. The cuddy might be just big enough for a portable toilet below the V-berth, and there will probably be room to put clothes and other items up forward out of the spray and wind.

If you want to lie down comfortably, you'll likely need a 24-foot-plus cuddy. The cockpit may be similar to the dual console's—open and accommodating. If looks count, the cuddy's low foredeck and raked windshield give the boat undeniable aesthetic appeal. When compared to the dual or center console, though, which put the boat's entire LOA to full-time use, the cuddy admittedly wastes space that could otherwise be used for passengers. But the cuddy layout works best for some families who value a dry, private space in a small boat.

The annual J.D. Power and Associates study divides runabouts into two segments: small (16 to 19 feet) and large (20 to 29 feet). With few exceptions (Cobalt, whose smallest boat is a 20-footer, is one), most boatbuilders that produce 16- to 19-footers also build boats in the 20- to 29-foot range.

Regal was rated highest by its owners in the small runabout segment, with its index score of 840 (on a 1,000-point scale) giving it a 31-point margin over second-ranked Crownline. Sea Ray, Stingray, and Chaparral follow in close succession. Maxum's 721-points was the lowest score across the marine industry, as well as in this segment, while Bayliner's 732 points made it the second-lowest across the industry.

Regal continued its standout status by earning five Power Circles, a measurement of customer satisfaction, in every category. Crownline received five Power Circles in quality and reliability, and in ride and handling, while Stingray was rated just as high in the engine category. Maxum earned just two Power Circles in each category. Bayliner had a mix of two and three Power Circle ratings, and Monterey (722 index score), which did comparatively well elsewhere, took a nosedive in product quality and reliability.

While Regal was a clear exception in 2007, the small runabout segment was the lowest ranked of the seven segments the study measures each year, with an average score of 756 (compared to 885 for the ski-wakeboard segment), in part because of the volume of low-scoring Maxums and Bayliners sold each year. But it also means the segment in general needs attention from boatbuilders.

Beyond design, construction, and component quality, one of the issues is that many small runabout owners are first-time boaters, and they often succumb to the lure of low pricing. This means they often get a boat with an engine that's too small to get up on plane easily (or at all) with a full load or to pull a wakeboarder or skier. The other problem is that the low-cost engine is often carbureted, which is harder to start, smokes, stalls, and sputters, and is generally a poor performer. Underpowering, and with a carbureted engine to boot, is one way to almost guarantee a low level of customer satisfaction. Add to that the fact that first-time buyers tend to rate their boats lower, and much of the reason for the segment's poor overall performance is clear. Buy the same boat with a larger electronically fuel-injected engine and you will almost certainly be more satisfied with it.

The large runabout segment award has been received by Cobalt every year that J.D. Power and Associates has conducted its study. In 2007, Cobalt with its 908 index score had a commanding 40-point advantage over Regal, which nonetheless improved remarkably over the previous year, and was also the leader in the small runabout and express cruiser segments in 2007. Regal in turn had a 23-point lead over

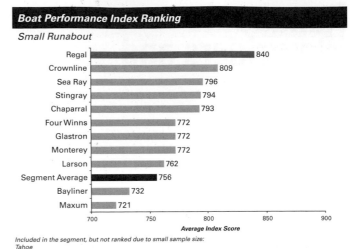

Boat Performance Index Ranking

Small Runabout

	Average Index Score
Regal	840
Crownline	809
Sea Ray	796
Stingray	794
Chaparral	793
Four Winns	772
Glastron	772
Monterey	772
Larson	762
Segment Average	756
Bayliner	732
Maxum	721

Included in the segment, but not ranked due to small sample size: Tahoe

Source: J.D. Power and Associates 2007 Boat Competitive Information Study SM

Power Circle Ratings™ ◉◉◉◉◉ JDPower.com

J.D. Power and Associates 2007 Boat Competitive Information Study SM

Small Runabout (16-19 ft.) Ratings

Company	Overall Rating	Quality & Reliability	Engine	Ride & Handling	Design & Style	Water Sports
Regal *Award Recipient*	○○○○○	○○○○○	○○○○○	○○○○○	○○○○○	○○○○○
Bayliner	○○○○○	○○○○○	○○○○○	○○○○○	○○○○○	○○○○○
Chaparral	○○○○○	○○○○○	○○○○○	○○○○○	○○○○○	○○○○○
Crownline	○○○○○	○○○○○	○○○○○	○○○○○	○○○○○	○○○○○
Four Winns	○○○○○	○○○○○	○○○○○	○○○○○	○○○○○	○○○○○
Glastron	○○○○○	○○○○○	○○○○○	○○○○○	○○○○○	○○○○○
Larson	○○○○○	○○○○○	○○○○○	○○○○○	○○○○○	○○○○○
Maxum	○○○○○	○○○○○	○○○○○	○○○○○	○○○○○	○○○○○
Monterey	○○○○○	○○○○○	○○○○○	○○○○○	○○○○○	○○○○○
Sea Ray	○○○○○	○○○○○	○○○○○	○○○○○	○○○○○	○○○○○
Stingray	○○○○○	○○○○○	○○○○○	○○○○○	○○○○○	○○○○○

SCORING LEGEND: ○○○○○ Among the best ○○○○○ Better than most ○○○○○ About average ○○○○○ The rest

third-place finisher Sea Ray. At the other end of the scale, Bayliner was rated lowest by its owners at 752 points, 43 points behind Stingray at 795 points.

One thing that becomes obvious in the large runabout segment is how closely many of the brands are ranked. Only 30 points separates seven boatbuilders. Stingray is certainly consistent, scoring 794 points, which is well above average, in small runabouts, and just a single point higher in large runabouts, running neck-and-neck with Rinker

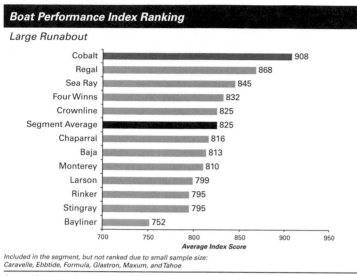

Boat Performance Index Ranking

Large Runabout

Brand	Average Index Score
Cobalt	908
Regal	868
Sea Ray	845
Four Winns	832
Crownline	825
Segment Average	825
Chaparral	816
Baja	813
Monterey	810
Larson	799
Rinker	795
Stingray	795
Bayliner	752

Average Index Score

Included in the segment, but not ranked due to small sample size:
Caravelle, Ebbtide, Formula, Glastron, Maxum, and Tahoe

Source: J.D. Power and Associates 2007 Boat Competitive Information Study ℠

and Larson. Of course, large runabout with an average index score of 825 points is a much more competitive segment than small runabout at 756 index points on average.

In Power Circle Ratings, Cobalt was rated five Power Circles in all six categories; in fact its lead in each category was so substantial that no other brand received five Power Circles in any category. Sea Ray came the closest, with four Power Circles in all six categories, and Regal earned five of six. Bayliner received two Power Circles in each category except watersports, in which it received three.

Power Circle Ratings™ ●●●●● JDPower.com

J.D. Power and Associates 2007 Boat Competitive Information Study℠

Large Runabout (20-29 ft.) Ratings

Company	Overall Rating	Quality & Reliability	Engine	Ride & Handling	Design & Style	Water Sports
Cobalt *Award Recipient*	●●●●●	●●●●●	●●●●●	●●●●●	●●●●●	●●●●●
Baja	●●●○○	●●●○○	●●●●○	●●●●○	●●●○○	●●○○○
Bayliner	●●○○○	●●○○○	●●●○○	●●●○○	●●○○○	●●●○○
Chaparral	●●●○○	●●●○○	●●●○○	●●●○○	●●●○○	●●●○○
Crownline	●●●○○	●●●●○	●●●○○	●●●○○	●●●○○	●●●●○
Four Winns	●●●○○	●●●●○	●●●○○	●●●○○	●●●○○	●●●●○
Larson	●●●○○	●●●○○	●●○○○	●●●○○	●●●○○	●●●○○
Monterey	●●●○○	●●●●○	●●●○○	●●●○○	●●●○○	●●●○○
Regal	●●●○○	●●●●○	●●●●○	●●●●○	●●●●○	●●●●○
Rinker	●●●○○	●●●○○	●●●○○	●●○○○	●●●○○	●●●○○
Sea Ray	●●●●○	●●●●○	●●●●○	●●●●○	●●●●○	●●●●○
Stingray	●●●○○	●●●○○	●●●○○	●●●●○	●●●○○	●●●○○
SCORING LEGEND:	●●●●● Among the best	●●●●○ Better than most	●●●○○ About average	●●○○○ The rest		

Azure, a new division of pontoon manufacturer Bennington Marine, builds fiberglass bowrider, deck boats, and express cruisers from 20 to 26 feet. Azure's 258 bowrider shown here, rated for up to 425 hp and 14 people, includes a few pontoon features, like a changing room, and also has a fishing option available. Stern-drive and outboard models are offered.

AZURE MARINE

Baja Marine builds high-performance boats as well as a series of Islander bowriders from 10 to 27 feet. The MerCruiser stern-drive-powered Islander series emphasizes speed. The needle bows in these sleek boats sacrifice some seating room forward; the fine bow sections below the chines provide an improved ride in a chop. The 277 shown is the biggest model in the series; it can handle 10 passengers and up to 600 hp.

BAJA MARINE

Bayliner builds bowriders from 17 to 24 feet. The 195 Classic shown offers excellent value with a low purchase price. Two seating plans are available. The aft jump seat converts to a sunpad, and standard power is a 190 hp MerCruiser V-6, decent power for a 19 footer.

BAYLINER

Chaparral builds a wide range of high-quality deck boats, runabouts, and express cruisers. The 236 shown has a large aft sunpad, in-deck wakeboard and ski storage, an enclosed head, and an optional wakeboard tower. Volvo and MerCruiser stern drives to 375 hp are available.

CHAPARRAL BOATS

Cobalt ranked highest in the annual J.D. Power and Associates study for highest customer satisfaction in the large runabout segment, builds a wide range of upscale runabouts from 20 to 34 feet. This 302 is the largest bowrider, with the large head compartment and topside entertainment center you'd expect of a 30-footer, and also with Cobalt's extra touches including double-stitched upholstery and precisely angled speaker flats. Up to twin 425 hp Volvo or MerCruiser stern-drive power is available.

COBALT BOATS

Crownline builds bowriders from 18 to 32 feet, as well as cuddy models. This middle-of-the-line 240LS comes with docking lights, shock-absorbing seats, an enclosed head and sink with shower, and recliner seats forward. Up to 425 hp Volvo or MerCruiser stern-drive power is available.   CROWNLINE BOATS

Formula builds high-end, race boat–derived bowriders starting at 24 feet, as well as cuddy models. The 260 shown has a good-running V-bottom hull, in-deck ski and wakeboard storage, premium upholstery and graphics, a power engine hatch, automatic fire-extinguishing system, and excellent helm station ergonomics. Single Volvo or MerCruiser stern-drive power is available. (See full-length Formula 240 review on pages 442–45.)   FORMULA BOATS

Donzi's smallest offering, the 16 Classic, has its origins in Jim Wynne's original deep-V racing designs dating to 1964. MerCruiser stern-drive options to 260 hp are available.   DONZI MARINE

Four Winns builds a wide range of Horizon series bowriders from 18 to 31 feet, along with cuddy models. Shown is the largest model in the class, the 310 Horizon. Included are a day berth with air conditioning belowdecks, an adjustable reclining sunpad, enclosed head, entertainment center, and a long list of options including Flexiteek aft. Power options range up to twin 320 hp Volvo or MerCruiser stern drives.   GENMAR HOLDINGS, INC.

Glastron builds moderate-priced bowriders from 17 to 25 feet, as well as cuddy models. This 205 is versatile, with a centerline walk-through to the cockpit from the swim platform with a filler cushion that converts to a full-beam sunpad. A large, two-level swim platform serves as a good staging area for tow sports. Single MerCruiser and Volvo stern-drive power options to 315 hp are available.

GENMAR HOLDINGS, INC.

Mariah builds moderately priced bowriders from 18 to 25 feet, as well as cuddies. This SX20 comes with a ski tow eye, boarding lad-der, flip-up bolster seat at the helm, bimini top, and tilt steering. Blue deck lights, pop-up cleats, and a wakeboard tower are among the options. MerCruiser stern-drive power to 260 hp is available.

MARIAH BOATS

Malibu, close to the top ranking in its segment in the annual J.D. Power and Associates study, is a ski and wakeboard boatbuilder specializing in high-end, inboard-powered competition towboats. They also build V-drive inboard bowriders like the Sunscape 25 LSV shown here. Due to the V-drive inboard's shaft angle, these boats come up on plane with little bow rise, and they do it quickly with deep-geared engines and acceleration-tuned props. Up to 450 hp is available.

MALIBU BOATS

MasterCraft, always near the top in the annual J.D. Power and As-sociates BCIS, builds high-end ski and wakeboard towboats pow-ered with inboard engines. The excellent Maristar line of family towboats and all-purpose bowriders runs from 20 to 28 feet. The 280 shown is the flagship, and it's a big, solidly built boat with strong acceleration, a good ride, a huge forward seating area thanks to the pickle fork bow design, lots of storage space below-decks, and plenty of room for a large crew. Up to two 5.7-liter V-drive gas inboards are available.

MASTERCRAFT BOATS

Maxum's Sportboat series of moderately priced bowriders and cuddies runs from 18 to 24 feet. The 1800 shown has a full fiberglass cockpit liner, which helps at cleanup and maintenance time, back-to-back seating that converts to a lounger, and standard power with a 135 hp MerCruiser stern drive. A trailer comes with the boat. Options include a wakeboard tower and full canvas.   MAXUM BOATS

Regal builds a series of excellent-running bowriders and cuddies from 19 to 27 feet. In fact, Regal received the J.D. Power and Associates award for highest customer satisfaction with small (16–20 foot) runabouts in 2006 and 2007 (Regal also won the express cruiser segment). The Regal 1900 is a beamy boat with a walkthrough transom and full fiberglass cockpit liner for easy cleanup and maintenance. The Regal 1900 has a 190 hp V-6 standard engine from Volvo or MerCruiser.   REGAL MARINE

Monterey builds a Sport Boat series of bowriders from 18 to 24 feet, as well as an upscale series of Super Sport models from 26 to 29 feet. This 298 SC Super Sport has a cuddy big enough to serve as a weekender. The cabin sleeps four, has a complete galley, convertible V-berth, and private head. The helm seat adjusts to allow the operator to drive standing up comfortably. Stern-drive power to twin 320 hp stern drives is available.   MONTEREY BOATS

Rinker builds a series of Captiva bowriders from 19 to 29 feet. This 296 is a big family day boat with a good ride in a light chop. Like Rinker cruisers and deck boats, it also comes well-equipped, with an enclosed head with toilet, holding tank and pumpout, multiple-position sun lounger, bimini top and full enclosure, dual batteries with switch, shore power, sink, transom shower, and a refrigerator.   RINKER BOATS

Sea-Doo builds personal watercraft (PWC) as well as a line of waterjet-powered Challenger sport boats. They range from 15-foot, multi-colored, oversized PWCs to true family waterjet-powered bowriders. The Challenger 230 shown is available with between 310 and 430 hp with a twin-engine propulsion system. The boat is well-equipped with standard features, can carry up to 12 passengers, and has a good-riding modified-V bottom.   SEA-DOO

Seaswirl is a saltwater fish boat builder that also produces a lineup of bowrider, fish-and-ski, and deck boats to 23 feet. The 175 shown comes with an AM-FM-CD stereo, swivel helm seat and port side sleeper seat, bimini top, and two seating options. The 175 is available with either stern-drive or outboard power.   GENMAR HOLDINGS, INC.

Sea Ray makes a series of nicely outfitted Sport Boats from 17 to 29 feet, as well as cuddy models. This bowrider lineup includes the top-of-the-line 290 Select EX shown here. Finished off and equipped to a high standard, standard equipment includes a bimini top and cockpit cover, carpet liner, head compartment with VacuFlush toilet, electric engine hatch, and Clarion stereo with six speakers. Both single and twin gas MerCruiser and Volvo diesel stern-drive power is available to a total of 640 hp.   SEA RAY BOATS

Tahoe builds a full line of fiberglass sport boats including this well-equipped Q8i. This 21-footer is rated for up to 320 stern-drive hp from MerCruiser and can carry up to 10 people. Boat, motor, and trailer are sold as a package with special pricing.   TAHOE

COBALT 222 BOWRIDER

Cobalt 222 Bowrider Specifications	
LOA:	22'6"
Beam:	8'6"
Deadrise:	21 deg.
Dry weight:	4,165 lb.
Cockpit depth:	32"
Draft:	36" (drive down)
Fuel capacity:	50 gal.
Maximum capacity:	12 people
Total capacity:	1,800 lb.

A new model in 2006, the Cobalt 222 has a number of features designed to meet ever-evolving customer tastes and needs: stainless steel–trimmed rubber footrests, push-button switches, and lots of storage and cooler capacity under the deck and inside the forward consoles. The 222 replaces the 226, with the new boat adding a little freeboard, which results in a higher cockpit coaming (it's a full 32 inches deep inside) and more internal volume for storage capacity.

The third-smallest bowrider (there are also 20- and 21-foot models in the builder's lineup), the same basic components and construction materials go into the 222 as Cobalt's larger models. A high-quality, thoughtfully designed boat, it serves as a good introduction to the line. The boat is rated for 12 people or a total of 1,800 pounds.

Construction

After the gelcoat is sprayed on the mold, Zycon, a hybrid of polyester and urethane, provides a barrier coat that's almost twice the thickness as the gelcoat that goes on the bottom (to protect against blistering) and the sides (to reduce print-through). The bottom is a solid-fiberglass laminate, while Spray-Core (more than 3 inches) is used on the sides to further prevent print-through.

The hull is supported by a network of high-hat hollow stringers that are flanged and bonded to the hull with a high-strength adhesive. The hull's molded- and bonded-in-place stringer system makes for a neat installation and a clean bilge presentation. Marine-grade XL-10 fiberglass-encapsulated plywood bulkheads are tabbed to the hull and the stringers. The single-piece deck liner goes on next, attached to the hull with a shoebox hull-to-deck joint, with stainless steel self-tapping screws every foot into a strip of pressure-treated plywood. Two more rows of screws follow, securing on the rubrail and stainless steel insert.

Hull Design

Cobalt designs its own running surfaces. The 222 has a modified-V bottom with reverse chines, running strakes, and a sharp entry tapering to a moderate, and appropriate, 20 degrees of transom deadrise. Cobalt does a good job building a good-looking boat with generous freeboard, more evidence that practicality and safety don't have to be at odds with attractive styling. The deeper cockpit also allows the low-profile windshield favored by the stylists, with the driver still getting decent protection from wind and spray.

Walkthrough

Cockpit and Topsides

Aft, the Cobalt has an extended swim platform with three features that add to the boat's practicality and passenger safety. First, the platform is surrounded by a heavy, 2-inch-diameter stainless steel pipe frame that adds strength and impact resistance to the structure. This includes resistance to docking damage from pilings when backing into a slip. Next, the platform extends aft past the propellers below, which is a critical safety feature. This pretty much eliminates the possibility of a swimmer or diver landing on the props and getting hurt, even if the lower unit is raised partially out of the water. Finally, the platform is close to the water, making it easy to climb back on board.

A telescoping ski pylon is easy to access at the aft edge of the sunpad, and it retracts out of the way when not needed. A raised walkthrough to starboard leads from the swim platform to the cockpit. A sunpad covers the engine compartment just aft of the cockpit.

The cockpit has a conventional layout, with an L-shaped lounge aft and to port, with storage space, including an insulated cooler, below to port. The battery switch is located under one of the cockpit seats by the stern walkthrough.

One feature not often seen in this size and class of boat is a deep insulated in-deck storage locker or cooler right in the inside corner of the L-shaped lounge. The deck hatch is tooled fiberglass on both sides, which looks great and is another example of the boat's overall build quality. There's another in-deck locker forward between the consoles; at 5 feet, 8 inches long and 15 inches deep it is is ideal for storing skis and wakeboards.

A pair of bucket pedestal seats is forward, one at either console. The seats are thickly contoured, offering excellent lateral support. One thing that jumps out during a walkthrough is the high quality of the upholstery, which has stitched patterns and embossing with the builder's logo. This upholstery, among other things, accounts for an aesthetic depth and substance lacking in some other brands. On a more practical note, Cobalt provides plenty of grab bars to hang onto, both on the backs of the pedestal seats and forward at the port passenger seat.

Helm

The helm is a classy affair, with more stitched upholstery lining the console. The tan color and the material's matte finish minimize windshield glare from sunlight or from the gauges during night running. Stainless steel–framed rubber mats on the footrests are comfortable and provide a secure nonskid surface when seated at either console. The well-padded tilt wheel, with its rounded spokes, feels very comfortable when driving, the side-mounted engine controls are well positioned, and the flip-up seat bolster provides room to stand while driving.

To port, the side console has a glove box storage compartment with the stereo mounted inside. This console is also covered with stitched upholstery, and a wide grab bar across it offers a handhold when under way.

The bow seating area has a U-shaped lounge with storage below. The area is surrounded by thick upholstered cushions and a coaming bolster. Handrails are provided along the gunwale, as are speakers and stainless steel cup holders. The lounges are designed for reclining while facing forward, with sculpted backrests built into the forward surface of the twin consoles. The same backrests hinge up and open for wide-open access to the cavernous storage compartments under the consoles. Even the undersides of the backrests are tooled fiberglass—attention to detail that we've come to expect from Cobalt. A two-piece door and the centerline windshield close to block off airflow to the cockpit. An anchor locker is forward, with the hatch lifting on a booster.

Engine

Engine access is good, with the entire sunpad and walkthrough lifting clear—a full 31 inches, with a pair of boosts making lifting the unit easy. A deep gutter surrounds the opening, keeping things dry and corrosion-free below. There's also a gasket along the perimeter to trap the engine noise and minimize rattling with the engine running. There's plenty of room on either side to access the engine for maintenance, and the bilge surfaces are smooth and white, making for good visibility and easy cleanup. Volvo and MerCruiser single stern-drive power options to 425 hp are available.

Sea Trial

The test boat was powered by a single 5.7-liter 280 hp Volvo DuoProp stern drive, and our test ride took place on Lake George in fairly calm conditions. Leaving the marina at 1,000 rpm in the no-wake zone, the boat handled well and shifted smoothly. The boat came up on plane with modest bow rise, so seated visibility ahead was quite acceptable.

We managed just over 51 mph on GPS. The boat handles well in a tight high-speed turn, with the boat's degree of heel well matched to the boat's turn rate, which in turn made it easy to stand up in a turn. While we only had a 6-inch chop and a few wakes to cross, the 222 ran smoothly and rode well.

Cobalt has obviously been in the business of matching power plants to hull designs for a while, since standard power is adequate on all of the Cobalts we've tested. On the same note, it was impossible to make this boat porpoise, which is a dynamic instability causing the bow to rise and fall repeatedly in the absence of corresponding waves, caused mostly by the center of gravity being too far aft for the running surface and too little hull in contact with the water. On this boat, there's no need to fuss around with trim tabs and drive angles to dial out porpoising. The power plant is nicely matched to the boat's size and weight, with strong acceleration throughout the rpm range, including from 4,000 to 5,000 rpm. Sound levels were moderate, just 83 dBA at a 3,500 rpm cruise speed.

The steering was crisp and precise at two-and-a-half turns lock-to-lock. Unlike some other boats, there was no unwelcome tendency for the steering wheel to pull to the side. The stern-drive trim gauge was well calibrated for the drive's actual range of trim, unlike some whose needles tend to bottom out too soon or too late for practical use. Back at the dock, the Volvo DuoProp backed very strongly— it was like hitting the brakes hard at idle speed. Those props really dig in. The boat also backs well with the MerCruiser Bravo 3's counterrotating props canceling out side force.

Cobalt 222 Bowrider Performance Results

RPM	Speed, mph	Noise Level, dBA
600	4.2	61
1,000	6.2	66
1,500	8.2	77
2,000	14.6	78
2,500	23.3	79
3,000	30	80
3,500	36.2	83
4,000	41.5	88
4,500	47.5	89
4,800	51.2	92

Test conditions: Two passengers, fuel tank half full, with a Volvo 280 hp 5.7 GLI DP. Six-inch chop.

The Cobalt 222 bowrider is an excellent day boat, with high build quality, a good-running hull form, and a practical, family-friendly layout that takes the inshore boating lifestyle into account. Cobalt is good at making the incremental change we see year-to-year in their models. They understand the need to get it right with the small boats so owners keep trading up, and the company executes its ideas accordingly.

Cobalt has become one the industry's masters at creating huge, easily accessible storage compartments seemingly everywhere on board, including combining what are ordinarily separate storage areas or voids into more useful large compartments.

FORMULA 240 BOWRIDER

Formula 240 BR Specifications	
LOA:	24'
Beam:	8'6"
Deadrise:	20 deg.
Dry weight:	5,000 lb.
Cockpit depth:	31"
Draft:	36" (drive down)
Fuel capacity:	60 gal.
Maximum capacity:	11 people
Total capacity:	1,490 lb.

Solidly built with its construction and hull design derived from the brand's FAS³Tech race boats, the 240 was a pleasure to drive during our month-long test period. We got to know the boat well and had plenty of time to put it through its paces. Designed to carry up to 11 passengers, this day boat includes a head compartment, sink with running water, lots of storage space below seats, and a great ride in rough water.

Construction

The Formula 240's construction starts with a 1½-ounce skin coat of chop wet out in vinylester resin to prevent osmotic blistering. It provides much better protection against blistering because this barrier coat is thicker than merely spraying a coat of vinylester resin over the gelcoat. A DCPD blend resin designed for minimal shrinkage on curing follows through the rest of the laminate. A series of stitched (versus woven) fiberglass reinforcements follow; the bottom is solid glass, while Coremat is added to the hull sides to prevent print-through, and also to increase laminate thickness, and therefore stiffness, at lighter weight than would be possible with solid fiberglass.

The stringer system is built using rot-proof high-density polyurethane foam composite board encapsulated in fiberglass. The transom is also high-density polyurethane foam, 26-pound density, which is designed to resist compression loads from the stern drive bolts. The boat's structural bulkheads are also fiberglass-encapsulated composite board.

The hull-to-deck joint is bonded with a Plexus adhesive that's stronger than the fiberglass itself. A bead of Plexus is applied to the hull's shoebox flange, the deck is lowered on the hull and the surfaces are mated up, screws are fastened to hold and clamp the joint, and then after curing, through-bolts are applied every 18 inches with metal backing plates. Self-tapping screws on 6-inch centers, used to attach the stainless steel rubrail, finish the job.

The 240 has a one-piece cockpit and deck liner that's bonded to the stringer system, adding structural integrity and making the inside of the boat easy to clean. All Formulas are painted with Imron polyethylene paint, which is much more durable than gelcoat, before leaving the factory. All hull and deck graphics are also painted on with Imron, which holds its color longer than gelcoat, and is more durable and damage-resistant than decals and pinstriping.

Hull Design

The 240 has a deep-V hull with a fine entry and high chines and spray strakes. The hull bottom running surface extends aft on either side of the stern-drive lower unit, adding buoyancy as well as dynamic lift at planing speeds; this in turn tends to improve ride quality (a longer boat is a smoother-riding boat, all else being equal) and helps the boat get on plane a little quicker and with less bow rise. Transom deadrise is 20 degrees.

Walkthrough

Cockpit

The first thing to mention regarding the Formula 240's cockpit is the plush quality of the upholstery. It's all white, with a red (matching the hull color) accent stripe, and it gives the boat an upscale look.

The 240 has an integral swim platform with a four-step boarding ladder concealed below a flush hatch. It's low to the water, so it's easy to climb up on. There is a grab bar at the ladder and another one forward at the transom. There is also a ski tow post receptacle, and a trunk storage locker to port of the sunpad-engine hatch that holds, among other things, the ski tow post, stern-drive tilt controls, as well as stereo remote controls. A walkthrough to the cockpit is on starboard. Next to the walkthrough is a sunpad extending forward over the cockpit seat, providing enough room for two people to stretch out.

Aft in the cockpit is an L-shaped lounge with a cooler and storage lockers below, and opposite is a small entertainment center with sink and storage below. Forward is a pair of pedestal seats for the skipper and first mate. The port console doubles as a roomy head.

No less than thirteen stainless cup holders can be found in the cockpit. Our boat also had a stainless steel forward-swept pipe radar arch as an option. This welded-pipe design is by far our favorite, as it does not interfere with sight lines from the helm (as is the case with a fiberglass arch). It also offers a convenient place for running lights; the higher they are, the better, as it increases the range at which you are likely to be seen at night by another boat. The arch can also be used as a wakeboard tow point, up high so the boarders in your family get plenty of air.

Between the port and starboard consoles, a door closes to block off the wind when underway, and the effect is completed with the center windshield closed as well. The bow has a U-shaped, wraparound lounge with storage below. A filler cushion to make the lounge into a sunpad is optional, as is a table supported by a stanchion receptacle built into the deck. Forward is a hatch with anchor locker below, along with a pair of pop-up bow cleats. A low handrail also wraps around the gunwale for the convenience and safety of the seat occupants. Finally, the nonskid pattern used by Formula is excellent and easy to clean with a brush, and offers a good grip underfoot when it's wet.

Helm

At the futuristic-looking helm, the bolstered pedestal seat includes a bolster that lifts up to provide more standing room at the wheel or to give you a higher seat. The instrumentation is high-end Livorsi, and the gauges are high in head-up-display fashion. A GPS display is front and center, also easy to read since Formula designed the 240's electronics flat specifically to hold it. Tilt steering, a small Ritchie compass, Bennett trim tab controls, a digital depth indicator, and a Kenwood CD-AM-FM stereo are all included as standard equipment. In a welcome, practical touch, the windshield is plenty high enough to offer good protection when sitting.

With the bolster raised, there's enough room to stand comfortably between the wheel rim and the seat. The wheel is high enough to reach comfortably, as is the single-lever engine control. The throttle, as we found out on our test ride, stays put wherever you set it, which is more than can be said for many engine controls.

Engine

The aft sunpad rises on a power lift, revealing excellent access to the well-lit engine room. The big-block 496 MerCruiser takes up a lot of room, but there's plenty of space to get around it and do maintenance. Wiring and plumbing are neatly routed and well fastened. Surfaces are smooth and finished in white for good visibility and easy cleanup. Engine room lighting, a remote oil filter for easier oil changes, and an automatic fire-extinguishing system are standard.

Sea Trial

We had the use of the Formula 240 for several weeks on Lake Champlain, our local test site. It's a big lake, so we were able to select the conditions we wanted to really test out the design. In this case, we chose a day when the wind was blowing at 20 knots, kicking up 3- to 4-footers. It was soon evident that Formula has given the 240 an excellent rough-water hull design. At 25 to 30 mph, the boat ran well in all directions to the seas. Running downsea, the boat tracked well, thanks to both a good hull design and spot-on weight distribution. Upsea in these demanding conditions, the 240 delivered a comfortably smooth and dry ride. We can't think of a better-running family boat in this size range in rough water.

On our speed run, with a 496 MerCruiser driving a Bravo 3 stern drive, the boat was a delight to drive. The boat ran 1 mile per hour or so faster in a slight (3- to 4-inch) chop than it did in glassy water, the chop aerating the bottom a bit more, reducing frictional drag. Optimum speed was pretty easy to dial in: just raise the drive using the throttle's trim switch until it starts to ventilate, then drop it back down a whisker. The trim tabs kicked in predictably and forcefully (when needed), either raising the stern (and dropping the bow) when used in tandem, or correcting for list when used one at a time. Running into the chop, as with any planing hull we've driven, the best way to soften the ride was to tuck the drive in a little, then drop the tabs a bit; you slow down as wetted hull surface increases, but the ride smoothes out as trim (running angle, or bow rise) decreases.

At full throttle, we managed just under 60 mph, an impressive speed for any bowrider. The boat ran beautifully at that speed, tracking well and under complete control. The MerCruiser power steering was responsive and fingertip easy, and the single-lever engine controls were a pleasure to operate.

A quick note on the Captain's Call exhaust. This is a popular feature on these boats, though making an engine sound louder than it has to may be a virtue that's just lost on some of us. Sound levels at 3,500 rpm went from 82 dBA with Captain's Call off to 85 dBA with it on, which allows exhaust to exit above the waterline. In any event, this big-block MerCruiser does not need the decreased exhaust backpressure, as we noticed no change in rpm with it open or closed.

The engine noise levels at 3,500 rpm—82 dBA—were as low as we've ever seen on a runabout, testimony to Formula's competence at sound-deadening engineering measures. We use 3,500 rpm as a reference as the boat runs comfortably at that speed, producing just under 40 mph.

Coming back to the dock, the Bravo 3 delivered strong backing power; traction at low speed was much like a tugboat, for lack of a better comparison. And the boat backs in whatever direction you point the lower unit, thanks to the counterrotating propellers. We also noticed that the boat has little tendency to drift sideways when shifting between forward and reverse; the MerCruiser Bravo 3 unit acts like a big rudder, even when the props stop turning.

Formula 240 BR Performance Results

RPM	Speed, mph	Noise Level, dBA
600	4.2	63
1,000	5.8	70
1,500	8.0	71
2,000	12.1	79 (tabs down)
2,500	22.5	79
3,000	31.4	81
3,500	39.3	85 (exhausts open)
4,000	46.6	88
4,500	54.8	89
4,800	58.7	91

Test Conditions: Two passengers, fuel tank three quarters full, with a 496 MerCruiser B3. Moderate seas.

Formula has succeeded in every way with the 240 Bowrider. Beautifully built with fiberglass tooling, outfitted with high-end components, and solidly engineered to last for years, the 240 is as good as it gets in the family bowrider market.

The 240 proved to be a superb performer, a genuine pleasure to be on in rough conditions, its ride and solidity especially reassuring for less experienced boaters. The family-friendly cockpit layout, enclosed head, and thickly cushioned seating made a long day out on the water a real treat.

FOUR WINNS 220 HORIZON

GENMAR HOLDINGS, INC.

Four Winns 220 Horizon Specifications	
LOA:	22'
Beam:	8'6"
Deadrise:	19 deg.
Dry weight:	3,800 lb.
Cockpit depth:	30"
Draft:	33" (drive down)
Fuel capacity:	50 gal.
Total capacity:	1,500 lb.

The Four Winns 220 Horizon bowrider is a family day boat well suited to inshore cruising and watersports. The open layout offers plenty of room for an average family, and Four Winns does a good job with all the basics, including a livable layout, a fairly smooth-riding hull design, and plenty of storage space.

Construction

The Four Winns 220 is conventionally solidly built, starting with a coat of vinylester resin sprayed on the gelcoat to help protect blsitering, followed by a 3-ounce layer of chop wet out in general-purpose resin. A DCPD is used in the rest of the laminate of mat and woven roving. The hull is supported by a fiberglass grid bonded to the hull and filled with foam. The hull-to-deck joint is secured with self-tapping screws driven into a plywood backing strip and sealed with caulking.

There were a few construction rough spots in the engine compartment of our test boat. One involved the rubber flap designed to deflect water leaking through the edge along the aft edge of the engine hatch that had come loose. Another was the poor fit of the fiberglass liner in the engine compartment, where two sections of hull liner met with large gaps at the outboard corner of the transom and the extended running surfaces.

Hull Design

The Four Winns 220 has a modified-V bottom with reverse chines and two running strakes per side. The hull's running surface is extended, with a slight step up, aft and outboard of the stern drive for added buoyancy as well as added dynamic lift, with a little added hook in the buttocks, on plane. The hull's fine entry delivered a smooth and dry ride in a light chop.

Walkthrough

Cockpit

The boat is comfortably boarded via the full-beam integral swim platform. A large sunpad covers the engine hatch just forward of the swim platform (with its concealed, retractable swim ladder), and very large (27-inch-deep) storage bins are provided to port and starboard. A walkthrough is also provided between the sunpad cushions on centerline to the cockpit, so you don't have to step on the upholstery to move around the boat. There are grab bars outboard of the sunpad, and head bolsters provide a place to rest your head.

Inside the cockpit is a U-shaped lounge aft, with more storage space and a portable cooler concealed below the seat cushion on port. Forward to port is a pedestal seat for a passenger with a flip-up bolster for added standing room, and a glove box storage area inside the console that also keeps the stereo dry. Opposite to starboard is the helm console, also with a pedestal seat with flip-up bolster. These pedestal seats offer good lateral support, a big help in the middle of a tight high-speed turn.

The in-deck storage locker offers plenty of room for skis (over 7 feet long) and wakeboards (17 inches deep, 19 inches wide). We didn't like the single-post cleats installed by Four Winns. Most cleats have two supports, which is stronger than one post, and also allows you to tie off two lines at once by dipping the lines over the horns of the cleats individually. These single-horn cleats remove that bit of mooring versatility.

Helm

The helm console is cleanly laid out. We found seated legroom to be on the tight side, even with the adjustable seat pushed back on its slides. The instruments are sensibly laid out, though we'd like to see the compass (it's right above the ignition switch) moved higher where it would be easier to see. The wood grain steering wheel looks great, and it feels good in the hands—no sharp spokes or corners to contend with. The dash gets a low-glare treatment, which is much appreciated on a sunny day, or at night running with the console lights illuminated. Forward, a door on centerline between the consoles closes to block off airflow at high speeds.

Foredeck

The forward seating area offers plenty of room for four people. There's more storage below the seats, grabrails are provided outboard along the gunwale, four stainless steel cup holders offer a place to put your drinks, and the combination of tooled fiberglass cockpit liner and thickly contoured upholstery lend an upscale look. There's yet more storage inside the consoles, and it's accessed by lifting the bow seat backrests. The bow ladder is also a nice touch, allowing you to climb back on board the boat when beached bow-in.

Engine

The engine hatch opens a full 38 inches, hinging at the stern to offer easy access to the single Volvo gas engine. The bilge is tooled white fiberglass, so it will be easy to keep clean. There's plenty of room all around the engine for routine maintenance. Engine mounts are through-bolted from the side, with the engines resting on heavy aluminum angle brackets. The battery is secured in the bilge aft to starboard, while the polypropylene fuel tank, plainly visible forward of the engine, is carefully secured against movement and chafe.

Sea Trial

Our test boat was powered by a single 280 hp Volvo 5.7-liter GI gas stern drive with an SX single-prop lower unit. Coming up on plane with the drive tucked in all the way, we lost sight of the horizon momentarily from our seated position. The ride in the light Lake George chop was fairly smooth and dry, though perhaps not quite as smooth as comparable boats from Cobalt and Regal.

In a hard high-speed turn, the boat tracked well and handled predictably, never hinting at losing control. When moving along at 6 or 7 mph, this boat seemed to have less bow steer, or yawing, than others in its class. We like to be able to stand and drive a boat, and for that you want plenty of room fore and aft between the seat and the wheel (it's tight on this boat), and the wheel and throttle at arm's length. We found the throttle and shift to be a little too low, as we had to lean over to reach it when standing. We don't feel that raising it a few inches would hurt the seated ergonomics, either. Even with the single prop, the boat backed well in any direction, including downwind.

We'd like to see more attention to some of the construction details on the Four Winns 220 Horizon and more standing room at the helm, but the boat offers a great layout, exceptional storage space, and versatility. It also looks more expensive than it is, with fiberglass tooling and thickly contoured upholstery. It will also be easy to maintain, with a full fiberglass cockpit liner and excellent engine room accessibility. We like the attention to detail Four Winns expends on areas like the cockpit cover: Four

Winns uses elastic ties aft, which are a lot easier to fasten than the snaps commonly seen, and the elastics also keep a steady strain on the canvas, helping to eliminate any rain-collecting pockets.

Four Winns 220 Horizon Performance Results

RPM	Speed, mph	Noise Level, dBA
650	3.6	65
1,000	5.8	67
1,500	6.9	72
2,000	9	77
2,500	23.3	79
3,000	30.1	81
3,500	35.3	84
4,000	42.7	88
4,500	51.9	91
5,200	49.4	91

Test conditions: Two passengers, fuel tank a quarter full, with a 280 hp 5.7-liter VolvoGi/SX single-prop stern drive.

YAMAHA SX230 HIGH OUTPUT

Yamaha SX230 High Output Specifications

LOA:	23'
Beam:	8'6"
Deadrise:	20 deg.
Dry weight:	3,170 lb.
Draft:	16"
Fuel capacity:	50 gal.
Maximum capacity:	10 people
Total capacity:	1,800 lb.

The 50 mph SX230 High Output is Yamaha's biggest news on the runabout scene. While it's bigger all over than the SX210, with a seating capacity of 10 people, the key advantage is the boat's enclosed head inside the port console. Yamaha says the 230 is already the best-selling runabout in the industry, including stern-drive models. The extra interior freeboard of the SX230 makes it even safer for kids, and it also makes it more comfortable to stand up and drive this boat with the raised throttles.

Yamaha's SX230 constitutes the company's frontal assault on the stern-drive runabout market. Laid out like the stern-drive-powered bowriders from Chaparral, Sea Ray, Four Winns, Regal, and others, the SX230 has a lot to offer. Its big differentiator is its propulsion system—a pair of high-rpm 160 hp four-stroke inboard engines driving 6-inch waterjets.

Construction

The SX230 High Output begins as a layer of gelcoat over the polished mold, followed by a 1½-ounce layer of fiberglass chop wet out in orthophthalic resin. Orthophthalic general-purpose resin is used in the rest of the laminate as well, which consists of a combination of nonwoven biaxial and woven reinforcements. Hulls are solid fiberglass (no coring is used), and they are stiffened and strengthened by a one-piece fiberglass grid.

The grid, which includes the stringer system, engine mounts, and a foundation for the cockpit, is laid up in a separate female mold, bonded with

polyurethane adhesive and fiberglassed in place to the hull, and then injected full of foam. A one-piece cockpit and deck liner is in turn bonded to the hull grid and stringer system. Balsa coring is used to stiffen the deck. The hull-to-deck joint is bonded with polyurethane adhesive and then clamped with self-tapping screws.

Hull Design

The SX230 has a conventional modified-V hull, with hard chines and running strakes and 20 degrees of transom deadrise. The hull form is more important to get right in some ways for a waterjet than for a propeller-driven boat, largely because the directional stability, or tendency to maintain course, is driven primarily by hull shape and the boat's weight distribution. Propeller-driven boats, including stern drives and outboards, have lower units that act as a rudder to control the direction of the stern, and act to resist lateral (sideways) movement brought from wind and sea. The only resistance the SX230 and most other waterjet boats have to lateral movement is provided by the hull's chines and deadrise. That's why a flat-bottom waterjet boat is a bear to keep on course, especially running downsea.

Walkthrough

Cockpit and Topsides

Starting our tour in the stern, the full-beam, two-level swim platform is covered with a rubber nonskid material that does a good job providing a nonslip surface and comfort for a swimmer. A large hatch opens to a storage compartment and a pair of cleanout ports for the twin waterjet impellers. Just raise the hatch, pull out the plugs, and reach down and get to work. There's also a cutout switch that prevents the engines from starting when the first impeller cleanout hatch is raised. There's also a deck socket for a table stanchion in the aft section of the swim platform, extending the cockpit all the way to the stern. A boarding ladder pulls out from below the platform when needed.

Passing from the integral swim platform forward through to the cockpit, the cockpit layout has a J-shaped lounge that starts to starboard aft of the helm seat, and continues across the stern and along the port side to the port console. The aft section of the seat, along with the entire aft deck, lifts up for access to the engines. Below the snap-in carpet, a large section of the cockpit deck lifts out (after removing 15 screws) for fuel tank access—a big plus eliminating the need for expensive fiberglass surgery in the event the tank needs replacing. A socket in this deck hatch accepts the cockpit table stanchion.

Below the cockpit deck, a large locker, 17 inches deep and over 6 feet long, offers space for skis and wakeboards. All hatches are tooled on both sides for a sharp appearance, thanks to Yamaha's closed-molding process, and are gasketed to help prevent rattling. To port, the forward end of the lounge seat folds up to create a pair of seat backs facing aft and forward just aft of the port console—a versatile and clever arrangement that lets the seating work as a recliner or a standard seat. Inside the port console is a head compartment with a portable toilet.

Walking forward between the consoles, a bifold door latches open to block off wind and spray, and it's held in the open position with a rubber retaining latch. The centerline windshield above also closes to seal off the wind. The bow seating area has a large U-shaped molded lounge with padded backrest bolsters, grab bars along the gunwales, and cup holders forward. There's storage space below the lounge seats, and an insulated cooler with a drain below the seat to starboard. Also at the bow is an anchor locker with anchor stock brackets and a pair of pop-up bow cleats. The bimini top is well proportioned, covering most of the cockpit for good sun and rain protection.

Helm

The helm has a well-padded pedestal seat with a flip-up bolster that adds standing room at the wheel. The dash area is finished in a brown color to minimize windshield glare. The wheel and engine controls are comfortably positioned, whether the driver is seated or standing. A cup holder and small fire extinguisher are provided next to the seat, as is an engine ignition cutoff lanyard for the driver to wear. The helm gives priority of place to the engine gauges, all positioned up high so they're easy to read, and the accessory rocker switches are also easy to reach. The compass is too small and situated off-center to the left and far forward for some reason; otherwise, the helm layout works well.

Engine

The SX230 is powered by a pair of 160 hp four-stroke, four-cylinder, 1052 cc EFI gas engines designed to turn 10,000 rpm—that's about twice the rpm of the automobile gas engines used to power stern drives. They each drive a 6-inch stainless steel impeller through a direct-drive drivetrain (no reduction gear). Engine access is good, with the aft cockpit seat and the aft sunpad riising as a unit out of the way. The hatch is surrounded by a gutter, which should help keep the machinery inside dry. The tooled fiberglass bilge should prove easy to keep clean, and the engines are neatly installed and plumbed. The engine mufflers are aft of the engine compartment below the swim platform.

Sea Trial

With its two 160 hp waterjets, the SX230 accelerated strongly and reached a top speed of 52 mph with one person on board. Unlike stern drives and inboards, which are more heavily loaded at the prop in the mid-rpm range, the waterjet engines themselves accelerate to their maximum rpm almost instantaneously. It's just a matter of waiting for the boat to catch up. One advantage of the waterjets is that their thrust line is at the transom rather than a foot or more below the bottom of the hull; this means the boat comes on plane with less bow rise and little subsequent interference with visibility ahead.

Steering is as responsive we've seen on any boat, and much more so than most, with only a three-quarter turn from lock-to-lock. Such a tight steering ratio is designed to compensate for the boat's propensity to wander about its heading (there's no running gear or keel below the hull to keep it going in a straight line), and it creates a tendency to oversteer, especially at low speeds.

As a result, the boat takes constant attention to keep on course. We'd like to see this steering ratio eased up to something like $1\frac{1}{2}$ to 2 turns, though it would take some testing to detemine an optimum ratio. At high speed, say above 20 mph, the boat tracked well and headed where we pointed it without deviating. The boat easily will twist (turn 360 degrees) in its own length at slow speeds, and it will also turn in its own length with both engines running slow ahead.

Running along at 8,000 rpm (about 35 mph), we put the wheel over hard and the boat just spun right around, easily in control, and started heading in the opposite direction about a boat-length-and-a-half from our original wake.

The boat had a fast idle setting, bringing the engine rpm from 1,800 up to 2,400, which makes handling at slow speeds a lot better, since the boat relies on continuous propulsion thrust to steer. The impellers don't start loading the engines until they reach high rpm, which is why they accelerate so rapidly, and it's also why the engines only slow 200 rpm or so in a hard turn, unlike an outboard that might slow 1,500 rpm or more with the rudder hard over. One feature that would make driving the boat more enjoyable would be a synchronizer to keep the engine running at the same speed; it's difficult and takes constant attention to do it manually.

If you lose an engine there will be no problem getting home on the other one. We made 26 mph running one engine at 10,000 rpm, although you may have to back off from that setting to prevent overheating the engine. We didn't run it long enough to find out, and given the impeller demand curve of a waterjet system, it might never overheat.

Like the SX210, the SX230 is loud! We'd definitely want to see better engine room insulation to bring these high-frequency (compared to a 5,000–6,000 rpm outboard or stern drive) noise levels from the high 90 dBA range down to the mid-80s, which is where most stern drives operate.

As with any waterjet-powered boat, count on losing power momentarily when the boat jumps over waves and wakes and loses contact with the water. The impeller intakes are flush with the bottom of the boat and, unlike propeller-driven craft,

need constant contact with the water to provide waterflow to the impellers. Also count on losing steering control when you cut the throttle suddenly from high speed because there's no running gear (like a lower unit or rudder) to offer steering control in the absence of prop or impeller thrust.

Compared to the SX210, the SX230 High Output is more comfortable to drive standing up because the throttles are mounted higher off the deck and are therefore easier to reach and there's more room between the wheel and the helm seat.

Yamaha SX230 Performance Results

RPM	Speed, mph	Noise Level, dBA
2,400	4.6	64
3,000	5.6	71
4,000	6.5	77
5,000	8.7	78
6,000	14.2	79
7,000	29.4	87 (levels off nicely)
8,000	35.8	89
9,000	42.8	94
10,050–10,200	52.5	97

Test conditions: One passenger, fuel tank half full, with twin 160 hp four-stroke engines driving waterjets.

The SX230's wandering at slow speeds makes paying close attention to your heading necessary, and the high engine noise levels definitely need addressing. But the SX230 is an attractive boat for a lot of reasons. A shallow draft lets you travel in under two feet of water, making more areas accessible and without the risk of dinging a prop. The lack of a propeller under the boat or projecting past the transom makes the boat safer for swimmers, for obvious reasons. It also means you won't have to dodge crab or lobster pot buoys. The high-speed maneuverability, including the tight turning capability, makes the boat a blast to drive. And the enclosed head compartment makes the boat much more practical for the whole family to spend a day out on the water.

Ski and Wakeboard Boats

Ski and wakeboard boats are highly specialized inboard-powered V-hull runabouts. They are designed to do one thing particularly well: pull a skier or wakeboarder while producing a wake of a certain characteristic preferred by the sport. The two sports favor different wake characteristics, which will be explained below. Many of these boats are used as general runabouts much of the time, but with prices generally higher than those of the typical runabout, and capable of lower top speeds, they make sense only to boat buyers with some serious interest in their primary calling.

Being inboard-powered, both ski and wakeboard boats lack the ability to adjust engine trim. And since they are designed to perform best at speeds favored by skiers or wakeboarders, top speed is lower than most inboards of comparable weight and power. But an inboard has stronger acceleration than a stern drive.

The annual J.D. Power and Associates study does not distinguish between ski and wakeboard towboats. It does not specify length, either, although most such boats are from 18 to 24 feet, and the majority are V-drive wakeboard boats, if you base the assertion solely on the number of completed surveys returned to J.D. Power and Associates by owners. Correct Craft (also known as Ski Nautique) has been at the top of this segment since it was added to the study in 2002, though in 2007 just a single point (on a 1,000-point scale) separates Correct Craft from Malibu. MasterCraft, in turn, is breathing down both brands' necks a few points back.

All of the boat brands in this segment are well worth considering. Keeping these scores in perspective, the lowest-ranked

brand, Moomba, scored 853, an excellent score which is on par with the highest-ranking pontoon boats, higher than any of the small runabouts or express cruisers, and much higher than the average large runabout or coastal fishing boat.

Most segment award recipients tend to get five Power Circles, a measurement of customer satisfaction within the study, in every category. However, the highest-rated manufacturer in the ski and wakeboard segment, Correct Craft, rated four Power Circles in design and styling and, surprisingly, only three in watersports. Like Correct Craft, second-ranked Malibu also earned five Power Circles in four of the six categories, lower than Correct Craft in quality and reliability (three circles), equal in ride and handling and in overall, and one circle higher in design and style. It received two Power Circles more in watersports.

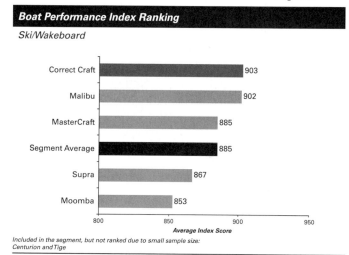

Boat Performance Index Ranking

Ski/Wakeboard

Brand	Average Index Score
Correct Craft	903
Malibu	902
MasterCraft	885
Segment Average	885
Supra	867
Moomba	853

Included in the segment, but not ranked due to small sample size: Centurion and Tige

Source: J.D. Power and Associates 2007 Boat Competitive Information Study ℠

Power Circle Ratings™ ○ ○ ○ ○ ○ JDPower.com

J.D. Power and Associates 2007 Boat Competitive Information Study ℠

Ski/Wakeboarding Boat Ratings

Company	Overall Rating	Quality & Reliability	Engine	Design & Style	Ride & Handling	Water Sports
Correct Craft **Award Recipient**	○○○○○	○○○○○	○○○○○	○○○○●	○○○○○	○○○●●
Malibu	○○○○○	○○○●●	○○○○○	○○○○○	○○○○○	○○○○○
MasterCraft	○○○●●	○○○○○	○○○●●	○○○●●	○○○●●	○○○○○
Moomba	○○●●●	○○○●●	○○●●●	○○●●●	○○●●●	○○○●●
Supra	○○●●●	○○○●●	○○●●●	○○●●●	○○●●●	○○●●●

SCORING LEGEND :	○○○○○ Among the best	○○○○● Better than most	○○○●● About average	○○●●● The rest

Ski Boats

The ski boat is highly specialized, since the hull design, propulsion system, and layout are all geared to snapping skiers up and out of the water in a heartbeat. Inboard power with an in-line transmission allows the engine to be mounted farther forward in the hull, which, along with a fairly flat bottom, produces the low, flat wake favored by tournament skiers. The driver, who sits on the starboard side, is supposed to keep his or her eyes on the road, so a rearview mirror and a portside aft-facing spotter seat next to the driver are provided. Optimal skiing speed is 28 to 36 mph and these boats reach that speed in seconds. Ski boat manufacturers stay close to their target market in many ways, heavily and visibly involved in tournaments, competitions, and ski-themed gatherings of all kinds.

Malibu's Response LXI has helped set a few ski records. This 20-footer is available with up to 400 hp and seats up to eight people. MALIBU BOATS

Correct Craft's high-end Ski Nautique line of ski boats ranked highest in the annual J.D. Power and Associates study ski and wakeboard segment for a number of years. The 206 shown is a good example of its excellent tournament ski boats. CORRECT CRAFT

MasterCraft's ProStar 190 is the smallest of their three ProStar ski boats, and it currently has set the slalom world record. The cuddy's closed bow presents a sharp appearance while adding interior storage space. Just under 20 feet, the 190 has seating for seven and is rated for up to 400 hp. MASTERCRAFT BOATS

Supra's Comp 20 is a three-event competition ski boat, fully certified. PerfectPass speed control is standard equipment. The bowrider layout adds seating forward, and ample aft-facing seating in the cockpit improves the view of the action. The boat is rated for 10 people and up to 340 hp.   SKIER'S CHOICE, INC.

Tige's 20i is a competition slalom ski boat with seating for eight and a deep cockpit for extra passenger security. The boat has a 340 hp in-line inboard and a TAPS trim control system that pulls the stern down for wakeboarding.   TIGE BOATS

MOOMBA OUTBACK

Moomba Outback Specificatioons	
LOA:	20'6"
Beam:	7'11"
Deadrise:	11 deg.
Dry weight:	2,750 lb.
Cockpit depth:	26"
Draft:	22"
Fuel capacity:	28 gal.
Maximum capacity:	10 people

Moomba's Outback is an entry-level ski boat that offers exceptional value and all the capabilities one would expect of a tournament-level towboat. With its in-line inboard gas powertrain, this is a purebred competition ski boat that has been certified as a three-event towboat by USA Water Ski. This certification consists of tests for power and acceleration, straight-line deviation, and handling. Power options range from 325 to 340 hp.

Construction

The Outback starts with a barrier coat of premium vinylester resin to prevent blistering followed by a ceramic coating to prevent print-through of the fiberglass reinforcement to the gelcoat. A laminate of solid fiberglass follows. The hull is supported by a pair of longitudinal stringers and interlocking bulkheads. The aluminum ski pylon structure is through-bolted to the bottom of the hull (with the tracking fins on the outside side of the hull) and supported on both sides by the stringers. Skier's Choice, Inc. has strain-tested these posts to 2,500 pounds of pull.

Hull Design

The Outback's hull has a modified-V bottom forward twisting to flat sections at the stern. The V-shaped bow sections deliver a smoother ride in a light chop, and the flat sections aft give the boat a low flat wake, and increased efficiency and speed for a given propulsion thrust. A pair of spray or lifting strakes on each side of the bottom keeps the boat a little drier than it would be without them. Deadrise varies, tapering to 11 degrees at the transom.

Walkthrough

Cockpit

Our test boat was equipped with a large bolt-on swim platform, low to the water for easy boarding. The rubberlike material covering the platform offered good grip to our boat shoes, and it would also be comfortable to sit on. Also at the transom is a long grab bar, giving a swimmer something to hold onto when climbing back into the boat. At the stern is a pair of gull-wing hatches that open to a storage compartment below. The floor of the compartment unscrews and lifts out for access to the steering gear below.

Inside the cockpit at the stern is a transom seat and a pair of cup holders. The transom seat has an upper and lower position, so it can either be used to extend the sunpad or serve as a lounge. Just make sure your passengers don't use the sunpad when the boat is underway. Forward of that is the engine box, which takes up the lion's share of the cockpit. Having the engine forward shifts the center of gravity forward as well, and that, along with the boat's flat bottom aft, delivers the tournament ski-quality wake geometry.

Forward to port is the aft-facing spotter's seat, where there is room for two to sit comfortably. Below the seat is a large storage area for skis, wakeboards, and other supplies that extends forward under the port console. The seat cushion lifts off and the seat back hinges open for access. The battery is

also found inside the port console, offsetting in part the driver's weight to starboard. On top of the port dash is a small glove box with the stereo inside. There's also an in-deck cooler between the helm and spotter seats under a deck hatch.

The centerline windshield opens for access to the bow seating area. There's storage below the seats, along with gunwale-mounted handrails and a pair of speakers.

Helm

The pedestal helm seat is thickly upholstered and well contoured to lock the driver into position, with those contours providing lots of side support, or lateral stability, a welcome feature for the driver in a hard turn at high speed. The seat also has a flip-up bolster, which increases the standing room between the seat and the wheel, though it's still pretty tight standing up. The dash is sensibly laid out for a ski boat, with the tachometer and the two speedometers front and center. The gray dash finish minimizes windshield glare on a sunny day.

The windshield on the Outback is generously proportioned. It's nice and high, offering more than token protection from the elements when blasting along. The corners are curved glass, and in general the mullions are narrow and interfere very little with sight lines to the horizon when seated. That, along with appropriate weight distribution and engine thrust lines, helps to account for the excellent seated visibility at the helm.

Engine

The single gas inboard is mounted in-line on the hull stringers, which means the transmission is on the aft end of the engine. The transmission is connected directly to the propeller shaft, which exits the hull through a packing gland and is supported on its underwater aft end by a shaft strut bolted to the hull. The hull is reinforced at the strut pad, which is subject to high grounding loads if the boat hits an underwater object at speed. The same goes for the rudderpost, with the hull beefed up there, too, for the same reason.

Access to the engine is excellent, afforded by opening the engine box, which lifts easily on boosts. All the daily maintenance points can be reached easily, and more extensive work can be accomplished by removing the deck-mounted collar the box is mounted on. The engine box is all fiberglass; fiberglass is definitely easier to clean and keep clean.

Sea Trial

Our test ride started with a speed run, recording speed and engine noise levels at the helm at intervals of 500 rpm. As with any ski or wakeboard towboat, acceleration with this 325 hp was this boat's strong suit as opposed to top speed. These boats are set up with low-pitch props so the engines can rev quickly under load. The trade-off, of course, is less top-end speed. The only way to have your cake and eat it too (strong acceleration, high top speed) is to install a two-speed gear. In the case of the Outback, acceleration off the line was strong, with the boat topping out at less than 43 mph with two people, a clean bottom, and little fuel in the tank.

The steering was responsive, just three-and-a-half low-effort turns lock-to-lock. We ran up to 4,000 rpm and put the rudder hard over a number of times, and the boat handled it just fine, turning in about 1 1/2 times the boat's length. Starting at 3,500 rpm, we put the wheel hard over, and a 360-degree turn took 8 or 9 seconds consistently—very impressive handling and responsiveness.

With a left-hand prop, the boat initially backs to starboard. But by revving the engine in reverse, initially, putting the rudder hard to port, gaining sternway, and then slowing the engine, the boat would consistently back to port, even downwind. That's impressive considering how small a ski boat's rudder is (smaller rudders produce less drag). The tracking fins along the keel forward help here, too, acting as a rudder at the bow, and offsetting the hull's tendency to walk sideways when backing.

The same tracking fins are critical to straight-line tracking when a skier is cutting from side to side. Properly placed tracking fins work with the boat's tow point forward of the engine box to minimize lateral lever arm from being created by the tow rope's strain, which makes steering the boat and maintaining course easier. And, like any keel, they work to minimize lateral motion in the water.

Sitting at the helm, there was plenty of legroom, and the seat was comfortable. The wheel and engine controls were well positioned for comfortable operation. We didn't lose the horizon coming up on plane, and this is without tabs or a stern drive's lower unit to trim the stern up. The boat handled well dockside, once you get the hang of an inboard. Just take a second to think through your approach in a current or wind, and boat handling will be a piece of cake. Even backing into a slip is straightforward if you approach from the right direction (which involves setting up for a port turn as you approach the slip, assuming a left-hand prop).

In a 6-inch chop, the Outback rode comfortably at 25 to 30 mph, running smooth, dry, and quite solid-feeling. This is a low-freeboard boat, and it has an open bow and a deck that drains to the bilge, all of which means it is a calm-water boat not meant for rough water.

Moomba Outback Performance Results

RPM	Speed, mph	Noise Level, dBA
700	5.1	64
1,000	6.8	66
1,500	9	79
2,000	15.5	82
2,500	24.4	86
3,000	30.1	88
3,500	33.8	89
4,000	37.7	91
4,500	41	96
5,000	42.9	101

Test conditions: Two passengers, fuel tank one-eighth full, with an inboard Indmar 325 hp MFI. Six-inch chop.

The Moomba Outback is an excellent choice for the ski enthusiast looking for performance and value. As a general-purpose runabout, the Outback would also do just fine, as long as the seaworthiness limitations of the low freeboard and open bow are taken into consideration. These should not be an issue if the boat is to be used on a small lake where the biggest waves are less than a foot high and the boat is prudently loaded (not bow heavy) and operated.

We like the inboard's generic simplicity and reliability. It's also relatively safe with the prop under the boat instead of sticking out at the transom. What you give up with any inboard is speed and propulsion efficiency, due to the less efficient running gear, and the lack of the stern drive or outboard's ability to adjust hull trim at speed for optimum lift and drag. It's also very loud at high rpm, like many ski boats, but it's a blast to drive.

The Outback can also be used for wakeboarding with the addition of a wakeboard tower offering a high tow point and a place to stow the boards and a ballast system adding displacement for a bigger wake.

Wakeboard Boats

Originally a take-off on the ski boat, the wakeboard boat has evolved to the point that it outsells ski boats by a factor of something like 6:1, depending on which manufacturer you talk to. The desired wake is high but smooth at the rooster tail, which takes a fairly flat bottom and a heavy, deeply immersed stern to produce. The wakeboard boat, therefore, has an inboard, V-drive engine mounted toward the stern, and water ballast tanks add still more weight aft. With this much rear weighting, the helm seat allows for standup operation so the driver can see over the bow. One manufacturer, Malibu, uses adjustable foils instead of ballast to pull the stern down at speed. They fold up out of the way when not in use.

Correct Craft's wakeboat series includes this top-of-the-line Crossover Nautique 236. With a LOA over 25 feet, a displacement of 4,300 pounds, 1,056 pounds of ballast, and a capacity of up to 14 people and up to 375 hp, this boat is capable of generating a seriously challenging wake. CORRECT CRAFT

Malibu's biggest boat is this Sunscape 25 LSV, a 450 hp V-drive with room for 16 people and a walkthrough transom. A sharp entry delivers a good ride in a chop. MALIBU BOATS

MasterCraft doesn't fool around when it comes to building big wakeboard boats. This yachtlike 28-footer with seating for 15 has a wet bar with Corian countertop, and includes a 1,000-pound ballast system (creating something like 9,000 pounds of wake-forming mass). Twin 350 hp V-drive inboards provide the juice. MASTERCRAFT BOATS

The 21-footer from Moomba offers lots of power, a trim tab to produce a lower wake for skiing, and enough deadrise forward to smooth out the ride. A 325 hp V-drive inboard is standard, and a 340 is optional. SKIER'S CHOICE, INC.

Supra's wakeboat series includes this open-bow Launch 21V, a 21-footer with 1,450 pounds of water ballast. The 21V is rated for up to 13 passengers and comes with a 325 hp V-drive inboard. SKIER'S CHOICE, INC.

Tige's pickle fork bow RZ2 is a 22-footer with lots of room forward thanks to the bow design. The RZ2 seats up to 14 people and is available with up to 400 hp. TIGE BOATS

Correct Craft 220 Specifications

LOA:	24'3" (22'1" w/out platform)
Beam:	96"
Deadrise:	Variable
Dry weight:	4,070 lb.
Cockpit depth:	28$\frac{1}{2}$"
Draft:	29"
Fuel capacity:	50 gal.
Maximum capacity:	12 people
Total capacity:	2,050 lb.

In production since 2006, the Correct Craft 220 is a tournament wakeboard boat with an aft-mounted V-drive engine, large cockpit, and open bow for additional passenger capacity. With the aft-mounted engine, the center of gravity is well aft, producing the large wake desired by wakeboarders. It also eliminates the in-line engine's engine box, creating a more open and useful cockpit configuration.

The 220 also has ballast that adds weight, mostly in the stern, further immersing the hull and increasing running angle, which creates a larger wake at a given speed. It is available with PCM gas V-drive engines of 330 or 375 hp. Though this is not a ski boat, the 220 can easily be skied from, as it has tremendous acceleration, an aft-facing spotter's seat, and excellent helm control with the forward rope attachment points. All it's missing, in fact, is the paper-thin wake skiing purists look for.

Construction

The boat starts off with a coat of chop wet out in vinylester resin to prevent osmotic blistering and cosmetic print-through. The hull is a solid laminate of fiberglass reinforcements wet out in general-purpose orthophthalic resin. Foam-core stringers used to strengthen the hull and support the cockpit deck liner above are encapsulated in fiberglass. The shoebox hull-to-deck joint is secured with self-tapping screws sealed with urethane adhesive.

Hull Design

Correct Craft calls its hull form a TWC (Total Wake Control) warped hull utilizing hydrogate—the hull is a modified-V with modest deadrise forward. There is possibly a little more deadrise than on a ski boat for a smoother ride, but much less than on a typical saltwater boat, so don't plan on taking a wakeboard boat out in rough water. Aft, the hull flattens out to maybe 10 degrees of transom deadrise, depending where you measure it. There's a keel pad, or flat area, about a foot wide at the transom. This pad makes installing the running gear easier, since the shaft through-hull, strut pad, and rudder all mount to it, and it also decreases draft. It also provides a little more lift aft, being flat. The chines curve inboard, in plan view, which, according to theories and observations prevalent in the ski and wakeboard industry, is supposed to decrease the size of the wake, particularly the rooster tail.

The rudders on these ski and wakeboard boats are supposed to pull to one side a bit to eliminate slack in the steering. Any slack would create less directional stability than is wanted, causing the boat to wander about its heading at speed. To get the rudder to pull to one side, ever so slightly, the manufacturer either grinds out one side of the aft end of the rudder, which creates a depression and therefore a low-pressure area, or they add a tab to the aft end of the rudder and point it off to the side a little, which does the same thing.

Walkthrough

Cockpit and Topsides

The 220 has a full-beam transom boarding platform, which gives something to step onto from the dock, and doubles as a staging area for wakeboarders or skiers aft. It's low to the water, and therefore easy to get back up on. Steps molded into the boat's transom make it easy to step up onto the engine hatch and sunpad aft and from there to the cockpit.

The three hatches to the engine compartment and outboard storage compartments are covered with a large full-beam sunpad in the stern. Here too are the first innovations we'll mention: The center sunpad cushion flips up to create a backrest, a clever design that adds a little sparkle back aft. Further, the whole engine hatch flips up to reveal a storage tray that's perfect for holding lines or fenders. Hopefully, people will have sense enough to use this area only when the boat is stopped. Outboard of the engine compartment is a pair of storage compartments—they're deep and long, providing tons of room for cockpit covers, coolers, wakeboards, and anything else. All these hatches, by the way, lift easily with boosts.

Inside the cockpit, the deck is low to the waterline, so the deck drains to the bilge. The deck is one-piece fiberglass under the snap-in carpet sections, making this an easy boat to maintain. The cockpit coaming is 28½ inches high, which provides a reasonable degree of safety for landlubbers unaccustomed to hard-turning, 30 mph plus boats. Just forward of the engine hatch is a retractable ski tow post, which would be used for skiing, or for wakeboarding in the absence of a tower. The tower is the preferred attachment point, since it's up higher, helping the wakeboarder jump higher and get more air.

Aft in the cockpit is a transom seat as well as port and starboard aft-facing side seats with storage space below. The transom seat can also be moved forward and turned around so it faces aft (just aft of the helm seat), too, making this into a U-shaped conversation area all its own. On both sides, separating the forward and aft cockpit seating areas, are integral coolers with cup holders; these also give you something to stand on when reaching for the tower board racks above.

Forward is a large lounge seat to port, with an aft-facing backrest making this the spot for the spotter. The seat flips up on boosts for access to a large storage compartment below and also forward under the port console. Inside the port console is the stereo amplifier and the subwoofer, indispensable equipment on the water today. Up on top is a glove box storage compartment with the Clarion stereo inside, as well as a cup holder on top of the dash.

The battery switch is under the seat, fairly easy to get to at the start and end of the day. Our elaborate wakeboard tower had a pair of swiveling board racks outboard that could be made to project outboard over the gunwales, freeing up room in the cockpit. The tower also holds an assortment of lights and speakers, the latter so the wakeboarder at the end of the rope can hear the tunes.

Helm

Opposite to starboard is the helm, with its thickly padded and upholstered pedestal seat sporting a flip-up bolster. The helm is functionally laid out, with the rpm and speed gauges front and center, and the other engine gauges off to the side. In addition to the analog readouts are digital displays that provide precise information as needed on everything from depth, speed, fuel level, and air and water temperatures, to engine oil pressure and engine hours.

The PerfectPass speed control was a pleasure to operate, and the controls are ergonomically situated at the helm. So are the helm station's remote controls for the Clarion stereo system in the opposite console. To start the boat, you have to enter a preprogrammed code, just like keyless entry on a car. Controls and tank level gauges for the three ballast tanks are in easy sight and reach below the dash. The dash has a flat gray treatment, which eliminates, or at least reduces, windshield glare. Correct Craft also makes it easy to service, with the whole dash lifting up for access after removing just four screws.

Bow Area

Between the consoles is a large in-deck storage compartment, well suited to holding skis and wakeboards. All the hatches on this boat were tooled on both sides, a nice touch reflective of the high quality evident everywhere onboard the 220. The hatches all lift easily, which means the builder took the time to find the right boosts for the job for each hatch, and they all have different requirements. Under the port console, and accessible from centerline through a fold-down door, is a large portable cooler.

Forward through the opening centerline windshield is the bow seating area. There's not a lot of room up here compared to some of the stern-drive bowriders, but there's plenty of room for three, and the seat cushions are well-padded and thickly upholstered, as on the rest of the boat. Correct Craft provides two grab handles, as well as four cup holders, speakers, and the combination running light in the bow. There's also more storage space below the seats, as well as a cockpit drain in the bow, and a removable snap-in carpet (one of the things that distinguishes this wakeboard boat from a ski boat).

Engine

The engine is accessed through an aft centerline hatch that lifts with little effort on boosts. There's plenty of room all around the engine for routine maintenance checks. The engine compartment is cleanly laid out, with gas and oil filters and water pumps within easy reach. About the only thing that would help visibility around the engine is using white gelcoat instead of black. PCM gas V-drive power options range from 30 to 275 hp.

Sea Trial

Our test ride on Lake George took place in an 8-inch chop, but judging from the light chop and the few wakes we crossed, the boat will deliver a decent ride in 1-footers at 25 or so mph. The boat felt solid underfoot, and acceleration was strong on our test boat, getting up to a regulation wakeboarding speed of 22 mph in under 4 seconds. Also while coming up on plane, bow rise was not that pronounced, so we didn't lose the horizon when seated at the helm. That makes the boat safer to operate.

The 1.42:1 transmission was as smooth as silk when shifting, and the engine control was at just the right height and distance forward for comfortable operation. So was the wheel, which was also comfortable to grip with no sharp edges anywhere. The boat turned well, generally making a 360-degree turn in under 10 seconds. Noise levels were moderate, which makes for a much more enjoyable boating environment. The stereo could easily produce more noise than the engine, in fact.

The windshield is nice and high, providing plenty of wind and spray deflection at speed. There's also a lot of legroom at the helm, and the seat was well-padded and offered great lateral support.

We found attention to detail everywhere we looked on the Correct Craft 220, from the two-sided

Correct Craft 220 Performance Results

RPM	Speed, mph	Noise Level, dBA
600	3.7	58
1,000	6.2	62
1,500	7.9	76
2,000	10.5	77
2,500	17.7	81
3,000	27.1	82
3,500	31.5	83
4,000	36	84
4,500	40.2	88
5,000	42.3	89
5,400	45.4	89

Test conditions: Two passengers, fuel tank one-third full, with PCM 6.0 375 hp V-drive engine. Light chop.

tooled hatches to the convertible cockpit seating. The boat was quiet, solid, and powerful off the line. As previously mentioned, Correct Craft ranked highest in annual J.D. Power and Associates study ski and wakeboard segment for highest in customer satisfaction for the last five years.

MASTERCRAFT X-STAR

MasterCraft X-Star Specifications

LOA:	24'5"
Beam:	8'4"
Deadrise:	0 deg.
Dry weight:	4,520 lb.
Draft:	30" (drive down)
Fuel capacity:	53 gal.
Maximum capacity:	12 people
Total capacity:	1,770 lb.

In production since 2002, the MasterCraft X-Star is a superb example of the wakeboard towboat genre. We had one for an extended testing period (six weeks) and became familiar with the boat and its capabilities. It's considered to be one of the best, and it has received official sanction, having been selected as the official towboat of the sport's premiere event, the X Games.

A 22-footer with all the bells and whistles, the X-Star stands out in a crowd with its pickle fork bow, hull graphics, multifunction tower with board brackets and tow point, and a space-age helm station with PerfectPass speed control. It's certainly one of the most nimble inboards I've ever handled, with fast-acting steering and engine controls. Even at low speeds, the X-Star turns on a dime and reacts immediately to throttle changes.

The X-Star is built to snap a boarder out of the water and up to 22 mph in seconds. This requires tremendous low-end acceleration and a perfectly tuned drivetrain. It also requires a prop with low pitch so the engine isn't loaded up in low- to midrange rpms—this is what allows the engine to accelerate so rapidly. The trade-off with any similarly setup boat is a lower top-end speed, in the case of the X-Star about 40 mph.

With a capacity of 12 persons or 1,770 pounds, and a total of 103 gallons of ballast water (859 pounds of fresh or 880 pounds of salt water) carried in three tanks in the bilge, the 350 hp Indmar MCX V-8 engine has its work cut out for it. Yet with its immediate and powerful acceleration, it proved to be more than up to the task. Up to 425 hp is available.

Construction

The X-Star starts with 2 ounces of chop over the gelcoat as a blister barrier, followed by multiple layers of 36-ounce knit reinforcement and 1-ounce mat on the hull sides. Over $3^{1}/_{2}$ inches of SprayCore is used to add bulk and stiffness to the hull between laminates. The stringers are fiberglass, with steel reinforcements used to support the engine and ski tow points. The hull-to-deck joint is bonded with adhesive and fastened with self-tapping screws sunk into a backing strip of HDPE plastic. AME 1000 vinylester resin, superior in physical properties to orthophthalic and isophthalic resins commonly used by boatbuilders, is used throughout the hull laminate.

Hull Design

The X-Star has a modified-V bottom with contoured cutouts in the chines aft that contribute to achieving the wake geometry, or shape, preferred by wakeboarders. Forward is a twin sponson, or gull-wing entry, that creates the pickle fork gunwale, opening up the beam at the gunwale and increasing the seating space in the bow. Three keel fins provide increased directional and steering control, especially in a turn with a wakeboarder under tow.

The inboard shaft is supported by a single strut at the prop. The precise and responsive steering can be attributed to a wedge-shaped ax head rudder directly aft of the left-hand, four-blade propeller. This inboard configuration produces agile and predictable handling, and draft is kept to a modest 28 inches at light load.

The X-Star's ballast system includes three water tanks, two aft to port and starboard, and one on centerline forward. Each has a pump with automatic shutoff (to prevent impeller burnout if left running dry) for filling and emptying.

Walkthrough

Cockpit

The cockpit is surrounded by U-shaped lounge seating, covered in heavy vinyl, with storage below. The port storage compartment continues under the windshield console up to the bow, so there's plenty of storage for wakeboards, skis, and other large objects. The two batteries are aft to port under the seat, making them easily accessible. On centerline is another hatch that opens to the engine transmission and the aft end of the 53-gallon polypropylene fuel tank.

The port lounge seat faces aft, making it comfortable for the spotter. Under the windshield to port, opposite the helm, is a cavernous glove box holding the AM-FM-CD stereo and plenty of room for cameras, purses, or other small items. The cockpit is loaded with speakers, including subwoofers and tweeters, and four aft-facing cannon speakers are mounted atop the tower so the rider, and anyone else on the lake, can hear the tunes.

Aft atop the engine and storage compartments is a sunpad for use when the boat is stopped. The swim platform at the transom is just a few inches off the waterline when the boat is loaded with people, fuel, ballast, and gear, so it's easy for a swimmer to get onto from the water. The platform's rubber nonskid is comfortable under bare feet and easy to keep clean. The platform can also be easily removed by disconnecting a couple of toggle pins when the boat is on the trailer.

The Zero Flex Flyer tower disassembles so the boat can fit in a garage, and it holds two wakeboards on either side on rotating brackets. It's an aluminum sculpture in its own right.

In the bow are port and starboard lounges that tilt clear, seat back and all, for excellent access to the storage space beneath. Between the seats in the bow is a self-draining insulated cooler. Forward of that is an anchor locker, complete with a molded support for the anchor stocks and rubber pads to keep anchor rattling to a minimum. Gunwale handrails add security for passengers forward.

Helm

A lot of thought and effort has gone into the X-Star's helm station, with the design team at MasterCraft achieving an unusually successful blend of form and function—the helm looks hip and works well from an operator's perspective. The carbon fiber helm instrument panel has bullet-shaped instrument pods, adding a decidedly space-age look, with the leather-wrapped wheel adding a further touch of class. Form doesn't get in the way of function: the instruments and gauges are clearly visible, and a stereo remote control is to starboard. The PerfectPass controls display the speed dialed in, the boat's actual speed, and the water temperature.

Engine

The X-Star's V-drive 350 hp 5.7-liter Indmar MCX inboard is mounted in the stern. The engine faces forward, with the V-drive transmission at the forward end of the engine and the propeller shaft exiting the hull below the engine. With the engine in the stern, there's more usable uncluttered cockpit space. And with the engine weight in the stern, the size of the wake increases due to deeper hull immersion aft. Shaft angle is 16 degrees, which is a lot compared to the 10 to 12 degrees seen in most larger inboards, but the steep angle also creates a slight vertical lift that helps drive the boat up on plane more efficiently and quickly. Once up and running, the boat runs with so little trim (bow rise) that the propeller's angle relative to the horizon (and surrounding waterflow) is not much different than a large convertible with 11-degree shafts running at 4 to 5 degrees of trim (which would be a total of 15 to 16 degrees from horizontal).

Port and starboard hatches lift on air springs for access to storage compartments outboard of the engine. There's lots of storage space inside, since the ballast tanks are under the deck, right in the bilge. Keeping the tanks low also lowers the center of gravity when the tanks are filled, improving stability and seaworthiness. Once the outboard hatches are raised, the centerline engine hatch also lifts up easily. Access to the engine is good, with all maintenance points in easy reach. Just forward of the engine hatch, the centerline cockpit seat cushion lifts out, along with a storage tub beneath, to provide access to the transmission and the aft end of the polypropylene fuel tank.

This fuel tank has port and starboard fills, making it convenient when you pull up to the pump in a gas station. You don't have to worry about whether the boat's fuel fill is on the same side as the SUV or truck pulling it. The same fueling flexibility also applies at the fuel dock, of course.

A pair of batteries is beneath the portside cockpit seat aft. Having the second battery is a nice touch, given the amperage pulled by the ballast tank pumps. You shouldn't have to worry about lacking the necessary power for the engine. The battery switch helps prevent accidental battery discharge if accessory switches are left on when the boat is left unattended.

Sea Trial

Considering its purpose-driven design, it should be no surprise to see so much discussion of the X-Star in the sea trial section. MasterCraft markets its wakeboard boats not only against other V-drive inboard competitors, but also against stern-drive-powered bowriders. So it's appropriate to make direct comparisons between inboard, stern-drive, and outboard power. How well the Master-Craft tracks at slow speed around the docks is very noticeable. There is little of the wandering seen in stern drives of this size.

The reason is two-fold: there's more directional stability provided by the three keel fins in the middle of the boat and the inboard running gear with its rudder and prop strut. And, the inboard's prop is farther forward, so there's less distance from the prop to the hull's pivot point, reducing the tendency to yaw at slow speeds. The V-drive also produces a lot less bow rise when climbing on plane, so visibility ahead is unrestricted, even when sitting and accelerating to wakeboard speed.

At dockside, or maneuvering to pick up a wakeboarder in the water, backing an inboard can be a problem, since the X-Star's left-hand prop tends to walk to starboard in reverse, and the stern will also seek the wind like any weathervane. As with most inboards, the rudder has little effect when backing since there is so little water pressure acting on it. That said, you can back and fill (using quick bursts of power, with the ahead bursts doing the steering for you) when maneuvering around the dock, and put the boat pretty much anywhere you want to once you get the hang of it. In fact, running an inboard dockside can be preferable in some circumstances since it's so predictable; just practice and get the hang of it, and plan your approaches.

The X-Star has a lot of low-end power, but don't expect all that power to translate into top-end speed. This boat is designed to tow wakeboarders and skiers, and that requires providing a lot of low-end torque to the prop, in a relatively low-speed rpm range. That means the engine has to be loaded lightly at top speed so propeller loading in the midrange is lessened, allowing it to accelerate quickly from a stop. The acceleration time from 0 to 22 mph is less than 4 seconds, and with 850 pounds of ballast on board that time changed very little. This speaks again to the finely calibrated gearing and propping, appropriately set for midrange performance.

Power steering lets you control the boat with your fingertips. The MasterCraft has a PerfectPass speed control system, and this is a great feature to have if you want to maintain a set speed, which is the whole point with wakeboard boats. Wakeboarders like to lock in at 22 mph, and it's simply a matter of dialing in the speed you want on the PerfectPass display, nailing the throttle, and off you go, with the engine slowing and adjusting automatically to keep you at a steady speed. Make a turn, and the engine speeds up automatically to keep the hull moving at the same speed through the water.

Considering that the Indmar engine turned up 5,300 rpm at wide-open throttle, the engine was just loafing at the 3,200 rpm needed to maintain 22 mph. In a hard turn, engine rpm picks up 500 rpm or so to maintain speed, but usually any rpm variation as you're running along is barely noticeable. In addition to the strong acceleration, the X-Star also turns on a dime, making a 360-degree turn in less than 10 seconds at high speed. With the prop's walking effect creating side force to port when running ahead, the turn to starboard is even faster than it is to port.

The MasterCraft is an exceptional boat that we were sorry to part with at the end of our test period. A classy, purpose-built towboat, the X-Star delivers strong acceleration, superb operator and wakeboarder ergonomics, and a stylish look and feel. You will find everything you're looking for in a wakeboard boat.

Attention to detail shows everywhere, from fit and finish to the boarding details that top-ranked wakeboarders expect: the tower with rotating board racks, the ballast system with its high-capacity tanks and low center of gravity, the sculpted yet businesslike helm, the stereo system, and the great hull graphics and gelcoat. We also give the PerfectPass speed control system high marks for its tenacity in keeping the boat in the dialed-in speed zone. It's easy to use and delivers as promised.

The X-Star will help you stand out in a crowded field. It got a lot of compliments and admiring looks whenever we pulled into a marina. The boat may look like it's ready to pounce when it's sitting on the trailer, but just wait until you get it on the water.

MasterCraft X-Star Performance Results

RPM	Speed, mph (ballast full)	Speed, mph (ballast empty)	Noise Level, dBA (at helm)
1,000	5.5	—	69
1,500	7.6	—	70
2,000	9.0	—	73
2,500	13.2	—	79
2,800	18.7	—	—
3,000	21.7	—	82
3,500	26.1	25.5	83
4,000	30.2	29.5	85
4,500	34	33.3	87
4,850	36.4	—	89
4,900	36.5	—	—
5,300	39.4	—	90

Test conditions: One passenger, full fuel tank. Six-inch chop. Note: Noise levels read high due to the exhaust, not radiated engine noise.

Art Bibliography

The following bibliography is for art reproduced in this book.

Armstrong, Bob. *Getting Started in Powerboating.* 2nd ed. Camden, Maine: International Marine, 1995.

Beebe, Robert P., Captain. *Voyaging under Power.* 3rd ed. Revised by James F. Leishman. Camden, Maine: International Marine, 1994.

Brewer, Ted. *Understanding Boat Design.* 4th ed. Camden, Maine: International Marine, 1994.

Gerr, Dave. *The Nature of Boats: Insights and Esoterica for the Nautically Obsessed.* Camden, Maine: International Marine, 1992, 1995.

Gerr, Dave. *Propeller Handbook: The Complete Reference for Choosing, Installing, and Understanding Boat Propellers.* Camden, Maine: International Marine, 1989, 2001.

Larsson, Lars, and Eliasson, Rolf E., *Principles of Yacht Design.* 2nd ed. Camden, Maine: International Marine, 2000.

Marchaj, Czeslaw A. *Seaworthiness: The Forgotten Factor.* Camden, Maine: International Marine, 1986.

Phillips-Birt, Douglas. *Naval Architecture of Small Craft.* New York: Philosophical Library, 1957.

Steward, Robert M. *Boatbuilding Manual.* 4th ed. Camden, Maine: International Marine, 1994.

Web Sites for Boat and Engine Manufacturers

A & M Manufacturing	www.ampontoons.com
AB Inflatables	www.abinflatables.com
Achilles	www.achillesinflatables.com/
Active Thunder Boats	www.activethunderboats.com
Advanced Marine Inflatables	www.amiboats.com
Albemarle Boats	www.albemarleboats.com
Albin Marine	www.albinmarine.com
Albury Brothers Boats	www.alburybrothers.com
Alden Yachts	www.aldenyachts.com
Almar Boats	www.almarboats.com
Aloha Pontoons/Waco Mfg.	www.alohapontoons.com
Altima Yachts	www.altimayachts.com
Alumacraft	www.alumacraft.com
Aluminum Chambered Boats, Inc.	www.acbboats.com
American Honda Motor Co. Inc.	www.honda.com
American Marine Holdings	www.prolineboats.com and www.donzimarine.com
American Marine Sports	www.americanmarinesports.com
American Tug	www.americantug.com
Andros Boatworks	www.androsboats.com
Angler Boat Corp.	www.anglerboats.com
APEX	www.apexinflatables.com
Apreamare	www.apreamare.it and www.ferrettigroup.com
Aquasport	www.aquasport.com
Atlantic Boat Company	www.atlanticboat.com
Avalon	www.avalonpoontoons.com
Avon Inflatables Ltd.	www.avonmarine.com
Azimut Yachts	www.azimutyachts.net
Azure	www.azureboats.com
Back Cove Yachts	www.backcoveyachts.com
Baha Cruisers	www.bahacruisers.com
Baja Marine	www.bajamarine.com
Bavaria Yachts USA	www.bavariayachts.com
Bayliner	www.bayliner.com
Beneteau USA	www.beneteauusa.com
Bennington Marine	www.benningtonmarine.com

The author wishes to thank NMMA for contributing to this list of manufacturers.

Bertram	www.bertram.com
Black Thunder Powerboats	www.blackthunder.com
Blazer Boats	www.blazerboats.com
Bluewater Sportfishing Boats, Inc.	www.bluewaterboats.com
Bluewater Yachts	www.bluewateryacht.com
Bombard	www.bombard.com/en
BRP USA	www.brp.com
Boston Whaler	www.whaler.com
Botewerks LLC	www.botewerks.com
Bryant Boats	www.bryantboats.com
Cabo Yachts	www.caboyachts.com
Calabria Genuine Ski Boats	www.calabriaboats.com
Camano Yachts	www.camanoyachts.com
Canaveral Custom Boats	www.deltaboats.com
Canyon Bay Boatworks	www.canyonboatworks.net
Caravelle Powerboats	www.caravelleboats.com
Caribe Inflatables USA, Inc.	www.caribeinflatables.com
Carolina Classic Boats	www.carolinaclassicboats.com
Carolina Skiff	www.carolinaskiff.com
Carrera Sport Fishing Boats	www.carrerapowerboats.com
Carver Yachts	www.carveryachts.com
Catalina Yachts	www.catalinayachts.com
Caterpillar	www.cat.com
Cavileer Yachts	www.cavileeryachts.com
C-Dory Marine Group	www.c-dory.com
Centurion Boats	www.centurionboats.com
Century Boats	www.centuryboats.com
Challenger Powerboats	www.challengerpowerboats.com
Champion Boats	www.championboats.com
Chaos Boatworks	www.chaosboatworks.com
Chaparral	www.chaparralboats.com
Checkmate	www.checkmatepowerboats.net
Chris-Craft	www.chriscraft.com
Cigarette Racing Team, LLC	www.cigaretteracing.com
Com-Pac Yachts	www.com-pacyachts.com
Cummins Mercruiser Diesel (CMD)	www.cmdmarine.com
CNB/Lagoon	www.cata-lagoon.com
Cobalt Boats	www.cobaltboats.com
Cobalt Yachts	www.cobaltyachts.com
Cobia	www.cobiaboats.com
Concept Boats	www.conceptboats.com
Contender Boats	www.contender.com
Correct Craft	www.correctcraft.com
Corsair Marine	www.corsairmarine.com

Crestliner	www.crestliner.com
Crownline	www.crownline.com
Cruisers Yachts	www.cruisersyachts.com
Crusader Engines	www.crusaderengines.com
CSI Marine	www.csimarine.com
Dakota	www.dakotaboats.com
Davis Boatworks	www.buddydavis.com
John Deere	www.deere.com
Delta Boats	www.delataboats.com
Destination Yachts, Inc.	www.destinationyachts.com
Dolphin Boats	www.dolphinboats.com
Donzi Marine	www.donzimarine.com
Donzi Yachts by Roscioli	www.donziyachts.com
Dorado	www.doradomarine.com
Doral	www.doralboat.com
Dufour Yachts USA, Inc.	www.boats.com/site/dufouryachtsusa
DURACRAFT Marine	www.duracraftmarine.com
Dusky Marine	www.dusky.com
Dyer Boats	www.dyerboats.com
Dyna Yachts	www.dynacraftyacht.com
Dynasty Boats	www.polarboats.com
Eastbay	www.grandbanks.com
Ebbtide Corporation	www.ebbtideboats.com
EdgeWater Power Boats	www.ewboats.com
Egg Harbor Yachts	www.eggharboryachts.com
Eliminator	www.eliminatorboat.com
Ellis Boat Company	www.ellisboat.com
Emerald Bay Custom Houseboats	www.emeraldbayhouseboats.com
Envision Boats	www.envisionboats.com
Ercoa	www.ercoa.com
Everglades Boats	www.evergladesboats.com
Evinrude	www.evinrude.com
Fairline Boats of North America	www.fairline.com
Famous Craft	www.famouscraftboats.com
Fathom Yachts	www.fathomyachts.com
Fearless Yachts	www.fearlessyachts.com
Ferretti Group USA	www.ferrettigroupusa.com
Fineline Industries	www.centurionboats.com
Fisher Boats	www.fisherboats.com
Forest River Marine	www.forestriverinc.com
Formula	www.formulaboats.com

Fountain Pajot	www.fountaine-pajot.com
Fountain Powerboats	www.fountainpowerboats.com
Four Winns	www.fourwinns.com
G3 Boats	www.g3boats.com
Galaxie Boat Works, Inc.	www.galaxieboatworks.com
Gibson Boats	www.gibsonboats.com
Glacier Bay	www.glacierbaycats.com
Glasstream	www.glasstream.com
Glastron Boats	www.glastron.com
Global Yacht Builders	www.globalyachtbuilders.com
Godfrey Marine	www.godfreymarine.com
Grady-White Boats	www.gradywhite.com
Grand Banks Yachts	www.grandbanks.com
Hann Powerboats, Inc.	www.hannpowerboats.com
HanseYachts	www.hanseyachts.com
Harbor Master Boats and Yachts	www.harbormasterboats.com
Harris Kayot	www.harriskayot.com
Hatteras Yachts	www.hatterasyachts.com
Hell's Bay Boat Works	www.hellsbayboatworks.com
Henriques Yachts	www.integritymarine.com
Hewes	www.pathfinderboats.com and
	www.maverickboats.com
Hinckley Company	www.hinckleyyachts.com
Hobie Cat Company	www.hobiecat.com
Holby Marine Company	www.holbymarine.com
Honda	www.honda.com
Hunt Yachts	www.huntyachts.com
Hunter Marine Corporation	www.huntermarine.com
Hurricane	www.hurricaneboats.com
Hustler Powerboats	www.hustlerpowerboats.com
Hutchins Company	www.com-pacyachts.com
Hydra-Sports Boats	www.hydrasports.com
IMAR Group/Sugar Sand	www.sugarsand.com
Impulse Marine	www.impulse-marine.com
Indmar Engines	www.indmar.com
Integrity Marine	www.integritymarine.com
Intrepid Powerboats	www.intrepidboats.com
Invincible Boat Company	www.invincibleboats.com
Island Packet Yachts	www.ipy.com
Island Pilot LLC	www.islandpilot.com
Island Runner	www.islandrunner.com

J-Boats	www.pearsoncomposites.com
Jeanneau	www.jeanneauamerica.com
Jefferson Yachts, Inc.	www.jeffersonyachts.com
Jersey Cape Custom Yachts	www.jerseycapeyachts.com
Jupiter Marine International	www.jupitermarine.com
Kadey-Krogen Yachts	www.kadeykrogen.com
Kal-Kustom Enterprises	www.reinell.com
Kawasaki	www.kawasaki.com
Kenner	www.kenner-boats.com
KEVCON Corporation	www.mistyharborboats.com
Kevlacat	www.kevlacat.com
Key West Boats	www.keywestboatsinc.com
Klamath Boat Company	www.klamathboats.com
Krogen Express	www.krogenexpress.com
Landau	www.landauboats.com
Larson Boats	www.larsonboats.com
Lazzara Yachts	www.lazzarayachts.com
Lear Boats	www.learboats.com
Legacy	www.freedomyachts.com
Leisure Pontoons	www.leisurepontoon.com
Lowe Boats	www.lowe.com
Luhrs Corporation	www.luhrs.com
Lund Boat Company	www.lundboats.com
Lyman Morse Boatbuilding	www.lymanmorse.com
Mainship Corporation	www.mainship.com
Mako	www.mako-boats.com
Malibu Boats	www.malibuboats.com
MAN Engines & Components, Inc.	www.man-mec.com
Manitou	www.manitouboats.com
Manitou Pontoon Boats	www.manitouboats.com
Mares Power Boats	www.maresmarine.com
Mariah Boats	www.mariah-boats.com
Marine Manufacturing	www.weeres.com
Maritec Industries	www.americanmarinesports.com
Maritimo	www.maritimo.com.au
Marlin Yacht, Mfg.	www.marlinyacht.com
Marlow Marine Sales, Inc.	www.marlowmarine.com
Marquis Yachts	www.marquisyachts.com
MasterCraft Boat Company	www.mastercraft.com
Maverick Boat Company, Inc.	www.maverickboats.com and www.pathfinderboats.com

Maxum	www.maxumboats.com
McAleer Marine	www.macmarineteam.com
McKee Craft	www.mckeecraft.com
Medeiros Boat Works Ltd.	www.medeiros-boatworks.com
Mercury Marine	www.mercurymarine.com
Mercury Inflatable Boats	www.mercurymarine.com
Meridian Yachts	www.meridian-yachts.com
Midnight Express	www.midnightboats.com
Mikelson Yachts	www.mikelsonyachts.com
MirroCraft Boats	www.mirrocraft.com
MJM Yachts, LLC	www.mjmyachts.com
Mochi Craft	www.mochicraft-yacht.com and ferrettigroupusa.com
Monark Marine	www.monarkmarine.com
Monterey Boats	www.montereyboats.com
Moomba	www.moomba.com
Mustang Marine	www.mustangmarine.com.au
Myacht Houseboats	www.myachtboats.com
Nauset Marine	www.nausetmarine.com
Nautic Star Boats	www.nauticstarboats.com
Nautica International, Inc.	www.nauticaintl.com
Nautic Star	www.nauticstar-marine.com
Navigator Yachts, Inc.	www.navyachts.com
Neptunus Yachts	www.neptunusyachts.com
Nitro	www.nitroboats.com
Nordhavn	www.nordhavn.com
Nordic Tugs	www.nordictugs.com
Nor-Tech Hi-Performance Boats	www.nor-techboats.com
NorthCoast Boats	www.northcoastboats.com
Northport Corporation of St. Cloud	www.mirrocraft.com
Novurania	www.novurania.com
Ocean Yachts	www.oceanyachtsinc.com
Outerlimits	www.outerlimitspowerboats.com
Pacific Skiffs, Inc.	www.pacificskiffs.com
Palm Beach Marinecraft	www.palmbeachmarine.com
Palmer Johnson	www.palmerjohnson.com
Palmer Marine	www.palmermarine.com
Palmetto Boats	www.palmettoboats.com
Panga	www.panga.com
Panther	www.airboats.com
Parker Marine Enterprises	www.parkerboats.net

Pathfinder	www.maverickboats.com and www.pathfinder.com
PCM Marine Engines	www.pcmengines.com
PDQ Yachts	www.pdqyachts.com
Pearson Yachts	www.pearsonyachts.com
Pegiva	www.pegiva.com
Peninsular Engines	www.peninsulardiesel.com
Post Yachts	www.postyachts.com
Premier	www.pontoons.com
Princecraft	www.princecraft.com
Princess	www.princessyachts.com
Procraft Boats	www.procraftboats.com
ProKat	www.prokatboats.biz
Pro-Line	www.prolineboats.com
Pronaubec	www.southlandboat.com
Pursuit	www.pursuitboats.com
Rampage	www.rampageyachts.com
Ranger Boats	www.rangerboats.com
Reinell	www.reinell.com
Regal	www.regalboats.com
Regulator	www.regulatormarine.com
Ribcraft USA	www.ribcraftusa.com
Rinker	www.rinkerboats.com
Riviera	www.rivierayachtsinc.com
Rivolta Yachts	www.rivoltayachts.com
Robalo	www.robalo.com
Roscioli	www.donziyachts.com
S1 Marine	www.seastrikeboats.com
S2 Yachts	www.s2yachts.com
Sabre Corporation	www.sabreyachts.com
Sailfish	www.sailfishboats.com
Salt Shaker Marine Custom Yachts	www.saltshakerboats.com
Savannah Yachts	www.savannahyachts.com
Scout Boats	www.scoutboats.com
Sea Ark Boats	www.seaark.com
Sea Boss Boats	www.seaboss.com
Sea Cat	www.seacatboats.com
SeaCraft	www.seacraft-boats.com
Sea Fox Boats	www.seafoxboats.com
Sea Pro Boats	www.seaproboats.com
Sea Quest	www.seaquestboats.biz
Sea Ray	www.searay.com

Seastrike	www.seastrikeboats.com
Sea Vee Boats	www.seaveeboats.com
Sea-Doo	www.seadoo.com
SeaHunter Boats	www.seahunterboats.com
Seaswirl Boats	www.seaswirl.com
Seawind Catamarans	www.seawindcats.com
Seminole Marine	www.sailfishboats.com
Sessa Marine	www.sessamarine.com
Shamrock Sport Fishing Boats	www.shamrockboats.com
Shannon Yachts	www.shannonyachts.com
Silver Marine	www.silvermarine.com
Silverton Marine Corporation	www.silverton.com
Skeeter Performance Fishing Boats	www.skeeterboats.com
Skier's Choice, Inc.	www.supraboats.com
SkipperLiner	www.skipperliner.com
Smoker Craft	www.smokercraft.com
Sonic Offshore Performance	www.sonicusaboats.com
Southland	www.southlandboat.com
Southport Boat Works	www.southport-boatworks.com
Southwind	www.southwindboats.com
Spectre Boats	www.spectresportfish.com
Spectrum Boats	www.trackermarine.com
Splendor Boats	www.splendorboats.com
Stabi-Craft	www.stabicraft.com
Stamas Yacht	www.stamas.com
Starcraft Marine	www.starcraftmarine.com
Starlite Luxury Houseboats	www.starlitehouseboats.com
Stingray Powerboats	www.stingrayboats.com
Stratos Boats	www.stratosboats.com
Strike Yachts	www.strikeyachts.com
Sumerset Houseboats	www.sumerset.com
Sun Chaser	www.sunchaserboats.com and www.smokercraft.com
Sunrunner Sport Cruisers	www.sunrunnercruises.com
Sunsation Performance	www.sunsationboats.com
Sunseeker	www.sunseeker.com
Suntracker	www.suntrackerboats.com
Supra	www.supraboats.com
Sylvan	www.sylvanmarine.com and www.smokercraft.com
Tahoe Pontoons	www.tahoepontoons.com
Tahoe	www.tahoesportboats.com
Team Kevlacat	www.kevlacat.com

Thoroughbred Houseboats	www.thoroughbredhouseboats.com
Thunderbird/Formula	www.formulaboats.com
Tiara Yachts	www.tiarayachts.com
Tige	www.tige.com
Tomco Marine Group, Inc.	www.americantug.com
Topaz Boats	www.topazboats.com
Tracker Marine Group	www.trackermarine.com
Trident Custom Boats	www.tridentboats.com
Triton Boats	www.tritonboats.com
Triumph	www.triumphboats.com
Trophy Sport Fishing Boats	www.trophyfishing.com
True North	www.tnyachts.com and
	www.pearsonyachts.com
True World Marine	www.trueworldmarine.com
Twin Anchors Houseboats	www.twinanchors.com
Twin Vee	www.twinvee.com
Valiant	www.valiant-boats.com
Vectra	www.vectraboats.com and
	www.smokercraft.com
Velocity Powerboats	www.velocityboats.com
Venture	www.venturemarine.com
Viking Sport Cruisers	www.vikingsportcruisers.com
Viking Yachts	www.vikingyachts.com
Visions Boatworks	www.visionboatworks.com
Volvo Penta	www.volvo.com/volvopenta
Walker Bay	www.walkerbay.com
Weeres	www.weeres.com
Wellcraft	www.wellcraft.com
Westerbeke	www.westerbeke.com
Whittley Marine Group International	www.whittley.com.au
Wilber Yachts	www.wilburyachts.com
Windsor Craft	www.windsorcraft.com
Windy USA	www.windy-usa.com
World Cat	www.worldcat.com
Xpress	www.xpressboats.com
Yamaha	www.yamaha-motor.com
Yanmar Marine	www.yanmarmarine.com
Yar-Craft Boats	www.yarcraft.com
Zodiac	www.zodiacmarineusa.com

J.D. Power and Associates
2007 Boat Competitive
Information Study℠

J.D. Power and Associates Boat Competitive Information Study℠, now in its sixth year, measures owner satisfaction with new boats among 76 boat brands in seven segments: ski/wakeboard, fiberglass bass boats, small runabouts (16 to 19 feet), large runabouts (20 to 29 feet), coastal fishing (17 to 28 feet), pontoons; and express cruisers (24 to 33 feet). Overall customer satisfaction index scores are based on performance in various categories including: cabin; engine; ride/handling; helm/instrument panel; design/styling; sound system; maintenance; water sports; and fishing.

What are Power Circle Ratings?

Power Circle Ratings (the Ratings) are an easy-to-use system developed by J.D. Power and Associates for JDPower.com. All Power Circle Ratings are based on the opinions of consumers who have actually used or owned the product or service being rated. Since the Ratings are based on J.D. Power and Associates research studies that survey a representative sample of owners, they are indicative of what typical buyers may experience.

High ratings for a particular product/service/company do not necessarily mean that every customer will have a positive experience. It simply indicates that, on average, consumer perceptions of the product/service/company indicate that it stands out when compared with competitive products/services/companies.

Please keep in mind that Power Circle Ratings measure consumer perceptions of product and service providers either at the brand level or at the segment level. In the automotive arena, for instance, this means that one particular SUV model is compared to other SUVs in its competitive segment or class.

How are Power Circle Ratings calculated?

J.D. Power and Associates assigns the highest-ranking company or brand in each segment five Power Circles, which equates to a rating of "among the best". Generally speaking, companies that receive five Power Circles represent the top performers within a segment (i.e., ski/wakeboard, small runaboats, pontoons), and companies that receive four Power Circles represent the next group of performers. If the highest-ranking company in a segment is "head and shoulders" above the remaining companies in that segment, it will be the only company to receive five Power Circles in that segment. In highly competitive segments, however, several companies can receive five Power Circles. The remaining companies in each segment receive four, three, or two Power Circles based on their performance.

What makes J.D. Power consumer ratings unique?

Power Circle Ratings are based on syndicated research from J.D. Power and Associates, a trusted source of market research information that is based on independent and unbiased feedback from verified product and service owners—meaning that the consumer actually owns or has owned or used the product or service being rated. Although many Web sites provide consumer ratings and feedback, in most cases product or service ownership is not verified. Verification of ownership is important because ratings on other sites may be based on information collected from discussion forums, blogs, or chat rooms. In some instances, respondents are providing feedback on products or services that they do not actually own.

Index

Numbers in **bold** indicate pages with illustrations

Boon, Dick, 123
Boston Whaler, 24–25, **51**; 19 Outrage, 220; 190 Montauk, **261**; 210 DC, **284**; 305 walkaround, **293**; 320 Outrage Cuddy, **274**; construction methods, **107**; foam flotation, **112**; J.D. Power and Associates ratings, 273; Unibond construction, 274
bottom loading, 18, **72**
bottom paint, 100–101
bottom strakes, 63, 64, 73
boundary layer of water, 17, 35, 53
bow diving, **69**
bowriders: fish-and-ski boats, **417–20**; runabouts, **431–50**, **434**, **435**, **436**, **437**, **438**, **439**, **442**, **445**, **447**
bow rise, 48
bow shapes: bulbous, 37, 38, **124**; displacement hulls, 37–38; pickle fork, **56**, **436**, **457**, **461**; ride quality and, 50–**51**
bow thrusters, 192
broaching, 15, **16**, 37–38, 71
brokers, 4–5, 237
Brunswick Corporation, 235. *See also* Baja Marine; Cabo; Crestliner Boats; Hatteras Yachts; Lowe Boats; Meridian Yachts; Princecraft Boats; Sea Pro Boats; Triton Boats; Trophy Sportfishing Boats
Buddy Davis. *See* Davis Yachts
bulbous bows, 37, 38, **124**
bulkheads, 23–25, **24**, 28, 105–**9**
bulking materials, 85
bulwarks, **22**
buoyancy, **8–10**; center of, **8–9**, 11; flare and, 52; longitudinal center of, 9, 46; reserve, 26, 27; rollover capability and, 14–15; transverse center of, 9, 12; vertical center of, 9
buttock lines: displacement hulls, **33**, **35**–36; planing hulls, 43, 48–49, 68–70, **69**

cabin design. *See* accommodations
Cabo Yachts: 40, 252; 40 Flybridge, **306–9**; 52 express sportfisherman, **205**, **326**
Camano Yachts: 31 Fast Trawler, **209**, **384–89**; 34, **188**; 41 cruiser, **235**
capsized vessels, 15–16, 18, 221
carbon fibers, 85–86
carbon monoxide (CO) poisoning, 231
carbureted engines, 148, 258
Carver Yachts: cruising yachts, **356**, **368**; head and shower, 226
catalytic converters, 149
catamarans, **74–79**; advantages and limitations, 74–75; hull design, **75–78**, 79; performance, 78; reviews, **267–73**; seaworthiness, 78–79; V-drive inboard, **157**
Caterpillar ACERT engine, **150**
Caterpillar Multi-Station Control System (MSCS), **202**
center consoles (CCs), 222, **274–84**
center of buoyancy (CB), **8–9**, 11
center of dynamic lift (CDL), 9, 28, 46–**48**
center of gravity (CG), 7–**8**, **9**, 14
Century Boats: 1850 DC, **284**; 2200 CC, **275**; 2202 Inshore, 133, **264–67**; 3200 Offshore, **226**, **327**; construction methods, **107**; J.D. Power and Associates ratings, 273
C-Flex, 117
Champion Boats: 21 Bay, **261**; 21SX, **418**; 210 Elite, **397**
Chaparral Boats: 236 bowrider, **434**; 27 Sunesta, **412**; 310 Signature express cruiser, **225**, **315**–18; 350 Signature express cruiser, **312**; J.D. Power and Associates

ratings, 431, 432, 433. *See also* Robalo
C-Hawk, 113
Checkmate boats, **343**
chine flats, **50**, 63, 64
chines: metal boats, **126–27**; planing hulls, **43**; purpose of, **50**; stability and, 14
chines, types of: double, 50, **52**; hard, 13, 14, 50, 62; radius, **126**; stepped, **57**
chine walking, 43, 70
chop and mat, 98
chopper guns, 82
Chris Craft, 56, 67
Cigarette Racing boats, **344**
Closed Cavity Bag Molding (CCBM), 103–4
coastal fishing boats, 273–303; center consoles (CCs), **274–84**; dual consoles (DCs), **284**–92; walkarounds, **293**–303
Cobalt Boats: 222 bowrider, **439–41**; 272 bowrider, **182**; 302 bowrider, **434**; 343 go-fast, **344**; helm station design, **200**; J.D. Power and Associates ratings, 312, 432, 433
Cobalt Yachts 45 express cruiser, **312**
Cobia Boats 27 walkaround, **293**
cockpit design, 26, 27, 207, **219–20**, 247
Codega, Lou, 69, 72
cold-molded construction, 118–**19**
COLREGS (International Regulations for Preventing Collisions at Sea), 194
companionways, 223–24
compartmentation, 23–25, **24**, 31
compass, 200
computer-aided design and computer-aided manufacturing (CAD-CAM), 97, 127, 128, 235
condition and value (C&V) survey, 240
constant dynamic instabilities, 71
Contender Boats 33T, **275**
controllable pitch propellers (CPPs), 159

convertible sportsfisherman: reviews, 303–9, **304**, **305**, **306**; scuppers, 220; stability of, 11
cooling systems: diesel engines, 153–54; failure of, 26; freshwater, 155; inboard engines, 155–56; outboard engines, 135; raw-water, 155–56, 190–91; stern drives, 141–43
Core-Cell, 92, 94
cored bottoms, 92, **94**
core materials: challenges of, 95–97; compression, **95**, **96**; delamination, 96; drilling and cutting, **95–96**; heat distortion temperature (HDT), 94–95; I-beams, **89**, 90; plywood, 110–11; properties by type, 92; purpose of, 81; sandwich laminate, 89–92, **90**; skin-to-core bond, 91–92; stiffness vs. strength, 89–**90**
core materials, types of: balsa, **89**, 92–93, **96**; foam, **89**, **91**, 92, **93**–95; honeycomb, **89**, 92, 95
Correct Craft: 206 Ski Nautique, **452**; 220 Super Air Nautique, **458–61**; Crossover Nautique 236, **456**; J.D. Power and Associates ratings, 451; swim platform, **213**
corrosion, 128–29, 191–92
course-keeping ability, 29–30, 51, 60–**61**
Covey Island 42 sportfisherman, **119**
Crestliner Boats: 1700 Fish Hawk, **390**; 1850 Sportfish, **390**; 1870 CJX, **391**
crew-overboard kit, **217**
Crownline Boats: 240LS cuddy, **435**; 252 EX, **412**; J.D. Power and Associates ratings, 431, 432, 433
Cruisers Yachts: 300 express, **312**; 447 Sport Sedan, **369**; 455 Express Motoryacht, **356**

Express, **56, 57**; J.D.
Power and Associates rat-
ings, 273
SCRIMP (Seemann Com-
posites Resin Infusion
Molding Process), 88,
100–102, **101**, 103
scuppers, 27, 29, **219**–20
Sea Boss Boats 190 DC, **286**
Sea Cat Boats 226 DC, **268**
sea cocks, **191**
Sea-Doo Challenger 230, **438**
Sea Fox Boats: 216 Pro Series
DC, **286**; J.D. Power and
Associates ratings, 273,
274
seakindliness, 6, 18–**19**
Sea Pro Boats: 1900 Bay, **263**;
270 CC, **277**
SeaQuest Boats 25 walka-
round, **296**
Sea Ray Boats: 240 Sundeck,
415–17; 270 Sundeck,
414; 290 Select EX, **438**;
310 express, **184**; 310
Sundancer, **231**; 40 aft-
cabin, **359**; 44 DA, 145;
58 Sedan Bridge, **371**; 60
Sundancer express
cruiser, **314**; Amberjack
series, 310, **328**; construction methods, **80,
84, 98, 109**; cruiser facility, **5**; J.D. Power and
Associates ratings, 310,
431, 432, 433; models
produced by, 359; out-
drive cover, **215**
Sea Sport 32 catamaran,
76
Seaswirl: 175 bowrider, **438**;
2901 walkaround, **296**
sea trial, 245–48
seaworthiness, **6**–7; catamarans, 78–79; deck
drainage and, 218–**20**;
factors, 27–32; flood prevention, 22–27, **23, 24,
26**; hull shape and, 6;
weight of vessel and, 13;
windows and, 14, **15**. See
also stability; stability,
types of
sectional view, **35, 52**
sedans, **368**–80
Sedona pontoon boats, 422
semicustom boats, 80

semidisplacement hulls, 18,
39–**42**
settees, **224**
Setzer, Ward, 54, 358
S-glass, 81, 85
shaft seals, **152**
shaft strut, **172**
shaft strut pads, **150, 163**
shear, 90
shower and head, 224–26,
225, 245
side decks, **206, 207,** 216–18,
217
Silverton Yachts: 42, **214**; 43
motor yacht, **359**; 45
convertible, **305**; safety
design features, **214**
sinks, 229
Skeeter Boats: 20i, **398,
408**–11; J.D. Power and
Associates ratings, 396;
SL210, **419**; SX200, **398**;
ZX 22 Bay, **263**
ski boats: J.D. Power and
Associates ratings,
254, 451; pontoon boats
as, 421; reviews, **452**–56.
See also fish-and-ski
boats
Skier's Choice: Moomba 21
wakeboard, **457**;
Moomba J.D. Power and
Associates ratings, 451;
Moomba Outback, **234,
453**–56; Supra J.D. Power
and Associates ratings,
451; Supra Comp 20,
453; Supra Launch 21V,
457
ski pad, 63
slamming loads, 48, **49**
Smoker Craft. See Vectra
Boats
Society of Accredited Marine
Surveyors (SAMS),
238
Southport Boatworks center
consoles, **236**, 277
Southwind Boats deckboats,
414, 422
Spectra, 86
speed: boat handling and,
30–31; deadrise vs., 59;
diesel engines and, 133,
155; dynamic instability,
70, **71**; factors that influence, 132; gas engines

and, 155; hull shape and,
133; low-speed instabili-
ties, 71–73; ratings for
engines, **132**–33; slow-
speed operation, 153;
speed vs. weight, 59–60
speed-to-length ratio (S/L),
30–31; displacement
hulls, 34–35, 36; planing
hulls, 44, 53; semi-
displacement hulls, 40,
41, 42
Spencer, Paul, 329–30
Spencer Yachts 43 Express,
147, **329**–34
sportsfisherman, 14, 216. See
also convertible sports-
fisherman; express
sportsfishermen
spray rails, 50, 63, **64**
spray strakes, 73
stability: above-water-to-
underwater profile ratio,
28; beam and, 18; buoy-
ancy and, **8**–10; center of
gravity and, 7–**8,** 9; freeboard and, 21–**22**, 28;
free-surface effect and,
27–28; hull shape and,
11; length-to-beam ratio
and, 18; metacentric
height (GM) and, 13;
reserve buoyancy and,
27; sea and weather con-
ditions and, 15–18,
21–**22**; trim and, **9**, 10,
21; weight distribution
and, 7, 28; weight of vessel and, 17
stability, types of: directional, **29**–30; dynamic,
12, 15–18; form, 11; initial, 7, 10–14, 15; reserve,
14, 16; static, **12**, 17, 21;
ultimate, 7, 10–14, 15, 19;
weight, 12
stability curves, **12**–13, 14,
15
stabilizing equipment, **17**,
18, **19**–**21**, 192
stagnation zone, 58, **69**
Starcraft Marine, 421, 422
static stability, **12**, 17, 21
static trim, 48
stations, 33, **43**, **52**
station-wagon effect, 231
steel boats, 31, **120**–30

steering responsiveness,
177–78
steering systems, **179**–81;
inspection, 241; Power
steering, 178, 180;
responsiveness and
speed, 30; wheel place-
ment, **200**–202
stepped hulls, **57**–58
steps and ladders, **208,**
213–16
stern drives, **141**–44; EFI recommendations, 258, 259;
monitoring and control
systems, 139–41, **140**;
steering, 180–81; trim-
ming with, 67–68; V-
drive inboard vs., 141–42
Stingray, 431, 432, 433
storage space, 230–31
stoves, 229, 231
strakes, running (bottom),
63, 64, 73
Stratos 176 XT, **398**
stray-current corrosion,
128–29
stringers, **80, 91, 93,** 105–11,
106, 107, 108, 109
styrene, 86, 87, 88
Sunseeker: cruiser, **169**;
Predator 80, 310
Sun Tracker 36 Megahut,
423
superchargers, 153
superstructures. See deckhouses and
superstructures
Supra: Comp 20, **453**; J.D.
Power and Associates
ratings, 451; Launch 21V,
457
surface-piercing propeller
drives, 132, **168**–71, 181
surge, **16**
surveys and surveyors,
237–41
survivability, 6
Suzuki outboard engines, 138
Suzuki Precision Control,
139
sway, **16**
swim ladders, **215**–16
swim platform, **213**

tabbing, **106**, 107–**9**
Tahoe: 265 deckboat, **414**;
Q6, **420**; Q8i, **438**